D0065456

THE PHILADELPHIA THEATRE
IN THE EIGHTEENTH CENTURY

For the BENEFIT of
Mr. Lewis Hallam,

By a Company of COMEDIANS from

LONDON,

At the NEW THEATRE, *in* Water-ftreet,

This prefent Evening (being the Twenty-feventh of *May*, 1754) will be prefented a COMEDY, called,

TUNBRIDGE WALKS:
OR,
The Yeoman of Kent.

The Part of *Woodcock* (the Yeoman of *Kent*) by Mr. *Malone*.

Reynard,	} by {	Mr. *Rigby*.
Loveworth,		Mr. *Miller*.

Captain *Squib*, by Mr. *Lewis Hallam*.
The Part of Mr. *Maiden*, by Mr. *Singleton*.

The Part of *Belinda*, by Mrs. *Becceley*.

Penelope,		Mrs. *Clarkfon*.
Lucy,	} by {	Mifs *Hallam*.
Mrs. *Goodfellow*,		Mrs. *Rigby*.

And the Part of *Hillaria*, to be perform'd by Mrs. *Hallam*.

To which will be added, a BALLAD OPERA, called,

The COUNTRY WAKE;
OR,
HOB in the WELL.

The Part of *Flora*, to be perform'd by Mrs. *Becceley*.

Sir *Thomas Tefty*,		Mr. *Clarkfon*.
Friendly,	} by {	Mr. *Adcock*.
Old *Hob*,		Mr. *Miller*.
Dick,		Mafter L. *Hallam*.

Hob's Mother,	} by {	Mrs. *Clarkfon*.
Betty,		Mifs *Hallam*.

And the Part of Young *Hob*, to be perform'd by Mr. *Hallam*.

Tickets to be had at Mrs. Bridges's, in Front-ftreet, and of Mr. Hallam.

BOX 6s.   PIT 4s.   GALLERY 2s. 6d.

N. B. The Doors will be open'd at Five, and the Play to begin at Seven a Clock. *VIVAT REX.*

THE PHILADELPHIA THEATRE
in the
EIGHTEENTH CENTURY

Together with the *Day Book* of the same period

By

THOMAS CLARK POLLOCK

GREENWOOD PRESS, PUBLISHERS
NEW YORK   1968

To Puck

FOREWORD

FROM THE point of view of chronology, Dr. Pollock's *History of the Philadelphia Theatre in the Eighteenth Century* is the beginning of a series in which the record of the Philadelphia stage is to be given with that authority which a detailed study alone permits. Circumstances dictated that the second period in the history of the Philadelphia stage should be the first to appear in print, Dr. James' *Old Drury,* which includes a facsimile reprint of the actual manuscript of William Wood, the manager of the Chesnut Street Theatre, having already been published. These two volumes will be followed by monographs already completed or in progress, dealing with the periods 1835–1855, 1855–1878, 1878–1900, 1900–1910, and it is hoped that the series will be continued until the present day is reached.

There are various ways in which the history of a city's theatrical life may be written. In this series an attempt has been made to combine accuracy with interest. Each of the contributing writers has examined the newspapers day by day, and checked this record by programs, diaries, and other theatrical material. The chronological account will be found to give the details of every performance of which record exists, while the chapters upon the plays, the actors, the theatres, and other matters will prove of interest to those who desire a composite picture of the stage. The indices will make it possible for the research worker to find at once complete information upon any performance given in Philadelphia during the period treated.

It has been a great pleasure for me to watch the growth of this series, and to witness the devotion of the scholars who have contributed to the record of a stage once the leading theatrical center of the United States. If that primacy has now passed away, it is pleasant to remember that in Philadelphia still stands the Walnut Street Theatre, the oldest in existence in the United States, and that in this city was produced *The Prince of Parthia,* the first play written by an American to be produced upon the professional stage.

ARTHUR HOBSON QUINN

University of Pennsylvania
1933

PREFACE

IN THE preparation of this volume I have been greatly helped by more men and more institutions than I can mention here. But I wish especially to record my gratitude to Professor Arthur Hobson Quinn, acknowledging the fact that this volume, as well as the series of which it is a part, has been inspired by his vision and generously informed by his scholarship; to Professor Schelling, for his careful critical reading of the manuscript; and to Professor Reese James, for his many valuable suggestions. I wish also to salaam to the shade of Charles Durang because he labored so patiently, if vainly, to get his valuable mound of work on the early Philadelphia stage between covers. A melancholy moment in the research for the present volume came when I saw a letter by Durang, preserved in the Shaw Theatre Collection, lamenting his failure to get his history published in book form. "I never," he wrote, "looked for *profit myself,* but, the satisfaction of seeing it out in a decent manner. Other writers, no doubt, will have hereafter the use of its facts and general matter." As those who have used it know, Durang's history, printed in the Philadelphia *Sunday Dispatch* in the middle of the last century and preserved in volumes of clippings, is, if not always finally reliable, invaluable. And I wish to acknowledge my special indebtedness to the libraries and librarians of the University of Pennsylvania, the Historical Society of Pennsylvania, the Library Company of Philadelphia, the Library of Congress, and the Shaw Theatre Collection.

THOMAS CLARK POLLOCK

Municipal University of Omaha

1932

CONTENTS

INTRODUCTION

PHILADELPHIA in the first half of the eighteenth century was a busily growing town. The forty-five hundred people and seven hundred houses of 1699, seventeen years after the founding of the city, had become by 1744 thirteen thousand people and fifteen hundred houses,[1] and the city kept steadily growing. William Penn's dream of saving the Delaware River waterfront as a place of beauty gave way before the rush of commerce, and Water Street, which fronted the river, became a hustling place of business, overlooking the wharves with their vessels arriving from England or spreading sail for the West Indies. Water Street, however, was not entirely devoted to business, and "all of the best and richest merchants dwelt under the same roofs with their stores, situated then in Water or Front street." [2]

The "People called Quakers," the earliest settlers, were soon followed by the Germans who founded Germantown. These two stocks were the backbone of early Philadelphia. In spite of opposition, the government was largely in their hands until the Revolution, and their somewhat narrow and practical, rather than artistic, attitude toward life was the background against which many of the less somber, perhaps more imaginative arrivals seemed unwontedly bright and gay. In its attitude toward the arts the Quaker and German majority was strengthened by the large Scotch-Irish immigration, which brought with it the Presbyterian fear of the arts as snares of the devil. But though this, in the broad sense puritan, majority was certainly not liberal, it was not fanatical, and the principles of tolerance on which Philadelphia was founded permitted the peaceful settling of many men of widely varying opinions. A large and important Church of England group made Philadelphia its home, and it was to the new freedom-promising city that young Benjamin Franklin, one of many attracted by the dream of liberty, came in 1723.

Something of the tone of the town in those early days is indicated in Franklin's *Autobiography* when he says, "In order to secure my credit and character as a tradesman, I took care not only to be in *reality* industrious and frugal, but to avoid all appearances to the con-

[1] Richard Peters' Letters to the Proprietors (ALS), p. 268, in Hist. Soc. of Pa.
[2] Watson, *Annals of Philadelphia*, I, 225.

trary. I dressed plainly; I was seen at no places of idle diversion. I never went a-fishing or shooting; a book, indeed, sometimes debauched me from my work, but that was seldom, snug, and gave no scandal, and, to show that I was not above my business, I sometimes brought home the paper I purchased at the stores through the streets on a wheelbarrow." [3] Of course, these are the words not merely of an early Philadelphian, but of a young man most determinedly on the make—whose virtues perennially consist in being unblushingly conservative and industrious. Yet it is noteworthy that when the young printer "debauched" himself with a book he did it "snug, and gave no scandal"! Many of Franklin's virtues, however, were largely his own: he drank sparingly, for example, while in 1728, when there were probably less than ten thousand people in Philadelphia, the consumption of rum alone (the West Indian beverage) in Pennsylvania was more than two hundred thousand gallons. [4]

Busily and peacefully growing as she was, Philadelphia was still far removed from the huge metropolis she has since become. In 1728 bears were killed in Germantown and Darby, and panthers seen; a woman killed a sleeping stag with a rock. In 1731 a court of admiralty was trying pirates, and a woman at New Castle was legally burnt alive for murdering her husband. Two years later a pair of whales are said to have come up the Delaware. "Decent citizens had a universal speaking acquaintance with each other, and everybody promptly recognized a stranger in the streets." [5] The line between the hereditary gentry and the tradesmen was distinct, and below the tradesmen were the slaves: negro, Indian, and "redemptioners"—white men and women who sold their services for a period, usually five years. Masters sent slaves to jail to be whipped. Most of the workingmen wore dingy, no longer yellow buckskin breeches, checked shirts, and red flannel jackets. People of fashion wore wigs; the men had cocked hats and sometimes gold-laced scarlet vests—all gentlemen wore laced ruffles and in winter little woolen muffs or "mufftees." The women wore hoopskirts and covered their hair with little caps. Fashionable young men sported swords, and if their honor was correctly attacked, dueled with them. Tailors, shoemakers, and hatters went to their customers' homes. The streets were

---

[3] *Autobiography of Benjamin Franklin,* Home Library Edition (A. L. Burt), p. 88.

[4] See *Pa. Gazette,* Vol. I, No. 3, 1728-9. By "consumption" I mean the difference between imports—224,500 gallons—and exports—11,400 gallons.

[5] Watson, *Annals of Phila.,* I, 175.

not paved; there were no curbs, and posts were put up to keep vehicles off the sidewalks. There was no provision for "enlightening the city" with public lamps till 1752, and highway robbery was common. In 1761 only twenty-nine people owned "chairs, chariots, or other wheeled vehicles for passenger transport," [6] and most traveling was done on horseback.

Andrew Bradford published the first Philadelphia newspaper, *The American Weekly Mercury,* in 1719. *The Pennsylvania Gazette* was begun nine years later by Samuel Keimer, and continued after 1729 by B. Franklin. The newspapers usually appeared once a week; unfortunately for our knowledge of the theatre, they lacked the modern paper's thirst for the extraordinary in contemporary life. Most of the space was given over to political news from Europe and dispatches from neighboring cities. The only newspaper mention of the second theatrical troupe known to have been in Philadelphia came as a New York notice, after the players had left Philadelphia. Indeed, almost the only local events to "make the news" before the Revolution were some especially exciting murders and the sermons of George Whitefield.

Fortunately, however, the papers ran advertisements or "notices," and we are able occasionally to find theatrical notes hidden among descriptions of runaway slaves and lists of goods for sale. But only one of these appeared before 1750, and for the first half of the century the newspapers yield, with this one important exception, nothing to our purpose save stray advertisements of what would now probably be vaudeville acts. This does not necessarily mean that no plays were given during the earlier period; in all probability many plays *were* given; but research has found a meager record. There is always the hope that some now unknown old letter or diary will further lighten this darkness—and the probability that we shall never certainly know.

But if it should be true that few plays were given in the city before 1750, one reason is apparent. Philadelphia was the most liberal and advanced city in the new world, "the city of firsts," but she was also a true child of the eighteenth century, and her young men divided their interest in the arts with their zest for the new science called "philosophy." They saw visions and dreamed dreams, but these were often connected with making experiments. B. Franklin "debauched" himself with electricity as well as books, and he had friends. In 1744 they "subscribed to *Dr. Spencer's* first course of EXPERIMENTAL PHILOS-

---

[6] John T. Faris, *The Romance of Old Philadelphia,* p. 249.

OPHY" in such numbers that they could not all "be conveniently accommodated," so that the scientific doctor had to give a second course, and three months later work up some new lectures.[7] A decade later Professor Kinnersley's scientific lectures and experiments drew crowds year after year. Fortunately, the Quakers and the Presbyterians had not inherited prejudices against this new science, as they had against the drama, and the experimenters encountered less opposition than the actors.

The quarter century before the Revolution was an era of strolling players. A small troupe of actors, "Comedians from London," later "The American Company," wandered along the Atlantic coast from Charleston to hopeful Annapolis, to prosperous Philadelphia, more and more their home, to Dutch New York, attempted Providence, were rebuffed at Boston. Those who loved the theatre gave the troupers eager welcome; those who feared the snares of Satan fought them bitterly. But the actors persevered with suppliant pride, obtained if they could permission to play, built theatres, unpacked their meager wardrobes, distributed handbills, and drew crowds. Three nights a week the theatre would be open. Beginning at six or seven o'clock, the players would give a five-act drama and a two-act farce, with singing and dancing in the intermission, and then work up a new bill for the next performance. The weeks would pass, actors would take their "benefits," often going to the homes of the leading citizens to solicit patronage, then pack Lear's crown and Yorick's skull in their boxes, and take the coach for another town, returning when they could. And they established the theatre in America.

With 1775 came the Revolution, and a change in the old order. Philadelphia found herself the focal point of the new nation. The First Continental Congress met, and the Second. Strong men peered somberly into the future as they signed the Declaration of Independence. The Liberty Bell rang. Families split, Loyalist and Whig. For a winter the British held the city and made it a gay camp, while the snow lay on the skeleton of Washington's army at Valley Forge. Business went from bad to worse. Prices rose; a good hat cost five hundred dollars, and the currency was inflated till the worthlessness of a "Continental" became proverbial.

When the Treaty of Peace was signed, Philadelphia emerged into a new world. The quiet provincialism of the colonial days was gone

---

[7] *Pa. Gazette,* Apr. 25, May 3, and July 26, 1744.

forever. The sober young printer of sixty years ago had become the almost legendary Dr. Franklin, idol of France. When he died in 1791, full of years and honor, the scientific spirit which he represented was beginning to bear its practical fruit. Fitch's first crude steamboat disturbed the waters of the Schuylkill in 1785, and in 1793 Blanchard was making exhibition flights in his balloon.

Philadelphia's trade reached to the ends of the earth. Stephen Girard was amassing a fortune with ships which sailed to India and China, bringing back teas and spices and silks. After the lean years of war, prosperity returned. The city went mad for luxury. Gay carriages crowded the streets, and Quarrier & Hunter did a thriving business in coaches, chariots, chaises, phaëtons, and sulkies. Thomas Jefferson's phaëton they painted green, and Robert Morris's chariot olive-green with vermilion and gilding. Washington lived in the city as President of the Constitutional Convention, and later as President of the United States, entertaining lavishly in his home and at the theatre. He "occasionally rode out to take the air with six horses to the coach, and always two footmen behind his carriage." The city flocked to his levees.

Fifty thousand people lived in Philadelphia during the last decade of the century, and the city was still growing rapidly. Twice it was racked by plague, and twice it recovered. The powder magazine of the French Revolution exploded, and French émigrés jostled each other in the Philadelphia streets—Talleyrand, the Vicomte de Noailles, the Duc de Liancourt, Louis Philippe. Followers of Jefferson sang *"Ça Ira,"* feared a monarchy, and called each other "Citizen." Democratic long trousers became popular. Though many "aristocrats" had their hair curled and powdered to the *macaroni* taste, the fashion for wigs was going out, and bald heads were being discovered.

Thomas Jefferson and Alexander Hamilton walked the streets of Philadelphia, struggling with the problems of the new nation. In the clash of party antagonisms many new journals sprang up. The daily paper became a habit of life, and local news was found to be of interest. The theatre no longer went without comment.

The days of the strolling player were passing, and the Old American Company retreated to New York (not yet the theatrical center of America), giving way before the permanent company at the splendid New Theatre in Chesnut Street, across the street from the Capitol. In the New Theatre, with its two thousand seats and excellent company of actors imported *en masse* from England, one could see James Fennell in *Lear,* John Bernard in *The School for Scandal,* or Mrs. Merry in *Othello.* But the noble roll of dramatic verse and the lilting ripple of high comedy alone did not satisfy the public. The taste of the new era demanded also musical entertainments, clever dances, new pantomimes—the ingredients which have since been formalized into musical comedy. Alexander Reinagle was kept busy writing new music, and William Francis composed ballets, harlequinades, spectacles. Great "circuses" sprang up, mixing musical comedy with horsemanship and acrobatics.

The theatrical infancy of the first half of the century had passed away. So, happily, had the newspaper reticence. The theatrical record of the last decade of the century, when Philadelphia was entering its golden age, is, for essential facts, very nearly complete.

In the pages which follow appears the full record, so far as research has been able to recover it, of the Philadelphia stage during the eighteenth century. The *Day Book* which forms the latter part of this volume gives a day-by-day statement of every known performance, with all known plays and casts. For convenience in reference these have been arranged chronologically, with a statement at the end of each season summarizing all the essential information concerning new and old plays and players. Following the *Day Book* are Indices of Plays, Players, and Playwrights. In the first part of the volume the attempt has been to make a clear and succinct statement of all the important theatrical developments in Philadelphia during the century.

There is a constant temptation in a history of this kind to elaborate the interesting non-essentials; and there is room for a later volume making some of these alluring bypaths, such as the lives of the actors in early America, a study in themselves. But in what follows the design has simply been to give, pruning the irrelevant, a brief view of the whole of the Philadelphia theatre for the eighteenth century, and a complete statement, day by day, of all pertinent records.

PART I

THEATRICAL HISTORY

CHAPTER I

THE COLONIAL PERIOD

1700–1775

THOUGH the record of the Philadelphia stage during the eighteenth century is of course primarily important as a keystone chapter in American theatrical annals, it also contributes a fundamental document to the history of American culture. The theatre's long struggle to final triumph throws light on many significant features of American civilization. In addition to illustrating the growth of our artistic life and its social methods, the account of that struggle reveals our religious organizations as militant social forces; mirrors the changes in population; indicates our interrelations with European cultures; shows the individualism of the American spirit, with its opposing surge toward mass action; and also affords what in the twentieth century is of extraordinary interest— a complete chapter in the history of legislative prohibitions. And the early theatrical history of Philadelphia is especially important because during the eighteenth century the Philadelphia stage was, on the whole, the most important in America. New York,[1] still a stubborn Dutch town, was important, but not yet the theatrical heart of the country. Charleston,[1] as well as other cities along the coast, had a brilliant stage. But Philadelphia, especially toward the end of the century, was unquestionably the leader.

For the first half of the century, however, when the growing town was still small, the record of the Philadelphia stage is significantly meager. Though the Quakers and Germans were not the only people in town— an increasingly large group, chiefly Church of England, was more interested in the arts—the Quakers controlled Philadelphia and gave it its official tone. They consistently fought the stage. And though, after 1719, newspapers were published once a week, they were not interested in local news. Save for one small advertisement, the papers made no mention of

---

[1] See Odell, *Annals of the New York Stage,* Vols. I and II, and Willis, *The Charleston Stage in the Eighteenth Century,* for detailed accounts of the early theatre in New York and Charleston.

players in Philadelphia till 1750, more than a quarter of a century after comedians are known to have been patronized by the Governor of Pennsylvania. So the theatrical record of the first half of the period is meager and accidental, with its most obvious facts concerning opposition to stage-playing rather than the theatre itself.

FIRST FACTS

As early as 1700 [2] the Assembly of Pennsylvania passed a law prohibiting "stage-plays, masks, revels" and other "rude and riotous sports." The immediate reason for this law is not certain. It is possible that the Quakers simply wished to fence their Eden as a sober precaution against riotous and alluring serpents. Or perhaps they feared the approach of players who were (probably) then in Virginia and New York, perhaps even in Boston.[3] Or it is quite possible that someone, perhaps the Richard Hunter who had a license to act in New York about the turn of the century, was already acting in or near Philadelphia. At any rate, the Assembly passed a prohibitory law, and an interesting struggle with the British government followed. In 1705 the law was repealed in England. When the Assembly heard the news, it set about passing the law again— this time with the prohibition extended, perhaps significantly, to "interludes." The new law was vetoed in England in 1709. Again the Quaker Assembly, in 1711, enacted a prohibition. When that law was repealed, in 1713, the Friends gave up the struggle till 1759, when, though partially outwitted by a governor favorable to the actors, they passed another law, in turn quickly vetoed.[4]

Denied legal prohibition, Yearly Meeting in 1716 advised Friends against "going to or being in any way concerned in plays, games, lotteries, music, and dancing." [5]

But at least by 1723, professional actors, led by "a Player who had Strowled hither to act as a Comedian," came to Philadelphia, "chose for their Stage a place just without the verge of the City," published "printed

[2] For the source of this and all other statements concerning the Philadelphia stage which are not supported by footnotes, see the *Day Book* of *The Philadelphia Theatre in the Eighteenth Century*, under the date mentioned.

[3] See Odell, *Annals of the New York Stage*, I, 3–9, for the earliest traces in other cities.

[4] For a fuller discussion of this subject, see W. S. Dye, "Pennsylvania versus the Theatre," *Pa. Mag. of Hist. and Biog.*, LX, 332–372 (Oct., 1931).

[5] Ezra Michener, *A Retrospect of Early Quakerism*, Phila., 1860, p. 361.

Bills," and went on "to act accordingly." James Logan, the Quaker mayor, wrote to a friend, "How grievous this proves to the sober people of the place, thou wilt easily judge, but it happens at p'sent to be more particularly so on me, having, unfortunately, been chosen Mayor of Philad[a] for this year, there is an expectation that I should exert that authority to suppress their acting. But as . . . ye Gov[r] [Sir William Keith] himself resorts thither, I can by no means think it advisable to embroil myself with the governour to no purpose"—especially as the governor had already "excused himself from prohibiting" the stage-playing.

The unhappy mayor's letter is, ironically, the only knowledge which has come to light of these "strowling" players, whose acting "just without the verge of the city" really opens our theatrical history. But it proves indubitably that there were professional *strolling players* in Philadelphia by 1723. And in the next year, 1724, a newspaper advertisement yields our first definite knowledge of a *theatre* in Philadelphia. It was "the New Booth on Society Hill." The single announcement tells of "Roap Dancing" and "your old friend Pickle Herring" [6]—possibly the leading comedian of 1723—who was in 1724 advertised for his "Comical Humour."

The "Roap Dancing" may be passed over, but the New Booth, the first theatre known in Philadelphia, is important. It was on Society Hill,[7] probably just to the south of the city limits, as two later theatres were to be, and across open fields from the built-up city. (Philadelphia in those days lay between the Delaware and Schuylkill Rivers, and Vine Street and Cedar, now South Street. North of Vine were the Northern Liberties, and South of Cedar lay Southwark.) All we know of the theatre itself is that there were "performances on the stage," that the prices were "on the stage 3s., in pit 2s., in gallery 1s. 6d.," and that it was called "the New Booth on Society Hill." These facts are meager. But they prove that Philadelphia, having received strolling players in 1723, could at least by 1724 [8] boast of a theatre, the New Booth on Society Hill.

---

[6] Dr. Schelling has suggested that this may indicate a German influence, as "Pickle Herring" was a German, as well as an Elizabethan, clown.

[7] Very possibly it was identical with the theatre which must have been used in 1723; C. P. Keith, *Chronicles of Pa.,* II, 671, says that the theatre of 1723 was "just below South Street." But he states no authority, and we must rely on probability and imagination.

[8] Knowledge of this theatre was of course wanted by Miss Willis when she

Between 1724 and 1749, when we get the next glimpse of Philadelphia comedians, the most important "firsts" (passing over the "Lyon
King of Beasts" and clock-work marvels) were of the first marionettes,
in 1742, when "A merry Dialogue between Punch and Joan his
wife . . . by changeable Figures of two Feet high" was given "At the
Sign of the Coach-and-Horses, against the State House, in Chesnut-
Street," and of Philadelphia's first "picture show," given by a "Magick
Lanthorn" at Joseph Barber's "at the Temple Bar in Second-Street" in
1743.

MURRAY AND KEAN AND NANCY GEORGE

In August, 1749, a "Company of Comedians" was in Philadelphia,
playing in a large warehouse owned by William Plumsted [9] in Water
(or King) Street between Pine and Lombard. The newspapers did not
mention the actors, but we know [10] that they gave *Cato* on August 22
or 23 and were still in the city in January, 1750, when the Common
Council attempted to "discourage" them. In February they went to
New York, and the *Pennsylvania Gazette* made history on March 6
by noting the arrival in the Dutch town of "a company of comedians
from Philadelphia"—the first time that a Philadelphia newspaper had,
save for one advertisement, mentioned the existence of actors in the
Quaker city. The comedians played two seasons in New York, from
March, 1750, to July, 1751. [11]

The origin of this company, led by Walter Murray and Thomas
Kean, is unknown, but the hypothesis is tenable that it was composed
in part of players from the West Indies who had come north to try

---

wrote that "Philadelphia did not have a playhouse until 1749." *The Charleston
Stage in the Eighteenth Century,* p. 7.

[9] Watson, *Annals of Phila.,* I, 101–2, testimony of Robert Venable.

[10] John Smith, son-in-law of James Logan, agent of William Penn, wrote in
his manuscript diary, in the volume covering the period from Third month, 20th,
1749, to Tenth month, 19th, 1749:

"6 mo. [August] 22.3. Jos: Morris & I happened in at Peacock Biggers, &
drank Tea there & his daughter being one of the Company who were going to
hear the Tragedy of Cato acted it Occasioned some Conversation in w'ch I Expressed my sorrow that any thing of the kind was encouraged."

This quotation is furnished by Dr. A. C. Myers, who has had access to the
privately owned manuscript.

[11] For this and other information as to their New York performances, see
Odell, I, 32–43.

their fortunes, as David Douglass and the nucleus of the American Company were to do ten years later. We know that a theatrical troupe which had been in Jamaica in 1745 was broken up in 1749.[12] The company in Philadelphia was professional (Dunlap to the contrary), though it recruited new blood—we know that a Nancy George, called "Gouge" by a negro servant decades later,[13] joined the players, though "many fell out" with her for so doing. The name of this one actress, Nancy George, of one play, *Cato,* of the theatre, in Plumsted's warehouse, and the dates August 22/3, 1749, and January 8, 1750, are, with the newspaper notice in March, our only definite knowledge of this early season. However, we know the names of some of the actors and some of the plays given by the Murray and Kean company in New York, where the papers were more informative. The plays known to have been given there were *The Beaux' Stratagem, The Beggar's Opera, A Bold Stroke for a Wife, The Busy Body, Cato, The Committee, The Distrest Mother, The Fair Penitent, George Barnwell, Love for Love, The Orphan, The Recruiting Officer, Richard III, Sir Harry Wildair,* and *The Spanish Fryar.* The known actors were the managers, Walter Murray and Thomas Kean, and Nancy George, Jago, Mrs. Leigh, Mr. Marks, Mr. Moore, Master Dicky Murray, Mrs. ("Widow") and Miss Osborne, Mr. Scott, Mr. Taylor, John Tremaine, and Charles Somerset Woodham.

With the appearance of this, the first theatrical troupe in America of which we have any detailed knowledge, the curtain hiding Philadelphia's stage, which had shed a little gleam through the peephole in 1723 and 1724, began slowly to rise.

THE COMEDIANS FROM LONDON

By 1754, when Hallam's "Company of Comedians from London" came to Philadelphia, the curtain was well up. The story of this adventurous troupe has often been told.[14] It originated in London, in the imagination of William Hallam, an actor-manager, who organized and equipped for America a company headed by his brother and sister-

[12] Odell, I, 69.

[13] Watson, *op. cit.*

[14] See Dunlap, Chaps. I and II, for an early and somewhat romanticized account, and Odell, I, 50–57, for scholarly corrections.

in-law, Mr. and Mrs. Lewis Hallam, he himself staying in London. The company was organized on a joint-stock or "sharing" basis, each of the twelve actors having one of eighteen shares, Lewis Hallam having two more for his services as manager and the work of his three children, and the remaining four shares being "assigned to the property"—that is, to the Hallam brothers for the use of their capital. (The old sharing system, modified by the introduction of salaried actors, remained in force till 1794.) Before the company left England, a number of plays were *"cast* and *put in study"*: Dunlap [15] records *The Merchant of Venice, The Fair Penitent, The Beaux' Stratagem, Jane Shore, The Recruiting Officer, Richard III, The Careless Husband, The Constant Couple, Hamlet, Othello, Theodosius, The Provoked Husband, Tamerlane, The Inconstant, Woman's Riddle, The Suspicious Husband, The Conscious Lovers, George Barnwell,* and *The Twin Rivals,* with the farces of *Miss in her Teens, The Mock Doctor, The Devil to Pay, Hob in the Well, Damon and Phillida, The Anatomist,* and the pantomime, *Harlequin Collector.* Thus equipped, the comedians set sail for America in *The Charming Sally* and arrived at York River, Virginia, on June 28, 1752. They opened in Williamsburg with *The Merchant of Venice,* and after a short season there and "wanderings through the southern commonwealth," [16] played in New York from September, 1753, to March, 1754.

While in New York, Dunlap tells us, Mr. Hallam was visited by "several gentlemen from Philadelphia" who urged him to bring the company to the Quaker city, and "pledged themselves for the success notwithstanding any opposition from the followers of Penn." Hallam sent Malone, heavy tragedian, to Philadelphia, but Malone found the Quakers too much for him, and sent for the manager. On his arrival Hallam "found the city of brotherly love and passive peace divided into two hostile factions, as violent as the green and red of Constantinople." Petitions and counter-petitions were presented to Governor Hamilton, who "gave permission to open a theatre and cause twenty-four plays with their attendant afterpieces to be performed, on condition that they 'offered nothing indecent and immoral,' and performed one night for the benefit of the city"—after having given adequate security for debts.[17]

[15] Dunlap's source was the verbal testimony of Lewis Hallam the Younger.
[16] Odell, I, 55.
[17] Dunlap, 15–17. See also allusion by "Y. Z." in the *Pa. Gazette,* March 26,

The Comedians from London opened on April 15 with *The Fair Penitent* and *Miss in her Teens,* and played on Mondays, Wednesdays, and Fridays till June 24, when the season closed with *The Provoked Husband* and the sprightly and popular *Miss in her Teens.* Governor Hamilton had granted "permission" for six additional nights,[18] so that in all, thirty performances were given, of which the newspapers and an extant playbill give record of only six, with five casts. It is interesting to note that of the six known plays of 1754, four were still being given in the city at the end of the century: *Tamerlane* appeared in 1795, *The Provoked Husband* in 1796, *The Fair Penitent* in 1798, and *The Gamester* in 1799; the pantomime, *Harlequin Collector,* was played in every Philadelphia season for the next fifteen years after 1754, the ballad-opera of *Flora, or Hob in the Well,* was still being given in 1796, and *Miss in her Teens* in the last year of the century.

The New Theatre in Water Street, at which the comedians appeared, was in William Plumsted's warehouse, which had housed the Murray and Kean players of 1749–50. This lofty building of "old-fashioned party-coloured or black glazed brick" [19] was fitted out with a gallery, pit, and stage, and was probably a much better theatre than the term "warehouse" would suggest; it was still standing in 1849. The company had brought new stage scenery and properties with it from England, "entirely new, extremely rich, and finished in the highest Taste." [20] A seat in the boxes cost six shillings, in the pit, four shillings, and in the gallery, two shillings sixpence. The performances began at seven o'clock, for the bills included a full-length play, an afterpiece of farce, pantomime, or ballad-opera, and often singing and dancing.

The leading actress, both in tragedy and comedy, was the "Queen-Mother" of the American stage, Mrs. Lewis Hallam (later Mrs.

1754, to the "express Conditions of the Permission lately granted." The fact that no record of the permission is to be found in *The Minutes of the Provincial Council, The Pennsylvania Archives,* or the *Votes of the Assembly* of this period has no significance, as there was no law against acting, and hence the governor's permission was simply a favorable gesture. For some hint of the bitter popular controversy, see, e. g., letters in the *Pa. Gaz.* for March 9 and 26, 1754. The verbal attacks on the stage in this early period were vitriolic.

[18] Durang, Series I, Chap. IX. The season included thirty-one playing nights, but no play was given on June 17.

[19] Durang, Series I, Chap. IV.

[20] P. L. Ford, *Washington and the Theatre,* p. 10, quoting the *Va. Gazette* of June 12, 1752.

David Douglass) ; [21] Rigby was the leading tragedian and light comedian, "a well bred professional man; and young [Lewis] Hallam [then a boy of fourteen playing servants] . . . said that he was indebted to Rigby for much valuable instruction in acting." [22] Malone was the heavy tragedian; Singleton, a light comedian; Mrs. Adcock played the walking ladies and smart chambermaids, "it is said with credit, and was a favorite"; [22] Miss Hallam took the girls, and Mrs. Becceley was the soubrette.[23]

Only the imagination and the extremities of research can attempt anything like a full reconstruction of the audiences in this early season, but it must have been a brilliant crowd (winnowed of Quaker drabness) of those to whom the arts, the amusements, and the beauty of life were important. We can feel quite sure, for example, that in the audiences were William Plumsted, who furnished the theatre, Provost William Smith, young Francis Hopkinson—the teacher and student worked on a play at the College two years later—and Thomas Godfrey. One can risk being more exact, and say that Godfrey, the young poet who was to write *The Prince of Parthia* (the first American play to be produced professionally) for the actors when they returned in 1759, was probably at the theatre on June 10, and heard Clarkson, as Omar in *Tamerlane,* call Tamerlane a "petty prince of Parthia." The produc-

[21] As there is apt to be confusion among the various Hallams, it is wise to differentiate them. Lewis Hallam the Elder, manager in 1754, never returned to the city, while his son, Lewis Hallam the Younger, became a leading actor and manager, appearing in the city as late as 1794, and again in the nineteenth century. Another son, Adam, played in 1759 (and probably in 1754), but is not important. A Master Hallam, child of Lewis the Younger, appeared in 1767. He may have been but probably was not Marvin Hallam, also son of Lewis the Younger, who played in 1794.

The Mrs. Lewis Hallam of 1754 was the Mrs. David Douglass of 1759 and later. Her daughter, Miss Hallam (whom Seilhamer, I, 144, calls Helen—the Christian name does not appear in the published Williamsburg, New York, or Philadelphia casts) did not appear after 1754, unless she was (as is unlikely) the Miss Nancy Hallam whose name appears only in 1759. A niece of Mrs. Hallam-Douglass, Miss Sarah Hallam, was a leading actress from 1766 to 1773. Miss Tuke, whose name first appears in 1789, married Lewis Hallam the Younger, and played here as Mrs. Hallam in the fall of 1794. The dates refer to the Philadelphia stage.

[22] Durang, Series I, Chap. II.

[23] For a complete list of the known actors and plays of this and every other season in Philadelphia during the eighteenth century, see the *Day Book* under the last playing date of the season.

tion of *The Careless Husband* and *Harlequin Collector* on June 19 was for the benefit of the Charity School which was to grow into the University of Pennsylvania. "Upwards of an Hundred Pounds" [24] was received by the trustees, it would seem in opposition to the desires of those who wished to protect the hems of their garments from the stage-players. Many prologues and epilogues [25] which have survived (because the newspapers were apparently more interested in them than in the plays and players) bear eloquent testimony, both solemn and sprightly, to the opposition the theatre was encountering, and to the support given it by the friends of the drama.

A prologue written by Francis Hopkinson for the opening of the Theatre on Society Hill next season [26] is typical of the more quietly serious verse. In form it is sixteen conventionally rigid iambic pentameter couplets; in content it is a plea that the stage may be tolerated and enjoyed for its moral influence as a school of virtue:

A PROLOGUE

Spoken by Mr. LEWIS HALLAM, at the opening of a Theatre at Philadelphia.

> To bid reviving virtue raise her head,
> And far abroad her heav'nly influence shed;
> The soul by bright examples to inspire,
> And kindle in each breast celestial fire:
> For injur'd innocence to waken fear;
> For suff'ring virtue swell the gen'rous tear;
> Vice to expose in each assum'd disguise,
> And bid the mist to vanish from your eyes,
> With keener passion, that you may detest
> Her hellish form, howe'er like virtue drest:
> The muse to cherish, genius to inspire,
> Bid fancy stretch the wing, and wit take fire—
> For these we come—for these erect our stage,
> And show the manners of each clime and age:
> For these we come—oh! may your smiles attend
> The pleasing task, and all our toils befriend.
> —Away ye senseless, ye whom nought can move,
> Vice to abhor, or virtue to approve;

[24] MS Minutes of the Board of Trustees of the College of Philadelphia for August 13, 1754.

[25] See *Pa. Gazette,* April 25, June 27.

[26] June 25, 1759. See note 40 on page 16.

Whose souls could ne'er enjoy the thought sublime,
Whose ears ne'er taste the muses' flowing rhime.

But ye whose breasts the pow'rs of softness know,
Who long have learnt to feel another's woe;
Nor blush to heave the sympathetic sigh,
Or drop the pious tear from pity's eye;
Attend our work, and may you ever find
Something to please and to improve the mind:
That as each diff'rent flow'r that decks the field
Does to the bee mellifluous sweetness yield:
So may each scene some useful moral show;
From each performance sweet instruction flow.
Such is our aim—your kind assent we ask,
That once obtain'd, we glory in the task.

THE FIRST AMERICAN COLLEGE PLAY

The comedians left the city after June 24, 1754, but their influence remained. In January 1757, during the Christmas holidays, the students at the College of Philadelphia produced a number of times *The Masque of Alfred the Great,* altered for use in the College by that admirable teacher, Provost William Smith: [27] the first drama at least partly American which has survived. Part of the prologue was spoken by W. Hamilton; S. Chew finished the prologue and acted the Danish King; and Jacob Duché took the part of Alfred and recited the epilogue. There is good reason to believe that Francis Hopkinson accompanied the songs, at least one of which he wrote, on the harpsichord.[28]

From the point of view of stage history, perhaps the most interesting part of the production was the dramatized criticism of the then prevalent custom of reciting prologues and epilogues whose spirit clashed with the play. While the overture was being played, "W. Hamilton, *entering hastily and interrupting the music,* began to speak a comedy overture." He was just getting in good breath when "Mr. S. Chew . . . enters hastily in a Students Garb, and driving him off speaks the Remainder *," which was fittingly serious. The asterisk called attention to the point: " * As the whole Piece is grave and moral, these lines

[27] See Quinn, *History of the American Stage from the Beginning to the Civil War,* p. 52; and also his "The First American College Play," *General Magazine,* Vol. XXVIII, 313–316 (April, 1926), for more recent light. For the contemporary account see *Pa. Gazette,* Jan. 20, 27, and Feb. 3, 10, 1757.

[28] O. G. Sonneck, *Francis Hopkinson,* p. 40.

in the Beginning were only introduced to give us an opportunity of disapproving such lighter Strains as on such Occasions serve too commonly to wipe off the virtuous Impression, which the chaste and sober Drama would otherwise leave on the Mind." This might well be called the first serious criticism of the theatre published in Philadelphia. The play was very well received, the young gentlemen meeting with applause "from crouded and discerning Audiences, during the several Nights of its Representation."

After this ambitious beginning, the students at the College of Philadelphia frequently gave dialogues at Commencement, though evidently none was quite so ambitious as *The Masque of Alfred*. We have record of six dialogues in the 1760's, two in the '70's, and one in 1790.

DOUGLASS AND THE THEATRE ON SOCIETY HILL

The Comedians from London had gone to the West Indies after their Philadelphia season of 1754, where they found a number of other actors, including David Douglass and Owen Morris. Lewis Hallam the Elder died soon after, and his widow became Mrs. David Douglass. A new company was formed, which, headed by Douglass, who was to be the most important theatrical manager in colonial America, came to the northern colonies in 1758. In New York it met with dogged antagonism, but succeeded in being allowed to play for thirteen nights between December 28, 1758, and February 7, 1759.[29] Then the company came to Philadelphia, where it enjoyed a brilliant season of over six months, from June 25 to December 28, 1759, presenting about eighty plays (not counting afterpieces) of which we have record of twenty-eight, including five by Shakespeare.

David Douglass, the new manager, appears from all accounts to have been a man of real ability, handling the theatre, the actors, and the public in a difficult period with a skill which approached genius, especially when compared with the botch his stepson and some others made of a less difficult task after the Revolution. Alexander Graydon, who had no connection with the theatre, and cared for words, called him "rather a decent than a shining actor, a man of sense and discretion." [30] His wife, earlier Mrs. Hallam, was still the leading lady of the company (though in a few more years she was to yield most of her youthful rôles), and

[29] Odell, I, 76–78.
[30] *Memoirs of a Life,* 76.

his stepson, Lewis Hallam, no longer called "the Younger," had now become at nineteen the leading juvenile actor in America, attempting all but the most mature rôles. Mr. Harman took the heavy leads and a various line of other parts, sharing honors with Lewis Hallam, as the very capable Mrs. Harman—a granddaughter of Colley Cibber—did to a lesser degree with Mrs. Douglass. Owen Morris took many of Malone's rôles, especially in low comedy. For a long time he was the comic idol of the Southwark gods, and as "Old Morris" was still playing in Philadelphia at the close of the century. The company was small and doubling was frequent. The only important addition as the season went on was a Mr. Palmer, whose name appeared for the first time on December 1, when he played Macbeth. The curious likelihood is that he was John Palmer the Younger, who "from 1761 to 1798 . . . was on the London stage, one of the best general actors it ever had." [31] John Palmer "had a good figure and finely cut features, a careless and easy going elegance of bearing, and the sort of insinuating amiability that rings a trifle false." [32] Before his London advent in 1761, "he had been told to go for a soldier. . . . He 'strolled,' struggled, starved," [31] and, I conjecture, came to America as a soldier, persuaded Douglass to let him appear in leading rôles (London later knew him as "Plausible Jack") ; and certainly *a* Mr. Palmer took a benefit as Romeo in Philadelphia on December 21.

This happened in the Theatre on Society Hill, which Douglass had, on April 5, 1759, got permission to build and act in. The theatre stood at Vernon and Cedar Streets, in Southwark, just across the line from the city. Plumsted's warehouse, which had housed the New Theatre in Water Street of 1754, was still standing, but Douglass' permit—and perhaps his sagacity, following an unfortunate experience in New York with civic authority—required that the company "Act without the bounds of the city." The Theatre on Society Hill was built and furnished by two men with curiously reduplicative names, Alexander Alexander erecting "a large building for the purpose" costing "£300 & upwards," and William Williams painting "a new set of scenes for the said theatre" which came to over £100. [33] Beyond the cost, little is known about the Theatre on Society Hill. Watson [34] says that it "was

[31] Doran, *Annals of the English Stage*, III, 101–4.
[32] Karl Mantzius, *A History of Theatrical Art*, VI, 14.
[33] *Pa. Archives*, III, 659–660.
[34] *Annals*, I, 472.

constructed of wood," but as at least seven other statements in the same paragraph are mistaken, this may not be the last word. The proprietor in 1930 of one of the three houses later built on the site said, on the basis of family tradition, that a brick wall running through the three houses was part of the old proscenium arch. If it was, the theatre was hardly of wood; yet a theatre with such a brick proscenium wall must have been at least comparable with the Theatre in Southwark, which Douglass saw fit to build when he returned to the city in 1766. If the Theatre on Society Hill was so well built in 1759 that its brick proscenium arch was standing in 1930, why was another theatre built next season? And if it was simply a soon-discarded wooden shanty, what explains the curious present brick wall? Of course, one guess is that the theatre was too small to hold the crowds that tried to get in. At any rate, it had a pit, a gallery, and boxes, and the prices were advanced to seven shillings sixpence, five, and three shillings, where they remained till after the Revolution. As far as we know, the Theatre on Society Hill was not used after 1759; but brick or wood, large or small, it housed one brilliant season.

Douglass had carefully got permission to play before starting his theatre, but the sight of the playhouse rising toward the sky down in Southwark roused the enemy, and the war for a prohibition of the drama, in abeyance since 1713, broke out afresh. Petitions beseeching "the House to frame and present to the Governor, for his Assent, a Bill to prohibit such ensnaring and irreligious Entertainments" [35] were presented by the Quakers, the Presbyterians,[36] the Lutherans,[37] and the Baptists [37] in quick order. In a very few days the Assembly drew up a bill "to prevent the Exhibition of theatrical Entertainments" and rushed it to the Governor. Governor Denny conferred with his council, some of whom "observed, that the Prohibition of plays was a most unreasonable restraint . . . from taking innocent Diversions," [38] and finally effected a wily compromise. He sent the law back so amended that it would not go into effect until the following year (January 1, 1760), thus giving the actors a clear six months. If the Assembly wanted any law, it was forced to accept this, though its chief object—to prohibit the use of the Theatre on Society Hill—was defeated. The law was passed

[35] *Votes of the Assembly,* May 22, 1759.
[36] *Ibid.,* May 23.
[37] *Ibid.,* May 26.
[38] *Minutes of the Provincial Council,* VIII, 339–40.

on June 20, and, as the canny Governor doubtless foresaw, was repealed by the King in Council the next year.

The opponents of the theatre were of course not silenced. One nameless upholder of virtue insisted on printing his belief that "the Playhouse, not only when some very prophane Play is on the Stage, but in its daily, common Entertainment, is as certainly the House of the Devil, as the Church is the House of God." [39]

But happily there were other beliefs. Francis Hopkinson wrote the prologue (quoted above) and one epilogue [40] for the production of *Tamerlane* which, on June 25, opened the Theatre, and with other "Gentlemen of this City" promoted a benefit "towards the raising a Fund for purchasing an Organ to the College-Hall in this City, and instructing the Charity Children in Psalmody" on December 27, when he quite probably played with the others in a concert "Before the Play and between the Acts," [41] and for which he certainly wrote a "Prologue in Praise of Music," spoken by Lewis Hallam. [42] His friend Thomas Godfrey, then temporarily in Wilmington, North Carolina, worked feverishly in an attempt to finish his blank-verse tragedy, *The Prince of Parthia,* so that Douglass' company could play it before they left Philadelphia. [43] *The Prince of Parthia* arrived too late for production this season, but was in time to be the first American drama produced when the American Company played it at the Theatre in Southwark on April 24, 1767—after its talented author had died.

The newspapers, published on Thursday, usually announced only the play for the following Friday. The announcements repeatedly said that Monday, Wednesday, and Friday were the "Days of Playing," as they continued to be, with a few exceptions, throughout the century, so we

---

[39] *Pa. Gazette,* August 30, 1759.

[40] They are included in his *Miscellaneous Essays and Occasional Writings,* Phila., 1792, III, Part 2, 50–53. There might be some doubt that the prologue was written for this particular opening, as the heading says only "A Prologue spoken by MR. LEWIS HALLAM, at the opening of a Theatre at Philadelphia," but as the epilogue given immediately after is entitled, "Epilogue for Tamerlane, Spoken by Mrs. Douglass," no reasonable doubt remains.

[41] A scrupulous scholar, Sonneck, *Francis Hopkinson,* p. 41, has no doubt of Hopkinson's participation.

[42] Hopkinson, *Miscellaneous Essays,* etc., III, Part 2, 54–56.

[43] N. Evans, Preface to Godfrey's *Juvenile Poems on Various Subjects, with the Prince of Parthia,* p. v, and Smith's letter used as postscript to the preface, p. xix.

know that our record of thirty performances is only about one-third complete. But that partial record shows that drama-loving Philadelphia was offered for the first known time *Hamlet, Lear, Richard III, Macbeth,* and *Romeo and Juliet,* as well as (for example) *The Beggar's Opera, The Recruiting Officer, The Drummer,* and *The Suspicious Husband.* Or one could have received edification—as the advertisements were careful to point out—from the Rev. Mr. Home's *Douglas,* or Lillo's lugubrious *George Barnwell.* For more frivolous amusement a number of new farces were offered, such as *Lethe, The Lying Valet,* and *The Virgin Unmasked.* The excellent season closed on December 24, when *Hamlet* was repeated for the benefit of the Pennsylvania Hospital. After the players had gone, the Managers of the Hospital felt called upon to say (though they had accepted the money, as their constitution, part of which they published, required) that the play had been given "without the consent of the said managers." [44] One of course does not doubt such an explicit statement, but, remembering that two of the hospital's managers,[45] Thomas Gordon and Evan Morgan, had been selling tickets for that last production of *Hamlet,*[46] one reads the colonial paper intelligently.

THE AMERICAN COMPANY AND THE THEATRE IN SOUTHWARK

Douglass and his company, leaving Philadelphia at the end of 1759, did not return till 1766. They spent their time till April, 1762, strolling in the colonies, playing at Annapolis, Williamsburg, Charleston, Providence, and New York, and then left the mainland for four years, probably going to the West Indies.[47] When they came back north in 1766, it was with the definite intention of making their home in the colonies, an intention thwarted only by the Revolutionary War. They now called themselves "The American Company" and built in Philadelphia a permanent theatre.

Just when in 1766 they came to Philadelphia is not clear. Durang [48] and Seilhamer [49] agree in saying that their first performance was on

[44] *Pa. Gazette,* Jan. 10, 1760.
[45] T. G. Morton, *The History of the Pennsylvania Hospital,* 405–6.
[46] *Pa. Gazette,* Dec. 27, 1759.
[47] Seilhamer, I, 153.
[48] Series I, Chap. VII.
[49] I, 153.

November 21.[50] However, the *Pennsylvania Journal* for November 6 advertised performances for November 12 and 14, and next week's *Journal,* for November 17 and 19. Furthermore, the advertisements of November 6 and 13 made no mention of the performances as opening the theatre, and there was no mention at all of the customary occasional prologue and epilogue. Accordingly, it seems quite possible that the Theatre in Southwark had been opened even before November 12, 1766. It is even possible that the players had arrived in the spring and opened the Theatre on Society Hill, which for some unknown reason they had abandoned. As early as June 27 the Quakers had "with real concern, heard that a Company of Stage Players are lately arrived in this City," [51] and of course prayed for the prohibition of "ensnaring and irreligious entertainments." Four days later, "E. F." wrote to the *Pennsylvania Journal* a letter which concluded with the blasting indictment (whose fearful irony is quite lost out of its context): "They forsooth are going to build a Playhouse at Philadelphia." Another letter (published in the *Gazette* for July 31) remarked bitterly the infatuation of those who "give encouragement to a Sett of strolling Comedians . . . lawless vagrants. . . . I suppose they are the same Sett of Gentry who attempted to exhibit in New York, and who were drove thence with righteous Indignation by the Inhabitants." This season heard a large number of similar tirades from those who were neither followers of the gentle Francis nor yet believers in letting the grain grow till the harvest.[52]

The playhouse whose erection was at least in part causing such an outcry was the New Theatre in Southwark,[53] built just outside the city limits, as the Theatre on Society Hill had been. "The lot which was selected for the theatre was in South [then Cedar] street, between Fourth and Fifth streets, at the corner of a small street, since called Apollo [later Charles, now Leithgow Street] in consequence of a minor

[50] Dunlap, p. 22, says that Douglass built and opened the Southwark Theatre in 1760. His statement, unsupported by any evidence or probability, deserves no further mention.

[51] The MS of their petition is in The Hist. Soc. of Pa.

[52] See, e. g., *Pa. Gazette,* Feb. 5, Mar. 12, Apr. 30, July 2, 1767; *Pa. Journal,* Feb. 19, Mar. 5; *Pa. Chronicle,* Feb. 9 (sequor), Feb. 23, Apr. 6, 1767.

[53] Interestingly enough, Southwark "was named after Southwark in London," to which a number of the Elizabethan theatres had gone to escape the city limits. It was incorporated as part of Philadelphia in 1794. A. H. Espenshade, *Pennsylvania Place Names,* p. 33.

theatre which was erected there in 1811. . . . On this lot [54] Douglass erected [a] large frame building" [55] with brick walls for its first story. "The framework was painted red, the prevailing color" for the theatres throughout the country. It "was well adapted for theatrical representations," Dunlap says,[56] and was ugly—"no ornament to the city"—in its physical appearance. Watson quotes "my friend Lang Syne" [57] as saying of it (as it was twenty years later), "The building, compared with the new houses, was an ugly, ill-contrived affair outside and inside. The stage lighted by plain oil lamps without glasses. The view from the boxes was intercepted by large square wooden pillars supporting the upper tier and roof. It was contended by many, at the time, that the front bench in the gallery was the best seat for a fair view of the whole stage." The New Theatre in Southwark was plain and lacked outward charm, but it was a substantial, permanent theatre, in use for over half a century (though not important after 1794), and holds a place of high honor in theatrical history.

Douglass had brought to Philadelphia a company largely new, with the famous Miss Cheer as leading woman. Miss Wainwright and Mr. Woolls, both singers, and Miss Sarah Hallam, later leading actress, were also important additions to the troupe. Lewis Hallam was still the leading man, now without the competition of Mr. Harman. One of the playgoers of the period, Graydon, has left in his *Memoirs* [58] an interesting criticism of the troupe. He says that Lewis Hallam, "then in full culmination, was the Roscius of the theatre. As the dramatic heroes were all *his* without a competitor, so the heroines were the exclusive property of Miss Cheer, who was deemed an admirable performer. The singing department was supplied and supported by the voices of Wools and Miss Wainwright, said to have been pupils of doctor Arne; while in the tremulous drawle of the old man, in low jest and buffoonery, Morris, thence the minion of the gallery, stood first and unrivalled. As for the Tomlinsons, the Walls, the Allens, &c. they were your Bonifaces, your Jessamys, your Mock Doctors, and what not. On the female side, Mrs. Douglass was a respectable, matron-like dame, stately

---

[54] Durang says, Series I, Chap. XVIII, that Douglass bought it from Richard Willing.

[55] Durang, Series I, Chap. VI.

[56] p. 22.

[57] *Annals,* I, 473.

[58] pp. 76–78.

or querulous as occasion required, a very good Gertrude, a truly appropriate lady Randolph with her white handkerchief and her weeds. . . . Mrs. Harman bore away the palm as a duenna, and Miss Wainwright as a chambermaid. Although these were among the principal performers at first, the Company was from time to time essentially improved by additions: Among these, the Miss Storers, Miss Hallam and Mr. Henry, were valuable acquisitions; as was also a Mr. Goodman, who had read law in Philadelphia with Mr. Ross. . . .

"Whether there may be any room for comparison between these . . . and the performers of the present day [1811], I venture not to say. Nothing is more subject to fashion than the style of public exhibitions. . . . I cannot but say, however, that in my opinion, the old company acquitted themselves with most animation and glee—they were a passable set of comedians."

The New Theatre in Southwark was opened at least by November 14, 1766, and the American Company played till July 6, 1767. As a new paper, the *Pennsylvania Chronicle,* printed on Mondays, appeared on and after January 26, 1767, we have after that date papers on Monday and Thursday, and hence usually record of two of the three weekly performances. For the entire season of about a hundred nights, we know definitely of fifty-nine bills, with forty different full-length plays, twenty-six of the plays new to the record in Philadelphia.

The most important historical events of the season were the announcement of Forrest's *The Disappointment* and the production of Godfrey's *The Prince of Parthia.* Though Forrest's comic opera had the honor of being the first American play announced for production (on April 20), it was happily withdrawn (as containing "personal reflections . . . unfit for the stage") just in time to give a superior play, *The Prince of Parthia,* the honor of being the first American drama produced on the stage. Unfortunately the actual cast for *The Prince of Parthia* was not published, though the names of the principal actors were. Seilhamer [59] has already suggested a cast which is probably about as close to the fact as we will get:

Artabanes	Mr. Douglass	Phraates	Mr. Greville
Vardanes	Mr. Tomlinson	Bethas	Mr. Morris
Arsaces	Mr. Hallam	Thermusa	Mrs. Douglass
Gotarzes	Mr. Wall	Evanthe	Miss Cheer

[59] I, 194.

Barzaphernes........	Mr. Allyn	Cleone......	Miss Wainwright
Lysias.........	Mr. Broadbelt	Edessa..........	Mrs. Morris

Among the other important productions new to the city were *Cymbeline* and *The Merchant of Venice, All for Love, The Beaux' Stratagem, The Conscious Lovers, Jane Shore, Love for Love* (with its "Luxuriances" prudently "cropped"), *Catherine and Petruchio*—Garrick's two-act farce from *The Taming of the Shrew*—and Thomson's *Coriolanus. Hamlet, Lear, Macbeth, Richard III,* and *Romeo and Juliet,* among others, reappeared.

Musical entertainments—"operas" and "ballad-operas"—were growing in popularity, a growth which continued throughout the century. A capable actor in those days had to be able to sing as well as act, and two of the new performers, Miss Wainwright and Mr. Woolls, were primarily vocalists. The production [60] of Bickerstaff's opera, *Love in a Village,* called forth the first newspaper theatrical criticism in Philadelphia, in the form of a letter by a "gentleman contributor" to the *Pennsylvania Gazette:*

As the Practice prevails in our Mother Country, I hope you will have no objections against inserting in your paper the observations that any gentleman may decently make concerning the Actors in our little Theatre here.

I do not relie wholly upon my own delicacy of Judgment in the following Remarks, for I have gathered and compared the Sentiments of many others, who have had good opportunities of improving their taste of both Plays and Players. The Practice of altering the Author's Expressions is so universally condemned by all Men of Sense, and leaves no excuse for the Vanity or Neglect of the Actor; and I hope this little Hint will be sufficient to guard our Actors against anything of the like Nature for the future; for they ought to consider that one indecent, unguarded, ill judged Expression, will do them inconceivable Mischief in this Country, and that no Advantage can arise from taking such a Liberty, but if they clearly avoid this Rock, and are prudent in the Choice of Plays, the rational Entertainment must, and will succeed, agreeable to the highest Wishes of those who are concerned in it.

I am sorry Mr. Hallam, who is genteel in his Person and Actions, could not take Copy from the inimitable Garrick, and speak plain English, whenever he assumes a character that may be supposed to understand the Language. There is no necessity of destroying the least articulate Beauty of Language, thro' Fury, Eagerness, or Passion;

[60] Sometime before the first newspaper announcement. See Jan. 22, 1767, for critical mention, and March 19, 1767, for the first announcement.

Miss Cheer never loses the sweetest Accent, or faulters in the Clearness of Expression, from any or all those Causes, though I believe she is equally delicate, and capable of feeling the Force of Passion.

I am not alone, when I pronounce her one of the best Players in the Empire; she appears to me, from that Ease of Behaviour which always shines through every Action, to have been much among People of Fashion, for she well fits the highest Character she ever assumes.

I must beg leave to inform the Public, that the pleasing LOVE IN A VILLAGE is done here beyond expectation, and must give real Delight to every Person void of Ill-Nature. . . . Miss Wainwright is a very good Singer, and her Action exceeds the famous Miss Brent. Mr. Hallam exceeds everything in the Character of Hodge; and Mr. Woolls almost equals Beard in Hawthorn. Miss Hallam deserves universal Applause and Encouragement. I could wish to see the House better filled whenever this justly applauded Entertainment is exhibited.

The small audiences during the winter are again referred to in a notice in the *Pennsylvania Journal* of January 8, 1767:

The Director of the Theatre begs leave to assure the Town that, for the future, no Audience, be it ever so small, will be disappointed, upon any account whatsoever, and that the Play advertised will be certainly performed.

One can easily imagine that on snowy nights in January Philadelphians may have preferred the warmth of their own firesides to a tramp across unpaved lanes to the wooden theatre.

The critical game having been started, a writer in the *Gazette* for January 29 continued it, mentioning again Hallam's bad habit of seeming "to suck in, or at least not to utter the first letters of the words he speaks," and the "justly celebrated and much admired Miss Cheer." From this time on there were occasional criticisms in the papers, though they did not become frequent till after the Revolution.

The war against the theatre was still on, and on February 17, 1767, "A Remonstrance from a Great Number of the Inhabitants of the City and County of Philadelphia, of several religious denominations, was presented to the House and read." [61] The House was moved to send to Governor John Penn a resolution which "respectfully sheweth" that it did not want the theatre, as too expensive, hurtful of business, and destructive of frugality.[62] But nothing came of it, and it is more pleasant

[61] *Votes of Assembly*, Feb. 17, 1767.
[62] *Ibid.*, Feb. 18.

to notice that there were men who rose in articulate defense of the stage.[63] Probably the most interesting defense was that of a clergyman recently out from England, who had sinned against a young lady's notions by going to the theatre. He [64] took the trouble to publish a thin volume with the delightful title, *True Pleasure, Chearfulness, & Happiness, the Immediate Consequence of* RELIGION *Fully and concisely proved With remarks on the* THEATRE *Addressed to a young Lady in Pennsylvania.* In it he explained his position wisely and irenicly, saying that he intended to continue enjoying the drama, and answering many of the theological and economic arguments against the theatre. "I am ashamed," he wrote, "to combat superstition; but . . . must Shakespeare, the immortal Shakespeare be destroyed—shall Molière be burnt—; shall Plautus, Terence, Euripides . . . be invólved in the horrid conflagration?" [65]

JOHN HENRY AND THE MISSES STORER

The American Company opened the Theatre in Southwark for a short supplementary season in the autumn of 1767, while waiting for the John Street Theatre in New York to be finished. This season extended from October 6 to November 23, with at least twelve different plays presented. Before the "legitimate" season began, Douglass and Hallam opened the theatre (on September 9 and 24) and offered Steven's very popular *Lecture on Heads,* with singing by various members of the company, "accompanied by the Band of his Majesty's Eighteenth Regiment." In the regular season, two plays new to Philadelphia were given: *Venice Preserved* (which has been overpraised as the best romantic tragedy since Shakespeare) and *The Clandestine Marriage.*

Another important event was the first appearance on the continent of John Henry, who at twenty-one [66] had already had a crowded life, and Miss Ann Storer, both "from the theatre in Jamaica." After the Revolution Henry shared the management of the Old American Company

[63] See *Pa. Journal,* Feb. 12, 19, Mar. 12, 1767.

[64] Probably, though the book is anonymous. But certainly if the clergyman did not write it, it was written for him. Published by Wm. and Thos. Bradford, Phila., 1767.

[65] Incidentally, this came seven years before Dr. Cooper's New York prologue, which Seilhamer (I, 323) says was the first time an American clergyman "gave the drama any recognition."

[66] See *Daily Advertiser,* Jan. 10, 1795.

with Hallam. "Tall and commanding in person," Henry must have been "as handsome an Aimwell as ever trod the stage"; [67] he was primarily a comedian. Dunlap tells us [68] that there were originally four Misses Storer with their mother in Jamaica. "Henry married the eldest, but during a voyage from Jamaica, the vessel in which she was a passenger . . . was burnt, and she with it." The other three sisters were Ann (or Nancy), Fanny, and Maria. Ann Storer appeared this season, and was known in the Philadelphia seasons of 1769–70, 1772–73, and 1773 as Mrs. Henry (later she became Mrs. Hogg). Fanny, not of immediate interest to our record, became Mrs. Mechtler, and so appeared here in 1796. Maria Storer, who played in Philadelphia from 1768 to 1773 under that name, became later the last Mrs. John Henry, and so the Philadelphia stage knew her from 1789 (or earlier) to 1793.

AUTUMN, 1768

The American Company went to New York after the fall season of 1767, where it opened the John Street Theatre, a replica of the Southwark. It did not return to Philadelphia till the fall of 1768; the exact date is uncertain. The *Chronicle* for September 19 reported "that the Theatre in Southwark will be opened, *for one Month only,* on Wednesday the 21st Instant, with a Comedy." However, the first announcement I have discovered is for October 4, when the company announced its stay "For one Month only," although the season, once started, extended to January 6, 1769. The advertisements this season were very meager, perhaps, as Seilhamer suggests, because the company was hard pressed for money after meeting with deadening opposition in New York.[69] Only thirteen announcements appeared in as many weeks (and there were papers on two different days), with only eight casts. Miss Maria Storer was the only important addition to the company; Darby, Parker, and Byerley replaced Greville, Malone, and Allyn in minor parts; Miss Wainwright, the singer, did not appear, and Miss Cheer and Lewis Hallam were still the leads.

Six new plays at least were given in this brief season: the rarely seen

[67] Seilhamer, I, 199, says that on this point "it is possible to agree with Dunlap for once."
[68] p. 29.
[69] Seilhamer, I, 234.

King John, Alexander the Great, The Busy Body (very popular to the end of the century), *False Delicacy, The Spanish Fryar,* and *Zara.* On December 9 and 14 Douglass introduced as an added attraction "Two Italian Brothers" who set off "An Elegant Sett of Fireworks," which were so good that the ceiling had to be "opened to carry off the Smoak." Mr. Douglass "with great Pleasure, observed the Satisfaction" which the fireworks gave the audience.

"SUMMER" AND YOUNG MANAGERS

The American Company went to New York in January, and returned in the autumn. In the spring of 1769, while the Theatre in Southwark was dark, the "Lovers of Elocution" were offered the chance to hear, at the Academy and the Assembly Room in Lodge Alley, a number of poems and speeches read, and operas read and their songs sung. The first of these performances came on May 23, when "a person who professes to teach with propriety to read any author in the English language" read Thomson's "Summer," and announced that "Proposals will shortly be published for the reading of Milton's Paradise Lost by subscription." When I first discovered this announcement, I hoped to learn that *Paradise Lost* had been read publicly in Philadelphia, but did not. However, Pope's "Sappho to Phaon," Demosthenes' Seventh Oration, and Voltaire's "Folly on Both Sides" were recited, and *Damon and Phillida, The Beggar's Opera, Love in a Village, The Maid of the Mill* (first act), and *The Musical Lady* were read, and their songs sung—all between May 23 and June 26. This interesting season (the readers and singers anonymous) was the only one of its kind I have discovered in the whole of the eighteenth century, though in the 1790's actors, especially James Fennell, gave readings from plays.

The Theatre in Southwark was opened on August 11, 1769, by Mr. Malone, with the American Company in New York in 1767, who promised that he would "exhibit several PERFORMANCES on the SLACK ROPE in FULL SWING."

The following letter from Manager Douglass, unaddressed, but doubtless to the Governor, John Penn, asking authority to open the theatre for a season, is now in the Shaw Theatre Collection. The mood of the letter is significant of the difficulties the colonial manager had to undergo; and it is significant, too, that in a time of distress the American Company turned to Philadelphia.

Sir

The great Indulgence, your Honour has, so often, been good enough to shew me, while it demands every grateful acknowledgement, a Breast, I hope, not insensible, can possibly entertain, covers me with Shame, when the Situation of our Affairs, make so frequent Applications absolutely necessary.

I had flatter'd myself, that I shou'd not, for a Year to come, at least, have given your Honour any Trouble, but a Disappointment at Carolina, and the recent loss of a great and honour'd Friend and Patron, whose Memory will be ever dear to the American Theatre, has made such a change in our Circumstances, that nothing but an exertion of that Humanity, which you possess in so eminent a Degree, can save us from Destruction.

Let my Situation speak for me, and, with your usual goodness, do not think me too importunate, if I sollicite your Honour for Permission to open the Theatre, for a short Time, this Winter, previous to my going to Annapolis, where I propose spending the Remainder of it.

The Maid of the Mill, the Padlock, and some other Pieces, not perform'd, hitherto, on this Stage, will, I flatter myself, give Your Honour some Entertainment.

I shou'd not have made my application in this Manner, but wou'd have waited on you myself, were not my feelings, upon the Occasion, too great, to permit me to say what I ought.

I shall intrude no farther upon your time, than to assure you, that it is impossible for any Person, among the Numbers who have been the Objects of your Benevolence, to have a more grateful sense of it, than

Sir

Your Honour's most

Obed^t and oblig'd hum. Serv.

DAVID DOUGLASS.

October 5th
1769

The permission was given, and the actors did not make the visit to Annapolis which Douglass mentioned, but stayed in Philadelphia all winter.

The American Company's season did not officially open till November 8. But on September 14 Lewis Hallam and John Henry, managers of the Old American Company after the Revolution, tried their hands as entrepreneurs, and announced at the Southwark a variety performance including the popular *Lecture on Heads,* singing, and a "Camera Obscura," which seems to have been some kind of magic lantern, and was "secured at considerable expence and trouble." Their inducement on September 25 was even more daring, if less mechanical—the young managers cut the prices to five, three, and two shillings! They also dreamed of "an Entertainment every Evening this Week," but admitted in the *Journal* of September 28 that it was "out of their power to fulfill that intention." On September 25 they gave *The Oracle* and *Harlequin Collector,* on September 29 *The Wrangling Lovers* and *The Dwarfs,* and on September 30 *The Oracle* and *The Dwarfs.*

AN ORCHESTRA AND THE GALLERY

On November 8, 1769, the American Company opened what was to be a brilliant season, playing at the Theatre in Southwark till the first of June, 1770. Our record, about three-fifths complete, shows forty-five performances, with thirty-three different full-length plays, thirteen of which were new, and nineteen afterpieces.

The American Company had now become established; it was in Philadelphia an accepted institution. We have no reason to believe that the anti-theatrical party had materially altered its attitude, but the columns of the newspapers for this season are pleasantly free from extravagant diatribes. Indeed, the company was so naturally accepted (according to another of Seilhamer's plausible conjectures) that it did not think it necessary to advertise its casts in the newspapers, so that for this season, though we have fuller knowledge than before as to the plays given, we do not know much about the assignment of parts. So far as we can tell, there was only one addition of any importance to the personnel of the company: Miss Richardson, whose name appears in a handbill for March 30, 1770, happily preserved in the Historical Society of Pennsylvania. It is possible that she was the "young gentlewoman" who played on December 12, 1769. "A young gentleman" appeared on June 1, 1770, who may have been Mr. Goodman, sometime a Philadelphia law student; Durang says [70] that Goodman "probably joined the company in 1770, when at Philadelphia." Miss Sarah Hallam was now the leading actress, Miss Cheer and Miss Wainwright both having left the stage.

The company now apparently had a regular orchestra, as the advertisement for December 1 said, "The Orchestra, on Opera Nights, will be assisted by some musical Persons, who, as they have no View but to contribute to the Entertainment of the Public, certainly claim a Protection from any Manner of Insult." Exactly what form of insult was feared is not clear. Seilhamer evidently assumes [71] that it was the social

[70] Series I, Chap. VIII.
[71] I, 275.

ostracism then supposedly endangering any one who associated with the players. This may have been true, but I find it difficult to believe that David Douglass would have thought his advertisement could have warded the amateur performers from the subtler forms of social insult. It is more likely that he feared trouble might come (perhaps it had already come, as it later came) in a more tangible form from the boys in the gallery, whose delicate sense of the incongruous might easily have been aroused by the spectacle of Philadelphia gentlemen seriously busy at their music in the orchestra pit, a fair target for oranges. It was late in 1769; the not very carefully analyzed notion of "liberty" was arousing the masses; and it is uncomfortably near the truth to realize that Francis Hopkinson, then a young vestryman of Christ Church, perhaps playing a "neat" harpsichord, would have been at a strategic disadvantage by being below, and within range of, the gallery.[72] But one hopes Douglass' advertisement had its effect, and is glad to know that the theatre now had a regular orchestra, even if it occasionally could use assistance.

After December 1 the normal days of playing (for this season only) were Tuesday and Friday, and in November the curtain rose at six; as the days grew longer, the time of opening grew later. A note on February 19 reminds us that we are thinking of the eighteenth century:

A Foot Way is made across the Common, to the Corner of Pine-Street, in Fourth-Street, on which those Ladies who are not provided with Carriages, may come to the House without dirtying their Feet.

Mr. Douglass will be extremely obliged to any Lady or Gentleman who will lend him the Burlesque Opera of the *Dragon of Wantley*.

Among the important new productions were *The Masque of Comus, Julius Caesar, The Merry Wives of Windsor, The Tempest* (in Shadwell's version, with the spectacular *Masque of Neptune and Amphitrite* —of course, all these Shakespearean plays were put through what Odell calls the eighteenth-century filter), *The Good-Natured Man,* and *The Tender Husband.* That charming "opera," *The Padlock,* was also new. "In the *Padlock,*" Dunlap says,[73] "Mr. Hallam was unrivalled to his

---

[72] See Sonneck, *Francis Hopkinson,* p. 50. It is merely possible that Hopkinson was one of the performers, but certain that a gentleman in the orchestra pit ran certain risks. In a later decade half the instruments in the orchestra were broken one night by missiles from the gallery. See, e. g., *General Advertiser,* Oct. 25, 1794.

[73] p. 31.

death, giving the Mungo with a truth derived from study of the negro slave character, which Dibdin the author [of the music] could not have conceived."

1772–1773

After leaving Philadelphia in 1770, the American Company went to the South, not returning to its northern empire till 1772,[74] when it began the last important season in Philadelphia before the Revolution, from October 28, 1772, to March 31,[75] 1773. It was a good season; though we know of only about two-thirds of the performances,[76] our record includes forty-five nights, with thirty-two different plays, ten of which were new. Among the new plays were *King Henry IV*, part one (with Mr. Douglass as Falstaff, Mr. Henry as Prince Hal, and Mr. Hallam as Hotspur), *Othello* (Mr. Hallam, the Moor), *The West Indian,* and *Lionel and Clarissa*. The performance for the first time on any stage of Cockings' *The Conquest of Canada* (which happily is not to be ranked as an American play) was made elaborately, the stage "much crouded with the ARTILLERY, BOATS, &c. necessary for the representation of the piece; and with the Men from both Corps, whose assistance the Commanding Officers are good enough to indulge us with." One hopes the spectacle was grand enough to overpower some of the most pedestrian verse in the language. It ran for three straight nights.

Among the new performers were the second Mrs. Morris, Goodman, the Philadelphia law student (we are sure of his appearance now), and Francis Mentges. The first Mrs. Morris had been drowned in December, 1767; the second, who was still on the Philadelphia stage at the end of the century, was a beautiful, stately, and pretentious woman, at times exceedingly popular. Francis Mentges appeared as a dancer; he was later a fencing master, and rose during the Revolution to be a Lieutenant Colonel, remaining in that rank as Inspector of Militia as

[74] In the American Company's absence, though there was no drama, there were occasional entertainments including *A Lecture on Heads* (*Chronicle,* August 1, 15, 22, 1772; *Journal,* Aug. 12); fireworks (*Chronicle,* Aug. 24, 1772); and "Equestrianism" (*Gazette,* Sept. 26, 1771, *Chronicle,* Aug. 29, Sept. 5, Sept. 12, Nov. 4, 1772.)

[75] The date of the last announcement, though as it says "The last night but one," the last performance was probably on Friday, April 2.

[76] Usually for Monday and Wednesday; this year the *Journal* and *Gazette* were published on Wednesday, leaving the performances of Friday unrecorded.

late as 1788.[77] Lewis Hallam and his cousin Sarah were still the leading performers—both at the height of their fame. Indeed, the company was, in the opinion of a competent judge, of high quality, "equal at least," wrote William Eddis, "to those who sustain the best of your [England's] characters in your most celebrated provincial theatres." [78]

The nuisance from the sons of liberty in the gallery was growing worse. "A most crouded and brilliant Audience" saw *A Word to the Wise* and *The Padlock* on the opening night, and Philo-Theatricus, "upon the Judgment of Gentlemen of undoubted Knowledge and Taste in theatrical Performances," said that Hallam's was "the best Mungo upon the British stage"; [79] but he asked indignantly if constables could not be secured to suppress the "Ruffians in the Gallery, who so frequently interrupted the Performance, committed repeated outrages upon that Part of the Audience who go there really to see the Play, and interrupted the Actors who are doing their best to please them." Perhaps the managers got a constable—the Southwark had one in the 90's; at any rate, no further protest was made in the papers as the season progressed.

THE LAST COLONIAL SEASON

The actors went to New York in April, returning to Philadelphia for a brief appearance—their last before the Revolution—from November 1 to 15, 1773. They had lost one of their most dependable actresses, Mrs. Catherine Maria Harman, granddaughter of Colley Cibber, who had died in New York on May 27. She was "a just actress, possessed much merit in low comedy . . . [and] in private life . . . was sensible, humane, and benevolent." [80] Otherwise the company was unchanged, though Miss Wainwright, who was living in Philadelphia, reappeared. No new plays were given.

In the *Packet* of Monday, November 15, Manager Douglass announced that "the PLAY on Saturday, was by him, really, absolutely, and *bona fide,* intended for the last performance," but that as many had asked for *The West Indian,* and the vessel which was to take the troupe to Carolina had been delayed, they would give one more performance.

---

[77] Graydon's *Memoirs,* 100; *Minutes of the Assembly of Penna.,* March 4, 1788; Seilhamer, III, 142.

[78] Quoted by Odell, I, 173.

[79] *Chronicle,* Oct. 31, 1772.

[80] Odell, I, 166, quoting obituary in *Rivington's Gazette* for June 3, 1773.

Trouble arose in the company over the casting of *The West Indian*. Mr. Goodman had played Major O'Flaherty in the previous season, but the part was announced for Mr. Henry, "being his third appearance in that character," and Mr. Goodman, a Philadelphian, was not cast at all. Parts were sacred property, and apparently Goodman was ready to fight for his rights. The manager felt it necessary to publish this broadside, happily preserved in the Shaw Theatre Collection:

Theatre,
Monday Morning, November 15, 1773.
Mr. Douglass having been informed that there is a Probability of a Disturbance happening in the House this Evening, occasioned by a Dispute that subsists between Mr. Goodman and Mr. Henry, concerning the part of Major O'Flaherty, thinks it a Duty incumbent upon him to do all he can to prevent it, and the only Method that suggests itself to him, is to give up the Play entirely, for this season, for should any Mischief happen, he would think himself accountable for the Consequences.

In a few hours another broadside, also preserved in the Shaw Theatre Collection, was printed:

The Town's Compliments to Mr. Douglass—are sorry that his apprehensions of a Disturbance in the House, should preclude them from the Pleasure they expected this Evening at the Representation of the West-Indian—Therefore desire, nay insist, that the Play shall go forward.

Whether or not *The West Indian* was given, one cannot be certain, though quite probably it was. For Mr. Goodman had another reason for wanting to appear that night. A farewell epilogue, very possibly the one announced for Mr. Hallam, had, so the *Packet* a week later said,[81] been "intended to be spoken by MR. GOODMAN the last night." The mention of "the last night" would indicate that there had been that last night. The epilogue rose to the climax:

Twas then he spoke aloud, this firm decree,
"My sons—be VIRTUOUS, *and my sons—be* FREE."

The Revolution was not far away, and the country was girding its loins for the contest. Douglass took his company to the south; then after a very successful season in Charleston,[82] the company came back north,

[81] Nov. 22, 1773. The epilogue is printed in full.
[82] See Willis, 74.

leaving Charleston in June, and in part at least returning to Philadelphia by September. Mr. Goodman and Mr. Allen (the latter a recent arrival from the Theatre Royal in Edinburgh) announced for September 19 at the Theatre in Southwark "An Attic Evening's Entertainment," composed of recitations and lectures, with an "Introductory Address to the town." Probably others of the company were in the city; Durang says that "At this eventful period the Thespians made a demonstration to act in Philadelphia." [83] But if they played at all, no record has survived.

The Revolution was too near, and the Continental Congress, then in session in Philadelphia, resolved on October 20, 1774, "That we will in our several stations encourage frugality . . . and discountenance and discourage, every species of extravagance and dissipation, especially all horse racing, and all kinds of gaming, cock fighting, exhibition of shews, plays, and other expensive diversions and entertainments." It is important to notice that the reason at this time for discouraging the theatre was not, at least on the surface, a continuation of the earlier opposition to the playhouse, but was a clearing of the social decks for action as the conflict with the mother country approached war. The recommendation of Congress was ratified by Pennsylvania in January of the next year (1775), when the convention for the province of Pennsylvania "Resolved Unanimously, that this convention most heartily approve of the conduct and proceedings of the Continental Congress, [and] That we will faithfully endeavour to carry into execution, the measures of the association entered into, and recommended by them."

COLONIAL RETROSPECT

The curtain was finally down on Philadelphia's, and America's, colonial stage. Of the players in the American Company just before the Revolution, only two, Mrs. Douglass (Hallam), the Queen Mother of that stage, and her son Lewis Hallam, its leading actor, had been with the original Company of Comedians from London. A number of the players never returned, so far as we know, to the city. Just when Mrs. Douglass died is a question complicated by a notice of her death appearing in *Rivington's Gazette* (New York) for September 23, 1773,[84] while she was demonstrably still alive. It is probable that she died in Philadel-

[83] Series I, Chap. IX.
[84] Quoted by Odell, I, 174.

phia in 1774. John North,[85] for many years caretaker of the Theatre in Southwark, said that she died in "a large frame house which stood nearly opposite the South street theatre" (it was a tavern), and that "she was buried in the Presbyterian ground corner of Fourth and Arch streets." Mr. Douglass, the leading theatrical manager in early America, left for Jamaica, married again,[86] and never returned to America, at least as an actor. Miss Sarah Hallam retired from the stage, becoming a teacher of dancing in Virginia.[87] But Lewis Hallam, John Henry and Maria Storer-Henry, Mr. and Mrs. Owen Morris, and Mr. Stephen Woolls were to return after a period of exile to the Philadelphia stage.

The plays given in the colonial city, from the time of *Cato* in August, 1749, to *The West Indian* in November, 1773, represented the best of the British theatre. The repertories of the Comedians from London and the American Company were well chosen, with little dead wood and many plays of real value. Not only in ratio to the number of performances, but in the actual count of good plays in a given season, our colonial theatre compares favorably with, if it does not surpass, the modern professional stage. Thirty-five or forty different plays, most of them quite good, with nearly as many farces, shorter comedies, musical plays, and pantomimes, were not unusual. The Shakespearean plays given before the Revolution may be taken as an index. Though our knowledge is far from complete, the record includes *Hamlet, Lear, Richard III, Macbeth, Romeo and Juliet, Cymbeline, The Merchant of Venice, King John, Julius Caesar, The Merry Wives of Windsor, The Tempest, Henry IV Part One,* and *Othello,* as well as such Shakespearean derivatives as Dryden's *All for Love,* Garrick's *Catherine and Petruchio,* and Thomson's *Coriolanus.*

[85] Quoted by Durang, Chap. XII, Series 1.
[86] Odell, I, 174.
[87] Odell, I, 173.

CHAPTER II

AN INTERLUDE BY MILITARY ACTORS

1776–1778

AND NOW, between the end of the colonial stage and the beginning of the national, there was an interlude—or rather, there were two interludes—by military actors. In Philadelphia the British officers, occupying the city during the winter of 1777–1778, were the players. And just outside the city the American Army, quartered at Valley Forge, improvised a theatre and gave plays during the spring of 1778.

HOWE'S THESPIANS

Shortly after the British had taken Philadelphia and settled down to a winter of gaiety, their officers opened the Theatre in Southwark, organized a company composed of British officers and soldiers' wives, and gave plays. Their first step was to get a staff for the theatre. On December 31, 1777, they advertised in the *Pennsylvania Ledger* that they "Wanted for the Play-house, a PERSON who writes quick, and a legible hand; also, a Person well versed in accounts, to act as Clerk and Vice-Treasurer. Any people that have ever been employed about the Play-House, as carpenters or scene-shifters, may get employment." They apparently secured a Mr. Smith as manager, as they announced later in the season that "Any person having any demands against the Theatre, ares requested to bring in, immediately their accounts to Mr. Smith at the office of the Theatre in Front street." [1]

They had difficulties in getting play-books. On January 3, 1778, the officers wrote to the *Pennsylvania Ledger* that "The COMEDY, called A Wonder or a Woman keeps a Secret is wanted for the use of the Theatre. Any person having it, that will either sell or lend it, is requested to apply to the Printer." John North, caretaker of the Theatre in Southwark, told Durang years later of the scarcity of play-books, and also that "Miss Hyde sang and acted with the British officers during

[1] *Pa. Ledger,* April 29, 1778.

[34]

the war. She belonged to one of the first companies that came here from the West Indies. [?] She sang 'Tally Ho' between the play and the farce. Many of the soldiers' wives helped the officers on the stage. They were generally of no character. They and the officers were about the theatre all day. When any piece was to be rehearsed, they all would flock about the back door, or the side lot." [2]

The leading spirits in this amateur corps were Major André and Captain Delancey. North said that Delancey was an excellent actor, and that André, in spite of his charming personality and other talents, was not. André was the scene painter, and a drop scene of his was part of the scenery of the theatre till the fire of 1821, hanging "about the middle of the third entrance, as called in stage directions. The name of André was inscribed in large black letters on the back of it; thus put, no doubt, on its completion, as is sometimes the custom with scenic artists." [3] It is a grim thought that less than twenty years later (May 14, 1798) *The Death of Major André* was an entertainment at the circus.

Altogether Howe's Thespians gave thirteen performances at the Southwark between January 19 and May 19, 1778, introducing to the city *The Lyar, The Minor,* and *No One's Enemy But His Own,* as well as the new farces, *Duke and No Duke* and *A Trip to Scotland.* Among their announcements is the curious note, in the *Ledger* of January 26:

Gentlemen are earnestly requested not to bribe the Door-keepers. The Foreign Gentleman who slipped a Guinea and a Half into the Hand of the Box-keeper, and forced his way into the House, is desired to send to the office of the Theatre in Front-street, that it may be returned.

Not content with managing the theatre, Major André and Captain Delancey were active in perfecting the chivalric splendor of the *Mischianza,* given on May 18, 1778.[4] Though not strictly dramatic, this spectacular and theatrical pageant in farewell to General Howe, who had been recalled to England, deserves to be mentioned if only for its theatrical exhibition of the old chivalry.

About half past four in the afternoon a grand flotilla of bedecked

---

[2] Durang, Chap. XII, Series 1.
[3] Durang, Chap. X, Series 1.
[4] See *Pa. Ledger,* May 18, 1778; *Gentleman's Magazine,* Aug., 1778, pp. 353–357; Watson, *Annals of Phila.,* II, 290–293.

galleys, barges, and smaller craft, led by three bands and guarded by ships of the navy, left Knight's Wharf, in the Delaware above Vine Street, and rowed down the river "regular to harmony." Near the old fort in Southwark the guests disembarked, and marched through an avenue of grenadiers to the large square lawn before the Wharton country mansion. There an elaborate tournament was held, with all the pomp of chivalry. The Knights of the Blended Rose, "habited in white and red silk and mounted on gray chargers, richly caparisoned," proclaimed by herald that "the Ladies of the Blended Rose excel in wit, beauty and every accomplishment, those of the *whole world.*" The Knights of the Burning Mountain, in black and orange, maintained that the damsels whose fame they defended were not excelled "by any in the universe." In the first onslaught spears were shivered; later pistols and swords were used. Finally the leaders fought in single combat till commanded by the Marshal of the Field instantly to desist, as honor, virtue, and beauty were satisfied.

Passing under a triumphal arch, the company entered the mansion, splendidly and elaborately furnished, and danced in the ball-room till ten, when the windows were thrown open and "a magnificent bouquet of rockets" blazed against the night. The display of fireworks continued till midnight. Then supper was announced, and "large folding doors, hitherto artfully concealed," opened to display the dining salon, which, with the officers and ladies, made "a *coup d'œil* beyond description magnificent." After supper and many toasts, the ball continued till four o'clock, when "the most splendid entertainment . . . ever given by an army to their general," as Major André called it, was over. After this farewell, General Howe sailed for England. A month later the American Army entered Philadelphia.

AMERICAN MILITARY ACTORS

While Howe's Thespians were playing in Philadelphia, the American Army was producing plays at Valley Forge. As soon as the critical winter of suffering was over, a theatre was opened, evidently at the "Bakehouse." No newspapers or play-bills have preserved the records of this season, so we have to rely on fugitive documents. But we know that a play was given on April 15, 1778, to a crowded house, and that *Cato* was produced on May 11, with other plays in preparation.

On April 15 George Ewing, a soldier of Valley Forge, made the following entry in his *Military Journal:*

15 . . . this afternoon I receivd a ticket for the Play to be acted this evening at the Bakehouse in the evening went down in company with Major Bloomfield Lieuts Curtis Wayman & Kessey but the house was so full that I could not get in then a number of Gent went to Major Parkers hut in the fourth where we spent the evening very merily.

And on the morning after, he wrote:

16 my head achd very badly this morning occasioned by my last nights frolic.

This shows definitely that a play was given on April 15 at the Bakehouse, which drew such a large crowd that George Ewing, who had a ticket, was not able to get in, and had to amuse himself otherwise. It is reasonable to suppose that plays were given between April 15 and May 11, when a letter tells of a performance of *Cato*—a fitting choice for an army of freedom, because of its strong republican sentiment.[5] On Thursday, May 14, William Bradford wrote to his sister Rachel:

The Camp could now afford you some entertainment. The manoeuvering of the Army is in itself a sight that would charm you— Besides these the Theatre is opened— Last Monday Cato was performed before a very numerous and splendid audience. His Excellency and Lady, Lord Sterling, the Countess and Lady Kitty, and Mrs. Green were part of the assembly. The Scenery was in Taste—and the performance admirable—Col George did his part to admiration—he made an excellent *die* (as they say)— Pray heaven, he dont *die* in earnest—for yesterday he was seized with the pleurisy and he's extremely ill— If the enemy does not retire from Philad[a]. soon, our Theatrical amusements will continue— The Fair Penitent with The Padlock will soon be acted. The 'recruiting officer' is also on foot.—I hope however we shall be disappointed in all these by the more agreeable Entertainment of taking possession of Philad[a]. There are strong rumors that the English are meditating a retreat— Heaven send it—for I fear we shall not be able to force them to go these two months.[6]

Six days later, on May 20, Bradford wrote to his sister, "I no longer invite you here—all is hurry and bustle—our plays and other amusements

---

[5] On the sesqui-centennial of this performance, a revival of *Cato* was given at Valley Forge, with appropriate historical pageantry, and with great success.

[6] ALS. Wallace Papers (Bradford), 1.58.

seem to be laid aside and every one is preparing for a sudden movement." [7]

From these happily preserved accidental records, one may conjecture that, in spite of the recommendations of Congress against "plays and other expensive Diversions and Entertainments," American officers were giving plays much of the time they were at Valley Forge.

When they took possession of Philadelphia, they resumed the production of plays. Again the record is haphazard. Durang, who apparently relied on the memory of John North, caretaker of the Southwark, says that the theatre was open in September and October, 1778, and that "a theatrical company performed there." Though the actors are unknown, "they were probably amateurs, with one or two of the old actors." Mr. and Mrs. Allen and Mr. Goodman are, Durang says, supposed to have stayed in Philadelphia during the Revolution.[8] A copy of *The Lying Valet* now in the Library of Congress, published in Philadelphia in 1778, says on its title page, "Printed at the Desire of some of the Officers in the American Army, who intend to exhibit at the Playhouse, for the Benefit of Families who have suffered in the War for American Liberty." And a letter from Gerard de Rayneval, first French Minister to the United States,[9] says, "The Philadelphia papers contain two resolutions passed by Congress. . . . The second is a renewal of the request made by the States to interdict dances, spectacles and races. The very day [October 12 [10]] this resolution was published a public (theatrical) performance, given by army officers and Whig citizens, was to take place. The following day the Governor of Philadelphia gave a ball, numerously attended. Congress, finding that its simple recommendation was not a law, prepared a resolution on the 16th to enforce it."

So it is obvious that American officers and others were producing plays at the Theatre in Southwark in the autumn of 1778. On October 16, Congress took the following action:

Whereas frequenting Play Houses and theatrical entertainments, has a fatal tendency to divert the minds of the people from a due attention to the means necessary for the defence of their country and preservation of their liberties:

[7] *Ibid.*, 1.59.

[8] Durang, Chap. XI, Series 1.

[9] Written Nov. 24, 1778; preserved in the French Archives; quoted here from John Durand, *New Materials for The History of the American Revolution*, N. Y., 1889, p. 166.

[10] *Journals of the Continental Congress*, Vol. XII, 1778, Oct. 12 and 16.

Resolved, that any person holding an office under the United States, who shall act, promote, encourage or attend such plays, shall be deemed unworthy to hold such office, and shall be accordingly dismissed.[10]

The newspapers mention the theatre only in a "human interest" story. The *Packet* said that on the very day of Congress's resolution, The Marquis de la Fayette, ignorant of that action, invited the President of Congress to go with him to the theatre. The President was sorry, but he had to refuse. Lafayette was urgent. But when the President finally told him that Congress had resolved to dismiss anyone who went to the theatre, the Frenchman took it with good grace. "Ah! replied the Marquis, have Congress passed such a resolution! Then I will not go to the play." Lafayette's patriotic abstinence may be said to be the final gesture of the first important epoch of Philadelphia's theatrical history.

CHAPTER III

PROHIBITIONS, THE OLD AMERICAN COMPANY AND THE NEW THEATRE

1779–1799

THE SECOND era of Philadelphia's stage history began, as did the first, with opposition to the theatre. We have seen that formerly, when the Assembly of the Province had passed prohibitive laws, the Crown in Council had promptly repealed them. Now, however, the crown had lost the power to veto the acts of Pennsylvania. The legislature took advantage of its new freedom, and on March 30, 1779, passed a law prohibiting the building of "any play house, theatre, stage or scaffold for acting, showing or exhibiting any tragedy, comedy or tragi-comedy, farce, interlude or other play or any part of a play whatsoever," and the acting or being "in any way concerned" in them or any of them. This law created a disturbing social situation, which lasted for ten years.

In 1779, however, the ethical and political problems raised were not acute. The war was on, and Pennsylvania had concerns more clamorous than that of preserving its right to be entertained. Though the Theatre in Southwark was opened from February 11 to April 28, 1780, by a Mr. Templeton, who gave performances on the slack wire, there was apparently no dramatic effort [1] until January 2, 1782, when a Frenchman, Alexander Quesnay, with a number of "young gentlemen, students" of the French language, presented Beaumarchais' *Eugénie* (in French) and *The Lying Valet* at the Southwark to a "brilliant assemblage" including George Washington and the Minister of France. The performance was successful, and Quesnay announced "by request" for January 11 a second night for *Eugénie,* with the farce of *The Cheat of Scapin:* for the benefit of "the virtuous American Soldiery in the Bar-

---

[1] Unless one chooses to classify Francis Hopkinson's "Oratorial Entertainment," *The Temple of Minerva,* as drama rather than music. It was given on Dec. 11, 1781, at the "hotel of the minister of France." See the *Freeman's Journal,* Dec. 19, 1781, and Sonneck, *Francis Hopkinson,* pp. 106–111.

racks of Philadelphia" and the poor in the Pennsylvania Hospital. But Mr. Quesnay reckoned without the blue laws. On January 8 he was forced to announce "that no public Play will be exhibited at the Theatre in Southwark, on Friday evening, nor any Exhibition made contrary to Law." He added the curious note that he "was also mistaken with respect to the Soldiery."

One "Maria Flutter," who had enjoyed *Eugénie,* wrote to the columnist of the *Freeman's Journal,* "But, O sir! judge what must have been my melancholy, when, as I afterwards heard, Mr. Quesnay was threatened with the law if he had any more plays acted. Do, sir, say something in favour of plays." The "Pilgrim," after ironically chiding her for simply enjoying the drama, and prohibiting her "from ever attending plays 'till she is able to collect a number of useful morals and rational sentiments," feared that the time was not yet ready for an open theatre: "Have patience, madam, 'till the war is successfully finished."

RETURNING ACTORS

There were others, however, who wanted the theatre opened. John Henry returned from Jamaica, and after a visit to Maryland came to Philadelphia armed with a letter of introduction to President Moore of the Supreme Executive Council, which he presented with a request on July 1, 1782. Finding "our Theatre here entirely out of repair, and a debt for ground rent and taxes incurred to the amount of £174/7/6," he asked permission "for one night only . . . to deliver a Lecture on Heads, . . . for the purpose of paying the above debt." His request was refused. A year later, in November, 1783, Dennis Ryan—who had succeeded to the management of the Baltimore theatre after Lindsay and Wall's régime, that is, early in 1783—attempted to open the Theatre in Southwark. His petition to the Assembly for a repeal of the prohibitory law was opposed by a "Memorial and Remonstrance from the people called Quakers." [2] The Assembly tabled Ryan's petition, so chloroforming it.

Early in 1784 Lewis Hallam returned to the city (he and John Henry had become separated during the Revolution) and, on behalf

[2] See *Minutes of the Supreme Executive Council,* Nov. 10, 1783, and *Pa. Archives,* Vol. X, 141–3. It is not quite clear whether there were two petitions, one from the Quakers and one from other "Inhabitants of the City" (as Seilhamer assumes, II, 162), or two records of the same petition.

of himself and "the comedians, commonly called the American Company," prayed for the repeal of the restraining law, and suggested that the theatre be taxed. His request was accompanied by "Divers recommendatory certificates, signed by a considerable number of the inhabitants of the city of Philadelphia and its vicinity." Counter-petitions from the Quakers (who I fear played the villains in this eighteenth-century drama) were promptly presented, and a motion in the Assembly "that a committee be appointed to bring in a bill, repealing" the anti-theatrical law, was defeated, 41 to 21, on February 18, 1784.

OUTSIDE THE LAW

The next five years, 1784–1789, constitute one of the most unfortunate and interesting periods in the history of our stage. The law prohibiting the theatre was in effect, and its supporters, numbering many of the most conspicuously moral citizens, intended to see that it stayed in effect. On the other hand, the number of those desiring the drama was increasing; and for a number of years the city was in an unfortunate situation. Many of the best citizens wanted to see plays; but there was a law against them. The result was perhaps inevitable. The law was evaded by garbling theatrical performances as concerts and obviously moral lectures, and the theatre was patronized by the best people in the city, from George Washington down. For years a seemingly futile struggle was kept up for the repeal of the prohibition, finally ending in victory in 1789.

Defeated in his purpose to get the theatre licensed for plays, Lewis Hallam opened the Theatre in Southwark between April 1 and June 9, 1784, and resorted to border-line performances. It is impossible to be sure exactly what was given this season, and the newspaper announcements were infrequent. There is, for example, no announcement between May 11 and June 9, though on May 22 General Washington "purchased four Play Tickets." The advertisements promised "A Lecture Upon Heads," or "Strictures upon the most eminent Dramatic Authors . . . diversified with Music, Scenery, and other Decorations." No actors' names appeared for a number of years. Durang says [3] that the company included (at least in 1785) John Durang (the historian's father), a dancer, "who, being a native citizen, was always received with applause," Mrs. Allen, "a pleasing vocalist," Charles Busselot,

[3] Chap. XI, Series 1.

"ex-officer in the guards of Louis XVI," who married Miss Caroline Durang, "a vocalist," and the then managers, Hallam and Allen. John Henry succeeded Allen as co-manager in 1785.

Leaving the city in June, the company returned in the winter and played from December 7, 1784, to July 29, 1785. The announcements were still carefully veiled, promising "Lectures," and occasionally a "pantomimical finale" or a "dialogue and dum shew [sic]." The announcement of the "Lectures" for December 7 repays reading as a literary puzzle.

LECTURES

Being a mixed Entertainment of Representation and Harmony, with the Monody divided into three parts:

First. A *serious* investigation of Shakespear's morality, illustrated by his most striking characters, faithfully applied to the test of *mingling profit with amusement*. On the first evening, the instability of human greatness; the unavoidable and miserable consequences of vice; the piercings of a wounded conscience, and the divine attributes of mercy, will be represented according to the animated descriptions of the illustrious bard.

Second. A poetical introduction to a display of characters, *comic* and *satyric;* in which those light follies and foibles that escape more serious animadversion, will be exposed to the lash of ridicule, and a science of innocent mirth opened to the heart, without sacrificing sense to laughter, or decency to wit. The impertinence of the fine gentleman, the profligacy of the rake, the humor of the low, and the vanity of the high will be ludicrously portrayed in a variety of shapes, and the forced satyr happily directed to the nobler purpose of admonition.

Third. A dissertation on the passions, shewing the different complexions they assume, and their various modes of expression, according to the circumstance of Character and situation.—Love and jealousy.—Humanity and libertinism.—Pride and poverty—often uniting in the same heart, but rarely appearing in the same garb.

The vocal part of the Monody by a LADY. And the whole Entertainment will be closed by

A RONDELAY

Celebrating the Independence of America. *Music,* Scenery and *other Decorations.*

The actors went to New York in August, 1785, and did not appear again in Philadelphia till January, 1787. While they were gone, the

Legislature, on September 25, 1786, conscious that the law had "not been fully and duly executed and enforced throughout this state," changed its form somewhat, the penalty now being two hundred pounds for every offense, and extended the prohibition to include pantomime.

The Old American Company, as the troupe, now managed by Hallam and Henry, was called (though it cautiously did not so advertise itself in the papers [4]) returned to the city in January, 1787, and though it at first said that it was here "For Six Nights Only," gave fifteen performances between January 15 and February 3. (The opening was postponed from January 8.) The entertainments were still veiled, announced as Concerts and Lectures, but the veil was thinner. Pantomimes were openly advertised, in spite of the new clause in the law, and when it was said, as on January 22, that in the pantomime would be "introduced a *Musical* Entertainment; called Darby and Patrick; With (by particular desire) the OVERTURE to the Poor Soldier," the initiated probably knew that O'Keeffe's musical farce, *The Poor Soldier,* was meant. The legal assumption evidently was that the law did not cover opera—later in the year the Southwark (this season called "the Theatre in South street") was called "The Opera House in Southwark." Among the new "operas" probably indicated by the announcements were *The Agreeable Surprize* and *Rosina;* soon afterwards, both were advertised for sale in book form.

On June 25, 1787, the Theatre in Southwark became "the Opera-House." Though the managers at first announced a stay of only a fortnight, the playhouse remained open till August 4. Each entertainment was announced as "Spectaculum Vitae," and the plays were called moral tales. For example, on July 25 "a Moral and Instructive TALE called FILIAL PIETY: Exemplified in the HISTORY of the Prince of Denmark" was promised. That the less well read might get the point, a passage beginning "What a Piece of Work is Man" was quoted, and as a final clue, there was the tag in very fine print, "Shakespear's Hamlet." This particular moral tale was later postponed "on account of the indisposition of Mr. Morris," which shows that he was with the company. There is little risk in assuming that *The School for Scandal* was produced during the season (for the first time in the city), though the tale advertised was *"The Pernicious Vice of Scandal."*

After this season, the Old American Company did not return to

4 See Seilhamer, II, 176.

Philadelphia till June, 1788. However, on December 1, 1787, Thomas Wignell, later co-manager of the New Theatre in Chesnut Street, gave a public reading of *The Contrast* at the City Tavern—thus introducing the first American comedy to Philadelphia. Its author, Royall Tyler, had given Wignell the copyright of the play.

In March, 1788, Hallam and Henry again petitioned the Assembly for a repeal of the law against acting. The Assembly appointed a committee of investigation, which brought back a report favorable to the petition. In so doing, the committeemen insisted that they were not "in the least influenced by any particular or personal wish for the establishment of a theatre." But they felt it "the part of integrity to propose their genuine sentiments" on such an important matter, though it was foreseen that those sentiments would differ from other beliefs held by "many persons truly estimable for their moral and religious virtues." The committee's most important conclusion was that, though the foreign yoke in government was cast off, we should "still be dependent for those productions which do most honor to human nature, until we can afford due protection and encouragement to every species of our own literature." They moved that a theatre be licensed. The motion was tabled.

The following summer, from June 23 to July 26, 1788, a season of fifteen nights was played at the theatre, with the announcements of the plays only slightly disguised. The most important new play was *She Stoops to Conquer,* or rather, *"A Lecture on the Disadvantages of Improper Education, Exemplified in the History of* TONY LUMPKIN." *"The Columbian Father;* Written by a Citizen of the United States" was also introduced. The season included *Hamlet, Richard III, The West Indian,* and *The School for Scandal.* While it was in progress, the Quakers did their duty by petitioning President Franklin to redeem the honor of the "righteous administration of government," which was being "insulted by the open contravention of the Law in the exhibition of Stage Plays, under whatsoever evasive name disguised." The Friends of course were quite right; the situation was intolerable, and its climax not distant.

Before the brief autumn season of 1788 at the "Opera-House in Southwark," *George Barnwell* was announced for October 25 at the "Concert Hall in the Northern Liberties." As the Old American Company opened in Southwark two days later, it is possible that some of its members offered *George Barnwell;* or the unannounced performers may have been led by Mr. Partridge, who appeared there in November, 1789.

The "Opera-House" was open for ten nights from October 27 to November 15, 1788. Those who patronized the law-breaking players, (and it was said that "not less than from 700 to 800 citizens . . . many . . . of rank the most respectable," [4a] did) saw the first Philadelphia productions of *The Rivals, The Countess of Salisbury,* and *The School for Wives,* as well as the reappearing *Henry IV, Lear, Richard III, The Beaux' Stratagem, The Provoked Husband, The West Indian,* and *The School for Scandal,* with several afterpieces.

THE DRAMATIC ASSOCIATION

The conflict caused by the law prohibiting plays now became acute. The war for independence had been won, no "emergency" existed, and the question as to whether a determined minority could write its notions of morality into the law of the state had to be faced. On November 7, 1788, the Quakers again recited their grievances, and remonstrated with the Assembly "against theatrical exhibitions being tolerated by law"; and on November 12, Hallam and Henry prayed that the committee's report from last March "be taken into consideration, and a license granted." Fuel was added to the fire by the Overseers of the Poor, who brought suit against the players as subject to fine for breaking the law. From one point of view their action was defensible, as any fines collected from the actors (£200 apiece per performance!) would have gone for poor relief; [5] on the other hand, as many of the citizens observed,[6] the prosecution came with particularly bad grace from the Overseers, as the company had made a practice of giving a benefit for the poor nearly every season.

At the height of the struggle, a Dramatic Association was formed "for the Purpose of obtaining the Establishment of a Theatre in Philadelphia, under a liberal and properly regulated plan." [7] The Dramatic

---

[4a] "Anti-persecutos" in *Pa. Packet,* Dec. 23, 1788.

[5] W. C. Heffner, *History of Poor Relief Legislation in Pennsylvania, 1682–1913,* p. 131. (Cleona, Pa., 1913.) The upshot of this suit was that the Overseers agreed to accept a benefit on April 10, 1790, "in lieu of any penalty that may have been incurred."

[6] See letters in *Pa. Packet,* Dec. 6, 23, 30, 1788.

[7] See *Packet,* Jan. 9, 19, Feb. 3, 17, 1789; *American Museum,* Feb., 1789; *Minutes of the General Assembly,* Feb. 16, 1789.

Association was a civic movement, the voice of the best liberal element in the growing city, of those interested in the arts and in political rights. On its active committee were General Walter Stewart, Major T. I. Moore, William Temple Franklin, Dr. Robert Bass, John Barclay, Jacob Barge, Dr. Joseph Redman, James Crawford, and John West. Mrs. Bingham was active in its support. "The characters of our most distinguished citizens were pledged for the respectable establishment of the Theatre." [8] Managers Hallam and Henry promised that, if the theatre were allowed to open legally, they would strengthen the company by the addition of "good performers from Europe." [9]

On February 16, 1789, the Dramatic Association gave to the Legislature a statement of rights which is one of the important social landmarks of America. Unfortunately it is much too long to be quoted here in full.[10] It argues that those opposed to the drama have no right to prohibit the theatre, and that those for whom drama does have intelligent meaning as artistic recreation should not "sacrifice that opinion, merely in compliment to the prejudices of those of their fellow citizens, who think this, as they do every other amusement, contrary to the laws of conscience and virtue." The heart of their statement is summed up in words which have not grown archaic:

While . . . we cannot admit, that a theatre is the temple of vice, we presume not to insist that it is the school of virtue. As a rational amusement, it is the object of our wishes; and the whole force of our reasoning is directed only to shew, that those who regard it in a contrary light, are not entitled to controul our sentiments or to compel the adoption of what they profess. If, indeed, a mere difference of opinion, shall be thought a sufficient foundation to curtail our rights, and diminish our enjoyments, the boasted liberality of the present age, will be eclipsed by a comparison with the furious bigotry of the middle centuries; and the same authority which proscribes our amusements may with equal justice, dictate the shape and texture of our dress, or the modes and ceremonies of our worship.

From the appeal to reason, the struggle went to the appeal to numbers. Petitions for and against the theatre circulated through the city, and, with long lists of signers, were presented to the legislature. Nineteen hundred names wanted the theatre on February 6; ten days later,

[8] *General Advertiser,* Feb. 23, 1791.
[9] *Federal Gazette,* Feb. 5, 1791.
[10] For the full text, see *Pa. Packet,* Feb. 17, 1789, and *Am. Museum,* Feb., 1789.

3446 names did not. In four more days, 3780 were for it, and 729 against. There were remonstrances and counter-remonstrances. Finally, on March 2, 1789, the Dramatic Association was successful, and "any act or part of an act which prohibits theatrical representations" was repealed "within the city of Philadelphia and the neighbourhood thereof." That the respectability of the stage might be assured, the executive and judicial heads of the state were given the power for the next three years to suppress any "exceptionable" plays.

UNVEILED PLAYS

During the struggle the Old American Company, under its own name, had given "An Entertainment" on January 9, and announced another for February 2, which it withdrew. As soon as the law was repealed, it opened the theatre and gave fifteen plays, again "By Authority," between March 9 and April 4, the company leaving then only because it was due at the John Street Theatre in New York. *Much Ado About Nothing,* "Never performed here," was given, as well as Burgoyne's *The Heiress,* also new. A number of dependable plays reappeared. For the first time in over fifteen years, casts were published, and we can be sure that Lewis Hallam, still the leading actor, played the Romeo and the Benedict. Mrs. Henry (it was Maria now) was the leading lady, when she appeared, as she did in Juliet. Mrs. Morris had more good parts (Beatrice, Maria, Lydia Languish, Lady Teazle), perhaps because she was more willing to work. Mr. Wignell, who was especially a broad comedian, and Mr. Henry took leading rôles, and Mr. Morris in low comedy again shook the gallery.

Late in 1789, five performances were given between November 4 and 30 in "Harmony Hall, Northern-Liberties, near Poole's Bridge," by a picked-up company led by a Mr. Partridge (or Patridge), and including John Durang, the dancer. It is not certain whether "Harmony Hall" was or was not another name for the Theatre in the Northern Liberties, also near Poole's Bridge, which was used in a long season during 1791–92. The only full-length play attempted during these five November nights was *The Beaux' Stratagem.*

CRITICAL AUDIENCES

The Old American Company reopened the Theatre in Southwark on January 6, 1790, and played a long season till July 19. The managers tried in a number of ways to make the old theatre more attractive. In January it was too cold, and they closed it for ten days for "Alterations and Improvements." They changed the pit entrance from the north side to the east. They made "a new brick Pavement . . . from Lombard street to the door of the theatre." They removed the gallery door "from the North side to the West side." In July, when it got too hot, they put up "A Wind Sail . . . for the purpose of keeping the House Cool." The next summer they had fire engines playing water on the roof.

In more significant matters, however, they were apparently not so active. In spite of their promise to the Dramatic Association that they would get new players from England, there was no improvement in the company. But the wrath of the public, happy in a fat season after so many lean, did not descend on them yet. Durang tells us [11] that "the business was excellent"— Mrs. Bingham and her coterie "often adorned the dingy-papered boxes of the old South." Four of the new plays produced were American: *The Contrast* (which Wignell had read to the city in 1787), Dunlap's *The Father,* John Henry's *The School for Soldiers* and Humphreys' *The Widow of Malabar.* There were newspapers every day now, and the record is without the colonial gaps, though the Old American Company did not often give casts in the papers—perhaps believing that silence was the better advertising.

At any rate, in the next season, December 8, 1790, to July 11, 1791, there were many complaints from the citizens that the company, only adequate at best, too often did not present its full strength. The criticisms were especially strong against Maria Henry, admittedly excellent in singing rôles and a great favorite when she wished to be, but capricious and disdainful of her public, often refusing to appear or playing negligently in minor parts. Just how much truth there was in the charges it is impossible now to say, especially in the absence of casts, but there is no doubt that many in the audience felt sure that her inattention was willful. A number of plays were postponed, and Hallam and Henry parried rather than met criticism. The truth seems to be that the managers had become so used to a grateful public's taking what it could get that they did not consider the rumblings of the storm serious. And good new actors might mean (when Hodgkinson came, they did mean) that Lewis Hallam, the theatrical idol of colonial

[11] Chap. XIV, Series 1.

America, would have to give up some of his youthful rôles—precious property. Henry was far from blameless, but there is no doubt that Hallam in especial (unlike his wise stepfather, David Douglass) was a penurious and time-serving manager, more interested in his own success than his company's. Toward the end of this turbulent season the managers put forward two new actresses, Mrs. Wilson and Mrs. Gee, who were well received, but were not important. There were spectators who, rather mildly, defended the managers, or attacked their attackers,[12] but when a meeting of those interested in subscribing to "building a Theatre in a central part of the city" was announced on May 2, the eventual result was the New Theatre in Chesnut Street.

Mr. Wignell, later the manager of the New Theatre, left the Old American Company at the end of this season, accompanied by Mr. and Mrs. Morris. Wignell was a very popular actor, and Henry was jealous.[13] There was strife, too, between the wives. Someone had to go to England to get new players. Hallam, it appears, had promised Wignell that he, Wignell, should go; then it was publicly announced that Henry, jealous of Wignell and one of the managers, would be the envoy. Wignell called for a showdown: he was a "sharer" and the treasurer, but at the mercy of the managers who controlled the casting: if co-manager Henry brought back a new comedian and gave him Wignell's parts, Wignell would be ruined. Either he must be allowed to buy into the management on a par with Hallam and Henry, or it must be he who was sent to England. Hallam and Henry refused the alternatives. Wignell resigned, joined with Alexander Reinagle as manager of the New Theatre, and the next year went to England for his own (the New Theatre's) company.

Wignell's leaving brought to an end the "sharing" system, which had been in force since the Comedians from London first reached America in 1752. The last sharing members were Hallam, Mr. and Mrs. Henry, Wignell, Mr. and Mrs. Morris, and Woolls.[14] In the future the actors (except, of course, the managers) were all on salary, though the system of actors' benefits was still in force, with its dangerously speculative influence on stage economics.

---

[12] For some of the letters pro and con this season see *The Federal Gazette,* Feb. 5, March 16; *General Advertiser,* Feb. 16, 18, 21, 23, 26, Mar. 1, 5, April 15, 21, 30, May 2, 9, 21, June 2, 13, 1791.

[13] Dunlap, 90–92, gives the story in some detail.

[14] Durang, Chap. XV.

The season of 1790–91 was also important for the theatrical criticism which was published. There had been sporadic criticism before, but from now on it grew to be a customary part of journalism. For example, the *General Advertiser* in reviewing *She Stoops to Conquer* (April 15) said:

Mrs. Morris performed in Miss Hardcastle with truth and great animation: We wish we could say as much of Miss Tuke in Miss Nevil. Nothing appeared to move her;—not even unexpectedly meeting with her lover. Mr. Wignell in Tony Lumpkin . . . entered fully into the spirit of the character, and performed every part of it with great humor.

Among the few new plays this season were *Constitutional Follies,* by Mr. Robinson, one of the actors, and Bickerstaff's *The Recess,* "Revised and altered by a Citizen of Philadelphia." (A long synopsis of the latter and a criticism of it as drama appeared in the *General Advertiser* for April 30 and May 2, 1791.)

THE "K" COMPANY

While the Old American Company was playing in Southwark a "New American Company" opened the Northern Liberty (or Liberties) Theatre on April 8, 11, 26, and 30. This was in Front Street, below Noble—"a small wooden theatre . . . on the wharf up at Noble street." [15] The title "New American Company" later disappeared, and as Mr. Kenna, Mrs. Kenna, Miss Kenna, Mr. Kelly, and Mr. and Mrs. Kedey, as well as the J. Kennas, appeared, it is simpler to follow Seilhamer in calling them the "K" company.

In July, when the Theatre in Southwark had closed, the "K" company began a season running from July 25, 1791, to May 16, 1792. (During the summer they appeared on alternate nights as actors at the Northern Liberties and as singers and dancers at George Esterly's Vauxhall Gardens, at "Harrowgate"—Broad and Walnut.) Mr., Mrs., and Miss Kenna, who had been with the Old American Company in New York in 1787,[16] before starting the new company, were the heart of the troupe, with Mrs. Kenna evidently the leading performer. A number of new actors appeared, many for a very short time and some

---

[15] Watson, *Annals,* I, 473.
[16] Odell, I, 254.

of them amateurs: on May 11, for example, "a Gentleman for his Amusement" was announced. During the season a company of French dancers, who occasionally gave pantomimes, appeared with the "K" Company, and later a company of tumblers, jugglers, and slack-wire performers led by a Mr. Donegani. Mr. Godwin, who had been with the American Company in 1766, turned up again on April 14, 1792, playing Jaffier in *Venice Preserved*. The list of plays given is quite respectable, including eight new titles, none very important, and nineteen old favorites, as well as a number of afterpieces, old and new.

NEW THEATRE BEGUN

Mr. Wignell had gone to England, and sent back "the most favourable accounts of his success in obtaining performers for the New Theatre." [17] A company of citizens had been formed to erect the building.[18] A lot on the north side of Chesnut above Sixth had been secured, and in February, 1792, some of the materials for building were already there, and the public was expectantly waiting "to see the Drama in a more perfect state than had hitherto been known in America." In June a model of the proposed theatre reached the city, and was "exhibited for the gratification of the curious." [19]

In the summer of 1792 the Old American Company gave a short season at the Southwark from May 28 to July 2. Without the services of Mr. Henry, who had gone to England for new performers (the secession of Mr. Wignell had finally forced the issue), Mr. and Mrs. Morris, and Mr. Wignell, the company was very weak, and relied on a French troupe of tumblers, dancers, and pantomimists, led by M. Placide, to draw the crowd. As a result, no new plays were given, but instead they offered a number of new pantomimes, ballets, and "dancing ballads"—which were becoming constantly more popular. The only new "legitimate" afterpiece was Robinson's farce (first given in New York in April), *The Yorker's Stratagem.*

[17] *Daily Advertiser,* Feb. 13, 1792.

[18] The original proposal, signed by the subscribers, is in the Historical Society of Pennsylvania. At first there were to be sixty shares at $300 each; on June 2, 1792, forty more shares were added (the first date is not distinguishable; it was probably late in 1791). Wignell and Reinagle were responsible for everything but the actual lot and building.

[19] *Pa. Gazette,* June 20, 1792.

After a brief season in Lancaster,[20] the Old American Company returned to the Southwark on September 26, 1792, playing through till January 12, 1793. On the opening night Mr. and Mrs. Hodgkinson, Mr. King, Mr. Prigmore, and Mr. West, some of the new performers John Henry had secured in England, appeared for the first time in America. John Hodgkinson was the most important—"a prodigy," Durang called him [21]—a fine actor, with boundless ambition, bottomless ignorance, and tremendous energy. The managers who had tried to suppress the competition of Wignell soon found themselves saddled with a popular actor who wanted to play all the good parts—theirs included—and trouble naturally followed. Mrs. Hodgkinson was also important. The *Aurora* of September 28 said that in her, "Mrs. Henry, at last, finds a rival worthy of her vocal abilities." She was a very capable general actress. Mrs. Pownall (sometime Mrs. Wrighten), who appeared ten days later, was an older actress, with an excellent singing voice. Prigmore, the buffoon, did not succeed as the managers had hoped in taking Wignell's place in popular favor. A few new plays were presented this season, with *The Road to Ruin, The Child of Nature,* and *He Would Be a Soldier* probably the best. At the close of the season, Lewis Hallam married Eliza Tuke,[22] and the backstage difficulties of the Old American Company grew yet more madly complicated.

In the meantime, with the public waiting impatiently, work was being pushed on the New Theatre. While Wignell was still in England getting his players, on February 2, 1793, the New Theatre in Chesnut Street, "nearly completed," was opened with "a grand Concert of Vocal and Instrumental Music." Five days later another concert was given, after which the theatre was closed "till further notice." (Its dramatic opening was on February 17, 1794.) All during the spring there was no drama, and the public was told of Wignell's strenuous efforts and asked to wait patiently if it wanted perfection.[23]

It was perfection Philadelphia sought, and the theatre rising west of Sixth and Chesnut was to be, as the Annalist of the New York Stage later said, "incomparably the finest home of the drama in America." Designed by Richards, a London artist (Wignell's brother-

---

[20] *Federal Gazette,* Oct. 10, 1792.
[21] Chap. XVII, Series 1.
[22] On January 14, 1793. See *Daily Adv.,* Jan. 17.
[23] *Daily Adv.,* May 6.

in-law), it was a copy of the Royal Theatre at Bath. A stately front stretched for ninety feet along Chesnut Street, flanked by two fifteen-feet wings. The extreme depth of one hundred and thirty-four feet allowed the stage to run back for seventy-one feet from the footlights. The interior, handsomely furnished, somewhat resembled a modern opera house, with two horseshoe tiers of boxes, or "lodges." The boxes accommodated nine hundred people, and when boxes, pit, and gallery were full, the house held an audience of two thousand. The stage, thirty-six feet wide between the front boxes, could be seen from any part of the house. The actors had a grateful number of dressing-rooms, two greenrooms (one for the youngsters and one more dignified), and, for the first time in America, there was a large and well-stocked wardrobe, with a wardrobe keeper.[24] From both sides of the footlights it was an excellent and spacious theatre.[25]

After a season in New York, the Old American Company opened the Southwark on July 1, 1793, but was compelled by the spread of yellow fever to close it on August 23. No casts were announced in the papers, but the company was doubtless much as it had been when it left in January, save that Hodgkinson was assuming more and more power. By next May in New York he had forced John Henry out entirely, buying his half interest in the company for £4000.[26] John Henry and Maria Storer Henry, who had been with the American Company a quarter of a century before, did not play in Philadelphia again.[27]

WIGNELL'S RECRUITS

When Thomas Wignell got back from England in the summer of 1793 with "a company of performers, consisting of fifty-six men, women,

---

[24] Durang, Chap. XXX, Series 1.

[25] For a contemporary account, see the *Daily Advertiser* for February 4, 1794.

[26] J. Hodgkinson, *Narrative of His Connection with the Old American Company,* N. Y., 1797, p. 5. Henry sold to Hallam, and Hallam to Hodgkinson. It appears that Hallam sold less than he bought, as the buyer later discovered. See Dunlap, 112–113.

[27] John Henry died at sea on his way to Rhode Island, Oct. 16, 1794, and after a hasty burial on the shore, his body was removed to "a vault in the graveyard of St. James Church at Bristol." *Daily Adv.,* Jan. 10, 1795. Mrs. Maria Henry died April 28, 1795, in her house back of the old Southwark Theatre. *Daily Adv.,* April 30.

and children," he found the city plagued by yellow fever, and took the players to Sandtown, New Jersey, till the danger was past.[28]

The plague in Philadelphia had been very bad, and the Quakers, suspecting its cause (with a huge new theatre going up and a load of stage-players ready to act in it), called on the Legislature when it met again (on December 2[29]) for "the absolute suppression and prohibition of those injurious and reproachful exhibitions" as a token of obedience to "the dispenser of life, health and happiness." They did their best to revive the war against the theatre,[30] but that fight had been fought, and "Plain Truth" reminded them bluntly that the Legislature had a duty to guard rights as well as morals.[31]

The New Theatre was finally opened with drama on February 17, 1794, and the season continued till July 18. Wignell's Company (which had played a few nights in Annapolis while waiting for the Philadelphia opening) was, with the exception of Mr. and Mrs. Morris and Mr. Wignell, entirely new. With James Fennell, a great tragedian and vagrant genius, at its head, it was in the opinion of all critics the finest dramatic and operatic corps that America had seen. In all, thirty-eight new actors appeared this season. Mrs. Oldmixon (the Miss George of the London stage) was one of the most distinguished, an excellent singing actress. John Pollard Moreton was the leading high comedian. John Harwood was (as both Durang and Dunlap phrase it) "one of the brightest ornaments" of the company. Mrs. Whitlock, a sister of Mrs. Siddons, was the leading tragic actress in the country—the Lady Macbeth to Fennell's Macbeth, the Imogen to his Posthumous. Mr. Chalmers, "engaged as the genteel comedian," though popular was not up to their level; however, he later took some excellent parts, both tragic and comic. ("Originally a Harlequin," Durang says,[32] he "never could play a part without a jump or turn in it.") Mrs. Marshall "was the *beau ideal* of a comic actress, and . . . *au fait* in every walk of the drama—nay, she was excellent. Her romps were a model of perfection." In the large company was Mrs. Susannah Haswell Rowson, the author of *Charlotte Temple;* for her benefit on June 30 she

[28] James Fennell, *An Apology for the Life of James Fennell*, Phila., 1814, p. 334.
[29] *Daily Adv.*, Dec. 13, 1793.
[30] See *Daily Adv.*, Dec. 23, 24, 31, 1793; Jan. 2, 1794.
[31] *Daily Adv.*, Dec. 18, 1793.
[32] Chap. XXI, Series 1.

wrote *Slaves in Algiers*. Her husband was the prompter this season.

The company, jointly managed by Thomas Wignell and Alexander Reinagle, the latter a musician and leader of the orchestra, was as strong in opera as in drama—it opened with O'Keeffe's comic opera, *The Castle of Andalusia*. Mr. Reinagle often contributed new music, and Mr. De Marque worked as compiler, while Mr. Milbourne was the scenic artist. Pantomime and ballet were also very popular. Mr. Francis, a dancer and pantomimist, and Mme. Gardie, danseuse from Paris, whose tragic end was not yet, delighted the audience. The company had been chosen so that it would be strong in all its departments. And it is important to notice that though James Fennell played all the tragic rôles and captured the imagination of the city, he was happily not yet a "star"; Wignell's was an excellent stock company.

Monday, Wednesday, and Friday were still the regular theatre nights, and a box seat cost one dollar, while a seat in the pit was "three-quarters of a dollar," and one in the gallery, half a dollar. Servants still came early to hold their masters' "lodge" seats. Much pertinent criticism was appearing. The critic of the *General Advertiser,* reviewing Kelly's *The School for Wives* on March 24, said that it, "like most of the modern English comedies, fails of interest through want of more unity, distinctness, and connection in the plot. The aim of the author has been to expose certain follies and vices; but he has undertaken the reformation of too many at a time. Besides, the play is not a mirrour for an American audience.—This to be sure is a fault common to most transatlantic productions of this nature," though of course "many good sentiments are introduced throughout the play, seasonable in all ages and climes, expressed with remarkable neatness."

Thirteen plays or "operas" were introduced to the city this season, including *As You Like It;* Mrs. Rowson's *Slaves in Algiers* has been mentioned. Among thirty-four reappearing plays were eight Shakespearean, as well as, for example, *Comus, The Provoked Husband, The Rivals,* and *The School for Scandal.* Of forty-seven afterpieces (farces, light operas, pantomimes, "comic ballads"), eighteen were new. It was the best season America had ever seen.

THE OLD AMERICAN COMPANY DEPARTS

At the close of their Philadelphia season, Wignell and Reinagle took the players to a new theatre they had built in Baltimore, which they were to use regularly in the summer and early fall. The Old American Company seized the chance to open the "Theatre, Cedar Street" (the old Southwark) from September 22 to December 4, 1794. It was to be their last appearance in Philadelphia.

A number of new performers were seen, the most important of whom was Mrs. Melmoth, a tragic actress of great power, though no longer young nor slender. Mme. Gardie, who had been at the New Theatre earlier in the year, "created quite a sensation in her pantomimic acting . . . the town were in extacies [sic] with her and this species of performance." [33] The only American plays new to the city were Dunlap's *The Fatal Deception* (later called *Leicester*) and Mrs. Hatton's *Tammany*. In all there were eleven new plays, and those which reappeared were, with a few exceptions, recent, and rather light. The crowd in the gallery was bad this season; anybody within beer-bottle range was in danger.[34] When Mr. and Mrs. Hallam took their benefit on December 4, the important history of the Theatre in Southwark was over. It was fitting that President George Washington should have been there on the last night "to honor the *Old American Company* with his presence." Nevertheless, Philadelphia was fortunate that it could surrender that strifeful company to New York and Dunlap, and turn its attention to the New Theatre in Chestnut Street.

The New Theatre had been reopened the day before, on December 3, 1794, and housed a long season till July 4, 1795. Unfortunately it had for a time lost Mr. Fennell, its leading tragedian; that restless gentleman was intent on making his own and Maryland's fortune with a salt-machine he had invented.[35] Chalmers attempted to take his place in tragic rôles; but he was not Fennell. Nevertheless, it was an excellent season, dramatic and musical, with seventy-four different standard plays and operas, thirteen of which were new—and this not counting afterpieces, which were often nearly as important as the main plays. On March 21, for example, *Comus* appeared as afterpiece to *The Rivals*. Interestingly enough, *A New Way to Pay Old Debts* was revived. Cumberland's *The Jew* was very popular, appearing six times. Most of the plays, old and new, were of course still English: Mrs.

[33] Durang, Series I, Chap. XXIV.

[34] See *Gen. Ad.*, Oct. 25, 1794.

[35] See J. Fennell, *Description of the Principles and Plan of Proposed Establishments of Salt Works; for the Purpose of Supplying the U. S. with Home Made Salt*, Phila., 1798.

Rowson's *The Female Patriot* and John Murdock's *The Triumphs of Love* were the only new American plays offered. Murdock, it seems, was a Philadelphia barber, and felt that there was foul play when the managers refused to revive his *The Triumphs of Love* next season, or produce his new farce.[36] There was undoubtedly too little emphasis on the development of American drama, but Murdock's was not a happy test case.

THE ART PANTHEON

Before Wignell's company returned from its season in Baltimore, The Art Pantheon, or Ricketts' Amphitheatre, was opened on the southwest corner of Sixth and Chesnut, just opposite the New Theatre. It was built like a huge circular tent of wood, ninety-seven feet in diameter, with white walls, straight for eighteen feet, slanting upward to make a conical roof fifty feet high. Primarily a circus with "equestrianism," tumbling, and pony races, it also attracted the public with a stage on which farces and pantomimes were given. "People of all classes thronged to the circus. From six to seven hundred persons filled the seats on every day of Ricketts' performances." [37] The Pantheon opened on October 19, 1795, but its stage performances this season were presented between December 22, 1795, and April 23, 1796. Five different harlequinades were given—one with the charming title, *The Triumph of Virtue, or Harlequin in Philadelphia.*

Soon after the New Theatre had opened its season from December 14, 1795, to July 1, 1796, it introduced Signior Joseph Doctor, an acrobat imported from Sadlers Wells to compete with the Pantheon across the street. His exhibitions were pointedly called "T'Other Side of the Gutter"—then later, "Both Sides of the Gutter." M. and Mme. Lege, pantomimists from the Italian Theatre in Paris, added strength to the musical and dancing departments. But in the more strictly dramatic part of the organization, no one had been secured to take Fennell's place, and in addition Chalmers, the substitute in tragedy, had left the company (though he rejoined it in May). There were no important recruits, and the public grumbled so distinctly that Manager Wignell, after taking a benefit on April 18, went to England for new actors. Though not a distinctive season, it was a good one; Philadelphia

[36] See the Introduction to J. Murdock, *The Beau Metamorphized,* Phila., 1800.
[37] Durang, Chap. XXV, Series 1. For an account of the circus as circus, see I. J. Greenwood, *The Circus, Its Origin and Growth prior to 1835,* N. Y., 1898.

was offered a large number of the best plays then on the English speaking stage, adequately presented in an excellent theatre. A "poor" season at the New Theatre in the 1790's meant simply that there was no great actor or striking success to catch the public's imagination.

The next "dramatic" season at the Pantheon extended from October 12, 1796, to February 23, 1797. Its repertory was much more ambitious than before. It gave thirty-two different entertainments, mostly panto-mimic, twenty of which were new to the city. A number of the standard farces were produced—*Catherine and Petruchio, The Lying Valet, Miss in Her Teens.* Its company also was stronger now, including Mr. Chambers, who had been with the Old American Company in 1792, and his wife—both later with Wignell and Reinagle's players.

When the New Theatre began its season from December 5, 1796, to July 14, 1797 (with an intermission from May 6 to July 5), an interesting struggle occurred. Ricketts, who had been playing on any day of the week that pleased him, announced that he would resume his former schedule of Tuesday, Thursday, and Saturday, thus leaving the New Theatre its regular nights of Monday, Wednesday, and Friday. But when Wignell and Reinagle saw the Saturday night crowds pouring into the Pantheon across the street and thought of the drains on their treasury, they opened the theatre on Saturday night, December 17, with a new French Company of Comedians giving two French comic operas in addition to the play by the regular actors. Ricketts immediately countered by announcing that as the Theatre chose to compete with him, he would be open on Monday, Wednesday, Friday, and Saturday nights till further notice. Accordingly, the Pantheon and the New Theatre divided the crowd for over three weeks; but Wig-nell and Reinagle finally gave up, and announced no play for Satur-day, January 14, when the old division of nights was resumed.

Wignell had been successful in England, bringing back with him Mrs. Ann Merry,[38] Thomas Abthorpe Cooper, and William Warren, as well as lesser figures. Mrs. Merry was one of the truly great actresses. John Bernard, comparing her with Mrs. Siddons (he was a good judge, and knew them both), said that Mrs. Siddons ascended to greatness in the "Queenly and thoughtful" Shakespearean heroines, while Mrs. Merry in "the loving and passionate . . . was equally perfect. . . .

[38] Sometime the Miss Brunton of the London stage; later Mrs. Thomas Wig-nell; later Mrs. William Warren.

With a voice that was all music, and a face all emotion, her pathos and tenderness were never exceeded." [39] Thomas A. Cooper, foster son of William Godwin and protégé of Thomas Holcroft, was at the time only twenty-one, with a genius more ambitious than developed, but he grew to be a great tragedian.[40] William Warren, later manager of the Chesnut Street Theatre, was an excellent comedian.

But on the other hand, Fennell and Chalmers were still away, and a number of other performers had gone to the new Boston Theatre— Mr. and Mrs. Whitlock, the Rowsons, Miss Broadhurst. The critics, enraptured by Mrs. Merry, strove to evaluate the new players with the old. It was an age of reason, and "Philo-Theatricus" attempted criticism as an exact science. Desiring to show that the managers had lost more than they had gained, he graded the players, "more from public, than private opinion," with 15 as an ideal score, thus:

Performers Absent		*New Performers*	
Mrs. Whitlock	13	Mrs. Merry	15
Shaw	10	Mechtler	4
Marshall	9	Miss L'Estrange	4
Cleveland	5	Mrs. L'Estrange	3
Green	4	Mr. Cooper	11
Rowson	3	Warren	9
Miss Broadhurst	10	Fox	6
Mr. Fennell	13	L'Estrange	4
Bates	12		
Chalmers	12		56
Whitlock	11		
Marshall	7		
Cleveland	5		
Green	5		
	119		

One notes Mrs. Merry's perfect 15. He graded some of the others: Mr. Moreton ("undoubtedly the only chaste male actor on the New Theatre stage"!) 13; Mr. Wignell 10; Mr. Harwood 13; Mr. Francis

[39] *Retrospections of the Stage,* N. Y., 1887.

[40] See J. N. Ireland, *A Memoir of the Professional Life of Thomas Abthorpe Cooper,* N. Y., 1888.

9; Mrs. Oldmixon 14; Mrs. Morris 8; and Mrs. Warren 9.[41] The greenroom comments on "Philo-Theatricus" must have been worth hearing.

The sensation of the season was Morton's *Columbus, or a World Discovered,* which, elaborately produced, was played nine times between January 30 and July 5—then a very long run (not, however, continuous). Morton's *The Way to Get Married* was given seven times, and a new American play, R. Merry's *The Abbey of St. Augustine,* ran for three nights. A number of new pantomimes and comic operas were given, featuring the French players and Mr. and Mrs. Byrne, who had been imported from Covent Garden.

In an effort to get their finances (which had never quite recovered from the necessity of paying full salaries to the actors in 1793, when the New Theatre could not be opened because of the yellow fever) in better shape, the managers raised the prices of the box seats to a dollar and a quarter, and of the pit to a dollar. But they did not make money, and next season had to go back to the old scale. The season was interrupted from May 6 to July 5 while the company rushed to Baltimore; a curious and temporary law there had banned the theatre for the summer, and the managers wanted to take at least the cream of a season.

A BIGGER CIRCUS

Another circus had been built—a huge place, "constructed on a scale of grandeur hitherto unknown in Philadelphia. From Fifth Street it extended westward along Prune Street to the jail wall, half a square in depth; along Fifth Street the front extended to the south wall of the present boundary of St. Thomas' Church. Above the building loomed up the mammoth proportions of a prodigious dome of large diameter, and extended in height to the altitude of ninety feet." [42] The New Theatre, which held two thousand people, looked to Dunlap "quite small after seeing Lailson's Circus." [43] The ambitious proprietor was a Frenchman, and had with him "the most splendid and well appointed double company (that is, for both stage and circus) which had ever come to America." [42] Its dramatic season extended from April 11

---

[41] The *Gazette of the United States,* Dec. 16, 1796. Could "Philo-Theatricus" have been the critic who used that name in 1772? See p. 30, above.

[42] Durang, XXXII, Series 1.

[43] 169.

to July 27, 1797, during which time eighteen new pantomimes, farces, and "comic ballads" were given. But Lailson's Circus was as transient as it was huge. The next spring Lailson opened on March 8 and kept going, in spite of difficulties, until April 7, when he finally realized that the enterprise was too vast, sold what he could, and returned to France. The histrionic members of his company stayed in the city [42] and joined other unattached actors (notably Chalmers) in giving scattered performances at the circuses and the Southwark between April 24 and June 8, 1798. And then one Sunday morning (July 8, 1798), "the immense dome of the circus gave way and fell to the ground between the walls, crushing the interior completely." [44]

The New Theatre began its season from December 11, 1797, to May 5, 1798, with its company further strengthened by the presence of John Bernard, an excellent comedian from England, who was an immediate success with the public.[45] James Fennell (who had given fifty-seven readings from plays at the College the winter before [46]) reappeared on January 3, as Zanga in *The Revenge,* "before as brilliant a Theatre as ever assembled in Philadelphia." [47] The boxes were crowded, the applause was long and sincere, and Philadelphia was his. The headstrong young Thomas Cooper, whose ambition had already been curbed by the managers, deserted the company on Fennell's approach, and went to New York, where he had friends who he knew would applaud the genius that was later to become great.[48] The managers had more trouble when Fennell grew capricious, and the theatre had to be closed from February 19 to 26 while he settled down.[49] (The tragedian himself said later that "Prudence . . . has always been with regard to me, so shy a goddess, that she never permitted me to touch

[44] Durang, XXXIII, Series 1.

[45] See, e. g., *Aurora,* Dec. 15, 1797. Bernard has left in his *Retrospections of America, 1797–1811,* N. Y., 1887, good accounts of other members of the company, as well as himself. His *Retrospections of the Stage,* 2 vols., London, 1830, is interesting for his life in England.

[46] See Fennell's *Apology,* 357, and the *Gazette of the United States,* Dec. 12, 1796, to April 11, 1797.

[47] *Gazette of the United States,* Jan. 4, 1798.

[48] See Dunlap, 214–221. Cooper was under contract to Wignell and Reinagle with a £500 forfeit; they forbade his New York appearance; he appeared anyway; when he returned to Philadelphia he was arrested; and his further history during the century belongs to New York. See Odell, II, 12, *et seq.*

[49] See Dunlap, 219–220, for the managers' statement.

the hem of her garment." [50] On April 2, the company lost John Pollard Moreton, who died of consumption and was buried from his house at 39 South Front Street.[51]

One of the most interesting events of the season came on April 25, when Gilbert Fox introduced for his benefit a new song written by Joseph Hopkinson—"Hail Columbia." "Hail Columbia" served a dual purpose. It filled the house for Mr. Fox's benefit, and it gave the Federalists words for their party tune, "The President's March," allowing them to compete on even terms in the current battle of music with the Republicans' *"Ça Ira."* Mr. Fox sang "Hail Columbia" to the accompaniment of a full band and a "grand chorous," brought the audience of the New Theatre cheering to its feet, and established the Federalist song in popular favor.[52]

Twelve new plays appeared this season, none very important; Mrs. Inchbald's *Wives as They Were* was given six times. It is significant that there were ten more new afterpieces than new plays. But a number of excellent plays reappeared: for example, *Lear, Othello, Hamlet, Henry IV, Venice Preserved,* and *The School for Scandal.*

THE LAST YEAR OF THE CENTURY

The yellow fever of 1798 prevented the New Theatre from being opened again till February 5, 1799. Ricketts' Circus started up a few weeks earlier, its dramatic season, comprising the usual new pantomimes and spectacles, extending to March 23.

On the first night of the season at the New Theatre from February 5 to May 27, 1799, William B. Wood, later an excellent comedian and the manager of the theatre, made his inauspicious entry on the Philadelphia stage.[53] Strong in comedy, with John Bernard at his best, the company was badly crippled in tragedy (Fennell was gone again, Cooper had deserted, Moreton was dead), and there was no one to play opposite Mrs. Merry in the great tragic rôles. As a consequence, the

---

[50] *Apology,* 340.

[51] *Gazette of the U. S.,* Apr. 2, 3, 1798.

[52] For a fuller account, see Burton Alva Konkle, *Joseph Hopkinson,* Phila., U. of Pa. Press, 1931.

[53] See his *Personal Recollections of the Stage,* Philadelphia, 1855, pp. 50–51, for his own account. He had not quite remembered the date: it was Feb. 5, 1799, not "December, 1798."

season was devoted to comedy, opera, and pantomime, and the fourteen new plays were nearly all comedies or Gothic mysteries. A young tragedian, Alexander Cain, was secured late in the season. ("Poor Cain," Durang lamented later, "with clever qualities and goodly prospects, was the author of his own mishaps. In juvenile tragedy he promised much excellence." [54]) Though at first announced (May 11) to make his début as Hamlet, he appeared first as Tancred to Mrs. Merry's Sigismunda, and was a success.

Earlier in the season Wignell had taken the dangerous step of attacking the newspapers, especially the *Philadelphia Gazette,* which had not been gentle in its criticisms.[55] That paper, hearing that "A new dramatic *trifle,* entitled 'RETALIATION, or A peg at the Printers,' is shortly to be brought forward at the New Theatre," advised:

> Good Tommy Wignell, don't attack the printers!
> As well might *drunkards* be revil'd by *vintners!*
> Believe me, friend, in spite of all your witticisms,
> They'll bear too hard upon you by their criticisms.
> 'Tis they can raise a player and a poet—
> You're wrong, believe me, and they'll let you know it.[56]
>
> Q

There is no record that *A Peg at the Printers* was enjoyed.

In 1798 Lailson's Circus had crashed down, and on December 17, 1799, Ricketts' Pantheon, which had begun its season on November 27, burned up. The spectacular pantomime of *Don Juan* had been announced, and the last scene, representing "the Infernal Regions with a view of the mouth of Hell," had been promised in realistic detail. The truth seems to be that the burning of the Pantheon had nothing to do with Don Juan's punishment, but the public was hard to convince.

The season at the New Theatre from December 4, 1799, to May 19, 1800, was just beginning when the nineteenth century, which ends the present record, came in. No important changes in the company had occurred over the summer. John Bernard was still the leading comedian, with Warren second only to him, and young Cain was again Tancred to Mrs. Merry's Sigismunda.

[54] Chap. XXXI, Series I.
[55] See, e. g., *Phila. Gazette,* Feb. 11, 26, 1799.
[56] February 23, 1799.

RETROSPECT

So by the end of the eighteenth century the Philadelphia stage had, after many decades of growth, achieved the vigor of manhood. Our knowledge of the first half of the century is cloudy, obscured by the fact that the newspapers, the first not appearing till 1719, gave almost no local news. But we know that from 1700 on there was strong opposition to the stage, expressed during the first two decades by repeated prohibitions. From an old letter we learn that strolling comedians were in town in 1723, and were patronized by the governor of the state. An advertisement in the next year tells of a theatre, "The New Booth on Society Hill." Then for a quarter of a century longer there is silence, broken only by the barkers for marionettes and a "magick lanthorn" show, till in 1749–50 a few whispers reveal that the Murray and Kean players, perhaps from the West Indies, were playing at Plumsted's warehouse in Water Street.

In 1754 Hallam's adventurous Comedians from London came to the city, and in 1759 David Douglass built the Theatre on Society Hill, and seven years later the Theatre in Southwark, which was to remain the most important theatre in the city for more than twenty-five years. Hallam's troupe had become the nucleus of the American Company, which, led by David Douglass, strolled along the Atlantic seaboard till the Revolution, with Philadelphia furnishing its most dependable audience. When the American Company was in Philadelphia, the Theatre in Southwark was open three nights a week, with a change of bill every night. The repertory included many of the best Shakespearean, Restoration, and early eighteenth century plays, and after each main play the entertainment was rounded out with an afterpiece of farce, pantomime, or ballad-opera. There were few purely American dramas to be seen during the century; only one, Godfrey's *The Prince of Parthia,* was produced in colonial Philadelphia.

In 1778, during the Revolution, the British officers gave plays at the Theatre in Southwark, as the American officers did at Valley Forge, and probably also at the Southwark. A law against plays which was passed in 1779 remained on the statute books for ten years, and made a great deal of trouble. When the actors returned after the war, they reopened the Theatre in Southwark, evaded the law by disguising plays as operas or moral lectures, and were patronized by the best people in

[65]

the city, including George Washington. Various efforts to repeal the prohibition failed till, in 1789, civic consciousness was at last thoroughly aroused, and a Dramatic Association formed which struck the law from the books.

In the last decade of the century the city outgrew the historic old Theatre in Southwark, and built the New Theatre in Chesnut Street, a spacious and excellent house, for which an admirable company was imported *en masse* from England. Dozens and scores of the best British plays were given every season, with operas and pantomimes, and new American plays as they were written. The growing taste for spectacle led to the building of two pantomimic-circuses, Ricketts' Art Pantheon and Lailson's Circus, both soon accidentally destroyed. So as the eighteenth century closed, the excellent New Theatre in Chesnut Street stood alone in Philadelphia, at the head of the American stage.

The following standard works have usually been referred to by the author's name, or by an abbreviated title:

Dunlap, William,
History of the American Theatre, N. Y., 1832.

Durang, Charles,
The Philadelphia Stage. From the Year 1749 to the Year 1855.
Partly compiled from the papers of his father, the late John
Durang; with notes by the editors [of the Philadelphia *Sunday*
Dispatch]. First series, 1749–1821, beginning in the issue of May
7, 1854. Complete files pasted in bound volumes are to be found
in the libraries of the University of Pennsylvania, the Philadelphia
Company, the Historical Society of Pennsylvania, and Harvard
University.

Odell, G. C. D.,
Annals of the New York Stage, Vols. I and II, New York, 1927.

Quinn, Arthur Hobson,
A History of the American Drama from the Beginning to the
Civil War, New York, 1923.

Seilhamer, George O.,
History of the American Theatre, 3 vols., New York 1888 (Vol.
I), 1889 (Vol. II), 1891 (Vol. III).

Watson, John F.,
Annals of Philadelphia and Pennsylvania in the Olden Time,
Philadelphia, 1879 (copyright 1857).

Willis, Eola,
The Charleston Stage in the Eighteenth Century, Columbia, S. C.,
1924.

PART II

DAY BOOK

1700–1800

INTRODUCTION TO THE DAY BOOK

IN THE following *Day Book* of the Philadelphia stage during the eighteenth century, the attempt has been made to record every production, every cast, and every performer, together with all relevant legislation. Gaps in the available documents, especially for the colonial period, have made this ideal unattainable; but the record includes all known information. The probable degree of completeness has been indicated at the end of the record of every colonial season. For the early national period from 1779 to 1789, when the presentation of plays was illegal in Pennsylvania, the record is too tenuous to make mathematical calculation helpful. For the period from 1789 to 1800, however, the record is presumably complete for the plays, and probably so for the actors, though the record of casts (and hence of actors) is dependent on the vagaries of advertising.

The following plan is used:

The arrangement is strictly chronological.

Note is made, on each date of playing, of the theatre, the known dramatic performances, and the known actors in both plays and afterpieces. An afterpiece is defined simply as a play, "opera," or pantomime immediately succeeding another play, "opera," or pantomime.

The beginning of each theatrical season is noted as it appears, and reference then made to the last playing date of the season.

Under the last date of the season, a summary is given of the new plays, the new afterpieces, and the new actors, and of the reappearing plays, afterpieces, and actors, for the entire season.

Each play is starred on its first known appearance, and its author, if known, then given.

The first known appearance of each actor is mentioned under the date of such appearance.

Unless otherwise noted, all dates and all statements of priority refer to the record of the Philadelphia stage. Thus a "new" play is one not previously recorded as on the Philadelphia stage; a "reappearing" actor is one who has appeared before in any Philadelphia theatre.

Unless otherwise noted, each documentary reference (given in the upper right-hand corner opposite the date) refers to the announcement of the bill.

The attempt has been made to preserve all significant idiosyncrasies of eighteenth century spelling and idiom, and not to reduce all terms to a modern norm. Thus "Mr. Hallam's Benefit," "Benefit of Mr. Hallam," and "Mr. Hallam's Night," all meaning the same thing, have not been standardized; and an actress may be "Mrs." at one time and "Mme." at another. On the other hand, the preservation of typographical errors has not been made an end in itself.

A Play Index, a Player Index, and a Playwright Index will be found immediately following the *Day Book*.

[71]

ABBREVIATIONS

THE following abbreviations for periodicals have been employed. The dates refer to the years for which the papers have been used.

1719–1745. "Mercury": *American Weekly Mercury.*
1728–1773. "Gazette": *Pennsylvania Gazette.*
1742–1790. "Journal": *Pennsylvania Journal or the Weekly Advertiser.*
1757–1758. "Am. Mag.": *American Magazine and Monthly Chronicle for the British Colonies.*
1767–1773. "Chronicle": *Pennsylvania Chronicle and Universal Daily Advertiser.*
1773–1790. "Packet": *Pennsylvania Packet and the General Advertiser.*
1776. *Pennsylvania Evening Post.*
1777–1778. "Ledger": *Pennsylvania Ledger.*
1781–1782. *Freeman's Journal.*
1789–1792. "Fed. Gaz.": *Federal Gazette and the Philadelphia Evening Post.*
1791–1799. "Daily Ad.": *Dunlap's [later Claypoole's] American Daily Advertiser.*
1791–1794. "Gen. Ad.": *General Advertiser and Political, Commercial, Agricultural, and Literary Journal.*
1792–1799. "G. U. S.": *Gazette of the United States, and Philadelphia Daily Advertiser.*
1795–1799. "Aurora": *Aurora General Advertiser.*
1795–1799. "Phila. Gaz.": *Philadelphia Gazette and Universal Daily Advertiser.*

OTHER SOURCES

"Acts Ass.": Acts of the Assembly of Pennsylvania.
"Votes Ass.": Votes of the Assembly of Pennsylvania.
"Min. Ass. Pa.": Minutes of the Assembly of Pennsylvania.
"Pa. Arch.": Pennsylvania Archives.
"H. S. P.": Historical Society of Pennsylvania.
"Min. Com. Coun.": Minutes of the Common Council of the City of Philadelphia, 1704–1776.
"J. Cont. Cong.": Journals of the Continental Congress.
"J. House Rep. Pa.": Journals of the House of Representatives of Pennsylvania.

DAY BOOK

1700–1800

DATE   COMPANY, THEATRE, PLAY, AUTHOR, CAST, NOTES   SOURCE

1700   Acts Ass., p. 1, and Statutes at
Large of Pennsylvania, II, 4

Law passed between October 24 and November 27, against "Stage plays, masks, and revels."

1705

Feb. 7   Acts Ass., p. 22

Law of 1700 repealed in England.

1706

Jan. 12   Votes Ass., pp. 80–81

Law against "Interludes, stage plays, masks, and revels" repassed.

1709

Oct. 24   Votes Ass., II, 76

Law of 1706 vetoed in England.

1711

Feb. 24   Votes Ass., II, 83

Law against sports passed.

1713

Feb. 20   Acts Ass., p. 60

Law of 1711 vetoed in England.

1723   Comedians in town before "9th 2mo."   Pa. Arch., 2nd
Series, VII, 70–72

These are the first actors known to have been in Philadelphia.

1724

April 30   "Roap dancing" at the "New Booth on   American Weekly
Society Hill."   Mercury, May 7

The "New Booth on Society Hill" is the first theatre known in Philadelphia. This is the first newspaper announcement of a theatrical performance.

1742   Punch and Joan "at the sign of the Coach and Horses."   Gazette, Dec. 30

The first marionettes on record in the city.

1743   "Magick Lanthorn" at Joseph Barber's,   Gazette, Jan. 27
        "at the Temple Bar in Second Street."

The first "picture show" on record in Philadelphia.

1749

Aug. 22/3   * *Cato*—Addison   Manuscript Diary of John Smith

This performance was given at Plumsted's (warehouse) Theatre, Water Street, probably by the Murray and Kean players. It was (there is little room for doubt) part of a season extending at least from August, 1749, to January, 1750.

The one play known to have been given this season is *Cato*. The following plays are known to have been given in New York after this season by the Murray and Kean company, and *may* have been given in Philadelphia: *The Beaux' Stratagem, The Beggar's Opera, A Bold Stroke for a Wife, The Busy Body, The Committee, The Distrest Mother, The Fair Penitent, George Barnwell, Love for Love, The Orphan, The Recruiting Officer, Richard III, Sir Harry Wildair,* and *The Spanish Fryar*. The only player known to have been with the company in Philadelphia was Nancy George. Other members of the company who appeared in New York: Walter Murray, Thomas Kean, Jago, Mrs. Leigh, Mr. Marks, Mr. Moore, Master Dicky Murray, Mrs. and Miss Osborne, Mr. Scott, Mrs. Taylor, John Tremaine, and Charles Somerset Woodham. (See Odell, I, 32–43.)

1750

Jan. 8   Min. Com. Coun., p. 523

The Common Council made a formal gesture attempting to "discourage" the actors.

Feb. 26   Gazette, March 26

A New York news item said, "Last week arrived here a company of comedians from Philadelphia." (See also Odell, I, 32.)

1754

March 26   Gazette

A letter from "Y.Z." refers to "one express condition of the Permission lately granted for the acting a few Plays here."

1754

HALLAM'S COMPANY—NEW THEATRE IN WATER STREET

April 15   * The Fair Penitent—Rowe   Gazette, April 11

Sciolto..............Mr. Malone	Altamount........Mr. Clarkson
Horatio.............Mr. Rigby	Lothario..........Mr. Singleton
Rossano............Mr. Adcock	Servant......Master L. Hallam
Calista............Mrs. Hallam	Lavinia...........Mrs. Adcock
Lucilla.............Mrs. Rigby	

* Miss in Her Teens—Garrick

Fribble..........Mr. Singleton	Capt. Loveit.........Mr. Adcock
Flash.............Mr. Clarkson	Puff................Mr. Miller
Jasper..............Mr. Rigby	Tagg.............Mrs. Adcock
Biddy Bellair....Miss [Helen?] Hallam	

This was the first appearance of Hallam's "Company of Comedians from London" in Philadelphia. The theatre used was the New Theatre in Water Street—sometime Plumsted's warehouse. All the actors were new to the Philadelphia record. "Master L. Hallam" was Lewis Hallam, the younger. The season ended June 24, 1754.

May 27   Benefit of Lewis Hallam   Play Bill in

* Tunbridge Walks—Baker   Pa. Hist. Soc.

Woodcock..........Mr. Malone	Raynard.............Mr. Rigby
Loveworth..........Mr. Miller	Capt. Squib....Mr. Lewis Hallam
Mr. Maiden.......Mr. Singleton	Belinda...........Mrs. Becceley
Penelope........Mrs. Clarkson	Lucy..............Miss Hallam
Hillaria...........Mrs. Hallam	Mrs. Goodfellow.....Mrs. Rigby

* Flora; or, Hob in the Well—Dogget

Sir Thomas Testy...Mr. Clarkson	Flora.............Mrs. Becceley
Friendly............Mr. Adcock	Old Hob............Mr. Miller
Dick..........Master L. Hallam	Hob's Mother.....Mrs. Clarkson
Betty.............Miss Hallam	Young Hob.Mr.[Adam?] Hallam

We have no record between the opening on April 15 and Lewis Hallam's benefit on May 27. This was the first known appearance of Mrs. Becceley, Mrs. Clarkson, Mr. [Adam?] Hallam, and Mr. Lewis Hallam, Sr.

June 10   Benefit of Miss Hallam and her Two Brothers   Gazette, June 6

* The Gamester—Moore
Miss in Her Teens

[75]

1754

June 12   Mr. Adcock's Benefit   Gazette, June 6

* *Tamerlane*—Rowe

Tamerlane........Mr. Singleton	Moneses............Mr. Rigby
Axalla...............Mr. Bell	Prince of Tanais.....Mr. Adcock
Stratocles..........Mr. Miller	Bajazet............Mr. Malone
Omar...........Mr. Clarkson	Dervise.......Mr. Lewis Hallam
Haly........Master L. Hallam	Selima...........Mrs. Becceley
Arpasia...........Mrs. Hallam	

* *A Wife Well Managed*—Mrs. Centlivre

First appearance of Mr. Bell.

June 19   Benefit of the Charity School   Gazette, June 13 and 20

* *The Careless Husband*—Cibber
* *Harlequin Collector* (pantomime)

Postponed from June 17. In the *Gazette* for June 20 appeared the first newspaper *notice* of a theatrical performance in Philadelphia.

June 24   * *The Provoked Husband*—Cibber   Gazette, June 27
                    Miss in Her Teens

The season from April 15 to June 24, 1754, ended with this night.
The season probably included 30 nights, of which we have record of only six. Six plays appeared for the first time on our record—*The Careless Husband, The Fair Penitent, The Gamester, The Provoked Husband, Tamerlane,* and *Tunbridge Walks.* The new afterpieces were *Flora; or, Hob in the Well, Harlequin Collector, Miss in Her Teens,* and *A Wife Well Managed.* New actors: Mr. and Mrs. Adcock, Mrs. Becceley, Mr. Bell, Mr. and Mrs. Clarkson, Mr. Adam Hallam, Miss [Helen?] Hallam, Mr. Lewis Hallam, Sr., Mrs. Lewis Hallam (later Mrs. Douglass), Mr. Lewis Hallam, Jr., Mr. Malone, Mr. Miller, Mr. and Mrs. Rigby, and Mr. Singleton.

1757

COLLEGE OF PHILADELPHIA

                                         Gazette

Jan.   * *The Masque of Alfred the Great*—   Jan. 20–Feb. 10
       Thomson & Mallet, as revised by Provost William Smith

This play was given by the students at the College of Philadelphia during the Christmas holidays. The new actors were W. Hamilton, S. Chew, Jacob Duché (see text p. 12).

1759

DOUGLASS COMPANY—THEATRE ON SOCIETY HILL

April 5   Pa. Arch. III, 659–660

Douglass got permission "To build a Theatre and Act Without the bounds of the City."

June 20   Min. Prov. Coun., 354

Law against theatres passed, but amended by Governor Denny so that it did not take effect till January 1, 1760. Repealed Sept. 2, 1760.

June 25   Opening of Theatre on Society Hill   Gazette, June 21

Tamerlane

Tamerlane.........Mr. Harman	Prince of Tanais......Mr. Horne
Bajazet............Mr. Hallam	Dervise.............Mr. Morris
Moneses..........Mr. Douglass	Haly.............Mr. A. Hallam
Axalla..............Mr. Reed	Arpasia..........Mrs. Douglass
Omar..........Mr. Tomlinson	Selima............Mrs. Harman

* *The Virgin Unmasked*—Fielding

Miss Lucy—Mrs. Harman

This is the first appearance of Mr. Douglass, Mr. and Mrs. Harman, Mr. Reed, Mr. Horne, Mr. Morris, Mr. Tomlinson; and Mrs. Love, who sang after the play. The Society Hill Theatre, used during this season, was at the southwest corner of Vernon and Cedar. Mrs. Douglass was the former Mrs. Hallam. This Lewis Hallam was "the Younger."

We have record of only about one-third of the plays probably produced in the season from June 25 to Dec. 28, 1759.

June 29   * *Richard III*—Shakespeare   Gazette, June 28

King Henry.......Mr. Douglass	Prince Edward....Mr. A. Hallam
Duke of York.Miss Nancy Hallam	King Richard.......Mr. Harman
Earl of Richmond....Mr. Hallam	Duke of Buckingham...Mr. Reed
Catesby.........Mr. Tomlinson	Lord Stanly........Mr. Morris
Oxford.............Mr. Horne	Queen Elizabeth...Mrs. Douglass
Lady Anne........Mrs. Harman	Dutchess of York......Mrs. Love

* *Lethe*—Garrick

Miss Nancy Hallam had not appeared before.

[77]

1759

July 6   *The Provoked Husband*   Gazette, July 5

Lord Townly......Mr. Douglass	Sir Francis Wronghead..........
Squire Richard.......Mr. Morris	Mr. Harman
Count Basset..........Mr. Reed	John Moody.....Mr. Tomlinson
Constable...........Mr. Horne	Lady Townly.....Mrs. Douglass
Lady Grace.......Mrs. Harman	Lady Wronghead......Mrs. Love
Miss Jenny........Mrs. Harman	Myrtilla........Mrs. Tomlinson
Manly.............Mr. Hallam	

* *The Wonder; an Honest Yorkshireman!*—Carey

Carey's farce is not to be confused with Mrs. Centlivre's comedy, *A Wonder, or a Woman Keeps a Secret*. Mrs. Tomlinson made her first Philadelphia appearance.

July 13   * *Douglas*—Home   Gazette, July 12

Lord Randolph.....Mr. Douglass	Old Norval........Mr. Harman
Glenalvon............Mr. Reed	Lady Randolph....Mrs. Douglass
Norval Douglas.....Mr. Hallam	Anna.............Mrs. Harman

* *The Mock Doctor*—Fielding

July 20   * *The Recruiting Officer*—Farquhar   Penna. Gazette,
                                                     July 19

Justice Ballance........Mr. Reed	Recruits.......Messieurs Allyn &
Captain Plume......Mr. Hallam	Harman
Captain Brazen.....Mr. Harman	Melinda..........Mrs. Harman
Worthy............Mr. Morris	Sylvia...........Mrs. Douglass
Serjeant Kite......Mr. Douglass	Rose...............Mrs. Love
Bullock..........Mr. Tomlinson	Lucy..........Mrs. Tomlinson
Constable...........Mr. Horne	

* *The Adventures of Half-an-Hour*—Bullock

First appearance of Mr. Allyn.

July 27   * *Hamlet*—Shakespeare   Gazette, July 26

King...........Mr. Tomlinson	Marcellus...........Mr. Allyn
Hamlet..........Mr. Hallam	Grave-Diggers...Messrs. Harman
Polonius..........Mr. Harman	& Allyn
Horatio...........Mr. Morris	Ghost...........Mr. Douglass
Laertes..............Mr. Reed	Queen..........Mrs. Douglass
Guildenstern........Mr. Horne	Ophelia..........Mrs. Harman
Osrick..........Mr. A. Hallam	Player Queen........Mrs. Love

1759

The Stage Coach—Farquhar

Aug. 3   *The Drummer*—Addison   Gazette, August 2

Sir George Truman.....Mr. Reed   Coachman.........Mr. Douglass
Fantom............Mr. Morris   Gardner.............Mr. Allyn
Tinfall............Mr. Hallam   Lady Truman.....Mrs. Douglass
Vellum............Mr. Harman   Abigail..........Mrs. Harman
Butler...........Mr. Tomlinson

The Anatomist, or The Sham-Doctor—Ravenscroft

Aug. 10   *Theodosius*—Lee   Gazette, August 9

Theodosius............Mr. Reed   Aranthes............Mr. Morris
Varamnes............Mr. Allyn   Pulcheria.........Mrs. Harman
Marcian............Mr. Hallam   Athenais.........Mrs. Douglass
Atticus............Mr. Harman   Marina.........Mrs. Tomlinson
Leontine.........Mr. Tomlinson   Flavilla.............Mrs. Love
Lucius...........Mr. Douglass

Lethe

Aug. 17   *George Barnwell*—Lillo   Gazette, August 16

Thorowgood.......Mr. Douglass   Blunt............Mr. Harman
Uncle.............Mr. Morris   Millwood.........Mrs. Douglass
George Barnwell.....Mr. Hallam   Marcia.............Mrs. Love
Truman.............Mr. Reed   Lucy............Mrs. Harman

Harlequin Collector

Aug. 24   *The Beggar's Opera*—Gay   Gazette, August 23

Capt. M'Heath.....Mr. Harman   Harry Paddington....Mr. Horne
Peachum.........Mr. Tomlinson   Filch............Mr. A. Hallam
Lockit................Mr. Scott   Mrs. Peachum.....Mrs. Harman
Mat of the Mint.......Mr. Reed   Polly...............Mrs. Love
Beggar............Mr. Morris   Lucy............Mrs. Harman
Player............Mr. Douglass   Mrs. Coaxer......Mrs. Douglass
Jemmy Twitcher......Mr. Allyn   Mrs. Slammekin..Mrs. Tomlinson

Lethe

This is the first recorded appearance of Mr. Scott, though he may have been in the Murray and Kean Company of 1749–50.

1759

Aug. 31   *The Fair Penitent*   Gazette, August 30

Sciolto..........Mr. Tomlinson		Rossano............Mr. Morris
Altamount............Mr. Reed		Calista............Mrs. Harman
Lothario...........Mr. Harman		Lavinia...........Mrs. Douglass
Horatio............Mr. Hallam		Lucilla..............Mrs. Love

* *The School-Boy*—Cibber

Sept. 7   *Douglas*   Gazette, Sept. 6

Sept. 14   *Hamlet*   Gazette, Sept. 13
The Adventures of Half-an-Hour

The cast for *Hamlet* is the same as that for July 27, save that Mr. Scott is now listed as the Player King (both Mr. Scott and the part were absent from the bill for July 27).

Sept. 21   *The Recruiting Officer*   Gazette, Sept. 20

Justice Ballance.......Mr. Reed		Recruits..Messieurs Tomlinson & Allyn
Captain Plume......Mr. Hallam		Bullock..........Mr. Tomlinson
Captain Brazen.....Mr. Harman		Melinda..........Mrs. Harman
Mr. Worthy........Mr. Morris		Sylvia...........Mrs. Douglass
Serjeant Kite......Mr. Douglass		Rose...............Mrs. Love
Mr. Scale.............Mr. Scott		Lucy..........Mrs. Tomlinson
Constable...........Mr. Allyn		

The Stage Coach

Sept. 28   * *King Lear*—Shakespeare   Gazette, Sept. 27

King Lear........Mr. Harman		Albany............Mr. Morris
Gloster..............Mr. Scott		Burgundy........Mr. Douglass
Kent...........Mr. Tomlinson		Gentleman Usher.....Mr. Allyn
Edgar..............Mr. Hallam		Goneril..............Mrs. Love
Bastard.............Mr. Reed		Regan.............Mrs. Harman
Cornwall...........Mr. Horne		Cordelia.........Mrs. Douglass

"Farce, as will be expressed in the Bills for the Day."

Oct. 5   *The Provoked Husband*   Gazette, Oct. 4

Lord Townly......Mr. Douglass		Lady Townly.....Mrs. Douglass
Manly...............Mr. Allyn		Lady Grace........Mrs. Harman
Sir Francis............Mr. Scott		Lady Wronghead.....Mrs. Love
Squire Richard.......Mr. Morris		Miss Jenny.......Mrs. Harman
Count Basset..........Mr. Reed		Myrtilla........Mrs. Tomlinson
John Moody.....Mr. Tomlinson		

1759

The Toy-Shop—Dodsley

Oct. 12   *The Provoked Husband*   Gazette, Oct. 11
                          Cast as for October 5.

Oct. 26   * *Macbeth*—Shakespeare   Gazette, Oct. 25

Duncan...........Mr. Harman   Seyton...........Mr. Tomlinson
Malcolm..............Mr. Reed   Flean.......Miss Nancy Hallam
Donaldbaine.....Mr. A. Hallam   Lady Macbeth....Mrs. Douglass
Lenox..............Mr. Morris   Lady Macduff........Mrs. Love
Macbeth...........Mr. Hallam   Hecate............Mrs. Harman
Banquo..............Mr. Scott   Witches..Messrs. Allyn, Harman,
Macduff.........Mr. Douglass   and Tomlinson

Nov. 2   * *Romeo and Juliet*—Shakespeare   Gazette, Nov. 1
                          Miss in Her Teens

Seilhamer (I, 105) gives the following cast for this production of *Romeo and
Juliet*. I have been unable to find it elsewhere:

Romeo............Mr. Hallam   Tybalt..............Mr. Reed
Mercutio..,......Mr. Harman   Apothecary..........Mr. Allyn
Montague........Mr. Douglass   Lady Capulet.......Mrs. Love
Capulet.........Mr. Tomlinson   Juliet............Mrs. Douglass
Friar Laurence.......Mr. Scott   Nurse...........Mrs. Harman
Paris..............Mr. Horne

Nov. 9   *The Beggar's Opera*   Gazette, Nov. 8

Peachum.........Mr. Tomlinson   Mrs. Peachum.....Mrs. Harman
Lockit..............Mr. Scott   Polly...............Mrs. Love
Capt. Macheath....Mr. Harman   Lucy...........Mrs. Harman
Filch..,..........Mr. Allyn   Mrs. Coaxer.....Mrs. Douglass
Mat of the Mint......Mr. Reed   Mrs. Slammekin..Mrs. Tomlinson
Harry Paddington....Mr. Horne   Diana Trapes.....Mrs. Harman
Beggar.........Mr. Tomlinson   Moll Brazen.....Mr. Douglass
Player...........Mr. Douglass

Harlequin Collector

Harlequin.........Mr. Hallam   Conjurer..........Mr. Harman
Miller.............Mr. Allyn   Doctor.........Mr. Tomlinson
Clown...........Mr. Douglass   Columbine.......Mrs. Douglass

1759

| Nov. 16 | Benefit of Mr. Scott | Gazette, Nov. 15 |

Theodosius

Cast as for August 10, except:

Theodosius........Mr. Douglass   Lucius.............Mr. Horne

* *The Lying Valet*—Garrick

| Nov. 23 | Benefit of Mr. Hallam | Gazette, Nov. 22 |

The Provoked Husband

Lord Townly.......Mr. Hallam	Constable............Mr. Horne
Manly..............Mr. Allyn	Lady Townly.....Mrs. Douglass
Sir Francis Wronghead..Mr. Scott	Lady Grace.......Mrs. Harman
Squire Richard......Mr. Morris	Lady Wronghead.....Mrs. Love
Count Basset.........Mr. Reed	Miss Jenny........Mrs. Harman
John Moody.....Mr. Tomlinson	Myrtilla........Mrs. Tomlinson

Harlequin Collector

| Dec. 1 | Mr. Allyn's Benefit | Gazette, Nov. 29 |

Macbeth

Macbeth...........Mr. Palmer   Lady Macbeth....Mrs. Douglass
Mr. Palmer's name had not previously appeared in the bills.

The Stage Coach

| Dec. 7 | Benefit of Mr. Adam Hallam | Gazette, Dec. 6 |

* *The Suspicious Husband*—Hoadly

Mr. Strickland......Mr. Palmer	Buckle..............Mr. Horne
Frankly..........Mr. Douglass	Chairman............Mr. Scott
Bellamy............Mr. Morris	Mrs. Strickland....Mrs. Harman
Ranger............Mr. Hallam	Jacintha.............Mrs. Love
Tester..........Mr. Tomlinson	Lucetta........Mrs. Tomlinson
Jack Maggot.........Mr. Reed	Clarinda.........Mrs. Douglass

The Virgin Unmasked

Miss Lucy.......Mrs. Harman

1759

| Dec. 14 | Benefit of Mr. Reed | Gazette, Dec. 13 |

The Gamester

Beverly	Mr. Hallam	Stukely	Mr. Palmer
Jarvis	Mr. Tomlinson	Dawson	Mr. Allyn
Lewson	Mr. Harman	Mrs. Beverly	Mrs. Douglass
Bates	Mr. Morris	Charlotte	Mrs. Harman

The School-Boy

| Dec. 21 | Benefit of Mr. Palmer | Gazette, Dec. 20 |

Romeo and Juliet

Romeo	Mr. Palmer	Benvolio	Mr. Morris
Montague	Mr. Douglass	Starved Apothecary	Mr. Allyn
Capulet	Mr. Tomlinson	Mercutio	Mr. Hallam
Paris	Mr. Horne	Juliet	Mrs. Douglass
Friar Lawrence	Mr. Scott	Lady Capulet	Mrs. Love
Tibalt	Mr. Reed	Nurse	Mrs. Harman

Harlequin Collector

Dec. 27   Gazette

"Towards the raising a Fund for purchasing an Organ to the College-Hall in this City, and instructing the Charity Children in Psalmody."

George Barnwell

Thorowgood	Mr. Douglass	Trueman	Mr. Tomlinson
Uncle	Mr. Morris	Millwood	Mrs. Douglass
George Barnwell	Mr. Hallam	Maria	Mrs. Love
Blunt	Mr. Harman	Lucy	Mrs. Harman

Lethe

"In which the Character of Lord Chalkstone will be introduced by Mr. Allyn."

| Dec. 28 | Benefit of the Pennsylvania Hospital | Gazette, Dec. 27 |

Hamlet

This ended (unless there was an unrecorded performance on December 29 or 31, which is not at all probable, after two charity benefits had been given) the brilliant season of June 25 to Dec. 28, 1759. We have record of twenty-eight performances having been given this season, of a probable eighty. Plays produced for the first time (as far as our record goes) in Philadelphia: *The Beggar's Opera, Douglas, The Drummer, George Barnwell, Hamlet, King Lear, King Richard III, Macbeth, The Recruiting Officer, Romeo and Juliet, The Suspicious Husband,* and *Theodosius.* The plays which reappeared were *The Fair Penitent, The Gamester, The Provoked Husband,* and *Tamerlane.* New after-

1759

pieces: *The Adventures of Half-an-Hour, the Anatomist, Lethe, The Lying Valet, The Mock Doctor, The School-Boy, The Stage-Coach, The Toy Shop, The Virgin Unmasked, The Wonder; An Honest Yorkshireman.* The repeated farces were *Harlequin Collector* (a pantomime) and *Miss in Her Teens.* The actors this season who had previously played in Philadelphia were Mrs. Douglass (in 1754, Mrs. Hallam), Adam and Lewis Hallam. (Scott *may* have been in the city in 1749–50, and Mrs. Love may have played here in 1754.) The new actors were Mr. Allyn; David Douglass, the manager; Miss Nancy Hallam (assuming her not to have been the Miss Hallam of 1754); Mr. and Mrs. Harman; Mr. Horne; Mrs. Love (?); Mr. Morris; (John?) Palmer; Mr. Reed; Mr. Scott (?); and Mr. and Mrs. Tomlinson.

1760

Jan. 1

Law against theatres went into effect. See June 20, 1759.

Sept. 2   Min. Prov. Coun. VIII, 552–7

Law of June 20, 1759, repealed in England.

1761

COLLEGE OF PHILADELPHIA

May 23   * *Dialogue*—Wm. Smith   Library, U. of Pa.
                            Ode—Francis Hopkinson

"Sacred to the Memory of His Late Gracious Majesty, George II."

1762

May 18   * *Dialogue*—Jacob Duché   Library, U. of Pa.

"On the Accession of His present gracious Majesty"—George III.

1763

May 17   * *Dialogue "On Peace"*—Nathaniel Evans   Library, U. of Pa.

1765

May 30   * *Dialogue*—Francis Hopkinson   Library, U. of Pa.

1766

May 20   * *Dialogue*—Francis Hopkinson   Library, U. of Pa. and
                                                             Pa. Journal, June 5

Celebrating the repeal of the Stamp Act.

1766

June 27   Ms. in H. S. P.

The Quakers petitioned Governor Penn to prevent the playing of "A Company of Stage Players [who] are lately arrived in this City." This is the first mention this season of the players being in town. It is possible that they opened the Theatre on Society Hill in the summer, though we have record of no performance before November at the Theatre in Southwark.

July 31   Journal

A letter says, "They forsooth are going to build a playhouse at Philadelphia."

SOUTHWARK THEATRE

Nov. 14   *The Provoked Husband*   Journal, Nov. 13
                       * *Thomas and Sally*—Bickerstaff

This bill was originally advertised in the Journal of November 6 for November 12. It is possible that it was given as first announced, but more probable that it was postponed to November 14. *Opening of the Theatre in Southwark.* First night of the season from Nov. 14 or earlier, 1766, to July 6, 1767.

Nov. 17   * *The Distressed Mother*—Phillips   Journal, Nov. 13
                           The Lying Valet

This was originally advertised in the Journal of November 6 as for November 14. (That is, for Friday, presumably after *The Provoked Husband,* which was announced for November 12.) I assume it was postponed till November 17.

Nov. 19   * *The Wonder*—Mrs. Centlivre   Journal, Nov. 13
                         * *The Citizen*—Murphy

Nov. 21   *Douglas*   Gazette, Nov. 20

Douglas............Mr. Hallam   Norval.............Mr. Morris
Lord Randolph.....Mr. Douglass   Anna..............Mrs. Harman
Glenalvon...........Mr. Wall

         * *Catherine and Petruchio*—Shakespeare—Garrick

Catherine...........Miss Cheer   Petruchio..........Mr. Hallam
First appearance of Miss Cheer.

Nov. 24   * *The School for Lovers*—Whitehead   Gazette, Nov. 20

Nov. 26   * *Jane Shore*—Rowe   Gazette, Nov. 20

[85]

1766

Nov. 28   *The Beggar's Opera*   Gazette, Nov. 27

Captain Macheath....Mr. Woolls	Mrs. Slammekin..Miss Dowthwait
Peachum.............Mr. Allyn	Beggar.............Mr. Morris
Lockit..........Mr. Tomlinson	Moll Brazen.......Mr. Douglass
Filch.................Mr. Wall	Mrs. Peachum.....Mrs. Harman
Jeremy Twitcher..Mr. Matthews	Polly.........Miss Wainwright
Lucy.............Mrs. Morris	

In Act 3 a Hornpipe, by Mr. Matthews

* The Old Maid—Murphy

The Old Maid.....Mrs. Harman	Captain Cape......Mr. Douglass
Cleremont.........Mr. Hallam	Mr. Harlow.........Mr. Allyn
Mr. Heartly.......Mr. Morris	Trifle.............Mrs. Morris
Mrs. Harlow.......Miss Cheer	

First appearance of Miss Wainwright, Mr. Wall, Mr. Woolls, Mr. Matthews, Mrs. Morris, and Miss Dowthwait.

Dec. 5   *Richard III*   Gazette, Dec. 4

King Richard.......Mr. Hallam	King Henry.........Mr. Morris
Richmond.........Mr. Douglass	Buckingham..........Mr. Wall
Prince Edward......Mr. Godwin	Duke of York...Miss Dowthwait
Lord Stanley........Mr. Allyn	Catesby..........Mr. Tomlinson
Ratcliffe............Mr. Woolls	Tressel..........Mr. Douglass
Lady Anne.........Miss Cheer	Duchess of York....Mrs. Harman
Queen Elizabeth.. Mrs. Douglass	

* The Oracle—Mrs. Cibber

Cinthia (with a song in Character) by Miss [Sarah] Hallam.
Oberon by Mr. Wall   Fairy Queen by Mrs. Douglass.

First appearance of Mr. Godwin and Miss Sarah Hallam.

Dec. 12   * The Merchant of Venice—Shakespeare   Gazette, Dec. 11

Shylock............Mr. Hallam	Bassanio..........Mr. Douglass
Anthonio........Mr. Tomlinson	Gratiano.............Mr. Allyn
Launcelot..........Mr. Morris	Lorenzo...........Mr. Woolls
Salanio.............Mr. Wall	Solarino.........Mr. Matthews
Jessica........Miss Wainwright	Portia.............Miss Cheer
Nerissa..........Mrs. Harman	

* The King and the Miller of Mansfield—Dodsley

1766

Dec. 19   * *The Constant Couple*—Farquhar   Gazette, Dec. 18

Sir Harry Wildair...Mr. Hallam	Colonel Standard...Mr. Douglass
Beau Clincher........Mr. Allyn	Young Clincher.......Mr. Wall
Alderman Smuggler..Mr. Morris	Vizard.........Mr. Tomlinson
Dickey.............Mr. Woolls	Angelica............Miss Cheer
Lady Darling....Mrs. Tomlinson	Parley........Miss Wainwright
Mob's Wife.......Mrs. Harman	Lady Lurewell....Mrs. Douglass

* *The Devil to Pay*—Coffey

Sir John Loverule....Mr. Woolls	Lucy..........Mrs. Tomlinson
(in which Character he will sing the	Nell..............Mrs. Morris
Early Horn)	Butler.............Mr. Morris
Jobson.........Mr. Tomlinson	Footman............Mr. Wall
Coachman...........Mr. Allyn	Lady Loverule.....Mrs. Harman
Doctor..........Mr. Douglass	Lettice........Miss Dowthwait

Dec. 26   *Theodosius*   Gazette, Dec. 25

Varanes............Mr. Hallam	Theodosius..........Mr. Morris
Marcian..........Mr. Douglass	Atticus..........Mr. Tomlinson
Leontine.............Mr. Allyn	Aranthes............Mr. Wall
Lucius.............Mr. Woolls	Pulcheria.........Mrs. Harman
Marina...........Miss Hallam	Flavilla........Miss Wainwright
Julia..........Miss Dowthwait	Delia..........Mrs. Tomlinson
Athenais...........Miss Cheer	

Lethe

Drunken Man......Mr. Hallam	Frenchman...........Mr. Allyn
Mercury...........Mr. Woolls	Old Man...........Mr. Morris
Fine Gentleman........Mr. Wall	Charon.........Mr. Tomlinson
Æsop............Mr. Douglass	Mrs. Tattoo.......Mrs. Harman
Mrs. Riot (with a song in character)...............Miss Wainwright	

1767

Jan. 2   *Tamerlane*   Journal, Jan. 1

Moneses by a Young Gentleman; being his first appearance on any stage.

Bajazet............Mr. Hallam	Tamerlane........Mr. Douglass
Axalla...............Mr. Wall	Dervise.............Mr. Morris
Omar..........Mr. Tomlinson	Zama................Mr. Platt
Prince of Tanais......Mr. Allyn	Mirvan.............Mr. Woolls
Haly.............Mr. Godwin	Selima.............Miss Cheer
Arpasia..........Mrs. Douglass	

[87]

1767

Jan. 2 (cont.)   *The Oracle*

Cinthia (with a Song).........   Oberon..............Mr. Wall
           Miss Hallam   Fairy Queen......Mrs. Douglass

This was Mr. Platt's first appearance.

Jan. 9   *Hamlet*   Journal, Jan. 8

Hamlet...........Mr. Hallam   King.............Mr. Douglass
Horatio.....A Young Gentleman   Laertes..............Mr. Wall
  (being his second appearance)   Ghost...........Mr. Tomlinson
Polonius...........Mr. Morris   Player King.........Mr. Allyn
Ostrick...........Mr. Godwin   Rosincrans..........Mr. Woolls
Bernardo............Mr. Platt   Grave-Diggers.Messrs. Morris and
Player Queen......Mrs. Harman   Tomlinson
Ophelia............Miss Cheer   Queen...........Mrs. Douglass

The Mock Doctor

Mock Doctor.........Mr. Allyn   Sir Jasper...........Mr. Morris
Leander............Mr. Woolls   Squire Robert........Mr. Wall
James..............Mr. Platt   Harry.............Mr. Godwin
Helebore.......Mr. Tomlinson   Charlotte...........Mrs. Wall
Dorcas............Mrs. Morris

First appearance of Mrs. Wall.

Jan. 16   * *The Orphan of China*—Murphy   Gazette, Jan. 15

Zamti...........Mr. Douglass   Zaphineri.........Mr. Hallam
Timurkan...........Mr. Allyn   Hamet..............Mr. Wall
Mirvan............Mr. Morris   Octar...........Mr. Tomlinson
Orasming.........Mr. Greville   Zimventi..........Mr. Woolls
Messenger........Mr. Godwin   Mandare........Mrs. Douglass

The Devil to Pay

Sir John Loverule....Mr. Woolls   Jobson.........Mr. Tomlinson
Butler..............Mr. Morris   Coachman...........Mr. Allyn
Footman............Mr. Wall   Doctor..........Mr. Douglass
Lady Loverule.....Mrs. Harman   Lucy..........Mrs. Tomlinson
Nell..............Mrs. Morris   Lettice........Miss Dowthwait

First appearance of Mr. Greville.

Jan. 22   Gazette

First theatrical criticism printed in a Philadelphia newspaper contained in a
letter to the editor. See March 19.

1767

Jan. 23   * *The Beaux' Stratagem*—Farquhar   Gazette, Jan. 22

Archer............Mr. Hallam	Aimwell.........Mr. Douglass
Sullen.............Mr. Wall	Foigard.............Mr. Allyn
Freeman..........Mr. Greville	Scrub..............Mr. Morris
Gibbet............Mr. Woolls	Boniface........Mr. Tomlinson
Hounslow.........Mr. Godwin	Bagshot.............Mr. Platt
Dorinda...........Miss Hallam	Lady Bountiful.....Mrs. Harman
Cherry.......Miss Wainwright	Gipsey.............Mrs. Wall
Mrs. Sullen........Miss Cheer	

* *The Upholsterer*—Murphy

Jan. 26   * *The Mourning Bride*—Congreve   Chronicle

Osmyn............Mr. Hallam	King..............Mr. Douglass
Gonsales...........Mr. Morris	Garcia..............Mr. Wall
Heli............Mr. Tomlinson	Selim..............Mr. Godwin
Alonzo...........Mr. Greville	Perez...............Mr. Allyn
Mutes....Messrs. Woolls & Platt	Attendants to Almeria. Miss Wain-
Attendants to Zara..Mrs. Tomlin-	wright and Miss Hallam
son and Mrs. Wall	Leonora..........Mrs. Harman
Zara............Mrs. Douglass	Almeria............Miss Cheer

* *High Life Below Stairs*—Townly

Lovel.............Mr. Hallam	Freeman.........Mr. Douglass
Lord Duke........Mr. Godwin	Kingston.............Mr. Allyn
Coachman.........Mr. Woolls	Tom...........Mr. Tomlinson
Philip.............Mr. Morris	Chloe.............Mr. Platt
Cook............Mrs. Harman	Lady Charlotte..Miss Wainwright
Kitty.............Miss Cheer	

This announcement is from the first issue of *The Pennsylvania Chronicle,*
which appeared on Mondays; from now on the record is somewhat fuller.

Jan. 30   *King Lear*   Gazette, Jan. 29

King Lear.........Mr. Hallam	Edgar............Mr. Douglass
Bastard.............Mr. Wall	Gloster............Mr. Morris
Albany.............Mr. Allyn	Cornwall.........Mr. Greville
Kent...........Mr. Tomlinson	Burgundy...........Mrs. Wall
Gentleman Usher....Mr. Godwin	Goneril.......Miss Wainwright
Regan...........Mrs. Harman	Arante........Mrs. Tomlinson
Cordelia...........Miss Cheer	

The Citizen

[89]

1767

Feb. 2   *Cato*   Chronicle

Cato.............Mr. Douglass
Portius..A Gentleman (being his
          first appearance)
Syphax..............Mr. Allyn
Lucius...........Mr. Tomlinson
Lucia...........Mrs. Harman

Sempronius.........Mr. Hallam
Juba................Mr. Wall
Marcus............Mr. Godwin
Decius............Mr. Woolls
Marcia.............Miss Cheer

* *The Reprisal*—Smollett

Mons. Champignon....Mr. Allyn
Ensign M'Claymore.Mr. Douglass
Lieut. Lyon......Mr. Broadbelt
Brush................Mr. Wall
Sailors......Messrs. Tomlinson,
          Godwin and Platt

Lieut O'Clabber.....Mr. Morris
Block..............Mr. Hallam
Heartly...........Mr. Greville
Hallyard...........Mr. Woolls
Miss Harriet.......Miss Hallam

This was Mr. Broadbelt's first appearance.

Feb. 6   *The Orphan of China*   Gazette, Feb. 5

Timurkan..........A Gentleman
    (being his second appearance)
Zamphineri........Mr. Hallam
Octar...............Mr. Allyn
Morat..........Mr. Tomlinson
Zimventi...........Mr. Woolls
Arsace.........Mrs. Tomlinson

Zamti.............Mr. Douglass
Hamet..............Mr. Wall
Mirvan............Mr. Morris
Orasming.........Mr. Greville
Messenger.........Mr. Godwin
Mandane........Mrs. Douglass

The original Epilogue by Mrs. Douglass

High Life Below Stairs

Feb. 9   * *The Miser*—Fielding   Chronicle

Miser...............Mr. Allyn
Cleremont...........Mr. Wall
Decoy.............Mr. Morris
Spartile............Mr. Woolls
Charles Bubbleboy...Mr. Godwin
Harriet...........Miss Hallam
Laffet............Mrs. Harman
Mariana............Miss Cheer

Frederick.........Mr. Douglass
James...........Mr. Tomlinson
Sattin............Mr. Greville
Furnish.............Mr. Platt
Ramillie...........Mr. Hallam
Mrs. Wisely.....Mrs. Tomlinson
Wheedle............Mrs. Wall

The Reprisal

1767

Feb. 13   *Romeo and Juliet*   Gazette, Feb. 12

Romeo............Mr. Hallam	Mercutio.........Mr. Douglass
Capulet............Mr. Morris	Montague.......Mr. Tomlinson
Fryar Laurence.......Mr. Allyn	Escalus...........Mr. Broadbelt
Tibalt................Mr. Wall	Paris...............Mr. Woolls
Benvolio..........Mr. Godwin	Balthazar.........Mr. Greville
Fryar John...........Mr. Platt	Nurse............Mrs. Harman
Lady Capulet......Mrs. Douglass	Juliet..............Miss Cheer

Catherine and Petruchio

Catherine...........Miss Cheer   Petruchio..........Mr. Hallam

Feb. 16   * *The Conscious Lovers*—Steele   Chronicle

Young Bevil........Mr. Hallam	Sealand...........Mr. Douglass
Myrtle..............Mr. Wall	Cimberton............Mr. Allyn
Sir John Bevil....Mr. Broadbelt	Tom...............Mr. Morris
Humphrey.......Mr. Tomlinson	Daniel.............Mr. Godwin
Isabella..........Mrs. Douglass	Phillis...........Mrs. Harman
Lucinda..........Miss Hallam	Indiana.............Miss Cheer

* *Damon and Phillida*—Cibber

Feb. 20   * *The Inconstant*—Farquhar   Gazette, Feb. 19

Young Mirabel......Mr. Hallam	Capt. Duretete.....Mr. Douglass
Durgard.............Mr. Wall	Old Mirabel.........Mr. Morris
Petit...........Mr. Tomlinson	First Bravo...........Mr. Allyn
Second Bravo......Mr. Broadbelt	Third Bravo.........Mr. Woolls
Fourth Bravo.......Mr. Greville	Oriana............Mrs. Harman
Lamorce.......Miss Wainwright	Bisarre..............Miss Cheer

Thomas and Sally

The Squire..........Mr. Woolls	The Sailor............Mr. Wall
Dorcas..............Miss Cheer	Sally.........Miss Wainwright

Feb. 23   *George Barnwell*   Chronicle

George Barnwell....Mr. Hallam	Thorowgood.......Mr. Douglass
Trueman............Mr. Morris	Uncle...............Mr. Allyn
Blunt...........Mr. Tomlinson	Maria.............Miss Hallam
Lucy.............Mrs. Harman	Niellwood..........Miss Cheer

1767

Feb. 23 (cont.)   * *The Mayor of Garratt*—Foote

Major Sturgeon	Mr. Hallam	Matthew Mug	Mr. Hallam
Jerry Sneak & Lint	Mr. Wall	Sir Jacob Jollup	Mr. Tomlinson
Bruin	Mr. Douglass	Crispin Heel-Tap	Mr. Morris
Roger	Mr. Godwin	Snuffle	Mr. Platt
First Mob	Mr. Woolls	Second Mob	Mr. Matthews
Third Mob	Mr. Broadbelt	Fourth Mob	Mr. Allyn
Mrs. Bruin	Mrs. Harman	Mrs. Sneak	Miss Cheer

Feb. 27   * *Love for Love*—Congreve   Gazette, Feb. 26

Valentine	Mr. Douglass	Miss Prue	Miss Cheer
Sir Sampson Legend	Mr. Tomlinson	Ben	Mr. Hallam
		Foresight	Mr. Morris
Scandal	Mr. Allyn	Tattle	Mr. Wall
Jeremy	Mr. Godwin	Buckram	Mr. Greville
Angelica	Miss Hallam	Mrs. Frail	Mrs. Douglass
Mrs. Foresight	Mrs. Wall	Nurse	Mrs. Harman

Damon and Phillida

Damon	Mr. Woolls	Mopfus	Mr. Hallam
Cimon	Mr. Wall	Orcas	Mr. Allyn
Corydon	Mr. Morris	Phillida	Miss Wainwright

A note was added:
"Mr. Congreve's Comedies are allowed to abound with genuine Wit, and true Humour; but, in compliance with the licentious Taste of the Times in which they were written, the Author has, in some places, given the rein to his wanton muse, and deviated from those Rules a more refined Age, and chaste Stage require: The Reviver of this Play has taken the Freedom to crop such Luxuriances, and expunge every Passage that might be offensive either to Decency or good Manners."

March 3   *The Provok'd Husband*   Chronicle, Mar. 2

Lord Townly	Mr. Hallam	Manly	Mr. Douglass
Sir Francis Wronghead	Mr. Morris	Squire Richard	Mr. Allyn
Count Barret	Mr. Wall	John Moody	Mr. Tomlinson
Lady Grace	Mrs. Douglass	Lady Wronghead	Mrs. Harman
Miss Jenny	Miss Hallam	Mrs. Motherly	Miss Wainwright
Myrtilla	Mrs. Wall	Trusty	Mrs. Morris
Lady Townly	Miss Cheer		

1767

March 3 (cont.) *Harlequin Collector*

Harlequin.........Mr. Hallam
Porter.............Mr. Morris
BABOON.............Mr. Wall
Miller's Man...Messrs. Broadbelt
   and Appleby
Columbine.........Miss Cheer
Doctor...........Mr. Douglass
CLOWN..........Mr. Tomlinson

SKELETON.......Mr. Matthews
Hay-Makers.....Messrs. Woolls,
   Wall, Godwin, Broadbelt,
   Matthews, Mrs. Harman,
   Miss Hallam, Miss Wain-
   wright, Mrs. Wall, Mrs.
   Morris, &c.

First appearance of Mr. Appleby.

March 5   *The Miser*   Gazette

Cast as for Feb. 9, 1767, except:

Mrs. Wisely......Mrs. Douglass

Harlequin Collector

Cast as for March 3, 1767, except:

Clown.............Mr. Morris   Porter..........Mr. Tomlinson

March 9   * *All for Love*—Dryden   Chronicle

Marc Antony.......Mr. Hallam
Dolabella.............Mr. Wall
Serapion.........Mr. Tomlinson
Octavia.........Mrs. Douglass
Cleopatra..........Miss Cheer

Ventidius..........Mr. Douglass
Alexas.............Mr. Morris
Neyris..............Mr. Woolls
Charmion......Miss Wainwright
Iras................Mrs. Wall

Antonius and Agrippine...........Master Hallam and Miss Tomlinson

"(being their first appearance on any stage.)"

Harlequin Collector

Cast as on March 5, 1767.

March 14   * *Love Makes A Man*—Cibber   Gazette, Mar. 12

Clodio, alias Don Dismallo Thickskulle De Half Witto..........Mr. Hallam

Carlos............Mr. Douglass

Antonio..............Mr. Allyn
Don Duart..........Mr. Wall
Monsieur.........Mr. Godwin
Page..........Miss Dowthwait
Louise..........Mrs. Douglass
Honoria............Mrs. Wall

Don Lewis, alias Don Cholerick
   Snapshorto de Teste.Mr. Morris
Charino.........Mr. Tomlinson
Governor.........Mr. Greville
Priest.............Mr. Woolls
Lawyer.............Mr. Platt
Elvira........Miss Wainwright
Angelina...........Miss Cheer

[93]

1767

March 14 (cont.)   *The Deuce is in Him*—Colman

Colonel Tamper.....Mr. Hallam	Major Belford.....Mr. Douglass
Prattle, with the Prologue.......	Mademoiselle Florival..........
Mr. Wall	Mrs. Harman
Bell..........Miss Wainwright	Emily............Miss Hallam

March 17   *King Richard III*   Chronicle, Mar. 16

Cast as for Dec. 5, 1766.

The Brave Irishman—Sheridan, Thomas

March 19   *Love in a Village*—Bickerstaff (see note)   Gazette

Justice Woodcock ..Mr. Douglass	Hawthorn..........Mr. Woolls
Young Meadows.......Mr. Wall	Hodge.............Mr. Hallam
Sir Wm. Meadows....Mr. Morris	Eustace..............Mr. Allyn
Lucinda..........Miss Hallam	Margery..........Mrs. Harman
Mrs. Deborah Woodcock.......	Rosetta........Miss Wainwright
Mrs. Douglass	

Servants at the Statute......Messrs. Tomlinson, Greville, Platt, Wall, etc.

The Mayor of Garratt

Love in a Village had been given earlier, as it was referred to in the criticism of January 22, 1767 (see above); this is its first announcement.

March 23   *The Earl of Essex*—Jones   Chronicle

The Earl of Essex....Mr. Hallam	Earl of Southampton. Mr. Douglass
Lord Burleigh.......Mr. Morris	Sir Walter Raleigh. Mr. Tomlinson
Lieutenant of the Tower........	Queen Elizabeth...Mrs. Douglass
Mr. Woolls	Countess of Rutland...Miss Cheer
Countess of Nottingham.........	
Miss Hallam	

Lords, Ladies, &c....Mr. Greville, Mr. Godwin, Mr. Platt, Miss Wainwright, Mrs. Morris, Mrs. Tomlinson, Mrs. Wall, etc.

Harlequin Collector

March 28   *Macbeth*   Journal, Mar. 26

Macbeth..........Mr. Hallam	Macduff..........Mr. Douglass
Duncan.............Mr. Allyn	Banquo............Mr. Morris
Lennox.............Mr. Wall	Seyton..........Mr. Tomlinson
Malcolm..........Mr. Godwin	Flean..........Miss Dowthwait
Donaldbain........Mr. Platt	Officer............Mr. Greville
First Murderer....Mr. Matthews	Hecate...........Mrs. Harman
Lady Macduff.....Mrs. Douglass	Attendant.........Mrs. Morris
Lady Macbeth.......Miss Cheer	

Witches...........Mrs. Harman, Miss Wainwright, Mrs. Tomlinson

1767

March 28 (cont.) *The Oracle*

Cinthia (with a Song)........... Oberon..............Mr. Wall
          Miss Hallam The Dance........Mr. Godwin
Fairy Queen.......Mrs. Douglass

March 30   *Macbeth*   Chronicle

Cast as for March 28, except:

Malcolm...........Mr. Greville

The Lying Valet

April 2   *The Gamester*   Gazette

Beverly............Mr. Hallam   Jarvis..............Mr. Morris
Lewson..............Mr. Wall   Bates............Mr. Tomlinson
Dawson..............Mr. Allyn   Lucy (with a song)............
Charlotte.........Mrs. Harman   Miss Wainwright
Mrs. Beverly.........Miss Cheer   The Epilogue........Miss Cheer
Stukely...........Mr. Douglass

* The Witches, or Harlequin Restored—Love

Harlequin..........Mr. Hallam   Statuary..........Mr. Douglass
Petit Maitre..........Mr. Allyn   Cook.............Mrs. Harman
Constable.........Mr. Broadbelt   Periot..............Mr. Tomlinson
Mercury............Mr. Woolls   Valet de Chambre......Mr. Wall
Necromancer........Mr. Woolls   Witches.......Miss Wainwright,
Colombine..........Miss Cheer   Mrs. Harman, Mrs. Tom-
Pantaloon..........Mr. Morris   linson, Mrs. Wall, Mr.
                   Broadbelt, Mr. Matthews

April 7   *Romeo and Juliet*   Chronicle, April 6

Cast as for February 13, 1767.

Lethe

April 9   *Hamlet*   Gazette

Cast as for January 9, except:

Horatio...........Mr. Greville

The Witches, or Harlequin Restored

Cast as for April 2.

April 13   Chronicle

Forrest's *The Disappointment* was announced for April 20, but was withdrawn

1767

in the Gazette for April 16, "as it contains personal reflections . . . unfit for the stage." This was the first American play announced for production.

April 20   Gazette, April 16

The Gazette which announced the withdrawal of *The Disappointment* said that for April 20 the bill would be:

The Mourning Bride
* *The Contrivances*—Carey

The gap between April 9 and April 20 (if it is real, and not simply a matter of our record) is to be explained by the fact that the company was busy preparing a new play, *The Disappointment,* and, having to withdraw that, put Godfrey's *The Prince of Parthia* into rehearsal.

April 24   * *The Prince of Parthia*—Godfrey   Journal, April 23

The Principal Characters by Mr. Hallam, Mr. Douglass, Mr. Wall, Mr. Morris, Mr. Allyn, Mr. Tomlinson, Mr. Broadbelt, Mr. Greville, Mr. Douglass, Mrs. Morris, Miss Wainwright, and Miss Cheer.

This was the first American drama to be professionally produced on the American stage. See text for probable cast, p. 20.

The Contrivances

April 27   * *A Bold Stroke for a Wife*—Mrs. Centlivre   Chronicle
                              The Devil to Pay

May 1   *All for Love*   Gazette, April 30
                        Flora; or, Hob in The Well

May 4   *A Bold Stroke for a Wife*   Chronicle
                         * *The Apprentice*—Murphy

May 7   Benefit of Miss Cheer   Gazette

* *The Jealous Wife*—Colman

The Jealous Wife.....Miss Cheer	Oakly..............Mr. Hallam
Major Oakly.......Mr. Douglass	Charles..............Mr. Wall
Sir Harry Beagle......Mr. Allyn	Russet..............Mr. Morris
Lord Trinket.......Mr. Hallam	Tom................Mr. Woolls
Captain O'Cutter......Mr. Allyn	John............Mr. Tomlinson
William.........Mr. Matthews	Harriet............Miss Hallam
Lady Freelove.....Mrs. Douglass	Toilet............Mrs. Harman
	Betty.........Miss Wainwright

1767

May 7 (cont.) *The Lying Valet*

Lying Valet........Mr. Hallam	Gayless.............Mr. Wall
Beau Trippet........Mr. Allyn	Justice Guttle.....Mr. Tomlinson
Drunken Cook......Mr. Morris	Melissa............Miss Cheer
Mrs. Gadabout...Mrs. Tomlinson	Mrs. Trippet........Mrs. Wall
Kitty Pry.........Mrs. Harman	

May 11   Benefit of Mr. Douglass   Chronicle

* The Committee—Howard

Teague.............Mr. Allyn	Ruth.............Miss Cheer
Colonel Careless....Mr. Douglass	Colonel Blunt.......Mr. Hallam
Committee-Men.....Messrs. Wall	Abel..............Mr. Woolls
and Greville	Bayliff.............Mr. Platt
Soldier..........Mr. Matthews	Mrs. Day........Mrs. Douglass
Arabella..........Miss Hallam	Mrs. Chat......Mrs. Tomlinson

* The Spirit of Contradiction—Rich

Randal.............Mr. Hallam	Steer.............Mr. Douglass
Lovewell............Mr. Wall	Mr. Partlet........Mr. Morris
Ruin...............Mr. Allyn	Miss Harriet...Miss Wainwright
Betty.............Mrs. Morris	Mrs. Partlet......Mrs. Harman

* The Picture of a Playhouse

May 14   Benefit of Mrs. Morris   Journal

Romeo and Juliet

Cast as Feb. 13, except:

Benvolio } ....Mr. Greville   Nurse............Mrs. Morris
Balthasar }

The Reprisal

May 18   Benefit of Mrs. Harman   Chronicle

The Drummer

Tinfil.............Mr. Hallam	Sir George Truman..Mr. Douglass
Vellum.............Mr. Allyn	Fantome........Mr. Tomlinson
Gardener..........Mr. Morris	Butler..............Mr. Wall
Coachman.........Mr. Greville	Abigail..........Mrs. Harman
Lady Truman.......Miss Cheer	

1767

May 18 (cont.)   *Catherine and Petruchio*

Catherine...........Miss Cheer	Petruchio............Mr. Hallam
Hortentio.........Mr. Douglass	Gumio..............Mr. Morris
Baptista.........Mr. Tomlinson	Biondello.............Mr. Wall
Music-Master........Mr. Allyn	Peter...............Mr. Woolls
Bianca..............Mrs. Wall	Curtis...........Mrs. Harman

May 21   *The Beaux' Stratagem*   Journal

Cast as for January 23, except:

Hounslow........Mr. Matthews   Cherry.............Mrs. Morris

* *Don Quixote in England*—Fielding

Don Quixote........Mr. Hallam	Sancho Panca........Mr. Morris
Guzzel...........Mr. Douglass	Sir Thomas.......Mr. Tomlinson
Squire Badge..........Mr. Wall	Fairlove...........Mr. Greville
John................Mr. Allyn	Cook..............Mr. Woolls
Jezebel...........Mrs. Morris	Dorothea.......Miss Wainwright

May 25   Benefit of Mr. Hallam   Chronicle

* *Cymbeline*—Shakespeare—Garrick

Posthumous.........Mr. Hallam	Imogen.............Miss Cheer
Cymbeline...........Mr. Allyn	Jachimo...........Mr. Douglass
Bellarius...........Mr. Morris	Cloten...............Mr. Wall
Guidenus..........Mr. Greville	Carius Luciers....Mr. Tomlinson
Pissanio..........Mrs. Harman	Arvinagus..........Mr. Woolls
Philario.............Mr. Morris	Doctor...............Mr. Platt
Ladies...Mrs. Morris, Mrs. Wall,	Lords...Messrs. Tomlinson, Platt,
Miss Wainwright, &c.	Matthews, &c.
Queen...........Mrs. Douglass	Helen.........Mrs. Tomlinson

The Mayor of Garratt

Cast as for February 23, 1767, except that the parts of Roger, Snuffle, and the Mobs are not mentioned.

May 28   Mr. Woolls' Benefit   Journal

Love in a Village

Cast as for March 19. "The fifth night."

High Life Below Stairs

June 1   Benefit of Mr. Wall   Chronicle

* *The Revenge*—Young
* *Tom Thumb the Great*—Fielding

1767

June 4	Benefit of Miss Wainwright	Journal

The Country Lasses—Johnson

Modely............Mr. Hallam	Heartwell.........Mr. Douglass
Sir John English.......Mr. Allyn	Freehold............Mr. Morris
Lurcher.............Mr. Wall	Vulture..........Mr. Tomlinson
Sneak..............Mr. Woolls	Longbottom........Mr. Greville
Carbuncle.........Mr. Broadbelt	Shacklefigure..........Mr. Platt
Country-Man.....Mr. Matthews	Flora.........Miss Wainwright
Aura...............Miss Cheer	

The Chaplet—Mendez

Damon.............Mr. Woolls	Palemon..............Mr. Wall
Pastora..........Mrs. Harman	Laura.........Miss Wainwright

June 8	Benefit of Mr. Tomlinson	Chronicle

Coriolanus—Shakespeare—Thomson
The Contrivances

June 12		Journal, June 11

The School for Lovers and *Neck or Nothing* were announced for Miss Hallam's Benefit, but postponed on account of the weather—Chronicle, June 15.

June 15	Benefit of Mr. Allyn	Chronicle

The Miser
Cast as for Feb. 9, 1767, except:

Decoy ⎫
Charles Bubbleboy ⎬ ..Mr. Morris   Mrs. Wisely......Mrs. Douglass

The Double Disappointment—Mendez

June 18	Benefit of Mrs. Douglass	Gazette

The Roman Father—Whitehead

The Roman Father...Mr. Hallam	Publius Horatius...Mr. Douglass
Tullus Hostilius.......Mr. Allyn	Valerius..............Mr. Wall
First Citizen........Mr. Morris	Second Citizen......Mr. Greville
Third Citizen.......Mr. Woolls	Fourth Citizen........Mr. Platt
Valeria..........Mrs. Douglass	Horatia............Miss Cheer

Neck or Nothing—Garrick

June 22	The Merchant of Venice	Chronicle

The Lying Valet

1767

June 25	Benefit of Mr. Greville	Gazette

The Wonder
The Citizen

June 29	Benefit of Miss Hallam	Chronicle

Cymbeline
Neck or Nothing

July 2	Benefit of Mr. Broadbelt	Gazette

The Gamester

Cast as for April 2, 1767, except:

Bates............Mr. Broadbelt

The Reprisal

Cast as for Feb. 2, 1767.

July 6	Benefit of Mrs. Wall	Chronicle

The Constant Couple
The Apprentice

"Last night of acting this season."

In the season from November 14, 1766, to July 6, 1767, we know of at least fifty-nine performances which were given, of a probable hundred. New plays: *The Prince of Parthia,* the first American play to be produced, and *All for Love, The Beaux' Stratagem, A Bold Stroke for a Wife, The Committee, The Conscious Lovers, The Constant Couple, Coriolanus* (Thomson), *The Country Lasses, Cymbeline, The Distressed Mother, The Earl of Essex, The Inconstant, Jane Shore, The Jealous Wife, Love for Love, Love in a Village, Love Makes a Man, The Merchant of Venice, The Miser, The Mourning Bride, The Orphan of China, The Revenge, The Roman Father, The School for Lovers,* and *The Wonder.* Otway's *The Orphan* also may have appeared this season—see January 9, 1770. Plays which had appeared in Philadelphia before: *The Beggar's Opera, Cato, Douglas, The Drummer, The Gamester, George Barnwell, Hamlet, King Lear, King Richard III, Macbeth, The Provoked Husband, Romeo and Juliet, Tamerlane,* and *Theodosius.* New afterpieces: *The Apprentice, The Brave Irishman, Catherine and Petruchio, The Chaplet, The Citizen, The Contrivances, Damon and Phillida, The Deuce is in Him, The Devil to Pay, Don Quixote in England, The Double Disappointment, High Life Below Stairs, The Mayor of Garratt, The Miller of Mansfield, Neck or Nothing, The Old Maid, The Oracle, The Reprisal, The Spirit of Contradiction, Thomas and Sally, Tom Thumb, The Upholsterer,* and *The Witches, or*

1767

Harlequin Restored. The five old afterpieces were *Harlequin Collector, Hob in the Well, Lethe, The Lying Valet,* and *The Mock Doctor.*

Of the twenty-seven different actors who appeared in the bills, eight had played in Philadelphia before: Lewis Hallam, Mr. and Mrs. Douglass, Allyn, Morris, Mr. and Mrs. Tomlinson, and Mrs. Harman. Eighteen were, according to our record, new to the city: Miss Cheer, Mr. Appleby, Mr. Broadbelt, Miss Dowthwait, Mr. Godwin, Mr. Greville, Miss Sarah Hallam, Master Hallam, Mr. Matthews, Mrs. Morris, Mr. Platt, Miss Tomlinson, Miss Wainwright, Mr. and Mrs. Wall, Mr. Woolls, and two unnamed "Gentlemen."

Sept. 9	"Messieurs Douglass & Hallam"	Chronicle, Sept. 7

*** A Lecture on Heads*—Stevens**

"Singing by Mr. Woolls and Miss Hallam, accompanied by the Band of His Majesty's Eighteenth Regiment." This was a pre-season entertainment. The fall season of the American Company opened on October 6.

Sept. 24	"Messieurs Douglass & Hallam"	Gazette

A Lecture on Heads

"A humorous Scene of a Drunken Man, by Mr. HALLAM. Singing by Mr. WOOLLS, Miss HALLAM, and Miss WAINWRIGHT, accompanied by a Band of Music."

Oct. 6	*The Roman Father*	Chronicle, Oct. 5

The Roman Father...Mr. Hallam	Publius Horatius.....Mr. Henry
Tullus Hostilius....Mr. Douglass	Valerius.............Mr. Wall
Citizens....Messrs. Morris, Tomlinson, Woolls, Roberts	Valeria..........Mrs. Douglass
	Horatia.............Miss Cheer

Miss in her Teens

Miss Biddy Bellair....Miss Storer	Capt. Flash.........Mr. Hallam
Capt. Lint......Mr. Tomlinson	Fribble.............Mr. Allyn
Jasper.............Mr. Woolls	Puff...............Mr. Morris
Tag..........Miss Wainwright	

First appearance of Mr. Henry, and Miss Ann Storer and Mr. Roberts. First night of the season from October 6 to Nov. 23, 1767, given by the American Company at the Theatre in Southwark.

Oct. 9	*The Jealous Wife*	Gazette, Oct. 8

Cast as for May 7, 1767, except:

Charles.............Mr. Henry	Lord Trinket.........Mr. Wall

(Part of William not mentioned)

[101]

1767

Oct. 9 (cont.)   *The Witches, or Harlequin Restored*
    Cast as for April 2, 1767, except that Matthews' name is omitted

Oct. 12   *Hamlet*   Chronicle
                          The Citizen

Oct. 16   *Romeo and Juliet*   Gazette, Oct. 15
                       The Mayor of Garratt

Oct. 19   *The Beaux' Stratagem*   Chronicle
                     High Life Below Stairs

Oct. 23   *The Gamester*   Gazette
              The Witches, or Harlequin Restored
(The *Pa. Journal* announced *Harlequin Collector* as the farce.)

Oct. 26   *Love in a Village*   Chronicle
                        The Oracle

Oct. 30   *The Wonder*   Gazette, Oct. 29
                      The Devil to Pay

Nov. 2   * *Venice Preserved*—Otway   Chronicle

Pierre.............Mr. Hallam   Jaffier.............Mr. Henry
Priuli............Mr. Douglass   Renault............Mr. Morris
Bedamar...........Mr. Wall   Duke..........Mr. Tomlinson
Spinosa...........Mr. Malone   Eliot............Mr. Greville
Theodore..........Mr. Woolls   Durand...........Mr. Roberts
Officer.............Mr. Allyn   Attendants....Mrs. Morris, Mrs.
Belvidera..........Miss Cheer   Tomlinson

Neck or Nothing

Slip..............Mr. Hallam   Mrs. Stockwell....Mrs. Douglass
Belford............Mr. Wall   Martin............Mr. Morris
Mr. Stockwell....Mr. Tomlinson   Sir William..........Mr. Allyn
Miss Nancy Stockwell..........   Jenny.........Miss Wainwright
                  Miss Hallam

Nov. 3–9
(The record of the next few days is confused. I have found no newspaper announcements for performances between November 2 and 13. Durang, Series I,
7, gives *The Wonder* and *The Devil to Pay* for November 3, but gives nothing
for October 30. For November 5 he gives *Venice Preserved* and *Neck or Noth-*

1767

ing, which I have found advertised for November 2. Seilhamer, I, 197, gives *Lear* and *The Miller of Mansfield* for November 9.)

Nov. 13   *Theodosius*   Gazette, Nov. 12
                                 The Chaplet

COLLEGE OF PHILADELPHIA

Nov. 17   * *Dialogue*—Thos. Coomb   Library, U. of Pa.

SOUTHWARK THEATRE

Nov. 19   * *The Clandestine Marriage*—Colman   Journal

Lord Ogleby........Mr. Hallam	Sir John Melvil.....Mr. Douglass
Lovewell...........Mr. Henry	Sterling............Mr. Morris
Canton.............Mr. Allyn	Brush...............Mr. Wall
Serjeant Flower...Mr. Tomlinson	Traverse...........Mr. Malone
Truman...........Mr. Greville	Mrs. Heidelberg...Mrs. Douglass
Fanny............Miss Hallam	Betty..............Miss Storer
Chambermaid...Miss Wainwright	Trusty.............Mrs. Morris
Miss Sterling........Miss Cheer	

The Brave Irishman

Nov. 23   *The Clandestine Marriage*   Chronicle
                         The Lying Valet

In this short Philadelphia season from Oct. 6, to Nov. 23, 1767, the American Company presented at the Theatre in Southwark two new plays: *The Clandestine Marriage* and *Venice Preserved;* ten old plays: *The Beaux' Stratagem, The Gamester, Hamlet, The Jealous Wife, King Lear, Love in a Village, The Roman Father, Romeo and Juliet, Theodosius,* and *The Wonder;* and twelve familiar afterpieces: *The Brave Irishman, The Chaplet, The Citizen, The Devil to Pay, High Life Below Stairs, The Lying Valet, The Mayor of Garratt, The Miller of Mansfield, Miss in Her Teens, Neck or Nothing, The Oracle,* and *The Witches, or Harlequin Restored.* The new actors were Mr. John Henry, and Miss Ann Storer, Messrs. Malone and Roberts. The other actors whose names appear were Mr. Allyn, Miss Cheer, Mr. and Mrs. Douglass, Mr. Greville, Mr. Lewis and Miss Sarah Hallam, Mr. and Mrs. Morris, Mr. and Mrs. Tomlinson, Miss Wainwright, Messrs. Wall and Woolls. Our record includes about two-thirds of the probable performances.

1768

Oct. 4   *The Provoked Husband*   Chronicle, Oct. 3

Lord Townly.......Mr. Hallam	Manly............Mr. Douglass
Sir Francis Wronghead.........	Count Basset.........Mr. Darby
Mr. Morris	John Moody......Mr. Tomlinson
Squire Richard......Mr. Woolls	Lady Wronghead...Mrs. Harman
Lady Grace.......Mrs. Douglass	Myrtilla............Miss Storer
Miss Jenny.........Miss Hallam	Lady Townly........Miss Cheer
Mrs. Motherly...Mrs. Tomlinson	

Miss in Her Teens

Mr. Fribble..Miss M[aria] Storer	Capt. Flash.........Mr. Hallam
Capt. Loveit.........Mr. Darby	Puff...............Mr. Morris
Jasper..............Mr. Woolls	Tag............Miss Ann Storer
Miss Biddy.........Miss Hallam	

First night of the season at the theatre in Southwark from October 4, 1768, to January 6, 1769. First appearance of Miss Maria Storer and Mr. Darby. No other notice appeared till October 20.

Oct. 21   * *The Spanish Fryar*—Dryden   Gazette, Oct. 20
                 The Honest Yorkshireman

Oct. 28   *The Mourning Bride*   Gazette, Oct. 27
                Miss in Her Teens

Nov. 4   *Cymbeline*   Gazette, Nov. 3
        * *Love à la Mode*—Kelly

Nov. 25   *The Clandestine Marriage*   Journal, Nov. 24
                   Lethe

Dec. 2   *Tamerlane*   Gazette, Dec. 1

Bajazet...........Mr. Hallam	Moneses............Mr. Henry
Axalla..............Mr. Parker	Omar...........Mr. Tomlinson
Dervise............Mr. Morris	Haly...............Mr. Wall
Tamerlane.........Mr. Douglass	Prince of Tanais......Mr. Darby
Mirvan............Mr. Woolls	Stratocles..........Mr. Byerley
Zama.............Mr. Raworth	Selima.............Miss Cheer
Arpasia...........Miss Hallam	

High Life Below Stairs

First appearance of Mr. Parker, Mr. Byerley, and Mr. Raworth.

1768

Dec. 9	* *The Busy Body*—Mrs. Centlivre	Gazette, Dec. 8
	The Contrivances	

"An ELEGANT SETT OF FIRE-WORKS
By the two Italian Brothers."

Dec. 12	* *King John*—Shakespeare	Gazette, Dec. 8

Dec. 14	*Macbeth*	Chronicle, Dec. 12

Macbeth..........Mr. Hallam   Lady Macbeth........Miss Cheer

Miss in her Teens

Fireworks by "Two Italian Brothers."

Dec. 16	* *False Delicacy*—Kelly	Journal, Dec. 15

Colonel Rivers.....Mr. Douglass   Cecil.............Mr. Hallam
Lord Winworth......Mr. Henry   Sidney.............Mr. Byerley
Sir Henry Newburg....Mr. Wall   Mrs. Halley.......Mrs. Douglass
Miss Marchmont....Miss Hallam   Miss Rivers.........Miss Storer
Lady Betty Lambton..Miss Cheer   Miss Sally........Mrs. Harman

Catherine and Petruchio

Dec. 22		Durang, Series I, 7

Durang gives a cast of *Tamerlane* which he says was given on December 22. It may easily have been given then; but as the cast is identical with that already given for December 2, it is also possible that the historian simply got one "2" too many in his date.

Dec. 26	* *Zara*—Hill	Journal, Dec. 22

Ozman...........Mr. Hallam   Lusigman.........Mr. Douglass
Zara..............Miss Cheer
"With a Farce"

Dec. 30	* *Alexander the Great*—Lee, Nathaniel	Journal, Dec. 29

Alexander.........Mr. Hallam   Clytus...........Mr. Douglass
Lysimachus........Mr. Henry   Hephestion.........Mr. Wall
Cossander.........Mr. Morris   Polyperchon........Mr. Parker
Philip.........Mr. Tomlinson   Thestalus.........Mr. Woolls
Perdiccas..........Mr. Byerley   Cumenus.........Mr. Roberts
Meleager.........Mr. Raworth   Aristander.........Mr. Darby
Statira...........Miss Hallam   Sysigambis.......Mrs. Douglass
Pariratis..........Miss Storer   Roxana...........Miss Cheer

1768

Dec. 30 (cont.)   * Fanny The Fantome

The Orator..........Mr. Wall   Sergeant Blarney....Mr. Douglass
Councellor Prosequi............   Shadrach Bodkin.....Mr. Morris
          Mr. Tomlinson   Justice.............Mr. Woolls
Clerk.............Mr. Raworth   Peter Paragraph.......Mr. Wall

"After which, Mr. Wall will deliver a Critical * Dissertation, upon NOSES."

Neck or Nothing

1769

Jan. 6   "Benefit of the Debtors"   Journal & Gazette, Jan. 5

Alexander the Great

Cast as for Dec. 30, 1768

Fanny the Fantome

Cast as for Dec. 30, 1768

A Dissertation upon Noses
The Contrivances

In this brief season from October 4, 1768, to January 6, 1769 by the American Company at the theatre in Southwark, the following new plays were produced: *Alexander the Great, The Busy Body, False Delicacy, King John, The Spanish Fryar,* and *Zara.* The plays seen before were *The Clandestine Marriage, Cymbeline, Macbeth, The Mourning Bride, The Provoked Husband,* and *Tamerlane.* New afterpieces: "A Dissertation upon Noses," *Fanny the Fantome,* and *Love à la Mode.* Reappearing afterpieces: *Catherine and Petruchio, The Contrivances, High Life Below Stairs, The Honest Yorkshireman, Lethe, Miss in Her Teens,* and *Neck or Nothing.* The personnel of the company was little changed, Miss Maria Storer, and Messrs. Byerley, Darby, Parker and Raworth being the only new members. Other actors known to have appeared this season: Miss Cheer, Mr. and Mrs. Douglass, Mr. Lewis Hallam, Miss Sarah Hallam, Mrs. Harman, Mr. John Henry, Mr. Owen Morris, Mr. Roberts, Miss (Ann) Storer, Mr. and Mrs. Tomlinson, Mr. Wall and Mr. Woolls. The record this season is especially meager; we have knowledge of less than a third of the probable performances.

May 23   * Summer—Thomson   Chronicle, May 22

This was *read* "At the Academy," "By a person who professes to teach with propriety to read any author in the English language."

May 29   * Sappho to Phaon—Pope   Chronicle
                    Demosthenes' Seventh Oration
                    * Folly on Both Sides—Voltaire

These, with other recitations, were given at the Academy.

1769

June 5	*Damon and Phillida*	Chronicle

Read and "All the songs . . . sung" at the Academy.

June 13	*The Beggar's Opera*	Chronicle, June 12

Read at Academy.

June 19	*Love in a Village*	Chronicle

Read and the songs sung at the Assembly Room in Lodge Alley.

June 23	* *The Maid of the Mill*—first act—Bickerstaff	Gazette, June 22

Read at the Assembly Room.

June 26	* *The Musical Lady*—Colman	Chronicle

Read at the Assembly Room, and the songs sung.

THEATRE IN SOUTHWARK

Aug. 11	Journal, August 10

Slack Rope Acrobatics by Mr. Malone.

Sept. 14	*A Lecture on Heads*	Journal
	"Camera Obscura"	

Lewis Hallam and John Henry appear for the first time as managers in a short season from Sept. 14 to 30, 1769, before the opening of the regular season from Nov. 8, 1769, to June 1, 1770. For summary, see June 1, 1770.

Sept. 25	*The Oracle*	Chronicle
	A Picture of a Play-House	
	Harlequin Collector	

Pre-season performance, under the management of Hallam and Henry.

Sept. 29	* *The Wrangling Lovers*—Lyon. This was quite possibly another title for *Lover's Quarrels*—Vanbrugh—King.	Journal

* *The Dwarfs*

Harlequin de Bergemasco........	Paiozo Neapolitano............
Mr. Hallam	"A Gentleman'
A Venetian Pantaloon..Mr. Henry	The Duenna......Mrs. Douglas
Cooper..........Mr. Broadbelt	Spaniolo Columbina..Miss Hallan

Pre-season performance, under the management of Hallam and Henry.

1769

Sept. 30   *The Oracle*   Play-bill in Shaw
                 Theatre Collection

Oberon............Mr. Hallam   Fairy Queen.......Mrs. Douglass
Cinthia (with a Song in Character).....................Miss Hallam

A Picture of a Play-House, given by Mr. Hallam
*The Dwarfs, or the Cascade Assignation, with the
Animating of Harlequin*

Cast as for Sept. 29, 1769.

Singing by Miss Hallam and dancing by "A Gentleman."

Pre-season performance, under the management of Hallam and Henry.
For summary of performances from Sept. 14 to 30, 1769, see June 1, 1770.

Oct. 5   ALS, Shaw Theatre Collection

David Douglass writes asking permission to open the theatre for a season, in
view of reverses suffered in Carolina.

Nov. 8   *The Busybody*   Chronicle, Nov. 6
        * *The Padlock*—Bickerstaff

The American Company opened its season from Nov. 8, 1769, to June 1, 1770.

Nov. 10   *Hamlet*   Gazette, Nov. 9
       The Musical Lady

First stage production of *The Musical Lady:* it had been *read* publicly on June
26, 1769.

Nov. 14   *The Gamester*   Chronicle, Nov. 13
       The Padlock

Nov. 17   *The Constant Couple*   Gazette, Nov. 16
       The Padlock

Nov. 20   *Romeo and Juliet*   Chronicle

"Juliet—Miss Hallam, being her second appearance in that Character."
Love à la Mode

Nov. 24   * *Midas*—O'Hara   Gazette, Nov. 23
       The Citizen

Dec. 1   *Douglas*   Gazette, Nov. 30
        Midas

[108]

1769

Dec. 5	*Love in a Village* *The Musical Lady*	Chronicle, Dec. 4
Dec. 8	*Cymbeline* *Midas*	Gazette, Dec. 7
Dec. 12	*The Beaux' Stratagem*	Chronicle, Dec. 11

Archer, by Mr. Hallam; Dorinda, by a young gentlewoman, being her first appearance [was this Miss Richardson?]; Mrs. Sullen, by Miss Hallam.

The Padlock

Dec. 15	*The Beggar's Opera*	Gazette, Dec. 14

Macheath, by Mr. Hallam.

Love à la Mode

Dec. 19	* *The Siege of Damascus*—Hughes *Harlequin Collector*	Chronicle, Dec. 18
Dec. 22	*The Suspicious Husband* *Midas*	Gazette, Dec. 21
Dec. 26	*The Clandestine Marriage* *Love à la Mode*	Chronicle, Dec. 25
Dec. 29	*George Barnwell* *The Witches, or Harlequin Restored*	Gazette, Dec. 28

1770

Jan. 2	*King John* *The Padlock*	Chronicle, January 1
Jan. 5	*The Maid of the Mill* *The Miller of Mansfield*	Gazette, January 9

(See June 23, 1769, for a reading of *The Maid of the Mill*.)

Jan. 9	* *The Orphan*—Otway *Flora*	Chronicle, Jan. 8

The Orphan is advertised as "not acted these three years." We have no record of its having been given previously in Philadelphia, though this evidently indicates that it had been. It was acted in New York, John Street Theatre, February 11, 1768. (*Odell* I, 127.)

Jan. 12	*The Maid of the Mill*	Gazette, January 11

The Witches, or Harlequin Restored "with alterations."

Jan. 19	* *The Tempest*—Shakespeare *Neptune and Amphritrite*	Gazette, Jan. 18

[109]

1770

This was Shadwell's drastic alteration of *The Tempest*. It was normally followed by the *Masque of Neptune and Amphitrite*.

Jan. 23	*The Tempest*	Chronicle, Jan. 22
	Neptune and Amphitrite	
	The Mayor of Garratt	

Jan. 29   *The Tempest*—"With Additions and Alterations"   Gazette, Jan. 25
Neptune and Amphitrite
The Mayor of Garratt

Feb. 2	*The Tempest*	Gazette, Feb. 1
	Neptune and Amphitrite	
	The Padlock	

Feb. 6	* *Edward, the Black Prince*—Shirley	Chronicle, Feb. 5
	The Citizen	

Feb. 9	* *The Funeral*—Steele	Gazette, Feb. 8
	Damon and Phillida	

Feb. 16	*The Orphan of China*	Gazette, Feb. 15
	The Upholsterer	

Feb. 19	*The Funeral*	Chronicle
	The Upholsterer	

March 2   * *The Merry Wives of Windsor*—Shakespeare   Journal,
High Life Below Stairs   March 1

I have found no advertisements between February 19 and March 2, but as this is advertised as "The Second Night" for *The Merry Wives*, the first American appearance of Shakespeare's comedy doubtless came a few days before March 2.

March 5	*The Tempest*	Chronicle
	Neptune and Amphitrite	
	The Padlock	

March 9	* *Comus*—Milton—Colman	Journal
	* *Edgar and Emmeline*—Hawkesworth	

March 12	*Edward, The Black Prince*	Chronicle
	Edgar and Emmeline	

March 16	*The Revenge*	Journal, March 15
	The Witches, or Harlequin Restored	

1770

March 20	*The Tempest*	Chronicle, Mar. 19
	Neptune and Amphitrite	
	The Devil to Pay	

"Jobson and Nell by Mr. Hallam and Miss Hallam, being their first appearance in that Character."

| March 22 | *The Beaux' Stratagem* | Gazette, March 22 |
| | *Edgar and Emmeline* | |

| March 30 | Benefit of Miss Storer | Handbill in H. S. P. |

* *The Tender Husband*—Steele

Humphrey Gubbin...Mr. Hallam		Sir Harry Gubbin...Mr. Douglass
Mr. Cleremont......Mr. Henry		Capt. Cleremont.....Mr. Byerley
Mr. Tipkin.........Mr. Morris		Mr. Pounce..........Mr. Wall
The Niece........Miss Hallam		Aunt..........Mrs. Tomlinson
Fainlove.........Mrs. Harman		Jenny.........Miss Richardson
Mrs. Cleremont......Mrs. Henry		

Miss in Her Teens

Mr. Fribble.........Miss Storer	Puff...............Mr. Morris
Capt. Flash.........Mr. Henry	Tag..............Mrs. Henry
Captain Lovet.......Mr. Parker	Jasper..............(torn off)
Miss Biddy..........(torn off)	

This Miss Storer was Maria, later Mrs. Henry. The current Mrs. Henry was *Ann* Storer. First recorded appearance of Miss Richardson.

April 5	Benefit of Mrs. Henry	Journal
	The Fair Penitent	
	Harlequin Collector	

Harlequin...........Mr. Henry

"(in which character he will run up a perpendicular
scene 20 Feet high)."

This performance was postponed from April 2.

April 16	Mrs. Harman's Benefit	Gazette, April 12
	Alexander the Great	
	Thomas and Sally	

April 20	Miss Hallam's Benefit	Journal, April 12
	Jane Shore	
	The Padlock	

1770

This is advertised as "The Tenth Night" for this popular opera—which indicates the unfortunate gaps in our record of this season. According to the record, it is the *eighth* night.

April 27	Mr. Morris's Benefit	Gazette, April 26
	* *The Good-Natured Man*—Goldsmith	
	The Devil to Pay	
May 3	Benefit of Mr. Tomlinson	Gazette
	The Good-Natured Man	
	Catherine and Petruchio	
May 10	Benefit of Mrs. Douglass	Gazette, May 10
	Love for Love	
	* *Wit's Last Stake*—King	

"To conclude with an Epilogue, to be spoken by Mr. Wall, Riding on an Ass."

Love for Love had been expurgated—"The Beauties of the Author are preserved, his Blemishes expunged."
We very evidently do not have record of all the benefits—since April 2 no advertisements had appeared in the *Chronicle,* published on Monday.

May 17	Benefit of Mr. & Mrs. Henry and Miss [Maria] Storer	Journal
	* *The Wild Irishman*	
	High Life Below Stairs	
May 24	Benefit of Mr. Parker and Mr. Broadbelt	Journal
	Cymbeline	
	* *The Guardian*—Garrick	
June 1	"The last Play Positively"	Journal, May 31
	* *Julius Cæsar*—Shakespeare	

"Mark Antony by a young Gentleman, being his first appearance on any Stage."

Harlequin Collector

Harlequin..........Mr. Hallam

First American production of *Julius Cæsar.*

In summary, the season of 1769–70 at the Theatre in Southwark opened with the first productions sponsored by Hallam and Henry (Sept. 14, 25, and 29, 1769), in which *The Dwarfs, Harlequin Collector, The Oracle,* and *The Wrangling Lovers* were given. The American Company then gave between Nov. 8, 1769, and June 1, 1770, these new plays: *Comus, Edward; The Black Prince, The Funeral, The Good-Natured Man, Julius Cæsar, The Maid of the Mill, The Merry Wives of Windsor, Midas, The Orphan* (this may have

1770

been given in 1767), *The Siege of Damascus, The Tempest, The Tender Husband,* and *The Wild Irishman.* Reappearing plays: *Alexander the Great, The Beaux' Stratagem, The Beggar's Opera, The Busy Body, The Clandestine Marriage, The Constant Couple, Cymbeline, Douglas, The Fair Penitent, The Gamester, George Barnwell, Hamlet, Jane Shore, King John, Love for Love, Love in a Village, The Orphan of China, The Revenge, Romeo and Juliet,* and *The Suspicious Husband.* New afterpieces: *Edgar and Emmeline, The Guardian, The Musical Lady, Neptune and Amphitrite, The Padlock,* and *The Wit's Last Stake.* Reappearing afterpieces: *Catherine and Petruchio, The Citizen, Damon and Phillida, The Devil to Pay, Harlequin Collector, Harlequin Restored, High Life Below Stairs, Hob in the Well, Love à la Mode, The Mayor of Garratt, The Miller of Mansfield, Miss in Her Teens, Thomas and Sally,* and *The Upholsterer.*

The only new actors were Miss Richardson, a "young gentleman," and a "young gentlewoman." Reappearing actors who were mentioned: Mr. Byerley, Mr. and Mrs. Douglass, Mr. Lewis and Miss Sarah Hallam, Mrs. Harman, Mr. and Mrs. (Ann) Henry, Mr. Owen Mooris, Mr. Parker, Miss Maria Storer, Mr. and Mrs. Tomlinson, Mr. Wall, and Mr. Woolls. We have record of about three-fifths of the probable performances.

COLLEGE OF PHILADELPHIA

June 5   * *Dialogue*   Library, U. of Pa.

THEATRE IN SOUTHWARK

June 6   *"A Rhapsody"*—Stevens   Chronicle, June 4

This was a post-season recitation given oy Mr. Wall at the "Lodge-room."

1772

Oct. 28   * *A Word to the Wise*—Kelly   Journal

Capt. Dormer	Mr. Hallam	Sir George Hastings	Mr. Henry
Sir John Dormer	Mr. Douglass	Villars	Mr. Goodman
Willoughby	Mr. Morris	Miss Dormer	Mrs. Henry
Mrs. Willoughby	Mrs. Morris	Miss Willoughby	Miss Storer
Miss Montagu	Miss Hallam	Lucy	Miss Richardson

The Padlock

Mungo	Mr. Hallam	Don Diego	Mr. Woolls
Leander	Mr. Wall	Ursula	Mrs. Morris
Leonora	Miss Hallam		

First appearance of the second Mrs. Morris (the first had been drowned in December, 1767—see Odell, I, 117) and of Mr. Goodman—sometime a Philadelphia law student.

[113]

1772

This opened the brilliant season from October 28, 1772, to March 31 (perhaps April 2), 1773.

Nov. 2   *The Roman Father*   Chronicle, Oct. 31

The Roman Father...Mr. Hallam
Publius...........Mr. Goodman
1st Citizen.........Mr. Morris
3rd Citizen.........Mr. Woolls
Soldier.............Mr. Parker
Horatia............Miss Hallam

Tullus Hostilius....Mr. Douglass
Valerius..............Mr. Wall
2nd Citizen.........Mr. Byerley
4th Citizen.........Mr. Johnson
Valeria.............Mrs. Henry

Midas

Midas............Mr. Goodman
Jupiter............Mr. Morris
Damaetas...........Mr. Wall
Juno...............Mrs. Henry
Daphne............Mrs. Morris

Apollo.............Mr. Woolls
Sileno.............Mr. Parker
Pan...............Mr. Byerley
Mysis............Mrs. Harman
Myra.............Miss Storer

Mr. Johnson made his first appearance on this night.

Nov. 4   *Love in a Village*   Journal

Justice Woodcock...Mr. Douglass
Young Meadows.....Mr. Morris
Lucinda............Miss Storer
Mrs. Deb. Woodcock...........
           Mrs. Douglass

Rosetta............Miss Hallam
Hawthorn..........Mr. Woolls
Eustace.............Mr. Byerley
Hodge..............Mr. Parker
Margery...........Mrs. Morris

Servants at the Statue....Messrs. Goodman, Wall, Johnson, Roberts, Mrs. Henry, Mrs. Harman, Miss Richardson, etc., etc.

The Old Maid

The Old Maid.....Mrs. Harman
Celeremont..........Mr. Wall
Mr. Heartly........Mr. Parker

Capt. Cape.........Mr. Morris
Mr. Harlow........Mr. Byerley
Mrs. Harlow........Mrs. Henry

Nov. 9   * *The West Indian*—Cumberland   Chronicle, Nov. 7

Belcour.............Mr. Henry
Mr. Stockwell.......Mr. Morris
Charles Dudley........Mr. Wall
Varland............Mr. Parker
Sailor..............Mr. Woolls
Louisa Dudley.......Miss Storer
Mrs. Fulmer........Mrs. Henry

Major O'Flaherty..Mr. Goodman
Captain Dudley.....Mr. Douglass
Fulmer.............Mr. Byerley
Stukely............Mr. Johnson
Lady Rusport.....Mrs. Douglass
Lucy...........Miss Richardson
Charlotte Rusport...Miss Hallam

1772

Nov. 9 (cont.)   *Miss in Her Teens*

Captain Flash........Mr. Henry	Mr. Fribble..........Mr. Wall
Capt. Loveit........Mr. Johnson	Puff..............Mr. Morris
Jasper.............Mr. Woolls	Tag..............Mrs. Henry
Miss Biddy.........Miss Storer	

Nov. 11   *The Mourning Bride*   Journal

Osmyn.............Mr. Hallam	King.............Mr. Douglass
Garcia.............Mr. Henry	Gonsalez............Mr. Morris
Heli................Mr. Parker	Selim...............Mr. Wall
Alonzo.............Mr. Byerley	Perez..............Mr. Woolls
Zara..............Mrs. Morris	Leonora............Miss Storer
Almeria...........Miss Hallam	Singing by Mr. Woolls

The Mayor of Garratt -

Major Sturgeon....Mr. Goodman	Sir Jacob Jollup.....Mr. Douglass
Sneak..............Mr. Morris	Lint.................Mr. Wall
Bruin..............Mr. Byerley	Roger.............Mr. Parker
Mrs. Bruin........Mrs. Hallam	Mrs. Sneak........Mrs. Henry

Nov. 16   *Hamlet*   Chronicle, Nov. 14

Hamlet............Mr. Hallam	King..............Mr. Douglass
Polonius...........Mr. Morris	Laertes..............Mr. Henry
Ghost...........Mr. Goodman	Horatio.............Mr. Parker
Marcellus..........Mr. Woolls	Bernardo..........Mr. Byerley
Player King..........Mr. Wall	Lucianus..........Mr. Roberts
Francisco.........Mr. Johnson	Guildenstern........Mr. Woolls
Rosincranz........Mr. Byerley	Player Queen....Miss Richardson
Queen..........Mrs. Douglass	Ophelia............Miss Hallam
Grave-Diggers ....Messrs. Morris and Byerley	

The Miller of Mansfield

King..............Mr. Henry	Miller.............Mr. Morris
Richard...........Mr. Byerley	Lord Lovewell........Mr. Wall
Joe...............Mr. Woolls	Peggy.........Miss Richardson
Kate...............Miss Storer	Margery..........Mrs. Harman

Nov. 18   * *The Shipwreck*—Cumberland   Journal

Young Belfield......Mr. Hallam	Belfield.............Mr. Henry
Capt. Ironsides.....Mr. Goodman	Sir Benjamin Dove....Mr. Morris
Paterson............Mr. Byerley	Skiff...............Mr. Woolls
Old Goodwin......Mr. Douglass	Philip................Mr. Wall
Jonathan...........Mr. Parker	Francis............Mr. Johnson

1772

Nov. 18 (cont.)

Sailors ....
Messrs. Parker, Roberts, etc.
Lady Dove.........Mrs. Morris
Lucy Waters........Miss Storer

Violetta...........Mrs. Henry
Kitty.............Mrs. Harman
Sophia............Miss Hallam
Fanny.........Miss Richardson

Lethe

Frenchman and Drunkenman.....
Mr. Hallam
Fine Gentleman.....Mr. Byerley
Tattoo..........Mr. Goodman
Æsop............Mr. Douglass

Mercury...........Mr. Woolls
Old Man..........Mr. Morris
Charon............Mr. Johnson
Mrs. Riot..........Miss Storer
Mrs. Tattoo.......Miss Hallam

Nov. 23   * A Way to Keep Him—Murphy   Chronicle, Nov. 21

Lovemore..........Mr. Hallam
Sir Brilliant Fashion...Mr. Henry
Sideboard..........Mr. Morris
Thomas..........Mr. Roberts
Lady Constant.......Miss Storer
Mignionet......Miss Richardson

Widow Belmour.....Miss Hallam
Sir Bashful Constant.Mr. Douglass
William.........Mr. Goodman
Richard............Mr. Parker
Mrs. Lovemore......Mrs. Henry
Fumish..........Mrs. Harman

An Honest Yorkshireman

Gaylove...........Mr. Woolls
Muckudow.........Mr. Morris
Slango............Mr. Byerley
Arabella............Miss Storer

Sapscul..............Mr. Wall
Blunder............Mr. Parker
Combrush.........Mrs. Morris

Nov. 25   The Maid of the Mill   Journal

Lord Aimworth......Mr. Hallam
Sir Harry Sycamore.Mr. Goodman
Lady Sycamore....Mrs. Douglass
Theodosia.......Miss Richardson
Patty.............Miss Hallam

Fairfield...........Mr. Douglass
Farmer Giles........Mr. Woolls
Ralph................Mr. Wall
Merwin.............Mr. Parker
Fanny.............Miss Storer

Gipsies....Messrs. Morris, Byerley, Roberts, Mrs. Henry, Mrs. Morris,
Mrs. Harmon, etc.

The Lying Valet

Sharp.............Mr. Morris
Justice Guttle......Mr. Goodman
Drunken Cook.......Mr. Parker
Mrs. Trippet....Miss Richardson
Kitty Pry..........Mrs. Henry

Gayless..............Mr. Wall
Beau Trippet........Mr. Byerley
Mrs. Gadabout.....Mrs. Harman
Melissa............Mrs. Morris

1772

Nov. 30   * *The Fashionable Lover*—Cumberland Chronicle,   Nov. 28

Mortimer...........Mr. Hallam	Tyrrel...........Mr. Goodman
Lord Abberville......Mr. Byerley	Dr. Druid...........Mr. Morris
Bridgemore..........Mr. Parker	Napthali.............Mr. Wall
Jarvis..............Mr. Woolls	LaJeunesse..........Mr. Roberts
Colin Macloid......Mr. Douglass	Lucinda...........Mrs. Henry
Mrs. Bridgemore...Mrs. Douglass	Betty..............Miss Storer
Mrs. Macintosh..Miss Richardson	Augusta Aubrey.....Miss Hallam
Aubrey.............Mr. Henry	

The Guardian

The Guardian.......Mr. Hallam	Lucy..............Mrs. Henry
Sir Charles Clochit....Mr. Morris	Miss Harriet........Miss Hallam
Young Clochit.........Mr. Wall	

Dec. 2   *George Barnwell*   Journal

George Barnwell.....Mr. Hallam	Thorowgood.......Mr. Douglass
Truman...........Mr. Parker	Uncle..............Mr. Henry
Blunt.............Mr. Morris	Maria.............Miss Storer
Lucy............Mrs. Harman	Millwood..........Mrs. Morris

Love à la Mode

Sir Callaghan O'Brallaghan...... Mr. Henry	Sir Theodore........Mr. Parker
	The Lady......Miss Richardson
Sir Archy Macsarcasm......... Mr. Douglass	'Squire Groom.........Mr. Wall
	Beau Mordecai.......Mr. Morris

Dec. 7   *Cymbeline*   Chronicle, Dec. 5

Posthumous.........Mr. Hallam	Cymbeline.........Mr. Douglass
Jachimo.............Mr. Henry	Bellarius..........Mr. Goodman
Guiderius...........Mr. Parker	Cloten..............Mr. Wall
Arvinagus..........Mr. Woolls	Caius Lucius........Mr. Byerley
Pisanio.............Mr. Morris	Philario.............Mr. Parker
Cornelius..........Mr. Roberts	Frenchman.........Mr. Woolls
Captain...........Mr. Johnson	Queen..........Mrs. Douglass
Imogen...........Miss Hallam	Helen..........Miss Richardson

The Upholsterer

Barker..............Mr. Wall	Quidnunc..........Mr. Byerley
Feeble.............Mr. Morris	Bellmore..........Mrs. Parker
Rovewell..........Mr. Woolls	Harriet.........Miss Richardson
Termagant.........Mrs. Henry	

1772

Dec. 9	*The West Indian*	Journal

Cast as for Nov. 9, 1772, except:

Charles Dudley......Mr. Hallam   Stukely.............Mr. Wall

The Devil to Pay

Sir John Loverule....Mr. Woolls   Jobson..............Mr. Henry
Butler..............Mr. Morris   Doctor.............Mr. Byerley
Coachman..........Mr. Johnson   Cook................Mr. Parker
Footman.............Mr. Wall   Blind Fiddler........Mr. Roberts
Lady Loverule.....Mrs. Harman   Lettice.............Mrs. Wall
Lucy..........Miss Richardson   Nell................Miss Storer

Dec. 14   * *Lionel and Clarissa*—Bickerstaff   Chronicle, Dec. 12

Col. Oldboy.......Mr. Goodman   Lionel..............Mr. Woolls
Sir John Flowerdale.Mr. Douglass   Mr. Jessamy.........Mr. Wall
Jenkins.............Mr. Parker   Harman.............Mr. Henry
Lady Mary Oldboy.Mrs. Harman   Clarissa............Miss Storer
Diana Oldboy.......Miss Hallam   Jenny..............Mrs. Henry

High Life Below Stairs

Lovell.............Mr. Hallam   Freeman............Mr. Parker
Lord Duke...........Mr. Wall   Sir Harry...........Mr. Henry
Philip.............Mr. Morris   Coachman..........Mr. Woolls
Kingston..........Mr. Byerley   Lady Bab..........Miss Storer
Lady Charlotte...Miss Richardson   Cook.............Mrs. Harman
Kitty..............Mrs. Henry   Chloe.............Mr. Roberts

Dec. 16	*Romeo and Juliet*	Journal

Romeo............Mr. Hallam   Mercutio..........Mr. Douglass
Capulet.............Mr. Henry   Fryer Lawrence......Mr. Morris
Escalus..........Mr. Goodman   Paris..............Mr. Woolls
Benvolio............Mr. Wall   Tibalt.............Mr. Parker
Montague.........Mr. Byerley   Apothecary........Mr. Roberts
Lady Capulet......Mrs. Douglass   Nurse...........Mrs. Harman
Juliet............Miss Hallam

The Old Maid

Cast as for Nov. 4, 1772.

Dec. 21	*Romeo and Juliet*	Packet

Cast as for Dec. 16, 1772.

The Old Maid

Cast as for Nov. 4, 1772.

1772

Dec. 23   *The Suspicious Husband*   Journal

Ranger............	Mr. Hallam	Strictland........	Mr. Douglass
Frankly...........	Mr. Henry	Jack Meggot.........	Mr. Wall
Tester............	Mr. Morris	Buckle............	Mr. Woolls
Simon............	Mr. Johnson	Mrs. Strictland......	Mrs. Henry
Jacintha..........	Mrs. Morris	Lucetta........	Miss Richardson
Milliner..........	Miss Storer	Landlady.........	Mrs. Harman
Maid.............	Mrs. Wall	Clarinda..........	Miss Hallam

Thomas and Sally

The Squire.........	Mr. Woolls	The Sailor.........	Mr. Henry
Dorcas...........	Mrs. Harman	Sally............	Miss Hallam

Dec. 28   *Richard III*   Chronicle, Dec. 26

King Richard.......	Mr. Hallam	Edward IV..........	Mr. Wall
Earl of Richmond.....	Mr. Henry	Henry VI..........	Mr. Morris
Duke of Buckingham.	Mr. Douglass	Duke of York....	Miss Richardson
Tressel............	Mr. Henry	Catesby............	Mr. Parker
Ratcliff............	Mr. Woolls	Oxford............	Mr. Johnson
Lady Ann..........	Mrs. Henry	Tyrrel............	Mr. Roberts
Duchess of York....	Mrs. Harman	Queen Elizabeth.....	Mrs. Morris

The Musical Lady

Old Mash..........	Mr. Morris	Mash...............	Mr. Wall
Freeman...........	Mr. Parker	Rosini............	Mr. Roberts
Lady Scrape........	Miss Storer	Laundress........	Mrs. Harman
Sophy............	Miss Hallam		

Dec. 30   "Not Acted these Five Years"   Journal

The School for Lovers

Modely...........	Mr. Hallam	Sir John Dorilant...	Mr. Douglass
Bellmour...........	Mr. Wall	Lady Beverly.......	Mrs. Morris
Steward...........	Mr. Morris	Araminta..........	Mrs. Henry
Celia............	Miss Hallam		

The Padlock

Cast as for October 28, 1772.

1773

Jan. 4   *Lionel and Clarissa*   Chronicle, Jan. 2

Cast as for December 14, 1772.

Love à la Mode

Cast as for December 2, 1772.

1773

Jan. 6 *Tamerlane* Journal

Bajazet............Mr. Hallam	Tamerlane.........Mr. Douglass
Moneses..........Mr. Goodman	Axalla...............Mr. Wall
Omar...............Mr. Henry	Dervise............Mr. Morris
Haly...............Mr. Parker	Prince of Tanais.....Mr. Woolls
Zama..............Mr. Johnson	Mirvan............Mr. Roberts
Selima............Mrs. Henry	Arpasia............Mrs. Morris

Catherine and Petruchio

Petruchio........Mr. Goodman	Grumio.............Mr. Morris
Biondello...........Mr. Wall	Hortentio..........Mr. Parker
Baptisa............Mr. Byerley	Taylor.............Mr. Roberts
Curtis............Mrs. Harman	Bianca.........Miss Richardson
Catherine..........Mrs. Morris	

Jan. 11 ** Henry IV—Part I*—Shakespeare Packet

Hotspur...........Mr. Hallam	King Henry.........Mr. Morris
Prince of Wales.....Mrs. Henry	Sir Walter Blunt..Mr. Goodman
Worcester..........Mr. Byerley	Vernon.............Mr. Parker
Westmoreland........Mr. Wall	Northumberland.....Mr. Woolls
Bardolph...........Mr. Johnson	Francis.............Mr. Roberts
Sir John Falstaff....Mr. Douglass	1st Carrier.......Mr. Goodman
Poins..............Mr. Byerley	Douglass............Mr. Woolls
2nd Carrier..........Mr. Parker	Peto................Mr. Wall
Prince John.........Mr. Roberts	Hostess Quickly....Mrs. Harman
Lady Percy........Mrs. Morris	

The Devil to Pay

Cast as for December 9, 1772.

Jan. 13 *Love for Love* Journal

Valentine..........Mr. Hallam	Sir Sampson Legend..Mr. Henry
Scandal...........Mr. Douglass	Tattle...............Mr. Wall
Foresight...........Mr. Morris	Jeremy............Mr. Byerley
Trapland..........Mr. Parker	Buckram...........Mr. Woolls
Ben..............Mr. Goodman	Miss Prue..........Miss Storer
Angelica...........Mrs. Henry	Nurse............Mrs. Harman
Mrs. Foresight...Miss Richardson	Mrs. Frail.........Mrs. Morris

High Life Below Stairs

Cast as for December 14, 1772.

Jan. 18 *The Conscious Lovers* Packet

Young Bevil.......Mr. Hallam	Mr. Sealand.......Mr. Douglass
Sir John Bevil.....Mr. Goodman	Myrtle.............Mrs. Wall

1773

Cimberton	Mr. Byerley	Humphrey	Mr. Parker
Daniel	Mr. Roberts	Tom	Mr. Morris
Mrs. Sealand	Mrs. Harman	Phillis	Miss Storer
Isabella	Mrs. Douglass	Lucinda	Miss Richardson
Indiana	Mrs. Morris		

"After the PLAY, a COMIC DANCE by Monsieur FRANCIS, from the THEATRE in AMSTERDAM."

Love à la Mode

Cast as for December 2, 1772.

"Monsieur Francis" was Francis Mentges, a fencing master, and later a colonel in the Army of the Revolution. This was his first appearance.

Jan. 20   *The Shipwreck*   Gazette

Cast as for November 18, 1772, except:

Sophia	Miss Storer	Fanny	Mrs. Wall
Lucy Waters	Miss Richardson		

* The Buck; or, The Englishman in Paris—Foote

Buck	Mr. Goodman	Sir John Buck	Mr. Morris
Mr. Subtle	Mr. Henry	Classic	Mr. Parker
Dauphine	Mr. Roberts	Solitaire	Mr. Wall
Gamut	Mr. Woolls	Roger	Mr. Johnson
Marquis	Mr. Byerley	Mrs. Subtle	Miss Richardson
Lucinda	Miss Storer		

Jan. 25   *False Delicacy*   Chronicle

Cecil	Mr. Hallam	Col. Rivers	Mr. Douglass
Lord Winworth	Mr. Henry	Sir Harry Newburg	Mr. Wall
Sidney	Mr. Byerley	Miss Betty Lambton	Mrs. Morris
Miss Marchmont	Miss Storer	Miss Rivers	Mrs. Henry
Sally	Miss Richardson	Mrs. Harley	Mrs. Douglass

Singing by Mrs. Stampfer, from the Theatre-Royal in Edinburgh.

Lethe

Cast as for Nov. 18, 1772, except:

Mrs. Tattoo........Mrs. Henry

First appearance of Mrs. Stampfer.

[121]

1773

Jan. 27   *Othello*—Shakespeare   Journal

Othello	Mr. Hallam	Iago	Mr. Douglass
Cassio	Mr. Goodman	Roderigo	Mr. Wall
Lodorico	Mr. Henry	Brabantio	Mr. Morris
Duke	Mr. Byerley	Montano	Mr. Parker
Officer	Mr. Johnson	Gratiano	Mr. Woolls
Messenger	Mr. Roberts	Desdemona	Mrs. Henry
Emilia	Mrs. Douglass		

Midas

Cast as for November 2, 1772, except:

Juno............Mrs. Wall   Mysis.........Miss Richardson

Feb. 1   *The Tempest*   Journal

Prospero	Mr. Douglass	Ferdinand	Mr. Hallam
Alonzo	Mr. Byerley	Antonio	Mr. Parker
Hypolito	Mr. Wall	Gonzalo	Mr. Johnson
Stephano	Mr. Morris	Trinculo	Mr. Henry
Ventoso	Mr. Johnson	Mustachio	Mr. Woolls
Ariel	Miss Storer	Miranda & Dorinda	Mrs. Henry
Caliban & Sycano	Messrs. Goodman and Roberts		and Miss Hallam

Neptune and Amphitrite

Neptune...........Mr. Woolls   Amphitrite.........Miss Storer

Miss in Her Teens

Cast as for Nov. 9, 1772, save that the part of Captain Loveit was not included.

Feb. 3   *The Tempest*   Journal
Neptune and Amphitrite

Repeated with no changes.

High Life Below Stairs

Cast as for December 14, 1772, except:

Freeman............Mr. Byerley   Cook..............Mrs. Wall
Kingston...........Mr. Parker

Feb. 8   *Beggar's Opera*   Chronicle

Capt. Macheath	Mr. Hallam	Peachum	Mr. Douglass
Mat o' th' Mint	Mr. Goodman	Lockit	Mr. Morris
Nimming Ned	Mr. Byerley	Filch	Mr. Wall
Jerry Twitcher	Mr. Johnson	Ben Budge	Mr. Parker
Mrs. Peachum	Mrs. Morris	Lucy	Miss Storer
Mrs. Coaxer	Mrs. Henry	Jenny Diver	Miss Richardson

1773

Feb. 8 (cont.)

Mrs. Slammekin......Mrs. Wall   Moll Brazen........Mr. Roberts
Diana Trapes....Miss Richardson   Polly.............Miss Hallam

The Mayor of Garratt

Cast as for Nov. 11, 1772.

Feb. 10   "Not Acted these Five Years"   Journal

Theodosius

Varanes...........Mr. Hallam   Theodosius..........Mr. Henry
Marcian.........Mr. Douglass   Leontine.........Mr. Goodman
Cetticus...........Mr. Woolls   Lucius.............Mr. Parker
Aranthes............Mr. Wall   Priests..Messrs. Morris & Byerley
Pulcheria..........Mrs. Morris   Marina...........Miss Storer
Julia..............Mrs. Wall   Flavilla........Miss Richardson
Athenais..........Miss Hallam

The Honest Yorkshireman

Cast as for November 23, 1772.

Feb. 15   *Lionel and Clarissa*   Chronicle

Cast as for January 4, 1773, except:

Lady Mary Oldboy.............Mrs. Douglass

Edgar and Emmeline

Edgar.............Mr. Hallam   Florimond...........Mr. Wall
First Aerial Spirit....Miss Storer   2nd Aerial Spirit.....Mrs. Henry
Woman to Elfida.....Miss Rich-   Emmeline.........Miss Hallam
             ardson
Other Spirits...Messrs. Goodman, Woolls, Byerley, Parker, Mrs. Morris,
             Mrs. Wall, &c. &c.

Feb. 17   * *The Conquest of Canada*—Cockings   Journal

General Wolfe......Mr. Hallam   Leonatus..........Mr. Douglass
Britannicus.........Mr. Henry   Montcalm.......Mr. Goodman
Bougainville.........Mr. Wall   Levi...............Mr. Morris
Peryton...........Mr. Byerley   First Caledonian Chief..A GENTLE-
Second Caledonian Chief.......   MAN
             Mr. Woolls   (Being his first appearance on any
                              Stage)
Jemmy Chaunter.....Mr. Woolls   Sailors.........Messrs. Johnson,
                              Roberts, etc.
Sophia.............Miss Hallam   Abers.............Mrs. Morris
First Nun..........Mrs. Henry   Second Nun........Miss Storer
Maid..........Miss Richardson   Sophronia........Mrs. Douglass

[123]

1773

Sea and Land Officers...Messrs. Byerley, Johnson, Parker, Woolls, Roberts, and a "YOUNG GENTLEMAN," (who never appeared on any Stage before)

No Farce

Feb. 22   "The THIRD, and positively the last Night"   Chronicle

The Conquest of Canada

Cast as on Feb. 17.

Love à la Mode

Cast as for January 4, 1773, except:

Sir Theodore........Mr. Byerley

The second appearance of *The Conquest of Canada* doubtless came on Friday, February 19.

Feb. 26   *A Word to the Wise*   Journal, Feb. 24

Cast as for October 28, 1772.

Catherine and Petruchio

Cast as for January 6, 1773, except:

Curtis..............Mrs. Wall

March 3   * *Cymon*—Garrick   Journal

Cymon............Mr. Hallam	Merlin..........Mr. Goodman
Linco.............Mr. Woolls	Dorus.............Mr. Morris
Damon.............Mr. Wall	Dorillas ....Mr. Byerley
First Demon of Revenge........	Cupid.............Miss Storer
Mr. Woolls	Urganda..........Mrs. Morris
Fatima............Mrs. Henry	Dorcas.........Miss Richardson
First Shepherdess.....Miss Storer	Second Shepherdess............
Sylvia.............Miss Hallam	Miss Richardson

March 8   Benefit of Mr. and Mrs. Douglass   Chronicle

The Fashionable Lover

Cast as for Nov. 30, 1772, except:

Lord Abberville.......Mr. Wall	Bridgemore.........Mr. Byerley
Napthali..........Mr. Roberts	Mrs. Bridgemore....Mrs. Morris

Edgar and Emmeline

Cast as for Feb. 15, 1773, except:

Another Spirit.......Mr. Roberts

("Woman to Elfrida" not mentioned)

[124]

1773

| March 10 | "Not Acted These Five Years" | Journal |

For the Benefit of Mr. and Mrs. Henry

The Merchant of Venice

Antonio............Mr. Hallam	Bassanio...........Mr. Douglass
Shylock............Mr. Henry	Gratiano..........Mr. Goodman
Lorenzo............Mr. Woolls	Duke..............Mr. Byerley
Salanio..............Mr. Wall	Solarino...........Mr. Dermot
Tubal.............Mr. Roberts	Gobbo.............Mr. Byerley
Lancelot...........Mr. Morris	Jessica............Miss Hallam
Nerissa.........Miss Richardson	Portia.............Mrs. Morris

Flora; or, Hob in the Well

Hob...............Mr. Hallam	Old Hob...........Mr. Byerley
Sir Thomas Tasty....Mr. Morris	Countrymen.......Messrs. Wall,
Dick..............Mr. Johnson	Roberts, Dermot
Hob's Mother....Miss Richardson	Betty.............Mrs. Henry
Friendly...........Mr. Woolls	Flora..............Miss Storer

As Mr. and Mrs. Henry again announced a benefit on March 29, this bill may have been postponed. First appearance of Mr. Dermot.

| March 15 | "Benefit of Mr. Hallam, and Co." | Chronicle |

The West Indian

Cast as for Nov. 9, 1772, except:

Belcour............Mr. Hallam	Charles Dudley......Mr. Henry
Varland............Mr. Woolls	The Sailor.........Mr. Roberts
Stukely..............Mr. Wall	Lady Rusport.......Mrs. Morris

The Padlock

Cast as for Oct. 28, 1772.

Bucks Have at Ye All

| March 17 | Benefit of Mr. and Mrs. Morris | Journal |

The Beaux' Stratagem

Archer.............Mr. Hallam	Aimwell..........Mr. Douglass
Sullen..............Mr. Henry	Forgard..........Mr. Goodman
Freeman..............Mr. Wall	Gibbet.............Mr. Woolls
Boniface...........Mr. Byerley	Bagshot............Mr. Dermot
Hounslow..........Mr. Roberts	Scrub..............Mr. Morris
Dorinda........Miss Richardson	Cherry.............Mrs. Henry
Lady Bountiful......Mrs. Wall	Gipsy..............Miss Storer
Mrs. Sullen........Mrs. Morris	

1773

March 17 (cont.)   *Catherine and Petruchio*

Cast as for Jan. 6, 1773, except:

Hortentio..........Mr. Dermot   Curtis..............Mrs. Wall

March 22   *The Earl of Essex*   Chronicle

Essex.............Mr. Hallam   Southampton.........Mr. Henry
Burleigh...........Mr. Morris   Lieutenant..........Mr. Woolls
Raleigh...........Mr. Byerley   Queen Elizabeth.....Mrs. Morris
Countess of Rutland..Miss Hallam Countess of Nottingham.........
                                                    Mrs. Henry

The Citizen

Young Wilding......Mr. Hallam   Young Philpot........Mr. Wall
Old Philpot........Mr. Morris   Beaufort............Mr. Woolls
Sir Jasper.........Mr. Byerley   Quildrive...........Mr. Roberts
Corinna........Miss Richardson   Maria.............Miss Hallam

March 24   Benefit of Messrs. Byerley, Parker and Johnson   Journal
The Recruiting Officer

Captain Plume......Mr. Hallam   Sergeant Kite......Mr. Douglass
Capt. Brayers.......Mr. Byerley   Mr. Worthy........Mr. Woolls
Justice Balance......Mr. Morris   Bullock...........Mr. Goodman
Justice Scale.......Mr. Dermot   1st Recruit...........Mr. Wall
Rose..............Miss Hallam   2nd Recruit........Mr. Roberts
Melinda...........Mrs. Henry   Lucy..........Miss Richardson
Sylvia (by particular desire)......
                  Mrs. Morris

Edgar and Emmeline

Edgar.............Mr. Hallam   Emmeline..........Miss Hallam
Florimond...........Mr. Wall

March 27   "The Last Benefit but One"   Play-bill in Shaw
                                                      Theatre Collection

For the Benefit of Mr. Woolls and Mr. Wall
The Earl of Essex
Cast as for March 22, 1773.

The Citizen
Cast as for March 22, 1773.
A Picture of a Play-House, by Mr. Hallam
[126]

1773

March 29   For the Benefit of Mr. and Mrs. Henry   Chronicle

"Not Acted these five Years"

The Wonder

Don Felix	Mr. Hallam	Colonel Briton	Mr. Henry
Don Pedro	Mr. Goodman	Don Lopez	Mr. Byerley
Frederick	Mr. Woolls	Lissando	Mr. Morris
Vasquez	Mr. Roberts	Gibby	Mr. Douglass
Donna Isabella	Miss Storer	Flora	Mrs. Henry
Inis	Miss Richardson	Donna Violante	Miss Hallam

* The Register Office—Reed

Capt. LeBrush	Mr. Hallam	Lord Brilliant	Mr. Goodman
Scotchman	Mr. Douglass	Irishman	Mr. Henry
Frenchman	Mr. Roberts	Harwood	Mr. Wall
Tricket	Mr. Morris	Gulwell	Mr. Beyerley
Frankly	Mr. Woolls	Williams	Mr. Johnson
Maria	Miss Storer	Margery Moorpont	Mrs. Henry

March 31   *The Tempest*   Journal

Cast as for Feb. 3, 1773, except:

Antonio.........Mr. Dermot

Neptune and Amphitrite
The Guardian

Cast as for Nov. 30, 1772.

"The last night but one." Probably the last night came on Friday, April 2, but we have no record.

During the American Company's season at the Theatre in Southwark from Oct. 28, 1772, to March 31, 1773, these new plays were given: *The Conquest of Canada, Cymon, The Fashionable Lover, King Henry IV (part one), Othello, The School for Fathers; or Lionel and Clarissa, The School for Libertines, The Shipwreck, The Way to Keep Him,* and *The West Indian.* The plays formerly seen were *The Beaux' Stratagem, The Beggar's Opera, Cymbeline, The Earl of Essex, False Delicacy, George Barnwell, Hamlet, King Richard III, Love for Love, Love in a Village, The Maid of the Mill, The Merchant of Venice, The Mourning Bride, The Recruiting Officer, The Roman Father, Romeo and Juliet, The School for Lovers, The Suspicious Husband, Tamerlane, The Tempest, Theodosius,* and *The Wonder.* New afterpieces: *The Buck,* and *The Register Office.* Reappearing afterpieces: *Catherine and Petruchio, The Citizen, The Devil to Pay, Edgar and Emmeline, The Guardian, High Life Below Stairs, Hob in the Well, The Honest Yorkshireman, Lethe, Love à la Mode, The Lying Valet, The Mayor of Garratt, Midas, The Miller of Mansfield, Miss in Her Teens, The Musical*

[127]

1773

Lady, The Old Maid, The Padlock, Thomas and Sally, and *The Upholsterer.* Our record is probably only two-thirds complete.

The new performers to appear were Mrs. Morris, Mr. Goodman, Mr. Johnson, Mr. Dermot, "A gentleman," "A young gentleman," Mr. Francis Mentges, and Mrs. Stampfer. Essentially the company was unchanged, consisting of Mr. and Mrs. Douglass, Mr. Lewis Hallam, Miss Sarah Hallam, Mr. and Mrs. Henry, Mr. Owen Morris, Miss Richardson, Miss Maria Storer, Mr. and Mrs. Wall, and Messrs. Woolls, Parker, Roberts, and Byerley.

May 12 (*et sequor*)   Journal

"New PROSPECTIVE THEATRE which the Sieur MERCIER has brought over" from London. At the Theatre in Southwark "on Mondays, Wednesdays, Fridays, and Saturdays."

This was apparently a combination of "magic lanthorn," marionettes, and panorama.

Nov. 1   *Lionel and Clarissa*   Packet
                          Love à la Mode

"The House [Southwark] will be open for a fortnight only." The last performance was on November 15.

Nov. 3   *The Earl of Essex*   Journal

Cast as for March 22, 1773, except:

Sir Walter Raleigh...Mr. Hughes   Countess of Nottingham.........
                                                    Miss Storer

The Citizen

The Citizen...........Mr. Wall   Beaufort............Mr. Woolls
Young Wilding......Mr. Hallam   Dapper............Mr. Douglass
Sir Jasper Wilding...Mr. Hughes   Corinna.........Miss Richardson
Old Philpot.........Mr. Morris
Maria.....Miss Wainright, being her first appearance these six years.

First appearance of Mr. Hughes.

Nov. 8   *Hamlet*   Packet
                    * *The Irish Widow*—Garrick

Nov. 10   *The Clandestine Marriage*   Journal

Lord Ogleby.......Mr. Hallam   Sir John Melville...Mr. Douglass
Lovewell...........Mr. Henry   Sergeant Flower....Mr. Goodman
Sterling.............Mr. Morris   Canton............Mr. Hughes
Traverse..........Mr. Dermot   Truman...........Mr. Woolls

1773

Miss Sterling......Miss Hallam		Betty..........Miss Richardson	
Miss Fanny.........Miss Storer		Chambermaid...Miss Wainwright	
Housekeeper.........Mrs. Wall		Mrs. Heidelberg...Mrs. Douglass	

The Padlock

Cast as for October 28, 1772.

Nov. 15   *The West Indian*   Packet

The West Indian....Mr. Hallam
  "being his fourth appearance in
  that character."
Capt. Dudley......Mr. Douglass
Varland............Mr. Woolls
Lady Rusport......Mrs. Douglass
Louisa Dudley.......Miss Storer
Lucy.........Miss Wainwright
Charles Dudley...a "young gentleman who never appeared on any stage
  before."

Major O'Flaherty....Mr. Henry
  "being his third appearance in
  that character."
Mr. Stockwell.......Mr. Morris
Fulmer............Mr. Hughes
Mrs. Fulmer....Miss Richardson
Charlotte Rusport...Miss Hallam

* *Cross Purposes*—O'Brien

Mr. Grub.........Mr. Morris
Chapeau.............Mr. Wall
Consol............Mr. Dermot
Mrs. Grub........Mrs. Morris

The Bevils......Messrs. Hallam,
                  Douglass, Henry
Robin.............Mr. Hughes
Emily.............Miss Storer

Prologue by the "Young Gentleman."
A farewell epilogue by Mr. Hallam.

This was the last performance of the American Company in Colonial Philadelphia. There is some doubt whether it was given, as a dispute arose between
Mr. Henry and Mr. Goodman as to the part of Major O'Flaherty. See
page 31.

We have record of five plays for this brief season from Nov. 1 to 15,
1773, by the American Company at the Theatre in Southwark: *The Clandestine Marriage, The Earl of Essex, Hamlet, Lionel and Clarissa,* and *The
West Indian;* and five afterpieces: *The Citizen, Love à la Mode, The Padlock, Cross Purposes,* and *The Irish Widow,* only the last two of which were
new.

The only new actors this season were Mr. Hughes and "A young gentleman."
Miss Wainwright reappeared. The other members of the company mentioned
in the casts were Mr. and Mrs. Douglass, Mr. Lewis and Miss Sarah Hallam,
Mr. and Mrs. Henry, Mr. and Mrs. Morris, Miss Richardson, Miss Maria
Storer, Messrs. Wall, Woolls, Dermot and Goodman.

1773

Nov. 22   *"A New Lecture"*—Stevens   Journal, Nov. 17

A post-season recitation, delivered by Mr. Wall at the "Long Room in Videll's Alley."

1774

Sept. 19   *A Lecture on Heads*   Packet
                Picture of a Playhouse, etc.

The Southwark Theatre was opened for one night by Messrs. Goodman and Allen. This is the first appearance of Mr. Allen. Many of the American Company were probably in Philadelphia at this time.

Oct. 20   J. Cont. Cong.
                             1774–1789, I, 78

Resolution of the Continental Congress against plays and "other expensive diversions."

1775

Jan. 23–28.   J. House Rep. Pa., I, 31–33

Convention for Pennsylvania approved the proceedings of the Continental Congress.

COLLEGE OF PHILADELPHIA

May 17   * *Dialogue*   Library, U. of Pa.

1778

HOWE'S THESPIANS—SOUTHWARK THEATRE

Jan. 19   * *No One's Enemy But His Own*—Murphy   Pa. Ledger
               The Deuce is in Him   Jan. 17

First performance of Howe's Thespians in Philadelphia, under the leadership of André and Delancey. They played till May 19.

Jan. 26   * *The Minor*—Foote   Playbill in Ridgeway
               The Deuce is in Him   Library, Philadelphia

Feb. 9   *The Minor*   Pa. Ledger, Feb. 7
          * *Duke and No Duke*—Tate

Feb. 16   *The Constant Couple*   Pa. Ledger, Feb. 14
           Duke and No Duke

March 9   *The Inconstant*   Pa. Ledger, March 7
           The Mock Doctor

("A Play" intended for February 27 and *The Constant Couple* and *The*

1778

Mock Doctor advertised for March 2 were postponed. See Pa. Ledger February 25 and 28, supplement.)

March 16	*The Inconstant* *Lethe*	Pa. Ledger, March 14
March 25	*King Henry IV, part I.* *The Mock Doctor*	Pa. Ledger

(Seilhamer, II, 29, gives *Lethe* as the farce, but the Pa. Ledger for March 21 and 25, and a playbill in the Ridgeway Library, Philadelphia, give *The Mock Doctor.*)

March 30	*King Henry IV, part I* *Lethe*	Pa. Ledger, March 28

VALLEY FORGE

April 15	The Military Journal of George Ewing, (1754–1824) a Soldier of Valley Forge, entry for April 15.

A Play was given "at the Bakehouse in the Evening." There is record of another production at Valley Forge on May 11.

HOWE'S THESPIANS

April 20	*The Wonder* * *A Trip to Scotland*—Whitehead	Playbill in Ridgeway Library
April 24	*The Wonder* *The Mock Doctor*	Pa. Ledger, April 22
May 1	* *The Lyar*—Foote *A Trip to Scotland*	Pa. Ledger, April 29
May 6	*The Lyar* *Duke and No Duke*	Pa. Ledger

VALLEY FORGE

May 11	*Cato*	A L S Wallace Papers (Bradford) 1, 58

On May 14: "If the Enemy does not retire from Philad^a. soon . . . The Fair Penitent with The Padlock will soon be acted. The 'recruiting officer' is also on foot." On May 20: "All is hurry and bustle—our plays and other amusements seem to be laid aside." Wallace Papers (Bradford) I, 59.

1778

WHARTON'S MANSION

May 18   *Mischianza*   Pa. Ledger

Elaborate pageantry farewell to General Howe, staged by his officers, particularly Major André and Captain Delancey.

HOWE'S THESPIANS

May 19   *Douglas*   Pa. Ledger, May 16
                                    The Citizen

Last performance by Howe's Thespians. Altogether they gave thirteen nights from Jan. 19 to May 19, 1778, at which eight full-length plays and six farces were presented. New plays: *The Lyar, The Minor,* and *No One's Enemy But His Own.* Reappearing plays: *Douglas, The Inconstant, King Henry IV (part one), The Constant Couple,* and *The Wonder.* New farces: *Duke and No Duke* and *A Trip to Scotland.* Reappearing farces: *The Citizen, The Deuce is in Him, Lethe,* and *The Mock Doctor.* The only known actors were a Miss Hyde (Durang, Chap. XII, Series 1), Major André, and Captain Delancey. Soldiers' wives are also said to have acted. André painted a drop curtain.

Sept.

Plays were probably given by American officers during September and October. See text, page 38.

Oct. 12   J. Cont. Cong. Vol.
                                                            XII, 1778, Oct. 12

Congress recommended to the states the suppression of theatrical entertainments, together with horses races, etc.

Oct. 16   J. Cont. Cong. Vol.
                                                            XII, 1778, Oct. 16

Congress resolved that office-holders who in any wise encouraged plays should be dismissed.

                                                            Pa. Packet, Oct. 17

"A play being to be performed . . . the Marquis de la Fayette" urged the President of Congress to attend it with him, but hearing of the resolution mentioned above, decided to stay away.

1779

March 30   Statutes at Large of Pa.,
                                                   Chap. 833 (Vol. 9)

Pennsylvania passed a law against the theatre, which remained in force till March 2, 1789.

1780

MR. TEMPLETON—SOUTHWARK THEATRE

Feb. 11	*Performances on Slack Wire*	Journal, Feb. 9

First appearance of Mr. Templeton.

Feb. 18	*Slack Wire*	Journal, Feb. 16
Feb. 25	*Slack Wire*	Journal, Feb. 23
Feb. 28	*Slack Wire*	Journal, Feb. 23
April 25	*Slack Wire*	Journal, April 19
April 28	*Slack Wire*	Journal, April 19

-Mr. Templeton's performances on the slack wire are interesting as they show that the Theatre in Southwark was open in 1780.

1782

SOUTHWARK THEATRE

Jan. 2	* *Eugènie*—Beaumarchais (in French) *The Lying Valet*	Freeman's Journal, Jan. 9

Given by Alexander Quesnay and "young gentleman, students in that [the French] language." In spite of the prohibition of the stage, George Washington and a number of others attended.

Jan. 5   Packet

Mr. Quesnay advertised for January 11 "a second Representation of *Eugènie,* with the Farce of *The Cheats of Scapin.*"

Jan. 8   Packet

Mr. Quesnay "inform[ed] the Public that no public Play . . . nor any Exhibition made contrary to Law" would be given.

July 1   Pa. Arch. IX, 573

John Henry petitioned President Moore, of the Supreme Executive Council of Pennsylvania, for permission to open the Theatre in Southwark.

July 2   Colonial Records, XIII, 324

John Henry's request refused.

Aug. 7   Journal

The Baltimore Theatre advertised in Philadelphia for actors.

1783

Nov. 10   Min. Ass. Pa. for Nov. 10, 1783

1783

"Dennis Ryan, in behalf of himself and a company of Comedians" petitioned the Assembly for a repeal of the law against plays. (They had been in New York in October, and opened in Baltimore in December. Seilhamer, II, Chaps. 7, 8, 9.) The Assembly tabled the appeal, and took no further action.

1784

Jan. 21

Min. Ass. Pa.
Jan. 21, 1784

Lewis Hallam, on behalf of himself and "The comedians, commonly called the *American* Company," asked for the repeal of the law against plays. "Recommendatory certificates, signed by a considerable number" of Philadelphians "were presented to the Assembly."

Feb. 3

Ibid., Feb. 3

The Quakers petitioned the Assembly *against* Hallam's request. Other petitions were read on Feb. 6, 9, and 18. (*Ibid.* on those dates.)

Feb. 18

Ibid., Feb. 18

The Assembly, 41 to 21, voted down a motion that a committee be appointed to draft a bill repealing the law against theatres.

Feb. 21

Packet

Lewis Hallam thanked those who had worked for the legal opening of the theatre in Philadelphia.

April 1   *Lecture Upon Heads*   Packet, Mar. 27

"Strictures upon the most eminent Dramatic Authors . . diversified with Music, Scenery, and other Decorations."

Mr. Hallam and (presumably) the remnant of the American Company presented "Lectures," which were in all probability disguised plays, or scenes from plays. For a number of years the advertisements simply announced, in roundabout language, "Lectures" on different subjects: there is usually no record of what actually was given. No actors names were mentioned. The first season was from April 1 to June 9.

April 19   *Lecture Upon Heads,*   Packet, April 17
                               etc.

April 26   *Lecture Upon Heads,*   Packet, April 24
                               etc.

May 11   *Lectures Upon Heads*   Packet
                            (New course)

"*Monody* in Honor of the Chiefs who have Fallen in the Cause of America."

1784

May 22 *Washington and the Theatre,* P. L. Ford, 28

George Washington, then in Philadelphia, "purchased four Play Tickets."

June 9 *Lecture Upon Heads* Packet, June 5

(New course)

Monody

"Last night of Performance"

This concluded the "Lecture" season at the Theatre in Southwark from April 1 to June 9, 1783. Our record is probably incomplete.

Dec. 7 *Lectures* Packet, Dec. 6
Monody

No names appear. Seilhamer (II, 165) says that the company, which had been in Baltimore, was under the management of Messrs. Hallam and Allen, and included also Mrs. Allen, Mr. John Durang, and his sister, Miss Caroline Durang. The season lasted from Dec. 7, 1784, to July 29, 1785, at the Theatre in Southwark.

Dec. 14 *Lectures* Packet
Picture of a Playhouse

Dec. 23 *Lectures* Packet
Monody

1785

Jan. 17 *Lectures,* including Packet
* "Garrick's *Ode on Dedicating a Building to Shakespeare*"

Jan. 24 *Lectures* Packet
Jan. 31 *Lectures* Packet
Feb. 21 Benefit of the Poor Packet, Feb. 14

Lectures
"*Pantomimical Finale*"

March 1 Benefit of the Poor Packet

Lectures

March 8 *Lectures* Packet, Mar. 5
March 15 *Lectures* Packet
March 17 *Lectures* Packet
"*Les Grandes Ombres Chinoises*"

[135]

1785

"Ombres Chinoises" were moving silhouettes, which had become fashionable in France. See Brander Matthews, "The Forerunner of the Movies," *Century Magazine,* 87, 916–24, Ap. '14.

March 29	*Lectures*	Packet
	Monody	
	Les Grandes Ombres Chinoises	
	Grand Pantomimical Finale	
April 2	*Lectures*	Packet
	Les Grandes Ombres Chinoises	
April 5	*Lectures*	Packet
April 9	*Lectures*	Packet
	Prologue in Character of Harlequin	
April 21	*Lectures*	Packet
	Garrick's *Ode on Shakespeare*	
	"The Skeleton Scene, from * *The Chase,* or *Merlin's Cave."*	
May 9	*Lectures*	Packet
May 11	*Lectures* as on April 21	Packet
May 16	*Lectures* as on April 21	Packet
May 19	*Lectures* as on April 21	Packet
May 26	*Lectures,* concluding with a "Mascherata al Fresco"	Packet
June 6	*Lecture,* the finale consisting of "Dialogue and dum shew [sic]."	Packet
June 8	*Lectures*	Packet
June 13	*Lectures*	Packet
June 29	*Lectures*	Packet
July 6	*Lectures*	Packet

Concluding with "A Pantomimical Flete [sic]. This Concluding Piece consists of the most favourite Scenes, selected from the Pantomimes already exhibited; so connected as to form a regular PLOT in dumb Shew."

"A ROUNDELAY celebrating American Independence."

July 9	"Positively the Last Time."	Packet
	Lectures	
July 29	"Grand Serenata"—*Peace and Liberty*	Packet
	Pantomimical Fête	

[136]

1785

"Eulogy on Freemasonry, by a *Brother* from the *Theatres* in *England,* being his *first appearance.*"

In all probability Hallam's company was giving the above entertainments, though there is no record in the announcements. Last night of the season from Dec. 7, 1784, to July 29, 1785, at the Theatre in Southwark.

1786

Sept. 25   Statutes at Large of Pennsylvania
                                         Chap. 1248 (vol. XII)

The law against theatres enlarged to include pantomimes.

1787

OLD AMERICAN COMPANY—SOUTHWARK THEATRE

Jan. 15   *Concert and Lectures*   Packet
             * *Robinson Crusoe* (pantomime)

The Old American Company (not advertising itself under that or any title) played from January 15 till February 3, 1787, at the Theatre in Southwark. The disguise of "concert" and "lectures" is somewhat less thin, and titles of pantomimes and "operas" emerge.

The performers mentioned in this "concert" were Messrs. Phile, Woolls, Harper, and Wolf.

Jan. 17   *Concert and Lectures*   Packet
          Hippersley's * *"Drunken Man"*
               Robinson Crusoe

Jan. 19   *Concert and Lectures*   Packet
        * *Harlequin's Frolics* (pantomime)
      * *Rosina, or The Reapers*—Mrs. Brooke

The advertisement said that in the pantomime would "be introduced a musical entertainment called the Reapers," but it is probable that the entire comic opera was given.

Jan. 20   *Concert and Lectures*   Packet

"The Reapers; or, Harlequin's Frolics with the overture to *Rosina* is promised for the last time."

Jan. 22   *Concert and Lectures*   Packet
       * *Harlequin and the Moon* (pantomime)

"In which will be introduced a musical entertainment; called * 'Darby &

[137]

1787

Patrick'; with (by particular desire) the OVERTURE to the Poor Soldier."
Again I imagine that the whole of O'Keeffe's musical farce, * *The Poor Soldier,* was given, as well as the overture. This was announced inaccurately "As the Last Week Of Performance."

Jan. 23   Packet

The same bill as for January 22—*perhaps* the performance had been post-poned.

Jan. 24   "For the Benefit of the Poor"   Packet
                          Concert and Lectures
                             The Reapers
                        Harlequin and the Moon
                    The Poor Soldier (?) (See Jan. 22)

The *Packet* for February 21 announced that "Part of the Donation of Messieurs Hallam and Henry will To-morrow Morning, at 10 o'clock, be distributed in BREAD, at the Court-House, to the Poor of this city and liberties."

Jan. 26   *Concert and Lectures*   Packet
                             The Padlock
                        Harlequin and the Moon
                    The Poor Soldier (?) (See Jan. 22)

Jan. 27   *Concert and Lectures*   Packet
                        Harlequin and the Moon
                    * *The Agreeable Surprise*—O'Keeffe

Jan. 29   *Concert and Lectures*   Packet
                               Rosina
                          Harlequin's Frolics
                               Midas

"Positively the last Week."

Jan. 30   *Concert and Lectures*   Packet
                        The Agreeable Surprise
                          Harlequin's Frolics

Jan. 31   *Concert and Lectures*   Packet
                          Love in a Village
                          Harlequin's Frolics

Feb. 1   *Concert and Lectures*   Packet
                          Love in a Village
                               Lethe
                                [138]

1787

Feb. 2   *Concert and Lectures*   Packet
                     Midas

Harlequin's Frolics—"In which will be introduced the Dog Scene from
* 'Perseus and Andromeda,' and the Dwarf Dance, with, by particular desire, Darby and Patrick" [*The Poor Soldier?*]

"Messrs. HALLAM and HENRY respectfully inform the gentlemen, who
have desired the *School for Scandal,* that in the present situation of the
Theatre, it is impossible to comply with their request."

Feb. 3   Lecture—with the prologue "in the Character of   Packet
                 an Impoverished Bard"
                    The Padlock
               * *Flitch of Bacon*—Bate
             A Picture of a Playhouse

"Positively the last Night."

In this brief season from Jan. 15 to Feb. 3, 1787, either fourteen or fifteen
(see January 22–23) performances were given. As the advertisements were
veiled we cannot be certain of the plays, but the following new plays (or
operas or farces) probably appeared: *The Agreeable Surprise, The Flitch of
Bacon, Harlequin and the Moon, Harlequin's Frolic, The Poor Soldier,
Robinson Crusoe,* and *Rosina.* Those reappearing were *Lethe, Love in a
Village, Midas,* and *The Padlock.* The only performers' names to appear were
those of Messrs. Hallam and Henry (the Managers), and Harper, Phile,
Wolf, and Woolls.

March 12   "Lectures on *Heads* and *Manners.*"   Packet

By Mr. Pursell at the Long Room, Corner of South and Front streets.

June 25   "*Spectaculum Vitae*"   Packet
            "For the Relief of our Fellow-
            Citizens enslaved at Algiers"
       "The Grateful Ward; or The Pupil in Love"
             [*The Poor Soldier*]

The Old American Company played in Philadelphia from June 25 to August
4, 1787, disguising the productions as "Concerts" and the theatre as the
"Opera-House in Southwark." They advertised each production as "Spectaculum Vitae." Though the disguise is thinner than before, it is not always
possible to tell just what was given. The titles in brackets indicate therefore
probable productions.

June 27   [*Love in a Village*]   Packet
June 29   *Rosina;* or *The Reapers*   Packet
     * *The Fairies;* or *Daphne and Amintor*—Bickerstaff

[139]

1787

July 3	*The Duenna*—Sheridan	Packet
July 5	"The Grateful Ward; or The Pupil in Love" * Love in a Camp—O'Keeffe	Packet
July 7	The Duenna	Pa. Herald
July 10	"The Detection, or the Servants' Hall in an Uproar" [High Life Below Stairs] Love in a Camp	Packet

George Washington attended this performance. P. L. Ford, *Washington and the Theatre*, p. 32.

July 11	* The Deserter—Dibdin "Darby and Patrick" [The Poor Soldier]	Pa. Journal
July 14	The Tempest ("an opera") Neptune and Amphitrite	Packet
July 17	The Tempest Neptune and Amphitrite "The Office for Hireing Servants" [The Register Office]	Packet
July 19	"A Serious and Moral LECTURE, (in Five Parts) on the VICE OF GAMING" [The Gamester]	Packet
July 21	"The CRUSADE; or The Generous Sultan" [* Edward and Eleanora—Thomson]	Packet
July 23	"The Penitent Wife, or The Fatal Indiscretion" [Jane Shore] [The Register Office]	Packet
July 25		Packet

Hamlet and *Lethe* were advertised, but the *Packet* of July 26 said they were "postponed on account of the indisposition of Mr. Morris."

July 26	[The Gamester] [High Life Below Stairs]	Packet
July 28	* Selima and Azor—Collier "Modern Lovers; or, Generosity Rewarded" [Lionel and Clarissa]	Packet
July 30	"The Pernicious Vice of Scandal" [* The School for Scandal—Sheridan]	Packet

1787

Aug. 4   Benefit of the Poor   Packet

"The Generous American"
[*The West Indian*]
The Padlock

Last night of playing.

The Southwark was open seventeen nights between June 25 and August 4, 1787. The new pieces: *Daphne and Amintor, The Deserter, The Duenna, Edward and Eleonora, "The Grateful Ward," Lionel and Clarissa, Love in a Camp, The School for Scandal,* and *Selima and Azor.* Those reappearing (longer plays—or operas): *The Gamester, Jane Shore, The Poor Soldier, Rosina, The Tempest,* and *The West Indian.* Afterpieces reappearing: *High Life Below Stairs, Neptune and Amphitrite, The Padlock, The Register Office.* Mr. Morris was the only actor mentioned (and that because he was ill!) See June 25, 1787, for note on the ambiguous advertisements this season.

Dec. 10   Packet

* *The Contrast*—Tyler—was *read* by Mr. Wignell at the City Tavern.

1788

March 18   Min. Ass. Pa.

Messrs. Hallam and Henry petitioned Assembly for repeal of the law against theatres.

March 28   *Ibid.*

The report of a committee favoring repeal was tabled. (For the full report, see the Minutes of the General Assembly for November 12, 1788, Reprinted by Seilhamer, II, 252.) This was the beginning of a decisive struggle for the legal opening of the theatre, which resulted in the law being repealed March 3, 1789.

June 23   "Improper Education"   Packet
[* *She Stoops to Conquer*—Goldsmith]

First night of the short season from June 23 to July 26, 1788, with the Old American Company offering slightly disguised plays at the Southwark.

June 25   "Impertinent Curiosity" [*The Busy Body*]   Packet
"Modern Love" [*Lionel and Clarissa*]

June 27   "Filial Piety" [*Hamlet*]   Packet

June 30   "On The Vice of Lying" [*The Liar*]   Packet
The Poor Soldier

July 2   * *The Columbian Father*   Packet
"Written by a Citizen of the United States."
* *The Madcap*—Fielding

[141]

1788

July 4	"Improper Education" [*She Stoops to Conquer*] * "The Fourth of July or THE Sailor's Festival"	Packet
July 7	"The Vice of Gaming" [*The Gamester*] The Padlock	Packet
July 9	"The Effects of JUVENILE INDISCRETION." [*The Clandestine Marriage.*]	Packet
July 11	"The Generous American" [*The West Indian*] "The CREDULOUS STEWARD; or, A new way to get Money." [* *A New Way to Pay Old Debts*—Massinger]	Packet
July 16	"The Penitent Wife" [*Jane Shore*] Love in a Camp	Packet
July 18		Pa. Arch. XI, 342–3

The Quakers petitioned President Franklin to do something about the law-breaking theatre.

July 18	"The Effects of Juvenile Indiscretion" [*The Clandestine Marriage*] The Musical Lady	Packet
July 21	The Maid of the Mill "The Fourth of July; or the Sailor's Festival"	Packet
July 23	"The Fate of Tyranny" [*Richard III*] The Credulous Steward [*A New Way to Pay Old Debts*]	Packet
July 25	"The Pernicious Vice of SCANDAL" [*The School for Scandal*] The Miller of Mansfield	Packet
July 26	"The first approaches of VICE" [*George Barnwell*] * *The True-Born Irishman*—Macklin	Packet

Last night of the season from June 23 to July 26, 1788, by the Old American Company at the Theatre in Southwark.

Fifteen performances were given. New to the record: *She Stoops to Conquer,* "*The Columbian Father,*" "*The Fourth of July,*" *The Madcap, A New Way to Pay Old Debts,* and *The True Born Irishman.* Reappearing plays: *The Busy Body, The Clandestine Marriage, The Gamester, George Barnwell, Hamlet, Jane Shore, The Liar, The Maid of the Mill, Richard III, The*

1788

School for Scandal, and *The West Indian.* Reappearing afterpieces: *Lionel and Clarissa, Love in a Camp, The Miller of Mansfield, The Musical Lady, The Padlock,* and *The Poor Soldier.* No actors' names appeared. Some of these titles are deduced from sham titles which were advertised.

CONCERT-HALL IN THE NORTHERN LIBERTIES

Oct. 25   A Concert of Music and   Packet
George Barnwell [disguised]
"An Humorous Lecture on Shaving, called, The
* *Vintner in the Suds"*

It is not known who gave this performance at "the Concert-Hall in the Northern Liberties." As the Old American Company opened at the Theatre in Southwark two days later, it is possible that some of its members offered *George Barnwell.*

SOUTHWARK THEATRE

Oct. 27   "The Vice and Folly of Fashionable Dissipation"   Packet
[*The Provoked Husband*]
"The RESOLUTION; or, *THE*
* *Widow's Vow"*—Mrs. Inchbald

First night of the season from October 27 to November 15, 1788. The plays were still slightly disguised, and the Old American Company did not advertise itself by name.

Oct. 29   "LONGSWORD—Earl of Salisbury"   Packet
[* *The Countess of Salisbury*—Hartson]
"The DETECTION, or the Servants' Hall in an Uproar"
[*High Life Below Stairs*]

Nov. 1   "The Fate of Tyranny" [*Richard III*]   Packet
* *Orpheus and Eurydice*—Theobold (?)

Nov. 3   "The Fortune Hunters" [*The Beaux' Stratagem*]   Packet
"The Office for Hiring Servants"
[*The Register Office*]

Nov. 5   "The Fortunate Son"   Packet
[*The West Indian*]
"The BANDITTI"
[* *The Castle of Andalusia*—O'Keeffe]

Nov. 7   Min. Ass. Pa.

The Quakers presented a memorial against the theatre.

1788

Nov. 8	"The Crime of Filial Ingratitude" [*King Lear*] *The True-born Irishman*	Packet

Nov. 10   "The Choleric Father,   Packet
or A
Trip to Bath" [* *The Rivals*—Sheridan]
The Banditti, or
The Castle of Andalusia—O'Keeffe

Nov. 12   "The Vanquished Veteran, or   Packet
The Termagant Triumphant"
[* *The School for Wives*—Kelly]
The Poor Soldier

Nov. 12   Min. Ass. Pa.

Hallam and Henry petitioned for repeal of the anti-theatrical law. The Assembly again considered it on November 20.

Nov. 14   *Henry IV* [slightly disguised]   Packet
The Guardian [slightly disguised]

Nov. 15   The Last Night   Packet

"The Pernicious Vice of Scandal"
[*The School for Scandal*]
"*Man and Wife;*
or, THE
* *Shakespeare Jubilee*"—Colman

In the ten nights at the Southwark between October 27 and November 15 the Old American Company obliquely announced three new full-length plays and four new afterpieces: *The Countess of Salisbury, The Rivals,* and *The School for Wives,* and *The Castle of Andalusia, Orpheus and Eurydice, The Shakespeare Jubilee,* and *The Widow's Vow.* Six plays and five afterpieces reappeared: *The Beaux' Stratagem, Henry IV (part I), Lear, Richard III, The Provoked Husband, The School for Scandal,* and *The West Indian;* and *The Guardian, High Life Below Stairs, The Poor Soldier, The Register Office,* and *The Trueborn Irishman.* No actors' names appeared.

Nov. 20   Min. Ass. Pa.

The Assembly reconsidered the petition of Hallam and Henry, and the counter-memorial of the Quakers. (See November 7 and 12.) Then on November 22 the Assembly adjourned till February 3, 1789.

1789   Packet

Jan. 9

The Old American Company (advertising now under its own name) an-

1789

nounced for one night only "An Entertainment, which may at the same time exercise the liberality of their friends, and disappoint the malignity of their enemies,"—A Concert, a Monody called "The Shadows of Shakespeare; or, Shakespeare's Characters paying homage to GARRICK," and a musical fête in which Messrs. Hallam, Harper, Henry, Wignell, Woolls, Mrs. Henry, and Mrs. Morris were to take part. A grand procession and Garrick's *Ode on Dedicating a Building to Shakespeare* were included.

Feb. 6   Min. Ass. Pa.

1900 citizens petitioned for repeal of the law against the theatres.

Feb. 16   *Ibid.*

3446 "inhabitants of the city and county" remonstrated against the petitions of the 1900.

The Committee of the Dramatic Association remonstrated against the petitions of the 3446 in an admirable defense of the liberty of the individual. It was signed by a committee composed of General Walter Stewart, Major T. I. Moore, William Temple Franklin, Dr. Robert Bass, John Barclay, Jacob Barge, Dr. Joseph Redman, James Crawford, and John West.

March 2   Statutes at Large
                                                                  of Pennsylvania
                                                            Chap. 1391 (Vol XIII)

The anti-theatrical law of September 25, 1786, was repealed, "within the city of Philadelphia or within one mile thereof," and the President of the Supreme Executive Council or the President of the Court of Common Pleas or the Chief Justice of the Supreme Court was empowered "within three years from and after the passing of this act" to license only such plays as he should think "unexceptionable." The penalty for "exceptionable" performances was "any sum not exceeding two hundred pounds," imprisonment, and giving security for good behavior.

March 9   By Authority   Packet, 7 and 9
                              The Roman Father
                    Occasional Prologue—Mr. Hallam
        In Act Fifth—"AN OVATION for Publius' Victory over
                    the Curatii." Hornpipe—Mr. Durang
                              The Lyar

The Theatre in Southwark opened legally—as the bills said, "By Authority" —on March 9. The Old American Company played till April 4. This is the first time that Mr. Durang has been mentioned in the announcements. (See 1784, Dec. 7.)

1789

March 11   "(Not performed here these Fifteen Years)"   Packet

The Fashionable Lover

Aubrey	Mr. Henry	Napthali	Mr. Ryan
Tyrrell	Mr. Wignell	Mortimer	Mr. Hallam
Lord Ciberville	Mr. Harper	Lucinda Bridgemore	Miss Tuke
Colin McCleod	Mr. Biddle	Mrs. Bridgemore	
Bridgemore	Mr. Woolls		Mrs. Williamson
Dr. Druid	Mr. Heard	Mrs. M'Intosh	Miss Durang
		Augusta Aubrey	Mrs. Morris

The True-Born Irishman

Murrough O'Dogherty		Lady Kinnegad	Mrs. Williamson
	Mr. Henry	Katy Farrel	Miss Tuke
Counsellor Hamilton	Mr. Harper	Mrs. Gazette	Mrs. Durang
Major Gamble	Mr. Morris	Mrs. O'Dogherty	Mrs. Morris
Count Mushroom	Mr. Wignell	(The Irish Fine Lady)	

The following names are new to our record (though probably most or all of the players had been with the company in Philadelphia when names were not mentioned): Mr. Biddle, Miss Durang, Mrs. John Durang, Mr. Heard, Mr. Ryan, Miss Tuke (later Mrs. Lewis Hallam), and Mrs. Williamson. Mr. Wignell had read *The Contrast* in 1787, but this is his first announced appearance in Philadelphia as an actor.

March 13   *The Busy Body*   Packet
     The Poor Soldier

March 16   "(Not performed here these twenty years)"   Packet

The Orphan of China
*** The Ghost**—Mrs. Centlivre

March 18   *** Much Ado About Nothing**—Shakespeare   Packet

Benedict	Mr. Hallam	Conrad	Mr. Ryan
Claudio	Mr. Harper	Bouchio	Mr. Lake
Don Pedro	Mr. Wignell	Leonardo	Mr. Henry
Dogberry	Mr. Morris	Hero	Miss Tuke
Balthasar	Mr. Woolls	Margaret	Mrs. Williamson
Don John	Mr. Heard	Ursula	Mrs. Durang
Antonio	Mr. Biddle	Beatrice	Mrs. Morris

The Register Office

Capt. LeBrush	Mr. Harper	Williams	Mr. Woolls
Scotchman	Mr. Biddle	Gulwell	Mr. Lake
		The Irishman	Mr. Henry

First appearance of Mr. Lake.

1789

March 20   *Cato*   Packet

Cato..............Mr. Hallam	Lucius..............Mr. Biddle
Portius.............Mr. Henry	Decius.............Mr. Woolls
Syphax............Mr. Morris	Juba..............Mr. Wignell
Marcus............Mr. Harper	Lucia.........Mrs. Williamson
Sempronius.........Mr. Heard	Marcia...........Mrs. Morris

Robinson Crusoe

Robinson Crusoe......Mr. Biddle	Pierrot.............Mr. Harper
Captain of the Ship...Mr. Woolls	Donna Pantalina..............
Sailors......Messrs. Heard, Lake,	Mrs. Williamson
Ryan, Gay, &c, &c.	Columbine.........Mrs. Durang
Pantaloon.........Mr. Wignell	Harlequin Friday....Mr. Durang

First appearance of Mr. Gay.

March 21   *The Fashionable Lover*   Packet
              High Life Below Stairs

March 23   *The Rivals*   Packet

Capt. Absolute.......Mr. Hallam	Faulkland..........Mr. Wignell
Sir Anthony Absolute..Mr. Morris	Mrs. Malaprop......Mrs. Harper
Bob Acres..........Mr. Harper	Julia..........Mrs. Williamson
Fag...............Mr. Woolls	Lucy...............Miss Tuke
David.............Mr. Heard	Lydia Languish......Mrs. Morris
Coachman...........**Mr. Ryan**	

Love a la Mode

Sir Callaghan O'Bralaghan......	Sir Theodore Goodchild.........
Mr. Henry	Mr. Woolls
Sir Archy M'Sarcasm..Mr. Biddle	Squire Groom.......Mr. Wignell
Beau Mordecai......Mr. Morris	Charlotte...........Miss Tuke

First appearance of Mrs. Harper.

March 25   *The Clandestine Marriage*   Packet

Lord Oglebey.......Mr. Hallam	Lovell.............Mr. Wignell
Sterling.............Mr. Morris	Mrs. Heidelburgh...Mrs. Harper
Sir John Melvill.....Mr. Harper	Fanny.........Mrs. Williamson
Brush.............Mr. Henry	Betty...............Miss Tuke
Sergeant Flower......Mr. Biddle	Nancy.............Mrs. Durang
Canton.............Mr. Ryan	Miss Sterling.......Mrs. Morris
Traverse...........**Mr. Heard**	

1789

March 25 (cont.)   *Love in a Camp*

Capt. Patrick........Mr. Harper	Rupert............Mr. Woolls
Marshal Fehrbellin............	Darby.............Mr. Wignell
Mr. Hallam	Flora..............Mrs. Harper
Olmutz.............Mr. Ryan	Miss Mable Flourish..Mr. Biddle
Quiz...............Mr. Heard	Nora..............Mrs. Morris

March 27   *The School for Scandal*   Packet

Sir Peter Teazle......Mr. Henry	Moses...............Mr. Ryan
Joseph Surface......Mr. Wignell	Snake...............Mr. Lake
Sir Oliver Surface....Mr. Morris	Charles Surface......Mr. Harper
Sir Benjamin Backbite...........	Mrs. Candover......Mrs. Harper
Mr. Biddle	Lady Sneerwell..Mrs. Williamson
Crabtree............Mr. Heard	Maria..............Miss Tuke
Dowley.............Mr. Woolls	Lady Teazle........Mrs. Morris

Robinson Crusoe

Cast as for March 20.

March 30

The Earl of Essex and *Cross Purposes,* announced by the *Packet* of March 28 for March 30, were postponed "on account of Mrs. Harper's indisposition." But neither play appeared later in the season.

March 31   "(Not performed here these Twenty years)"   Packet,

* *The English Merchant*—Colman, Jr.   Mar. 30

Sir Wm. Douglass....Mr. Henry	Spatter............Mr. Wignell
Lord Falbridge......Mr. Harper	Amelia.............Mrs. Henry
Freeport............Mr. Morris	Molly..............Miss Tuke
State Messenger......Mr. Biddle	Mrs. Goodman..Mrs. Williamson
Le France...........Mr. Ryan	Lady Alton........Mrs. Morris

The Citizen

"(Not performed here these twenty-eight years)"

Young Philpot......Mr. Wignell	Quildrive............Mr. Lake
Young Wilding......Mr. Harper	Old Philpot.........Mr. Morris
Beaufort............Mr. Woolls	Corinna..........Mrs. Durang
Sir Jasper Wilding....Mr. Biddle	Maria..............Mrs. Henry
Dapper..............Mr. Ryan	

The announcement that *The English Merchant* was "not performed here these twenty years" is interesting, as there is no earlier record of its production in the city. On the other hand, the announcement that *The Citizen* was

1789

"not performed here these twenty-eight years" is also interesting as it is recorded for 1766, 1767, 1769, 1770, 1773, and 1778!

April 2   *Romeo and Juliet*   Packet

Romeo............	Mr. Hallam	Montague...........	Mr. Lake
Capulet...........	Mr. Henry	Peter...............	Mr. Ryan
Tibalt............	Mr. Wignell	Friar John............	Mr. Gay
Friar Laurence......	Mr. Morris	Mercutio...........	Mr. Harper
Benvolio...........	Mr. Biddle	Nurse..........	Mrs. Williamson
Paris..............	Mr. Woolls	Lady Capulet........	Miss Tuke
		Juliet.............	Mrs. Henry

The Madcap

Bister.............	Mr. Harper	Thomas.............	Mr. Biddle
Quaver...........	Mr. Woolls	Coupee.............	Mr. Hallam
Goodwill..........	Mr. Morris	Miss Lucy.........	Mrs. Henry

April 3   "(Not performed here these twenty years)"   Packet

The Siege of Damascus

Christians

Phocyas...........	Mr. Wignell	Artamon.............	Mr. Lake
Eumenes...........	Mr. Morris	Sergius..............	Mr. Ryan
Herbis.............	Mr. Woolls	Eudocia...........	Mrs. Morris

Saracens

Abudah...........	Mr. Harper	Caled..............	Mr. Henry
Daran.............	Mr. Biddle		

The Poor Soldier

April 4   * *The Heiress*—Burgoyne   Federal Gazette

Sir Clement Flint....	Mr. Henry	Chignon.............	Mr. Ryan
Lord Gayville.......	Mr. Harper	Clifford............	Mr. Hallam
Alscrip.............	Mr. Morris	Miss Alscrip........	Miss Tuke
Blandish...........	Mr. Biddle	Miss Alton..........	Mrs. Henry
Rightly.............	Mr. Heard	Mrs. Blandish...	Mrs. Williamson
Prompt.............	Mr. Woolls	Lady Emily........	Mrs. Morris

The Citizen

Cast as for March 31, except: Corinna........ Miss Tuke.

Fifteen performances were given between March 9 and April 4, 1789. Three new plays appeared: *The English Merchant* (which had probably been here

1789

earlier—see March 31, 1789), *The Heiress,* and *Much Ado About Nothing;* and one new afterpiece: *The Ghost.* Reappearing plays: *The Busy Body, Cato, The Clandestine Marriage, The Fashionable Lover, The Orphan of China, The Rivals, The Roman Father, Romeo and Juliet, The School for Scandal,* and *The Siege of Damascus.* Reappearing afterpieces: *The Citizen, High Life Below Stairs, Love à la Mode, Love in a Camp, The Lyar, The Madcap, The Poor Soldier, The Register Office, Robinson Crusoe,* and the *Trueborn Irishman.* The actors new *to our record* (with the many years of veiled announcements, we dare not say they were new to the city): Mr. Biddle, Miss Caroline Durang, Mr. and Mrs. John Durang, Mr. Gay, Mrs. Harper, Mr. Heard, Mr. Lake, Mr. Ryan (*not* Dennis Ryan, who wrote the petition of November 10, 1783), Miss Tuke, Mr. Wignell, and Mrs. Williamson. The actors certainly in the city before were Lewis Hallam, Mr. Harper, John Henry, and Mrs. *Maria* Henry (in 1773 Miss Maria Storer), Mr. and Mrs. Morris, and Mr. Woolls.

HARMONY HALL

Nov. 4   * The Devil Upon Two Sticks   Packet
"*or, The Droll Examination of Doctor Last before the College of Physicians.*"—Foote
Dr. Last.......... Mr. Partridge
"The rest of the characters by the Gentlemen of the Faculty, for their Amusement."

This is the first of a number of performances (the last on November 30) sponsored by Mr. Partridge (the name is also spelled Patridge). This is his first appearance in our record. The performances were held at "Harmony Hall, Northern-Liberties, near Poole's Bridge," which *may* have been the Northern Liberties Theatre. They seem to have been partly amateur and partly professional. On this evening there was also to be singing and dancing, and Mr. Partridge announced that he would "exhibit his Horse of Knowledge, which is greatly improved since the last exhibition."

Nov. 7   *The Devil Upon Two Sticks*   Packet, 6 and 7
Dr. Last.......... Mr. Partridge

The Devil: "A Gentleman from London who will eat real red-hot fire and blue flaming Brimstone matches, and show some other Devilish Tricks." Mr. Riley, Mr. Durang, Mrs. Stewart, and "A young Lady only 11 years old" were mentioned for dancing. "Mr. Durang will dance a Hornpipe on 13 Eggs, blindfolded, without breaking one."

First appearance of Mr. Riley and Mrs. Stewart.

[150]

1789

Nov. 11   "(Never performed before)"—2 acts   Packet

The Manager Out-Witted

Principal Characters by Partridge, Mr. Riley, Mr. Vaughan &c.
A Dance by Mr. Durang and Miss Apker

The Wapping Landlady, or
Jack in Distress (pantomimic dance)

Landlady........Mr. Partridge		Jack in Distress.......Mr. Riley
Harry...........Mr. Durang		Mrs. Friskey.......Mrs. Stewart
Tom............Mr. Vaughan		Miss Friskey........Miss Apker
Dick.............Mr. Dickson		

First appearance of Miss Apker and Messrs. Dickson and Vaughan (or Vaughn).

Nov. 14   *The Devil Upon Two Sticks*   Packet

Devil...."Gentleman who played it last week"		Camphor..........Mr. Wright
		Jallap..............Mr. Smith
Calomel..........Mr. Vaughan		Dr. Last.........Mr. Partridge

The Wapping Landlady

Landlady........Mr. Partridge		Dick...............Mr. Smith
Harry............Mr. Durang		Jock..............Mr. Wright
Tom............Mr. Vaughan		

(Women not mentioned.)

First appearance of Mr. Smith.

Nov. 30   *The Beaux' Stratagem*   Packet, Nov. 27

Archer...........Mr. Vaughan		Scrub...........Mr. Partridge
Aimwell...........Mr. Gilliam		Dorinda ....
Bonnyface........Mr. Dickson		Mrs. Osmond, from Baltimore
Sullen.............Mr. Smith		Cherry........."A young Lady"
Gibbet............Mr. Parker		Mrs. Sullen.......Mrs. Stewart

The Wapping Landlady

Landlady........Mr. Partridge		Jack in Distress......Mr. Parker
Tom.............Mr. Vaughan		Mrs. Friskey.......Mrs. Stewart
Dick.............Mr. Dickson		Miss Friskey........Miss Apker

etc.

First appearance of Mr. Gilliam, Mrs. Osmond, Mr. Wright, and possibly of Mr. Parker—though he *may* have been the Mr. Parker of the Colonial American Company.

On their five nights between November 4 and November 30, 1789, Mr.

1789

Partridge's Company produced *The Devil Upon Two Sticks, The Manager Out-Witted,* and *The Wapping Landlady,* all new. Their only full-length play, *The Beaux' Stratagem,* had been given in Philadelphia before. The new actors were Miss Apker, Messrs. Dickson, and Gilliam, Mrs. Osmond, perhaps Mr. Parker, Messrs. Partridge, Riley, and Smith, Mrs. Stewart, Messrs. Vaughan and Wright, "a Gentleman from London," "A young lady only 11 years old," and "a young Lady." Mr. Durang and perhaps Mr. Parker had appeared before.

1790

SOUTHWARK THEATRE

Jan. 6	*The Rivals*	Packet
	* *The Critic*—Sheridan	

The Old American Company opened the Theatre in Southwark on January 6, 1790, and played till July 19.

Jan. 8	*The Rivals*	Packet
	The Critic	

The theatre was closed till January 18 while the managers made "Alterations and Improvements" "to prevent the Complaints made of the Coldness of the Theatre." (Packet, January 13.)

Jan. 18	*The Miser*	Packet
	The Old Maid	

"The Public are respectfully informed that the Entrance into the PITT is altered from the North to the East Side of the Theatre."

Jan. 20	*The Clandestine Marriage*	Packet

Lord Ogleby.......Mr. Hallam   Trueman..............Mr. Gay
Sterling...........Mr. Morris   Lovell..............Mr. Morris
Sir John Melvill.....Mr. Harper   Mrs. Heidelburgh...Mrs. Harper
Brush............Mr. Wignell   Fanny.............Mrs. Henry
Canton..............Mr. Ryan   Betty...........Mrs. Hamilton
Sergeant Flower.....Mr. Woolls   Nancy.............Miss Tuke
Traverse............Mr. Lake   Miss Sterling.......Mrs. Morris

Dancing by Mr. Durang

Miss in Her Teens

Capt. Flash........Mr. Wignell   Fribble.............Mr. Harper
Capt. Loveit.......Mr. Hallam   Tag...............Mrs. Harper

1790

Puff..............Mr. Morris   Miss Biddy Bellair....Miss Tuke
Jasper..............Mr. Woolls

First appearance of Mrs. Hamilton.

| Jan. 22 | *The Gamester* | Packet |

Who's the Dupe?—Mrs. Cowley

| Jan. 25 | **All in the Wrong*—Murphy* | Packet |

Catherine and Petruchio

"A new brick Pavement continued from Lombard street to the door of the Theatre."

| Jan. 27 | *She Stoops to Conquer* | Packet |

Hardcastle..........Mr. Morris   Tony.............Mr. Wignell
Marlow...........Mr. Harper   Mrs. Hardcastle....Mrs. Harper
Hastings..........Mr. Hallam   Constance..........Mrs. Morris

(This cast from a rimed criticism in *The Independent Gazetteer,*
quoted by Seilhamer, II, 289.)

High Life Below Stairs

| Jan. 29 | *The Beaux' Stratagem* | Packet |
| | *The Musical Lady* | |

| Feb. 1 | *The Wonder* | Packet |
| | *The Musical Lady* | |

| Feb. 3 | *The Provoked Husband* | Packet |

** The Prisoner at Large*—O'Keeffe*

| Feb. 5 | | Packet |

"A COMEDY (never performed here) written by a CITIZEN
of the United States"—"Called—* *The FATHER*—or
American Shandy-ism"—Dunlap

Prologue.......... Mr. Wignell

Epilogue.......... Mrs. Henry

The Lyar

| Feb. 8 | *The School for Scandal* | Packet |
| | *The Prisoner at Large* | |

| Feb. 10 | *Love in a Village* | Packet |

End of Act I

[153]

1790

"A Statue Scene and Dance. Servants at the Statue, Mr. Ryan, Mr. Vaughan, Mr. Lake, Mr. Claypit, &c."

Robinson Crusoe

"With entire new SCENERY, MACHINERY, MUSIC, &c, &c.
The former (save a View of the Falls of Passaick) taken from
Captain Cooke's Voyage to Otaheite, New Zealand, &c.
WITH A SOLEMN Indian Incantation. The SINGING and
RECITATION by Messrs. Harper, Wignell, and Henry.
AND a Allegorical Finale."

First appearance of Mr. Claypit.

Feb. 12	*The Brothers* [*The Shipwreck*] *Robinson Crusoe*	Packet
Feb. 15	*The Heiress* *The Musical Lady*	Packet
Feb. 17	*The Jealous Wife* *Who's The Dupe?*	Packet
Feb. 19	"(Not performed here these twenty years)"	Packet

The Earl of Essex
* *The Dead Alive*—O'Keeffe

"With Alterations, as performed at New York."

Feb. 22	* *Gustavus Vasa*—Brooke *Who's The Dupe?*	Packet
Feb. 24	*The Constant Couple* *Love in a Camp*	Packet
Feb. 26	*Hamlet* *The Wrangling Lovers*	Packet

"The Gallery Door is removed from the North to the West side of the theatre."

Feb. 27	*The Constant Couple* *Love in a Camp*	Packet

"Hallam and Henry respectfully inform the Public, the above Pieces are brought forward out of the common Nights of Performance, to accommodate several Friends of the Drama, who are leaving town, and were disappointed of seeing them on Wednesday last."

March 1	*Venice Preserved* *The Poor Soldier*	Packet
March 3	*The Merry Wives of Windsor* *The Miller of Mansfield*	Packet

[154]

1790

March 5	The West Indian	Packet
	The Citizen	
March 8	Richard III	Packet
	The Prisoner at Large	
March 10	The English Merchant	Packet

"The original Epilogue by Mr. Wignell and Mrs. Morris."

The Lyar

| March 13 | Douglas | Packet |

"(Douglas, by a Young Gentleman, being his first Appearance on
any stage)"

The Dead Alive

| March 15 | Douglas | Packet |

"(The Young Gentleman made his second appearance)"

Cross Purposes

March 17	Love Makes a Man	Packet
	Miss in Her Teens	
March 19	Love Makes a Man	Packet
	Miss in Her Teens	
March 24	Love Makes a Man	Packet
	Miss in Her Teens	
March 26	Selima and Azor	Packet
	The Prisoner at Large	
March 27	George Barnwell	Packet
	Love in a Camp	

"The Public are respectfully informed the ensuing being Passion Week, there
will be no Performance till Easter Monday."

| April 5 (Easter Monday) | Macbeth | Packet |

"With Original Songs, Chorusses, and Incantations Composed by
Doctor MATHEW LOCKE."

The Wrangling Lovers

April 6	George Barnwell	Packet
	Love in a Camp	
April 8	George Barnwell	Packet
	The Ghost	
April 10	"For the Benefit of the Poor,	Packet

1790

The Overseers have recently agreed to accept [this benefit] in lieu of any Penalty that may have been incurred, before the liberal Exertions of a generous Public had obtained a legal Sanction for Theatrical Performances."

The Toy—O'Keeffe
The Wrangling Lovers

April 14	*The School for Scandal* *The Poor Soldier*	Journal
April 16	*Zara* *Rosina*	Packet
April 19	*The Toy* *The Critic*	Packet
April 22	*Tamerlane* *The Apprentice*	Packet
April 24	*The Tempest* *Neptune and Amphitrite* *The Prisoner at Large*	Packet
May 3	*Alexander the Great* *Love à la Mode*	Packet, April 27 and May 3
May 5	*Alexander the Great* *The Poor Soldier*	Packet
May 7		Packet

"A Tragedy, never performed, written by a citizen of the United States"

* *The Widow of Malabar*—Humphreys.

"In Act 5th, a representation of the Funeral Pile [sic!] in Flames. The Prologue by Mr. Hallam, and the Epilogue by Mrs. Henry."

* *The Invasion*—Pilon

May 10	*The Widow of Malabar* *The Devil to Pay*	Packet
May 13	*Othello* *The Padlock*	Packet
May 17	"Mr. Henry's Night"	Packet

* *The School for Soldiers*—Henry
* *Half an Hour after Supper*
* *Inkle and Yarico*—Colman, Jr.

John Henry added a note, saying that a number of his fellow citizens in the militia "would help to make the 'military scene' surpass anything previously seen on that stage."

1790

May 20

The Maid of the Mill, The Monody on the Chiefs, and *Cymon and Sylvia* announced in the *Packet* of May 20 for "Mrs. Henry's Night" were post-poned to June 7 "on account of her Indisposition." (Her enemies often suggested that her postponements were usually on account of her disposition.)

May 24   "Mrs. Morris's Night"   Packet

* *The Belle's Stratagem*—Mrs. Cowley
* *"Darby's Return to his Own Potatoe Ground
with a Description of the Countries he has Visited,
Particularly America."*—Dunlap
The True-Born Irishman

May 27   "Mr. Harper's Night"   Packet
The Rivals

"An Interlude from *The Devil on Two Sticks,* called *Dr. Last's Examination.*"

* *Barataria* or, *Sancho Panca Turn'd Governor*—Pilon
with a grand procession—Sancho Panca "riding on his FAVOURITE
DAPPLE"

May 31   "Mr. Morris's Night"   Packet
* *The Grecian Daughter*—Murphy
Midas

June 3   "Mrs. Harper's Night"   Packet
The School for Wives

"Between the Play and Farce the favourite Sea-Song of the Storm, by Mr. Harper. Scene,—View of the Vessel riding the Sea, a Tempest, Thunder, Lightening, and the different situations of the Ship from her first striking on the Rock till her release from thence, as alluded to in the Song."

* *All the World's a Stage*—Jackman

June 7   "Mrs. Henry's Night"   Packet

*The Maid of the Mill
A Monody to the Chiefs
Cymon and Sylvia*

UNIVERSITY OF PENNSYLVANIA

June 7   * *Dialogue*   Library, U. of Pa.

[157]

1790

SOUTHWARK THEATRE

June 10

The Duenna, and *Man and Wife* were advertised for Mr. Woolls' night, but as the same bill for his benefit was advertised on June 17, this bill was probably postponed.

June 14   "Mr. Wignell's Night"   Packet
Theodosius
The Miser
Darby's Return

June 17   "Mr. Woolls' Night"   Packet
The Duenna
Man and Wife, or the Shakespeare Jubilee

June 24   "Mr. Hallam's Night   Packet
The Suspicious Husband
* *The Medley; or, Harlequin's Invasion of the Realms of Shakespeare*
"a SPEAKING PANTOMIME (never performed here) written on the Model of the Italian Comedy, by David Garrick."

Mr. Lewis Hallam's Benefit was postponed from June 21.

July 1   "Mr. Martin, Mrs. Hamilton, Mr. Heard and   Packet
Mr. Biddle's Night"

The Clandestine Marriage
The Banditti, or *The Castle of Andalusia*
* *Harlequin Cook; or, The Enchanted Pye*
"a new Pantomime, in one Act"

"A Wind Sail is erected for the purpose of keeping the House Cool."

First mention of Mr. Martin, though evidently not his first appearance, as he got part of a benefit.

July 7   "Mr. Ryan, Mr. Robinson, Mr. Durang and   Packet
Mr. Gay's Night"

The Contrast
The Agreeable Surprise

A "Miscellaneous entertainment, with transparent Scene of *Les Petites Ombres Chinoises,* or CHINESE SHADES, in which will be exhibited a variety of Picturesque Characters."

* *Harlequin Skeleton*

First mention of Mr. Robinson.

[158]

1790

July 12   "Mr. Morris and Mrs. Harper's Night"   Packet

The Merchant of Venice

"A COMIC OLIO, chiefly selected from the Lecture on Heads, with a Word, or two, about HEARTS, And (by particular desire)—The remarkable LAW CASE 'Bullum versus Boatum' will be delivered by Mr. Wignell."

The Lying Valet

"The emoluments of Mr. Morris' and Mrs. Harper's former nights, having fallen considerably short of the expectations of their Friends, they are induced once more jointly to solicit . . . partronage."

July 19   "Mr. Woolls' Night"   Packet

Tamerlane
The Deserter

"Mr. Woolls respectfully acquaints his Friends and the Public, that his former Night having failed altogether as to Emolument, he is induced again to solicit their Patronage."

In the Old American Company's season from January 6 to July 19, 1790, the following new plays (or operas) appeared: *All in the Wrong, The Belle's Stratagem, The Contrast* (which Mr. Wignell had *read* in 1787), *The Father, The Grecian Daughter, Gustavus Vasa, The School for Soldiers, The Toy,* and *The Widow of Malabar.* The new afterpieces: *All the World's a Stage, Barataria, The Critic, Darby's Return, The Dead Alive, Half an Hour After Supper, Harlequin's Invasion of the Realms of Shakespeare, Harlequin Skeleton, Inkle and Yarico, The Invasion, The Prisoner at Large,* and *Who's The Dupe?* The reappearing plays were: *Alexander The Great, The Clandestine Marriage, The Constant Couple, Douglas, The Duenna, The Earl of Essex, The English Merchant, The Gamester, George Barnwell, Hamlet, The Heiress, The Jealous Wife, Love in a Village, Love Makes a Man, Macbeth, The Maid of the Mill, The Merchant of Venice, The Merry Wivs of Windsor, Othello, The Provoked Husband, Richard III, The Rivals, The School for Scandal, The School for Wives, Selima and Azor, She Stoops to Conquer, The Shipwreck, The Suspicious Husband, Tamerlane, The Tempest, Theodosius, Venice Preserved, The West Indian, The Wonder,* and *Zara.* The reappearing afterpieces: *The Agreeable Surprise, The Apprentice, The Banditti; or the Castle of Andalusia, Catherine and Petruchio, The Citizen, Cross Purposes, Cymon and Sylvia, The Devil to Pay, The Ghost, High Life Below Stairs, The Lyar, Love à la Mode, Love in a Camp, The Lying Valet, Man and Wife; or the Shakespeare Jubilee, The Miller of Mansfield, The Miser, Miss in Her Teens, The Musical Lady, Neptune and Amphitrite, The Old Maid, The Padlock, Robinson Crusoe, Rosina, The Trueborn Irishman,* and *The Wrangling Lovers.*

The new actors mentioned were Messrs. Claypit, Martin, and Robinson,

1790

Mrs. Hamilton, and a "Young Gentleman." The reappearing players: Messrs. Biddle, Durang, Gay, and Hallam, Mr. and Mrs. Harper, Mr. Heard, Mr. and Mrs. Henry, Mr. Lake, Mr. and Mrs. Morris, Mr. Ryan, Miss Tuke, and Messrs. Vaughan, Wignell, and Woolls.

Dec. 8	Occasional Prologue by Mr. Hallam	Packet
	The Clandestine Marriage	
	Who's The Dupe?	

The Old American Company opened the Theatre in Southwark on December 8, 1790, and played till July 11, 1791. (Before they had closed, the "Kenna" Company opened the Northern Liberties Theatre, on April 8.)

Dec. 10	*The Busy Body*	Packet
	High Life Below Stairs	
Dec. 13	*The Suspicious Husband*	Packet
	The Poor Soldier	
Dec. 15	*Douglas*	Packet
	The Prisoner at Large	
Dec. 16	*Douglas*	Packet
	The Prisoner at Large	

(This performance may have been a postponement from December 15, though nothing was said about it.)

Dec. 20	* *More Ways than One*—Mrs. Cowley	Packet
	"A Farce as will be expressed in the Bills of the Day."	
Dec. 22	*Romeo and Juliet*	Packet
	The Miller of Mansfield	
Dec. 27	*Romeo and Juliet*	Packet
	The Miller of Mansfield	
Dec. 29	*The Wonder*	Packet
	Hob in the Well	
Dec. 31	*Henry IV, Part I*	Packet
	The Prisoner at Large	

1791

Jan. 3	*The Roman Father*	Gen. Ad.
	The True-Born Irishman	
Jan. 5	*The School for Scandal*	Journal
	The Poor Soldier	

1791

Jan. 7	*She Stoops to Conquer* *Flora*	Gen. Ad.

A criticism in the *General Advertiser* of February 23 said that in *She Stoops to Conquer* Mr. Robinson played Marlowe, and Mr. Martin, Hastings.

Jan. 10	*The Mourning Bride* *The Apprentice*	Gen. Ad.
Jan. 12	*The Miser* *High Life Below Stairs*	Journal
Jan. 14	*The Miser* *The Citizen*	Gen. Ad.
Jan. 17	*The West Indian* *Catherine and Petruchio*	Fed. Gaz., Jan. 15
Jan. 19	*The School for Scandal* *Rosina, or The Reapers*	Journal

A criticism in the *General Advertiser* of February 23 says that Mr. Harper doubled Charles and Crabtree in *The School for Scandal,* and that "the President of the United States and his Lady attended."

Jan. 21	*The West Indian* *Catherine and Petruchio*	Gen. Ad.

A criticism in the *General Advertiser* of February 23 said that Mrs. Hamilton doubled Lady Rusport and Mrs. Fulmer ("her Ladyship" Mrs. Henry not appearing) and that Mr. Robinson played Capt. Dudley. It *may* not have been for this production of *The West Indian* (see Jan. 17).

Jan. 24 "By Desire, For the Entertainment of the Seneca Chiefs" Gen. Ad.

Richard III
The Mayor of Garratt

Jan. 26	*The Father*	Journal

"End of the Play, DANCING by a GENTLEMAN from Europe, being his first appearance on this Stage."

The Dead Alive

Jan. 29	*Julius Cæsar* *Hob in the Well*	Gen. Ad.
Jan. 31	*The English Merchant* *The Ghost*	Gen. Ad.
Feb. 2	*The Tempest* *Neptune and Amphitrite* *The Musical Lady*	Journal

1791

Feb. 4 *Douglas* Gen. Ad.

"Dancing by Mr. André"

* *Patie and Roger; or, The Gentle Shepherd*—Tickell

"A Scots Pastoral, in two Acts, altered from Allan Ramsay, by Mr. Tickell, Author of *Anticipation,* never performed here, with (by permission of the Patentees) the overture and Accompaniments, as performed at the Theatre Royal, Drury Lane."

First appearance of Mr. André.

Feb. 5 Fed. Gaz.

There was much dissatisfaction with the actors this season. Many claimed (as did "Z" on February 5) that the managers had not kept their promise, made when the prohibitory law was being repealed, to improve their company, even though opportunity had been offered. Much controversy followed.

Feb. 7 *The Orphan of China* Gen. Ad.
The Guardian

Feb. 9 *The Widow of Malabar* Journal
The Padlock

Feb. 11 *The Beaux' Stratagem* Gen. Ad.
The Guardian

A criticism in the *General Advertiser,* February 23, says that in *The Beaux' Stratagem* Mrs. Hamilton played Dorinda; Mrs. Durang, Lady Bountiful; and Miss Tuke, Cherry.

Feb. 14 *She Stoops to Conquer* Gen. Ad.
The Ghost

Feb. 18 * *Isabella*—Southerne Journal, Feb. 16
"In Act 3d. An Epithalamium, by Mr. WOOLLS"
The Prisoner at Large

A criticism in the *General Advertiser* for Feb. 21 gave the following parts in *Isabella:*

Isabella............Mrs. Henry   Carlos..............Mr. Harper
Baldwin............Mr. Henry   Bison..............Mr. Hallam
Villeroy..........Mr. Wignell

Feb. 23 * *The Chances*—Garrick Journal
Love in a Camp

Feb. 25 *The Busy Body* Gen. Ad.
The Guardian

1791

| March 2 | *The Grecian Daughter*
 * *The Rival Fools*—Cibber | Journal |

March 4 — Gen. Ad.

"On account of the Indisposition of Mrs. HENRY, there will be no performance this Evening."

| March 7 | *The Chances*
 Catherine and Petruchio | Gen. Ad. |

| March 14 | *More Ways than One*
 * *Seeing's Believing*—Joddrell | Journal |

"(never performed in America)"

This bill first appeared for March 11, then for March 12, and finally for March 14, the farce still "never performed." It is of course barely possible that it appeared on March 11 and (or) 12, and that the "never performed" was a copy-reader's mistake; but more probably the play was postponed, especially as Mrs. Maria Henry was being "indisposed" this season rather often.

| March 16 | *Tamerlane*
 The Irish Widow | Gen. Ad. |

"The Widow Brady, with the Epilogue song, by Mrs. Wilson."

A criticism in the *General Advertiser* of March 31 said that in *Tamerlane* Mrs. Henry played Selima and Mrs. Morris, Arpasia, and that Mrs. Henry was hissed on her first appearance, whereupon she went literally quite upstage.

First appearance of Mrs. Wilson.

| March 18 | *The Recruiting Officer*
 The Apprentice | Gen. Ad. |

"The Original Prologue spoken by Mr. WIGNELL."

| March 23 | *The Orphan*
 The Rival Fools | Journal |

March 25 — See March 28, 1791

| March 28 | *The Suspicious Husband*
 The Irish Widow | Gen. Ad. |

The Widow.........Mrs. Wilson

This was announced for March 25, but postponed "on account of the indisposition of Mrs. Morris." (*Fed. Gazette,* March 25.)

| April 1 | *Hamlet*
 Seeing's Believing | Gen. Ad. |

"(never performed in America)"

[163]

1791

Again *Seeing's Believing* is announced as "never performed in America," and again we may believe this note to be simply an example of careless copy-reading (which very often happened in these announcements), or that none of the performances advertised for March 11, 12, and 14 was given.

| April 5 | The Drummer | Gen. Ad. |
| | The Poor Soldier | |

NORTHERN LIBERTY THEATRE

| April 8 | * Clementina—Kelly | Daily Adv. |
| | * The Waterman—Dibdin | |

The first appearance of the Northern Liberty [or Liberties] Theatre, in Front Street, below Noble. The production was doubtless managed by the Kennas, whose names appear later: it was advertised as by the "New American Company," but as the name later disappeared, and Mr. Kenna, Miss Kenna, Mrs. Kenna, Mr. J. Kenna, Mr. Kelly, *et al.,* appeared, it is simpler to follow Seilhamer in calling them the "K" Company. They appeared on April 8, 11, 26, and 30, and then on July 25, *sequor.*

SOUTHWARK THEATRE

| April 9 | The Gamester | Gen. Ad. |
| | * The Two Misers—O'Hara | |

NORTHERN LIBERTY THEATRE

| April 11 | Jane Shore | Fed. Gaz. |
| | The Waterman | |

Presumably by the "K" Company.

SOUTHWARK THEATRE

| April 12 | The West Indian | Gen. Ad. |
| | The Two Misers | |

April 15	"Last Night before Easter"	Gen. Ad.
	She Stoops to Conquer	
	The Two Misers	

In an excellent criticism in the *General Advertiser* of April 15, these parts in *She Stoops to Conquer* appear:

Tony Lumpkin.....Mr. Wignell		Hastings...........Mr. Martin
Hardcastle.........Mr. Morris		Mrs. Hardcastle...Mrs. Hamilton
Miss Hardcastle.....Mrs. Morris		Marlowe...........Mr. Harper
Miss Nevil..........Miss Tuke		

[164]

1791

April 15 (cont.) *The Two Misers*

Harriet...............Mrs. Gee
Jenny.............Mrs. Wilson

The Two Misers................
    Messrs. Hallam and Wignell
Lively.............Mr. Harper

First appearance of Mrs. Gee.

NORTHERN LIBERTY THEATRE

April 26   *Clementina*   Fed. Gaz., April 25

Anselmo..........Mr. J. Kenna
Palermo...........Mr. Vaughan
Officer..............Mr. Allen

Granville............Mr. Kenna
Elizara..........Mrs. J. Kenna
Clementina........Mrs. Kenna

The Guardian

Mr. Heartly.......Mr. Vaughan
Young Clachit......Mr. J. Kenna
John...............Mr. Allen

Old Clachit..........Mr. Kenna
Lucy............Mrs. J. Kenna
Harriet............Miss Kenna

This is the first record in Philadelphia of Mr., Mrs., and Miss Kenna, of Mr. and Mrs. J. Kenna, and perhaps of Mr. Allen, though he may have been the Allen who was here in 1774 and perhaps in 1785. (See Seilhamer, II, 165.)

SOUTHWARK THEATRE

April 27   Mr. Hallam's Night   Gen. Ad.

"A Comedy (never performed in America) Revised and altered by a Citizen of Philadelphia; called

* *The Recess; or, The Mask'd Apparition"*—Bickerstaff

A criticism in the *General Advertiser* of April 30 and May 2 gives these parts:

Don Guzman........Mr. Harper
Don Ferdinand......Mr. Martin
Don Pedro.......Mr. Hammond
Don Carlos........Mr. Wignell

Muskato...........Mr. Hallam
Donna Marcella......Miss Tuke
Donna Aurora.........Mrs. Gee
Beatrice............Mrs. Morris

Inkle and Yarico

(same source for casting)

Yarico..............Miss Tuke
Sir Christopher.......Mr. Henry

Narcissa...............Mrs. Gee
Wowsky..........Mrs. Wilson

First appearance of Mr. Hammond.

[165]

1791

NORTHERN LIBERTY THEATRE

April 30   *Douglas*   Fed. Gaz., April 29

"Noble" Douglas......Miss Kenna   Lady Randolph......Mrs. Kenna

The Miller of Mansfield

For further performances at the Northern Liberties, see July 25, *sequor*.

May 2   Gen. Ad. April 25

A meeting of those interested in subscribing to "building a Theatre in a central part of the city" was announced. The final result was the New [or Chesnut Street] Theatre.

SOUTHWARK THEATRE

May 2   Mr. Harper's Night   Gen. Ad.

The Recess
* The Little Hunch Back—O'Keeffe

(Seilhamer, II, 321, has this bill for May 27, but the *General Advertiser* and the *Daily Advertiser* say May 2.)

May 5   Mrs. Morris's Night   Gen. Ad.

"A Comic Sketch, Partly original and partly compiled from the works of the most celebrated Dramatic Humorists, called

The Gallery of Portraits; or, The World as it Goes

The Belle's Stratagem

Mrs. Gee, in masquerade, Act. IV, singing as Diana.

The Two Misers

May 9   Mrs. Harper's Night   Gen. Ad.

The Chances
The Deserter

May 12   "For the Benefit of the Unhappy Sufferers by   Gen. Ad.
the late FIRE"

The West Indian
The Poor Soldier

May 19   Mr. Henry's Night   Gen. Ad.

Selima and Azor
* The Death of Harlequin
* As It Should Be—Oulton

[166]

1791

May 23

Mr. Morris's benefit, announced for this date, was postponed (*General Advertiser,* May 23) "on account of the continued indisposition of Mr. Hallam." Mrs. Rankin (mentioned for the first time) was to have sung, and Mr. and Mrs. Durang danced. *Cymbeline* and *Neck or Nothing* were to have been the plays. Mr. Morris's benefit came on June 6.

May 26   Mr. Wignell's Night   Gen. Ad.

* *The Dramatist; or Stop Him Who Can*—Reynolds
The Critic

May 30. See June 2.

June 2   Mr. Woolls' Night   Gen. Ad.
The Dramatist

Prologue...........Mr. Harper   Epilogue...........Mr. Wignell
Thomas and Sally
The True-Born Irishman

This was first announced for May 30—Fed. Gaz.

June 6   Mr. Morris's Night   Gen. Ad.
The Rivals
Rosina
Darby's Return

June 9   Mr. Hammond's Night   Daily Ad.
The School for Scandal
The Invasion

June 13   Mr. Martin's Night   Daily Ad.
The Toy

Sophia Seymour......Mrs. Henry

* *Harlequin Shipwrecked*
* *The Rival Candidates*—Bate

June 16   Mrs. Gee's Night   Daily Ad.
The Belle's Stratagem
The Rival Candidates

June 20   Mrs. Hamilton's Night   Daily Ad.
A Word to the Wise, or The School for Libertines
Harlequin Shipwrecked
Patie and Roger

[167]

1791

June 23	Miss Tuke's Night	Daily Ad.

The Conscious Lovers
Inkle and Yarico

June 30	Mr. Robinson's Benefit	Daily Ad.

* *"Constitutional Follies—or, A Trip to Demerara*—written by
Mr. Robinson—'never performed' "
The Deserter

July 7	Messrs. Durang, Vaughan, Heard, and Mrs. Rankin's Night	Daily Ad.

The Provoked Husband
* *The Birth of Harlequin*

July 11	Mr. Hammond's Night	Daily Ad.

The Clandestine Marriage

Lord Ogleby........Mr. Hallam	Trueman..........Mr. Vaughan
Sterling...........Mr. Morris	Mrs. Heidelberg....Mrs. Rankin
Sir John Melville....Mr. Harper	Fanny...............Mrs. Gee
Brush.............Mr. Martin	Betty............Mrs. Hamilton
Canton..........Mr. Robinson	Nancy..............Miss Tuke
Serg't Flower........Mr. Woolls	Miss Sterling.......Mrs. Morris

(This and the following *cast* from Seilhamer, II, 322: I have not found them elsewhere.)

The Birth of Harlequin

Dismal............Mr. Harper	Enchanter..........Mr. Woolls
Pantaloon........Mr. Robinson	Harlequin..........Mr. Durang
Fop.............Mr. Hammond	Market Woman.....Mr. Martin
Harlequin Pigmy..Master Durang	Airy Spirit...........Mrs. Gee
Enchanter..........Mr. Woolls	Columbine........Mrs. Durang

First mention of Master [Ferdinand] Durang. Last night of the season.

Between December 8, 1790, and July 11, 1791, the Old American Company produced at the Southwark Theatre these new plays: *The Chances, Constitutional Follies, The Dramatist, Isabella, More Ways Than One,* and *The Recess;* new afterpieces: *As It Should Be, The Birth of Harlequin, Harlequin Shipwrecked, The Little Hunchback, Patie and Roger, The Rival Candidates, The Rival Fools, Seeing's Believing,* and *The Two Misers.* Reappearing plays: *The Beaux' Stratagem, The Belle's Stratagem, The Busy Body, The Clandestine Marriage, The Conscious Lovers, Douglas, The Drummer, The English Merchant, The Gamester, The Grecian Daughter, Henry IV, Julius Cæsar, The Miser, The Mourning Bride, The Orphan, The Orphan of China, The Provoked Husband, The Recruiting Officer, Richard III, The*

1791

Rivals, The Roman Father, Romeo and Juliet, The School for Scandal, Selima and Azor, She Stoops to Conquer, The Suspicious Husband, The Tempest, The Toy, The West Indian, The Wonder, and *A Word to The Wise.* Reappearing afterpieces: *The Apprentice, Catherine and Petruchio, The Citizen, Darby's Return, The Death of Harlequin, The Deserter, The Ghost, The Guardian, High Life Below Stairs, Hob in the Well* (or *Flora*), *Inkle and Yarico, The Invasion, The Irish Widow, Love in a Camp, The Mayor of Garratt, The Miller of Mansfield, The Musical Lady, Neptune and Amphitrite, The Poor Soldier, The Prisoner at Large, Rosina, Thomas and Sally, The True-born Irishman,* and *Who's the Dupe?*

Actors new to our record: Master Ferdinand Durang, Mr. André, Mrs. Gee, Mr. Hammond, Mrs. Rankin, Mrs. Wilson, and "a gentleman from Europe." Reappearing players: Mr. and Mrs. Durang, Mr. Hallam, Mrs. Hamilton, Mr. and Mrs. Harper, Mr. Heard, Mr. and Mrs. Henry, Mr. Martin, Mr. and Mrs. Morris, Mr. Robinson, Mr. Vaughan, Miss Tuke, Mr. Wignell, and Mr. Woolls.

NORTHERN LIBERTY THEATRE

July 25   "That Elegant and Fashionable PASTICCIO—Called   Daily Ad.
THE BROOM; OR, A new Way for rubbing off the Rust of Care"
"SATAN'S ADDRESS TO THE SUN, from Milton's Paradise Lost
By Mrs. Kenna, which she had the honor to deliver
before the Literati of Trinity College, Dublin."

The "K" Company, which had played at the Northern Liberties Theatre on April 8, 11, 26, and 30, now began a season which lasted till May 16, 1792.

Aug. 1   "By Particular Desire"   Daily Ad.

The Broom
* Sir Flimsy Nervous, or a Trip to Harrowgate

Sir Flimsy Nervous....Mr. Kenna   Miss Flirt..........Miss Kenna
Landlady..........Mrs. Kenna

Aug. 8   *George Barnwell*   Daily Ad.

Thoroughgood.......Mr. Kenna   Maria.............Miss Kenna
Freeman....."A gentleman (being   George Barnwell......."A young
    his first appearance in that   gentleman, being his first ap-
    character)"   pearance on any stage."
Uncle..............Mr. Smyth   Lucy & Millwood....Mrs. Kenna

Cross Purposes

Old Grub..........Mr. Kenna   George Bevel....."by the Gentle-
Consul............Mr. Smyth   man who performs Barnwell."
Harry Bevel...."by the gentleman   Emily......"by a Young Lady, for
    that plays Trueman."   that Night only"

1791

Aug. 8 (cont.)

Frank Bevel..........Mr. Brett   Betty.........Mrs. Bra[dshaw]
                                   Mrs. Grub.........Mrs. Kenna

First appearance of Mrs. Bradshaw and Mr. Brett. Mr. Smyth is probably the Mr. Smith who appeared with Mr. Partridge on November 14, 1789.

Aug. 15   *George Barnwell*   Daily Ad.

Same cast as for August 8

Cross Purposes

Same cast as for August 8, save that Mrs. "Bra" is now Mrs. Bradshaw

Aug. 22   *A Trip to Scotland*   Daily Ad.
                     The Poor Soldier

Patrick............Mrs. Kenna   Norah.....Miss Hughes, being her
Kathleen.....by a Lady, being her   first appearance on any stage
              first appearance   Darby.............:Mrs. Kenna

Aug. 27   *Isabella*   Daily Ad.

Carlos.............Miss Kenna   Isabella............Mrs. Kenna
Biron..............Mr. Kenna

The Poor Soldier

Patrick............Miss Kenna   "Kathleen, by a lady; second appear-
                                              ance"

Aug. 31   *The Provoked Husband*   Daily Ad.
                    "(altered by Sheridan)"

Lord Townly........Mr. Kenna   Lady Grace.........Mrs. Ratlief
John Moody......by a gentleman   [Ratcliff]
Lady Townly........Mrs. Kenna   Songs.......Mr. and Mrs. Kenna

The Mayor of Garratt

Jerry Sneak....."by the gentleman   Major Sturgeon......Mr. Kenna
          who plays John Moody"   Mrs. Sneak.........Miss Kenna
Roger......Mr. Ratlief [Ratcliff]

The unnamed gentleman may have been Mr. Kenny—See Sept. 24.
First appearance of Mr. and Mrs. "Ratlief": the names soon become (in the bills) "Ratcliff," and it is probable that the names rather than the performers changed.

1791

Sept. 3   *Douglas*   Daily Ad.

Norval Douglas......Miss Kenna   Old Norval..........Mr. Kenna
Glenalvon........by a gentleman   Anna.....Mrs. Ratlief [Ratcliff]
Lord Randolph....by a gentleman   Lady Randolph......Mrs. Kenna
Officer.............Mr. Smith

* *The Intriguing Chambermaid*—Fielding

Col. Bluff..........Mr. Kenna   Lettice (the intriguing chamber-
Valentine...Mr. Ratlief [Ratcliff]   maid)............Miss Kenna
Mrs. Highman.......Mrs. Kenna

Sept. 9   * *The Earl of Warwick*—Francklin   Daily Ad.

Earl of Warwick......Mr. Kenna   Lady Elizabeth Gray..Miss Kenna
King Edward........Mr. Kenna   Margaret...........Mrs. Kenna

* *Polly Honeycombe*—Colman

Mr. Honeycombe.....Mr. Kenna   Mrs. Honeycomb.....Mrs. Kenna
Ledger............Mr. Ratcliff   Nurse..........Mrs. Bradshaw
Scribble..........Mrs. Ratcliff   Polly Honeycomb....Miss Kenna

Sept. 14   *A Trip to Scotland*   Daily Ad.

Old Gustein........Mr. Kenna   Miss Gustein.......Miss Kenna
Tillagree..........Mrs. Kenna

The Devil to Pay

Sir John Loverule...Mrs. Ratcliff   Lady Loverule......Miss Kenna
Doctor..........by a gentleman   Lettice..........Mrs. Bradshaw
Butler.............Mr. Ratcliff   Nell..............Mrs. Kenna
Jobson.............Mr. Kenna

Sept. 17   *Isabella*   Daily Ad.

Carlos.............Miss Kenna   Biron..............Mr. Kenna
Viceroy..........by a gentleman   Nurse..........Mrs. Bradshaw
Count Baldwin......Mr. Derrick   Isabella............Mrs. Kenna

The Intriguing Chambermaid

Colonel Bluff........Mr. Kenna   Lettice............Miss Kenna

First appearance of Mr. Derrick.

Sept. 21   *The Beaux' Stratagem*   Daily Ad.

"Aimwell, by a gentleman, being his first appearance on this Stage. Dorinda,
by a Lady, being her first appearance on any Stage."

[171]

1791

Sept. 21 (cont.)   *The Poor Soldier*

Patrick............Mrs. Kenna   Norah.............Miss Kenna
Darby.............Mr. Kenna   Kathleen..........Mrs. Ratcliff

Sept. 24   *Douglas*   Daily Ad.

Norval Douglass.....Miss Kenna   Old Norval.........Mr. Kenne
Glenalvon..........Mr. Kenna   Anna.............Mrs. Ratcliff
Lord Randolph......Mr. Derrick   Lady Randolph......Mrs. Kenna
Officer............Mr. Ratcliff

Polly Honeycomb

Cast as for Sept. 9

Mr. "Kenne," is probably Mr. Kenny, whose name appears with a "y" on
September 28. He has not been recorded before, unless on August 31.

Sept. 28   *The Beaux' Stratagem*   Daily Ad.

Archer.............Mr. Kenny   Dorinda...."The Young lady who
Aimwell...........Mr. Ratcliff   performed Cupid"
Scrub..............Mr. Kenna   Mrs. Sullen........Miss Kenna
Cherry............Mrs. Kenna

The Mayor of Garratt

Major Sturgeon......Mr. Kenna   Mrs. Sneak.........Miss Kenna
Jerry Sneak.........Mr. Kenny

Oct. 1   *The Earl of Warwick*   Daily Ad.

Earl of Warwich......Mr. Kenny   Lady Eliz. Gray......Miss Kenna
Earl of Suffolk......Mr. Derrick   Lady Clifford.......Mr. Ratcliff
Earl of Pembroke..Mrs. Bradshaw   Margareta Oriyon....Mrs. Kenna
King Edward........Mr. Kenna

The Virgin Unmasked

Coape (Dancing Master)........   Old Goodwill.....Mrs. Bradshaw
                Mrs. Ratcliff   Blister.............Mr. Kenna
Quaver............Mr. Kenny   Miss Lucy..........Mrs. Kenna
Mr. Thomas.......Mr. Derrick

Oct. 5   *The Old Maid*   Daily Ad.

Cleremont........Mrs. Ratcliff   Mrs. Harlow.......Miss Kenna
Mr. Harlow.......Mr. Derrick   Trifle.........by a Young Lady
John............Mrs. Bradshaw   Miss Harlow.......Mrs. Kenna
Captain Cape........Mr. Kenna

1791

Oct. 5 (cont.) *Thomas and Sally*

'Squire.............Mr. Kenny   Dorcas............Mrs. Ratcliff
Thomas.............Mr. Kenna   Sally...............Mrs. Kenna

Oct. 10 *The Citizen* Daily Ad.

Young Philpot........Mr. Kenna   Old Philpot......Mrs. Bradshaw
Young Wilding.....Mrs. Ratcliff   Corinna............Miss Kenna
Beaufort...........Mr. Derrick   Maria..............Mrs. Kenna

Thomas and Sally

'Squire............Mrs. Ratcliff   "Sally, by a Lady of well-known
Thomas.............Mr. Kenna   abilities, being her first ap-
Dorcas.............Mrs. Kenna   pearance on this Stage."

Oct. 14 *Jane Shore* Daily Ad.

Dumont...."by a Gentleman from   Belmour...."by a Gentleman from
    the Theatre Royal, Drury-   the Theatre Royal, Hay-
    Lane, London (being his first   Market, London (being his
    Appearance on this Stage)"   first Appearance on this
Ratcliff............Mr. Ratcliff   Stage)"
Catesby............Mrs. Ratcliff   Jane Shore..........Miss Kenna
Duke of Glouster....Mr. Derrick   Alicia..............Mrs. Kenna
Lord Hastings........Mr. Kenna

Cross Purposes

Old Grub...........Mr. Kenna   George Bevil........Mr. Derrick
Consul...."by the Gentleman who   Betty............Mrs. Bradshaw
    plays Shore"   Emily.........by a Young Lady
Harry Bevil.....by the Gentleman   Mrs. Grub..........Miss Kenna
    who plays Belmour

The new actors were probably Mr. Freeman and Mr. Holman, whose names
appear on October 19.

Oct. 19 *The Countess of Salisbury* Daily Ad.

Raymond...........Miss Kenna   Knights............Mr. Derrick
Lord Salisbury.......Mr. Kenna   Gray...............Mr. Kenny
Morton...........Mr. Holman   Eleanor...........Mrs. Ratcliff
Lerocher...........Mr. Freeman   Countess of Salisbury..Mrs. Kenna

The Intriguing Chambermaid

Col. Bluff...........Mr. Kenna   Security...........Mr. Derrick
Col. Oldcastle......Mr. Freeman   Miss Highman......Mrs. Ratcliff
Valentine.........Mr. Holman   Charlotte.......by a young Lady
Goodal.........Mrs. Bradshaw   Lettice............Miss Kenna

First mention of Mr. Freeman and Mr. Holman. See Oct. 14.

1791

Oct. 22   *The Beaux' Stratagem*   Daily Ad.

Archer..............Mr. Kenny   Sullen.............Mr. Freeman
Aimwell..........Mrs. Ratcliff   Scrub & Bonaface [sic].Mr. Kenna
Gibbit.............Mr. Holman

The Old Maid

Cleremont........Mrs. Ratcliff   Mrs. Harlow........Miss Kenna
Capt. Cape..........Mr. Kenna   Miss Harlow........Mrs. Kenna

Oct. 26   *The Countess of Salisbury*   Daily Ad.

Cast as for October 19

The Old Maid

Cast as for October 22, with the addition of

Mr. Harlo[w]......Mr. Holman   Trifle.........by a Young Lady

Nov. 5   "For the Benefit of Brother Kenna"   Daily Ad.

The Earl of Essex

Earl of Essex........Mr. Kenna   Earl of Southampton..Mr. Kenny
Lord Burleigh......Mr. Holman   Queen Elizabeth.....Miss Kenna
Sir Walter Raleigh.Mrs. Bradshaw   Countess of Nottingham.........
Lieutenant of the Tower.......   Mrs. Ratcliff
         by a Gentleman   Countess of Rutland..Mrs. Kenna

Thomas and Sally

Cast as for October 5, with the addition of

Sailor.............Mr. Holman

Nov. 14   Benefit of Mrs. Ratcliff   Daily Ad.

The Fair Penitent

Altamont......."by Mr. Stewart,   Rossanno........Mrs. Bradshaw
     from N. York, being his first   Lothario............Mr. Kenny
     appearance on this stage."   Lavinia.............Miss Kenna
Horatio.............Mr. Kenna   Lucilla............Mrs. Ratcliff
Sciolto.............Mr. Holman   Calista.............Mrs. Kenna

The Poor Soldier

Patrick.............Mrs. Kenna   Capt. Fitzroy.......Mr. Stewart
Father Luke........Mr. Kenny   Norah....."by the lady who per-
Dermot...........Mr. Holman   formed Sally"
Bogabell........Mrs. Bradshaw   Kathleen..........Mrs. Ratcliff
Darby.............Mr. Kenna

1791

Nov. 18   Benefit of Mrs. Kenna   Daily Ad.

The Countess of Salisbury

Lord Raymond	Miss Kenna	Lord Salisbury	Mr. Kenna
Gray	Mr. Kenny	Eleanor	Mrs. Ratcliff
Moreton	Mr. Holman	Countess of Salisbury	Mrs. Kenna
Knight	Mrs. Bradshaw		

* Three Weeks after Marriage—Murphy

Lovelace	Mrs. Ratcliff	Divinity	Miss Kenna
Woodley	Mr. Holman	Mrs. Drugget	Mr. Bradshaw
Old Drugget	Mr. Kenny	Lady Rachet	Mrs. Kenna
Sir Charles Rachet	Mr. Kenna		

Nov. 26 "A Company of French Dancers on the Tight Rope"— Daily Ad.
including "The Young Florentine," and Mr. Du Moulain.

"The Clown's Abilities are so well known to the Public, there needs no comment on them."

The Devil to Pay

Sir John Loverule	Mrs. Ratcliff	Jobson	Mr. Kenna
Conjuror	Mr. Kenny	Lady Loverule	Miss Kenna
Butler	Mr. Kelly	Lucy	by a Young Lady
Cook	Mrs. Bradshaw	Nell	Mrs. Kenna

First appearance of Mr. Du Moulain and the other French Dancers, and of Mr. Kelly.

Nov. 29   French Dancers   Daily Ad.

Three Weeks after Marriage

Cast as for November 18, save

Woodley.............Mr. Kelly

* Harlequin Barber

Harelequin	Mr. LaValet	Pantaloon	Mr. Anderson
Pero [sic]	Mr. Du Moulain	Columbine	Mrs. Ratcliff

First mention of Mr. LaValet (later Lavalet) and Mr. Anderson.

Dec. 1   French Dancers   Daily Ad.

The Deuce is in Him

Col. Tamper	Mr. Kenny	Maids	Mrs. Bradshaw, Miss Kenna
Major Belford	Mr. Kelly		
Dr. Prattle	Mr. Kenna	Florival	Mrs. Ratcliff
Emily	Mrs. Kenna		

[175]

1791

Dec. 1 (cont.)   *Harlequin Magician*

Harlequin.........Mr. LaValet   Pero [sic].....Mr. Du Moulain
Pantaloon........Mr. Anderson   Columbine........Mrs. Ratcliff

Dec. 3   French Dancers   Daily Ad.
The Fair Penitent

Cast as for November 14, except:

Altamount........Mrs. Ratcliff   Lothario...........Mr. Kenna
Sciolto.............Mr. Kelly   (The newspaper printing is in-
Lucilla..........A Young Lady   distinct—*perhaps* Mr. Kenny
                                as before)

Harlequin Dead or Alive

Harlequin.........Mr. LaValet   "Pero".........Mr. Du Moulain
Pantaloon........Mr. Anderson   Columbine........Mrs. Ratcliff

Dec. 6   French Dancers   Daily Ad.
The Fair Penitent

Cast as for December 3

Harlequin Dead or Alive

Cast as for December 3

Dec. 10   French Dancers   Daily Ad.
The Padlock

Don Diego..........Mr. Kenny   Mungo.............Mr. Kenny
Leander.............Mr. Kelly   Ursula...........Mrs. Ratcliff
Scholar.......Master Anderson   Leonora...........Miss Kenna
First appearance of Master Anderson.

Dec. 13   Benefit of Mr. Kenna   Daily Ad.
French Dancers
Isabella

Carlos.............Miss Kenna   Biron.............Mr. Kenna
Villeroy............Mr. Kenny   Isabella...........Mrs. Kenna

Harlequin turn'd Doctor

Harlequin.........Mr. LaValet   Pero...........Mr. Dumoulain
Pantaloon........The Florentine   Columbine........Mrs. Ratcliff

[176]

1791

Dec. 17   French Dancers   Daily Ad.
                        The Deuce is in Him

Col. Tamper.........Mr. Kenny   Maid...........Mrs. Bradshaw
Major Belfor.........Mr. Kelly   Bell...............Miss Kenna
Doctor Prattle........Mr. Kenna   Florival...........Mrs. Ratcliff
Emily...............Mrs. Kenna

*   * Linco's Travels—Garrick

Linco..............Mr. Kenna   Flora..............Mrs. Kenna
Cymon..............Mr. Kelly   Diana.............Mrs. Ratcliff
Clown.............Mr. Lavalet   Ceres...........A Young Lady
Cuddy.............Mr. Kenny   Old Woman......Mrs. Bradshaw
Mopsus..........Mr. Anderson   Clarissa.............Miss Kenna
Light-Foot........Mr. Dumulain

Dec. 20   Benefit of Mr. Dumoulain   Daily Ad.
                        French Dancers
                   * *Florizel and Perdita*—Garrick

Florizel.............Miss Kenna   Autolicus............Mr. Kenna
King...............Mr. Kenny   Dorcas...........A Young Lady
Antigonus............Mr. Kelly   Mopsa.............Mrs. Ratcliff
Clown............Mr. Anderson   Perdita.............Mrs. Kenna
Camillo.........Mrs. Bradshaw

                        Linco's Travels

Linco..............Mr. Kenna   Flora..............Mrs. Kenna
Cymon..............Mr. Kelly   Diana.............Mrs. Ratcliff
Cuddy.............Mr. Kenny   Ceres...........A Young Lady
Pedro...........Mr. Anderson   Old Woman......Mrs. Bradshaw
Clown............Mr. Lavalet   Clarissa.............Miss Kenna

Dec. 23   Donegani's Tumblers   Daily Ad.
                        Harlequin Skeleton

Harlequin..........Mr. Dumont   Clown.............Mr. Clumsy
Porter............Mr. Dellroy   Columbine......Madam Vil[l]er
Beaux...........Mr. Partridge

"This Company [has] performed in the most populous Cities in Europe, and
some in America."

N.B. "Two large Stoves are erected in the Play-house, which make it very
comfortable to the Audience."

[177]

1791

Mr. Donegani's company of acrobats had appeared at the Northern Liberties on November 8 and 25, and December 2, 16, and 19, but this pantomime is the first dramatic production they had announced.

Messrs. Dumont, Dellroy, Clumsy, and Madame Viller are new to our record. Mr. Patridge is probably the Mr. Patridge or Partridge of 1789.

Dec. 27   Daily Ad.

For "the immediate relief of distressed Masons, Widows and Orphans—This evening being the anniversary of St. John the Evangelist."

Venice Preserved

Dec. 31   French Dancers   Daily Ad.
                          Florizel and Perdita

Florizel	Miss Kenna	Autolicus	Mr. Kenna
King	Mr. Kenny	Mopsa	Mrs. Ratcliff
Camillo	Mr. Rankin	Dorcas	A Young Lady
Antigonus	Mr. Kelly	Perdita	Mrs. Kenna
Clown	Mr. Anderson		

First appearance of Mr. Rankin.

1792

Jan. 4   "By Desire of the Indian Chiefs"   Daily Ad.

French Dancers
Douglas

Norval Douglas	Miss Kenna	Old Norval	Mr. Kenna
Glenalvon	Mr. Kenny	Anna	Mrs. Ratcliff
Officer	Mr. Rankin	Lady Randolph	Mrs. Kenna
Lord Randolph	Mr. Kelly		

* *The French Shoemaker*

This bill was "By Desire of the Indian Chiefs," but the *Daily Advertiser* of January 9 said that "the only reason of the *Indian Chiefs* not being at the Play on *Wednesday* last, was on account of their dining with a large Company, and not breaking up till it was too late."

Jan. 7   French Dancers   Daily Ad.
                          Beaux' Stratagem

Aimwell	Mrs. Ratcliff	Sir Chas. Freeman	Mr. Rankin
Scrub	Mr. Kenna	Archer	Mr. Kenny
Sullen	Mr. Kelly	Cherry	Mrs. Kenna
Foigard	Mrs. Bradshaw	Dorinda	A Young Lady
Gibbit	Mrs. Rankin	Mrs. Sullen	Miss Kenna
Boniface	Mrs. Kenna		

[178]

1792

Jan. 12. See Jan. 14, 1792.

Jan. 14   French Dancers   Daily Ad.
Jane Shore

Hastings............Mr. Kenny	Dumont, alias Shore...Mr. Kenna
Duke of Glouster......Mr. Kelly	Jane Shore..........Miss Kenna
Catesby............Mrs. Ratcliff	Alicia..............Mrs. Kenna
Belmour............Mr. Rankin	

Linco's Travels

Linco..............Mr. Kenna

This was first announced for January 12, but was "postponed on account of bad weather" till January 14, when it would be "positively presented." In the *Daily Advertiser* for January 14 the following bill *also* is announced; probably it was postponed, but we have no further record.

French Dancers
Florizel and Perdita

Cast as for December 31, except:

Camillo........Mrs. Bradshaw

The Intriguing Chambermaid

Valentine...........Mr. Kenny	Security.........Mrs. Bradshaw
Goodall.............Mr. Kelly	Drunken Coll.......Mr. Kenna
Oldcastle...........Mr. Kenna	

Jan. 17   *The Agreeable Surprise*   Daily Ad.

Sir Felix Friendly......Mr. Kelly	Lingo "The pedantic schoolmaster"
Campton............Mr. Rankin	Mr. Kenna
Eugene..........Mr. Anderson	Laura..............Mrs. Kenna
Chicane............Mr. Kenny	Mrs. Cheshire......Mrs. Ratcliff
Cudden.............Mr. Brett	Fringe...........A Young Lady
Stump............Mr. Jackson	Cowslip............Miss Kenna
John............Mrs. Bradshaw	

The Intriguing Chambermaid

Cast as for January 14, with addition of

Slap..............Mr. Rankin	Lettice...........A Young Lady
Mrs. Highman......Mrs. Ratcliff	Charlotte..........Miss Kenna

"Security" is not mentioned

First appearance of Mr. Jackson.

1792

Jan. 21   "By Desire of the Indian Chiefs"   Daily Ad.

The Earl of Essex

Earl of Essex.........Mr. Kenna	Queen Elizabeth.....Miss Kenna
Lord Burleigh.........Mr. Kelly	Countess of Nottingham.........
Raleigh..........Mr. Bradshaw	Mrs. Ratcliff
Earl of Southampton...Mr. Kenny	Countess of Rutland..Mrs. Kenna

Florizel and Perdita

Cast as for December 31, except:

Camillo.........Mrs. Bradshaw   Ceres...........A Young Lady

"Dorcas" was not mentioned

Jan. 23   *The Tempest of Harlequin, or The Clown*   Daily Ad.
turned Miller

Harlequin.......Mr. Dumoulain	Sepon...............Mr. Leroy
Panterloon [sic].....Mr. Velleroy	Clown.............Mr. Clumsy
Beau................Mr. Palo	Columbine..........Mrs. Viller

"Mr. Patridge" said that he had been "at considerable expence" for machinery, dresses, etc., and hoped the public would like it. He talked as if he were the manager of the French Company. First dramatic appearance of Mr. Velleroy, Mr. Palo, and Mr. Leroy.

Jan. 26   "For the Benefit of the Young Florentine"   Daily Ad.

Mr. Dumoulain's Acrobats
A Pantomime

Columbine.........Mrs. Ratcliff	Pantaloon.........Mr. Anderson
Harlequin..........Mr. LaValet	Jew...........Young Florentine
Pero...........Mr. Dumoulain	Dancing Master.....Mr. Barnard

First appearance of Mr. Barnard.

Jan. 27   Benefit of Miss Kenna   Daily Ad.

The Suspicious Husband

Bellamy...........A Gentleman	Simon...............Mr. Kelly
(For that Night only)	Ranger............A Gentleman
Mr. Strickland......Mr. Kenna	(For that Night only)
Jack Megot........A Gentleman	Jacintha...........Mrs. Kenna
(For that Night only)	Mrs. Strickland.....Mrs. Ratcliff
Frankly.............Mr. Kenny	Landlady........Mrs. Bradshaw
Tester.............Mr. Rankin	Lucetta..........A Young Lady
Buckle...........A Gentleman	Clarinda............Miss Kenna
(For that Night only)	

1792

Jan. 27 (cont.)   *Thomas and Sally*

Thomas............Mr. Kenna   Dorcas...........Mrs. Ratcliff
'Squire.............Mr. Kenny   Sally..............Mrs. Kenna
Huntsmen & Sailors.........Mr. Kelly, Mr. Rankin, and Mrs. Bradshaw

Jan. 28   Benefit of Mr. Clumsy   Daily Ad.

Acrobatics
*The Tempest of Harlequin, or
The Clown Turned Miller*

Cast as for January 23, except:

Harlequin. . . . Mr. Dumont

Jan. 31   "By Desire of the Indian Chiefs"   Daily Ad.

Dumoulain's Company
Harlequin Barber

Cast as for November 29, 1791

Feb. 1   Benefit of Miss Kenny   Daily Ad.
The Grecian Daughter

Evander............Mr. Kenny   Dionisius...........Mr. Kenna
Melanthon..........Mr. Kelly   Philotas............Miss Kenna
Calipus............Mr. Rankin   Erixene..........A Young Lady
Arcas...............Mr. Kelly   Euphrasia..........Mrs. Kenna
Phocian...........Mrs. Ratcliff   (The Grecian Daughter)

Mayor of Garratt

Major Sturgeon.......Mr. Kenna   Jerry Sneak.........Mr. Kenny
Bruin...........Mrs. Bradshaw   Mrs. Bruin........Mrs. Ratcliff
Sir Jacob Jollup........Mr. Kelly   Mrs. Sneak.........Mrs. Kenna
Roger.............Mr. Rankin

"The Indian Chiefs will attend the Theatre This Evening, dressed in their Robes."

This is the first mention of Miss Kenny; she was very possibly the "young lady" so frequently mentioned.

Feb. 4   Mr. Dumoulain's Company—Acrobatics   Daily Ad.
The French Shoemaker
Feb. 6   *The Grecian Daughter*   Daily Ad.

Cast as for Feb. 1, except:

Phocian.........."a Gentleman"

[181]

1792

Feb. 6 (cont.)   *The Deuce is in Him*

Cast as for Dec. 17, 1791, except:

Florival..............."a Lady"

"Benefit of Mr. Kelly"

Feb. 10   "(never on this Continent)"   Daily Ad.

* *The Hypocrite*—Bickerstaff

Col. Lambert.......Mrs. Ratcliff   Seyward............Miss Kenna
Sir John Lambert......Mr. Kelly   Young Lady Lambert...........
Dr. Cantwell........Mr. Kenna   A Young Lady
Darnley............Mr. Kenny   Old Lady Lambert. Mrs. Bradshaw
Mauworm.........A Gentleman   Charlotte............Mrs. Kenna
        (for that night only)

The Poor Soldier

Capt. Fitzroy.......A Gentleman   Bagatelle.........Mrs. Bradshaw
        (for that night only)   Patrick.............Mrs. Kenna
Darby.............Mr. Kenna   Kathleen..........Mrs. Ratcliff
Dermot.............Mr. Kelly   Norah.............Miss Kenna
Father Luke........Mr. Kenny

Feb. 11   Mr. Dumoulain's Company—"POSITIVELY the   Daily Ad.
            last night in this city"—Acrobatics
                The French Shoemaker

Feb. 14   *George Barnwell*   Daily Ad.

George Barnwell....A Gentleman   Uncle.............A Gentleman
    from London, being his First   Thoroughgood........Mr. Kenna
    Appearance on any stage.   Maria.............Miss Kenna
Trueman............Mr. Kenny   Lucy.............A Young Lady
Blunt...............Mr. Kelly   Millwood...........Mrs. Kenna

"A Farce—as in Bills of the Day"

Feb. 20   *The Hypocrite*   Daily Ad.

Cast as for February 10, except:

Darnley..........A Gentleman   Col. Lambert........Miss Kenna
Mow-worm.......Mr. Partridge   Seyward...........A gentleman

* *Like Master like Man*—Vanbrugh—King

Carlos.............Mr. Kenny   Leonora...........Mrs. Kenna
Lopez............Mr. Patridge   Jacinta.............Mrs. Kenna
Sancho.............Mr. Kenna

[182]

1792

Feb.25   *The Revenge*   Daily Ad.

Zanga......."A Gentleman from Dublin, being his first Appearance on this Stage."
Carlos..............Mr. Kenny
Don Manuel..........Mr. Kelly
Don Alvares..........Mr. Kenna

Captain of the Procession......"A Gentleman for his Amusement"
Isabella.............Miss Kenna
Leonora............Mrs. Kenna

The Miller of Mansfield

King.....by Gentleman who plays Alonzo
Richard..............Mr. Kelly
Lord Lurewell.......Mr. Kenny
Miller..............Mr. Kenna

Peggy.............Miss Kenna
Madge...........Mrs. Bradshaw
Kate..............Mrs. Kenna

The "gentleman from Dublin" was probably Mr. Kedey; the "gentleman" played Romeo on February 29, and Mr. Kedey played it on March 13, when his name first appears.

Feb. 29   *Romeo and Juliet*   Daily Ad.

Romeo......by the gentleman who performed Zanga
Capulet..............Mr. Kenny
Benvolio.............Mr. Kelly
Tibalt & Friar Laurence....... Mr. Vaughan

Paris..............A Gentleman
Peter..........Master Bradshaw
Mercutio............Mr. Kenna
Nurse..........Mrs. Bradshaw
Juliet..............Miss Kenna
Balthasar...........Mr. Kenna

The Irish Widow

Whittle...........Mr. Vaughan
Kechsey............Mr. Kenny
Bates......Gentleman who plays Romeo
Thomas..............Mr. Kelly

Nephew.....Gentleman who plays Paris
Pompey........Master Bradshaw
Sir Patrick O'Neale....Mr. Kenna
Irish Widow.........Mrs. Kenna

First appearance of Master Bradshaw.

March 3   *The Grecian Daughter*   Daily Ad.
                Florizel and Perdita

March 6   *She Stoops to Conquer*   Daily Ad.

Miss Neville....."Miss Hopkins from Dublin, being her first appearance on any Stage."

The Irish Widow

March 12. See March 13

[183]

1792

March 13   *Romeo and Juliet*   Daily Ad.

Cast as for Feb. 29, except:

Romeo.............Mr. Kedey

The Agreeable Surprise

Sir Felix Friendly......Mr. Kelly	Chicane............Mr. Kenny
Compton............Mr. Kedey	Lingo..............Mr. Kenna
Eugene............Mr. Fowler	Cowslip.........A Young Lady
Cudden..........Mr. Vaughan	Mrs. Cheshire.......Miss Kenna
Thomas.............Mr. Brett	Laura.............Mrs. Kenna

First mention of Mr. Kedey, who was probably the "gentleman from Dublin" of February 25. This bill was postponed from March 12.

March 16   *Clementina*   Daily Ad.

Alselmo [sic].........Mr. Kedey	Guards & Attendants........Mr.
Palesmo...........Mr. Vaughan	Fowler, Mr. Kenny, etc.
Adorno.............Mr. Kelly	Granville............Mr. Kenna
Capt. of the Guards...Mr. Kenny	Elizara.............Miss Kenna
	Clementina.........Mrs. Kenna

The Wrangling Lovers, or Like Master Like Man

Carlos.............Mr. Kenny	Jacintha............Miss Kenna
Lopez...............Mr. Kelly	Leonora...........Mrs. Kenna
Sancho.............Mr. Kenna	

First appearance of Mr. Fowler.

April 9   "By Request of the FARMER'S BROTHER,   Daily Ad.
              Head Chief of the Five Nations"

The Jealous Wife
The Ghost

April 14   *Venice Preserved*   Daily Ad.

"Jaffier by Mr. Godwin (formerly of the Old American Company) with an Address relative to his performing in this city twenty years past."

The Citizen

Old Philpot........Mr. Godwin

April 19   Benefit of Mrs. Kenna   Daily Ad.

* *Percy*—Miss More
Catherine and Petruchio

Petruchio......Mr. Godwin

[184]

1792

| April 21 | *The Miser* | Daily Ad. |

Lovegold..........Mr. Godwin   Lappet.............Mrs. Kenna

The Miller of Mansfield

| April 23 | *A Lecture on Heads* | Daily Ad. |
(or, "Theatrical Evening Brush")—by Mr. Godwin

Lethe

Old Man
Drunken Man } ...Mr. Godwin   Fine Lady..........Mrs. Kenna

"On this occasion, Mr. Godwin respectfully solicits the Presence of the 'Friends to his Endeavours.'"

| April 26 | Mr. Kenny's Benefit | Daily Ad. |

The Orphan

Chamont...........Mr. Godwin   Castalio.............Mr. Kenny
Acasto and Ernesto.....Mr. Kelly Serina.............Mrs. Ratcliff
Chaplain............Mr. Kedey   Florella..........Mrs. Bradshaw
Polydore..........Mr. Vaughan   Monimia............Mrs. Kenna
Page..............Young Lady

The Deuce Is in Him

Col. Tamper.........Mr. Kenny   Florival..........Mrs. Ratcliff
Major Belford.......Mr. Kelly   Bell..............A Young Lady
Prattle.............Mr. Godwin   Emily.............Miss Kenna

| April 30 | Benefit of Mr. Kedey | Daily Ad. |

* *Oroonoko*—Southerne

Aboan..............Mr. Kenny   Captain Driver.....Mr. Vaughan
Blanford...........Mrs. Ratcliff   Oroonoko...........Mr. Kedey
Stanmore...........Miss Kenna   Imoinda...........Mrs. Kenna
Governor............Mr. Kelly

Polly Honeycomb

Mr. Honeycomb......Mr. Kenny   Nurse...........Mrs. Bradshaw
Ledger..............Mr. Kelly   Polly Honeycomb.....Miss Kenna
Scribble...........Mrs. Ratcliff

[185]

1792

May 4	Benefit of Mrs. Ratcliff	Daily Ad.

The Miser

Lovegold..........Mr. Godwin	Ramilie............Mr. Kenny
Frederick.........Mr. Vaughan	Mariana............Miss Kenna
Cleremont..........Mr. Kedey	Harriot...........Mrs. Ratcliff
Deeney..............Mr. Kelly	Wheedle.......[Mrs?] Bradshaw
Cook and Taylor.............	Lapet..............Mrs. Kenna

[blank given]

The Lying Valet

Sharp.............Mr. Godwin	Melissa.............Mrs. Kenna
Gayless...........Mr. Vaughan	Kitty Pry...........Miss Kenna
Justice Guttle........Mr. Kelly	Miss Trippet......A Young Lady
Cook...............Mr. Kenny	Mrs. Gadabout....Mrs. Bradshaw

May 11	Benefit of Mr. Kelly	Daily Ad.

* The New Peerage—Miss Lee

Mr. Vandercrab.....Mr. Godwin	Virtu......."A Gentleman for his
Charles..............Mr. Kedey	Amusement."
Sir John Lovelace...Mr. Vaughan	Lord Melville........Mr. Kenny
Medley & Allen........Mr. Kelly	Miss Vandercrab.....Mrs. Kenna
Kitty............A Young Lady	Miss Harley........Mrs. Ratcliff

"The Elopement" (cut from The Duenna)

Isaac Mendoza......Mr. Godwin	Don Jerome..........Mr. Kenny
Don Carlos..........Mr. Kelly	Margaretta.........Mrs. Ratcliff
Don Antonio........Mr. Kedey	Louisa..............Mrs. Kenna
Sancho...........Mr. Vaughan	

"A full Band of Music"

May 16	"Benefit of Mrs. Kedey"	Daily Ad.

* Which is the Man—Mrs. Cowley

Fitzherbert........Mr. O'Reiley	Dobby Pendragon.....Mr. Kenny
"(Late of the Theatre Royal,	Julia...............Mrs. Kedey
Crow Street, Dublin) first ap-	Clarinda...........Mrs. Ratcliff
pearance on this Stage"	Sophy Pendragon...A Young Lady
Lord Sparkle.......Mr. Vaughan	Kitty..........."Mr." Bradshaw
Belville.............Mr. Kelly	[was this Master Bradshaw?]
Beauchamp..........Mr. Kedey	Lady Bell Bloomer....Mrs. Kenna

1792

May 16 (cont.)   *The Agreeable Surprise*

Sir Felix Friendly	Mr. Kelly	Lingo	Mr. O'Reilly
Compton	Mr. Kedey	Laura	Mrs. Kenna
Eugene	Mr. Vaughan	Mrs. Cheshire	Mrs. Ratcliff
Chicane and Cudden	Mr. Kenny	Fringe	A Young Lady
John	Mr. Bradshaw	Cowslip	Mrs. Kedey

This is the first mention of Mrs. Kedey and Mr. O'Reilly. I assume that the "Mr." Bradshaw who played "Kitty" was Master Bradshaw, previously noted.

The Northern Liberties Theatre was open from April 8 to 30, 1791, and from July 25, 1791, to May 16, 1792. In it appeared the so-called "K" Company, the French Dancers, led by Mr. Dumoulain, and Donegani's Acrobats or Tumblers. The dancers and tumblers are noted only when they appeared on a bill which included drama.

New plays produced: *Clementina, The Earl of Warwick, Florizel and Perdita, The Hypocrite, The New Peerage, Oroonoko, Percy,* and *Which is the Man.* New afterpieces: *"The Broom," The Duenna* (cut to *"The Elopement"*), *Sir Flimsy Nervous, A* (or *The*) *French Shoemaker, Harlequin Barber, Harlequin Dead and Alive, Harlequin Magician, Harlequin Turned Doctor, The Intriguing Chambermaid, Like Master Like Man, Linco's Travels, Polly Honeycomb, The Tempest of Harlequin, Three Weeks after Marriage,* and *The Waterman.*

Reappearing plays: *The Agreeable Surprise, The Beaux' Stratagem, The Countess of Salisbury, Douglas, The Earl of Essex, The Fair Penitent, George Barnwell, Isabella, Jane Shore, The Jealous Wife, The Orphan, The Miser, The Provoked Husband, The Revenge, The Grecian Daughter, Romeo and Juliet, She Stoops to Conquer, The Suspicious Husband,* and *Venice Preserved.* Reappearing afterpieces: *Catherine and Petruchio, The Citizen, Cross Purposes, The Deuce is in Him, The Devil to Pay, The Ghost, Harlequin Skeleton, The Irish Widow, Lethe, The Mayor of Garratt, The Miller of Mansfield, The Old Maid, The Padlock, The Poor Soldier, Thomas and Sally, A Trip to Scotland, The Virgin Unmasked,* and *The Wrangling Lovers.*

A number of new actors appeared, many for a very short time. In addition to the unnamed "Gentlemen" and "Ladies," the new actors were Mr. Allen (presuming him not to have been the Mr. Allen who had appeared in 1774), Mr. and Master Anderson, Mr. Barnard, Mrs. and Master Bradshaw, Messrs. Brett, Clumsy, Dellroy, Derrick, Dumont, Dumoulain, Freeman, Fowler and Holman, Miss Hopkins, Miss Hughes, Mr. Jackson, Mr. and Mrs. Kedey, Mr. Kelly, Mr., Mrs., and Miss Kenna, Mr. and Mrs. J. Kenna, Mr. and Miss Kenny, Messrs. Lavalet, Leroy, Palo, and Rankin, Mr. and Mrs. Ratcliff, Messrs. O'Reilly, Stewart, Velleroy, Mrs. Viller

1792

and the "Young Florentine." Reappearing actors: Messrs. Godwin, Partridge, Smith (presumably), Vaughan, and *perhaps* Mr. Allen.

SOUTHWARK THEATRE

May 28   *The New Peerage*   Daily Ad.

Mr. Vandercrab	Mr. Hallam	Charles Vandercrab	Mr. Harper
Lord Melville	Mr. Martin	Miss Harley	Miss Tuke
Sir John Lovelace	Mr. Hammond	Miss Vandercrab	Mrs. Rankin
Medley	Mr. Ashton	Kitty	Mrs. Hamilton
Allen	Mr. Ryan	Lady Charlotte Courtley	
Virtu	Mr. Durang		Mrs. Henry
James	Mr. Robinson		

Acrobatics by M. Placide, "The Little Devil," and Mr. Simonette.

("Dancing Ballet")
* *The Bird Catcher*

Bird Catcher	Mr. Placide	Rosetta	Madame Placide
Hunters	Messrs. Duran[g], Martin, Ryan, Robinson, &c.		

The Old American Company played at the Theatre in Southwark from May 28 to July 2, 1792. The Placide troupe of tumblers and dancers was with it. First appearance of Mr. Ashton, M. and Mme. Placide, "The Little Devil" (perhaps a Mr. Martin—see Odell, I, 338), and Mr. Simonette.

May 30   *The Recess*   Daily Ad.

Muskato	Mr. Hallam	Octavio	Mr. Ashton
Don Guzman de Ribbera		Lopez	Mr. Durang
	Mr. Heard	Don Carlos	Mr. Harper
Don Ferdinand	Mr. Martin	Dona Marcella	Miss Tuke
Don Pedro	Mr. Hammond	Dona Aurora	Mrs. Rankin
Lazarillo	Mr. Ryan	Leonarda	Mrs. Hamilton
Alguazil	Mr. Woolls	Beatrice	Mrs. Henry

The Placides—Acrobatics
* *The Old Soldier* ("Historic Pantomime")

Old Soldier	M. Placide	Clown	Mr. Durang
Two Thieves	M. Dumas	Lord of the Manor	Mr. Harper
	and The Little Devil	Milk Maid	Mrs. Hamilton
Lucas	Mr. Martin	Collate	Madame Placide

First appearance of M. Dumas.

June 2   *The Busy Body*   Daily Ad.
* *King of the Genii, or*
Harlequin Neptune (pantomime)

Originally for June 1.

[188]

1792

June 5	*The Beaux' Stratagem* * *The Enchanted Nosegay* (pantomime)	Daily Ad.
June 7	*The Wonder* * *The Dutchmen, or The Merry Girl* (dancing Ballet) "by the Little Devil and M. Placide."	Daily Ad.
June 9	(By Desire) *The New Peerage* * *Columbine Invisible* (pantomime)	Daily Ad.
June 13	(By Desire) *The New Peerage* *Columbine Invisible*	Daily Ad.
June 15	*The Clandestine Marriage* * *The Yorker's Stratagem,* or *Banana's Wedding*—Robinson	Daily Ad.
June 18	*The Maid of the Mill* *The Mock Doctor*	Daily Ad.
June 20	Benefit of Mme. Placide *Love Makes a Man* "(never here)" * *Harlequin [Balloonist]* or *Pierot in the Clouds* (pantomime)	Daily Ad.

I assume that this pantomime was *Harlequin Balloonist,* as the Placides had given such a pantomime with the second title *Pierot in the Clouds,* in New York, May 3, 1792. (Odell, I, 306.) The announcement of June 19 said "Harlequin Tobacconist," and that of June 20, "Harlequin Babouist."—both times "or Pierot in the Clouds."

June 22	*The Roman Father* *All The World's a Stage*	Daily Ad.
June 25	*Love in a Village* *The Bird Catcher* *Love à la Mode*	Daily Ad.
June 27	*The Provoked Husband* *Inkle and Yarico*	Daily Ad.
June 29	*The School for Wives* * *The Return of the Labourers* ("dancing ballad") *The Padlock*	Daily Ad.

[189]

1792

July 2   "Benefit of the Little Devil"   Daily Ad.

The Miser
* The Sorcerer's Apprentice, or
Harlequin Wood-Cutter (pantomime)

"Positively the Last Night."

In the brief season from May 28 to July 2, 1792, there were no new full-length plays, but these new afterpieces (with the exception of *The Yorker's Stratagem,* all pantomimes or ballets) were produced: *The Bird Catcher, Columbine Invisible, The Dutchmen; or the Merry Girl, The Enchanted Nosegay, Harlequin* [*Balloonist*—see June 20]; *or Pierot in the Clouds, The King of the Genii; or Harlequin Neptune, The Old Soldier, The Return of the Labourers,* and *The Yorker's Stratagem.*

Reappearing plays: *The Beaux' Stratagem, The Busy Body, The Clandestine Marriage, Love in a Village, The Maid of the Mill, The Miser, The New Peerage, The Provoked Husband, The Recess, The Roman Father, The School for Wives,* and *The Wonder.* Reappearing afterpieces: *All The World's a Stage, Inkle and Yarico, Love à la Mode, The Mock Doctor,* and *The Padlock.*

The new performers: Mr. Ashton, M. Dumas, "The Little Devil," M. and Mme. Placide, and Mr. Simonette. Reappearing actors: Mr. Durang, Mr. Hallam, Mrs. Hamilton, Mr. Hammond, Mr. Harper, Mr. Heard, Mrs. Henry, Mr. Martin, Mrs. Rankin, Mr. Robinson, Mr. Ryan, Miss Tuke, and Mr. Woolls.

NORTHERN LIBERTY THEATRE

July 11   Benefit of Mrs. Kenna   Daily Ad.

Venice Preserved

"The principal characters by gentlemen of the Old American Company" and Belvidera—Mrs. Kenna.

** The Old Schoolmaster Grown Young*

Old Schoolmaster	M. Placide	Jeanette	Mrs. Rankin
Lucas	M. Placide	Rosetta	Mme. Placide

Thomas and Sally

Thomas	Mr. Harper	Squire	Mr. Woolls
Sailors	Messrs. Robinson,	Dorcas	Miss Kenna
	Kedey, etc.	Sally	Mrs. Rankin

An isolated performance at the Northern Liberties Theatre.

Mrs. Kenna said that "Mr. Harper and Placide, with the other gentlemen" had promised to exert themselves "in extricating her from a truly embarrassed situation."

SOUTHWARK THEATRE

Sept. 26   *The Wonder*   Daily Ad.

"—An Introductory Address by Mr. Hodgkinson, written by himself"

The Padlock

Seilhamer, III, 56, gives the following cast for *The Wonder*:

Don Felix.......Mr. Hodgkinson	Vasquez..........Mr. Durang
(His first appearance in America)	Lissardo..........Mr. Prigmore
Col. Briton...........Mr. King	(His first appearance in America)
(His first appearance in America)	Isabella.............Miss Tuke
Don Pedro.........Mr. Ashton	Flora..............Mrs. Rankin
Don Lopez..........Mr. Ryan	English Soldier.....Mr. Robinson
Gibby..............Mr. Bisset	Ines.............Mrs. Hamilton
Alguazil........Mr. Hammond	Violante............Mrs. Henry

and for *The Padlock* (*ibid.*)

Mungo.............Mr. Hallam	Ursula..........Mrs. Hamilton
Don Diego.........Mr. Woolls	Leonora.......Mrs. Hodgkinson
Leander.............Mr. West	(Her first appearance in America)
(His first appearance in America)	

First night of the Old American Company's season at the Theatre in Southwark from September 26, 1792, to January 12, 1793. (A number of casts for this season which Seilhamer gives, III, 56–64, I have not been able to find in *The Daily Advertiser, The General Advertiser, The National Gazette, The Federal Gazette, The Pennsylvania Journal, The Pennsylvania Gazette, The Gazette of the United States,* or the *Columbian Centinel.*) First appearance of Mr. Bisset, Mr. and Mrs. Hodgkinson, Mr. King, Mr. Prigmore, and Mr. West.

Sept. 28   *The West Indian*   Daily Ad.
                           The Padlock

Seilhamer, III, 57, gives the following parts in *The West Indian*:

Belcour.........Mr. Hodgkinson	Major O'Flaherty......Mr. King
Varland.........Mr. Prigmore	Charlotte..........Mrs. Henry

Oct. 1   *The Clandestine Marriage*   Daily Ad.
                          The Flitch of Bacon

Oct. 3   *She Stoops to Conquer*   Daily Ad.
                          The Deserter

1792

Seilhamer, III, 57, gives the following parts for *She Stoops to Conquer:*

Hardcastle........Mr. Prigmore	Tony Lumpkin......Mr. Hallam
Young Marlow..Mr. Hodgkinson	Miss Hardcastle.....Mrs. Henry

Oct. 5	*The Beaux' Stratagem*	Daily Ad.
	The Flitch of Bacon	

Seilhamer, III, 62, gives the following parts for the *Beaux' Stratagem:*

Archer.........Mr. Hodgkinson	Mrs. Sullen.........Mrs. Henry
Aimwell.............Mr. West	Dorinda...........Mrs. Kenna
Scrub..............Mr. Hallam	Cherry...........Mrs. Pownall

First appearance of Mrs. Pownall.

Oct. 8	*The School for Scandal*	Daily Ad.
	The Deserter	
Oct. 10	*Love in a Village*	Daily Ad.
	Catherine and Petruchio	
Oct. 12	*Jane Shore*	Daily Ad.
	The Lying Valet	
Oct. 15	*The Maid of the Mill*	Daily Ad.
	Love à la Mode	

Seilhamer, III, 60, gives the following cast for *The Maid of the Mill:*

Aimworth.......Mr. Hodkinson	Ralph..............Mr. Hallam
Sir Harry Sycamore.Mr. Prigmore	Lady Sycamore....Mrs. Hamilton
Merwyn.............Mr. West	Fanny.............Mrs. Kenna
Fairfield...........Mr. Ashton	Theodosia...........Miss Tuke
Giles...............Mr. Woolls	Patty.............Mrs. Pownall

Oct. 17	*The Maid of the Mill*	Daily Ad.
	The Mayor of Garratt	
Oct. 19	*Richard III*	Daily Ad.
	The Devil to Pay	
Oct. 22	*The Busy Body*	Daily Ad.
	* *The Romp*—Bickerstaff	

Seilhamer, III, 58, gives the following parts for *The Romp:*

Watty Cockney.....Mr. Prigmore	Priscilla Tomboy.Mrs. Hodgkinson
Barnacle..............Mr. King	Penelope.............Miss Brett
Old Cockney........Mr. Ashton	Miss LaBlond.......Mrs. Rankin
Capt. Sightly........Mr. West	

First mention of Miss Brett.

[192]

1792

| Oct. 24 | *The Miser* | Daily Ad. |
| | *Rosina* | |

Seilhamer, III, 58, gives the following parts for *Rosina*:

Belville...........Mr. Chambers   Rosina.........Mrs. Hodgkinson
Capt. Belville.........Mr. West   Phoebe............Mrs. Pownall
William..........Mr. Prigmore   Old Woman......Mrs. Hamilton
Irishman..............Mr. King

First mention of Mr. Chambers.

| Oct. 26 | *The Clandestine Marriage* | Daily Ad. |
| | *The Romp* | |

| Oct. 29 | *Othello* | Daily Ad. |
| | *The Romp* | |

Seilhamer, III. 61, gives the following parts for *Othello*:

Othello.........Mr. Hodgkinson   Cassio................Mr. King
Iago..............Mr. Hallam   Desdemona...........Miss Tuke

| Oct. 31 | *The Dramatist* | Daily Ad. |
| | *The Devil to Pay* | |

Seilhamer, III, 60, gives this cast for *The Dramatist*:

Vapid..........Mr. Hodgkinson   Peter................Mr. Ryan
Lord Scratch.......Mr. Prigmore   Marianne...........Miss Tuke
Ennui...............Mr. King   Lady Waitford....Mrs. Hamilton
Floriville..........Mr. Hallam   Louisa...............Miss Brett
Willoughby......Mr. Hammond   Letty.............Mrs. Rankin
Neville............Mr. Martin

| Nov. 2 | *The Dramatist* | Daily Ad. |
| | *Rosina* | |

| Nov. 5 | *Henry IV—Part I* | Daily Ad. |
| | *The Padlock* | |

| Nov. 7 | *The Dramatist* | Daily Ad. |
| | *The Romp* | |

| Nov. 9 | *Love in a Village* | Daily Ad. |
| | *The Lying Valet* | |

The following parts are given by Seilhamer, III, 59:

1792

Nov. 9 (cont.)   *Love in a Village*

Young Meadows...Mr. Chambers		Hodge.............Mr. Hallam
Woodcock.........Mr. Ashton		Madge...........Mrs. Pownall
Sir William......Mr. Hammond		Rosetta........Mrs. Hodgkinson

Lying Valet

Sharp.............Mr. Hallam		Beau Trippet.....Mr. Hammond
Guttle.............Mr. Ashton		Kitty Pry...........Miss Tuke

Nov. 12   * *The Mysterious Husband*—Cumberland   Daily Ad.
The Prisoner at Large

But see November 28, when *The Mysterious Husband* was announced as "never performed here."

Nov. 14   *The Maid of the Mill*   Daily Ad.
The Romp

Nov. 16   *The Miser*   Daily Ad.
* *The Farmer*—O'Keeffe

Seilhamer, III, 59, gives this cast for *The Farmer:*

Farmer Blackberry.....Mr. King		Rundy.............Mr. Martin
Valentine.............Mr. West		Stubble.............Mr. Woolls
Fairly..............Mr. Heard		Louisa..............Mrs. Kenna
Col. Dorimont.......Mr. Ashton		Molly........Mrs. Hodgkinson
Jemmy Jumps.....Mr. Chambers		Betty Blackberry....Mrs. Pownall
Flummery...........Mr. Ryan		Landlady...........Mrs. Rankin

Nov. 17   *The Dramatist*   Daily Ad.
The Romp

Nov. 19   *Othello*   Daily Ad.
The Farmer

Nov. 21   *The Busy Body*   Daily Ad.
Midas

Nov 23   *The Busy Body*   Daily Ad.
Midas

Nov. 24   *Douglas*   Daily Ad.
Rosina

Nov. 26   *The School for Scandal*   Daily Ad.
The Flitch of Bacon
"Never performed here"

[194]

1792

Nov. 28   *The Mysterious Husband*   Daily Ad.
           The Prisoner at Large

A note before *The Mysterious Husband* says "never performed here": the performance announced for November 12 may have been postponed, or the note may have been a (not uncommon) clerical error.

Nov. 30   *More Ways than One*   Daily Ad.
        * *No Song No Supper*—Hoare

Seilhamer, III, 59, gives the following cast for *No Song No Supper:*

Robin	Mr. Hodgkinson	William	Mr. Robbins
Endless	Mr. Martin	Margaretta	Mrs. Hodgkinson
Crop	Mr. Prigmore	Dorothy	Mrs. Pownall
Frederick	Mr. West	Nelly	Mrs. Rankin
Thomas	Mr. Ryan	Louisa	Miss Brett

First mention of Mr. Robbins.

Dec. 3   *All in the Wrong*   Daily Ad.
           The Poor Soldier

Seilhamer, III, 62, gives the following parts:

All in the Wrong

Sir John Restless	Mr. Hodgkinson	Lady Restless	Mrs. Pownall
Beverly	Mr. Hallam	Belinda	Miss Tuke
Sir William Belmont	Mr. Prigmore	Clarissa	Miss Brett
Young Belmont	Mr. Martin	Tattle	Mrs. Hamilton

The Poor Soldier

Patrick	Mr. Hodgkinson	Darby	Mr. Prigmore
Capt. Fitzroy	Mr. West	Norah	Mrs. Pownall
Father Luke	Mr. King	Kathleen	Mrs. Hodgkinson

Dec. 5   *Romeo and Juliet*   Daily Ad.

Vocal parts in Dirge by Mrs. Pownall, Mr. Chambers, Mr. West, Mr. Robbins, Mrs. Kenna, and Mrs. Hodgkinson.

No Song No Supper

Dec. 7   *More Ways than One*   Daily Ad.
           No Song No Supper

Dec. 10   * *The Road to Ruin*—Holcroft   Daily Ad.
           The Romp

[195]

1792

Seilhamer, III, 63, gives the following cast for *The Road to Ruin:*

Goldfinch	Mr. Hallam	Smith	Mr. Ashton
Mr. Dornton	Mr. Henry	Jacob	Mr. Ryan
Harry Dornton	Mr. Hodgkinson	Widow Warren	Mrs. Pownall
Milford	Mr. Martin	Sophia	Miss Tuke
Silky	Mr. Prigmore	Jenny	Mrs. Hamilton
Sulky	Mr. King	Mrs. Ledger	Mrs. Kenna

Dec. 12	The Road to Ruin No Song No Supper	Daily Ad.
Dec. 14	The Fair Penitent The Agreeable Surprise	Daily Ad.
Dec. 17	The Road to Ruin No Song No Supper	Daily Ad.
Dec. 20	The Dramatist * Don Juan—Delpini	Daily Ad.

Seilhamer, III, 64, gives this cast for *Don Juan:*

Don Juan	Mr. Hodgkinson	Scaramouch	Mr. Prigmore
Don Guzman	Mr. Hallam	Confidante	Mrs. Hamilton
Don Ferdinand	Mr. Chambers	Donna Anna	Mrs. Henry

This bill was postponed from December 19.

Dec. 22	All in the Wrong Don Juan	Daily Ad.
Dec. 26	The Earl of Essex Don Juan	Daily Ad.

Seilhamer, III, 61, gives the following parts for *The Earl of Essex:*

Essex	Mr. Hodgkinson	Queen Elizabeth	Mrs. Kenna
Lord Burleigh	Mr. King	Countess of Nottingham	
Sir Walter Raleigh	Mr. Ashton		Mrs. Hamilton
Lieutenant	Mr. Woolls	Countess of Rutland	Mrs. Henry
Southampton	Mr. Martin		

Dec. 28	* He Would be a Soldier—Pilon The Agreeable Surprize	Daily Ad.

Seilhamer, III, 63, gives the following casts:

He Would be a Soldier

Colonel Talbot	Mr. Henry	Amber	Mr. Ryan
Capt. Crevalt	Mr. Hodgkinson	Harriet	Miss Tuke

[196]

1792

Caleb	Mr. Hallam	Lady Oldstock	Mrs. Rankin
Mandeville	Mr. Martin	Mrs. Wilkins	Mrs. Hamilton
Sir Oliver Oldstock	Mr. Ashton	Betty	Mrs. Kenna
Johnson	Mr. Hammond	Nancy	Miss Brett
Wilkins	Mr. Woolls	Charlotte	Mrs. Henry

The Agreeable Surprize

Lingo	Mr. Hodgkinson	John	Mr. Martin
Eugene	Mr. West	Harry	Mr. Hammond
Compton	Mr. Chambers	Laura	Mrs. Kenna
Sir Felix Friendly	Mr. King	Mrs. Cheshire	Mrs. Rankin
Chicane	Mr. Ashton	Fringe	Mrs. Hamilton
Cudden	Mr. Ryan	Cowslip	Mrs. Hodgkinson

Dec. 29 "For the Entertainment of the Wabash Indian Chiefs" Daily Ad.

The Fashionable Lover
Don Juan

Dec. 31 *He Would be a Soldier* Daily Ad.
No Song No Supper

1793

Jan. 2 Benefit of Mr. Hodgkinson and Mr. King Daily Ad.
Hamlet
The Agreeable Surprize

Jan. 4 Benefit of Mrs. Pownall and Mr. Chambers Daily Ad.
Venice Preserved
The Farmer

Jan. 7 Benefit of Mrs. Hodgkinson and Miss Brett Daily Ad.
* *The Child of Nature*—Mrs. Inchbald
Cymon [*and Sylvia*]

Seilhamer, III, 64, gives these parts for *The Child of Nature:*

Duke Mercia	Mr. Prigmore	Seville	Mr. Ryan
Marquis Almanza	Mr. King	Marchioness Merida	Mrs. Pownall
Count Valentia	Mr. Hodgkinson	Amanthis	Mrs. Hodgkinson
Granada	Mr. Martin		

Jan. 9 Benefit of Mr. West and Mr. Prigmore Daily Ad.
* *Ways and Means*—Colman, Jr.
The Romp

[197]

1793

Seilhamer, III, 64, gives this cast for *Ways and Means:*

Sir David Dunder...Mr. Prigmore	Paul Perry..........Mr. Ashton
Random........Mr. Hodgkinson	Lady Dunder.......Mrs. Rankin
Scruple..............Mr. West	Harriet..............Miss Brett
Tiptoe..............Mr. King	Kitty..........Mrs. Hodgkinson

Jan. 11   *The Fair Penitent*   Daily Ad.
Rosina

Jan. 12   *More Ways than One*   Daily Ad.
The Prisoner at Large

"The Last Night Positively"

The new plays presented by the Old American Company at the Theatre in Southwark between September 26, 1792, and January 12, 1793, were *The Child of Nature, The Mysterious Husband, He Would be a Soldier, The Road to Ruin,* and *Ways and Means.* New afterpieces: *Don Juan, The Farmer, No Song No Supper,* and *The Romp.*

Reappearing plays: *All in the Wrong, The Beaux' Stratagem, The Busy Body, The Clandestine Marriage, Douglas, The Dramatist, The Earl of Essex, The Fair Penitent, The Fashionable Lover, Hamlet, Henry IV (part one), Jane Shore, Love in a Village, The Maid of the Mill, The Miser, More Ways than One, Othello, Richard III, Romeo and Juliet, The School for Scandal, She Stoops to Conquer, Venice Preserved, The West Indian,* and *The Wonder.* Reappearing afterpieces: *The Agreeable Surprise, Catherine and Petruchio, Cymon (and Sylvia), The Deserter, The Devil to Pay, The Flitch of Bacon, Love à la Mode, The Lying Valet, The Mayor of Garratt, Midas, The Padlock, The Poor Soldier, The Prisoner at Large,* and *Rosina.* The new actors were Mr. Bisset, Miss Brett, Mr. Chambers, Mr. and Mrs. Hodgkinson (their first season in America), Mr. King, Mrs. Pownall, and Messrs. Prigmore, Robbins, and West. Reappearing actors: Mr. Ashton, Mr. Durang, Mr. Hallam, Mrs. Hamilton, Mr. Hammond, Mr. and Mrs. Henry, Mrs. Kenna, Mr. Martin, Mrs. Rankin, Mr. Robinson, Mr. Ryan, Miss Tuke, and Mr. Woolls.

NEW THEATRE

Feb. 2   Daily Ad.

The New Theatre in Chesnut Street was opened with a "Grand Concert of Vocal and Instrumental Music." The theatre was at this time "nearly completed." Its first regular season (owing to the yellow fever epidemic of 1793) did not begin till February 17, 1794.

Feb. 7   "A Grand Concert" was given at the New Theatre.   Daily Ad.
"Last Time till Further Notice."

1793

SOUTHWARK THEATRE

July 1	*The Road to Ruin* *Love à la Mode*	Daily Ad.

First night of the Old American Company's season at the Theatre in South-wark from July 1 to August 23, 1793. No casts appeared for this season.

July 3	*The Maid of the Mill* * *The Irishman in London*—Macready	Daily Ad.
July 5	* *Such Things Are*—Mrs. Inchbald *The Devil to Pay*	Daily Ad.
July 8	*George Barnwell* *The Irishman in London*	Daily Ad.
July 10	"(Never here)"	Daily Ad.
	* *Notoriety*—Reynolds *The Prisoner at Large* Dancing by Mr. Durang.	

This was probably postponed to July 12, as then *Notoriety* was announced as "never here," and on July 18 as "Performed but once."

July 12	"(Never here)"	Daily Ad.
	Notoriety *Prisoner at Large*	

This was probably the first appearance of *Notoriety*—see July 10.

July 15	* *The Chapter of Accidents*—Miss Lee *The Lying Valet*	Daily Ad.
July 18	"Performed here but once"	Daily Ad.
	Notoriety *No Song No Supper*	
July 20	* *Wild Oats*—O'Keeffe *The Padlock*	Daily Ad.
July 23	*Wild Oats* *The Romp*	Daily Ad.
July 25	* *Animal Magnetism*—Mrs. Inchbald *Rosina*	Daily Ad.
July 27	"(Not performed in twenty years)"	Daily Ad.
	Lionel and Clarissa *The Register Office*	

[199]

1793

This was probably postponed till August 5, when the same bill, with the note, "Not performed in twenty years" was given. On August 12 *Lionel and Clarissa* was announced as "here but once."

July 29	Benefit of the Distressed French Emigrants	Daily Ad.
	The Clandestine Marriage	
	The Romp	
July 31	*The School for Scandal*	Daily Ad.
	The Deserter	
Aug. 2	*Richard III*	Daily Ad.
	The Rival Candidates	
Aug. 5	"Not performed in twenty years"	Daily Ad.
	Lionel and Clarissa (see July 27)	
	The Register Office	
Aug. 7	*Wild Oats*	Daily Ad.
	* *St. Patrick's Day*—Sheridan	
Aug. 9	"Benefit of the Distressed Emigrants from Hispaniola"	Daily Ad.
	More Ways Than One	
	The Agreeable Surprize	
Aug. 10	"By Desire of the Patriotic Society"	Daily Ad.
	Cato	
	The Irishman in London	
Aug. 12	"Here but once"	Daily Ad.
	Lionel and Clarissa	
	The Critic	
Aug. 14	*The Tempest*	Daily Ad.
	Neptune and Amphitrite	
	Catherine and Petruchio	
Aug. 16	*The Dramatist*	Daily Ad.
	The Farmer	
Aug. 19	*The Child of Nature*	Daily Ad.
	Ways and Means	
Aug. 23	Mrs. Pownall's Benefit	Daily Ad.
	Wild Oats	
	No Song No Supper	

"Mrs. Henry being obliged to go to Bristol for her health, Mrs. Hodgkinson has undertaken the Part of Lady Amaranth at a short notice."

1793

Last night of the Old American Company's season at the Theatre in Southwark from July 1 to August 23, 1793. (*I'll Tell You What* and *Comus* were announced for Mr. Hodgkinson's Benefit on August 26, then postponed till August 28, and then "The Indisposition of Part of the Company still continuing," postponed "till further notice." Before that notice was given, Philadelphia was in the grip of the yellow fever.)

New plays: *Animal Magnetism, The Chapter of Accidents, Notoriety, Such Things Are,* and *Wild Oats.* New afterpieces: *The Irishman in London,* and *Saint Patrick's Day.*

Reappearing plays: *Cato, The Child of Nature, The Clandestine Marriage, The Dramatist, George Barnwell, Lionel and Clarissa, The Maid of the Mill, More Ways than One, Richard III, The Road to Ruin, The School for Scandal,* and *The Tempest.* Reappearing afterpieces: *The Agreeable Surprize, The Critic, The Deserter, The Devil to Pay, The Farmer, Love à la Mode, The Lying Valet, Neptune and Amphitrite, No Song No Supper, The Padlock, The Prisoner at Large, The Register Office, The Rival Candidates, The Romp, Rosina,* and *Ways and Means.*

The only actors' names preserved were Mrs. Henry, Mr. and Mrs. Hodgkinson, Mr. Durang, and Mrs. Pownall. The company doubtless was, however, essentially the same as it had been in the previous season (see January 12, 1793).

NEW THEATRE

1794

| Feb. 17 | *The Castle of Andalusia* | Daily Ad. |

Don Scipio	Mr. Finch	Phillipo...... Mr. Darley, Jun.
Don Caesar	Mr. Darley	Banditti...... Messrs, Harwood,
Don Fernanda	Mr. Marshall	Francis, Cleveland, Warrell,
Don Juan	Mr. Morris	Blisset, etc., etc.
Don Alphonso	Mr. Moreton	Victoria.......... Mrs. Warrell
Pedrillo	Mr. Bates	Lorenza.......... Mrs. Marshall
Spado	Mr. Wignell	Isabella............. Mrs. Bates
Sanguino	Mr. Green	Catalina....... Miss Broadhurst

Who's the Dupe?

Doiley	Mr. Morris	Gradus.......... Mr. Harwood
Sandford	Mr. Moreton	Miss Doiley........ Mrs. Francis
Granger	Mr. Cleveland	Charlotte.......... Mrs. Rowson

"—Previous to the opera, an occasional address."

This was the opening night of Wignell and Reinagle's New Theatre (in Chesnut Street). (Concerts had been given in it before it was completed—see Feb. 2, 1793.) The first season lasted from February 17 to July 18, 1794.

1794

With the exception of Mr. Morris and Mr. Wignell, all the actors were new to the city.

Feb. 19   *Isabella*   Gen. Ad.

Count Baldwin	Mr. Whitlock	Belford	Mr. Cleveland
Biron	Mr. Fennell	Pedro	Mr. Green
Carlos	Mr. Marshall	Officer	Mr. Warrell
Villeroy	Mr. Wignell	Isabella	Mrs. Whitlock
Sampson	Mr. Francis	Nurse	Mrs. Rowson

Rosina

Belville	Mr. Marshall	2nd Irishman	Mr. Blissett
Capt. Belville	Mr. Moreton	Rosina	Mrs. Warrell
William	Mr. Francis	Dorcas	Mrs. Bates
Rustic	Mr. Warrell	Phoebe	Miss Broadhurst
1st Irishman	Mr. Green		

First appearance of Mr. Fennell and Mr. and Mrs. Whitlock.

Feb. 21   *The Dramatist*   Gen. Ad.

Lord Scratch	Mr. Bates	Vapid	Mr. Chalmers
Neville	Mr. Cleveland	Mrs. Courtney	Mrs. Francis
Floriville	Mr. Moreton	Lady Waitford	Mrs. Shaw
Willoughby	Mr. Green	Letty	Mrs. Rowson
Ennui	Mr. Finch	Marianne	Mrs. Marshall
Peter	Mr. Francis		

HighlandReel—Mr. Francis, Miss Williams, & Mrs. De Marque

The Flitch of Bacon

Justice Benbow	Mr. Warrell	Tipple	Mr. Francis
Major Benbow	Mr. Harwood	Eliza	Miss Broadhurst
Captain Greville	Mr. Marshall	Kilderkin	Mr. Warrell
Captain Wilson	Mr. Darley	Ned	Mr. Blissett

First appearance of Mr. Chalmers, Mrs. Cleveland, Mrs. De Marque, Mrs. Shaw, and Miss Williams (or Willems—later Mrs. Green).

Feb. 24   *Venice Preserved*   Daily Ad.

Duke of Venice	Mr. Finch	Spinosa	Mr. Harwood
Priuli	Mr. Whitlock	Elliot	Mr. Moreton
Bedamar	Mr. Marshall	Durand	Mr. Warrell
Pierre	Mr. Fennell	Officer	Mr. Francis
Jaffier	Mr. Wignell	Belvidera	Mrs. Whitlock
Renault	Mr. Green		

1794

Feb. 24 (cont.)   *The Lying Valet*

Sharp	Mr. Bates	Melissa	Mrs. Francis
Gargle	Mr. Moreton	Mrs. Gadabout	Mrs. Bates
Justice Guttle	Mr. Warrell	Mrs. Trippet	Mrs. Rowson
Beau Trippet	Mr. Harwood	Betty Pry	Mrs. Shaw
Drunken Cook	Mr. Francis		

Feb. 26   *Love in a Village*   Daily Ad.

Sir William Meadows	Mr. Morris	Hodge	Mr. Francis
Justice Woodcock	Mr. Bates	Deborah	Mrs. Shaw
Hawthorn	Mr. Darley	Lucinda	Mrs. Warrell
Young Meadows	Mr. Marshall	Rosetta	Mrs. Marshall
Eustace	Mr. Darley, Jr.	Madge	Miss Broadhurst

"Servants at Statue—Messrs. Warrell, Blissett, Rowson, Mrs. Rowson, Mrs. Bates, and Mrs. De Marque, etc."

The Guardian

Mr. Heartly	Mr. Whitlock	Servant	Master Warrell
Sir Charles Clackit	Mr. Morris	Lucy	Mrs. Rowson
Young Clackit	Mr. Finch	Harriet	Mrs. Marshall

* *The Caledonian Frolic*

First appearance of Mr. Rowson (the prompter) and Master [T] Warrell.

Feb. 28   *The Jealous Wife*   Daily Ad.

Oakly	Mr. Fennell	John	Mr. Warrell
Major Oakly	Mr. Whitlock	Tom	Mr. Francis
Charles	Mr. Moreton	Servant	Master Warrell
Russet	Mr. Wignell	Mrs. Oakly	Mrs. Whitlock
Sir Harry Beagle	Mr. Chalmers	Lady Freelove	Mrs. Shaw
Lord Trinket	Mr. Finch	Harriet	Mrs. Francis
Captain O'Cutter	Mr. Bates	Toilet	Mrs. Rowson
William	Mr. Darley, Jr.	Chambermaid	Miss Willems

"A new Comic Dance, composed by Mr. Francis, called
* *The Scheming Clown,* or the Sportsman deceived—by
Mr. Francis, Mr. Darley, Jun., & Mrs. De Marque."

The Liar

Old Wilding	Mr. Whitlock	Miss Granthan	Mrs. Francis
Young Wilding	Mr. Chalmers	Miss Godfrey	Mrs. Cleveland
Sir James Elliot	Mr. Cleveland	Kitty	Mrs. Rowson
Papillion	Mr. Finch		

[203]

1794

March 3   *School for Scandal*   Daily Ad.

Sir Peter Teazle	Mr. Bates	Moses..............Mr. Francis
Sir Oliver Surface	Mr. Morris	Snake...............Mr. Green
Joseph Surface	Mr. Wignell	Trip...............Mr. Moreton
Charles Surface	Mr. Chalmers	Lady Teazle........Mrs. Morris
Sir Benj. Backbite	Mr. Finch	Lady Sneerwell......Mrs. Francis
Crabtree	Mr. Harwood	Mrs. Candour........Mrs. Shaw
Rowley	Mr. Warrell	Maria...........Mrs. Cleveland

The Poor Soldier

Captain Fitzroy	Mr. Darley	Bagatelle..........Mr. Marshall
Father Luke	Mr. Finch	Boy...........Master J. Warrell
Dermot	Mr. Darley, Jr.	Norah..........Miss Broadhurst
Patrick	Mr. Moreton	Kathleen..........Miss Willems
Darby	Mr. Wignell	

First appearance of Master J. Warrell (or "Mr. Warrell, Jr.").

March 5   * *The Carmelite*—Cumberland   Daily Ad.
               * *The Spoiled Child*—Bickerstaff

March 7   * *Every One Has His Fault*—Mrs. Inchbald   Daily Ad.

Lord Norland	Mr. Whitlock	Porter.............Mr. Warrell
Sir Robert Ramble	Mr. Chalmers	Edward..........Mrs. Marshall
Mr. Solus	Mr. Morris	Lady Eleanor......Mrs. Whitlock
Mr. Harmony	Mr. Bates	Mrs. Placid........Mrs. Rowson
Capt. Irwin	Mr. Fennell	Miss Spinster.........Mrs. Bates
Mr. Placid	Mr. Moreton	Miss Wooburn......Mrs. Morris
Hammond	Mr. Green	

* *The Village Lawyer*—Macready

Scout	Mr. Harwood	Charles...........Mr. Cleveland
Snarl	Mr. Francis	Mrs. Scout.........Mrs. Rowson
Sheepface	Mr. Bates	Kate...............Mrs. Bates
Justice Mittimus	Mr. Warrell	

March 8   *Every One Has His Fault*   Daily Ad.

Cast as for March 7.

The Poor Soldier

"The Characters the same as on Monday Last." [March 3]

March 10   * *Robin Hood*—MacNally   Daily Ad.

Robin Hood	Mr. Darley	Rutlekin.............Mr. Bates
Little John	Mr. Wignell	Friar Tuck........Mr. Whitlock

1794

Scarlet............Mr. Francis	Edwin............Mr. Marshall
Bowman..........Mr. Warrell	Clorinda..........Mrs. Warrell
Allan-a-Dale.....Mr. Darley, Jr.	Annette..........Mrs. Marshall
Stella............Miss Willems	Angelina.......Miss Broadhurst

Archers..........Messrs. Blissett, Warrell Jun., DeMoulin, Lee, Bason, etc.

Who's the Dupe?

Cast as for February 17, save—

Charlotte..........Mrs. Marshall

First appearance of Messrs. Bason, and Lee. Mr. DeMoulins (or De Moulin) is doubtless the Mr. DuMoulin of 1791.

March 12   *Douglas*   Daily Ad.

Lord Randolph......Mr. Green	Young Norval......Mr. Moreton
Glenalvon.........Mr. Fennell	Lady Randolph....Mrs. Whitlock
Old Norval.......Mr. Whitlock	Anna...........Mrs. Cleveland

The Farmer

Colonel Dormant.....Mr. Green	Rundy.............Mr. Francis
Valentine.........Mr. Marshall	Farmer Stubble......Mr. Morris
Fairly.............Mr. Warrell	Louisa...........Mrs. Warrell
Flummery..........Mr. Blissett	Betty Blackberry....Mrs. Rowson
Farmer Blackberry....Mr. Darley	Mollie Maybush..Miss Broadhurst
Jemmy Jumps........Mr. Bates	Landlady..........Mrs. Bates

March 14   *Robin Hood*   Daily Ad.

Cast as for March 10, except:

Annette—Mrs. Francis

and in addition—

Shepherdesses..........Mrs. Bates, Mrs. Cleveland, Mrs. Rowson, Mrs. De Marque, Mrs. Finch, and Miss Rowson.

The Liar

Cast as for February 28.

First appearance of Mrs. Finch and Miss Rowson.

March 17   *Isabella*   Gen. Ad.

Cast as for February 19, except:

Carlos..............Mr. Green   Pedro.............Mr. Francis

1794

March 17 (cont.)   *Saint Patrick's Day*

Lieut. O'Conner....Mr. Whitlock
Justice Credulous......Mr. Bates
Dr. Rosy...........Mr. Francis
Trounce.............Mr. Green
Flint.............Mr. Harwood
Blacksmith.........Mr. Moreton

Servant........Master J. Warrell
Bridget............Mrs. Rowson
Laura............Mrs. Francis
Soldiers........Messrs. Finch, de
    Moulin, Darley, Jr., and Cleveland.

March 19   *The Castle of Andalusia*   Gen. Ad.

Cast as for February 17, save that Mr. Francis was
not mentioned in Banditti.

* *The Sailor's Landlady*—Francis (pantomimical dance)

Jack...............Mr. Francis
Ned Halyard....Mr. Darley, Jun.
Sailors...Messrs. Warrell, Blissett,
    Warrell, Jun., Lee, Bason, and
    De Moulin

Lasses......Mrs. Cleveland, Mrs.
    Bates, Miss Rowson, and Miss
    Willems
Landlady...........*Mr.* Rowson
Orange Girl.....Mrs. DeMarque

The Spoiled Child

Little Pickle.......Mrs. Marshall
Old Pickle...........Mr. Finch
Tag................Mr. Francis
John..............Mr. Blissett
Thomas............Mr. Darley

Miss Pickle........Mrs. Rowson
Maria..........Mrs. Cleveland
Margery............Mrs. Bates
Susan............Miss Willems

March 21   *The School for Wives*   Gen Ad.

General Savage.......Mr. Bates
Belville...........Mr. Chalmers
Torrington.........Mr. Morris
Leeson...........Mr. Moreton
Captain Savage....Mr. Cleveland
Connolly.........Mr. Whitlock
Spruce.............Mr. Francis
Leech..............Mr. Green
Crow..............Mr. Blissett

Wolf..............Mr. Warrell
Miss Walsingham....Mrs. Morris
Mrs. Belville......Mrs. Whitlock
Lady Rachel Mildew............
    Mrs. Rowson
Mrs. Tempest........Mrs. Bates
Miss Leeson.......Mrs. Francis
Maid.............Miss Willems

The Deserter

Henry............Mr. Marshall
Russet.............Mr. Darley
Skirmish.............Mr. Bates
Simkin.............Mr. Francis

Flint................Mr. Green
Louisa..........Mrs. Marshall
Jenny..........Miss Broadhurst
Margaretta..........Mrs. Bates

1794

| March 22 | *The Jealous Wife* | Gen. Ad. |

Oakly.............Mr. Fennell
Major Oakly......Mr. Whitlock
Charles............Mr. Moreton
Russet.............Mr. Wignell
Sir Harry Beagle...Mr. Chalmers
Lord Trinket........Mr. Finch
Capt. O'Cutter.......Mr. Bates
William..........Mr. Darley, Jr.

John..............Mr. Warrell
Tom...............Mr. Francis
Servant.........Master Warrell
Mrs. Oakly.....Mrs. Whitlock
Lady Freelove......Mrs. Morris
Harriet............Mrs. Rowson
Toilet............Miss Willems

The Sailor's Landlady

Cast as for March 19

The Virgin Unmasked

Goodwill...........Mr. Warrell
Coupee............Mr. Francis
Quaver...........Mr. Marshall

Blister...............Mr. Bates
Thomas.............Mr. Green
Lucy.............Mrs. Marshall

March 24   "Benefit of American Citizens, Captives in Algiers"   Gen. Ad.

Every One Has His Fault

Cast as for March 7.

The Sailor's Landlady

Cast as for March 19

The Poor Soldier

Cast as for March 3.

| March 26 | *The Fair Penitent* | Gen. Ad. |

Sciolto............Mr. Whitlock
Altamont............Mr. Green
Horatio.............Mr. Fennell
Lothario...........Mr. Moreton

Rossano.............Mr. Francis
Calista..........Mrs. Whitlock
Lavinia............Mrs. Francis
Lucilla............Mrs. Rowson

The Sailor's Landlady

Cast as for March 19.

Catherine and Petruchio

Petruchio.........Mr. Chalmers
Baptista............Mr. Warrell
Hortensio........Mr. Cleveland
Grumio.............Mr. Morris
Music Master.......Mr. Francis
Biondello.........Mr. Harwood

Pedro..............Mr. Green
Tailor.............Mr. Blissett
Catherine..........Mrs. Morris
Bianca..........Mrs. Cleveland
Curtis..............Mrs. Bates

1794

March 28   *The Dramatist*   Daily Ad.

Cast as for February 21, except:

Lady Waitford......Mrs. Rowson   Letty...........Mrs. Cleveland

The Sailor's Landlady

Cast as for March 19.

The Farmer

Cast as for March 12.

March 29   *Love in a Village*   Gen. Ad.

Cast as for February 26:

Sir Wm. Meadows..Mr. Warrell   Deborah..........Mrs. Rowson
Eustace..........Mr. Cleveland   Madge...........Miss Willems

And Warrell is not mentioned as a servant, while Miss Rowson is.

The Village Lawyer

Cast as for March 7, except:

Charles.........Mr. Darley, Jr.

March 31   *The Grecian Daughter*   Gen. Ad

Evander...........Mr. Whitlock   Arcas..............Mr. Francis
Philotas...........Mr. Moreton   Greek Herald........Mr. Finch
Melanthon...........Mr. Green   Greek Officer.....Mr. Harwood
Phocion.........Mr. Cleveland   Euphrasia.......Mrs. Whitlock
Dionysius..........Mr. Fennell   Erixene.........Mrs. Cleveland
Calippus..........Mr. Warrell

The Sailor's Landlady

Cast as for March 19.

The Spoiled Child

Cast as for March 19.

April 2   *The Grecian Daughter*   Daily Ad.

Cast as for March 31.

* *The Son-in-Law*—O'Keeffe

Cranky.............Mr. Finch   Landlord..........Mr. Warrell
Bowkit.............Mr. Francis   John...........Mr. Darley, Jr.
Bouquet..........Mr. Moreton   Sig. Arionelli......Mr. Marshall
Vinegar.............Mr. Bates   Cecilia...........Mrs. Warrell
Idle..............Mr. Harwood   Dolce............Miss Willems
Orator Mum........Mr. Blissett

1794

April 4   * The Highland Reel—O'Keeffe   Gen. Ad.

Croudy	Mr. Harwood	Capt. Dash	Mr. Moreton
Laird of Col	Mr. Green	Serjt. Jack	Mr. Darley
Raasay	Mr. Warrell	Apie	Mr. Blissett
MacGilpin	Mr. Finch	Benin	Master J. Warrell
Sandy	Mr. Marshall	Moggy	Mrs. Marshall
Charley	Mr. Francis	Jenny	Mrs. Warrell
Shelty	Mr. Bates		

The Lying Valet

Cast as for February 24, except: "Gargle" is not cast, and

Drunken Cook	Mr. Blissett	Mrs. Trippet	Mrs. Bates
Mrs. Gadabout	Mrs. Cleveland	Kitty Pry	Mrs. Rowson

Added: "Gayless" .... Mr. Green

April 5   *The Highland Reel*   Daily Ad.
               Catherine and Petruchio

April 7   *Macbeth*   Gen. Ad.

Macbeth	Mr. Fennell	Seyton	Mr. Francis
Duncan	Mr. Green	Doctor	Mr. De Moulin
Malcolm	Mr. Cleveland	Messenger	Mr. Blissett
Donalbane	Master Warrell	Lady Macbeth	Mrs. Whitlock
Banquo	Mr. Whitlock	Gentlewoman	Mrs. Cleveland
Macduff	Mr. Moreton	Hecate	Mr. Darley
Lenox	Mr. Harwood	First Witch	Mr. Bates
Fleance	Master T. Warrell	Second Witch	Mr. Finch
Siward	Mr. Warrell	Third Witch	Mr. Wignell

The Flitch of Bacon

Cast as for February 21, except:

Major Benbow .... Mr. Bates

April 9   *The Rivals*   Gen. Ad.

Sir Anthony Absolute	Mr. Morris	David	Mr. Francis
Capt. Absolute	Mr. Moreton	Coachman	Mr. Warrell
Faulkland	Mr. Fennell	Mrs. Malaprop	Mrs. Shaw
Acres	Mr. Bates	Lydia Languish	Mrs. Marshall
Sir Lucius O'Trigger		Julia	Mrs. Francis
	Mr. Whitlock	Lucy	Mrs. Rowson
Fag	Mr. Marshall	Boy	Master T. Warrell

The Sailor's Landlady

Cast as for March 19.

1794

April 9 (cont.) *The Agreeable Surprize*

Sir Felix Friendly.....Mr. Finch	Cudden.............Mr. Blissett
Compton............Mr. Darley	Lingo...............Mr. Bates
Eugene............Mr. Marshall	Laura.........Miss Broadhurst
Chicane...........Mr. Warrell	Mrs. Cheshire........Mrs. Shaw
John..............Mr. Francis	Cowslip..........Mrs. Marshall
Thomas.............Mr. Green	Fringe.............Mrs. Rowson
Farmer Stump....Mr. De Moulin	

April 11 *The Gamester* Gen. Ad.

Beverly.............Mr. Fennell	Dawson...........Mr. Moreton
Stukely............Mr. Wignell	Waiter..........Mr. De Moulin
Lewson..........Mr. Cleveland	Mrs. Beverly.....Mrs. Whitlock
Jarvis.............Mr. Whitlock	Charlotte..........Mrs. Francis
Bates..............Mr. Green	Lucy............Mrs. Cleveland

The Sailor's Landlady

Cast as for March 19.

The Guardian

Cast as for February 26, except:

Servant.........Mr. Blissett

April 12 *Macbeth* Daily Ad.

Cast as for April 7.

Miss in Her Teens

Captain Loveit........Mr. Green	Jasper..............Mr. Francis
Fribble............Mr. Marshall	Tag...............Mrs. Rowson
Captain Flash......Mr. Chalmers	Miss Biddy........Mrs. Marshall
Puff...............Mr. Morris	

April 14 *The Road to Ruin* Daily Ad.

Dornton..........Mr. Whitlock	Sheriff's Officer.....Mr. Warrell
Harry Dornton.......Mr. Green	Jacob.............Mr. Blissett
Sulky..............Mr. Finch	Marker.........Master Warrell
Silky................Mr. Bates	Postillion......Master T. Warrell
Goldfinch.........Mr. Chalmers	Mrs. Warren........Mrs. Shaw
Milford..........Mr. Cleveland	Sophia............Mrs. Marshall
Smith.............Mr. Moreton	Jenny.............Mrs. Francis
Hosier............Mr. Harwood	Mrs. Ledger.........Mrs. Bates

The Sailor's Landlady

Cast as for March 19.

[210]

1794

The Agreeable Surprize
Cast as for April 9.

April 16   *The Belle's Stratagem*   Gen. Ad.
               Saint Patrick's Day

April 17   *The Highland Reel*   Daily Ad.

Cast as for April 4.

Miss in Her Teens

Cast as for April 12, except:

Fribble.........Mr. Finch

April 21   *Richard III*   Gen. Ad.

King Henry VI....Mr. Whitlock	Oxford.............Mr. Blissett
Prince Edward....Master Warrell	Lieutenant of the Tower.........
Duke of York..Master T. Warrell	Mr. Finch
Duke of Gloster....Mr. Chalmers	Lord Stanley........Mr. Green
Duke of Buckingham...........	Lord Mayor.........Mr. Bates
Mr. Wignell	Tyrell..........Mr. DeMoulin
Earl of Richmond....Mr. Fennell	Blunt.............Mr. Warrell
Duke of Norfolk....Mr. Moreton	Queen Elizabeth....Mrs. Morris
Ratcliff............Mr. Francis	Lady Anne........Miss Oldfield
Catesby.........Mr. Cleveland	Duchess of York......Mrs. Shaw
Tressel...........Mr. Marshall	

The Sailor's Llandlady

Cast as for March 19.

The Son-in-Law

Cast as for April 2.

First appearance of Miss Oldfield.

April 23   *The School for Scandal*   Gen. Ad.
     * *Peeping Tom of Coventry*—O'Keeffe

April 25   *Hamlet*   Gen. Ad.
       The Wrangling Lovers

April 26   *The Rivals*   Gen. Ad.
       * *La Forêt Noire*

(pantomime—"originally at the Theatre in Paris")

See April 30 for a cast.

[211]

1794

April 28   *Hamlet*   Daily Ad.

Hamlet............Mr. Fennell		Bernardo...........Mr. Warrell
King...............Mr. Green		Marcellus........Mr. Harwood
Ghost...........Mr. Whitlock		Osric...............Mr. Finch
Horatio..........Mr. Marshall		Officer.............Mr. Blissett
Laertes...........Mr. Moreton		Gravediggers...... { Mr. Bates
Polonius...........Mr. Morris		Mr. Wignell
Rosencranz.........Mr. Francis		Queen..............Mrs. Shaw
Guildenstern......Mr. Cleveland		Ophelia..........Mrs. Marshall
Player King......Mr. DeMoulin		Player Queen......Mrs. Rowson
Francisco........Mr. Darley, Jr.		

La Forêt Noire

April 30   *The Highland Reel*   Daily Ad.

Cast as for April 4.

La Forêt Noire

Geronte............Mr. Green	Lucille....Madame Gardie, "from
Lanzedan..........Mr. Moreton	the Theatre at Paris, being her
Adolphe......Master T. Warrell	second appearance on this
Pince..............Mr. Francis	Stage."
Lubin..........Master Warrell	Le Terreur........Mr. Marshall
Fronte.............Mr. Warrell	Sans Quartier......Mr. Cleveland
Pasquin............Mr. Darley	Robbers......Messrs. Blissett, De
	Moulin, Lee, Bason, &c.

"Books, descriptive of the Pantomime, to be had at the Theatre."

First *mention* of Mme. Gardie, though "her second appearance." Her first appearance was probably on April 26, when *La Forêt Noire* was first produced.

May 2   *Othello*   Gen. Ad.
         Peeping Tom of Coventry

May 3   *The Dramatist*   Gen. Ad.
         La Forêt Noire

May 5   *Inkle and Yarico*   Gen. Ad.
       The Wrangling Lovers

May 7   *The Provoked Husband*   Gen. Ad.

Lord Townly.......Mr. Fennell		Servant.........Mr. Darley, Jr.
Manly..............Mr. Green		Lady Townly.......Mrs. Morris
Sir Francis..........Mr. Morris		Lady Grace........Mrs. Francis
Count Basset.........Mr. Finch		Lady Wronghead......Mrs. Shaw
Squire Richard......Mr. Blissett		Jenny...........Miss Broadhurst
John Moody.........Mr. Bates		Trusty............Miss Willems

1794

Poundage........Mr. DeMoulin
Constable.........Mr. Warrell
James..........Master Warrell

Mrs. Motherly.......Mrs. Bates
Myrtilla.........Mrs. Cleveland

La Forêt Noire

May 9
Inkle and Yarico
The Wrangling Lovers
Gen. Ad.

May 10
Othello
Peeping Tom of Coventry
Gen. Ad.

May 12
The Recruiting Officer
La Forêt Noire
Gen. Ad.

May 14
Robin Hood
Gen. Ad.

Cast as for March 10, except:

Clorinda..........Mrs. Oldmixon (late Miss George, from
The Theatre Royal, Drury Lane, London, being her
first appearance in America).

Who's the Dupe?

Cast as for February 17.

May 16   *The Maid of the Mill*
Gen. Ad.

Lord Aimworth....Mr. Marshall
Sir Harry Sycamore....Mr. Bates
Mervin..........Mr. Cleveland
Fairfield.........Mr. Whitlock
Giles.............Mr. Darley

Ralph.............Mr. Wignell
Lady Sycamore.......Mrs. Shaw
Theodosia.........Miss Willems
Patty.............Mrs. Warrell
Fanny..........Mrs. Oldmixon

* *The Fruitless Precaution* ("comic pastoral Ballet")—Francis
by M. Bellona, Messrs. Blissett, Darley, Jr., T. Warrell,
Francis, Mrs. De Marque, and Madame Gardie.

* *The Quality Binding*—Rose

Mr. Level..........Mr. Green
Col. Modish......Mr. Harwood
Lord Simper.......Mr. Moreton
Sir Wm. Wealthy....Mr. Francis
First appearance of M. Bellona.

Mr. Plainwell.......Mr. Bates
John...............Mr. Blissett
William.........Mr. Darley, Jr.
Mrs. Level........Mrs. Francis

May 19   Mr. Fennell's Benefit
Gen. Ad.
* *The Surrender of Calais*—Colman, Jr.

King Edward......Mr. Moreton
Sir Walter Many....Mr. Warrell
Ribemont..........Mr. Fennell

Crier...............Mr. Blissett
First Gallowsmaker............
Mr. Harwood

[213]

1794

May 19 (cont.)

LeGloire..............Mr. Bates
St. Pierre.........Mr. Whitlock
John de Vienne......Mr. Green
Old Man........Mr. DeMoulin
Sergeant...........Mr. Wignell
O'Carrol.........Mr. Marshall

Second Gallowsmaker...........
          Mr. Darley, Jr
Queen..............Mrs. Shaw
Madelon.........Mrs. Marshall
Julia...............Mrs. Francis
John D'Aire......Mr. Cleveland

* The Sultan—Bickerstaff

Solyman...........Mr. Moreton
Osmyn...........Mr. Harwood
Elmira............Mrs. Francis

Ismene..........Miss Broadhurst
Roxalana.........Mrs. Oldmixon

May 21   Mr. Chalmer's Benefit   Gen. Ad.

The West Indian

Stockwell..........Mr. Fennell
Belcour..........Mr. Chalmers
Capt. Dudley.........Mr. Finch
Charles Dudley....Mr. Cleveland
Maj. O'Flaherty...Mr. Whitlock
Stukely..........Mr. DeMoulin
Fulmer.............Mr. Green
Varland.............Mr. Bates

Sailor..............Mr. Blissett
Lady Rusport........Mrs. Shaw
Charlotte........Mrs. Marshall
Louisa Dudley.....Miss Willems
Mrs. Fulmer.......Mrs. Rowson
Lucy...........Mrs. Cleveland
Housekeeper.........Mrs. Bates

* The Triumph of Mirth

Harlequin........Mr. Chalmers
Don Pasticio......Mr. DeMoulin
Don Ronando Songrado.........
         Mr. Cleveland
Stridero.............Mr. Green
Magician...........Mr. Warrell

Waiter..........Master Warrell
Statuary.........Mr. Darley, Jr.
Clown............Mr. Blissett
Mirth..........Miss Broadhurst
Colombine.........Miss Willems

May 23   Mr. Bates' Benefit   Gen. Ad.

The Duenna

Don Jerome..........Mr. Finch
Don Ferdinand.....Mr. Marshall
Antonio............Mr. Francis
Carlos.........Mr. Darley, Jr.
Lopez.............Mr. Blissett
Father Paul........Mr. Darley
Father Frank.......Mr. Warrell

Starved Friar......Mr. DeMoulin
Isaac Mendoza........Mr. Bates
Clara...........Miss Broadhurst
Louisa............Mrs. Warrell
Flora............Mrs. Cleveland
Margaret............Mrs. Shaw

1794

May 23 (cont.) *Robinson Crusoe*

Robinson Crusoe....Mr. Whitlock	Spaniard.........Mr. Cleveland
Pantaloon.......Mr. DeMoulin	Captain............Mr. Darley
Pierot.........Mr. Darley, Jr.	Friday..............Mr. Bates
Clown.............Mr. Blissett	Columbine.........Miss Willems

"Mr. Quesnay, from the Opera-House in Paris, will dance
Une Entre Pastorale, Being his first Appearance in America"

May 26 Mr. Morris's Night Gen. Ad.

She Would and She Would Not—Cibber

Don Manuel........Mr. Morris	Diego...........Mr. DeMoulin
Don Philip........Mr. Fennell	Vasquez........Master Warrell
Don Lewis......Mr. Cleveland	Hypolita.........Mrs. Marshall
Octavio.............Mr. Green	Rosara............Mrs. Morris
Trapanti.........Mr. Chalmers	Flora.............Mrs. Francis
Soto...............Mr. Bates	Villetta.............Mrs. Shaw
Corrigidore........Mr. Warrell	

The Fruitless Precaution

The Prize—Hoare

Dr. Lenitive.......Mr. Harwood	Boy.........Master T. Warrell
Mr. Heartwell.....Mr. Moreton	Juba............Miss Broadhurst
Mr. Caddy..........Mr. Finch	Mrs. Caddy.......Mrs. Rowson
Label.............Mr. Wignell	Caroline........Mrs. Oldmixon

May 28 Mr. Whitlock's Night Gen. Ad.

Julia—Jephson

Duke of Guise........Mr. Finch	Manon...........Mr. Whitlock
Durazzo.............Mr. Green	Servant.........Master Warrell
Mentevole.........Mr. Fennell	Fulvia.............Mrs. Shaw
Marcellus.........Mr. Moreton	Julia.............Mrs. Whitlock
Camillo.........Mr. Cleveland	Olympia...........Mrs. Francis
Officer.........Mr. De Moulin	Nerina..........Mrs. Cleveland

Bon Ton—Garrick

Sir John Trotley...Mr. Whitlock	Mignon.............Mr. Blissett
Lord Minikin......Mr. Moreton	Lady Minikin........Mrs. Shaw
Col. Tivy........Mr. Cleveland	Miss Tittup......Mrs. Oldmixon
Jessamy..........Mr. Harwood	Gymp.............Mrs. Rowson
Davy..............Mr. Bates	

Julia was advertised on June 23 as "never here," which, if true, would in-

[215]

1794

dicate that *Julia* was not given on May 28. However, as Mr. Whitlock had no later benefit, the "never here" of June 23 was probably a mistake.

May 30   Mr. Marshall's Benefit   Daily Ad.

* As You Like It—Shakespeare

Orlando...........Mr. Moreton	Charles.............Mr. Rowson
Adam.............Mr. Whitlock	Touchstone...........Mr. Bates
Duke Senior.......Mr. Harwood	Corin.............Mr. De Moulin
Duke Frederick......Mr. Warrell	Sylvius...........Mr. Cleveland
Amiens..........Mr. Marshall	William.............Mr. Francis
Jaques...........Mr. Chalmers	Rosalind..........Mrs. Marshall
Le Beau............Mr. Finch	Celia..............Mrs. Francis
Oliver..............Mr. Green	Phoebe...........Mrs. Cleveland
Jaques De Bois....Mr. Darley, Jr.	Audrey..............Mrs. Shaw
Dennis.......Master T. Warrell	

* Hartford Bridge—Pearce

June 2   Mrs. Warrell's Benefit   Gen. Ad.

Lionel and Clarissa

Sir John Flowerdale............ Mr. Whitlock	Jenkins..............Mr. Darley
	Lady Oldboy.........Mrs. Shaw
Colonel Oldboy........Mr. Bates	Clarissa..........Mrs. Warrell
Jessamy..........Mr. Moreton	Diana...........Mrs. Oldmixon
Lionel...........Mr. Marshall	Jenny.............Miss Willems
Harman..........Mr. Cleveland	

* Modern Antiques—O'Keeffe

Cockletop...........Mr. Francis	Mrs. Cockletop.......Mrs. Shaw
Frank..............Mr. Green	Mrs. Camomile.....Mrs. Rowson
Joey.................Mr. Bates	Belinda..........Mrs. Cleveland
Napkin.............Mr. Blissett	Nan...............Mrs. Francis
Hearty..........Mr. DeMoulin	Flounce..............Mrs. Bates
Thomas............Mr. Warrell	Betty..............Miss Rowson

June 4   Mrs. Marshall's Benefit   Gen. Ad.

Romeo and Juliet

Romeo.............Mr. Fennell	Friar John..........Mr. Warrell
Escalus..............Mr. Finch	Balthazar........Mr. Darley, Jr.
Paris..............Mr. Moreton	Apothecary..........Mr. Francis
Montagu........Mr. De Moulin	Peter...............Mr. Blissett
Mercutio..........Mr. Chalmers	Page........Master T. Warrell
Benvolio..........Mr. Cleveland	Juliet............Mrs. Marshall
Tybalt............Mr. Harwood	Lady Capulet.......Mrs. Rowson

[216]

1794

Capulet..............Mr. Green   Nurse..............Mrs. Shaw
Friar Laurence....Mr. Whitlock

The Romp

Watty Cockney......Mr. Francis   Priscilla Tomboy...Mrs. Marshall
Barnacle.............Mr. Finch   Penelope..........Miss Willems
Old Cockney......Mr. DeMoulin   Mme. Le Blond...Mrs. Cleveland
Capt. Sightly.......Mr. Marshall   Quasheba.........Miss Rowson

June 6   Mr. Darley's Night   Gen. Ad.

Every One Has His Fault

Cast as for March 7, except:

Edward..........Master Warrell

No Song No Supper

Frederick.........Mr. Marshall   Dorothy.............Mrs. Shaw
Crop..............Mr. Darley   Louisa..........Miss Broadhurst
Endless..........Mr. Harwood   Margaretta......Mrs. Oldmixon
Robin...............Mr. Bates   Nelly.............Miss Willems
William.........Mr. J. Darley

(Mr. J. Darley was Mr. Darley, Jr.)

June 9   Mrs. Morris's Benefit   Gen. Ad.

* The Battle of Hexham—Colman, Jr.

Montague...........Mr. Green   Barton............Mr. Whitlock
Warwick........Mr. Cleveland   Gondibert..........Mr. Fennell
Somerset.........Mr. Warrell   Gregory Gubbins......Mr. Bates
Le Varenne.......Mr. Moreton   Prince Edward................
Corporal.........Mr. Harwood   Master. T. Warrell
Drummer..........Mr. Francis   Margaret of Anjou.............
Fifer.............Mr. Blissett   Mrs. Whitlock
Fool..............Mr. Wignell   Adeline..........Mrs. Marshall

The True Born Irishman

Murrough O'Dougherty........   James..........Mr. De Moulin
                Mr. Whitlock   Mrs. Diggerty.....Mrs. Morris
Count Mushroom....Mr. Wignell   Lady Kennigad.......Mrs. Bates
Counsellor Hamilton...Mr. Green   Lady Bab Frightful..Mrs. Rowson
Major Gamble.......Mr. Morris   Mrs. Gazette:....Mrs. Cleveland
John..............Mr. Blissett   Kitty Farrell.......Miss Willems
William..........Mr. Darley, Jr.

[217]

1794

June 11   Mrs. Whitlock's Night   Gen. Ad.

The Mourning Bride

Manuel...........Mr. Whitlock   Selim............Mr. Harwood
Osmyn............Mr. Fennell   Alonzo...........Mr. Warrell
Gonzales.........Mr. Green   Almeria..........Mrs. Morris
Garcia...........Mr. Wignell   Zara.............Mrs. Whitlock
Heli.............Mr. Cleveland   Leonora..........Mrs. Francis
Perez............Mr. Francis

Three Weeks after Marriage

Sir Charles Racket..Mr. Chalmers   Lady Racket......Mrs. Whitlock
Drugget..............Mr. Bates   Mrs. Drugget.....Mrs. Rowson
Lovelace.........Mr. Moreton   Nancy............Mrs. Francis
Woodley..........Mr. Cleveland   Dimitry..........Mrs. Shaw
Servant..........Mr. Darley, Jr.

June 13   Mr. Finch's Benefit   Gen. Ad.

The Merchant of Venice

Duke.............Mr. Green   Launcelot........Mr. Bates
Antonio..........Mr. Whitlock   Old Gobbo........Mr. Francis
Bassanio.........Mr. Moreton   Leonardo.........Mr. Blissett
Gratiano.........Mr. Finch   Balthazar........Mr. Darley, Jr.
Lorenzo..........Mr. Marshall   Stephano.........Mr. Warrell
Salerino.........Mr. Cleveland   Portia...........Mrs. Whitlock
Solanio..........Mr. De Moulin   Jessica..........Miss Broadhurst
Shylock..........Mr. Chalmers   Nerissa..........Mrs. Francis
Tubal............Mr. Harwood

Embargo—by "a citizen of Philadelphia."

Mr. Neverfret........Mr. Bates   Patrick O'Flanagan....Mr. Finch
Capt. Standby........Mr. Darley   Mrs. Neverfret.......Mrs. Shaw
Ben Standby..........Mr. Green   Lucy.............Mrs. Warrell
Jack Mainstay........Mr. Francis   Ruth Doublescore.....Mrs. Bates
Bob Overhaul.........Mr. Blissett

The Embargo of 1794 is not to be confused with J. N. Barker's *The Embargo,
or What News,* produced at the same theatre March 16, 1808. However,
as Blissett, who acted in *The Embargo* of 1794, later suggested the subject
to Barker (see Quinn, *American Drama from The Beginning to the Civil
War,* p. 138), there was probably some relationship between the plays.

[218]

1794

June 16   Mr. and Mrs. Francis's Benefit   Gen. Ad.

Gustavus Vasa

Christian..........Mr. Marshall	Arnoldus..........Mr. Harwood
Trollio..............Mr. Green	Siward.............Mr. Warrell
Peterson............Mr. Francis	Christiana........Mrs. Whitlock
Laertes...........Mr. Cleveland	Augusta.............Mrs. Shaw
Gustavus............Mr. Fennell	Marianne........Mrs. Cleveland
Arvida.............Mr. Wignell	Gustava..............."a child"
Anderson........Mr. De Moulin	

Harlequin Shipwrecked

Harlequin...........Mr. Francis	Pantaloon..........Mr. Warrell
Leo (The Lion)..Master Warrell	Billy Whipple........M. Bellona
Captain of ship.....Mr. Cleveland	Whimsical...........Mr. Green
Savages...Messrs. Darley, Lee, etc.	The Clown..........Mr. Blissett
Sailors..........Messrs. Bason &	Taylor...........Mr. DeMoulin
DeMoulin	Hair Dresser...Master T. Warrell
Cobler..........Mr. Darley, Jr.	Farmer............Mr. Rowson

June 18   Miss Broadhurst's Benefit   Gen. Ad.

* The Woodman—Dudley

Sir Walter Waring....Mr. Finch	Filbert..............Mr. Blissett
Wilford...........Mr. Marshall	Emily..........Miss Broadhurst
Capt. O'Donnell......Mr. Green	Dolly............Mrs. Oldmixon
Medley..............Mr. Bates	Polly..............Young Lady
Bob................Mr. Francis	Miss Di Clackit......Mrs. Shaw
Fairlop.............Mr. Darley	Bridget...........Mrs. Francis

The Critic

Dangle............Mr. Wignell	Leicester..........Mr. Cleveland
Sneer..............Mr. Fennell	Sir Walter Raleigh....Mr. Green
Sir Fretful Plagiary.............	Sir. C. Hatton......Mr. Francis
Mr. Harwood	Master of Horse....Mr. Warrell
Sig. Pasticio.......Mr. Marshall	First Niece........Mr. Cleveland
Interpreter...........Mr. Finch	Second Niece.......Miss Willems
Puff..............Mr. Chalmers	Confidant..........Mrs. Rowson
Mrs. Dangle........Mrs. Francis	Tilburina............Mrs. Shaw
Lord Burleigh.........Mr. Bates	Don Whiskerandos..Mr. Moreton
Governor...........Mr. Darley	Prompter..........Mr. Rowson

1794

June 20   Mr. Green's Benefit   Gen. Ad.

How to Grow Rich—Reynolds

Pave............	Mr. Chalmers	Plainly.........	Mr. De Moulin
Smalltrade...........	Mr. Bates	Nab..............	Mr. Rowson
Roundhead..........	Mr. Finch	Formal............	Mr. Warrell
Latitat..............	Mr. Green	Lady Henrietta....	Mrs. Whitlock
Hippy.............	Mr. Francis	Rosa.............	Mrs. Marshall
Warford...........	Mr. Moreton	Miss Dazzle........	Mrs. Francis
Sir Chas. Dazzle...	Mr. Cleveland	Betty,...........	Mrs. Cleveland

La Forêt Noire

Cast as for April 30, except:

Pasquin........Mr. Darley, Jr.   Le Fronte..........Mr. Blissett

June 23   Mrs. Shaw's Night   Gen. Ad.

("never here"—but see May 28)

Julia

Cast as for May 28, except:

Servant.........Master Warrell

The Waterman

Mr. Bundle........	Mr. Francis	Mrs. Bundle........	Mrs. Shaw
Tug..............	Mr. Darley	Wilhelmina......	Miss Broadhurst
Robin..............	Mr. Bates		

June 25   Messrs. Moreton and Harwood's Benefit   Daily Ad.

The Wonder

Don Lopez..........	Mr. Finch	Alguazil..........	Mr. Warrell
Don Felix.........	Mr. Moreton	Vasquez........	Master Warrell
Frederick...........	Mr. Green	Soldier..........	Mr. Darley, Jr.
Don Pedro.........	Mr. Francis	Violante..........	Mrs. Whitlock
Colonel Briton.......	Mr. Fennell	Isabella............	Mrs. Francis
Gibby..............	Mr. Bates	Flora..............	Mrs. Shaw
Lissardo..........	Mr. Harwood	Inez.............	Mrs. Rowson

Comus

Comus............	Mr. Fennell	Sabrina........	Miss Broadhurst
First Spirit..........	Mr. Green	Pastoral Nymph...	Mrs. Marshall
Elder Brother......	Mr. Moreton	Bacchante........	Mrs. Warrell
Younger Brother...	Mr. Cleveland	Euphrosyne.......	Mrs. Oldmixon
Lady...........	Mrs. Whitlock		

Mr. Munto, new to our record, is mentioned among the "Bacchanals."

1794

June 27   Madame Gardie's and Miss Willems' Benefit   Gen. Ad.

Macbeth

Cast as for April 7.

* *Female Heroism,* or
The Siege of Orleans (pantomime)

Jeanne d'Arc.....Madame Gardie   Porte Guidon........Mr. Darley
St. Denis.........Mr. Cleveland   Chandos...........Mr. Moreton
Dunois............Mr. Marshall   Officer...........Mr. DeMoulin
Le Tremouille.......Mr. Bellona   Padlock............Mr. Francis

June 30   Mrs. Rowson's Night   Gen. Ad.

* *Slaves in Algiers*—Mrs. Rowson

Muley Muloch.......Mr. Green   Sadi............Master Warrell
Frederick..........Mr. Moreton   Selim.............Mr. Blissett
Henry..........Mr. Cleveland   Zorianna..........Mrs. Warrell
Constant.........Mr. Whitlock   Fetnah..........Mrs. Marshall
Sebastian.............Mr. Bates   Rebecca.........Mrs. Whitlock
Ben Hassan........Mr. Francis   Selima..........Mrs. Cleveland
Mustapha........Mr. Darley, Jr.   Olivia.............Mrs. Rowson

The Citizen

Old Philpot........Mr. Morris   Dapper............Mr. Francis
Young Philpot.....Mr. Chalmers   Quilldrive..........Mr. Blissett
Sir Jasper.........Mr. Warrell   Maria.............Mrs. Rowson
Young Wilding.......Mr. Green   Corinna..........Miss Rowson
Beaufort.........Mr. Cleveland

July 2   Mr. and Mrs. Cleveland's Night   Gen. Ad.

The Widow of Malabar

Raymond..........Mr. Moreton   Young Bramin.....Mr. Cleveland
Albert............Mr. Harwood   Narrain.............Mr. Green
Chief Bramin.......Mr. Fennell   Indamora.........Mrs. Whitlock
Second Bramin......Mr. Warrell   Fatima..........Mrs. Cleveland

* *L'Americain* (farce)

Jacques Splin.....Mrs. Cleveland   Loyer.....Mr. Bologna [Bellona]
Jacquot..............Mr. Finch   L'Huissier.........Miss Rowson

Selima and Azor

Azor............Mr. Marshall   Fatima...........Mrs. Rowson
Scander...........Mr. Darley   Lesbia.........Miss Broadhurst
Ali................Mr. Bates   Selima..........Mrs. Marshall

[221]

1794

July 4   *Romeo and Juliet*   Gen. Ad.

Cast as for June 4.

The Critic

Cast as for June 18.

July 7   *Mrs. Oldmixon's Night*   Gen. Ad.

* *The Spanish Barber*—Colman, Jr.

Count Almavia	Mr. Moreton	Notary	Mr. Warrell
Dr. Bartholo	Mr. Green	Tallboy	Mr. Francis
Bazil	Mr. Darley	Argus	Mr. Blissett
Lazarillo	Mr. Bates	Rosina	Mrs. Oldmixon
Alcaide	Mr. Darley, Jr.		

The Prisoner at Large

Lord Osmond	Mr. Fennell	Tough	Mr. Morris
Old Dowdle	Mr. Bates	Trap	Mr. Darley, Jr.
Count Fripon	Mr. Finch	Muns	Mr. Wignell
Jack Conner	Mr. Harwood	Adelaide	Mrs. Cleveland
Father Frank	Mr. Blissett	Rachel	Mrs. Marshall
Frill	Mr. Francis	Mary	Mrs. Rowson
Phelim	Master Warrell	Landlady	Mrs. Bates

* *The Scheming Milliners*—Francis

July 9   Mr. Blissett's and Mrs. De Marque's Benefit   Gen. Ad.

Cymbeline

Cymbeline	Mr. Green	Pisanio	Mr. Marshall
Cloten	Mr. Blissett	Frenchman	Mr. Finch
Posthumous	Mr. Fennell	Cornelius	Mr. Warrell
Arviragus	Mr. Harwood	Second Gentleman	Mr. DeMoulin
Guiderius	Mr. Cleveland	First Gentleman	Mr. Francis
Belarius	Mr. Whitlock	Roman Captive	Mr. Darley, Jr.
Philario	Mr. Darley	Queen	Mrs. Shaw
Iachimo	Mr. Moreton	Helena	Mrs. Cleveland
Caius Lucius	Mr. Bates	Imogen	Mrs. Whitlock

The Devil Upon Two Sticks

Devil	Mr. Wignell	Dr. Last	Mr. Blissett
Sir Thomas	Mr. Finch	Forceps	Mr. Darley, Jr.
Invoice	Mr. Cleveland	Secretary	Mr. Harwood
Julep	Mr. Bates	Printer's Devil	Master Warrell
Apoxem	Mr. Francis	Mrs. Marg. Maxwell	Mrs. Shaw

1794

Dr. Calomel......Mr. De Moulin   Harriet.........Miss Broadhurst
Dr. Camphire.......Mr. Warrell

The Irish Lilt—Francis

July 11   Mr. Franklin's Benefit   Gen. Ad.

[Mr. Franklin was the "box-keeper"]

Comus

Cast as for June 25.

Ways and Means

Sir David Dunder..Mr. Harwood   Boundfee............Mr. Finch
Random...........Mr. Moreton   Bailiff.............Mr. Warrell
Scruple..........Mr. Cleveland   Lady Dunder.........Mrs. Shaw
Old Random......Mr. Whitlock   Harriet............Mrs. Francis
Carney............Mr. Blissett   Kitty..............Young Lady
Tiptoe...............Mr. Bates   Mrs. Perry.........Mrs. Rowson
Paul Peery.........Mr. Francis

The Prize

Cast as for May 26.

July 14   Mr. Milbourne's Benefit   Gen. Ad.

[Mr. Milbourne was the scene painter.]

The Tempest

Alonzo.............Mr. Green   Mustachio.......Mr. De Moulin
Ferdinand........Mr. Moreton   Ventoso........Mr. Darley, Jr.
Prospero..........Mr. Whitlock   Triculo..............Mr. Bates
Antonio...........Mr. Warrell   Caliban............Mr. Darley
Gonzalo...........Mr. Finch   Miranda.........Mrs. Cleveland
Hippolito.........Mr. Francis   Dorinda.........Mrs. Marshall
Stephano.........Mr. Harwood   Ariel..........Miss Broadhurst

The Birth of Harlequin

Harlequin Skip....Mr. Milbourne   Pantaloon.........Mr. Bellano
Bob Saunter.......Mr. Cleveland   Clown..........Mr. Milbourne
Maid.............Mrs. Rowson   Columbine......Madame Gardie
Skip Harlequin......Mr. Francis

First appearance of Mr. Milbourne as an actor.

July 16   Gen. Ad.

Benefit of Mr. Blissett, Mr. De Moulin, Mrs. De Marque, and Madame
Gardie.

1794

July 1 (cont.) *The Gamester*

Beverly	Mr. Fennell	Dawson	Mr. Moreton
Stukely	Mr. Wignell	Waiter	Mr. De Moulin
Lewson	Mr. Cleveland	Mrs. Beverly	Mrs. Whitlock
Jarvis	Mr. Whitlock	Charlotte	Mrs. Francis
Bates	Mr. Green	Lucy	Mrs. Cleveland

The Sultan

Cast as for May 19.

The Irish Litt

The benefit for Mr. Blissett, Mrs. De Marque, and Mme. Gardie was "in Consequence of the ill success of their former nights."

July 18   "Positively the Last Night"   Gen. Ad.

Benefit of a fund for aged and infirm actors.

Every One Has His Fault

Cast as for March 7, except:

Edward	Mrs. Francis	Mrs. Placid	Mrs. Shaw

The Birth of Harlequin

Harlequin	Mr. Francis	Clown	Mr. Milbourne
Pantaloon	Mr. Bologna	Maid	Mrs. Cleveland
	[Mr. Bellona]	Columbine	Mme Gardie
Miser	Mr. Blissett		

The new plays of this first season at the New Theatre (Chesnut Street) from February 17 to July 18, 1794, were *As You Like It, The Battle of Hexham, The Carmelite, Everyone Has His Fault, The Highland Reel, How to Grow Rich, Julia, Robin Hood, She Would and She Would Not, Slaves in Algiers, The Spanish Barber, The Surrender of Calais,* and *The Woodman.* New afterpieces: *L'Americain, Bon Ton, The Caledonian Frolic, The Embargo, Female Heroism; or the Siege of Orleans, The Fruitless Precaution, Hartford Bridge, La Forêt Noire, The Irish Lilt, Modern Antiques, Peeping Tom of Coventry, The Prize, The Quality Binding, The Sailors' Landlady, The Scheming Clown, The Son-in-Law, The Spoiled Child, The Sultan, The Triumph of Mirth,* and *The Village Lawyer.*

Reappearing plays: *The Belle's Stratagem, The Castle of Andalusia, Comus, Cymbeline, Douglas, The Dramatist, The Duenna, The Fair Penitent, The Gamester, The Grecian Daughter, Gustavus Vasa, Hamlet, Isabella, The Jealous Wife, Lionel and Clarissa, Love in a Village, Macbeth, The Maid of the Mill, The Merchant of Venice, The Mourning Bride, Othello, The*

Provoked Husband, The Recruiting Officer, Richard III, The Rivals, The Road to Ruin, Romeo and Juliet, The School for Scandal, The School for Wives, The Tempest, Venice Preserved, The West Indian, The Widow of Malabar, and *The Wonder.* Reappearing afterpieces: *The Agreeable Surprize, The Birth of Harlequin, Catherine and Petruchio, The Citizen, The Critic, The Deserter, The Devil Upon Two Sticks, The Farmer, The Flitch of Bacon, The Guardian, Harlequin Shipwrecked, Inkle and Yarico, The Liar, The Lying Valet, Miss in Her Teens, No Song No Supper, The Poor Soldier, The Prisoner at Large, Robinson Crusoe, The Romp, Rosina, Saint Patrick's Day, Selima and Azor, Three Weeks after Marriage, The True Born Irishman, The Virgin Unmasked, The Waterman, Who's the Dupe?* and *The Wrangling Lovers.*

The only reappearing actors were Mr. De (or Du) Moulin(s), Mr. and Mrs. Morris, and Mr. Wignell. New actors: Mr. Bason, Mr. and Mrs. Bates, Mr. Bellona (or Bologna), Mr. Blissett, Miss Broadhurst, Mr. Chalmers, Mr. and Mrs. Cleveland, Mr. Barley, Mr. J. Darley, Jr., Mrs. De Marque, Mr. Fennell, Mr. and Mrs. Finch, Mr. and Mrs. Francis, Mme. Gardie, Messrs. Green, Harwood, and Lee, Mr. and Mrs. Marshall, Mr. Milbourne, Mr. Moreton, Mr. Munto, Miss Oldfield, Mrs. Oldmixon, Mr. Quesnay, and Mr., Mrs., and Miss Rowson, Mrs. Shaw, Mr. and Mrs. Warrell, Master J. Warrell (or Mr. Warrell, Jr.), Master T. Warrell, Mr. and Mrs. Whitlock, Miss Willems (or Williams—later Mrs. Green), and a "Young Lady."

SOUTHWARK THEATRE

Sept. 20   Gen. Ad.

Hallam and Henry advertised that they would open on September 22, "when Mrs. MELMOUTH, formerly of Drury Lane and Covent Garden, and last from Dublin," would make her first appearance. A few days later Mons. Quenet, principal ballet master from Paris, and Madame Gardie would appear "in a new grand Pantomime"—also Mr. and Mrs. Marriott, from the Theatre Edinburgh, Mr. Richards from Dublin, Mr. Nelson from the Theatre Richmond, Mr. Munto from Goodman's Fields, and Mr. Carr of the Antient Concerto, London.

This is the first mention of Mrs. Melmoth, Mr. Carr, Mr. and Mrs. Marriott, Mr. Nelson, Mr. Quenet (perhaps the Mr. Quesnay who had appeared at the New Theatre), and Mr. Richards (Richard Crosby). Mme. Gardie, Mr. Munto, and perhaps Mr. Quenet, had been at the New Theatre (Chesnut Street) earlier in the year.

Sept. 22   *Old and New Houses*   Gen. Ad.

"an occasional Prelude . . . Characters by Mr. Hodgkinson, Mr. King, Mr. Ryan, Mr. Martin, Mrs. Miller, &c."

1794

Sept. 22 (cont.) *The Grecian Daughter*
The Romp

"Open for a few weeks only."

The last season of the Old American Company at the "Theatre, Cedar Street"—the Theatre in Southwark—was from September 22 to December 4, 1794.

First mention of Mrs. Miller.

Sept. 24 *Love in a Village* Gen. Ad.
* *The Midnight Hour*—Mrs. Inchbald

First appearance of Mr. Berwick? (See Sept 26, which is said to be his *second* appearance.)

Sept. 26 * *The Young Quaker*—O'Keeffe Phila. Gazette

Young Sadboy...Mr. Hodgkinson Twig..............Mr. Durang
Chronicle.........Mr. Prigmore Goliah............Miss Hatton
Clod..............Mr. Hallam Spatterdark..........Mr. King
Capt. Ambush.......Mr. Martin Araminta.......Mrs. Hodgkinson
Shadrack Boaz.....Mr. Hammond Pink............Mrs. Pownall
(for that night only) Lady Rounceval......Mrs. Miller
Old Sadboy.......Mr. Richards Mrs. Millefleur....Mrs. Hamilton
Malachi...........Mr. Woolls Judith..............Mrs. King
Lounge............Mr. Munto Dinah Primrose.....Mrs. Hallam

The Midnight Hour

Marquis........Mr. Hodgkinson General..........Mr. Richards
Sebastian..........Mr. Martin Julia.............Mrs. Marriott
Nicholas.........Mr. Prigmore (her second appearance)
Mathias..........Mr. Berwick Cicily..........Mrs. Hamilton
(his second appearance) Flora.............Mrs. Pownall
Ambrose............Mr. Ryan

First mention of Mr. Berwick, Miss Hatton, and Mrs. King.

Sept 29 *The Fair Penitent* Gen. Ad.
No Song No Supper

Oct. 1 *The Young Quaker* Gen. Ad.
The Padlock

Oct. 3 *Percy* Gen. Ad.
The Highland Reel

Oct. 6 * *I'll Tell You What*—Mrs. Inchbald Gen. Ad.
* *The Quaker*—Dibdin

1794

| Oct. 8 | *The Dramatist* | Gen. Ad. |

    The Danaides—Quenet and Pelisier (pantomime)

In which were to appear Madame Gardie, M. Quenet, Mr. Mariot [Marriott] and Mr. Prigmore.

"The Scenery executed by Mr. Ciceri."

| Oct. 10 | *Robin Hood* | Gen. Ad. |
| | *The Danaides* | |

| Oct. 13 | *A Bold Stroke for a Husband*—Mrs. Cowley | Gen. Ad. |
| | *The Danaides* | |

| Oct. 15 | *Macbeth* | Gen. Ad. |
| | *The Rival Candidates* | |

| Oct. 17 | *The Beggar's Opera* | Gen. Ad. |

"Never performed here" [sic!]

"Altered, revised, and corrected."

Three Weeks after Marriage

The announcement of the same bill for October 20 with the statement "never performed here" indicates that these plays may have been postponed.

| Oct. 18 | *Tammany*—Mrs. Hatton | Gen. Ad. |
| | *A Bold Stroke for a Wife* | |

"Reduced to an Afterpiece of two Acts"—and "expunged" of indelicacy.

Oct. 20	("Never performed here")	Gen. Ad.
	The Beggar's Opera	
	Three Weeks after Marriage	

| Oct. 22 | *The World in a Village*—O'Keeffe | Gen. Ad. |
| | *High Life Below Stairs* | |

"A Mock Minuet by Mrs. Solomons and Mr. Prigmore." First mention of Mrs. Solomons.

Oct. 24	*Barbarossa*—Brown	Gen. Ad.
	No Song No Supper	
	The Two Philosophers	

| Oct. 27 | *Wild Oats* | Gen. Ad. |
| | *Don Juan* | |

| Oct. 29 | *The Fatal Deception*—Dunlap | Gen. Ad. |
| | *Rosina* | |

[227]

1794

| Oct. 30 | *The Belle's Stratagem* | Gen. Ad. |
| | *The Agreeable Surprize* | |

Oct. 31   *The Carmelite*   Gen. Ad.
A Bold Stroke for a Wife
(reduced to two acts)

Nov. 1   *The West Indian*   Gen. Ad.
* *Sophia of Brabant*

Nov. 3   Benefit of Messrs. Ashton and Woolls   Gen. Ad.
Such Things Are

A Eulogium—and an ode to Masonry—Messrs. Ashton, Carr, Martin, Woolls, Solomons, Richards, Prigmore, Barkwick [or Berwick or Barwick], Ryan, Lee, and Munto.

* *The Intrigues of a Morning*—Mrs. Parsons

First mention of Mr. Solomon.

Nov. 5   Benefit of Mr. King and Mr. Richards   Gen. Ad.
The Young Quaker
The Highland Reel

Nov. 7   Benefit of Mr. Munto and Mrs. Solomons   Phila. Gazette, Nov. 6
The Battle of Hexham—"with alterations by Mr. Hodgkinson"

"After the play, will be delivered an Address, written by a citizen of the United States, called the THREE REASONS, by Mrs. Solomons and Mr. Munto." Masonic Song by "Brother Solomons," "Brothers Carr, Martin, Woolls, Richards, Prigmore, and Barwick."

Song of "the WAXEN DOLL by Miss Solomons."

The Citizen

First mention of Miss Solomons.

Nov. 10 Benefit of Mrs. Miller, Mrs. Hamilton, and Mr. Ryan   Gen. Ad.
Tammany
The True-Born Irishman

Nov 12   Benefit of Mrs. Melmoth and Mrs. Pownall   Gen. Ad.
The Gamester
* *The Wedding Ring*—Dibdin

[228]

1794

Nov. 14   Benefit of Mr. and Mrs. Hallam   Gen. Ad.

Love's Frailties—Holcroft
The Busy Body

(reduced to two acts)

Nov. 17   Benefit of Mr. and Mrs. Marriott   Gen. Ad.

Alexander the Great

("never acted")
* *The Chimera*—Mrs. Marriott

Nov. 19   Benefit of Mr. King, Mr. Durang, and Mr. Barwick   Gen. Ad.

* *The Country Girl*—Garrick
The Birth of Harlequin

Nov. 21   Benefit of Mr. Ashton and Mme. Gardie   Gen. Ad.

(On account of bad weather, Mr. Ashton did not get enough in his benefit with Mr. Woolls, so he "purchased a share" of Madame Gardie's Night.)

Love's Frailties
The Bird Catcher (Ballet Dance)
* *Harlequin Pastry Cook* (pantomime)

Nov. 24   Benefit of Mr. Hallam, Jr., and Mr. Carr.   Gen. Ad.

The Suspicious Husband
* *The Children in the Wood*—Morton

First mention of Mr. [Marvin] Hallam—though it is within the range of possibility that he was the "Master Hallam" of March 9, 1767. But he is of no importance, save as a link in the Hallam chain.

Nov. 26   Benefit of Mr. Prigmore and Mr. Martin   Gen. Ad.

Notoriety
Children in the Wood

(*Hunt the Slipper,* which Seilhamer, III, 103, gives, was advertised on November 25 for November 26—but on November 26, *Children in the Wood* was announced "By Particular Desire.")

Nov. 28   Benefit of Mr. Nelson and Mrs. Wilson   Gen. Ad.

Wild Oats
The Romp

Dec. 2   Benefit of Mr. and Mrs. Hodgkinson   Gen. Ad.

* *The Haunted Tower*—Cobb
The Lyar

[229]

1794

NEW THEATRE

Dec. 3   *Every One Has His Fault*   Daily Ad.

Lord Norland......Mr. Whitlock	Porter.............Mr. Warrell
Sir Robert Ramble..Mr. Chalmers	Edward..........Mrs. Marshall
Mr. Solus...........Mr. Morris	Lady Eleanor Erwin..Mrs. Whit-
Mr. Harmony........Mr. Green	lock
Mr. Placid.........Mr. Wignell	Mrs. Placid..........Mrs. Shaw
Mr. Irwin.........Mr. Moreton	Miss Spinster.........Mrs. Bates
Hammond.......Mr. Cleveland	Miss Wooburn......Mrs. Morris

The Prize

First night of the season at the New Theatre (Chesnut Street) from Dec. 3, 1794, to July 4, 1795.

SOUTHWARK THEATRE

Dec. 4   Benefit of Mr. and Mrs. Hallam   Gen. Ad.
               Last Night this Season

The Young Quaker
Children in the Wood
The Two Philosophers

"We are happy in announcing to the public that the President of the United States means to honor the *Old American Company* with his presence at the Theatre this evening."

December 4, 1794, finished an era in the history of the Philadelphia—of the American—stage, when the last regular dramatic season (Sept. 22–December 4) at the Theatre in Southwark ended. The Old American Company was never again in the city, and Lewis Hallam, who had first appeared in 1754, made his final bow to eighteenth-century Philadelphia. Stephen Woolls, the only other actor of the Old American Company who had played in the colonial days, also played his last Philadelphia season.

New plays produced this season: *Barbarossa, A Bold Stroke for a Husband, The Carmelite, The Country Girl, The Fatal Deception, The Haunted Tower, I'll Tell You What, Love's Frailties, Tammany, The World in a Village,* and *The Young Quaker.* New afterpieces, *The Children in the Wood, The Chimera, Harlequin Pastry Cook, The Danaides, The Intrigues of a Morning, The Midnight Hour, The Quaker, Sophia of Brabant, The Two Philosophers,* and *The Wedding Ring.*

Reappearing plays: *Alexander the Great, The Battle of Hexham, The Beggar's Opera, The Belle's Stratagem, The Dramatist, The Fair Penitent, The Gamester, The Grecian Daughter, Love in a Village, Macbeth, Notoriety, Percy, Robin Hood, Such Things Are, The Suspicious Husband, The West*

1794

Indian, and *Wild Oats.* Reappearing afterpieces: *The Agreeable Surprize, The Bird Catcher, The Birth of Harlequin, A Bold Stroke for a Wife* (cut to two acts), *The Busybody* (cut to two acts), *The Citizen, Don Juan, The Highland Reel, High Life Below Stairs, The Liar, The Padlock, The Rival Candidates, The Romp, Rosina, Three Weeks after Marriage,* and *The True-Born Irishman.*

The new actors: Mr. Berwick (or Barwick or Barkwick), Mr. Carr, Mr. Marvin Hallam, "Jr.," Miss Hatton, Mrs. King, Mr. and Mrs. Marriott, Mrs. Melmoth, Mrs. Miller, Mr. Nelson, Mr. Quenet (unless he was Mr. Quesnay), Mr. Richards (Richard Crosby), and Mr., Mrs., and Miss Solomons (or Solomon). Reappearing actors: Mr. Ashton, Mr. Durang, Mme. Gardie, Mr. Hallam, Mrs. Hallam (formerly Miss Tuke), Mrs. Hamilton, Mr. Hammond, Mr. and Mrs. Hodgkinson, Mr. King, Mr. Lee, Mr. Martin, Mr. Munto, Mrs. Pownall, Mr. Prigmore, perhaps Mr. Quesnay, Mr. Ryan, Mrs. Wilson, and Mr. Woolls.

NEW THEATRE

Dec. 5	*The Highland Reel*	Daily Ad.
	The Lyar	

Dec. 8	*Venice Preserved*	Daily Ad.

Duke of Venice...... Mr. Morris	Elliot............ Mr. Cleveland
Priuli........... Mr. Whitlock	Theodore......... Mr. Warrell
Pierre........... Mr. Chalmers	Officer............ Mr. Francis
Renault............ Mr. Green	Belvidera........ Mrs. Whitlock
Spinosa.......... Mr. Harwood	

The Birth of Harlequin

Harlequin........... Mr. Francis	1st Witch.......... Mr. Darley
Pantaloon........... Mr. Green	2nd Witch........ Mr. Marshall
Miser............. Mr. Blissett	3rd Witch...... Miss Broadhurst
Clown.......... Mr. Milbourne	Maid........... Mrs. Cleveland
Lawyer.......... Mr. J. Darley	Columbine...... Mrs. De Marque

Dec. 10	*As You Like It*	Daily Ad.

Orlando.......... Mr. Moreton	Charles........... Mr. Rowson
Adam........... Mr. Whitlock	Touchstone.......... Mr. Bates
Duke Senior....... Mr. Harwood	Corin............. Mr. Darley
Duke Frederick..... Mr. Warrell	Sylvius.......... Mr. Cleveland
Amiens.......... Mr. Marshall	William........... Mr. Blissett
Jacques.......... Mr. Chalmers	Rosalind......... Mrs. Marshall
Le Beau........... Mr. Francis	Celia............. Mrs. Francis
Oliver............. Mr. Green	Phoebe......... Mrs. Cleveland
Jacques de Bois.... Mr. Darley, Jr.	Audrey............. Mrs. Shaw
Dennis......... Master Warrell	

1794

The Birth of Harlequin
Cast as on December 8, except:
3rd Witch...Mr. Warrell

Dec. 12   *Romeo and Juliet*   Daily Ad.

Romeo	Mr. Moreton	Friar Laurence	Mr. Whitlock
Esculus	Mr. Warrell	Balthasar	Mr. Darley, Jr.
Paris	Mr. Marshall	Apothecary	Mr. Francis
Montague	Mr. Morris	Peter	Mr. Blissett
Capulet	Mr. Green	Page	Master T. Warrell
Mercutio	Mr. Wignell	Juliet	Mrs. Marshall
Benvolio	Mr. Cleveland	Lady Capulet	Mrs. Rowson
Tibalt	Mr. Harwood	Nurse	Mrs. Shaw

The Sultan

Soloman	Mr. Moreton	Ismene	Miss Broadhurst
Osmyn	Mr. Harwood	Roxalana	Mrs. Oldmixon
Elmira	Mrs. Francis		

Dec. 15   *Lionel and Clarissa*   Daily Ad.

Sir John Flowerdale	Mr. Whitlock	Jenkins	Mr. Darley
Col. Oldboy	Mr. Bates	Lady Oldboy	Mrs. Shaw
Jessamy	Mr. Moreton	Clarissa	Mrs. Marshall
Lionel	Mr. Marshall	Diana	Mrs. Oldmixon
Harman	Mr. Cleveland	Jenny	Miss Broadhurst

Ways and Means

Sir David Dunder	Mr. Harwood	Paul Peery	Mr. Francis
Random	Mr. Moreton	Lady Dunder	Mrs. Shaw
Scruple	Mr. Cleveland	Harriet	Mrs. Francis
Tiptoe	Mr. Bates	Kitty	Mrs. Marshall

Dec. 17   *Isabella*   Daily Ad.

Count Baldwin	Mr. Green	Belford	Mr. Cleveland
Biron	Mr. Whitlock	Pedro	Mr. Francis
Carlos	Mr. Marshall	Officer	Mr. Warrell
Villeroy	Mr. Moreton	Isabella	Mrs. Whitlock
Sampson	Mr. Bates	Nurse	Mrs. Rowson

Rosina

Belville	Mr. Marshall	2nd Irishman	Mr. Blissett
Capt. Belville	Mr. Moreton	Rosina	Mrs. Warrell
William	Mr. Francis	Dorcas	Mrs. Bates
Rustic	Mr. Warrell	Phoebe	Miss Broadhurst
1st Irishman	Mr. Green		

[232]

1794

Dec. 19   *The Maid of the Mill*   Daily Ad.

Lord Aimworth....Mr. Marshall	Ralph.............Mr. Wignell
Sir Harry Sycamore....Mr. Bates	Lady Sycamore........Mrs. Shaw
Mervin..........Mr. Cleveland	Theodosia.......Miss Broadhurst
Fairfield..........Mr. Whitlock	Patty.............Mrs. Warrell
Giles..............Mr. Darley	Fanny..........Mrs. Oldmixon

The Village Lawyer

Scout.............Mr. Harwood	Sheep-face............Mr. Bates
Snarl.............Mrs. Francis	Kate.................Mrs. Bates
Charles.........Mr. Darley, Jr.	Mrs. Scout..........Mrs. Shaw
Justice Mittimus....Mr. Warrell	

Dec. 22   *Slaves in Algiers*   Gen. Ad.

(with Alterations)

Moley Moloch........Mr. Green	Fetnah...........Mrs. Marshall
Constant..........Mr. Whitlock	Selima...........Mrs. Cleveland
Sebastian.............Mr. Bates	Frederick..........Mr. Moreton
Ben Hassen.........Mr. Francis	Henry............Mr. Cleveland
Mustapha........Mr. Darley, Jr.	Augustus......Master T. Warrell
Sadi..............Mr. Blissett	Rebecca..........Mrs. Whitlock
Selim..........Master Warrell	Olivia.............Mrs. Rowson
Zoriana..........Mrs. Warrell	

The Critic

Dangle............Mr. Wignell	Governor............Mr. Darley
Sneer.............Mr. Moreton	Leicester..........Mr. Cleveland
Sir Fretful Plagiary.Mr. Harwood	Sir Walter Raleigh....Mr. Green
Signior Pasticio.....Mr. Marshall	Sir Christopher Hatton..........
Interpreter..........Mr. Blissett	Mr. Francis
Prompter..........Mr. Rowson	Master of the Home..Mr. Warrell
Puff..............Mr. Chalmers	Don Ferollo Whiskerandos......
Miss Dangle........Mrs. Francis	Mr. Bates
Italian Girls...Mrs. Oldmixon &	1st Niece.........Mrs. Cleveland
Miss Broadhurst	2nd Niece..........Miss Rowson
Lord Burleigh.......Mr. Blissett	Confidant..........Mrs. Rowson
	Tilburina...........Mrs. Shaw

Dec. 24   * *The Natural Son*—Cumberland   Gen. Ad.

Sir Jeffrey Latimer..Mr. Harwood	David..............Mr. Francis
Blushenly..........Mr. Moreton	Thomas........Mr. Darley, Jr.
Rueful..............Mr. Green	William.............Mr. Price
Jack Hastings......Mr. Chalmers	Mrs. Phoebe Latimer..Mrs. Shaw
Major O'Flaherty..Mr. Whitlock	Lady Paragon.....Mrs. Whitlock
Dumps..............Mr. Bates	Penelope.........Mrs. Cleveland

[233]

1794

Dec. 24 (cont.) *The Flitch of Bacon*

Major Benbow.....Mr. Harwood	Tipple.............Mr. Francis
Justice Benbow.......Mr. Green	Kilderkin..........Mr. Warrell
Capt. Greville.....Mr. Marshall	Ned................Mr. Blissett
Capt. Wilson........Mr. Darley	Eliza...........Miss Broadhurst

First appearance of Mr. Price.

Dec. 26   *George Barnwell*   Gen. Ad.
The Birth of Harlequin

Dec. 27   *Lionel and Clarissa*   Gen. Ad.

Cast as for December 15, save that Jenkins is not mentioned

Modern Antiques

Dec. 29   *The Natural Son*   Gen. Ad.
Peeping Tom of Coventry

Dec. 31   *Macbeth*   Gen. Ad.

Duncan.............Mr. Green	Seyton.............Mr. Francis
Malcolm.........Mr. Cleveland	Doctor.........Mr. De Moulin
Donalbaine......Master Warrell	Messenger..........Mr. Blissett
Macbeth..........Mr. Chalmers	Lady Macbeth.....Mrs. Whitlock
Banquo...........Mr. Whitlock	Gentlewoman.....Mrs. Cleveland
Macduff...........Mr. Moreton	Hecate..............Mr. Darley
Lenox...........Mr. Harwood	1st Witch.........Mr. Bates
Fleance.....Master T. Warrell	2nd Witch........Mr. Warrell
Siward............Mr. Morris	3rd Witch.........Mr. Wignell

Peeping Tom of Coventry

Peeping Tom........Mr. Bates	Count Lewis......Mr. Cleveland
Mayor of Coventry..Mr. Harwood	Maud..........Mrs. Marshall
Harold...........Mr. Darley, Jr.	Emma..........Miss Broadhurst
Crazy.............Mr. Francis	Lady Godiva......Mrs. Cleveland
Earl of Mercia.......Mr. Green	Mayoress...........Mrs. Shaw

1795

Jan. 2   *The Rivals*   Daily Ad.

Sir Anthony Absolute..Mr. Morris	David.............Mr. Francis
Capt. Absolute......Mr. Moreton	Coachman.........Mr. Warrell
Faulkland........Mr. Cleveland	Boy.........Master T. Warrell
Acres.................Mr. Bates	Mrs. Malaprop.......Mrs. Shaw
Sir Lucius O'Trigger..Mr. Whitlock	Lydia Languish....Mrs. Marshall
	Julia.............Miss Francis
Fag.............Mr. Marshall	Lucy.............Mrs. Rowson

1795

Jan. 2 (cont.)   *Harlequin Shipwrecked*

Harlequin..........Mr. Francis
Leo (the Lion)..Master Warrell
Indian Chief........Mr. Nugent
Capt. of Ship.....Mr. Cleveland
Cobler.........Master Warrell
Taylor.........Mr. De Moulin
Barber.......Master T. Warrell
Sawyers...Messrs. Gibbon & Price

Pantaloon..........Mr. Warrell
Tippy Bob.......Mr. Darley, Jr.
Clown............Mr. Blissett
Savage Princess..(afterwards Columbine) Miss Milbourne (being her first appearance on any stage.)

First mention of Mr. Gibbon, Miss Milbourne, and Mr. Nugent. As there are three Master Warrells mentioned, one is probably Master *Harry* Warrell, so that this may be taken as his first appearance.

Jan. 3   *The Spanish Barber*   Daily Ad.

Jan. 5   *The Countess of Salisbury*   Daily Ad.
                    The Poor Soldier

Jan. 7   *The Dramatist*   Daily Ad.

Lord Scratch.........Mr. Bates
Neville..........Mr. Cleveland
Fronville.........Mr. Moreton
Willoughby.........Mr. Green
Ennui...........Mr. Marshall
Peter.............Mr. Francis

Vapid...........Mr. Chalmers
Miss Courtney......Mrs. Francis
Lady Waitfort........Mrs. Shaw
Letty..........Mrs. Cleveland
Marianne.......Mrs. Marshall

The Sailor's Landlady

Jack..............Mr. Francis
Mate..............Mr. Nugent
Ned Halyard....Mr. Darley, Jr.

Landlady..........Mr. Rowson
Orange girl.....Mrs. De Marque

* *The Purse*—Cross

Baron...........Mr. Whitlock
Theodore.........Mr. Moreton
Edmund.........Mr. Marshall

Will Steady.......Mr. Harwood
Page...........Mrs. Marshall
Sally..........Mrs. Oldmixon

Jan. 9   *Hamlet*   Daily Ad.

Hamlet..........Mr. Chalmers
King............Mr. Green
Ghost............Mr. Wignell
Horatio.........Mr. Marshall
Laertes..........Mr. Moreton
Polonius..........Mr. Morris
Rosencrans......Master Warrell

Marcellus.........Mr. Harwood
Bernardo..........Mr. Warrell
Osric.............Mr. Francis
Officer...........Mr. Blissett
Grave-Diggers..Mr. Bates & Mr. Milbourne
Queen............Mrs. Shaw

[235]

1795

Guildenstern......Mr. Cleveland   Ophelia..........Mrs. Marshall
Player King......Mr. De Moulin   Player Queen.......Mrs. Rowson
Francisco........Mr. Darley, Jr.

The Purse

Cast as for January 7, 1795, except:

Baron....Mr. Green

Jan. 10   *The Castle of Andalusia*   Phila. Gaz.

Don Scipio..........Mr. Francis   Sanguino............Mr. Green
Don Caesar..........Mr. Darley   Phillipo..........Mr. Darley, Jr.
Don Fernando.....Mr. Marshall   Victoria...........Mrs. Warrell
Don Juan...........Mr. Morris   Lorenza..........Mrs. Marshall
Don Alphonso......Mr. Moreton   Isabella............Mrs. Bates
Pedrillo.............Mr. Bates   Catalina........Miss Broadhurst
Spado.............Mr. Wignell

The Lying Valet

Sharp...............Mr. Bates   Melissa...........Mrs. Francis
Gayless.............Mr. Green   Mrs. Gadabout.......Mrs. Bates
Justice Guttle.......Mr. Francis   Mrs. Trippet.....Mrs. Cleveland
Beau Trippet......Mr. Cleveland   Kitty Pry...........Mrs. Shaw
Drunken Cook......Mr. Blissett

Jan. 12   *The Merchant of Venice*   Aurora

Duke...............Mr. Morris   Tubal..........Mr. Milbourne
Antonio..........Mr. Whitlock   Old Gobbo..........Mr. Francis
Bassanio..........Mr. Moreton   Launcelot...........Mr. Bates
Gratiano..........Mr. Wignell   Leonardo..........Mr. Blissett
Lorenzo..........Mr. Marshall   Balthazar........Mr. J. Darley
Solarino..........Mr. Cleveland   Portia..........Mrs. Whitlock
Salanio.............Mr. Green   Jessica.........Miss Broadhurst
Shylock..........Mr. Chalmers   Nerissa..........Mrs. Francis

The Spoiled Child

Little Pickle......Mrs. Marshall   Miss Pickle........Mrs. Rowson
Old Pickle..........Mr. Green   Maria..........Mrs. Cleveland
Tag...............Mr. Francis   Margery............Mrs. Bates
John..............Mr. Blissett   Susan............Miss Rowson
Thomas........Mr. Darley, Jr.

1795

Jan. 14   *The School for Scandal*   Daily Ad.

Sir Peter Teazle......Mr. Bates   Rowley...........Mr. Warrell
Sir Oliver Surface....Mr. Morris   Moses.............Mr. Francis
Joseph Surface......Mr. Wignell   Snake..............Mr. Green
Charles Surface....Mr. Chalmers   Trip.............Mr. Moreton
Sir Benjamin Backbite..........   Lady Teazle........Mrs. Morris
          Mr. Marshall   Lady Sneerwell.....Mrs. Rowson
Crabtree.........Mr. Harwood   Mrs. Candour.......Mrs. Shaw
Careless..........Mr. Cleveland   Maria............Mrs. Francis
Sir Harry..........Mr. Darley

The Purse

Cast as for Jan. 7, 1795.

Jan. 16   *The Gamester*   Daily Ad.

Beverly..........Mr. Chalmers   Dawson...........Mr. Moreton
Stukely...........Mr. Wignell   Waiter.........Mr. Darley, Jr.
Lewson.........Mr. Cleveland   Mrs. Beverly......Mrs. Whitlock
Jarvis.............Mr. Morris   Charlotte..........Mrs. Francis
Bates...............Mr. Green   Lucy...........Mrs. Cleveland

The Romp

Watty Cockney......Mr. Francis   Priscilla Tomboy..Mrs. Marshall
Barnacle..........Mr. Harwood   Penelope..........Miss Rowson
Old Cockney.......Mr. Warrell   Madame Le Blond.Mrs. Cleveland
Capt. Slightly......Mr. Marshall   Quasheba.....Master T. Warrell

Jan. 17   *Inkle and Yarico*   Aurora

Inkle............Mr. Marshall   3rd Planter.........Mr. Warrell
Sir Christopher Curry...........   Waiter.......Master T. Warrell
          Mr. Whitlock   Mate..............Mr. Darley
Medium...........Mr. Francis   Yarico..........Mrs. Marshall
Campley..........Mr. Moreton   Narcissa.........Miss Willems
Trudge...........Mr. Wignell   Wowski.......Miss Broadhurst
1st Planter.......Mr. Harwood   Patty..............Mrs. Shaw
2nd Planter......Mr. Cleveland

The Critic

Cast as for Dec. 22, 1794, except:

Lord Burleigh........Mr. Bates   Whiskerandos......Mr. Harwood

[237]

1795

Jan. 19   *The Surrender of Calais*   Daily Ad.

King Edward.......Mr. Moreton
Sir Walter Manny..Mr. Warrell
Ribemont.........Mr. Chalmers
La Gloire.........Mr. Harwood
Eustace de Saint Pierre..........
              Mr. Whitlock
John de Vienne........Mr. Green
Citizens.........Messrs. Francis,
            Morris, &c.
Old Man.......Mr. De Moulin

Sergeant..........Mr. Wignell
O'Carrol..........Mr. Marshall
John D'Aire......Mr. Cleveland
1st Gallows Maker..Mr. Blissett
2nd Gallows Maker............
              Mr. Darley, Jr.
Queen.............Mrs. Shaw
Madelon.........Mrs. Marshall
Julia............Mrs. Whitlock

The Wrangling Lovers

Don Carlos.......Mr. Moreton
Don Lorenzo.........Mr. Green
Lopez...........Mr. Harwood

Sancho............Mr. Wignell
Leonora..........Mrs. Francis
Jacintha..........Mrs. Rowson

Jan. 21   *The Gamester*   Daily Ad.

Cast as for January 16, except:

Jarvis............Mr. Whitlock

* *The Volunteers*—Mrs. Rowson

Trueman..........Mr. Marshall
Manly............Mr. Darley
Milikin............Mr. Francis
Jerry...............Mr. Bates
Grumble...........Mr. Blissett
Adams.............Mr. Green
Thomas.........Mr. Darley, Jr.
Jacob..........Mr. De Moulin

Soldiers......Messrs. Warrell, J.
       Warrell, Mitchell, etc.
Miss Aura........Mrs. Marshall
Mrs. Grumble........Mrs. Shaw
Jemima.........Miss Broadhurst
Rosalind...........Miss Rowson
Ruth............Mrs. Cleveland
Omeeah.........Mrs. Oldmixon

First appearance of Mr. Mitchell.

Jan. 23   *Richard III*   Phila. Gaz.

Henry VI.........Mr. Whitlock
Prince Edward....Master Warrell
Duke of York..Master T. Warrell
Duke of Gloucester..Mr. Chalmers
Duke of Buckingham............
              Mr. Wignell
Earl of Richmond..Mr. Moreton
Duke of Norfolk....Mr. Warrell
Ratcliff............Mr. Francis
Catesby..........Mr. Cleveland

Tressel..........Mr. Marshall
Oxford............Mr. Blissett
Lieut. of Tower....Mr. Harwood
Lord Stanley........Mr. Green
Lord Mayor..........Mr. Bates
Tyrrel..........Mr. De Moulin
Queen Elizabeth.....Mrs. Morris
Lady Anne.........Mrs. Francis
Duchess of York......Mrs. Shaw

[238]

1795

Jan. 23 (cont.) *The Deserter*

Henry	Mr. Marshall	Soldiers	Messrs. Rowson, War-
Russet	Mr. Darley		rell, Darley, Jr.
Skirmish	Mr. Bates	Louisa	Mrs. Marshall
Simkin	Mr. Francis	Jenny	Miss Broadhurst
Flint	Mr. Green	Margaretta	Mrs. Bates

Jan. 24   *The Clandestine Marriage*   Daily Ad.

Lord Ogleby	Mr. Chalmers	Trueman	Mr. Warrell
Sir John Melville	Mr. Green	Servant	Mr. Darley, Jr.
Sterling	Mr. Morris	Mrs. Heidelberg	Mrs. Shaw
Lovewell	Mr. Marshall	Miss Sterling	Mrs. Morris
Canton	Mr. Harwood	Fanny	Mrs. Marshall
Brush	Mr. Moreton	Betty	Mrs. Rowson
Sergeant Flower	Mr. Francis	Chambermaid	Mrs. Francis
Traverse	Mr. Cleveland	Trusty	Mrs. Bates

The Purse

Cast as for January 7.

Jan. 26   *The Road to Ruin*   Phila. Gaz.

Dornton	Mr. Whitlock	Tradesmen	Messrs. De Moulin,
Harry Dornton	Mr. Green		Darley, Jr., Price
Sulky	Mr. Francis	Jacob	Mr. Blissett
Silky	Mr. Bates	Marker	Master Warrell
Goldfinch	Mr. Chalmers	Postillion	Master T. Warrell
Milford	Mr. Cleveland	Mrs. Warren	Mrs. Shaw
Smith	Mr. Moreton	Sophia	Mrs. Marshall
Hosier	Mr. Harwood	Jenny	Mrs. Francis
Sheriff's Officer	Mr. Warrell	Mrs. Ledger	Mrs. Bates

The Volunteers

Cast as for January 21, except:

Adams......Mr. Warrell

The part of Jacob is not mentioned, and De Moulin is one of the soldiers. The part of Rosalind not mentioned.

"We hear the President and his Lady intend to honour the Theatre with their Presence this evening."

Jan. 28   *The Country Girl*   Daily Ad.

Moody	Mr. Bates	2d Servant	Mr. Darley, Jr.
Harcourt	Mr. Marshall	Miss Peggy	Mrs. Marshall
Sparkish	Mr. Moreton	Alithea	Mrs. Francis

[239]

1795

Jan. 28 (cont.)

Belville..........Mr. Cleveland   Lucy...............Mrs. Shaw
1st Servant.........Mr. Blissett

Comus

Comus...........Mr. Chalmers   Sabrina.........Miss Broadhurst
1st Spirit............Mr. Green   Pastoral Nymph...Mrs. Marshall
Elder Brother......Mr. Moreton   Euphrosyne.......Mrs. Oldmixon
Younger Brother...Mr. Cleveland   Bacchante.........Mrs. Warrell
Lady...........Mrs. Whitlock

Jan. 30   *The Natural Son*   Daily Ad.

Cast as for December 24, 1794.

No Song No Supper

Frederick.........Mr. Marshall   Dorothy.............Mrs. Shaw
Crop..............Mr. Darley   Louisa............Miss Willems
Endless..........Mr. Harwood   Margaretta.......Mrs. Oldmixon
Robin..............Mr. Bates   Nelly...........Miss Broadhurst
William........Mr. Darley, Jr.

Jan. 31   *Every One Has His Fault*   Phila. Gaz.

Cast as for December 3, 1794, except:

Mrs. Placid.......Mrs. Rowson   Hammond..........Mr. Green
Mr. Harmony........Mr. Bates

Robinson Crusoe

Robinson Crusoe......Mr. Bates   Capt. of Ship........Mr. Darley
Pierot..........Mr. Darley, Jr.   Friday.............Mr. Francis
Pantaloon.......Mr. De Moulin

Feb. 4   *The Clandestine Marriage*   Daily Ad.

Cast as for January 24.

Robinson Crusoe (pantomime under direction of Mr. Bates)

Cast as for January 31.

Feb. 6   *The Country Girl*   Daily Ad.

Cast as for January 28, except that Blissett's part is called "Countryman,"
and Darley, Jr.'s, "Thomas:
William.....Master T. Warrell

Rosina

Cast as for December 17, 1794.

[240]

1795

Feb. 7 *Cymbeline* Aurora

Cymbeline..........Mr. Green	Caius Lucius.........Mr. Bates
Cloten............Mr. Wignell	Frenchman.......Mr. Marshall
Posthumous......Mr. Chalmers	1st Gentleman......Mr. Francis
Arviragus........Mr. Harwood	2d Gentleman....Mr. De Moulin
Guiderius........Mr. Cleveland	Queen..............Mrs. Shaw
Belarius..........Mr. Whitlock	Helena.........Mrs. Cleveland
Philario............Mr. Darley	Imogen.........Mrs. Whitlock
Iachimo..........Mr. Moreton	

The Romp

Cast as for January 16.

Feb. 9 *The Highland Reel* Phila. Gaz.

Laird of Col.........Mr. Green	Capt. Dash.......Mr. Moreton
Laird of Ramsay....Mr. Warrell	Sergeant Jack........Mr. Darley
M'Gilpin.........Mr. Harwood	Apie.........Master T. Warrell
Sandy............Mr. Marshall	Benin..........Master Warrell
Charley............Mr. Francis	Moggy..........Mrs. Marshall
Shelty..............Mr. Bates	Jenny............Mrs. Warrell
Crowdy...........Mr. Blissett	

* *The East Indian*

Sir Hector Strangeways......... Mr. Bates	Buflora..........Mr. Harwood
Col. Ormsby.........Mr. Green	James..........Master Warrell
Brownlow........Mr. Marshall	Zelide............Mrs. Marshall
Orson.............Mr. Blissett	Lady Di Strangeways..Mrs. Shaw
	Jenny............Miss Rowson

Feb. 11 * *The Jew*—Cumberland Daily Ad.

Sir Stephen Berham............. Mr. Whitlock	Jabal............Mr. Harwood
Frederick.........Mr. Moreton	Waiter.........Mr. Darley, Jr.
Chas. Ratcliffe.....Mr. Chalmers	Mrs. Ratcliffe.......Mrs. Shaw
Saunders............Mr. Green	Eliza Ratcliffe.....Mrs. Whitlock
Sheba.............Mr. Wignell	Mrs. Goodison.......Mrs. Bates
	Dorcas............Mrs. Francis

The Purse

Cast as for February 11, except:

Baron...Mr. Green

The Sailor's Landlady

[241]

1795

Feb. 13   *Romeo and Juliet*   Aurora

Cast as for December 12, 1794, except:

Mercutio.........Mr. Chalmers

The Padlock

Don Diego.........Mr. Darley	Mungo..............Mr. Bates
Leander...........Mr. Marshall	Leonora.........Miss Broadhurst
Scholars......Mr. J. Warrell, and	Ursula..............Mrs. Shaw
Mr. Darley, Jr.	

Feb. 14   *Robin Hood*   Daily Ad.
               Ways and Means

Feb. 16   *Douglas*   Daily Ad.
            Ways and Means
            The Irish Lilt

Feb. 18   *The Haunted Tower*   Daily Ad.

Lord William......Mr. Marshall	De Courcy........Mr. Cleveland
Baron of Oakland...Mr. Harwood	Martin............Mr. Warrell
Edward............Mr. Francis	Hubert............Mr. Mitchell
Lewis..............Mr. Blissett	Lady Elinor.......Mrs. Warrell
Robert...........Mr. Darley, Jr.	Adela...........Mrs. Oldmixon
Charles............Mr. Darley	Cicely.........Miss Broadhurst
Hugo..............Mr. Green	Maud..............Mrs. Bates

The Miller of Mansfield

King.............Mr. Whitlock	2nd Courtier.....Master Warrell
Miller.............Mr. Morris	3rd Courtier........Mr. Mitchell
Richard..........Mr. Moreton	Keeper..............Mr. Price
Lord Lurewell.....Mr. Cleveland	Peggy.............Miss Oldfield
Joe..............Mr. Darley, Jr.	Margery............Mrs. Bates
1st Courtier........Mr. Warrell	Kate.............Miss Willems

Feb. 20   *The English Merchant*   Daily Ad.
      Three Weeks After Marriage
        The Irish Lilt

Feb. 21   *The Jew*   Phila. Gaz.

Cast as for Feb 11.

The *Philadelphia Gazette* said that *The Flitch of Bacon* was the farce, but the *Aurora* announced *The Prize*.

The Tempest

[242]

1795

Feb. 24   *Neptune and Amphitrite*   Daily Ad.
The Critic

Feb. 25   *The Haunted Tower*   Daily Ad.
The East Indian

Feb. 27   *The Country Girl*   Daily Ad.

Cast as for Feb. 6, 1795.

La Forêt Noire

Geronte............Mr. Green	Pasquin..........Mr. Darley, Jr.
Lanzedan..........Mr. Moreton	Lucille.............Mrs. Francis
Adolphe.......Master T. Warrell	Martin............Miss Rowson
Prince..............Mr. Francis	Le Terreur........Mr. Marshall
Lubin..........Master Warrell	Sans Quartier......Mr. Cleveland
Fronte............Mr. Warrell	Le Fourbe...........Mr. Blissett

Feb. 28   *The Fair Penitent*   Daily Ad.

Sciolto............Mr. Whitlock	Rosano.............Mr. Warrell
Altamount...........Mr. Green	Calista...........Mrs. Whitlock
Horatio..........Mr. Chalmers	Lavinia............Mrs. Francis
Lothario..........Mr. Moreton	Lucilla............Miss Oldfield

Peeping Tom of Coventry

Cast as for Dec. 31, 1794.

March 2   *Lionel and Clarissa*   Daily Ad.
La Forêt Noire

March 4   *Isabella*   Daily Ad.

Cast as for Dec. 17, 1794, except that Mr. Francis as Pedro is not mentioned.

* *The Farm House*—Kemble

Medley...........Mr. Cleveland	1st Constable........Mr. Blissett
Freehold..........Mr. Whitlock	2nd Constable.....Mr. Darley, Jr.
Shacklefigure.......Mr. Francis	Aurra............Mrs. Marshall
Heartwell.........Mr. Moreton	Flora..............Mrs. Francis
Sir John English.....Mr. Warrell	

The Caledonian Frolic

March 6   *She Would and She Would Not*   Daily Ad.

Don Manuel.........Mr. Morris	Diego...........Mr. De Moulin
Don Philip........Mr. Cleveland	Vasquez.........Master Warrell
Don Lewis.........Mr. Moreton	Hypolita..........Mrs. Marshall
Octavio.............Mr. Green	Rosana.............Mrs. Morris

1795

Traffonti.........Mr. Chalmers	Flora.............Mrs. Francis
Soto.................Mr. Bates	Villetta............Mrs. Shaw
Corrigidore........Mr. Warrell	

The Waterman

Bundle............Mr. Francis	Mrs. Bundle.........Mrs. Shaw
Tug...............Mr. Darley	Wilhelmina......Miss Broadhurst
Robin..............Mr. Bates	

March 7   The Jew   Daily Ad.
                 The Prize

March 9   The Haunted Tower   Phila. Gaz.

Cast as for February 18.

The Farm House

Cast as for March 4, except:

Modely.......Mr. Chalmers

March 11   Every One Has His Fault   Daily Ad.

Cast as for December 3, 1794, except:

Mr. Harmony........Mr. Bates	Hammond..........Mr. Green
Mr. Placid.......Mr. Cleveland	

The Poor Soldier

Capt. Fitzroy.......Mr. Moreton	Bagatelle.........Mr. Marshall
Father Luke........Mr. Blissett	Boy.........Master T. Warrell
Dermot.........Mr. Darley, Jr.	Norah........Miss Broadhurst
Patrick............Mr. Darley	Kathleen.........Miss Willems
Darby............Mr. Wignell	

March 13   * Fontainville Forest—Boaden   Aurora

Marquis of Montault...Mr. Green	Jacques...........Mr. Warrell
Lamotte..........Mr. Chalmers	Nemours.........Mr. Cleveland
Louis............Mr. Moreton	Hortensia..........Mrs. Shaw
Peter............Mr. Whitlock	Adeline.........Mrs. Whitlock

The Agreeable Surprize

Sir Felix Friendly....Mr. Francis	Cudden.............Mr. Blissett
Compton..........Mr. Darley	Lingo................Mr. Bates
Eugene.........Mr. Darley, Jr.	Laura.........Miss Broadhurst
Chicane...........Mr. Warrell	Mrs. Cheshire........Mrs. Shaw
John............Mr. Cleveland	Cowslip.........Mrs. Solomons
Thomas............Mr. Green	(first appearance on this stage)
Farmer Stump.....Mr. DeMoulin	Fringe...........Miss Willems

1795

March 14	*The Tempest*	Phila. Gaz.
	The Spoiled Child	
March 16	*Fontainville Forest*	Phila. Gaz.
	The Prisoner at Large	
March 18	*The School for Wives*	Daily Ad.

General Savage........Mr. Bates   Crow..............Mr. Blissett
Belville...........Mr. Chalmers   Wolf..............Mr. Warrell
Torrington..........Mr. Morris   Miss Walsingham....Mrs. Morris
Leeson.............Mr. Moreton   Mrs. Belville......Mrs. Whitlock
Capt. Savage.......Mr. Cleveland   Lady Rachel Mildew. Mrs. Rowson
Connolly..........Mr. Whitlock   Mrs. Tempest.....Mrs. Solomons
Spruce.............Mr. Francis   Miss Leeson.........Mrs. Francis
Leech..............Mr. Green   Maid.............Miss Willems

The Children in the Wood

Sir Rowland.........Mr. Green   Helen............Mrs. Solomons
Lord Alford........Mr. Marshall   Josephine.........Mrs. Marshall
Walter..........Mr. Harwood   Winifred..........Mrs. Rowson
Apathy...............Mr. Bates   Boy..............Master Parker
Gabriel...........Mr. Moreton   Girl.............Miss Solomons
Oliver..........Mr. Darley, Jr.   (being her first appearance on this
Russian..........Mr. De Moulin   stage)

The Irish Lilt

First appearance of Master Parker.

| March 20 | *The Busy Body* | Phila. Gaz. |

Marplot...........Mr. Chalmers   Butler............Mr. Warrell
Sir George Airy.....Mr. Moreton   Miranda..........Mrs. Marshall
Charles.............Mr. Green   Isabinda...........Mrs. Francis
Sir Francis Gripe.....Mr. Morris   Patch..............Mrs. Shaw
Sir Jealous Traffic....Mr. Francis   Scentwell........Mrs. Cleveland
Whisper...........Mr. Blissett

The Children in the Wood

Cast as for March 18, except:

Russian............Mr. Blissett

March 21	*The Rivals*	Daily Ad.
	Comus	
March 23	*Fontainville Forest*	Phila. Gaz., Mar. 21
	Hartford Bridge	

[245]

1795

March 25   *The Belle's Stratagem*   Phila. Gaz.

Doricourt........Mr. Chalmers	Gentleman........Mr. Harwood
Hardy.............Mr. Morris	Gibson............Mr. Warrell
Sir George Touchwood........ Mr. Whitlock	Dick..............Mr. Blissett
	Letitia Hardy......Mrs. Morris
Flutter...........Mr. Marshall	Mrs. Racket.........Mrs. Shaw
Saville.............Mr. Green	Lady Frances Touchwood....... Mrs. Cleveland
Saville's Servant...Mr. Darley, Jr.	
Villers...........Mr. Cleveland	Miss Ogle........Mrs. Solomons
Courtail..........Mr. Moreton	Kitty Willis........Mrs. Rowson

The Children in the Wood

Cast as for March 18, except:

Russian............Mr. Blissett

March 27   *The West Indian*   Daily Ad.

Stockwell...........Mr. Morris	Varland.............Mr. Bates
Belcour..........Mr. Chalmers	Sailor.............Mr. Blissett
Capt. Dudley.........Mr. Green	Lady Rusport.........Mrs. Shaw
Chas. Dudley......Mr. Cleveland	Charlotte Rusport..Mrs. Marshall
Major O'Flaherty..Mr. Whitlock	Louisa Dudley......Miss Willems
Stukely...........Mr. Moreton	Mrs. Fulmer........Mrs. Rowson
Fulmer..........Mr. Harwood	Lucy..............Miss Rowson

The Devil to Pay

Sir John Loverule...Mr. Marshall	Jobson..............Mr. Bates
Butler.............Mr. Francis	Lady Loverule.......Mrs. Francis
Cook..............Mr. Blissett	Lucy..............Miss Willems
Footman.........Mr. Solomons	Lettice..........Mrs. Cleveland
Coachman.......Mr. Darley, Jr.	Nell.............Mrs. Marshall
Conjurer..........Mr. Warrell	

March 28   *The Jew*   Aurora
                  The Purse

The *Daily Advertiser* gives *Poor Vulcan* as the afterpiece, but as that burletta is advertised for April 6 as "never performed in America," *The Purse* was probably the afterpiece for March 28.

March 30   *The Orphan*   Phila. Gaz.
                  The Devil to Pay

March 31   *The Busybody*   Daily Ad.
                  The Deuce is in Him

1795

April 1	*Love in a Village*	Daily Ad.
	The Critic	
April 2	*The Haunted Tower*	Daily Ad.
	Ways and Means	
April 6	* *The Box-Lobby Challenge*—Cumberland	Phila. Gaz.,
	* *Rural Revels*—Francis	April 4
	* *Poor Vulcan* (burletta)—Dibdin	

Of *Poor Vulcan* it says—"never performed in America"—See March 28.

| April 8 | *The Woodman* | Aurora |
| | *The Devil to Pay* | |

Sir John Loverule...Mr. Marshall | Jobson............Mr. Harwood
Butler.............Mr. Francis | Lady Loverule......Mrs. Francis
Cook..............Mr. Blissett | Lucy.............Miss Willems
Footman.........Mr. Solomons | Lettice..........Mrs. Cleveland
Coachman.......Mr. Darley, Jr. | Nell.............Mrs. Marshall
Conjurer..........Mr. Warrell

April 10	*The Jealous Wife*	Daily Ad.
	Rural Revels	
	The Liar	

| April 13 | *Percy* | Daily Ad. |

Percy............Mr. Moreton | Sir Hubert.......Mr. Cleveland
Earl Douglass........Mr. Green | Messenger.......Mr. Darley, Jr.
Earl Raby........Mr. Whitlock | Elvina..........Mrs. Whitlock
Edric............Mr. Harwood | Bertha..........Mrs. Cleveland
Harcourt.......Mr. Warrell, Jr.

High Life Below Stairs

Lovel............Mr. Marshall | Robert.............Mr. Blissett
Trueman........Mr. Cleveland | Tom............Mr. Darley, Jr.
Sir Harry..........Mr. Francis | Kitty.............Mrs. Morris
Lord Duke........Mr. Harwood | Lady Bab.........Mrs. Rowson
Philip............Mr. Wignell | Lady Charlotte......Mrs. Francis
Coachman..........Mr. Warrell | Cook...............Mrs. Bates
Kingston.......Mr. Warrell Jr. | Chloe............Miss Rowson

| April 15 | *The Beaux' Stratagem* | Daily Ad. |

Aimwell............Mr. Green | Bonniface..........Mr. Darley
Archer...........Mr. Chalmers | Scrub..............Mr. Morris
Sullen...........Mr. Whitlock | Lady Bountiful.....Mrs. Rowson
Sir Charles Freeman.Mr. Cleveland | Dorinda...........Mrs. Francis

[247]

1795

April 15 (cont.)

Foigard	Mr. Marshall	Mrs. Sullen	Mrs. Whitlock
Gibbett	Mr. Francis	Gipsey	Miss Willems
Hounslow	Mr. Solomons	Cherry	Mrs. Cleveland
Bagshot	Mr. Darley, Jr.		

The Children in the Wood

April 17   *The Carmelite*   Daily Ad.

Saint Valori	Mr. Whitlock	Gyfford	Mr. Harwood
Lord de Courci	Mr. Green	Fitz-Allan	Mr. Warrell, Jr.
Lord Hildebrand	Mr. Moreton	Raymond	Mr. Warrell
Montgomeri	Mr. Cleveland	Matilda	Mrs. Whitlock

The Two Misers

Gripe	Mr. Francis	Osman	Mr. Darley, Jr.
Hunks	Mr. Wignell	Mustapha	Mr. Blissett
Lively	Mr. Marshall	Harriet	Miss Broadhurst
Ali	Mr. Darley	Jenny	Mrs. Oldmixon

April 18   *The English Merchant*   Daily Ad.
The Two Misers

April 20

There is a confusion as to the play, *The Aurora* and *The Daily Advertiser* giving *The English Merchant,* and *The Philadelphia Gazette* announcing *The Carmelite.* They agree on *The Two Misers* as afterpiece. No casts were given.

April 22   *Tamerlane*   Aurora

Tamerlan	Mr. Whitlock	Mirvan	Mr. Mitchell
Bajazet	Mr. Chalmers	Zama	Mr. Darley, Jr.
Axalla	Mr. Cleveland	Hali	Mr. Warrell, Jr.
Moneses	Mr. Moreton	Dervise	Mr. Morris
Prince of Tanais	Mr. Warrell	Arpasia	Mrs. Whitlock
Omar	Mr. Harwood	Selima	Mrs. Marshall

Tom Thumb the Great

Tom Thumb	Miss Solomons	Queen Dollalolla	Mrs. Warrell
King Arthur	Mr. Bates	Princess Huncamunca	
Lord Grizzle	Mr. Marshall		Mrs. Oldmixon
Noodle	Mr. Francis	Cleora	Miss Oldfield
Doodle	Mr. Darley, Jr.	Mustacha	Miss Willems
Merlin & Ghost of Gaffer Thumb	} Mr. Darley	Glumdalca	Mr. Rowson

1795

April 24   *Inkle and Yarico*   Aurora

Cast as for Jan. 17, except:

Trudge...........Mr. Bates

Tom Thumb

Cast as for April 22, except:

Lord Grizzle.......Mr. Harwood   Doodle............Mr. Blissett

April 27   *She Stoops to Conquer*   Aurora

Sir Chas. Marlow....	Mr. Warrell	Landlord...........	Mr. Darley
Young Marlow.....	Mr. Chalmers	Jeremy.............	Mr. Blissett
Hardcastle.........	Mr. Morris	Mrs. Hardcastle......	Mrs. Shaw
Hastings..........	Mr. Cleveland	Miss Hardcastle...	Mrs. Marshall
Tony Lumpkin........	Mr. Bates	Miss Neville.......	Mrs. Francis
Diggory............	Mr. Francis	Maid..............	Miss Willems

* *My Grandmother*—Hoare

Sir Mathew Medley...	Mr. Francis	Souffrance........	Mr. Harwood
Vapour...........	Mr. Moreton	Tom..............	Mr. Blissett
Woodney...........	Mr. Darley	Florella.........	Mrs. Oldmixon
Gossip..............	Mr. Bates	Charlotte.......	Miss Broadhurst

April 29   *The Heiress*   Aurora

Sir Clement Flint...	Mr. Whitlock	Rightly...........	Mr. Cleveland
Clifford..........	Mr. Chalmers	Lady Emily........	Mrs. Morris
Lord Gayville......	Mr. Moreton	Miss Alscript.....	Mrs. Whitlock
Alscript............	Mr. Morris	Miss Alton........	Mrs. Marshall
Chignon...........	Mr. Marshall	Mrs. Sagely.........	Mrs. Bates
Blandish..........	Mr. Harwood	Tiffany..........	Mrs. Cleveland
Prompt............	Mr. Francis	Mrs. Blandish......	Mrs. Rowson

The Two Misers

Cast as for April 17.

May 1   *The Jew*   Aurora

Cast as for February 11, except:

Mrs. Goodison....Mrs. Cleveland   Dorcas...........Mrs. Rowson

The Sailor's Landlady
Tom Thumb

Cast as for April 22, except:

Lord Grizzle.......Mr. Harwood

1795

May 4   Mrs. Marshall's Night   Daily Ad.

Know Your Own Mind—Murphy

Millamour	Mr. Moreton	Charles	Mr. Francis
Dashwood	Mr. Chalmers	Lady Bill	Mrs. Marshall
Malvil	Mr. Whitlock	Lady Jane	Mrs. Cleveland
Bygone	Mr. Bates	Mrs. Bromley	Mrs. Shaw
Capt. Bygone	Mr. Cleveland	Madame Le Rouge	Mrs. Rowson
Sir John Millamour	Mr. Warrell	Miss Neville	Mrs. Francis
Sir Harry Lovewit	Mr. Harwood		

Rural Revels
Auld Robin Gray—Arnold

Auld Robin Gray	Mr. Bates	Jamie	Mr. Marshall
Donald	Mr. Francis	Dorcas	Mrs. Rowson
M. Fracas	Mr. Harwood	Jennie	Mrs. Marshall

May 6   Mrs. Morris's Night   Aurora

The Child of Nature

Marquis of Almanza	Mr. Whitlock	2d Peasant	Mr. Warrell
Count Valantia	Mr. Chalmers	Marchioness of Merida	
Duke of Mercia	Mr. Bates		Mrs. Morris
Seville	Mr. Cleveland	Amanthis	Mrs. Marshall
Grenada	Mr. Wignell	Attendant	Miss Oldfield
1st Peasant	Mr. Marshall		

The Sicilian Romance—Siddons

Ferrand	Mr. Moreton	Gerbin	Mr. Wignell
Don Lope de Viega	Mr. Morris	Julia	Miss Solomons
Lindor	Mr. Marshall	Alinda	Miss Broadhurst
Martin	Mr. Harwood	Clara	Mrs. Oldmixon
Jacques	Mr. Blissett	Adelaide	Mrs. Whitlock
Sancho	Mr. Warrell		

May 8   Mrs. Oldmixon's Night   Aurora

The Noble Peasant—Holcroft

Leonard	Mr. Moreton	Will Clowdeslee	Mr. Darley, Jr.
Earl Walter	Mr. Whitlock	Fool	Mr. Bates
Earl Egbert	Mr. Francis	Dwarf	Miss Solomons
Annloff	Mr. Rowson	Edwitha	Mrs. Marshall
Harold	Mr. Cleveland	Adela	Mrs. Oldmixon
Adam Belt	Mr. Darley	Alice	Miss Broadhurst
Clym O' The Cleugh	Mr. Marshall		

1795

May 8 (cont.)   *The Apprentice*

Wingate	Mr. Morris	Scotchman	Mr. Darley, Jr.
Dick	Mr. Chalmers	President of Club	Mr. Darley
Gargle	Mr. Harwood	Bailiff	Mr. Warrell
Simon	Mr. Bates	Watchman	Mr. Francis
Irishman	Mr. Blissett	Charlotte	Mrs. Francis

May 11   Benefit of Mr. Bates   Aurora

A New Way to Pay Old Debts

Sir Giles Overreach	Mr. Chalmers	Allworth	Mr. Cleveland
Lord Lovell	Mr. Moreton	Marrall	Mr. Harwood
Justice Greedy	Mr. Bates	Order	Mr. Warrell
Tapwell	Mr. Wignell	Fumace	Mr. Francis
Amble	Mr. Blissett	Lady Allworth	Mrs. Shaw
Waitwell	Mr. Warrell	Margaretta	Mrs. Marshall
Wellborn	Mr. Whitlock	Froth	Mrs. Rowson

* *Set a Beggar on Horseback*—O'Keeffe

Old Codger	Mr. Francis	Scout	Mr. Harwood
Cosey	Mr. Warrell	Master Billy	Mr. Darley
Bamey Vag	Mr. Blissett	James	Mr. Warrell, Jr.
Music Master	Mr. Darley, Jr.	Nancy Buttercup	Mrs. Marshall
Comey	Mr. Bates	Mrs. Mummery	Mrs. Shaw
Horace	Mr. Cleveland	Miss Bamey Vag	Miss Rowson

May 13   Mr. Darley's Night   Aurora

The Brothers (*The Shipwreck*)

Sir Benjamin Dove	Mr. Morris	Francis	Mr. Darley, Jr.
Belfield, Sr.	Mr. Moreton	Jonathan	Mr. Darley
Belfield, Jr.	Mr. Marshall	Lady Dove	Mrs. Shaw
Capt. Ironsides	Mr. Chalmers	Sophia	Mrs. Marshall
Skiff	Mr. Francis	Violetta	Mrs. Morris
Patterson	Mr. Cleveland	Fanny	Mrs. Cleveland
Old Goodwin	Mr. Warrell	Lucy Waters	Mrs. Francis
Philip	Mr. Harwood	Kitty	Miss Willems

* *The Sailor's Return*—Francis
The Quaker

Steady	Mr. Darley	Gillian	Mr. Marshall
Solomon	Mr. Bates	Floretta	Miss Broadhurst
Lubin	Mr. Marshall	Cecily	Mrs. Solomons
Farmer Casey	Mr. Warrell		

[251]

1795

May 15   Mrs. Whitlock's Night   Aurora

The Roman Father

Tullus Hostilius.... Mr. Moreton	1st Citizen........ Mr. Mitchell
Horatius......... Mr. Whitlock	2d Citizen.......... Mr. Blissett
Publius.......... Mr. Chalmers	3d Citizen......... Mr. Solomon
Valerius......... Mr. Cleveland	Horatia.......... Mrs. Whitlock
Valscinius....... Mr. Darley, Jr.	Valeria.......... Mrs. Cleveland
Roman Soldier...... Mr. Warrell	

The Midnight Hour

Marquis......... Mr. Marshall	Ambrose.......... Mr. Warrell
General.......... Mr. Harwood	Julia.............. Mrs. Francis
Sebastian........... Mr. Francis	Cicely.............. Mrs. Bates
Nicholas............. Mr. Bates	Flora........... Mrs. Whitlock
Mathias........... Mr. Blissett	

May 18   Mr. Chalmers' Night   Aurora

The Suspicious Husband

Ranger.......... Mr. Chalmers	Simon............. Mr. Warrell
Strictland........ Mr. Whitlock	Ranger's Servant. Mr. Warrell, Jr.
Frankly.......... Mr. Moreton	Mrs. Strictland.... Mrs. Cleveland
Bellamy......... Mr. Cleveland	Jacintha............ Mrs. Francis
Jack Meggotts..... Mr. Harwood	Lucetta............. Mrs. Shaw
Tester.............. Mr. Bates	Landlady........... Mrs. Bates
Buckle............ Mr. Blissett	Clarinda......... Mrs. Marshall

* The Roman Actor ("from Massinger")

Paris............. Mr. Chalmers	Lictors...... Mr. J. Darley & Mr. Mitchell
Aretimus......... Mr. Whitlock	
Asopus............ Mr. Warrell	Senators....... Mr. Solomons, etc.
Latimus............. Mr. Price	

Duke and No Duke

Lavinio........... Mr. Moreton	Trapolin............ Mr. Bates
Barbarino.......... Mr. Francis	Isabella.......... Mrs. Cleveland
Alberto........... Mr. Warrell	Prudentia......... Mrs. Francis
Brunetta......... Mr. Cleveland	Flametto......... Miss Willems
Puritan.......... Mr. Harwood	Mob Woman........ Mrs. Bates
Conjurer........... Mr. Blissett	

[252]

1795

May 20   Mr. Moreton's Night   Daily Ad.

A Bold Stroke for a Husband

Don Julio..........Mr. Chalmers
Don Carlos..........Mr. Moreton
Don Vincentio.....Mr. Harwood
Don Caesar...........Mr. Bates
Don Garcia.......Mr. Cleveland
Don Vasquez........Mr. Francis
Don Gasper........Mr. Whitlock

Pedro..............Mr. Blissett
Olivia............Mrs. Marshall
Victoria..........Mrs. Whitlock
Laura..............Mrs. Francis
Minette.............Mrs. Shaw
Marcella.........Mrs. Cleveland
Inis..............Mrs. Solomons
Sancho..............Mrs. Bates

The Scheming Milliners

(a comic dance)

Old M'Donald.......Mr. Blissett
Patie...............Mr. Francis
Billy Whiffle.......Mr. Warrell

Milliners.....{ Miss Milbourne
              { Mrs. De Marque

Hob in the Well

Sir Thomas Trusty....Mr. Francis
Friendly..........Mr. Marshall
Hob................Mr. Bates
Old Hob...........Mr. Warrell
Rich.............Mr. Harwood

Roger..............Mr. Blissett
Flora.............Mrs. Warrell
Betty............Mrs. Solomons
Hob's Mother.........Mrs. Bates

May 22   * *The Triumphs of Love*—"by a Citizen   Daily Ad.
              of Philadelphia"—Murdock

George Friendly, Sr..Mr. Whitlock
Jack Friendly, Sr. ....Mr. Morris
George Friendly, Jr..Mr. Moreton
Jack Friendly, Jr. ....Mr. Francis
Major Manly.....Mr. Chalmers
Peevish............Mr. Wignell
Beauchamp........Mr. Cleveland
Triple............Mr. Marshall
Careless............Mr. Green
Patrick..........Mr. Harwood

Sambo...............Mr. Bates
Dick...............Mr. Blissett
Watchman.......Mr. Darley, Jr.
Constable.........Mr. Mitchell
Hannah Friendly......Mrs. Shaw
Rachel Friendly....Mrs. Marshall
Mrs. Peevish......Mrs. Whitlock
Clementina........Miss Willems
Jenny..............Mrs. Francis

* *The Wedding Day*—Mrs. Inchbald

Lord Rakeland......Mr. Moreton
Sir Adam Contest...Mr. Harwood
Mr. Milden.........Mr. Warrell
Mr. Contest.......Mr. Cleveland
Lady Autumn.......Mrs. Rowson

Lady Contest........Mrs. Hervey
(From the Hay-market Thea-
tre, being her first appearance
in America)
Mrs. Hamford........Mrs. Shaw
Hannah...........Miss Rowson

[253]

1795

May 22 (cont.)   *Tom Thumb The Great*

Tom Thumb......Miss Solomons	Queen Dollalolla...Mrs. Warrell
King Arthur..........Mr. Bates	Princess Huncamunca..........
Lord Grizzle.......Mr. Harwood	Mrs. Oldmixon
Noodle............Mr. Francis	Cleora...........Miss Oldfield
Doodle............Mr. Blissett	Mustacha........Miss Willems
Merlin &	Glumdalca.........Mr. Rowson
Ghost of Gaffer Thumb..........	
Mr. Darley	

First appearance of Mrs. Hervey.

May 25   Mr. Marshall's Night   Daily Ad.

The Conscious Lovers

Young Bevil.......Mr. Chalmers	Tom.............Mr. Marshall
Myrtle..........Mr. Cleveland	Indiana..........Mrs. Marshall
Amberton...........Mr. Bates	Mrs. Sealand......Mrs. Rowson
Sealand.........Mr. Whitlock	Isabella.............Mrs. Bates
Sir John Bevil.......Mr. Green	Lucinda.........Mrs. Cleveland
Humphrey.........Mr. Warrell	Phyllis.............Mrs. Hervey
Daniel.............Mr. Blissett	

* *Harlequin Hurry Scurry*—Francis (pantomime)

Harlequin..........Mr. Francis	Tailor..........Mr. J. Warrell
Farmer............Mr. Rowson	Sawyers........Mr. Price & Mr.
Cobbler.........Mr. Darley, Jr.	Mitchell
Clown.............Mr. Blissett	Columbine......Mrs. De Marque
Barber.........Mr. T. Warrell	

Midas

Jupiter............Mr. Warrell	Midas...............Mr. Bates
Apollo...........Mr. Marshall	Dametas............Mr. Blissett
Momus..........Mr. Solomons	Sileno..............Mr. Darley
Mercury.........Mr. J. Darley	Myrio............Mrs. Rowson
Pan...............Mr. Francis	Daphne.........Mrs. Oldmixon
Juno.............Miss Willems	Myra...........Mrs. Marshall

May 27   Mrs. Warrell's Night   Daily Ad.

The Duenna

Don Jerome.......Mr. Harwood	Porter...........Mr. Milbourne
Ferdinand........Mr. Moreton	Friars.....Messrs. Mitchell, Solo-
Antonio........Mr. Darley, Jr.	mons, Price, &c.
Carlos............Mr. Marshall	Clara............Mrs. Warrell

1795

Isaac.............Mr. Wignell
Lopez.............Mr. Blissett
Father Paul.........Mr. Darley

Louisa.........Miss Broadhurst
Duenna.............Mrs. Shaw

Fruitless Precaution

(comic dance)

The Little Yankee Sailor

Jack Worthy........Mr. Darley
Harding..........Mr. Cleveland
Hatchway..........Mr. Francis
Capt. Bowling.......Mr. Warrell
Tango.............Mr. Green

William (the Little Yanky Sailor).
Master T. Warrell
Mary.............Mrs. Warrell
Emily...........Mrs. Marshall
Arra..........Miss Broadhurst

May 29   *The Toy*   Daily Ad.

Sir Carol O'Donovan............
Mr. Whitlock
Young Kavenagh....Mr. Moreton
Alibi..............Mr. Morris
Larry.............Mr. Wignell
Metheglin...........Mr. Bates
Aircourt..........Mr. Chalmers
Nol Pros...........Mr. Warrell
Decroteur..........Mr. Blissett

1st Waiter.......Mr. Darley, Jr.
2d Waiter........Mr. Solomons
Footman.......Mr. Warrell, Jr.
Boy.........Master T. Warrell
Lady Arable.........Mrs. Shaw
Lady Jane.........Mrs. Morris
Sophia...........Mrs. Marshall
Fib..............Miss Willems
Katy Kavenagh.....Mrs. Rowson

The Prisoner—Rose

Marcos..........Mr. Marshall
Bernardo...........Mr. Darley
Pasqual.........Mr. Darley, Jr.
Roberto.........Mr. Harwood
Lewis............Mr. Moreton
Theresa..........Mrs. Hervey

Narcisso...."A Young Gentleman,
being his first appearance on
this stage."
Clara..........Miss Broadhurst
Nina.............Mrs. Marshall
Juliana..........Miss Solomons

June 1   Mr. Whitlock's Night   Daily Ad., May 30

The Merry Wives of Windsor

Falstaff...........Mr. Whitlock
Fenton...........Mr. Cleveland
Justice Shallow.....Mr. Harwood
Master Slender.....Mr. Moreton
Page...............Mr. Green
Ford...........Mr. Chalmers
Sir Hugh Evans........Mr. Bates
Dr. Caius.........Mr. Marshall

Nym..............Mr. Warrell
Pistol.............Mr. Francis
Robin (Falstaff's page).........
Miss Solomons
Simple.............Mr. Blissett
Rugby...........Mr. J. Warrell
Mrs. Page........Mrs. Whitlock
Mrs. Ford.........Mrs. Morris

[255]

1795

June 1 (cont.)

Host..............Mr. Wignell   Ann Page.........Miss Willems
Bardolf..........Mr. Darley, Jr.   Mrs. Quickly.......Mrs. Rowson

* *The Jubilee*—Garrick

June 3   Mr. Green's Night   Daily Ad.

The Constant Couple

Sir Harry Wildair..*Mrs.* Marshall   Young Clincher........Mr. Bates
  (being her first appearance in   Tom Errand.........Mr. Francis
  that character, and for that   Dicky..............Mr. Blissett
  night only)   Constable........Mr. Darley, Jr.
Col. Standard......Mr. Moreton   Angelica...........Mrs. Hervey
Vizard...........Mr. Cleveland   Lady Lurewell......Mrs. Francis
Alderman Smuggler...Mr. Morris   Parly..............Mrs. Shaw
Beau Clincher........Mr. Green   Tom Errand's Wife....Mrs. Bates

The Sailor's Return
The Sicilian Romance

Cast as for May 6.

June 5   Mr. Harwood's night   Daily Ad.

* *The Next Door Neighbours*—Mrs. Inchbald

Sir George Splendorville........   Bluntly...........Mr. Harwood
                Mr. Moreton   Shopman........Mr. Darley, Jr.
Manly..............Mr. Green   Lady Car. Seymour..Mrs. Francis
Backman............Mr. Bates   Lady Squander......Mrs. Rowson
Lucre.............Mr. Wignell   Evans...........Mrs. Solomons
Welford.........Mr. Whitlock   Eleanor.........Mrs. Marshall
Henry...........Mr. Marshall

The Prisoner

Cast as for May 29.

The Mayor of Garratt

(reduced to one act)

Sir Jacob Jollup......Mr. Francis   Roger..............Mr. Blissett
Major Sturgeon....Mr. Chalmers   Mrs. Sneak...........Mrs. Shaw
Jerry Sneak.......Mr. Harwood   Mrs. Bruin......Mrs. Cleveland
Bruin..............Mr. Green

June 8   Miss Broadhurst's Night   Aurora

The Beggar's Opera

Peachum............Mr. Bates   Robin of Bagshot..Mr. Darley, Jr.
Lockit.............Mr. Francis   Nimming Ned.....Mr. J. Warrell

[256]

1795

June 8 (cont.)

Macheath.........Mr. Marshall	Harry of Paddington.Mr. Warrell
Filch...............Mr. Blissett	Mrs. Peachum........Mrs. Shaw
Jemmy Twitcher...Mr. Cleveland	Polly Peachum...Miss Broadhurst
Mat O' The Mint.....Mr. Darley	Lucy Lockit......Mrs. Oldmixon
Ben Budge..........Mr. Green	

* The First Floor—Cobb

Whimsey...........Mr. Green	Frank...........Mr. J. Warrell
Monford.........Mr. Cleveland	Snap...........Mr. Darley, Jr.
Young Whimsey....Mr. Moreton	Landlord...........Mr. Warrell
Fumish..............Mr. Bates	Post Boy........Master Warrell
Simon.............Mr. Blissett	Mrs. Patty Pan.....Mrs. Rowson
Tim Tartlett......Mr. Harwood	Charlotte.........Miss Oldfield
	Nancy.............Mrs. Hervey

June 10   Mrs. Shaw's Night   Aurora

The Chapter of Accidents

Lord Glenmore.....Mr. Marshall	Jacob.............Mr. Harwood
Governor Harcourt....Mr. Green	Servant..........Mr. J. Warrell
Woodville.........Mr. Chalmers	Cecilia.........Mrs. Marshall
Capt. Harcourt....Mr. Cleveland	Miss Mortimore...Mrs. Cleveland
Gray.............Mr. Whitlock	Wamer...........Mr. Solomons
Vane..............Mr. Francis	Bridget.............Mrs. Shaw

Linco's Travels

Linco...............Mr. Bates	Dorcas..............Mrs. Bates

The Children in the Wood

Cast as for March 18, except:

Oliver.............Mr. Darley	Helen...........Mrs. Solomons
Russian............Mr. Blissett	

June 12   Mr. and Mrs. Francis's Night   Daily Ad.

* Better Late Than Never—Andrews

Saville...........Mr. Moreton	Lawyer Clerk........Mr. Blissett
Flurry..............Mr. Francis	Richard.........Mr. J. Warrell
Sir Chas. Chouse......Mr. Green	Charles.........Mr. Darley, Jr.
Grump..............Mr. Bates	Augusta.........Mrs. Whitlock
Litigamus........Mr. Harwood	Mrs. Flurry.......Mrs. Hervey
Pallet............Mr. Marshall	Diary.............Mrs. Francis

* Les Armans d'Arcade—Francis

"a new divertisement"

[257]

1795

June 12 (cont.) * *The Guardian Outwitted*—Francis

The Guardian	Mr. Nugent	Alonzo	Mr. Francis
Orsini	Mr. Warrell, Jr.	Marcella	Mrs. De Marque

Harlequin's Invasion

"a speaking pantomime"

(this cast in *Aurora*)

Harlequin	Mr. Francis	Crier	Master Warrell
Mercury	Mr. Marshall	Padlock	Mr. J. Warrell
Forge	Mr. Moreton	Fairy	"A Young Lady"
Bounce	Mr. Green	Fairy Harlequin	Master Parker
Frontin	Mr. Harwood	Fairy Columbine	Miss Solomons
Taffy	Mr. Cleveland	Dolly Snip	Mrs. Francis
Bog	Mr. Darley, Jr.	Mrs. Snip	Mrs. Rowson
Simon (the Clown)	Mr. Wignell	Sukey Chitterlie	Miss Willems
Snip	Mr. Bates	Old Woman	Mr. Marshall
Abraham	Mr. Blissett	Tragic Nurse	Mrs. Cleveland
Justice	Mr. Warrell	Comic Nurse	Miss Milbourne

June 15   Mr. and Mrs. Cleveland's Night   Aurora

* *The Follies of a Day*—Holcroft

Count	Mr. Chalmers	Page	Mrs. Marshall
Figaro	Mr. Harwood	Countess	Mrs. Cleveland
Antonio	Mr. Bates	Marcelina	Mrs. Rowson
Basil	Mr. Francis	Agnes	Miss Rowson
Courier	Mr. Darley, Jr.	Susan	Mrs. Whitlock

* *The Devil in the Wine Cellar*—Hill

Sir Timothy Tough	Mr. Morris	Sprightly	Mr. Green
Toby	Mr. Wignell	Leonore	Miss Rowson
Custom	Mr. Francis		

Florizel and Perdita

Polixines	Mr. Green	Pedlar	Mr. Bates
Florizel	Mr. Moreton	Perdita	Mrs. Marshall
Camillo	Mr. Warrell	Mopsa	Miss Rowson
Antigonus	Mr. Whitlock	Dorcas	Mrs. Bates
Clown	Mr. Blissett		

June 17   Miss Solomon's Benefit   Aurora

The Prisoner

Cast as for May 29, except:

Bernardo	Mr. Darley, Jr.	Pasqual	Mr. Darley

1795

June 17 (cont.)

The Midnight Hour

Cast as for May 15.

Les Armans D'Arcade
The Purse

Cast as for Jan. 7, except:

Bason..............Mr. Green   Page............Miss Solomons

June 19   Mr. and Mrs. Rowson's Night   Daily Ad.

The Female Patriot—Mrs. Rowson—
"altered from Massinger's *Bondman*."

Timolson..........Mr. Whitlock   Cymbio.............Mr. Blissett
Archidamus..........Mr. Green   Pirander..........Mr. Chalmers
Leorthenes.........Mr. Moreton   Cleora...........Mrs. Whitlock
Hernando..........Mr. Francis   Olympio..........Mrs. Marshall
Diphilus..........Mr. Warrell   Statilla............Mrs. Rowson
Jailer..........Mr. Darley, Jr.   Xanthia...........Mrs. Francis
Graculo...........Mr. Wignell

The Travellers Preserved (pantomime)

Banditti........Mr. Blissett, Mr.   Romirez............Mr. Rowson
              Solomons, etc.   Old Woman........Mrs. Francis
Alberto...........Mr. Moreton   Rosalie..........Miss Milbourne
La Fleur..........Mr. Marshall   Jacqualina........Miss Solomons
Gerald.............Mr. Warrell

All The World's a Stage

Sir Gilbert Pumpkin..Mr. Francis   Cymon.............Mr. Blissett
Charles Stanley.....Mr. Marshall   Wat.............Mr. Darley, Jr.
Harry Stukely........Mr. Green   Hostler...........Mr. Solomons
William......Master T. Warrell   Miss Bridget.......Mrs. Rowson
Waiter..........Mr. J. Warrell   Miss Kitty........Mrs. Marshall
Diggory.............Mr. Bates   Jane...............Mrs. Francis

June 22   Mrs. Hervey and Miss Willem's Night   Daily Ad.

The Rage—Reynolds

Gingham..........Mr. Wignell   Waiter............Mr. J. Darley
Darnley..........Mr. Moreton   Richard..........Mr. J. Warrell
Sir George Gauntlet....Mr. Green   William.........Mr. T. Warrell
Mr. Savage.......Mr. Harwood   Groom............Mr. Mitchell
Sir Paul Perpetual......Mr. Bates   Lady S. Savage......Mrs. Hervey
Flush.............Mr. Francis   Clara Sidley.......Miss Willems
Ready............Mr. Warrell   Mrs. Darnley......Mrs. Whitlock

1795

June 22 (cont.) *The Guardian Outwitted*

Cast as for June 12.

The Irish Widow

Sir Patrick O'Neale.Mr. Whitlock   Thomas............Mr. Blissett
Nephew..........Mr. Marshall   Footman........Mr. Warrell, Jr.
Whittle ....[blank]   Widow Brady.....Mrs. Marshall
Kicksey............Mr. Francis

June 24   Benefit of Mr. Warrell, Mr. Warrell, Jr., and   Daily Ad.
Master Warrell

Every One Has His Fault

Cast as for December 3, 1794, except:

Harmony............Mr. Bates   Hammond..........Mr. Green
Placid...........Mr. Cleveland   Mrs. Placid.......Mrs. Rowson

The Sailor's Landlady

Jack..............Mr. Francis   Midshipman...Master T. Warrell
Mate...........Mr. J. Warrell   Landlady..........*Mr.* Rowson
Ned Halyard.....Mr. Darley, Jr.   Orange Girl.....Mrs. De Marque

Tom Thumb

Cast as for May 22

Note: As this benefit, with the same bill, is also given for July 3, very possibly it was postponed from June 24, though I have found no definite statement to this effect.

June 26   Mr. Blissett and Mrs. De Marque's Night   Daily Ad.

The Farm House

Modely...........Mr. Chalmers   1st Constable........Mr. Blissett
Freehold..........Mr. Whitlock   2d Constable......Mr. Darley, Jr.
Shacklefigure.......Mr. Francis   Aura.............Mrs. Marshall
Heartwell.........Mr. Moreton   Flora..............Mrs. Francis
Sir John English.....Mr. Warrell

* *The Miraculous Mill*—Francis
(pantomimical dance)

Gaffer Thoughtless...Mr. Francis   Goody Benson....Mrs. DeMarque
The Miller..........Mr. Nugent   Patty...........Miss Milbourne
Bab............Mr. Warrell, Jr.

1795

June 26 (cont.) *The Irishman in London*

Capt. Seymour.....Mr. Cleveland	Cymon............Mr. Blissett
Frost.............Mr. Francis	Louisa............Mrs. Hervey
Colooney..........Mr. Moreton	Caroline..........Miss Willems
Murtock Delaney...Mr. Marshall	Cubba............Mrs. Francis
Edward..........Mr. Harwood	

The Travellers Preserved

Cast as for June 19.

June 29　　　　　Mr. Milbourne's Night　　　　　Daily Ad.

The Midnight Hour

Marquis..........Mr. Marshall	Ambrose..........Mr. Warrell
General..........Mr. Harwood	Julia.............Mrs. Francis
Sebastian.........Mr. Francis	Cecily.............Mrs. Bates
Nicholas.........Mr. Bates	Flora...........Mrs. Whitlock
Mathias..........Mr. Blissett	

Love in a Camp

Capt. Patrick.......Mr. Marshall	Drummers.......Messrs. J. & T.
Marshall Fehrbellin....Mr. Green	Warrell
Father Luke......Mr. Harwood	Darby............Mr. Wignell
Oldmutz..........Mr. Rowson	Flora..........Miss Milbourne
Quiz..............Mr. Blissett	Miss Mable Flourish...........
Rupert...........Mr. Moreton	Mr. Darley, Jr.
Adjutant.........Mr. Cleveland	Norah.........Miss Broadhurst

* *The Elopement; or,*
Harlequin's Tour through the Continent of America

Harlequin..........Mr. Francis	Caesar.......Master J. Warrell
Pantaloon.........Mr. Warrell	Dennis...........Mr. Mitchell
Scaramouch.....Mr. Darley, Jr.	Watchman........Mr. Solomon
Lover.............Mr. Blissett	Colombine.......Miss Milbourne
Clown..........Mr. Milbourne	

"A Grand Display of the Great Falls of Niagara, etc."

July 1　　　　　Mr. Wells' Night　　　　　Daily Ad.

The Rage

"never performed here" (?) but cast as for June 22, 1795, except:

Sir Paul Perpetual..Mr. Whitlock	Clara Sedley.........Miss Wells
Richard............Mr. Blissett	(that night only)
Thomas..........Mr. Mitchell	Mrs. Damley......Mrs. Marshall
Groom.......Master J. Warrell	

[261]

1795

July 1 (cont.)   *The Miraculous Mill*
Cast as for June 26.

Peeping Tom of Coventry
Cast as for December 31, 1794, except:

Lady Godiva.......Miss Willems   Mayoress.........Mrs. Rowson
First appearance of Miss Wells.

July 3   Benefit of Mr. Warrell, Mr. Warrell, Jr., and   Daily Ad.
Master Warrell

The same bill as for June 24.

July 4   "Last Night this Season"   Daily Ad.

The Next Door Neighbours
The Irishman in London
The Elopement, or Harlequin's Tour Through
the Continent of America

In the season from December 3, 1794, to July 4, 1795, at the New Theatre, these new plays were given: *Better Late Than Never, The Female Patriot, The First Floor, The Follies of a Day, Fontainville Forest, The Jew, Know Your Own Mind, The Natural Son, The Next Door Neighbours, The Noble Peasant, The Rage* and *The Triumphs of Love.* New afterpieces: *Auld Robin Gray, The Devil in the Wine Cellar, The East Indian, The Elopement; or Harlequin's Tour Through the Continent of America, The Farm House, The Guardian Outwitted, Harlequin Hurry Scurry, The Jubilee, Les Armans d'Arcade, The Little Yankee Sailor, The Miraculous Mill, My Grandmother, A New Way to Pay Old Debts, The Prisoner, The Purse, The Roman Actor, Rural Revels, The Scheming Milliners, Set a Beggar on Horseback, The Sicilian Romance, The Travellers Preserved, The Volunteers,* and *The Wedding Day.*

Reappearing plays: *As You Like It, The Beaux' Stratagem, The Beggar's Opera, The Belle's Stratagem, A Bold Stroke for a Husband, The Brothers (The Shipwreck), The Busy Body, The Carmelite, The Castle of Andalusia, The Chapter of Accidents, The Child of Nature, The Clandestine Marriage, The Conscious Lovers, The Country Girl, Cymbeline, Douglas, The Dramatist, The Duenna, Duke and No Duke, The English Merchant, Every One Has His Fault, The Fair Penitent, The Gamester, George Barnwell, Hamlet, The Haunted Tower, The Heiress, The Highland Reel, Inkle and Yarico, Isabella, The Jealous Wife, Lionel and Clarissa, Love in a Village, Macbeth, The Maid of the Mill, The Merchant of Venice, The Merry Wives of Windsor, The Orphan, Percy, Richard III, The Rivals, The Road to Ruin, Robin Hood, The Roman Father, Romeo and Juliet, The School for Scandal,*

1795

*The School for Wives, She Stoops to Conquer, She Would and She Would
Not, Slaves in Algiers, The Spanish Barber, The Surrender of Calais, The
Suspicious Husband, Tamerlane, The Tempest, The Toy, Venice Preserved,
The West Indian*, and *The Woodman*. Reappearing afterpieces: *The Agree-
able Surprize, All the World's a Stage, The Apprentice, The Birth of Har-
lequin, The Caledonian Frolic, The Children in the Wood, Comus, The
Critic, The Deserter, The Deuce is in Him, The Devil to Pay, The Flitch
of Bacon, Florizel and Perdita, La Forêt Noire, The Fruitless Precaution,
Harlequin's Invasion, Harlequin Shipwrecked, Hartford Bridge, High Life
Below Stairs, Hob in the Well, The Irish Lilt, The Irish Widow, The
Irishman in London, The Liar, Linco's Travels, Love in a Camp, The
Lying Valet, The Mayor of Garratt, Midas, The Midnight Hour, The
Miller of Mansfield, Modern Antiques, Neptune and Amphitrite, No Song
No Supper, The Padlock, Peeping Tom of Coventry, The Poor Soldier, The
Prize, The Quaker, Robinson Crusoe, The Romp, Rosina, The Sailor's Land-
lady, The Spoiled Child, The Sultan, Three Weeks after Marriage, Tom
Thumb The Great, Two Misers, The Village Lawyer, The Waterman,
Ways and Means*, and *The Wrangling Lovers*.

New actors: Mr. Gibbon, Mrs. Hervey, Miss Milbourne, Mr. Mitchell,
Mr. Nugent, Master Parker, Mr. Price, Master Harry Warrell (?), Miss
Wells, and a "young lady" and "young gentleman." Reappearing actors:
Mr. and Mrs. Bates, Mr. Blissett, Miss Broadhurst, Mr. Chalmers, Mr.
and Mrs. Cleveland, Mr. Darley, Mr. J. Darley, Jr., Mrs. De Marque,
Mr. and Mrs. Francis, Mr. Green, Mr. Harwood, Mr. and Mrs. Marshall,
Mr. Milbourne, Mr. Moreton, Mr. and Mrs. Morris, Miss Oldfield, Mrs.
Oldmixon, Mr., Mrs., and Miss Rowson, Mrs. Shaw, Mr. and Mrs. Warrell,
Mr. J. Warrell, Jr. (often called "Master Warrell"), Master T. Warrell,
Mr. and Mrs. Whitlock, Mr. Wignell, and Miss Willems.

PANTHEON

Oct. 19   Phila. Gaz.

The Pantheon, or Ricketts' Amphitheatre, was opened at Sixth and Chesnut,
just opposite the New Theatre, by Mr. John Bill Ricketts, formerly proprietor of Ricketts' Circus at Thirteenth and Market (with which his new
Amphitheatre is not to be confused). The Pantheon was of wood, and burned
down December 17, 1799. In it were given regular circus performances of
"Equestrianism," tumbling, pony races, and so on (in which the present
record is not interested), and also often farces and pantomimes. This list
includes only such dramatic productions. See Dec. 22, 1795.

NEW THEATRE

Dec. 14   *The Carmelite*   Daily Ad.

A new pantomime Ballet "Composed and under the direction of Mons.
LEGE, from the Italian Theatre in Paris, called"

[263]

1795

Dec. 14 (cont.)   *La Boiteuse*

"By Mons. Lege (being his first appearance on this Stage), Mrs. De Marque, &c."

The Romp

First night of the season at the New Theatre (Chesnut Street) from December 14, 1795, to July 1, 1796. First appearance of M. Lege.

Dec. 16   *The Highland Reel*   G. U. S.

Cast as for Feb. 9, 1795.

The Irishman in London

Capt. Seymour	Mr. Green	Cymon	Mr. Blissett
Mr. Frost	Mr. Francis	Louisa	Mrs. Hervey
Mr. Callooney	Mr. Moreton	Caroline	Miss Willems
Murtoch Delaney	Mr. Marshall	Cubba	Mrs. Francis
Edward	Mr. Harwood		

Dec. 18   *The Rage*   G. U. S.

Cast as for June 22, 1795, except:

Richard	Mr. Blissett	Groom	Master T. Warrell
Thomas	Mr. Mitchell	Lady Savage	Mrs. Shaw
	(not cast before)	Clara Sedley	Mrs. Marshall
William	Mr. Warrell, Jr.	Mrs. Darnley	Mrs. Whitlock

Les Armans D'Arcade
The Children in the Wood

Cast as for March 18, 1795, except:

Apathy	Mr. Francis	Boy	Miss Gillespie
Russian	Mr. Blissett		

First appearance of Miss Gillespie (or Gilaspie).

Dec. 21   *The Child of Nature*   G. U. S.

Marquis of Almanza	Mr. Whitlock	1st Peasant	Mr. Green
Count Valantia	Mr. Moreton	2nd Peasant	Mr. Warrell
Duke Marcia	Mr. Bates	Marchioness Merida	Mrs. Morris
Seville	Mr. Beete	Amanthis	Mrs. Marshall
Grenada	Mr. Warrell, Jr.		

1795

Dec. 21 (cont.)   "As Performed in Paris"

* *Les Deux Chasseurs:*
or *The Death of the Bear*—M. Lege

(comic ballet)

Colas...............	Mr. Francis	Magistrate.........	Mr. Warrell
Guillot...............	M. Lege	Perritte.........	Mrs. De Marque

The Midnight Hour

Marquis..........	Mr. Marshall	Ambrose..........	Mr. Warrell
General..........	Mr. Harwood	Julia..............	Mrs. Francis
Sebastian..........	Mr. Francis	Cecily..............	Mrs. Bates
Nicholas............	Mr. Bates	Flora............	Mrs. Whitlock
Mathias..........	Mr. Blissett		

First appearance of Mr. Beete.

PANTHEON

Dec. 22   Phila. Gaz., Dec. 21

Ricketts announced "Equestrian Exercises and stage performances, by Mr. Ricketts and his celebrated company."

Act 1—"Horsemanship"
Act 2—"Stage Performances"
Act 3—"Equestrian Exercises"
Act 4—"Stage Performances"
Act 5—"Lofty Vaulting."

"To Conclude with a very humorous exhibition."

Days of Performance—Tues. Thur. & Sat.

The season extended to April 23, 1795. See Oct. 19, 1795.

NEW THEATRE

Dec. 23   *Percy*   G. U. S.

Cast as for April 13, except:

Sir Hubert..........	Mr. Warrell	Birtha............	Mrs. Hervey

The Sailor's Landlady
Cast as for June 24.

Cross Purposes

Grub..............	Mr. Morris	Robin..............	Mr. Blissett
Consol..............	Mr. Francis	Thomas...........	Mr. Mitchell
Francis Bevil......	Mr. Darley, Jr.	Mrs. Grub..........	Mrs. Shaw
Harry Bevil..........	Mr. Green	Emily............	Miss Williams
George Bevil.......	Mr. Moreton	Housemaid.........	Mrs. Hervey
Chapeau..........	Mr. Marshall		

[265]

1795

PANTHEON

Dec. 24   Circus and   Phila. Gaz.
Harlequin Statue

Harlequin........Mr. Sully, Jr.   Ariel.............Master Sully
Pantaloon............Mr. Reano   Clown...........Mr. Spinacuta
Lover........Mr. [Mc]Donald   Columbine.......Mrs. Spinacuta

First definite announcement of all the above actors in a dramatic production here (a number of them had been seen before as circus performers).

NEW THEATRE

Dec. 26   *George Barnwell*   G. U. S.

Thorowgood.......Mr. Whitlock   Gaoler.............Mr. Warrell
Uncle.............Mr. Wignell   Maria............Mrs. Whitlock
George Barnwell....Mr. Moreton   Millwood...........Mrs. Shaw
Trueman............Mr. Green   Lucy..............Mrs. Francis
Blunt.............Mr. Francis

Harlequin Shipwrecked

Harlequin..........Mr. Francis   Tippy Bob..........Mr. Robbins
Indian Chief.....Mr. Warrell, jr.   Whimsical..........Mr. Green
Captain of Ship.....Mr. Solomon   Drowsy..........Mr. Darley, jr.
Pantaloon.........Mr. Warrell

"A Grand Exhibition of Scenery, Action, Spectacle, Dance, and FEATS of ACTIVITY, called

* T'Other Side of the Gutter"

In which Signior JOSEPH DOCTOR from Sadler's Wells made his first appearance.

Signior Doctor's feats in *T'Other Side of the Gutter* were in competition with the circus in the Pantheon, just across Chesnut Street.

PANTHEON

Dec. 26   Circus and Horsemanship   G. U. S.
Harlequin Statue

Cast as for Dec. 24.

NEW THEATRE

Dec. 28   *The Haunted Tower*   G. U. S.

Cast as for Feb. 18, except:

De Courcy.........Mr. Moreton   Cicely..............Mrs. Hervey

1795

Dec. 28 (cont.)   *T'Other Side the Gutter,* with Sig. Joseph Doctor
Lovers' Quarrels

Don Carlos........Mr. Moreton	Sancho............Mr. Wignell
Don Lorenzo........Mr. Green	Leonora...........Mrs. Francis
Lopez...........Mr. Harwood	Jacintha..........Mrs. Rowson

PANTHEON

Dec. 29   Circus   G. U. S.
Harlequin Statue

Cast as for December 24.

NEW THEATRE

Dec. 30   *The Jew*   G. U. S.

Cast as for Feb. 11, 1795, except:

Chas. Ratcliffe........Mr. Green	Dorcas............Mrs. Rowson
Saunders..........Mr. Warrell	

La Boiteuse
Tom Thumb

Cast as for May 22, except:

Princess Hunca Munca.........   Mustachia.........Miss Rowson
Miss Willems

PANTHEON

Dec. 31   Circus   G. U. S.
Harlequin Statue

1796

NEW THEATRE

Jan. 1   * *The Bank Note*—Macready   G. U. S.
Dec. 31, 1795.

Sir Charles Leslie....Mr. Moreton	William........Mr. Darley, Jr.
Bloomfield..........Mr. Wignell	James..........Mr. Warrell, Jr.
Bloomfield, Sr........Mr. Morris	Cook..............Mr. Mitchell
Lieut. Selby.........Mr. Green	Butler............Mr. Solomon
Neddy Dash.......Mr. Harwood	Lady Suffle........Mrs. Rowson
Hale................Mr. Bates	Mrs. Bloomfield.....Mrs. Morris
Killeavy..........Mr. Marshall	Miss Russell......Mrs. Marshall
Tim...............Mr. Blissett	Miss Emma Hale...Miss Oldfield
Young Bloomfield..Miss Solomon	Sally Flounce........Mrs. Francis
Careful...........Mr. Warrell	Maid.............Miss Rowson
Porter............Mr. Morgan	

1796

Jan. 1 (cont.) *The Purse*

Cast as for Jan. 7, 1795, except:

Bason.............Mr. Green   Page.............Miss Solomon

T'Other Side of the Gutter

First appearance of Mr. Morgan.

Jan. 4   *Fontainville Forest*   G. U.S.

Marquis of Montault..Mr. Green	Jacques.............Mr. Warrell
Lamotte..........Mr. Whitlock	Nemours.........Mr. Harwood
Louis.............Mr. Moreton	Hortensia...........Mrs. Shaw
Peter.............Mr. Morris	Adeline..........Mrs. Whitlock

* *Rural Merriment* (pantomime)—Francis
High Life Below Stairs

Lovel.............Mr. Marshall	Robert.............Mr. Blissett
Freeman.............Mr. Beete	Tom...........Mr. Darley, Jr.
Sir Harry..........Mr. Francis	Kitty.........Mrs. Morris
Lord Duke........Mr. Harwood	Lady Bab.........Mrs. Rowson
Philip.............Mr. Wignell	Lady Charlotte......Mrs. Francis
Coachman.........Mr. Warrell	Cook...............Mrs. Bates
Kingston........Mr. Warrell, Jr.	Chloe............Miss Rowson

PANTHEON

Jan. 5   Circus   G. U. S.
Harlequin Statue

NEW THEATRE

Jan. 6   *Next Door Neighbours*   Phila. Gaz.

Sir George Splendorville........ Mr. Moreton	Bluntly..........Mr. Harwood
	Shopman........Mr. Darley, Jr.
Manly.............Mr. Green	Lady Carol Seymour........... Mrs. Francis
Blackman............Mr. Bates	
Lucre.............Mr. Wignell	Lady Squander.....Mrs. Rowson
Lord Hazard....Mr. Warrell, Jr.	Evans............Mrs. Solomon
Welford.........Mr. Whitlock	Eleanor..........Mrs. Marshall
Henry............Mr. Marshall	

Harlequin Shipwrecked

Cast as for December 26, 1795, with addition of:

Genius of Liberty...Mrs. Warrell   Columbine.......Miss Milbourne
Primrose Girl......Miss Solomon

1796

Both Sides of the Gutter—Blissett
(with a pantomimic prologue by Mr. Blissett)

Jan. 8 *The Natural Son* G. U. S.
The Farmer

Col. Dormant........Mr. Green
Valentine..........Mr. Marshall
Fairly.............Mr. Warrell
Counsellor Flummery..Mr. Blissett
Farmer Blackberry....Mr. Darley
Jemmy Jumps.........Mr. Bates

Rundy..............Mr. Francis
Farmer Stubble......Mr. Morgan
Louisa.............Mrs. Hervey
Betty Blackberry....Miss Willems
Molly Maybush.....Mrs. Warrell
Landlady............Mrs. Bates

The Bank Note, which had been announced, was postponed on account of the illness of Mrs. Marshall.

PANTHEON

Jan. 9 Circus G. U. S.
Harlequin Statue

NEW THEATRE

Jan. 11 *The School for Scandal* G. U. S.

Sir Peter Teazle.......Mr. Bates
Sir Oliver Surface....Mr. Morris
Joseph Surface.......Mr. Wignell
Charles Surface.....Mr. Moreton
Sir Benj. Backbite...Mr. Marshall
Crabtree.........Mr. Harwood
Careless.............Mr. Beete
Sir Harry...........Mr. Darley

Rowley...........Mr. Warrell
Moses.............Mr. Francis
Snake..............Mr. Green
Trip...........Mr. Warrell, Jr.
Lady Teazle........Mrs. Morris
Lady Sneerwell......Mrs. Rowson
Mrs. Candour........Mrs. Shaw
Maria............Mrs. Francis

The Bird Catcher—M. Lege
The Poor Soldier

Capt. Fitzroy......Mr. Moreton
Father Luke........Mr. Morgan
Dermot.........Mr. Darley, Jr.
Patrick.............Mr. Darley
Darby...........Mr. Wignell

Bagatelle.........Mr. Marshall
Boy............Master Warrell
Norah.............Mrs. Warrell
Kathleen.........Miss Willems

PANTHEON

Jan. 12 Circus G. U. S.
Harlequin Statue

[269]

1796

NEW THEATRE

Jan. 13   *The Wheel of Fortune*—Cumberland   Phila. Gaz.

Sir David Daw	Mr. Francis	Jenkins	Mr. Darley, Jr.
Tempest	Mr. Bates	James	Mr. Warrell, Jr.
Penruddock	Mr. Whitlock	Richard	Mr. Morgan
Woodville	Mr. Green	Harry	Mr. Mitchell
Sydenham	Mr. Wignell	Thomas	Master Warrell
Henry Woodville	Mr. Moreton	Mrs. Woodville	Mrs. Morris
Weazle	Mr. Harwood	Emily Tempest	Mrs. Marshall
Woodville's Servant	Mr. Beete	Dame Dunckley	Mrs. Rowson
Officer	Mr. Warrell	Maid	Miss Rowson

The Prize

Doctor Lenitive	Mr. Harwood	Boy	Master T. Warrell
Heartwell	Mr. Moreton	Juba	Miss Milbourne
Caddy	Mr. Green	Mrs. Caddy	Mrs. Bates
Label	Mr. Francis	Caroline	Mrs. Oldmixon

Jan. 15   *The Rage*   G. U. S.

Cast as for Dec. 18, 1795.

Peeping Tom of Coventry

Cast as for Dec. 31, 1794, except:

Count Lewis	Mr. Blissett	Emma	Miss Broadhurst
Maud	Miss Willems	Lady Godiva	Miss Oldfield

Jan. 18   *Douglas*   G. U. S.

Lord Randolph	Mr. Green	Officers	Mr. Warrell,
Glenalvon	Mr. Wignell		Mr. Darley, Jr., etc.
Old Norval	Mr. Whitlock	Lady Randolph	Mrs. Whitlock
Young Norval	Mr. Moreton	Anna	Mrs. Francis

La Boiteuse
The Deaf Lover—Pilon

Meadows	Mr. Green	William	Mr. Warrell, Jr.
Young Wronghead	Mr. Beete	Joe	Mr. Mitchell
Old Wronghead	Mr. Francis	Bob	Mr. Darley, Jr.
Canteen	Mr. Harwood	John	Mr. Warrell
Stemhold	Mr. Blissett	Sophia	Miss Willems
Groom	Mr. Bates	Betty Blossom	Mrs. Francis
Cook	Mr. Morgan	Chambermaid	Mrs. Bates

1796

PANTHEON

Jan. 19	Circus	G. U. S.
	Harlequin Statue	

NEW THEATRE

Jan. 20	*The Rivals*	G. U. S.

Sir Anthony Absolute..Mr. Morris
Captain Absolute....Mr. Moreton
Faulkland..........Mr. Wignell
Acres...............Mr. Bates
Sir Lucius O'Trigger...........
          Mr. Whitlock
Fag..............Mr. Marshall

David.............Mr. Francis
Coachman.........Mr. Warrell
Boy..........Master T. Warrell
Lydia Languish....Mrs. Marshall
Julia.............Mrs. Francis
Lucy (first time)...Mrs. Doctor

Harlequin's Invasion

Harlequin..........Mr. Francis
Mercury.........Mr. Marshall
Forge............Mr. Moreton
Bounce............Mr. Green
Frontin..........Mr. Harwood
Taffy..............Mr. Beete
Bog...........Mr. Darley, Jr.
Simon............Mr. Wignell
Snip.................Mr. Bates
Abraham..........Mr. Blissett

Justice............Mr. Warrell
Crier........Master T. Warrell
Padlock.......Mr. Warrell, Jr.
Fairy............Miss Solomon
Columbine........Miss Gillespie
Dolly Snip.........Mrs. Francis
Mrs. Snip........Mrs. Rowson
Sukey Chitterlin....Miss Willems
Old Woman........*Mr.* Darley

First appearance of Mrs. Doctor.

Jan. 22	*Romeo and Juliet*	G. U. S.

Romeo...........Mr. Moreton
Escalus.............Mr. Beete
Paris..........Mr. Darley, Jr.
Montague.........Mr. Warrell
Capulet............Mr. Morris
Mercutio..........Mr. Wignell
Benvolio...........Mr. Green
Tibalt...........Mr. Harwood

Friar Laurence........Mr. Bates
Balthazar.........Mr. Whitlock
Apothecary......Mr. Warrell, Jr.
Peter.............Mr. Francis
Page.............Mr. Blissett
Juliet...........Mrs. Marshall
Lady Capulet......Mrs. Solomon
Nurse.............Mrs. Rowson

The Midnight Hour

Cast as for Dec. 21, 1795.

PANTHEON

Jan. 23	Circus	G. U. S.
	Harlequin Statue	

[271]

1796

NEW THEATRE

Jan. 25   *Robin Hood*   G. U. S.

Robin Hood........Mr. Darley   Ruttekin............ Mr. Bates
Little John.......Mr. Wignell   Friar Tuck...... Mr. Whitlock
Scarlet............Mr. Francis   Edwin...........Mr. Marshall
Bowman..........Mr. Warrell   Clorinda..........Mrs. Warrell
Allen a Dale....Mr. Darley, Jr. Annette........Miss Milbourne
Stella............Miss Willems   Angelina.........Mrs. Marshall

Harlequin's Invasion

Cast as for Jan. 20, 1796.

PANTHEON

Jan. 26   Circus   G. U. S.
                          Harlequin Statue

NEW THEATRE

Jan. 27   *The Country Girl*   G. U. S.

Moody..............Mr. Bates   William......Master T. Warrell
Harcourt.........Mr. Marshall   Thomas.........Mr. Darley, Jr.
Sparkish..........Mr. Moreton   Miss Peggy.......Mrs. Marshall
Belville.............Mr. Green   Alithea...........Mrs. Francis
Countryman.......Mr. Mitchell   Lucy...............Mrs. Shaw

Ways and Means

Sir David Dunder..Mr. Harwood   Sir Paul Peery......Mr. Francis
Random...........Mr. Moreton   Lady Dunder......Mrs. Rowson
Scruple.............Mr. Green   Harriet...........Miss Oldfield
Tiptoe..............Mr. Bates   Kitty..........Miss Milbourne

T'Other Side of the Gutter

PANTHEON

Jan. 28   Circus   G. U. S.
                       "Stage Performances"

NEW THEATRE

Jan. 29   *The Wheel of Fortune*   G. U. S.

Cast as for Jan. 13, 1796.

The First Floor

Whimsey..........Mr. Francis   Snap...........Mr. Darley, Jr.
Monfort............Mr. Beete   Landlord..........Mr. Warrell

1796

Young Whimsey...Mr. Moreton
Fumish..............Mr. Bates
Simon..............Mr. Blissett
Tim Bartlett......Mr. Harwood
Frank..........Mr. Warrell, Jr.

Post Boy.......Master Warrell
Mrs. Pattypan......Mrs. Rowson
Charlotte.........Miss Oldfield
Nancy............Mrs. Hervey

PANTHEON

Jan. 30   Circus   G. U. S.
Harlequin Statue

NEW THEATRE

Feb. 1   *Isabella*   G. U. S.

Cast as for Dec. 17, 1794, except:

Belford............Mr. Warrell
Pedro...............Mr. Beete

Officer............Mr. Mitchell

and in addition:

Child............Miss Solomon

Rural Merriment
The Devil to Pay

Sir John Loverule..Mr. Marshall
Butler...............Mr. Francis
Cook...............Mr. Blissett
Footman.........Mr. Darley, Jr.
Coachman.........Mr. Morgan
Conjurer..........Mr. Warrell

Jobson..............Mr. Bates
Lady Loverule......Mrs. Francis
Lucy.............Miss Willems
Lettice...........Mrs. Solomon
Nell.............Mrs. Marshall

PANTHEON

Feb. 2   Circus   G. U. S.
"Stage Performance"

NEW THEATRE

Feb. 3   *The Bank Note*   G. U. S.

Cast as for Jan. 1.

Hob in the Well

Sir Thomas Trusty...Mr. Francis
Friendly..........Mr. Marshall
Hob.................Mr. Bates
Old Hob..........Mr. Warrell
Dick.........Mr. Warrell, Jr.

Roger..............Mr. Blissett
Flora............Mrs. Warrell
Betty............Mrs. Hervey
Hob's Mother.......Mrs. Bates

[273]

1796

Feb. 5   *The Married Man*—Mrs. Inchbald   G. U. S.

Lord Lovemore.....Mr. Moreton	William............Mr. Blissett
Sir John Classick....Mr. Wignell	Lady Classick.....Mrs. Marshall
Clarrick..........Mr. Marshall	Emily.............Mrs. Francis
Tradewell Classick.....Mr. Bates	Lucy.............Mrs. Hervey
Dorimont...........Mr. Green	

La Rose et le Bouton (pantomime)

Priestess..........Mrs. Warrell	Agatha.........Miss Milbourne
Colin.............Mr. Francis	

The Widow's Vow

Don Antonio........Mr. Morris	Countess..........Mrs. Morris
Marquis..........Mr. Moreton	Donna Isabella.....Mrs. Hervey
Carlos.........Mr. Darley, Jr.	Inis..............Mrs. Rowson
Servant...........Mr. Mitchell	Ursula............Mrs. Doctor
Jerome.............Mr. Bates	Flora.............Mrs. Francis

PANTHEON

Feb. 6   Circus   G. U. S.

*The Triumph of Virtue, or
Harlequin in Philadelphia* (pantomime)

("with an Equestrian Statue composed and executed by
Mr. Joseph Perosiani, painter & architect from Italy.")

Harlequin...........Mr. Sully	Piero............Mr. Spinacuta
Pantaloon..........Mr. Reano	Columbine.......Mrs. Spinacuta
Lover..........Mr. M'Donald	Chinese....."Masters Deforrests"
Magicians.....Messrs. M'Donald	"Masters M'Elroys"
and Sully	Master Grant
Punchinello........Miss Rickson	Master Snider
(being her first appearance)	Master Mills
Dwarf............Mr. Langley	Master Frost
Palliasa........Mr. F. Ricketts	

First definite mention as dramatic performers of the Masters Deforrest,
Master Frost, Master Grant, Mr. Langley, The Masters M'Elroy, Master
Mills, Mr. F. Ricketts, Miss Rickson, Master Snider (or Snyder or Schny-
der), and Mr. Sully.

NEW THEATRE

Feb. 8   *The Woodman*   G. U. S.

Sir Walter Waring....Mr. Bates	Filbert............Mr. Blissett
Wilford..........Mr. Moreton	Emily...........Mrs. Marshall

1796

Feb. 8 (cont.)

Capt. O'Donnell....Mr. Marshall	Dolly...........Mrs. Oldmixon
Medley..............Mr. Francis	Miss Di Clockit......Mrs. Shaw
Bob............Mr. Darley, Jr.	Polly.............Miss Solomon
Fairlop.............Mr. Darley	Bridget............Mrs. Francis

All the World's a Stage

Sir Gilbert Pumpkin..Mr. Francis	Watt.............Mr. Darley, Jr.
Chas. Stanley......Mr. Marshall	Hostler.............Mr. Solomon
Harry Stukely.......Mr. Green	Miss Bridget Pumpkin..........
William.........Master Warrell	Mrs. Rowson
Waiter........Mr. Warrell, Jr.	Miss Kitty Sprightly...........
Diggory..............Mr. Bates	Mrs. Marshall
Cymon.............Mr. Blissett	Jane...............Mrs. Francis

PANTHEON

Feb. 9	Circus	G. U. S.

Harlequin in Philadelphia

Cast as for Feb. 6.

NEW THEATRE

Feb. 10	The Provoked Husband	G. U. S.

Lord Townly......Mr. Whitlock	Lord Townly's Servant.........
Manly..............Mr. Green	Mr. Darley, Jr.
Sir Francis Wronghead.........	Lady Townly......Mrs. Morris
Mr. Morris	Lady Grace........Mrs. Francis
Count Basset......Mr. Marshall	Lady Wronghead.....Mrs. Shaw
Squire Richard.....Mr. Blissett	Miss Jenny........Miss Willems
John Moody.........Mr. Bates	Myrtilla...........Mrs. Rowson
Poundage.........Mr. Mitchell	Trusty............Miss Rowson
Constable.........Mr. Warrell	Mrs. Motherly.......Mrs. Bates
James........Mr. Warrell, Jr.	

* The Warrior's Welcome Home—Francis
("Divertissement")

The Children in the Wood

Cast as for March 18, 1795, except:

Apathy.............Mr. Francis	Helen...............Mrs. Shaw
Russian.............Mr. Blissett	Boy..............Miss Gilaspie

PANTHEON

Feb. 11	Circus	G. U. S.

Harlequin in Philadelphia

Cast as for Feb. 6.

1796

NEW THEATRE

Feb. 12   *The Roman Father*   G. U. S.

Tullus Hostilius......Mr. Green		1st Citizen.........Mr. Mitchell
Horatius.........Mr. Whitlock		2nd Citizen.........Mr. Blissett
Publius............Mr. Moreton		3rd Citizen.......Mr. Solomon
Valerius...........Mr. Wignell		Horatia..........Mrs. Whitlock
Volscinius.......Mr. Darley, Jr.		Valeria............Mrs. Hervey
Roman Soldier......Mr. Warrell		

The Warrior's Welcome Home
The Spoiled Child

Little Pickle......Mrs. Marshall	Miss Pickle........Mrs. Rowson
Old Pickle.......Mr. Harwood	Maria.............Mrs. Francis
Tag................Mr. Francis	Margery.............Mrs. Bates
John..............Mr. Blissett	Susan.............Miss Willems
Thomas........Mr. Darley, Jr.	

PANTHEON

Feb. 13   Circus   G. U. S.
Harlequin in Philadelphia

Cast as for February 6, except:

Punchinello.........Mr. Crump

First appearance of Mr. Crump.

NEW THEATRE

Feb. 15   *Every One Has His Fault*   G. U. S.

Cast as for December 3, 1794, except:

Sir Robert Ramble...Mr. Wignell	Placid...............Mr. Green
Harmony............Mr. Bates	Hammond......Mr. Warrell, Jr.

The Warrior's Welcome Home
The Poor Soldier

Cast as for Jan. 11, except:

Father Luke.........Mr. Blissett

PANTHEON

Feb. 16   Circus   G. U. S.
Harlequin in Philadelphia

[276]

1796

NEW THEATRE

Feb. 17 *She Stoops to Conquer* G. U. S.

Sir Chas. Marlow...Mr. Warrell
Young Marlow....Mr. Moreton
Hardcastle.........Mr. Morris
Hastings............Mr. Green
Tony Lumpkin.......Mr. Bates
Diggory...........Mr. Francis

Landlord............Mr. Darley
Jeremy.............Mr. Blissett
Mrs. Hardcastle......Mrs. Shaw
Miss Hardcastle...Mrs. Marshall
Miss Neville.......Mrs. Francis
Maid.............Miss Willems

Un Divertissement Pastoral—M. Lege
The Midnight Hour

Cast as for Dec. 21, 1795.

PANTHEON

Feb. 18 Circus G. U. S.
Harlequin in Philadelphia

NEW THEATRE

Feb. 19 *The Castle of Andalusia* G. U. S.

Don Scipio.........Mr. Francis
Don Fernando......Mr. Marshall
Don Caesar.........Mr. Darley
Don Juan..........Mr. Morris
Don Alphonso....Mr. Darley, Jr.
Pedrillo..............Mr. Bates
Spado.............Mr. Wignell

Sanguino............Mr. Green
Philippo.......Mr. Warrell, Jr.
Victoria..........Mrs. Warrell
Lorenza..........Mrs. Marshall
Isabel...............Mrs. Bates
Catalina.........Miss Willems

Un Divertissement Pastoral
As It Should Be

Lord Megrim......Mr. Moreton
Fidget..............Mr. Francis
Winworth..........Mr. Green

Sparkle...........Mr. Harwood
Lucy..............Miss Willems
Celia..............Mrs. Francis

PANTHEON

Feb. 20 Circus G. U. S.
Harlequin in Philadelphia

NEW THEATRE

Feb. 20 *The English Merchant* G. U. S.

Lord Fallbridge....Mr. Moreton
Sir Wm. Douglas...Mr. Whitlock
Freeport...........Mr. Morris

Officer.............Mr. Warrell
Lady Alton........Mrs. Morris
Amelia..........Mrs. Marshall

[277]

1796

Feb. 20 (cont.)

Spatter............Mr. Wignell   Mrs. Goodman......Mrs. Shaw
Owen..............Mr. Green   Molly............Mrs. Francis
La France.......Mr. Harwood

The Warrior's Welcome Home
Tom Thumb

Cast as for May 22, 1795, except:

Princess Huncamunca...........   Mustachia........Miss Rowson
      Miss Willems

Feb. 23   *Zara*   G. U. S.

Osman............Mr. Moreton   Orasmin.............Mr. Beete
Lusignan..........Mr. Whitlock   Melidor........Mr. Darley, Jr.
Nereston.........Mr. Marshall   Zara.............Mrs. Whitlock
Chatillon...........Mr. Green   Selima............Mrs. Hervey

The Agreeable Surprize

Sir Felix Friendly....Mr. Francis   Cudden............Mr. Blissett
Compton...........Mr. Darley   Lingo...............Mr. Bates
Eugene..........Mr. Darley, Jr.   Laura............Mrs. Marshall
Chicane...........Mr. Warrell   Mrs. Cheshire......Miss Willems
John............Master Warrell   Cowslip............Mrs. Shaw
Thomas............Mr. Green   Fringe............Mrs. Rowson
Farmer Stump.....Miss Solomon

Feb. 24   *The Dramatist*   G. U. S.

Lord Scratch........Mr. Bates   Vapid............Mr. Harwood
Neville..............Mr. Green   Miss Courtney......Mrs. Francis
Floriville..........Mr. Moreton   Lady Waitfor't.......Mrs. Shaw
Willoughby......Mr. Darley, Jr.   Letty..............Mrs. Hervey
Ennui............Mr. Marshall   Marianne........Mrs. Marshall
Peter..............Mr. Francis

The Sailor's Landlady

Cast as for Jan. 7, 1795, except:

Mate..........Mr. Warrell, Jr.
and add: Midshipman........Master Warrell

The Padlock

Don Diego.........Mr. Darley   Mungo..............Mr. Bates
Leander..........Mr. Marshall   Leonora.........Mrs. Marshall
1st Scholar......Mr. Warrell, Jr.   Ursula............Mrs. Rowson
2d Scholar......Mr. Darley, Jr.

1796

PANTHEON

Feb. 24   Circus   G. U. S.
"Stage Performances in Honor of 'The President's
Birth-Night' "
Harlequin in Philadelphia

Feb. 25   Circus   G. U. S.
Harlequin in Philadelphia

NEW THEATRE

Feb. 26   *Jane Shore*   G. U. S.

Duke of Gloster......Mr. Green	Dumont..........Mr. Whitlock
Lord Hastings......Mr. Wignell	Earl of Derby........Mr. Francis
Catesby...........Mr. Harwood	Alicia..............Mrs. Morris
Sir Richard Ratcliffe..Mr. Warrell	Jane Shore........Mrs. Whitlock
Belmour............Mr. Beete	

** The Witches of the Rock; or
Harlequin Everywhere*—"Compiled by Mr. Millbourne"
("partly new & partly compiled")

Harlequin...........Mr. Francis	Miser.............Mr. Moreton
1st Witch.........Mr. Darley	Pompey........Mr. Warrell, Jr.
2nd Witch.......Mrs. Warrell	Tinker...........Mr. Mitchell
Pantaloon.........Mr. Warrell	Bricklayer.......Master Warrell
Lawyer..........Mr. Darley, Jr.	Fruit Woman......Mrs. Rowson
Drunken Valet....Mr. Milbourne	Columbine.......Miss Milbourne
Surveyor............Mr. Beete	Old Lady.........Miss Solomon
Pero........Mr. Joseph Doctor	

PANTHEON

Feb. 27   Circus   G. U. S.
Harlequin in Philadelphia

NEW THEATRE

Feb. 29   *The Rage*   G. U. S.

Cast as for Dec. 18, 1795.

The Spoil'd Child

Cast as for February 12, 1796.

News item:
"The President of the United States intends visiting the Theatre this
Evening; and the Entertainments are by his particular desire."

[279]

1796

PANTHEON

March 1   Circus   G. U. S.
Harlequin Statue
"with alterations"

NEW THEATRE

March 2   *The Gamester*   Aurora

Beverly..........Mr. Whitlock   Dawson..............Mr. Beete
Stukely...........Mr. Wignell   Waiter........Mr. Warrell, Jr.
Lewson...........Mr. Moreton   Mrs. Beverly.....Mrs. Whitlock
Jarvis..............Mr. Morris   Charlotte..........Mrs. Francis
Bates..............Mr. Green   Lucy..............Miss Oldfield

The Witches of the Rock

Cast as for Feb. 26, 1796.

PANTHEON

March 3   Circus   G. U. S.
Harlequin Statue

NEW THEATRE

March 4   *The Married Man*   G. U. S.

Cast as for Feb. 5, except:

Classick..........Mr. Whitlock   William.......Mr. Warrell, Jr.

Les Deux Chasseurs

"never here"—"as performed at Paris"

[but see Dec. 21, 1795]

Colas.............Mr. Francis   Magistrate.........Mr. Warrell
Guillot...............M. Lege   Perrite........Mrs. De Marque

The Prisoner

Marcos..........Mr. Marshall   Clara.............Mrs. Warrell
Bernardo.......Mr. Darley, Jr.   Theresa..........Miss Willems
Pasquel............Mr. Darley   Nina.............Mrs. Marshall
Roberto..........Mr. Harwood   Juliana..........Miss Solomon
Lewis.............Mr. Moreton
Narcisso.........Miss Gillespie

PANTHEON

March 5   Circus   G. U. S.
Harlequin in Philadelphia
[280]

1796

NEW THEATRE

March 7   *The Merry Wives of Windsor*   G. U. S.

Falstaff..........Mr. Whitlock	Bardolph...........Mr. Warrell
Fenton.........Mr. Warrell, Jr.	Pistol...........Mr. Darley, Jr.
Justice Shallow....Mr. Harwood	Robin............Miss Solomon
Master Slender.....Mr. Moreton	Scruple...........Mr. Mitchell
Page...............Mr. Green	Rugby............Mr. Solomon
Ford..............Mr. Wignell	Mrs. Page........Mrs. Whitlock
Sir Hugh Evans.......Mr. Bates	Mrs. Ford.........Mrs. Morris
Doctor Caius......Mr. Marshall	Ann Page.........Miss Oldfield
Host..............Mr. Darley	Mrs. Quickly.......Mrs. Rowson

* The Egyptian Festival—M. Lege
"Divertissement"

Who's The Dupe?

Doily.............Mr. Morris	Servant.... ....Mr. Darley, Jr.
Sandford..........Mr. Moreton	Miss Doily........Mrs. Francis
Granger............Mr. Green	Charlotte.........Mrs. Rowson
Gradus..........Mr. Harwood	

PANTHEON

March 8   Circus   G. U. S.
Harlequin in Philadelphia

NEW THEATRE

March 9 *A Bold Stroke for a Husband* G. U. S.

Cast as for May 20, 1795, except:

Don Julio............Mr. Green	Don Gasper.......Mr. Whitlock
Don Garcia..........Mr. Beete	Marcella.........Miss Oldfield
Don Vasquez.......Mr. Warrell	Inis............Miss Milbourne

Florizel and Perdita

Polixenes............Mr. Green	Pedlar...............Mr. Bates
Florizel...........Mr. Moreton	Perdita...........Mrs. Marshall
Camillo............Mr. Warrell	Mopsa.............Mrs. Bates
Antigonus.........Mr. Whitlock	Dorcas..........Miss Milbourne
Clown.........Mr. Darley, Jr.	

PANTHEON

March 10   Circus   G. U. S., March 9
Harlequin in Philadelphia

1796

NEW THEATRE.

March 11   *The Orphan*   G. U. S.

Acasto............Mr. Whitlock	Cordelio..........Miss Solomon
Castalio..........Mr. Moreton	Chaplain.............Mr. Beete
Polydore............Mr. Green	Monimia........Mrs. Whitlock
Chamont.........Mr. Wignell	Serina...........Miss Willems
Ernesto............Mr. Warrell	Florella............Mrs. Hervey
Paulino.......Mr. Warrell, Jr.	

* The Mogul Tale—Mrs. Inchbald

Great Mogul......Mr. Moreton	Johnny Atkins.........Mr. Bates
Doctor Pedant......Mr. Wignell	Zaphira...........Miss Oldfield
Omar..............Mr. Green	Irene............Mrs. Hervey
Selim...............Mr. Beete	Sheba.............Miss Willems
1st Guard......Mr. Darley, Jr.	Fanny Atkins.....Mrs. Marshall
2nd Guard........Mr. Mitchell	

PANTHEON

March 12   Circus   G. U. S.
* Vulcan's Gift

Harlequin............Mr. Sully	Piero.............Mr. Spinacuta
Old Man............Mr. Reano	Columbine........Mrs. Spinacuta
Sportsman.......Mr. Macdonald	Vulcan................Mr. Sully
Game Keeper..........Mr. Price	Cyclops......Mr. F. Ricketts, etc.
Hymer..........Master Snyder	Cottage Keeper......Mr. Langley

NEW THEATRE

March 14   *The Road to Ruin*   G. U. S.

Cast as for Jan. 26, 1795, except:

Goldfinch.........Mr. Harwood	Smith...........Mr. Darley, Jr.
Milford..............Mr. Beete	Tradesmen.......Messrs. Darley,
	Solomon, Mitchell, etc.

* The Lucky Escape (pantomime—"founded on Dibdin's" ballad of that name)—Francis

Ploughman..........Mr. Francis	Peggy Perkins....Mrs. DeMarque
Jack...........Mr. Warrell, Jr.	Anna............Miss Milbourne
Ben Block..........Mr. Doctor	Kate..............Miss Willems
Bill Babler.............M. Lege	Sally..............Miss Gilaspie

The Mogul Tale

Cast as for March 11.

[282]

1796

PANTHEON

March 15   Circus   G. U. S.
Vulcan's Gift

Cast as for March 12.

NEW THEATRE

March 16   * *The Suicide*—Colman, Jr.   G. U. S.

Tobine............Mr. Moreton	1st Watchman......Mr. Warrell
Tabby..............Mr. Green	2d Watchman......Mr. Solomon
Dr. Truby........Mr. Whitlock	Anthony.............Mr. Beete
Ranter............Mr. Marshall	Tom Cellarman....Mr. Mitchell
Catchpenny........Mr. Harwood	Bolus..............Mr. Morgan
Bounce.........Mr. Darley, Jr.	Members of Club........Messrs.
Squib.............Mr. Blissett	Darley, Robbins, Rowson, etc.
Juggins............Mr. Francis	Mrs. Grogram......Mrs. Rowson
John.........Mr. Warrell, Jr.	Nancy............Mrs. Marshall
Wingrave............Mr. Bates	Peggy.............Mrs. Hervey

The Lucky Escape

Cast as for March 14.

The Deaf Lover

Cast as for Jan. 18, except that:

"Groom" is not cast.

PANTHEON

March 17   Circus   G. U. S.
Vulcan's Gift

Cast as for March 12.

NEW THEATRE

March 18   *Inkle and Yarico*   G. U. S.

Inkle............Mr. Marshall	3d Planter........Mr. Warrell
Sir Christopher Curry..........	Waiter..........Master Warrell
Mr. Whitlock	Mate...............Mr. Darley
Medium...........Mr. Francis	Yarico..........Mrs. Marshall
Crampey.........Mr. Moreton	Narcissa.........Miss Willems
Trudge...........Mr. Wignell	Wowski........Mrs. Oldmixon
1st Planter.........Mr. Beete	Patty...............Mrs. Shaw
2d Planter........Mr. Blissett	

* *The Shamrock*—Francis
"Comic Irish Dance"

[283]

1796

March 18 (cont.)   *The Irishman in London*
Cast as for Dec. 16, 1795

PANTHEON

March 19   Circus   G. U. S.
Vulcan's Gift
Cast as for March 12.

NEW THEATRE

March 21   *Zara*   G. U. S.
Cast as for Feb. 23.
The Lucky Escape
Cast as for March 14.
The Deserter
Cast as for Jan. 23, 1795, except:

Flint..............Mr. Blissett   Jenny.............Mrs. Warrell

PANTHEON

March 22   Circus   G. U. S.
Vulcan's Gift

NEW THEATRE

March 23   *The Duenna*   G. U. S.
Cast as for May 27, 1795, except:

Isaac................Mr. Bates   Louisa............Mrs. Warrell
Friars.........Messrs. Mitchell,   Clara............Mrs. Oldmixon
    Solomon, Morgan, Robbins,
             Warrell
Nun................Mrs. Bates   Floretta...........Miss Oldfield
Lauretta..........Mrs. Rowson

The Widow's Vow
Cast as for February 5.
* *The Fandango Dance*—Francis

PANTHEON

March 24   Circus   G. U. S.
Vulcan's Gift

1796

NEW THEATRE

March 24	*The Tempest*	G. U. S.
	The Mogul Tale	

PANTHEON

March 26	Circus	G. U. S.
	Vulcan's Gift	

"A New Pantomime" (probably *Harlequin's Renovations* mentioned on March 28.)

March 28	Circus	G. U. S.

* *Harlequin's Renovations*—Compiled by Messrs. Ricketts, Sully, and Spinacuta

(See March 26)

NEW THEATRE

March 28	*The Earl of Essex*	G. U. S.

Earl of Essex......Mr. Wignell   Queen Elizabeth.....Mrs. Morris
Earl of Southampton...........   Countess of Rutland...........
                Mr. Moreton   Mrs. Whitlock
Lord Burleigh........Mr. Green   Countess of Nottingham........
Sir Walter Raleigh..Mr. Harwood   Mrs. Shaw
Lieut. of The Tower..Mr. Beete

* *The Easter Gift*—Francis and Milbourne
The Warrior's Welcome Home

PANTHEON

March 29	Circus	G. U. S.
	Vulcan's Gift	

NEW THEATRE

March 30	*George Barnwell*	G. U. S.

Cast as for Dec. 26, 1795.

T'Other Side of the Gutter
—Joseph Doctor in "New Performances"
Love in a Camp

Cast as for June 29, 1795, except:

Rupert........Mr. Warrell, Jr.   Drummers........Mr. Mitchell
Adjutant..........Mr. Warrell   and Mr. T. Warrell
Norah...........Miss Willems

1796

April 1	*The Jealous Wife*		G. U. S.

Oakly.............Mr. Green		William.........Mr. Darley, Jr.	
Major Oakly......Mr. Whitlock		John..............Mr. Warrell	
Charles...........Mr. Moreton		Tom...............Mr. Francis	
Russet............Mr. Wignell		Mrs. Oakly......Mrs. Whitlock	
Sir Harry Beagle...Mr. Harwood		Lady Freelove.......Mrs. Shaw	
Lord Trinket......Mr. Marshall		Harriet...........Mrs. Francis	
Capt. O'Cutter.......Mr. Bates		Toilet............Mrs. Rowson	
Paris.............Mr. Blissett		Chamber Maid....Miss Willems	

The Prize

Cast as for Jan. 13.

PANTHEON

April 2	Benefit of Mr. Francis Ricketts	G. U. S.

Circus
Vulcan's Gift

NEW THEATRE

April 2	*The Jew*	G. U. S.

Cast as for Dec. 30, 1795.
The Witches of the Rock
Cast as for February 26.

April 4	*All in the Wrong*	G. U. S.

Sir John Restless...Mr. Whitlock	James.........Mr. Warrell, Jr.
Beverly...........Mr. Moreton	John...........Mr. Darley, Jr.
Sir Wm. Bellmont..Mr. Warrell	Lady Restless....Mrs. Whitlock
Young Bellmont......Mr. Green	Belinda...........Mrs. Morris
Blandford..........Mr. Francis	Clarissa...........Mrs. Francis
Robert.............Mr. Beete	Tattle............Mrs. Rowson
Brush.............Mr. Blissett	Tippet...........Miss Oldfield
Richard...........Mr. Mitchell	Marmalet.........Mrs. Hervey

No Song No Supper

Frederick.........Mr. Marshall	William........Mr. Darley, Jr.
Crop..............Mr. Darley	Dorothy............Mrs. Shaw
Endless...........Mr. Harwood	Louisa............Miss Rowson
Thomas............Mr. Blissett	Margaretta.......Mrs. Oldmixon
Robin..............Mr. Bates	Nelly.............Miss Willems

[286]

1796

PANTHEON

April 5   Benefit of Mr. Sully   G. U. S.

Circus
Harlequin's Olio

Harlequin............Mr. Sully
Pantaloon............Mr. Reano
Lover...........Mr. Macdonald
Dwarf.........Master Schnyder

Genius...........Master Sully
Clown............Mr. Spinacuta
Columbine........Mrs. Spinacuta

NEW THEATRE

April 6   *The Rage*   G. U. S.

Cast as for Dec. 18, 1795.
The Shipwreck'd Mariners Preserved

Capt. Hatchway........M. Lege
Jack Ratling........Mr. Blissett
Gerald.............Mr. Warrell
Ramisey............Mr. Doctor
Banditti.....Messrs. Warrell, Jr.,
Morgan, Mitchell, Beete, etc.

Sailors.......Messrs. Darley, Jr.,
Solomon, &c.
Rosalie..........Miss Milbourne
Jacqualine.........Miss Solomon
Leonardo...........Mr. Francis

T'Other Side of the Gutter

PANTHEON

April 7   Benefit of Mr. Reano   G. U. S.

Circus
Harlequin's Olio

NEW THEATRE

April 8   *The Miser*   G. U. S.

Lovegold.............Mr. Bates
Frederick.........Mr. Marshall
Clerimont...........Mr. Green
Ramilie...........Mr. Wignell
Decoy.............Mr. Warrell
Fumish...............Mr. Beete
Sparkle........Mr. Darley, Jr.
Sattin.............Mr. Mitchell
List................Mr. Blissett

Lawyer............Mr. Morgan
Thomas........Master Warrell
James..............Mr. Francis
Harriet...........Mrs. Francis
Mrs. Wisely.......Mrs. Rowson
Mariana.........Mrs. Oldmixon
Wheedle..........Mrs. Solomon
Lappett............Mrs. Morris

[287]

1796

April 8 (cont.) *The Jubilee*

Irishman	Mr. Whitlock	2nd Waiter	Mr. Warrell, Jr.
Ralph	Mr. Bates	3rd Waiter	Master Warrell
1st Serenade	Mr. Marshall	1st Pedlar	Mr. Blissett
2nd Serenade	Mr. Darley	2nd Pedlar	Mr. Warrell
3rd Serenade	Mr. Darley, Jr.	Trumpeter	Mr. Rowson
1st Gentleman	Mr. Moreton	Showman	Mr. Morgan
2nd Gentleman	Mr. Beete	Goody Benson	Mrs. Bates
Ostler	Mr. Blissett	Goody Jarvis	Mrs. Rowson
Cook	Mr. Morris	1st Country Girl	Mrs. Oldmixon
Man Ballad Singer	Mr. Harwood	2nd Country Girl	Miss Willems
Woman Ballad Singer	Mr. Bates	Tragic Muse	Mrs. Whitlock
1st Waiter	Mr. Francis	Comic Muse	Miss Willems

PANTHEON

April 9 Circus G. U. S.
Harlequin's Olio

Cast as for April 5.

NEW THEATRE

April 11 *All in the Wrong* G. U. S

Cast as for April 4, 1796.

The Sicilian Romance

Marquis of Otranto	Mr. Moreton	Gerbin	Mr. Wignell
Don Lope de Viega	Mr. Morris	Julia	Miss Solomon
Lindor	Mr. Marshall	Alinda	Mrs. Warrell
Martin	Mr. Harwood	Clara	Mrs. Oldmixon
Jacques	Mr. Mitchell	Lady of Otranto	Mrs. Whitlock
Sancho	Mr. Warrell		

PANTHEON

April 12 Benefit of Mr. Spinacuta G. U. S.

Circus
* Harlequin in the Sun

Harlequin	Mr. Simonet	Columbine	Mrs. Spinacuta
	(this night only)	Magician	Mr. Macdonald
Old Man	Mr. Reano	Servant	Mr. Price
Lover	Mr. Sully	Cottager	Mr. Langley
Piero	Mr. Spinacuta		

[288]

NEW THEATRE

April 13   *Hamlet*   G. U. S.

Hamlet ("first time").........
               Mr. Moreton
King................Mr. Green
Ghost............Mr. Whitlock
Horatio...........Mr. Marshall
Laertes............Mr. Wignell
Polonius............Mr. Morris
Rosencrans......Mr. Warrell, Jr.
Guildenstern..........Mr. Beete
Francisco........Mr. Darley, Jr.

Marcellus.........Mr. Harwood
Bernardo...........Mr. Warrell
Ostric..............Mr. Francis
Officer.............Mr. Blissett
Grave-Diggers...Mr. Bates & Mr.
                    Milbourne
Queen...............Mrs. Shaw
Ophelia..........Mrs. Marshall
Player Queen.......Mrs. Rowson

The Village Lawyer

Scout.............Mr. Harwood
Snarl...............Mr. Francis
Charles.........Mr. Darley, Jr.
Justice Mittimus....Mr. Warrell

Sheep-face............Mr. Bates
Kate................Mrs. Bates
Mrs. Scout..........Mrs. Shaw

PANTHEON

April 14   Benefit of Mr. Collet   G. U. S.

Circus
Harlequin in the Sun

NEW THEATRE

April 15   *The Maid of the Mill*   G. U. S.

Lord Aimworth....Mr. Marshall
Sir Harry Sycamour....Mr. Bates
Merwin........Mr. Darley, Jr.
Fairfield.........Mr. Whitlock
Giles..............Mr. Darley

Ralph..............Mr. Francis
Lady Sycamour.......Mrs. Shaw
Theodosia.........Miss Willems
Patty.............Mrs. Warrell
Fanny..........Mrs. Oldmixon

La Forêt Noire

Cast as for Feb. 27, 1795, except:

Adolphe..........Miss Solomon
Pasquin...........Mr. Mitchell

Martin...........Miss Oldfield
Sans Quartier....Mr. Darley, Jr.

PANTHEON

April 16   Benefit of Messrs. Macdonald, Langley, and   G. U. S.
                    Master C. Sully

Circus

[289]

1796

Harlequin's Olio

Cast as for April 5.

NEW THEATRE

April 18   Mr. Wignell's Night   G. U. S.

* *The Mountaineers*—Colman, Jr.

Octavian.........Mr. Moreton	Pacho.........Mr. Darley, Jr.
Virolet..............Mr. Green	Sadi..............Mr. Harwood
Killmalloch.......Mr. Marshall	Moors.......Messrs. Solomon &
Rogue.............Mr. Wignell	Mitchell
Lope Tocho.........Mr. Francis	Zorayda.........Mrs. Whitlock
Perequillo....Master T. Warrell	Floranthe..........Mrs. Francis
Bulcazin Muley....Mr. Whitlock	Agnes...........Mrs. Oldmixon
Ganem..............Mr. Beete	

High Life Below Stairs

Cast as for Jan. 4, 1796, except:

Lovel............Mr. Wignell   Philip...............Mr. Green

April 20   *Hamlet*   G. U. S.

Cast as for April 13.

Robinson Crusoe

(reduced to one act)

Robinson Crusoe.......Mr. Bates	Will Atkins.........Mr. Beete
Pantaloon.........Mr. Warrell	Sam Stern.........Mr. Mitchell
Pierot..........Mr. Darley, Jr.	Friday.............Mr. Francis
Capt. of Ship........Mr. Darley	

PANTHEON

April 21   Circus   G. U. S.

Harlequin's Olio

NEW THEATRE

April 22   Mr. Harwood's Night   G. U. S.

* *Rule a Wife and Have a Wife*—Garrick-Beaumont-Fletcher

Duke of Medina...Mr. Whitlock	Lorenzo.......Mr. Warrell, Jr.
Don Juan............Mr. Green	Margaretta.........Mrs. Shaw
Sanchio..............Mr. Beete	Altea.............Mrs. Francis
Alonzo........Mr. Darley, Jr.	Clara.............Mrs. Hervey
Cacosogo..........Mr. Darley	Estisania........Mrs. Marshall

1796

Leon..............Mr. Moreton
Michale Perez.....Mr. Harwood
Lopez.............Mr. Mitchell

Old Woman..........Mr. Bates
Maid..............Mr. Francis

Harlequin Hurry Scurry

Colin................M. Lege
Heeltap.........Mr. Darley, Jr.
Cabbage........Mr. Warrell, Jr.
Billy Puff.......Master Warrell
Farmer Sturdy......Mr. Rowson
Sawyers......Messrs. Mitchell &
Solomon

Bumkin.............Mr. Doctor
Lucy............Miss Milbourne
Milliner..........Miss Willems
Sempstress...........Mrs. Lege
Washer Woman....Mrs. Hervey,
&c.
Columbine......Mrs. DeMarque

* Two Strings to Your Bow—Jephson

Don Pedro..........Mr. Francis
Don Sancho........Mr. Warrell
Octavio..............Mr. Beete
Ferdinand...........Mr. Green
Borachio...........Mr. Morgan
Lazarillo.............Mr. Bates

Drunken Porter.....Mr. Blissett
Waiters.....Messrs. J. Warrell &
Mitchell
Donna Clara.......Mrs. Francis
Leonora...........Miss Willems
Maid.............Miss Rowson

First mention of Mrs. Lege.

PANTHEON

April 23

"Last Night This Season"

G. U. S.

Circus
Harlequin's Olio

Between December 22, 1795, and April 23, 1796, the following new panto-mimes were presented at The Pantheon (or Ricketts' Amphitheatre): *Harle-quin in the Sun, Harlequin's Olio, Harlequin Statue, The Triumph of Virtue; or Harlequin in Philadelphia* [sic!], and *Vulcan's Gift.*

The only performers who had been seen before (in dramatic productions) were Mr. Price and M. Simonette. The new performers: Mr. Crump, the Masters Deforrest, Master Frost, Master Grant, Mr. Langley, Mr. M'Donald, The Masters M'Elroy, Master Mills, Mr. Reano, Mr. J. B. Ricketts, Mr. F. Ricketts, Miss Rickson, Master Snider (or Snyder or Schnyder), Mr. and Mrs. Spinacuta, and Mr. Sully, Mr. Sully, Jr., and Master Sully.

NEW THEATRE

April 25

The Mountaineers

G. U. S.

Cast as for April 18.

[291]

1796

Ways and Means
Cast as for Jan. 27.
Mr. Harwood's "Last Appearance."

April 27 Benefit of Philadelphia Dispensary and of Sunday Schools G. U. S.
Every One Has His Fault
Cast as for Dec. 3, 1794, except:

Sir Robert Ramble..Mr. Wignell   Placid...............Mr. Green
Harmony............Mr. Bates   Hammond......Mr. Warrell, Jr.

* *The Irish Vagary* (Comic Dance)—Francis
The Romp

Watty Cockney......Mr. Francis   Priscilla Tomboy..Mrs. Marshall
Barnacle...........Mr. Blissett   Penelope.........Miss Willems
Old Cockney.......Mr. Warrell   Madame Le Blond..Mrs. Hervey
Capt. Slightly.....Mr. Marshall

                                                      G. U. S.
April 29   * *The Deserted Daughter*—Holcroft

Mordent............Mr. Green   Donald..............Mr. Bates
Cherril............Mr. Moreton   Joanna...........Mrs. Marshall
Lennox...........Mr. Marshall   Mrs. Sarsnet.......Mrs. Francis
Item..............Mr. Francis   Mrs. Enfield......Mrs. Solomon
Grime.............Mr. Beete   Betty.............Mrs. Doctor
Clement......Mr. Warrell, Jr.   Lady Ann........Mrs. Whitlock

The Prisoner

Cast as for March 4, except:

Bernardo..........Mr. Darley   Roberto...........Mr. Blissett
Pasquel........Mr. Darley, Jr.

"After the Play Mr. Wignell made a handsome address to the audience, intimating his intention of leaving this country, in order to recruit his Theatrical Corps." (G. U. S., April 30.)

                               Mr. Moreton's Night   G. U. S.
May 2
The Way to Keep Him

Lovemore.........Mr. Whitlock   John............Mr. Darley, Jr.
Sir Bashful Constant...Mr. Bates   Mrs. Lovemore....Mrs. Whitlock
Sir Brilliant Fashion............   Widow Belmour...Mrs. Marshall
           Mr. Moreton   Lady Constant......Mrs. Francis
William..........Mr. Marshall   Muslin............Mrs. Morris
Sideboard..........Mr. Francis   Mignionet.........Mrs. Hervey
Pompey.......Mr. Warrell, Jr.   Fumish.............Mrs. Bates

1796

May 2 (cont.)   * *The Rival Knights* ("serious Ballet")

Duke	Mr. Doctor	Chamont	Mr. Warrell
Pierre de Province	Mr. Moreton	Dumont	Mr. Mitchell
Ferriers	M. Lege	St. Creux	Mr. Beete
Clermont	Mr. Francis	La Belle Magulonne	
La Gloire	Mr. Robbins		Mrs. Francis
Belmonte	Mr. Green	Elize	Mrs. De Marque
Ribemonte	Mr. Darley, Jr.	Sophie	Miss Willems

May 4   Mrs. Warrell's Night   G. U. S.

Know Your Own Mind

Millamour	Mr. Moreton	Dashwood	Mr. Marshall
Sir John Millamour	Mr. Warrell	Capt. Bygrove	Mr. Beete
Sir Harry Loveit	Mr. Francis	Lady Jane	Mrs. Morris
Malvil	Mr. Green	Mrs. Bromley	Mrs. Shaw
Charles	Mr. Warrell, Jr.	Miss Neville	Mrs. Warrell
Bygrove	Mr. Bates	Mme. Le Rouge	Miss Oldfield

* *The Motley Group, or Harlequin's Invitation*—Francis

Harlequin	Mr. Warrell, Jr.	Punch	Mr. Francis
Pierot	Mr. Doctor	Clown	Master T. Warrell
Scaramouch	Mr. Darley, Jr.		

The Poor Soldier

Fitzroy	Mr. Darley	Darby	Mr. Moreton
Father Luke	Mr. Blissett		(that night only)
Patrick	Mrs. Warrell	Boy	Master Warrell
	(that night only)	Norah	Mrs. Oldmixon
Bagatelle	Mr. Marshall	Kathleen	Miss Willems

May 6   *The Deserted Daughter*   G. U. S.

Cast as for April 29.

The Jubilee

May 9   Mrs. Marshall's Night   G. U. S

Alexander the Great

Alexander	Mr. Moreton	Perdiccas	Mr. Beete
Hephestion	Mr. Warrell, Jr.	Eumenes	Mr. Francis
Lysimachus	Mr. Marshall	Slave	Mr. Mitchell
Cassandre	Mr. Green	Roxana	Mrs. Shaw
Polyperchon	Mr. Darley, Jr.	Sysigambis	Mrs. Rowson
Philip	Mr. Morgan	Parasatis	Miss Willems
Clitus	Mr. Whitlock	Statira	Mrs. Marshall
Thessalus	Mr. Warrell		

[293]

1796

May 9 (cont.)   *The Deserter of Naples ("serious pantomime")

General	Mr. Doctor	Jailor	Mr. Blissett
Russett	Mr. Warrell	Margaret	Mrs. Rowson
Henry	Mr. Marshall	Jenny	Miss Milbourne
Skirmish	Mr. Bates	Louisa	Mrs. Marshall
Simkin	Mr. Francis		

May 11   Mr. Darley's Benefit   G. U. S.

Such Things Are

Sultan	Mr. Green	1st Keeper	Mr. Warrell
Lord Flint	Mr. Beete	2nd Keeper	Mr. Mitchell
Sir Luke Tremor	Mr. Bates	1st Prisoner	Mr. Blissett
Twincall	Mr. Moreton	2nd Prisoner	Mr. Morgan
Harwell	Mr. Whitlock	Messenger	Mr. Warrell, Jr.
Elvirus	Mr. Marshall	Lady Tremor	Mrs. Shaw
Meanright	Mr. Darley, Jr.	Aurelia	Mrs. Francis
Zedan	Mr. Darley	Female Prisoner	Mrs. Whitlock

The Mogul Tale

Cast as for March 11, except:

Dr. Pedant.........Mr. Francis

May 13   Mr. Whitlock's Benefit   G. U. S.

*Henry II, or The Fall of the Fair Rosamond—Hull

Henry	Mr. Moreton	Servant	Mr. Mitchell
Clifford	Mr. Whitlock	Abbot	Mr. Green
Prince	Mr. Warrell, Jr.	Queen	Mrs. Shaw
Salisbury	Mr. Beete	Ethelinda	Mrs. Hervey
Leicester	Mr. Warrell	Rosamond	Mrs. Whitlock
Verulam	Mr. Morris		

The Miraculous Mill

Gaffer Thoughtless	Mr. Francis	Goody Benson	Mrs. DeMarque
Old Rowly Powly	Mr. Doctor	Patty	Miss Milbourne
The Miller	Mr. Rowson	Lucy	Miss Gillaspie
Bob	Mr. Warrell, Jr.		

Love à la Mode

Sir Callaghan O'Brallaghan	Mr. Whitlock	Sir Theodore Goodchild	Mr. Beete
Sir Archy Macsarcasm	Mr. Bates	Servant	Mr. Mitchell
Squire Groom	Mr. Marshall	Charlotte	Miss Willems
Beau Mordecai	Mr. Francis		

[294]

1796

May 16   Mr. Bates' Benefit   G. U. S.

The Patriot—Bates

["As altered from the Play of *Helvetic Liberty,* and compressed
into Three Acts, by Mr. Bates"]

Albert	Mr. Green	Werner	Mr. Beete
Oscar	Mr. Moreton	Walter of Vri	Mr. Warrell
Provost	Mr. Francis	Old Man of the Mountains	
Edwald	Mr. Warrell, Jr.		Mr. Morgan
Corporal Popgun	Mr. Blissett	Count Fool	Mr. Bates
1st Citizen	Mr. Mitchell	Marina	Mrs. Whitlock
William Tell	Mr. Whitlock	Serena	Miss Willems
Tell's Son	Miss Solomon		

Barnaby Brittle—Betterton

Barnaby Brittle	Mr. Bates	Jeffrey	Mr. Warrell, Jr.
Clodpole	Mr. Blissett	Mrs. Brittle	Mrs. Marshall
Jeremy	Mr. Francis	Lady Pride	Mrs. Shaw
Sir Peter Pride	Mr. Morgan	Damaris	Mrs. Rowson
Lovemore	Mr. Green		

Gil Blas (pantomime)—Bates

[As originally produced by Mr. Bates at the Royalty Theatre,
in London]

Gil Blas	Mr. Bates	Domingo	Mr. Morgan
His Father	Mr. Warrell	Post Boy	Master Warrell
Gil Perez	Mr. Blissett	Dorothea	*Mr.* Rowson
Young Spaniard	Mr. Green	Spanish Lady	Miss Willems
Captain of Banditti	Mr. Moreton	Gil Blas' Mother	Mrs. Solomon
Pompey	Mr. Mitchell		

May 18   Mr. Marshall's Benefit   G. U. S.

The Count of Narbonne—Jephson

[from *The Castle of Otranto*]

Raymond	Mr. Whitlock	Hortensia	Mrs. Whitlock
Austin	Mr. Green	Adelaide	Mrs. Marshall
Theodore	Mr. Moreton	Jacqueline	Miss Willems
Fabian	Mr. Beete		

The Lucky Escape
The Farm House

[295]

1796

May 20 Mrs. Oldmixon's Night G. U. S.

Speculation—Reynolds

Sir Frederick Faintly...........
Mr. Francis
Project..............Mr. Bates
Vickery.............Mr. Blissett
Alderman Arable...Mr. Whitlock
Jack Arable.......Mr. Marshall
Tanjore...........Mr. Moreton
Capt. Arable........Mr. Green

Promptly..........Mr. Morgan
Meanwell............Mr. Beete
John..........Mr. Warrell, Jr.
Waiter...........Mr. Mitchell
Lady Project........Mrs. Shaw
Emmeline........Mrs. Whitlock
Cecilia..........Mrs. Marshall

The Miraculous Mill

Cast as for May 13.

The Doctor and the Apothecary—Cobb

Thomaso...........Mr. Green
Sturmwald..........Mr. Bates
Carlos...........Mr. Marshall
Juan..............Mr. Francis
Gusman...........Mr. Darley

Dr. Bilioso..........Mr. Morris
Perez..............Mr. Blissett
Anna...........Mrs. Oldmixon
Isabella.........Mrs. Marshall
Theresa..........Mrs. Rowson

May 23 Mrs. Whitlock's Benefit G. U. S.

First Love—Cumberland

Frederick Mowbray............
Mr. Moreton
David Mowbray......Mr. Bates
Sir Miles Mowbray..Mr. Whit-
lock
Billy Blinter.......Mr. Francis
Wrangle.............Mr. Green
Robin..............Mr. Blissett
Servant to Lady Ruby.........
Mr. Warrell, Jr.

Servant to Lady Wrangle.......
Mr. Darley, Jr.
Lord Sensitive......Mr. Marshall
Sabina Rosny.....Mrs. Marshall
Mrs. Wrangle........Mrs. Shaw
Mrs. Kate........Mrs. Rowson
Waiting Woman....Miss Oldfield
Lady Ruby.......Mrs. Whitlock

The Maid of the Oaks—Burgoyne

Oldworth...........Mr. Green
Old Groveby......Mr. Whitlock
Sir Harry Groveby..Mr. Marshall
Dupely...........Mr. Moreton

Hurry..............Mr. Bates
Lady Bab Lardoon.............
Mrs. Whitlock
Maria...........Miss Willems

1796

May 25   *The Road to Ruin*   G. U. S.

Cast as for Jan. 26, 1795, except:

Milford..............Mr. Beete	Marker.......Mr. Warrell, Jr.
Smith...........Mr. Darley, Jr.	Postillion........Master Warrell
Tradesmen......Messrs. Darley, Solomon, Mitchell, Morgan	

The Critic

Dangle..............Mr. Green	Lord Burleigh......Mr. Morgan
Sneer.............Mr. Moreton	Earl of Leicester....Mr. Blissett
Sir Fretful Plagiary............. Mr. Marshall	Sir Walter Raleigh....Mr. Beete
	Sir Chris. Hatton....Mr. Francis
Pasticcio Ritomello............. Mr. Darley, Jr.	Master of Horse....Mr. Warrell
	Beef-Eater.......Mr. Darley, Jr.
Interpreter.........Mr. Doctor	Whiskerandos.........Mr. Bates
Prompter.........Mr. Rowson	1st Niece......Mrs. Rowson [sic]
Puff..............Mr. Chalmers	2nd Niece.........Miss Oldfield
Mrs. Dangle.......Mrs. Francis	Tilburina............Mrs. Shaw
Italian Girl.......Miss Willems	Confidante....Mrs. Rowson [sic]
Gov. of Tilbury Fort..Mr. Darley	

Mr. Chalmers rejoined the company.

May 27   Mr. Morris' Benefit   G. U. S.

The Suspicious Husband

Ranger..........Mr. Chalmers	Ranger's Servant.............. Mr. Warrell, Jr.
Strictland.........Mr. Whitlock	Mrs. Strictland......Mrs. Shaw
Frankly.........Mr. Moreton	Jacintha...........Mrs. Francis
Bellamy.........Mr. Green	Lucetto...........Mrs. Rowson
Jack Meggott.......Mr. Francis	Landlady...........Mrs. Bates
Tester..............Mr. Bates	Milliner...........Miss Willems
Buckle............Mr. Blissett	Clarinda..........Mrs. Morris
Simon.............Mr. Warrell	

Comus

Comus...........Mr. Chalmers	The Lady........Mrs. Marshall
1st Spirit...........Mr. Green	Sabrina...........Mrs. Hervey
Elder Brother......Mr. Moreton	Pastoral Nymph..Miss Milbourne
Younger Brother.............. Mr. Warrell, Jr.	Euphrosyne......Mrs. Oldmixon
	Principal Bacchante............ Mrs. Warrell
Principal Bacchanals......Messrs Marshall & Darley.	
Bacchanals. Messrs. Warrell, Darley, Jr., Solomon, & Mitchell	Bacchantes.......{ Mrs. Solomon / Mrs. Bates / Miss Oldfield

1796

The Warrior's Welcome Home—Daily Ad.

May 30   Mr. Green's Benefit   G. U. S.

Macbeth

Macbeth..........Mr. Chalmers
Malcolm.......Mr. Warrell, Jr.
Lenox............Mr. Marshall
Fleance..........Miss Solomon
Seyton...............Mr. Beete
Duncan..............Mr. Green
Donalbaine......Master Warrell
Macduff..........Mr. Moreton

Banquo...........Mr. Whitolck
Siward.............Mr. Morris
Murderers....Messrs. Darley, Jr.
        Morgan, & Solomon
Lady Macbeth....Mrs. Whitlock
Hecate..............Mr. Darley
Witches..Messrs. Bates, Warrell,
        & Francis

* *Harlequin's Club* (pantomime ballet)—Francis

Harlequin......Mr. Warrell, Jr.
Pierrot.............Mr. Doctor
Scaramouch......Mr. Darley, Jr.
Bumpkin..........Mr. Blissett

Waiter..........Master Warrell
Punch..............Mr. Francis
Landlady...........Mr. Rowson

The Ghost

Sir Jeffery Constant..Mr. Warrell
Captain Constant..Mr. Darley, Jr.
Clinch..............Mr. Green
Trusty.............Mr. Francis

Roger...............Mr. Bates
Belinda...........Mrs. Hervey
Dorothy...........Mrs. Shaw

June 1   Mrs. Shaw's Benefit   G. U. S.

The Busy Body

Marplot..........Mr. Chalmers
Sir George Airy....Mr. Moreton
Charles..............Mr. Green
Sir Francis Gripe....Mr. Morris
Sir Jealous Traffic...Mr. Francis
Whisper...........Mr. Blissett

Butler.............Mr. Warrell
Miranda.........Mrs. Marshall
Isabinda...........Mrs. Francis
Patch..............Mrs. Shaw
Scentwell.........Miss Oldfield

*The Motley Groupe, or
Harlequin's Invitation*

Cast as for May 4.

* *The Midnight Wanderers*—Pearce

Marquis de Morelle....Mr. Bates
Julian...........Mr. Marshall
Don Pedrozzo......Mr. Warrell
Gasper............Mr. Francis

Guide.............Mr. Morgan
Adelaide..........Mrs. Warrell
Jacquelin...........Mrs. Shaw
Maresa.........Mrs. Oldmixon

[298]

1796

Dennis............Mr. Blissett   Berilla.........Miss Milbourne
Mendicant..........Mr. Beete

June 3   Mr. and Mrs. Francis's Benefit   G. U. S.
Coriolanus—Shakespeare (as altered by Kemble)

Caius Marcius......Mr. Moreton   Young Marcius....Miss Solomon
Tullus Aufidius......Mr. Green   Roman Officer...Mr. Darley, Jr.
Menenius...........Mr. Bates   Volscian Officer.....Mr. Morgan
Cominius.........Mr. Whitlock   Virgilia............Mrs. Francis
Sicinius Velutus....Mr. Marshall   Valeria.............Mrs. Shaw
Junius Brutus........Mr. Beete   Gentlewoman.......Miss Rowson
Volusius........Mr. Darley, Jr.

Harlequin Dr. Faustus—Francis (pantomime)

Azuria............Mrs. Francis   Miller.............Mr. Warrell
Harlequin Dr. Faustus.........   Miller's Son......Mr. Darley, Jr.
             Mr. Francis   Miller's Wife.......Mme. Lege
Mephistopheles.......Mr. Darley   Clown..............Mr. Blissett
Good Spirit.......Mrs. Warrell   Columbine.......Miss Milbourne
Evil Spirit......Mr. Darley, Jr.   Scaramouch........Mr. Doctor
Helen of Troy....Mrs. Marshall

This is the first appearance of Shakespeare's *Coriolanus* (as altered by Kemble), though Thomson's play had been produced on June 8, 1767.

June 6   Mrs. Harvey & Miss Willem's Night   G. U. S.
Richard III
Cast as for Jan. 23, 1795, except:

Prince Edward.....Mrs. Harvey   Lieut. of Tower..Mr. Warrell, Jr.
Duke of York.....Miss Solomon   Lord Stanley..........Mr. Beete
Buckingham..........Mr. Green   Tyrrell............Mr. Morgan
Catesby.........Mr. Darley, Jr.   Lady Anne........Miss Willems

Barnaby Brittle
Cast as for May 16, except:

Mrs. Brittle.........Mrs. Shaw   Damaris..........Mrs. Harvey
Lady Pride........Mrs. Rowson

[299]

1796

June 8   G. U. S.

Mr. Warrell, Mr. Warrell, Jr., & Master Warrell's Benefit

Romeo and Juliet

Cast as for Jan. 22, except:

Mercutio.........Mr. Chalmers	Friar Laurence.....Mr. Whitlock
Tibalt..............Mr. Beete	Apothecary..........Mr. Francis
Balthazar......Mr. Warrell, Jr.	Peter...............Mr. Blissett
(and Escalus is not cast)	Page............Master Warrell

The Liar

Old Wilding......Mr. Whitlock	Servant.........Master Warrell
Young Wilding....Mr. Chalmers	Mrs. Grantham.....Mrs. Francis
Sir James Elliot......Mr. Green	Miss Godfrey........Mrs. Harvey
Papillion..........Mr. Marshall	Kitty.............Mrs. Rowson
Waiter.............Mr. Blissett	

June 10   M. Lege and Sig. Doctor's Benefit   G. U. S.

The Merchant of Venice

Duke..............Mr. Morris	Tubal.............Mr. Morgan
Antonio..........Mr. Whitlock	Launcelot...........Mr. Bates
Bassanio..........Mr. Moreton	Old Gobbo.........Mr. Francis
Gratiano...........Mr. Green	Leonardo..........Mr. Blissett
Lorenzo..........Mr. Marshall	Balthazar........Mr. Darley, Jr.
Solarino...........Mr. Warrell	Jessica...........Mrs. Warrell
Salanio..............Mr. Beete	Nerissa............Mrs. Francis
Shylock..........Mr. Chalmers	Portia..........Mrs. Whitlock

* *The Merry Girl*—Lege (Pantomimical Ballet)
* *The Valiant Officer, or*
The Rescue of Columbine (pantomime)

June 13   Mrs. and Miss Solomon's Night   G. U. S.

Three Weeks After Marriage

Sir Chas. Rackett...Mr. Chalmers	Lady Rackett......Mrs. Whitlock
Drugget.............Mr. Green	Mrs. Drugget......Mrs. Rowson
Woodley.............Mr. Beete	Nancy............Mrs. Francis
Servant.........Mr. Darley, Jr.	Dimity..........Mrs. Solomon

The Children in the Wood

Sir Rowland.........Mr. Green	Helen............Mrs. Solomon
Lord Alford......Mr. Marshall	Josephine.........Mrs. Marshall
Walter...........Mr. Moreton	Winifred.........Mrs. Rowson

1796

Apathy	Mr. Francis	Boy	Miss C. Solomon (being her first appearance on any stage)
Gabriel	Mr. Blissett		
Oliver	Mr. Darley, Jr.	Girl	Miss Solomon
Russian	**Mr. Morgan**		

The Spoiled Child

Cast as for Feb. 12, 1796, except:

Little Pickle	Miss Solomon	Maria	Miss Gilaspie
Old Pickle	Mr. Green	Susan	Miss Rowson

First appearance of Miss C. Solomon (s).

June 15 Mr. Blissett, Mrs. De Marque, and Mrs. Bates' Night G. U. S.

The School for Soldiers

Major Bellamy	Mr. Green	Hector	Mr. Francis
Bellamy	Mr. Moreton	Frederick	Master Warrell
Col. Valentine	Mr. Beete	Mrs. Mildmay	Mrs. Hervey
Capt. Valentine	Mr. Warrell, Jr.	Clara	Mrs. Marshall

The Purse

Bason	Mr. Green	Page..Miss Gillespie—"Being her last appearance on any stage." [sic!]	
Theodore	Mr. Green		
Edmund	Mr. Darley, Jr.	Sally	Mrs. Oldmixon
Will Steady	Mr. Bates		

* Les Deux Sœurs

June 17 * The Disbanded Officer—Johnstone G. U. S., June 16

[translated from Lessing's *Minna Von Barnhelm*]

Col. Holberg	Mr. Moreton	Boy	Master Warrell
Paul Warmans	Mr. Green	Baroness of Brucksal	
Katzenbuckle	Mr. Francis		Mrs. Whitlock
Rohf	Mr. Bates	Lisetta	Mrs. Rowson
Count Bellair	Mr. Marshall	Mrs. Marloff	Mrs. Shaw
Messenger	Mr. Warrell, Jr.		

* The American Tar, or
The Press Gang Defeated—Francis

(ballet "founded on a recent fact at Liverpool")

Will Steady	Mr. Francis	Jane	Miss Milbourne
Tom Capstan	Mr. Warrell, Jr.	Capt. Trunnion	Mr. Beete
Dick Hauser	Mr. Rowson	Midshipman	Mr. Darley, Jr.
Susan Steady	Miss Rowson		

[301]

1796

June 17 (cont.) *Catherine and Petruchio*

Petruchio........Mr. Chalmers
Baptista..........Mr. Warrell
Hortensio...........Mr. Beete
Grumio............Mr. Morris
Music Master......Mr. Francis
Biondello.........Mr. Mitchell

Pedro...........Mr. Darley, Jr.
Taylor............Mr. Blissett
Catherine.........Mrs. Rowson
Bianca............Mrs. Hervey
Curtis..............Mrs. Bates

June 20 Mr. Chalmers' Benefit G. U. S.

The Revenge

Don Alonzo.......Mr. Moreton
Don Carlos.........Mr. Green
Don Alvarez........Mr. Beete
Don Manuel.....Mr. Darley, Jr.

Zango............Mr. Chalmers
Leonora.........Mrs. Whitlock
Isabella...........Mrs. Hervey

The Mock Doctor

Sir Jasper...........Mr. Beete
Leander........Mr. Darley, Jr.
Gregory.............Mr. Bates
Esquire Robert..Mr. Warrell, Jr.
James.............Mr. Blissett

Harry...........Mr. .Mitchell
Davy..............Mr. Morgan
Hellbore..........Mr. Warrell
Dorcas...........Mrs. Rowson
Charlotte.........Mrs. Hervey

June 22 Mr. Darley, Jr., and Miss Milbourne's Benefit G. U. S.

The Dramatist

Cast as for Feb. 24, except:

Vapid...........Mr. Chalmers
Letty.............Mrs. Solomon

Marianne.......Miss Milbourne

The Prisoner

Cast as for March 4, except:

Narcisso.......Master R. Bates
"(first time)"

Roberto...........Mr. Blissett
Theresa...........Mrs. Harvey

First appearance of Master R. Bates.

June 24 Mrs. Francis's Benefit G. U. S.

(A second benefit because of the great expense and small
receipts on her former night—June 3.)

The West Indian

Stockwell..........Mr. Morris
Capt. Dudley........Mr. Beete

Fulmer.............Mr. Green
Varland.............Mr. Bates

1796

June 24 (cont.)

Belcour...........Mr. Chalmers
("being his last appearance this
season")
Chas. Dudley......Mr. Marshall
Major O'Flaherty..Mr. Whitlock
Stukely.........Mr. Warrell, Jr.

Sailor.............Mr. Mitchell
Lady Rusport........Mrs. Shaw
Charlotte Rusport..Mrs. Mitchell
Louisa Dudley......Mrs. Francis
Mrs. Fulmer.......Mrs. Rowson
Lucy..............Miss Oldfield

* *Crotchet Lodge*—Hurlstone

Nimble...........Mr. Moreton
Timothy Truncheon..Mr. Francis
Dashley.............Mr. Green
Squire Shrinken ApLloyd........
Mr. Blissett
Dr. Chronic.........Mr. Beete
Paddy.............Mr. Morgan
Waiter.........Mr. Darley, Jr.
Bootcatcher.......Mr. Mitchell

Hostler.........Master Warrell
Sam..............Mr. Solomon
Florella...Mrs. Green, late Miss
Willems
Miss Crotchet......Mrs. Rowson
Mrs. Truncheon......Mrs. Bates
Chambermaid.......Miss Rowson
Thisbe.............Mrs. Francis

June 27   Mr. Milbourne's Night   G. U. S.

The Contrast

Col. Manly.........Mr. Green
Dimple ....Mr. Marshall
Vanrough...........Mr. Morris
Jessamy............Mr. Francis
Jonathan.............Mr. Bates

Charlotte...........Mrs. Morris
Maria.........Miss Milbourne
Letitia.............Mrs. Francis
Jenny.............Mrs. Harvey

The Rival Knights

Cast as for May 2, except:

Ferriers.............Mr. Green
Belmonte.......Mr. Warrell, Jr.

La Belle Magulonne...........
Miss Milbourne
"La Gloire" not in bill

[Miss Willems now Mrs. Green]

June 29   *The Carmelite*   G. U. S.

Montgommeri..A Young Gentleman (first appearance on any
stage)
St. Valori........Mr. Whitlock
Lord Hildebrand....Mr. Moreton

Lord De Courci.......Mr. Green
Gyfford..............Mr. Beete
Fitzallen........Mr. Warrell, Jr.
Raymond.........Mr. Warrell
Matilda.........Mrs. Whitlock

The Mock Doctor

Cast as for June 20.

[303]

1796

July 1   Benefit of Mr. Wells, "Box-Booth-Keeper"   G. U. S.

The Deserted Daughter

Cast as for April 29, except:

Lady Ann..........Mrs. Shaw

Rosina

Belville...........Mr. Marshall	2nd Irishman.......Mr. Blissett
Capt. Belville....Mr. Darley, Jr.	Rosina............Mrs. Warrell
William............Mr. Francis	Dorcas.............Mrs. Bates
Rustic.............Mr. Warrell	Phoebe.............Mrs. Green
1st Irishman........Mr. Green	

In the season at the New Theatre (Chesnut Street) from December 14, 1795, to July 1, 1796, these new plays were offered: *The Bank Note, Coriolanus* (Kemble's version of Shakespeare—Thomson's play had appeared in 1767), *The Count of Narbonne, The Deserted Daughter, The Disbanded Officer, First Love, Henry II, The Married Man, The Mogul Tale, The Mountaineers, The Patriot, Rule a Wife and Have a Wife, Speculation, The Suicide,* and *The Wheel of Fortune.* New afterpieces: *The American Tar, Barnaby Brittle, La Boiteuse, Both Sides of the Gutter, Crotchet Lodge, The Deaf Lover, The Deserter of Naples, Les Deux Chasseurs, Les Deux Sœurs, Un Divertissement Pastoral, The Fandango Dance, The Doctor and the Apothecary, The Easter Gift, The Egyptian Festival, Gil Blas, Harlequin Dr. Faustus, Harlequin's Club, Harlequin's Invitation, The Irish Vagary, The Lucky Escape, The Maid of the Oaks, The Merry Girl, The Midnight Wanderers, T'Other Side of the Gutter, The Rival Knights, La Rose et le Bouton, Rural Merriment, The Shamrock, The Shipwrecked Mariners Preserved, Two Strings to Your Bow, The Valiant Officer, The Warrior's Welcome Home, The Widow's Vow,* and *The Witches of the Rock.*

Reappearing plays: *Alexander the Great, All in the Wrong, A Bold Stroke for a Wife, The Busy Body, The Carmelite, the Castle of Andalusia, The Child of Nature, The Contrast, The Country Girl, Douglas, The Dramatist, The Duenna, The Earl of Essex, the English Merchant, Everyone Has His Fault, Fontainville Forest, The Gamester, George Barnwell, Hamlet, The Haunted Tower, The Highland Reel, Inkle and Yarico, Isabella, Jane Shore, The Jealous Wife, The Jew, Know Your Own Mind, Macbeth, The Maid of the Mill, The Merchant of Venice, The Merry Wives of Windsor, The Miser, The Natural Son, Next Door Neighbours, The Orphan, The Provoked Husband, The Rage, The Revenge, Richard III, The Rivals, The Road to Ruin, the Roman Father, Romeo and Juliet, The School for Scandal, The School for Soldiers, She Stoops to Conquer, Such Things Are, The Suspicious Husband, Three Weeks After Marriage, A Way to Keep Him, The West Indian, The Woodman, The Wrangling Lovers* (or *Lovers' Quarrels*), and *Zara.* Reappearing afterpieces: *The Agreeable Surprize, All the*

1796

World's a Stage, Les Armans d'Arcade, As it Should Be, The Bird Catcher, Catherine and Petruchio, The Children in the Wood, Comus, The Critic, The Devil to Pay, The Farm House, The Farmer, The First Floor, Florizel and Perdita, La Forêt Noire, The Ghost, Harlequin Hurry-Scurry, Harlequin Shipwrecked, Harlequin's Invasion, High Life Below Stairs, Hob in the Well, The Irishman in London, The Jubilee, The Liar, Love à la Mode, Love in a Camp, The Midnight Hour, The Miraculous Mill, The Mock Doctor, No Song No Supper, The Padlock, Peeping Tom of Coventry, The Poor Soldier, The Prisoner, The Prize, The Purse, Robinson Crusoe, The Romp, Rosina, The Sailor's Landlady, The Sicilian Romance, The Spoiled Child, Tom Thumb The Great, The Village Lawyer, Ways and Means, and *Who's the Dupe?*

New actors: Master R. Bates, Mr. Beete, Sig. Joseph Doctor, Mrs. Doctor, Miss Gillespie (or Gilaspie), M. Lege, Mrs. Lege, Mr. Morgan, Miss C. Solomon, and a "Young Gentleman." Reappearing actors: Mr. and Mrs. Bates, Mr. Blissett, Mr. Chalmers, Mr. Darley, Mr. Darley, Jr., Mrs. De Marque, Mr. and Mrs. Francis, Mr. Green, Mrs. Green (earlier Miss Willems), Mr. Harwood, Mrs. Hervey, Mr. and Mrs. Marshall, Mr. and Miss Milbourne, Mr. Mitchell, Mr. Moreton, Mr. and Mrs. Morris, Miss Oldfield, Mrs. Oldmixon, Mr. Robbins, Mr., Mrs., and Miss Rowson, Mrs. Shaw, Mr., Mrs., and Miss Solomon (or Solomons—they had earlier been with the Old American Company), Mr. and Mrs. Warrell, Mr. Warrell, Jr., Master T. Warrell, Mr. and and Mrs. Whitlock, Mr. Wignell, and Miss Willems (later Mrs. Green).

PANTHEON

Oct. 10   G. U. S.

Ricketts' Amphitheatre, called "the Pantheon," opened.

The season lasted till February 23, 1797.

No mention of any definite performance.

Oct. 12   *The Two Philosophers* (Ballet)   G. U. S.

Two Philosophers..........Messrs. Durang and Tompkins
Merry Girl..........Mrs. Tompkins

* The Death and Renovation of Harlequin

Harlequin............Mr. Sully   Clown...........Mr. Spinacuta
Old Man..........Mr. Durang   Ariel............Miss Robinson
Lover..........Mr. Tompkins   Columbine........Miss Spinacuta

First appearance of Miss Robinson, Miss Spinacuta, and Mr. and Mrs. Tompkins.

[305]

1796

Oct. 13   Circus   G. U. S.
The Two Philosophers

Cast as for October 12.

The Death and Renovation of Harlequin

Cast as for October 12.

Oct. 15   The*Distressed Sailor* (Pantomimic dance)   G. U. S.

Poor Jock.........Mr. Durang   Mrs. Casey......Mrs. Tompkins
Ned Halyard........Mr. Coffie   "The Wapping Landlady"
Orange Girl......Mrs. Durang

The Death and Renovation of Harlequin

Cast as for October 12.

The Distressed Sailor was probably simply another title for *The Wapping Landlady,* or *The Sailor's Landlady*: but as it is impossible now to determine the exact nature of the pantomime, I give the title as it appeared.

First appearance of Mr. Coffie.

Oct. 19   Circus   G. U. S.
* *The Country Frolic*
or, *The Merry Haymakers* (Comic Ballet)—Durang

William...........Mr. Durang   Rosina..........Mrs. Tompkins
Rustic..............Mr. Sully   Dorcas..........Miss Robinson
Father Frank......Mr. Tompkins   Phoebe...........Mrs. Durang
Old Man...........Mr. Coffie

Vulcan's Gift

Harlequin...........Mr. Sully   Pierrot..........Mr. Spinacuta
Pantaloon.........Mr. Durang   Fille de Chambre..Miss Robinson
Sportsman Lover...Mr. Tompkins   Columbine........Mrs. Spinacuta
Gamekeeper.........Mr. Coffie   Vulcan..............Mr. Sully

Oct. 22   Circus   G. U. S.
* *Mirth's Medley* (pantomime)   .

Harlequin...........Mr. Sully   1st Speaking Witch............
Pantaloon.........Mr. Durang   Mrs. Tompkins
Lover...........Mr. Tompkins   Clown...........Mr. Spinacuta
Dwarf........Master Hutchins   Columbine........Mrs. Spinacuta
2nd Speaking Witch..Mr. Coffie

First appearance of Master Hutchins.

[306]

1796

Oct. 24   Circus   G. U. S.
The Valiant Soldier (pantomime)

Capt. of Banditti..Mr. Spinacuta		Valiant Soldier.......Mr. Sully	
2d Thief............Mr. Coffie		Milkmaid..........Mrs. Durang	
Lucas.............Mr. Durang		Colette.........Mrs. Tompkins	
Clown.........Mr. F. Ricketts			

Oct. 26   Circus   G. U. S.
Harlequin Everywhere (pantomime)

Harlequin...........Mr. Sully		Palliaso........Mr. F. Ricketts	
Lover............Mr. Tompkins		Piero.............Mr. Spinacuta	
Pantaloon..........Mr. Durang		Arsel..........Mrs. Tompkins	
Punch..............Mr. Coffie		Columbine........Mrs. Spinacuta	

Oct. 27   Circus   G. U. S.
Harlequin Everywhere

Cast as for Oct. 26.

Oct. 29   Circus   G. U. S.
Don Juan

Don Juan...........Mr. Sully		Scaramouch......Mr. Spinacuta	
Commandant......Mr. Tompkins		1st Fisherwoman....Mrs. Durang	
Lover.............Mr. Durang		2nd Fisherwoman..Miss Robinson	
Fisherman...........Mr. Coffie		Donna Anna.....Mrs. Spinacuta	
Sailor..........Mr. F. Ricketts			

Oct. 31   Circus   G. U. S.
Don Juan

Cast as for Oct. 29.

Nov. 2   Circus   G. U. S.
Don Juan

Cast as for Oct. 29.

Nov. 3   Circus   G. U. S.
The Two Huntsmen (comic ballet)

Gillot..............Mr. Durang		Country Girl.....Mrs. Tompkins	
Colas...............Mr. Sully		Milk Girl........Mrs. Durang	
Lawyer.............Mr. Coffie			

The Valiant Soldier

Cast as for Oct. 24, save that the part of Lucas is omitted, and there is added:

Lord of the Manor..Mr. Tompkins

1796

Nov. 5   Circus   G. U. S.

The Two Huntsmen

Cast as for November 3.

Don Juan

Nov. 7   Circus   G. U. S.

* *The Death of Capt. Cook*—"Grand Serious Pantomime"

Capt. Cook..........Mr. Sully	Perea............	} Mr. Durang
1st Lieutenant......Mr. Ricketts	Priest............	
Midshipman.....Mr. F. Ricketts	Koah.............Mr. Spinacuta	
Tereboa.........Mr. Tompkins	Emai............Mrs. Spinacuta	

Nov. 9   Circus   G. U. S.

The Death of Captain Cook

Cast as for Nov. 7.

Nov. 10   Circus   G. U. S.

The Death of Captain Cook

Cast as for Nov. 7.

Nov. 12   Circus   G. U. S.

The Death of Captain Cook

Cast as for Nov. 7.

Nov. 14   Circus   G. U. S.

The Death of Captain Cook

Cast as for Nov. 7.

Nov. 16   Circus   G. U. S.

The Wapping Landlady, or Poor Jack

Poor Jack.........Mr. Durang	Mrs. Casey......Mr. Tompkins
Ned Halyard........Mr. Sully	Orange Girl......Mrs. Durang
Boatswain...........Mr. Coffie	

Don Juan

Cast as for Oct. 29, 1796.

Nov. 19   Circus   Aurora, Nov. 19

* *The Milliners*

Abbot.............Mr. Durang	Valet..........Mr. F. Ricketts
Officer..............Mr. Sully	Tiffany.............Mr. Coffie
Countryman......Mr. Tompkins	Miss Sarsnet......Mrs. Tompkins
Wigmaker........Mr. Spinacuta	Miss Pink........Miss Robinson
Dancing Master.....Mr. Durang	Fille de Chambre...Mrs. Durang
Singing Master.....Mr. Franklin	

1796

Nov. 23   Circus   G. U. S.
               The Two Philosophers
               The Death of Captain Cook

Nov. 24   Circus   Aurora
                Miss in Her Teens

Capt. Flash..........Mr. Sully   Capt. Loveit......Mr. Tompkins
Puff..............Mr. Durang   Fribble..........Mr. Chambers
Jasper..............Mr. Jones   Tag.............Mrs. Durang
  ("first appearance on the stage")   Miss Biddy.......Mrs. Chambers

First appearance of Mrs. Chambers and Mr. Jones.

Nov. 26   Circus   G. U. S.
                Miss in Her Teens

               Cast as for Nov. 24.

Nov. 28   Circus   G. U. S.
        Poor Jack (The Wapping Landlady)
                  Don Juan

Don Juan........Mr. Chambers   1st Fisherwoman..Mrs. Chambers

Nov. 30   Circus   Aurora
                Miss in Her Teens

               Cast as for Nov. 24.

Dec. 3   Circus   G. U. S.
                The Bird Catcher
 * *Oscar and Malvina, or The Hall of Fingal* (from Ossian)—Byrne

For the remainder of the season, the days of performance were to be Tuesday, Thursday, and Saturday. This was on the supposition that the New Theatre (Chesnut Street) would be open on Monday, Wednesday, and Friday.

NEW THEATRE

Dec. 5   *Romeo and Juliet*   G. U. S.

Romeo...........Mr. Moreton   Friar John........Mr. Warrell
Paris.........Mr. Warrell, Jr.   Balthazar.........Mr. Mitchell
Montague..........Mr. Morris   Apothecary.........Mr. Francis
Capulet.....M. L'Estrange (from Peter.............Mr. Blissett
    the Theatre, Covent-Garden) Page...........Master Warrell
Mercutio.........Mr. Wignell   Juliet....Mrs. Merry (being her
Benvolio.............Mr. Fox   first appearance in America)
Tybalt.........Mr. Darley, Jr.   Lady Capulet......Mrs. Harvey

1796

Dec. 5 (cont.)

Friar Laurence......Mr. Warren   Nurse.........Mrs. L'Estrange
    (from the Theatre, York)

(In the vocal parts....Mrs. Gillingham, and Miss L'Estrange are
                mentioned.)

The Waterman

Bundle.............Mr. Warren   Mrs. Bundle.....Mrs. Oldmixon
Tug...............Mr. Darley   Wilhelmina........Mrs. Warrell
Robin.............Mr. Francis

First appearance of Mrs. Merry, Mr., Mrs., and Miss L'Estrange, Mrs.
Gillingham, Mr. Fox, and Mr. Warren.

First night at the New Theatre (Chesnut Street) of the season from December 5, 1796, to July 14, 1797 (with an intermission from May 6 to July 5).

PANTHEON

Dec. 7   Circus   Aurora
        The Hall of Fingal, or Oscar and Malvina

NEW THEATRE

Dec. 7   Inkle and Yarico   G. U. S.

Inkle.............Mr. Moreton   3d Planter.........Mr. Warrell
Sir Christopher Curry..........   Walter.........Master Warrell
                Mr. Warren   Mate..............Mr. Darley
Medium...........Mr. Francis   Yarico...........Mrs. Warrell
Compley.......Mr. Darley, Jr.   Narcissa.........Mrs. Mechtler
Trudge............Mr. Wignell   (first appearance on this stage)
1st Planter.......Mr. Mitchell   Wowski.........Mrs. Oldmixon
2d Planter.........Mr. Blissett   Patty.............Mrs. Harvey

Dermot and Kathleen (pantomimic ballet dance)—Byrn[e]

Patrick.........Mr. Warrell, Jr.   Dermot......Mr. Byrn [e] (first
Darby.............Mr. Blissett   appearance in America)
Father Luke........Mr. Doctor   Kathleen....Mrs. Byrn [e] (first
Mother Kathleen.....Mr. Francis   appearance in America)
Norah.........Miss Milbourne

The Village Lawyer

Scout.............Mr. Harwood   Sheep-Face..........Mr. Blissett
Snarl.............Mr. Francis   Kate..............Mrs. Doctor
Charles.........Mr. Darley, Jr.   Mrs. Scout......Mrs. L'Estrange
Justice Mittimus....Mr. Warrell

First appearance of Mr. and Mrs. Byrne and Mrs. Mechtler.

1796

PANTHEON

Dec. 8   Circus   Aurora
The Ghost

Clinch	Mr. Chambers	Roger	Mr. Sully
Capt. Constant	Mr. Jones	Belinda	Miss Robinson
Sir Jeffery Constant	Mr. Durang	Dolly	Mrs. Chambers
Trusty	Mr. Coffie		

NEW THEATRE

Dec. 9   *Macbeth*   G. U. S.

Macbeth	Mr. Cooper	Siward	Mr. Morris
(from Covent-Garden—first appearance here)		Seyton	Mr. Darley, Jr.
		Doctor	Mr. Warrell
Duncan	Mr. L'Estrange	Messenger	Mr. Mitchell
Malcolm	Mr. Fox	Lady Macbeth	Mrs. Morris
Donalbaine	Master Warrell	Gentlewoman	Miss Oldfield
Macduff	Mr. Moreton	Hecate	Mr. Darley
Banquo	Mr. Warren	1st Witch	Mr. Wignell
Lenox	Mr. Warrell, Jr.	2nd Witch	Mr. Francis
		3rd Witch	Mr. Harwood

The Prize

Dr. Lenitive	Mr. Harwood	Boy	Master Warrell
Heartwell	Mr. Fox	Juba	Miss Milbourne
Caddy	Mr. Warrell	Mrs. Caddy	Mrs. L'Estrange
Label	Mr. Francis	Caroline	Mrs. Oldmixon

First appearance of Mr. Cooper.

PANTHEON

Dec. 10   Circus   Aurora
Oscar and Malvina

NEW THEATRE

Dec. 12   *The Fair Penitent*   G. U. S.

Sciolto	Mr. Warren	Rossano	Mr. Darley, Jr.
Altamount	Mr. Fox	Calista	Mrs. Merry
Horatio	Mr. Cooper	Lavinia	Mrs. Francis
Lothario	Mr. Moreton	Lucilla	Mrs. Hervey

1796

Dec. 12 (cont.) *Who's the Dupe?*

Doiley.............Mr. Morris
Sandford..........Mr. Wignell
Granger...........Mr. Moreton
Gradus...........Mr. Harwood

Servant.........Master Warrell
Miss Doiley........Mrs. Francis
Charlotte.........Mrs. Hervey

Dec. 13   Circus   G. U. S., Dec. 12
The Wapping Landlady
Harlequin Everywhere

NEW THEATRE

Dec. 14   *Henry IV, Part I*   G. U. S.

King Henry......Mr. L'Estrange
Prince of Wales....Mr. Moreton
Prince John of Lancaster........
            Master Warrell
Worcester............Mr. Fox
Northumberland......Mr. Darley
Hotspur...........Mr. Cooper
Douglas........Mr. Darley, Jr.
Sir Richard Vernon............
            Mr. Warrell, Jr.
Westmoreland......Mr. Warrell

Sir Walter Blunt....Mr. Wignell
Falstaff............Mr. Warren
Poins.............Mr. Harwood
Peto..............Mr. Mitchell
Bardolph..........Mr. Morgan
Francis............Mr. Blissett
Carriers......Mr. Morris & Mr.
            Francis
Lady Percy.........Mrs. Morris
Hostess Quickly..Mrs. L'Estrange

The Widow's Vow

Don Antonio........Mr. Morris
Marquis..............Mr. Fox
Carlos...........Mr. Darley, Jr.
Servant..........Master Warrell
Jerome...........Mr. Harwood

Countess..........Mrs. Morris
Donna Isabella......Mrs. Hervey
Inis..............Miss Oldfield
Ursula.............Mrs. Doctor
Flora.............Mrs. Francis

PANTHEON

Dec. 15   Circus   G. U. S., Dec. 14
The Ghost
The Death of Captain Cook

NEW THEATRE

Dec. 16   *The Child of Nature*   G. U. S.

Marquis of Almanza............
            Mr. Wignell
Count Valantia.....Mr. Moreton
Duke Marcia.......Mr. Warren
Seville............Mr. Warrell

Grenada........Mr. Warrell, Jr.
1st Peasant.........Mr. Cooper
2nd Peasant........Mr. Mitchell
Marchioness Merida..Mrs. Morris
Amanthis..........Mrs. Merry

[312]

1796

Dec. 16 (cont.) *Dermot and Kathleen*

Patrick	Mr. Warrell, Jr.	Norah	Miss Milbourne
Darby	Mr. Blissett	Dermot	Mr. Byrne
Father Luke	Mr. Doctor	Kathleen	Mrs. Byrne
Mother Kathleen	Mr. Francis		

Animal Magnetism

Marquis de Lancy	Mr. Moreton	François	Mr. Warrell, Jr.
La Fleur	Mr. Harwood	Jeffery	Mr. Blissett
Doctor	Mr. Francis	Constance	Mrs. Harvey
Picard	Mr. M'Donald	Lisette	Mrs. Francis

Mr. M'Donald had played in Rickett's Pantheon the season before.

Dec. 17   G. U. S.

The managers announced the engagement of a French Company of Comedians, making their first appearance.

* *Le Tableaux Parlant* (French Comic Opera)

Cassander	M. St. Mare	Isabella	Mlle. Tesseire
Leandre	M. Viellard	Colombine	Mlle. Sophie
Pierrot	M. Bouchoni		

Next Door Neighbours

Sir George Splendorville	Mr. Moreton	Bluntly	Mr. Harwood
Manly	Mr. Warrell	Shopman	Mr. Morgan
Blackman	Mr. Francis	Lady Caroline Seymour	Mrs. Francis
Lucre	Mr. Blissett	Lady Squander	Mrs. Mechtler
Lord Hazard	Mr. Darley, Jr.	Evans	Mrs. Doctor
Wilford	Mr. Warren	Eleanor	Miss L'Estrange
Henry	Mr. Fox		

Lex Deux Chasseurs et la Laitiere ("French Comic Opera")

Guillot	M. Viellard	Pierette	Mlle. Tesseire
Colas	M. St. Mare		

First appearance of all the members of the French Company.

PANTHEON

Dec. 17   Circus   G. U. S.
                 The Purse

Will Steady	Mr. Chambers	Edmond	Mr. Tompkins
Page	Miss Sully	1st Servant	Mr. Coffie

1796

Dec. 17 (cont.)

Bason	Mr. Durang	2nd Servant	Mr. F. Ricketts
Theodore	Mr. Jones	Sally	Mrs. Chambers

First mention of Miss Sully.

Both the New Theatre and the Pantheon were open this Saturday Night—December 17. On Monday (December 19, *G. U. S.*) Mr. Ricketts announced that as the New Theatre chose to compete with him on Saturday night he would change his nights to Monday, Wednesday, Friday (the Theatre nights), and Saturday. The New Theatre was open on Saturday nights and the theatres competed till January 11, 1797, after which the Pantheon returned to Tuesday, Thursday, and Saturday nights, and the New Theatre to Monday, Wednesday, and Friday.

NEW THEATRE

Dec. 19   *Hamlet*   G. U. S.

(As Mr. Moreton was ill, Mr. Cooper took Hamlet)

Hamlet	Mr. Cooper	Bernardo	Mr. Warrell
King	Mr. Warren	Ostric	Mr. Francis
Ghost	Mr. L'Estrange	Lucianus	Mr. Blissett
Horatio	Mr. Wignell	Grave Diggers	Mr. Harwood
Polonius	Mr. Morris		and Mr. Blissett
Rosencrans	Mr. Warrell, Jr.	Queen	Mrs. L'Estrange
Guildenstern	Mr. Mitchell	Ophelia	Mrs. Oldmixon
Francisco	Mr. Darley, Jr.	Player Queen	Mrs. Harvey
Marcellus	Mr. Fox		

The Purse

Bason	Mr. Warrell	Will Steady	Mr. Harwood
Theodore	Mr. Fox	Page	Miss L'Estrange
Edmond	Mr. Darley, Jr.	Sally	Mrs. Oldmixon

PANTHEON

Dec. 21   Circus   G. U. S.

The Lying Valet

Sharp	Mr. Chambers	Melissa	Miss Robinson
Gayless	Mr. Jones	Mrs. Gadabout	Mrs. Durang
Justice Guttle	Mr. Durang	Mrs. Trippet	Mrs. Tompkins
Beau Trippet	Mr. Tompkins	Kitty Pry	Mrs. Chambers
Dick	Mr. Sully		

* *The Dwarf* (Comic Dance)

[314]

1796

NEW THEATRE

Dec. 21   *The Road to Ruin*   G. U. S.

Dornton............Mr. Warren	Sheriff's Officer......Mr. Warrell
Harry Dornton.......Mr. Cooper	Jacob..............Mr. Blissett
Sulky...........Mr. L'Estrange	Marker.........Mr. Warrell, Jr.
Silky..............Mr. Francis	Postillion........Master Warrell
Goldfinch.........Mr. Harwood	Mrs. Warren.....Mrs. Oldmixon
Milford...............Mr. Fox	Sophia..............Mrs. Merry
Smith..........Mr. Darley, Jr.	Jenny.............Mrs. Francis
Tradesmen.....Messrs. Mitchell, Morgan, etc.	Mrs. Ledger.......Mrs. Doctor

The Irishman in London

Capt. Seymour.........Mr. Fox	Cymon.............Mr. Blissett
Frost..............Mr. Francis	Louisa.............Mrs. Hervey
Callooney........Mr. Darley, Jr.	Caroline........Miss L'Estrange
Murtoch Delaney....Mr. Warren	Cubba.............Mrs. Francis
Edward..........Mr. Harwood	

PANTHEON

Dec. 23   "Benefit of the Sufferers by the Fire at Savannah"   Aurora

Circus
The Lying Valet
Harlequin Statue

NEW THEATRE

Dec. 23   *The Orphan*   G. U. S.

Acasto.............Mr. Warren	Cordelio........Miss L'Estrange
Castalio..........Mr. Moreton	Chaplain.........Mr. L'Estrange
Polydore..........Mr. Wignell	Monimia..........Mrs. Merry
Chamont...........Mr. Cooper	Serina............Mrs. Francis
Ernesto..........Mr. Warrell	Florella...........Mrs. Hervey
Paulino........Mr. Warrell, Jr.	

The Mayor of Garratt

Sir Jacob Jollup......Mr. Francis	Bruin..............Mr. Warrell
Major Sturgeon....Mr. Warren	Roger.............Mr. Blissett
Jerry Sneak.......Mr. Harwood	Mrs. Sneak........Mrs. Francis
Crispin Heeltap...Mr. Darley, Jr.	Mrs. Bruin......Mrs. Mechtler

PANTHEON

Dec. 24   Circus   G. U. S.
New Hay at the Old Market—Colman, Jr.

[315]

1796

NEW THEATRE

Dec. 24   *She Stoops to Conquer*   G. U. S.

Sir Chas. Marlow....Mr. Warrell	Landlord...........Mr. Darley
Young Marlow.....Mr. Moreton	Jeremy............Mr. Blissett
Hardcastle.........Mr. Morris	Mrs. Hardcastle..Mrs. L'Estrange
Hastings.............Mr. Fox	Miss Hardcastle.....Mrs. Morris
Tony Lumpkin......Mr. Wignell	Miss Neville........Mrs. Francis
Diggory...........Mr. Francis	Maid............Mrs. Mechtler

(French Company—second appearance)

* Les Souliers Mordores

Le Baron de Piecourt. M. Bouchoni	Hans.............M. Poignand
Sock..............M. Viellard	Le Brigadier.......M. Lavancey
Michel............M. St. Mare	Odile...........Mlle. Tesseire

First appearance of M. Lavancey and M. Poignand.

Dec. 26   *Romeo and Juliet*   G. U. S.

Cast as for December 5.

Dermot and Kathleen

Cast as for December 16.

PANTHEON

Circus
New Hay at the Old Market

Doggerwood......Mr. Chambers	Carpenter............Mr. Sully
Fustian............Mr. Durang	Mrs. Biezom.......Mrs. Durang
Manager's Servant..Mr. Tompkins	Molly Biezom.....Mrs. Chambers
Prompter...........Mr. Jones	

Harlequin in Philadelphia
The Valiant Soldier (the *Aurora* announced)

NEW THEATRE

Dec. 27   *George Barnwell*   G. U. S.

Thorowgood........Mr. Warren	Gaoler............Mr. Morgan
Uncle..........Mr. L'Estrange	Maria.........Miss L'Estrange
George Barnwell....Mr. Moreton	Millwood.........Mrs. Francis
Trueman.............Mr. Fox	Lucy.............Mrs. Harvey
Blunt.............Mr. Francis	

1796

Dec. 27 (cont.) *Harlequin's Invasion*

Harlequin...........Mr. Francis	Justice.............Mr. Warrell
Mercury.........Mr. Darley, Jr.	Crier...........Master Warrell
Forge.............Mr. Moreton	Padlock.........Mr. Warrell, Jr.
Bounce.............Mr. Warren	Dolly Snip.........Mrs. Francis
Frontier...........Mr. Blissett	Mrs. Snip.........Mrs. Doctor
Bog..............Mr. Morgan	Sukey Chitterlin.....Mrs. Harvey
Simon............Mr. Wignell	Old Woman.........Mr. Darley
Snip.............Mr. Harwood	Tragic Muse.......Miss Oldfield
Abraham........Mr. Warrell, Jr.	Comic Muse......Miss Milbourne

Dec. 28   Benefit of the Savannah Sufferers   G. U. S.

The Child of Nature

Cast as for Dec. 16.

The Agreeable Surprize

Sir Felix Friendly....Mr. Warren	Cudden.............Mr. Blissett
Compton...........Mr. Darley	Lingo............Mr. Moreton
Eugene........Mr. Darley, Jr.	Laura..........Mrs. Oldmixon
Chicane...........Mr. Warrell	Mrs. Cheshire....Mrs. L'Estrange
John..........Mr. Warrell, Jr.	Cowslip..........Mrs. Warrell
Thomas..........Mr. Mitchell	Fringe............Mrs. Harvey
Farmer Stump.......Mr. Morgan	

PANTHEON

Dec. 30   Circus   Aurora

Oscar and Malvina

NEW THEATRE

Dec. 30   *The Wheel of Fortune*   Aurora

Sir David Daw.......Mr. Francis	Jenkins.........Mr. Darley, Jr.
Tempest..........Mr. Harwood	James..........Mr. Warrell, Jr.
Penruddock.........Mr. Cooper	Richard...........Mr. Morgan
Woodville.........Mr. Warren	Harry..........Mr. M'Donald
Sydenham.........Mr. Wignell	Thomas........Master Warrell
Henry Woodville....Mr. Moreton	Mrs. Woodville......Mrs. Morris
Weazle.............Mr. Blissett	Emily Tempest.......Mrs. Merry
Woodville's servant..Mr. Mitchell	Dame Dunckley......Mrs. Doctor
Officer............Mr. Warrell	Maid..........Miss Milbourne

* La Melomanie (French Co.)

Geronte.............M. Viellard	Chrisante..........M. Poignand
St. Real............M. Lavency	Elsie............Mlle. Tesseire
Crispin............M. St. Mare	Lisette............Mlle. Sophie

[317]

1797

Jan. 2 *Richard III* Aurora

Henry VI.........Mr. Warren	Tressel...............Mr. Fox
Prince Edward...Miss L'Estrange	Earl of Oxford......Mr. Blissett
Duke of York..Master L'Estrange	Lieut. of Tower..Mr. Warrell, Jr.
Duke of Gloster......Mr. Cooper	Lord Stanley.....Mr. L'Estrange
Duke of Buckingham.Mr. Wignell	Lord Mayor........Mr. Warrell
Earl of Richmond...Mr. Moreton	Tyrrel............Mr. Morgan
Duke of Norfolk.....Mr. Francis	Queen Elizabeth.....Mrs. Morris
Ratcliffe...........Mr. Morris	Lady Ann.........Mrs. Francis
Catesby.........Mr. Darley, Jr.	Duchess of York..Mrs. L'Estrange

* The New Year's Gift
(or Highland Frolicks) (Pantomime Ballet)—Byrne

Sandy..............Mr. Byrne	Mother Gibby.......Mr. Francis
Jamie.........Mr. Warrell, Jr.	Peggie..........Miss Milbourne
Young Pedler......Master Bates	Annie..............Mrs. Byrne
Father Gibby.......Mr. Blissett	

Animal Magnetism

Cast as for December 16, 1796.

First appearance of Master L'Estrange.

PANTHEON

Jan. 2 Circus Aurora
The Death of Captain Cook

Jan. 3 Circus Aurora
* The Ruins of Troy, or The World Turn'd Upside Down
The Death of Captain Cook

NEW THEATRE

Jan. 4 *The Wheel of Fortune* Aurora

Cast as for December 30, 1796.

* Lock and Key—Hoare

Brummagem........Mr. Francis	Florella..........Mrs. Warrell
Cheerly.........Mr. Darley, Jr.	Fanny..........Mrs. Oldmixon
Capt. Vain............Mr. Fox	Selina............Mrs. Harvey
Ralph...........Mr. Harwood	Dolly..........Miss Milbourne

PANTHEON

Jan. 5 Circus Aurora
Poor Jack (The Wapping Landlady)

1797

Jan. 5 (cont.)   * *The Siege of Troy*
                        * *Harlequin's Medley*

NEW THEATRE

Jan. 6   *The Fair Penitent*   Aurora

Cast as for Dec. 12, 1796.

Lock and Key

Cast as for January 4.

Jan. 7   *The Rage*   G. U. S.

Gingham...........Mr. Wignell	Richard.............Mr. Blissett
Darnley...........Mr. Moreton	Thomas............Mr. Morgan
Sir George Gauntlet.....Mr. Fox	William........Mr. Warrell, Jr.
Savage...........Mr. Harwood	Groom.........Master Warrell
Sir Paul Perpetual....Mr. Warren	Lady Sarah Savage. Mrs. Oldmixon
Flush..............Mr. Francis	Clara Sedley.....Miss L'Estrange
Ready.............Mr. Warrell	Mrs. Darnley.......Mrs. Morris
Waiter..........Mr. Darley, Jr.	

* *Blaize et Babet* (French Co.—comic opera)

Le Seigneur.........M. Viellard	Delome............M. Poignand
Blaize.............M. St. Mare	Louiz.............M. Lavency
Mathusin........."un Amateur"	Babet...........Mlle. Tesseire
Jacquiere......M. Bouchony [sic]	Alie..............Mlle. Sophie

PANTHEON

Jan. 7   Circus   Aurora
           The Siege of Troy

Jan. 9   Circus   Aurora
           The Siege of Troy
* *Harlequin's Rambles, or The Absurdities of Mankind* (pantomime)

NEW THEATRE

Jan. 9   *The Child of Nature*   G. U. S.

Cast as for December 16, 1796, except:

Marchioness Merida..Mrs. Merry   Amanthis..........Mrs. Morris

Lock and Key

Cast as for January 4.

[319]

1797

PANTHEON

Jan. 11   Circus   Aurora
Harlequin's Rambles

NEW THEATRE

Jan. 11   *The Wonder*   G. U. S.

Don Lopez	Mr. Warrell	Alguazil	Mr. Warrell, Jr.
Don Felix	Mr. Moreton	Vasquez	Master Warrell
Frederick	Mr. Fox	Soldier	Mr. Darley, Jr.
Don Pedro	Mr. Francis	Donna Violante	Mrs. Merry
Col. Briton	Mr. Warren	Donna Isabella	Mrs. Warrell
Gibby	Mr. Blissett	Flora	Mrs. Francis
Lissardo	Mr. Harwood	Inis	Mrs. Harvey

The Mogul Tale

Great Mogul	Mr. Moreton	Johnny Atkins	Mr. Bates
Dr. Pedant	Mr. Francis	("first appearance this season")	
Omar	Mr. Fox	Zaphira	Miss Oldfield
Selim	Mr. Warrell	Irene	Mrs. Harvey
1st Guard	Mr. Darley, Jr.	Sheba	Miss Milbourne
2nd Guard	Mr. J. Warrell	Fanny Atkins	Mrs. Francis

This was the last night of competition between the Pantheon and the New Theatre. See Dec. 17.

PANTHEON

Jan. 12   Benefit of Francis Ricketts   Aurora

Circus
Oscar and Malvina

NEW THEATRE

Jan. 13   *The School for Scandal*   G. U. S.

Sir Peter Teazle	Mr. Bates	Rowley	Mr. Warrell
Sir Oliver Surface	Mr. Morris	Moses	Mr. Francis
Joseph Surface	Mr. Wignell	Snake	Mr. Darley, Jr.
Charles Surface	Mr. Moreton	Trip	Mr. Warrell, Jr.
Sir Benjamin Backbite	Mr. Fox	Lady Teazle	Mrs. Morris
Crabtree	Mr. Harwood	Lady Sneerwell	Mrs. Harvey
Careless	Mr. Blissett	Mrs. Candour	Mrs. Oldmixon
Sir Harry	Mr. Darley	Maria	Mrs. Francis

1797

Jan. 13 (cont.)   *Peeping Tom of Coventry*

Peeping Tom..........Mr. Bates
Mayor of Coventry...Mr. Warren
Harold..........Mr. Darley, Jr.
Crazy..............Mr. Francis
Earl of Mercia..........Mr. Fox

Count Lewis......Mr. J. Warrell
Maud..........Mrs. Oldmixon
Emma............Mrs. Warrell
Lady Godiva.......Miss Oldfield
Mayoress........Mrs. L'Estrange

PANTHEON

Jan. 14   Circus   Aurora
The Magic Feast (comic pantomime)

NEW THEATRE

Jan. 16   The French Company's Night   G. U. S.

La Melomanie

Cast as for Dec. 30, 1796, except:

Geronte..............M. Fieron
Chrisante..........M. Viellard

The Married Man

Lord Lovemore.....Mr. Moreton
Sir John Classick....Mr. Wignell
Classick..........Mr. Warren
Tradewell Classick.....Mr. Bates
Dorimont.............Mr. Fox

William........Mr. Warrell, Jr.
Lady Classick....Miss L'Estrange
Emily.............Mrs. Francis
Lucy.............Mrs. Harvey

* Deux Petits Savoyards

Le Seigneur.........M. St. Mare
Clermont.........M. Poignand
Le Vailly..........M. Viellard

Jaque..............M. Lavancey
Michell.........Mlle. Tesseire
Joset..............Mlle. Sophie

First advertised for January 14.

First appearance of M. Fieran.

Jan. 18   *Every One Has His Fault*   G. U. S.

Lord Norland.......Mr. Warren
Sir Robert Ramble...Mr. Wignell
Solus..............Mr. Morris
Harmony............Mr. Bates
Capt. Irwin.........Mr. Cooper
Placid.............Mr. Moreton
Hammond......Mr. Warrell, Jr.

Porter............Mr. Warrell
Edward........Miss L'Estrange
Lady Eleanor Irwin...Mrs. Merry
Mrs. Placid......Mrs. Oldmixon
Miss Spinster....Mrs. L'Estrange
Miss Wooburn......Mrs. Morris

1797

Jan. 18 (cont.)   *Lock and Key*

Cast as for Jan. 4, 1797.

PANTHEON

Jan. 19   Circus   Aurora
                              Oscar and Malvina

NEW THEATRE

Jan. 20   *The Mountaineers*   G. U. S.

Octavian..........Mr. Moreton	Ganem.........Mr. Warrell, Jr.
Virolet................Mr. Fox	Pacha..........Mr. Darley, Jr.
Kilmallock..........Mr. Warren	Sadi..............Mr. Harwood
Rogue.............Mr. Wignell	Moors.........Mr. Mitchell, etc.
Lope Tocho........Mr. Francis	Zorayda...........Mrs. Warrell
Perequillo.......Master Warrell	Floranthe.........Mrs. Francis
Bulcazin Muley.....Mr. Cooper	Agnes..........Mrs. Oldmixon

Seeing is Believing

Sir Credule.........Mr. Francis	Porter...........Mr. Darley, Jr.
Capt. Nightshade.....Mr. Francis	Miss Di............Mrs. Harvey
Sceptic.............Mr. Warren	Kitty..............Mrs. Francis
Simon...........Mr. Harwood	

Jan. 21   *Venice Preserved*   G. U. S.

Duke of Venice....Mr. Warrell	Spinosa..........Mr. Darley, Jr.
Priuli..............Mr. Warren	Elliott...........Mr. M'Donald
Bedamar...............Mr. Fox	Theodore...........Mr. Blissett
Pierre.............Mr. Cooper	Officer.........Mr. Warrell, Jr.
Jaffier............Mr. Moreton	Belvidera..........Mrs. Merry
Rennault........Mr. L'Estrange	

Le Tableau Parlant

Cassandre...........M. Viellard	Isabelle............Mlle. Sophie
Leandre.............M. Glaize	Colombine.........Mlle. Tesseire
Pierot.............M. St. Mare	

First appearance of M. Glaize (or Gleise).

PANTHEON

Jan. 21   Circus   Aurora
                        The Death of Captain Cook

[322]

1797

NEW THEATRE

Jan. 23

The Aurora announced

The Road to Ruin
The Flitch of Bacon

"In which Mr. PRIGMORE will make his first appearance at this Theatre."
—But the *G. U. S.,* January 23, said "The entertainments of the New Theatre postponed till Monday the 30th Inst. on account of the preparations . . . for . . . *Columbus.*"

PANTHEON

Jan. 24	Circus	Aurora
	Oscar and Malvina	
Jan. 28	Circus	Aurora
	Catherine and Petruchio	
	* *Harlequin Mariner*	

NEW THEATRE

Jan. 30   * *Columbus*—Morton   Aurora

Columbus	Mr. Cooper	1st Spaniard	Mr. Darley, Jr.
Alonzo	Mr. Moreton	2d Spaniard	Mr. Morgan
Harry Herbert	Mr. Wignell	Orozimbo	Mr. Warren
Dr. Dolores	Mr. Harwood	Solasco	Mr. L'Estrange
Briton	Mr. Francis	Catalpe	Mr. Warrell
Roldan	Mr. Fox	Cuto	Mr. Warrell, Jr.
Valverdo	Mr. Darley	Cora	Mrs. Merry
Moscoso	Mr. Blissett	Nelti	Mrs. Francis
Captain	Mr. Macdonald		

[Scene painter—J. Richards, Esq., R.A., principal Scene Painter to the Covent Garden Theatre. Machinist—Mr. Lenthall. Dresses by Mr. Gibbons.]

The Purse

Cast as for Dec. 19, 1796, except:

Baron............Mr. Warren

PANTHEON

Jan. 31   Benefit of Mr. and Mrs. Tompkins   G. U. S.

Don Juan
Robinson Crusoe

[323]

1797

NEW THEATRE

Feb. 1   *Columbus*   G. U. S.
The Flitch of Bacon

Wilson...........Mr. Darley	Major Benbow........Mr. Bates
Greville.......Mr. Darley, Jr.	Kilderkin..........Mr. Morgan
Tipple...........Mr. Prigmore	Putty............Mr. Mitchell
(first appearance at this Theatre)	Justice Benbow......Mr. Warrell
Ned...........Mr. J. Warrell	Eliza............Mrs. Warrell

Feb. 3   *Venice Preserved*   G. U. S.

Cast as for Jan. 21, except:

Rennault..........Mr. Wignell   Elliott............Mr. Mitchell

* *The Drunken Provençal (or The Sailor's Return)*—Byrne (Ballet Dance)

Ivre...............Mr. Byrne	Moses.............Mr. Blissett
Will..........Mr. Warrell, Jr.	Dicky Gossip...Mr. Mitchell
Vicar..............Sig. Doctor	Susan..........Miss Milbourne

Animal Magnetism

Cast as for Dec. 16, 1796, except:

Marquis De Lancy.......Mr. Fox

PANTHEON

Feb. 4   ("By particular Desire of the Druid's Lodge")   Aurora
Benefit of Mr. Coffie and Miss Robinson

Circus

Poor Jack (The Wapping Landlady)

Poor Jack........Miss Robinson

Robinson Crusoe

NEW THEATRE

Feb. 6   *Columbus*   G. U. S.

Cast as for Jan. 30.

Barnaby Brittle

Barnaby Brittle........Mr. Bates	Jeffery.........Mr. Warrell, Jr.
Clodpole...........Mr. Blissett	Mrs. Brittle........Mrs. Francis
Jeremy............Mr. Francis	Lady Pride.......Mrs. Mechtler
Sir Peter Pride......Mr. Morgan	Damaris..........Mrs. Harvey
Lovemore.............Mr. Fox	

1797

PANTHEON

Feb. 7   Mr. and Mrs. Durang's Night   Aurora

Circus

* *The Independence of America, or*
The ever memorable Fourth of July, 1776.

NEW THEATRE

Feb. 8   *Columbus*   G. U. S.

Cast as for Jan. 30.

Love à la Mode

Sir Calaghan O'Bralaghan....... Mr. Warren	Sir Theodore Goodchild........ Mr. Warrell
Sir Archy Macsarcasm..Mr. Bates	Servant...........Mr. Mitchell
Squire Groom......Mr. Harwood	Charlotte...........Mrs. Hervey
Beau Mordecai.......Mr. Francis	

PANTHEON

Feb. 9   *"Infant Jockies Night"*   Aurora

Circus

* *Harlequin's Revenge*

NEW THEATRE

Feb. 10   *Columbus*   Aurora

Cast as for Jan. 30.

Lock and Key

Cast as for Jan. 4.

PANTHEON

Feb. 11   Benefit of Mr. Franklin, Riding-Master   G. U. S., Feb. 10

Circus

* *The Dutch Wake, or, The Sailor's Return from Algiers.* (Comic Ballet)

NEW THEATRE

Feb. 13   * *The Way to Get Married*—Morton   Aurora

Tangent...........Mr. Moreton	Undertaker......Mr. Macdonald
Toby Alspice.......Mr. Harwood	Jailer.............Mr. Mitchell
Capt. Faulkner.......Mr. Cooper	Solicitor............Mr. Morgan
Caustic.............Mr. Warren	Officer.............Mr. Warrell
Dick Dashall........Mr. Wignell	William.........Mr. Darley, Jr.

[325]

1797

Feb. 13 (cont.)

M'Queery.........Mr. Prigmore
Landlord............Mr. Darley
Shopman........Mr. Warrell, Jr.
Ned...............Mr. Blissett
Postillion........Mr. T. Warrell

Julia Faulkner.......Mrs. Merry
Clementina.........Mrs. Francis
Lady Sorrell.....Mrs. L'Estrange
Fanny..............Mrs. Doctor

The Irishman in London

Cast as for Dec. 21, 1796.

PANTHEON

Feb. 14   Benefit of Mr. and Mrs. Spinacuta   G. U. S.

Circus
** The Dressing Room
or The Intriguing Friseur* (Comic Burletta)

Sir Jeremy.......Mr. Chambers
Puff................Mr. Sully

Lady Jeremy.......Miss Robinson
Betty...........Mrs. Chambers

** The Magic Fight
or The Little Cripple Devil* (pantomime) "Got up by Mr. Spinacuta"

Harlequin.............Mr. Sully
Don Ferdinand......Mr. Durang
Alphonso............Mr. Jones
Pierrot..........Mr. Spinacuta
Donna Elenna.....Mrs. Spinacuta

Little Cripple Devil....Miss Sully
Benevolent Witch......Mr. Coffie
Gunners.....Mr. F. Ricketts, and
                  Mr. Coffie

NEW THEATRE

Feb. 15   *Columbus*   Aurora

Cast as for Jan. 30.

The Ghost

Sir Jeffery Constant..Mr. Warren
Capt. Constant....Mr. Darley, Jr.
Clinch.............Mr. Morris
Trusty.............Mr. Francis

Roger...............Mr. Bates
Belinda............Miss Oldfield
Dorothy...........Mrs. Francis

PANTHEON

Feb. 16   Benefit of Mrs. Chambers and Miss Sully   Aurora

Circus
Neptune and Amphitrite
The Magic Fight

Cast as for Feb. 14.

[326]

1797

NEW THEATRE

Feb. 17   *The Way to Get Married*   G. U. S.

Cast as for Feb. 13.

The Padlock

Don Diego...........Mr. Darley   Mungo...............Mr. Bates
Leander.........Mr. Darley, Jr.   Leonora...........Mrs. Warrell
1st Scholar......Mr. Warrell, Jr.   Ursula...........Mrs. Metchler
2d Scholar........Mr. Mitchell

PANTHEON

Feb. 18   "Last Night at the Pantheon" [see Feb. 23]   Aurora

"Benefit of Mr. Jones—Acting Manager"

Circus
Harlequin's Revenge

NEW THEATRE

Feb. 20   *The Way to Get Married*   G. U. S.

Cast as for February 13.

The Village Lawyer

Cast as for December 7, 1796.

Feb. 23   *Jane Shore*   Aurora

Duke of Gloster......Mr. Warren   Dumont...........Mr. Moreton
Lord Hastings.......Mr. Wignell   Earl of Derby......Mr. Warrell
Catesby........Mr. Warrell, Jr.   Alicia..............Mrs. Merry
Sir Richard......Mr. Darley, Jr.   Jane Shore.........Mrs. Morris
Belmour..............Mr. Fox

The Death of Captain Cook

Principal Characters by Messrs. Byrne, Francis, Warren, Darley, Moreton, Fox, Warrell, and Mrs. Byrne.

("as performed in Covent Garden Theatre, under the direction of Mr. Byrne.")

PANTHEON

Feb. 23   Aurora

"At the request of several Ladies and Gentlemen" at "The New Rotunda at Mr. Rickett's Amphitheatre."

[327]

1797

Feb. 23 (cont.)   Circus
Poor Jack (The Wapping Landlady)
The Death of Captain Cook

"brought out first in America by Mr. Ricketts"—and being played on
February 23 on both sides of Chesnut Street.

This was the last dramatic performance at the Pantheon of the season from
October 10, 1796, to February 23, 1797. (The Pantheon ended its circus
season on February 28.) These new afterpieces were produced: *The Country
Frolic, The Death of Captain Cook, The Death and Renovation of Harlequin, The Distressed Sailor* (probably *The Wapping Landlady, or Poor
Jack*), *The Dressing Room, The Dutch Wake, Harlequin Mariner, Harlequin's Rambles, Harlequin's Revenge, The Independence of America, The
Magic Feast, The Magic Fight, The Milliners, Mirth's Medley, New Hay
at the Old Market, Oscar and Malvina (or the Hall of Fingal), Poor Jack*
(but this is probably *The Wapping Landlady*), *The Ruin of Troy, The Two
Huntsmen,* and *The Valiant Soldier.* Reappearing afterpieces: *The Bird
Catcher, Catherine and Petruchio, Don Juan, The Ghost, Harlequin Everywhere, Harlequin in Philadelphia, The Lying Valet, Miss in Her Teens,
Neptune and Amphitrite, The Purse, Robinson Crusoe The Two Philosophers,* and *Vulcan's Gift.*

New performers: Mrs. Chambers, Mr. Coffie, Master Hutchins, Mr. Jones,
Miss Robinson, Miss Spinacuta, Miss Sully, and Mr. and Mrs. Tompkins,
Reappearing performers: Mr. Chambers, Mr. and Mrs. Durang, Mr. F.
Ricketts, Mr. J. B. Ricketts, Mr. and Mrs. Spinacuta, and Mr. Sully.

NEW THEATRE

Feb. 24   *Every One Has His Fault*   G. U. S.
Cast as for Jan. 18, except:

Mrs. Placid.........Mrs. Francis
The Death of Captain Cook
Cast as for Feb. 23.

Feb. 25   *The Wheel of Fortune*   G. U. S.
Cast as for Dec. 30, 1796, except:

Tempest.............Mr. Bates   Weazle..........Mr. Harwood
The Death of Captain Cook
Cast as for Feb. 23.

Feb. 27   *The Way to Get Married*   G. U. S.
Cast as for Feb. 13.

[328]

1797

Feb. 27 (cont.)   *Dermot and Kathleen*
                          Animal Magnetism

March 1   *Henry IV*   G. U. S.
                  Cast as for Dec. 4, 1796, except:
                  Sir Walter Blunt...Mr. Prigmore
                      The Death of Captain Cook
                      Cast as for Feb. 23.

March 3   *The Grecian Daughter*   G. U. S.

Dionysius...........Mr. Cooper   Greek Herald.....Mr. Darley, Jr.
Philotas...........Mr. Moreton   Greek Soldier...........Mr. Fox
Melanthon........Mr. Warren   Perdiccas.......Mr. MacDonald
Phocion...........Mr. Prigmore   Evander..........Mr. Wignell
Arcas..........Mr. Warrell, Jr.   Erixene...........Miss Oldfield
Calippus...........Mr. Warrell   Euphasia...........Mrs. Merry

                        * *The Enchanted Flute*
            ("written in America—never performed")

Codgerly.............Mr. Bates   Jeweller...............Mr. Fox
Raymond..........Mr. Moreton   Tradesmen.....Mr. Mitchell, etc.
Sir Horace Hustle...Mr. Harwood   Harriet Bloomley.Miss L'Estrange
Dr. Endless........Mr. Francis   Dinah..........Mrs. L'Estrange
Giles..............Mr. Blissett   1st Lady...........Mrs. Doctor
Landlord..........Mr. Warrell   2d Lady.........Mrs. Mechtler

March 4   *Next Door Neighbours*   G. U. S.
                     Dermot and Kathleen
                     Peeping Tom of Coventry

March 6   *The Way to Get Married*   G. U. S.
                      Cast as for Feb. 13.
                      The First Floor

March 8   *The Revenge*   G. U. S.

Don Alonzo........Mr. Moreton   Zanga..............Mr. Cooper
Don Carlos............Mr. Fox   Leonora...........Mrs. Francis
Don Alvarez........Mr. Warren   Isabella...........Mrs. Harvey
Don Manuel......Mr. Darley, Jr.

                     The Drunken Provençal
                     The Enchanted Flute
                  Cast as for March 3.

[329]

1797

March 10   *The Merry Wives of Windsor*   Aurora

Falstaff	Mr. Warren	Pistol	Mr. Darley, Jr.
Fenton	Mr. Warrell, Jr.	Nym	Mr. Morgan
Shallow	Mr. L'Estrange	Robin	Master L'Estrange
Slender	Mr. Francis	Simple	Mr. Blissett
Page	Mr. Prigmore	Rugby	Master Warrell
Ford	Mr. Wignell	Mrs. Page	Mrs. Warrell
Sir Hugh Evans	Mr. Bates	Mrs. Ford	Mrs. Morris
Dr. Caius	Mr. Harwood	Ann Page	Miss Oldfield
Host	Mr. Darley	Mrs. Quickly	Mrs. L'Estrange
Bardolph	Mr. Warrell		

The Son-in-Law

Old Cranky	Mr. Prigmore	Orator Mum	Mr. Blissett
Bowkit	Mrs. Francis	Sig. Arionelli	Mr. Darley, Jr.
Bouquet	Mr. Fox	Cecilia	Mrs. Warrell
Vinegar	Mr. Bates	Dolce	Mrs. Doctor
Idle	Mr. Harwood		

March 11   *The Tempest*   Aurora
The Midnight Hour

March 13   *The Mountaineers*   G. U. S.

Cast as for January 20.

The Deaf Lover

March 15   *Venice Preserved*   G. U. S.

Cast as for Feb. 3.

The Drunken Provençal

Cast as for Feb. 3, with addition of

Jenny.............Mrs. Byrne

The Poor Soldier

Capt. Fitzroy	Mr. Darley	Bagatelle	Mr. Fox
Father Luke	Mr. Warren	Boy	Master T. Warrell
Dermot	Mr. Darley, Jr.	Norah	Mrs. Warrell
Patrick	Mr. Prigmore	Kathleen	Mrs. Harvey
Darby	Mr. Blissett		

March 17   *The Way to Get Married*   G. U. S.

Cast as for February 13.

[330]

1797

March 17 (cont.) *La Forêt Noire*

Geronte............Mr. Francis	Martin............Miss Oldfield
Lancedan.......Mr. Warrell, Jr.	Le Terreur...........Mr. Byrne
Prince.............M. St. Mare	Sans Quartier....Mr. Darley, Jr.
Adolph.........Master Warrell	Le Fourbe...........Mr. Blissett
Fronte.............Mr. Warrell	Cartouche..........Sig. Doctor
Pasquin............Mr. Mitchell	Mandrain.........M. Lavancey
Lucille.............Mrs. Byrne	Briseur.........Mr. Macdonald

March 20   **The Abbey of St. Augustine*—Merry   G. U. S.

Principal Characters by:

Mr. Moreton	Mr. Darley, Jr.
Mr. Cooper	Miss L'Estrange
Mr. L'Estrange	Mrs. Merry
Mr. Warren	(see March 22 for a cast)

High Life Below Stairs

Lovell.............Mr. Wignell	Robert.............Mr. Blissett
Freeman..........Mr. Warren	Tom............Mr. Darley, Jr.
Sir Harry..........Mr. Francis	Kitty.............Mrs. Morris
Lord Duke........Mr. Harwood	Lady Bab.........Mrs. Harvey
Philip............Mr. Prigmore	Lady Charlotte......Mrs. Francis
Coachman.........Mr. Warrell	Cook...........Mr. L'Estrange
Kingston.......Mr. Warrell, Jr.	Chloe..........Miss Milbourne

March 22   *The Abbey of St. Augustine*   G. U. S.

Lorenzo..........Mr. Moreton	Theodore........Mr. Darley, Jr.
Vancenza..........Mr. Cooper	Laura.........Miss L'Estrange
Abbot..........Mr. L'Estrange	Julia...............Mrs. Merry
Albert............Mr. Warren	

La Forêt Noire

March 24   *Columbus*   G. U. S.
          The Midnight Hour

March 25   *The Abbey of St. Augustine*   G. U. S.
          The Farmer

March 27   *The Merchant of Venice*   G. U. S.

Duke..............Mr. Morris	Tubal..........Mr. Milbourne
Antonio...........Mr. Warren	Launcelot.............Mr. Bates
Bassanio..........Mr. Moreton	Old Gobbo.........Mr. Francis
Gratiano..........Mr. Wignell	Leonardo..........Mr. Blissett
Lorenzo.............Mr. Fox	Balthazar.....Master T. Warrell

[331]

1797

March 27 (cont.)

Solarino	Mr. Warrell, Jr.	Portia	Mrs. Merry
Solanio	Mr. Darley, Jr.	Jessica	Mrs. Warrell
Shylock	Mr. Cooper	Nerissa	Mrs. Francis

Lock and Key

March 29   Mrs. Merry's Night   G. U. S.

* *The Ransomed Slave*—Merry

"Altered by Mr. Merry, from his play of Lorenzo, performed at Covent Garden Theatre."

Don Guzman	Mr. Wignell	Gaspero	Mr. Darley, Jr.
Count Lorenzo	Mr. Moreton	Servant	Mr. Macdonald
Don Fabio	Mr. Warren	Zeraphine	Mrs. Merry
Garcias	Mr. Fox	Zoriana	Mrs. Francis

The Drunken Provençal
The Sultan

Soliman	Mr. Moreton	Elmira	Miss Oldfield
Osmyn	Mr. Harwood	Ismene	Mrs. Warrell

March 31   Mr. Moreton's Night   G. U. S.

Hamlet

Cast as for Dec. 19, 1796, except:

Hamlet	Mr. Moreton	Queen	Mrs. Merry

* *The Doldrum, or 1804*—O'Keeffe

Sir Marmaduke	Mr. Warren	Looby	Mr. Blissett
Septimus	Mr. Harwood	Porter	Mr. Macdonald
Capt. Septimus	Mr. Fox	Drummer Boy	Master L'Estrange
Capt. Slash	Mr. Darley, Jr.	Emmeline	Miss L'Estrange
Flam	Mr. Wignell	Mrs. Auburn	Mrs. Oldmixon
Gyp	Mr. Francis	Maid	Mrs. Doctor

April 3   Mr. Cooper's Night   G. U. S.

Alexander the Great

Alexander	Mr. Moreton	Perdicas	Mr. Blissett
Hephestion	Mr. Warrell, Jr.	Eumenes	Mr. Francis
Lysimachus	Mr. Fox	Soldier	Mr. Mitchell
Cassander	Mr. Wignell	Statira	Mrs. Merry
Polyperchon	Mr. Darley, Jr.	Sysigambis	Mrs. L'Estrange
Philip	Mr. Macdonald	Roxana	Mrs. Morris

1797

April 3 (cont.)

Clytus	Mr. Warren	Parisatis	Mrs. Harvey
Thessalus	Mr. Warrell		

(In Act 2 a real elephant was introduced—there had been one in town all winter.)

The Drunken Provençal

* *The Adopted Child*—Birch

Sir Bertram	Mr. Warren	Boy	Miss L'Estrange
Michael	Mr. Cooper	Flint	Mr. Blissett
Record	Mr. Harwood	Clara	Mrs. Warrell
Spruce	Mr. Fox	Nelly	Mrs. Oldmixon
Le Sage	Mr. Darley	Lucy	Mrs. Harvey

April 5   Mrs. Oldmixon's Night   G. U. S.

Love's Frailties

Sir Gregory Oldwort	Mr. Francis	Lady Louisa Campton	
Charles Seymour	Mr. Fox		Mrs. Francis
Muscadel	Mr. Moreton	Mrs. Wilkins	Mrs. Doctor
Craig Campbell	Mr. Warren	Nannette	Mrs. Oldmixon
James	Mr. Blissett	Julette	Miss Milbourne
Footman	Master T. Warrell	Paulina	Mrs. Merry
Lady Fancourt	Mrs. Morris		

The Adopted Child

Cast as for April 3.

April 10   Mr. Harwood's Night   G. U. S.

* *Werter* [*and Charlotte*]—Reynolds

Albert	Mr. Cooper	Lenthrop	Mr. Warren
Werter	Mr. Moreton	Charlotte	Mrs. Merry

* *Highland Festivity* (pantomimic Ballet)—Byrne

Sandy	Mr. Byrne	Mother Gibby	M. St. Mare
Jamie	Mr. Warrell, Jr.	Poggy	Miss Milbourne
Young Pedlar	Master Bates	Annie	Mrs. Byrne
Father Gibby	Mr. Blissett		

The Little Hunchback

Bassa of Bagdad	Mr. Warren	Crank	Mr. Moreton
Crumpy	Mr. Blissett	Absolom	Mr. Warrell, Jr.
Cross Leg	Mr. Harwood	Dominique	Mr. Mitchell
Zebede	Mr. Francis	Crier	Mr. Warrell
Baboric	Mr. Darley, Jr.	Dora	Miss L'Estrange
Cadi	Mr. Macdonald	Juggy	Mrs. L'Estrange
Dr. Quinvina	Mr. Fox		

[333]

1797

LAILSON'S CIRCUS

April 11   Circus   G. U. S.
"Pantomime on Horseback"—
* *The Death of Bucephalus*

* *Les Quatre Fils Aymond*
(heroic pantomime as in Paris—direction of Mr. Jaymond)

Charlemagne	Mr. Prouble	Clare	Mme. Douvilliers
Roland	Mr. Jaymond	Aymonret	Mlle. Lailson
Renaud	M. Douvilliers	Yonnet	Mlle. Douvilliers
Richard	M. Poignard	Officers of Charlemagne	Messrs.
Alard	Mr. Langley	Vandevelde, Viellard, M'Donald	
Guichard	Mr. Sully		

First night at Lailson's Circus. The season extended to July 27.

First appearance of M., Mme., and Mlle. Douvilliers, Mr. Jaymond, Mlle. Lailson, Mr. Prouble (or Pouble), and Mr. Vandevelde. Mr. M'Donald (unless there were two performers of that name) played on alternate nights at the New Theatre and Lailson's Circus.

April 13   Circus   G. U. S.
Les Quatre Fils Aymond

Cast as for April 11.

April 15   Circus   G. U. S.
Les Quatres Fils Aymond

Cast as for April 11.

NEW THEATRE

April 17   * *The Iron Chest*—Colman, Jr.   G. U. S.

Sir Edward Mortimer	Mr. Cooper	Orson	Mr. Francis
Fitzarding	Mr. Wignell	1st Robber	Mr. Darley
Wilford	Mr. Moreton	2d Robber	Mr. Darley, Jr.
Adam Winterton	Mr. Morris	3d Robber	Mr. Blissett
Rowbold	Mr. Warren	4th Robber	Mr. Warrell
Samson	Mr. Harwood	Helen	Mrs. Merry
Armstrong	Mr. Prigmore	Blanch	Mrs. Francis
Boy	Master Warrell	Barbara	Mrs. Oldmixon
Peter	Mr. M'Donald	Judith	Mrs. Harvey

* *Alonzo and Imogen*—Dibdin

"Grand, Serious Pantomime" from the poetic tale of that name in the novel of *The Monk*.

Alonzo............Mr. Byrne   Priest............Mr. Warrell

1797

April 17 (cont.)

Baron St. Clare......Mr. Francis
Lorenzo.........Mr. Darley, Jr.
Ambrosis........Mr. Warrell, Jr.

Imogen............Mrs. Byrne
Leonora...........Mrs. Harvey

LAILSON'S CIRCUS

April 18   Circus   G. U. S.
(with Miss Vanice, "first female performer in America").
The Four Sons of Aymond

Cast as for April 11

NEW THEATRE

April 19   Mrs. Warrell's Night   G. U. S.

King Lear

Lear..............Mr. Warren
Burgundy......Mr. Warrell, Jr.
Cornwall........Mr. Darley, Jr.
Albany.................Mr. Fox
Gloster..........Mr. L'Estrange
Kent..................Mr. Bates
Edgar.............Mr. Wignell

Edmund...........Mr. Moreton
Gentleman Usher....Mr. Francis
Old Man..........Mr. Warrell
Goneril...........Mrs. Warrell
Regan.............Mrs. Harvey
Arante...........Miss Oldfield
Cordelia...........Mrs. Merry

Tom Thumb the Great

LAILSON'S CIRCUS

April 20   Circus   G. U. S.
* The American Heroine (Historical Pantomime)

Yarico..........Mrs. Douvilliers
English Captain.....Mr. Prouble
Indian Chief......Mr. Jaymond

Inkle............M. Douvilliers
English Officers...Messrs. Viellard
                        and Poignard

NEW THEATRE

April 21   Mr. Bates' Night   G. U. S.

Much Ado About Nothing

Don Pedro........Mr. Warren
Leonato............Mr. Wignell
Don John.............Mr. Fox
Claudio...........Mr. Moreton
Benedict...........Mr. Cooper
Balthazar.......Mr. Darley, Jr.
Antonio........Mr. L'Estrange
Borachio........Mr. Warrell, Jr.
Conrade..........Mr. Mitchell

Dogberry.............Mr. Bates
Verges..............Mr. Blissett
Town Clerk.......Mr. Prigmore
Friar...............Mr. Warrell
1st Watchman.......Mr. Francis
Hero..............Mrs. Francis
Margaret.........Mrs. Harvey
Beatrice...........Mrs. Merry
Ursula..........Mrs. Mechtler

1797

April 21 (cont.) *Gil Blas*

Gil Blas............Mr. Bates
Father.............Mr. Warrell
Gil Perey..........Mr. Blissett
Young Spaniard......Mr. Francis
Captain of Banditti.............
　　　　　　Mr. Moreton
Pompey..........Mr. Mitchell

Domingo...........Mr. Morgan
Post Boy.........Master Warrell
Dorothea..........Mr. Prigmore
Spanish Lady....Miss L'Estrange
Gil Blas' Mother..............
　　　　　　Mrs. L'Estrange

LAILSON'S CIRCUS

April 22　　　　　Circus　　　　　G. U. S.
The Two Philosophers (pantomimic ballet)

NEW THEATRE

April 24　　　　Mr. Francis' Night　　　　G. U. S.

* *Heigh ho! for a Husband!*—Waldron

General Fairlove....Mr. Warren
Justice Racket........Mr. Bates
Squire Edward......Mr. Moreton
Frank............Mr. Harwood
Timothy...........Mr. Francis
Player..............Mr. Fox

William............Mr. Warrell
Charlotte..........Mrs. Merry
Maria..........Mrs. Oldmixon
Mrs. Milclock...Mrs. L'Estrange
Dorothy..........Mrs. Francis
Chambermaid......Mrs. Doctor

* *Harlequin Conqueror* (pantomime)

Harlequin Enchanter..Mr. Francis
Magician..........Mr. Warrell
Old Woman.....Mr. Darley, Jr.
Fernando.......Mr. Warrell, Jr.
Sancho.........Master Warrell

Pantaloon..........M. Lavancey
Clown.............Mr. Blissett
Pero..............Sig. Doctor
Columbine.......Miss Milbourne

April 26　　　　Mr. Darley's Night　　　　G. U. S.

Love in a Village

Sir Wm. Meadows...Mr. Warrell
Young Meadows..Mr. Darley, Jr.
Justice Woodcock.....Mr. Bates
Hawthorn..........Mr. Darley
Eustace..............Mr. Fox
Hodge.............Mr. Francis
Carter...........Mr. Mitchell

Footman.......Mr. Warrell, Jr.
Countryman.........Mr. Blissett
Rosetta.........Mrs. Oldmixon
Lucinda..........Mrs. Warrell
Deborah Woodcock..Mrs. Francis
Margery..........Mrs. Hervey
Country Girl.....Miss Milbourne

The Sailor's Landlady

1797

April 26 (cont.)   *All The World's a Stage*

Sir Gilbert Pumpkin..Mr. Francis		Wat............Mr. Darley, Jr.	
Charles Stanley.....Mr. Warren		Hostler....,....Mr. Macdonald	
Harry Stukely..........Mr. Fox		Miss Bridget.,..,Mrs. L'Estrange	
William........Master Warrell		Miss Kitty......Miss L'Estrange	
Diggory........Mr. Warrell, Jr.		Jane.............Mrs. Francis	
Cymon...............Mr. Bates			

LAILSON'S CIRCUS

April 27   Circus   Aurora
* Le Marechal des Logis
or The Two Thieves ("Historical pantomime")

NEW THEATRE

April 28   *The Jew*   G. U. S.

Sir Stephen Bartram..Mr. Warren	Waiter..........Mr. Darley, Jr.
Frederick..........Mr. Moreton	Mrs. Ratcliffe....Mrs. L'Estrange
Chas. Ratcliffe..........Mr. Fox	Eliza Ratcliffe......Mrs. Francis
Saunders..........Mr. Warrell	Mrs. Goodison.....Mrs. Doctor
Sheva..............Mr. Cooper	Dorcas............Mrs. Harvey
Jubal............Mr. Harwood	

The Critic

Dangle............Mr. Moreton	Governor............Mr. Darley
Sneer..............Mr. Warren	Leicester..............Mr. Fox
Sig. Pasticio.....Mr. Darley, Jr.	Raleigh...........Mr. Prigmore
Interpreter.........Sig. Doctor	Master of Horse....Mr. Warrell
Prompter.........Mr. Mitchell	Beef Eater......Mr. Darley, Jr.
Mrs. Dangle.......Mrs. Francis	Whiskerandos........Mr. Bates
Italian Girls........Mrs. Harvey	1st Niece.........:.Miss Oldfield
& Miss Milbourne	2nd Niece.......Miss L'Estrange
Sir Fretful Plagiary and Puff.....	Confidant.........Mrs. Harvey
Mr. Harwood	Tilburina........Mrs. Oldmixon
Lord Burleigh.......Mr. Blissett	

LAILSON'S CIRCUS

April 29   Circus   G. U. S.
Le Marechal des Logis

NEW THEATRE

May 1   Mr. Warren's Night   G. U. S.

All for Love

Mark Antony......Mr. Moreton	Antony's Gentleman...........
Ventidius..........Mr. Warren	Mr. Warrell, Jr.

1797

May 1 (cont.)

Dollabella...........Mr. Cooper	Egyptians.......Messrs. Morgan,
Alexis.................Mr. Fox	Macdonald, etc.
Serapion.........Mr. L'Estrange	Octavia...........Mrs. Morris
Myris.............Mr. Warrell	Charmion..........Mrs. Harvey
Cleopatra...........Mrs. Merry	Iris...............Miss Oldfield

The Dead Alive

Sir Walter Weathercock......... Mr. Warren	Coachman...........Mr. Darley
Edward........Mr. Darley, Jr.	Hannibal........Master Warrell
Sable..............Mr. Morris	Grizley...........Mr. Morgan
Sheers...........Mr. Harwood	Miss Hebe Wintertop........... Mrs. L'Estrange
Motley..............Mr. Bates	Comfit..........Mrs. Oldmixon
Dennis.............Mr. Warrell	Caroline..........Mrs. Warrell
Degagee.............Mr. Fox	

LAILSON'S CIRCUS

May 2   *The American Heroine*   G. U. S.

Cast as for April 20.

Circus

NEW THEATRE

May 3   Mr. and Mrs. Byrne's Night   G. U. S.

Alonzo and Imogen

Cast as for April 17.

* An Ancient Day

(A New Play in Three acts, written by "a Citizen of Philadelphia.")

Baron..............Mr. Warren	George.........Miss L'Estrange
Frederick.........Mr. Moreton	Clarintha...........Mrs. Merry
Adolphus..........Mr. Harwood	Lauretta...........Mrs. Harvey
Jailor...............Mr. Bates	

* Blue Beard—Byrne

("A new Pantomime . . . from an old Story")

Blue Beard........Mr. Francis	Indian Chief....Mr. Warrell, Jr.
Fernando.......Mr. Macdonald	Leonora.............Mrs. Byrne
Bardenio......Master T. Warrell	Sister Ann..........Mrs. Harvey
Leander...........Mr. Byrne	Assassins.......Messrs. Lavancey,
Pedro............Mr. Mitchell	Morgan, Blissett, &c.

[338]

1797

LAILSON'S CIRCUS

May 4   *Blaise and Babet* (opera)   G. U. S.
      * *La Quinquette, or, The Good Humored Girl* (ballet)

NEW THEATRE

May 5   Mr. Prigmore's Night   G. U. S.

* The School for Citizens

Lovemore	Mr. Moreton	Servant	Mr. Warrell, Jr.
Oldworth	Mr. Cooper	Julianna	Mrs. Francis
Rosewell	Mr. Fox	Mariana	Mrs. Morris
Firelock	Mr. Harwood	Susan	Miss L'Estrange
Seagar	Mr. Prigmore	Polly	Mrs. Oldmixon
1st Indian	Mr. Warren	Patty	Mrs. Harvey
2d Indian	Mr. Darley, Jr.	Dorcas	Mrs. L'Estrange
3d Indian	Mr. Warrell		

The Sailor's Landlady

Jack	Mr. Warrell, Jr.	Lasses	Mrs. Harvey,
Midshipman	Master T. Warrell		Mrs. Doctor, &c.
Ned Haulyard	Mr. Darley	Landlady	Mr. Doctor
Sailors	Messrs. Mitchell,	Orange Girl	Miss Milbourne
	Morgan, &c.		

No Song No Supper

(this cast in *G. U. S.*, May 4)

Frederick	Mr. Darley. Jr.	Sailors	Messrs. Mitchell,
Crop	Mr. Darley		Macdonald, &c.
Endless	Mr. Harwood	Dorothy	Mrs. Warrell
Robin	Mr. Bates	Louisa	Miss Milbourne
William	Mr. Warrell	Margaretta	Mrs. Oldmixon
Thomas	Mr. Blissett	Nelly	Mrs. Harvey

May 6   *The Way to Get Married*   G. U. S.
      Lock and Key

"The last night of performing this season."

"The Engagements of the Managers, rendering it necessary, from recent occurrences, that they should open the Theatre at Baltimore, so as to close the season there on the tenth of June next, they have thought it expedient, (with the approbation of the individual performers, who are particularly interested) to discontinue the present course of Benefits until that period has elapsed."

The theatre was reopened on July 5, and closed on July 14. See July 14

1797

for summary of the entire season at the New Theatre from December 5, 1796, to July 14, 1797.

LAILSON'S CIRCUS

May 6   Circus   G. U. S.

Harlequin Restored

Harlequin..............Mr. Sully	Magician........Mr. Vandevelde
Pierot..........[no name given]	Lover..............Mr. Langley
Pantaloon............Mr. Reano	Columbine..........Miss Sophie
Cobler.............Mr. Viellard	Columbine's Mother............
	Miss Robinson

Four Witches   A Chimney Sweep
A Barber   Six Sailors
A Servant   Six Young Ladies

May 9   Circus   G. U. S.

Les Quatre Fils Aymond

Cast as for April 11.

May 10   "For the benefit of the Company"   G. U. S.

Circus
Les Quatre Fils Aymond

May 12   * *The Four Travelling Brothers*   G. U. S.

"A Comic Scene on horseback, in one act."

Rognollet........Mr. M'Donald	Cassaco............Mr. Nicholas
Courte Mesure.....Mr. Langley	Driver............Mr. Webber
Sans Couture......Mr. Herman	Director...........Mr. Lailson

Le Tableau Parlant

"With elegant new scenery executed by Mr. Perouany."

Cassandre.........Mr. St. Marc	Pierot...........Mr. Douvilliers
(formerly St. Mare)	Isabella........Mrs. Douvilliers
Leandre...........Mr. Prouble	Columbine........Miss Tesseire

First appearance of Messrs. Lailson, Herman, Nicholas, and Webber.

May 13   Circus   G. U. S.

* *The Despairing Lover, or The Ghost*

Le Grime...........Mr. Reano	C'Est Moi........Mr. St. Marc
Ghost...............Mr. Sully	Attend...............Mr. Leger
Pierot.............Mr. Lailson	Margot.............Mr. Saroie

1797

May 13 (cont.)

Leandre............Mr. Langley   Little Devils.....Messrs. Herman
Grifford..........Mr. Viellard   and Berg
Asmodeus........Mr. Vandevelde   La Belle Agathe.....Miss Sophie

First appearance of Mr. Berg, Mr. Leger, and Mr. Saroie.

May 16   Circus   G. U. S.
The Two Huntsmen and The Milkmaid

Guillot.............Mr. Viellard   Perrete............Miss Tesseire
Colas............Mr. St. Marc

Harlequin Restored

Cast as for May 6—again no name is given for Pierot

May 18   Circus   G. U. S.
The American Heroine

May 20   Circus   G. U. S.
Les Deux Petits Savoyards

Lord............Mr. Douvilliers   ⌈ Michael...........
Clermont.........Mr. Poignard   The Sweeps ⟨   Miss Tesseire
Judge.............Mr. Viellard   │ Joseph...........
James............Mr. St. Marc   ⌊   Miss Sophie

La Quinquette

May 23   Circus   G. U. S.
* *The Fusilier; or, The Clown Outwitted*—Dibdin
* *Harlequin's Whim; or, The Doctor Outwitted*

("New pantomime") see May 27 for a cast.

May 25   Circus   G. U. S.
La Melomanie

May 27   Circus   G. U. S.
Le Marechal des Logis
Harlequin's Whim

Harlequin.........Mr. Sully, Jr.   Lover.............Mr. Langley
The Magician......Mr. Sully, Sr.   Clown.........Mr. Vandeveldt
Pantaloon...........Mr. Reano   Colombine.........Miss Sophie
Valet...............Mr. Saroie

May 30   Circus   G. U. S.
Les Deux Petits Savoyards

Cast as for May 20.

The Four Travelling Brothers

1797

June 1	Circus *The American Heroine*	G. U. S.
June 3	Circus *Harlequin Mariner*	G. U. S.

"Colombine, Mrs. Rowson, from the Theatre Royal, Covent Garden, being her first appearance in America."

This Mrs. J. Rowson is not Mrs. Susanna Haswell Rowson, earlier with the New Theatre (Chesnut Street) Company.

June 6	Circus * *Pierre de Provençe and The Beautiful Maguelone.*	G. U. S.

"An heroical, historical Pantomime, in three acts." (See June 15 for cast)

June 8	Circus *Le Tableau Parlant* *Harlequin Mariner*	G. U. S.
June 10	Circus * *Harlequin Triumphant*	G. U. S.
June 13	Circus *Pierre de Provençe, and The Beautiful Maguelone*	G. U. S.
June 15	Circus *Pierre de Provençe*	G. U. S.

Pierre de Provençe. . . . .
             Mr. Douvilliers
Ferrieres. . . . . Mr. Jaymond
King of Naples. . . . . Mr. Prouble
Capt. of the Guards. . Mr. Poignard

Maguelone. . . . . . Mrs. Douvilliers
Knights of the Tournament. . . . . .
    Messrs. Sully, St. Marc, Vande-
    velde, Jaymond, Douvilliers

June 17	Circus *The Four Travelling Brothers* * *Pantaloon Duped, or, The Forced Marriage* "in which Mrs. Devan will perform in the Character of the Goddess Calypse"—her first appearance.	G. U. S.
June 20	Miss Vanice's Benefit Circus *The Four Travelling Brothers* Cast as for May 12.	G. U. S.
June 24	Circus *The American Heroine*	Aurora
June 27	Mr. Sully's Benefit	Aurora

1797

June 27 (cont.)   Circus
    * *The Weird Sisters, or The Adoption of Harlequin*

June 29   Benefit of Mr. Langley   G. U. S.
                    Circus
              Pierre de Provençe

July 1   Mr. Herman's Benefit   Aurora
                    Circus
    The Weird Sisters, or The Adoption of Harlequin

NEW THEATRE

July 5   G. U. S.

"The Public are respectfully informed, that the Entertainments of the New Theatre will recommence with a Dramatic Trifle,"

               Seeing is Believing
                   Columbus
            Dermot and Kathleen

July 7   *The Way to Get Married*   G. U. S.
                Lock and Key

July 10   Mr. Fox's Night   G. U. S.
             Romeo and Juliet

Cast as for Dec. 5, 1796, except:

Romeo	Mr. Cooper	Page	Master L'Estrange
Mercutio	Mr. Moreton	Lady Capulet	Mrs. L'Estrange
Tybalt	Mr. Warrell, Jr.	Nurse	Mrs. Harvey

The Anatomist, or The Sham Doctor

M. Le Medicin	Mr. Fox	Martin	Mr. Blissett
Crispin	Mr. Bates	Doctor's Wife	Mrs. L'Estrange
Old Gerald	Mr. Francis	Beatrice	Mrs. Francis
Young Gerald	Mr. Warrell, Jr.	Angelica	Miss L'Estrange
Simon Burley	Mr. Warren	Waiting Woman	Mrs. Doctor

LAILSON'S CIRCUS

July 11   Benefit of Mr. Jaymond   G. U. S.
                    Circus
  * *La Belle Dorothé; or, Maternal Affection* ("Heroic Pantomime")
              * *Les Preux Chevaliers*

1797

NEW THEATRE

July 12   "Last Night but one!"   G. U. S.

Mrs. Francis's Night

The Rivals

Sir Anthony Absolute..Mr. Morris
Capt. Absolute.....Mr. Moreton
Faulkland..........Mr. Cooper
Acres...............Mr. Bates
Sir Lucius O'Trigger...........
                    Mr. Warren
Fag.................Mr. Fox

David..............Mr. Francis
Coachman..........Mr. Warrell
Boy.........Master T. Warrell
Mrs. Malaprop...Mrs. Oldmixon
Julia..............Mrs. Merry
Lydia Languish.....Mrs. Francis
Lucy..............Mrs. Harvey

* The Savoyard, or, The Repentant Seducer (Musical Farce)

Belton...............Mr. Fox
Front..........Mr. Harwood
Simond..........Mr. Warren
Father Bertrand...Mr. L'Estrange
Benjamin....Master H. Warrell
Jaques............Mr. Moreton

Banditti........Messrs. Francis,
        Warrell, and Blissett
Countess..........Mrs. Francis
Nannette........Mrs. Oldmixon
Claudine..........Mrs. Warrell
[this part from *Aurora*, July 12]

LAILSON'S CIRCUS

July 13   Circus   G. U. S.
La Belle Dorothé
Les Preux Chevaliers

NEW THEATRE

July 14   Last Night this Season   Aurora

Benefit of Mr. Blissett and Mrs. Harvey

The Road to Ruin

Dornton..........Mr. Warren
Harry Dornton.....Mr. Moreton
Sulky.............Mr. Francis
Silky.............Mr. Blissett
Goldfinch........Mr. Harwood
Milford.............Mr. Fox
Smith.... ....Mr. Warrell

Tradesmen..Messrs. Mitchell, &c.
Jacob..........Mr. Warrell, Jr.
Postillion........Master Warrell
Widow Warren...Mrs. Oldmixon
Sophia..............Mrs. Merry
Jenny.............Mrs. Harvey
Mrs. Ledger........Mrs. Doctor

The Magician of the Enchanted Castle;
or, Harlequin Conqueror

Harlequin Enchanter..Mr. Francis
Magician of The Castle........
                Mr. Warrell

Sancho..........Master Warrell
Pantaloon.........Mr. Lavancey
Clown..............Mr. Blissett

[344]

1797

July 14 (cont.)

Old Woman.......Mr. Mitchell	Pero...............Sig. Doctor
Fernando......Mr. Warrell, Jr.	Columbine.......Miss Milbourne

"The Pantomime partly compiled from the most favourite Pantomimes."

At the New Theatre (Chesnut Street) from December 5, 1796, to July 14, 1797 (with an intermission from May 6 to July 5) these new plays were presented: *The Abbey of St. Augustine, Columbus, Heigh Ho! for a Husband, The Iron Chest, The Ransomed Slave, The School for Citizens, The Way to Get Married,* and *Werter* [*and Charlotte*]. New afterpieces: *The Adopted Child, Alonzo and Imogen, An Ancient Day, Blaize et Babet, Blue Beard, Dermot and Kathleen, Les Deux Petits Savoyards, The Doldrums, The Drunken Provençal, The Enchanted Flute, Harlequin Conqueror; or The Magician of the Enchanted Castle, The Highland Festivity, Lock and Key, La Melomanie, The New Year's Gift, Les Souliers Mordores, Le Tableau Parlant.*

Reappearing plays: *All for Love, The Child of Nature, Every One Has His Fault, The Fair Penitent, George Barnwell, The Grecian Daughter, Henry IV, (part one), Inkle and Yarico, The Jew, King Lear, Love in a Village, Love's Frailties, Macbeth, The Merchant of Venice, The Merry Wives of Windsor, The Mountaineers, Much Ado About Nothing, The Orphan, The Rage, The Revenge, The Road to Ruin, Romeo and Juliet, The School for Scandal, She Stoops to Conquer, Venice Preserved, The Wheel of Fortune,* and *The Wonder.* Reappearing afterpieces: *The Agreeable Surprize, All the World's A Stage, The Anatomist, Animal Magnetism, Barnaby Brittle, The Critic, The Dead Alive, Les Deux Chasseurs, The First Floor, The Flitch of Bacon, Harlequin's Invasion, La Forêt Noire, The Ghost, Gil Blas, High Life Below Stairs, The Irishman in London, The Little Hunchback, Love à la Mode, The Married Man, The Mayor of Garratt, The Mogul Tale, Next Door Neighbours, The Padlock, Peeping Tom of Coventry, The Prize, The Purse, The Sailor's Landlady, Seeing is Believing, The Son-in-Law, The Sultan, The Village Lawyer, The Waterman, Who's the Dupe?* and *The Widow's Vow.*

New actors: M. Bouchoni, Mr. and Mrs. Byrne, Mr. Cooper, M. Fieron, Mr. Fox, Mrs. Gillingham, M. Glaize (or Gleise), M. Lavencey, Mr., Mrs., Miss, and Master L'Estrange, Mrs. Mechtler, Mrs. Merry, M. Poignand (or Poignard), Mlle. Sophie, M. St. Mare (or St. Marc), Mlle. Tesseire, M. Viellard, and Mr. Warren. Reappearing actors: Mr. Bates, Mrs. Blissett, Mr. Darley, Mr. Darley, Jr., Sig. and Mrs. Doctor, Mr. and Mrs. Francis, Mr. Harwood, Mrs. Hervey (or Harvey), Mr. M'Donald, Mr. and Miss Milbourne, Mr. Mitchell, Mr. Moreton, Mr. Morgan, Mr. and Mrs. Morris, Miss Oldfield, Mrs. Oldmixon, Mr. Prigmore, Mr. and Mrs. Warrell, Master H. Warrell, Mr. Warrell, Jr., Master T. Warrell, and Mr. Wignell.

1797

LAILSON'S CIRCUS

July 18   Benefit of Mr. Collet, Leader of the Band   G. U. S.

Circus

* *Mirza and Lindor* ("historical and heroical pantomime")

Governor of Martinique.........	Maître d'Hotel.....Mr. Viellard
Mr. Pouble	Lindor...........Mr. Douvilliers
English Officer......Mr. Jaymond	Elene.............Miss Tesseire
Officer and Corporal of the	Zoé...............Mrs. Rowson
Guard...........by Amateurs	Mirza..........Mrs. Douvilliers

"A regiment of infantry, By Amateurs of this city.
Hired troops,   By ditto."

July 20   Messrs. Vandevelde & Viellard's Benefit   G. U. S.

Circus
The Four Travelling Brothers

Timothy Plumpjug............	Jonathan Plumpjug............
Mr. M'Donald	Mr. N. Corre[y]
Dicky Plumpjug..Mr. Vandevelde	Nathan Plumpjug...Mr. Herman

Don Juan—"Tragi-comic Pantomime"

Don Juan.......Mr. Douvilliers	Three Musicians..Messrs. Mengui
Commandant.......Mr. Jaymond	Moran, &c.
Don Carlos.........Mr. Pouble	Tavern Keeper.....Mr. Vieillard
Scaramouche.......Mr. Sully, Jr.	Fisherman........Mr. Sully, Sr.
Four Servants....Messrs. Martin,	Old Man.........Mr. Vieillard
Challet, etc.	Two Fisherwomen..Mrs. Kendery
Two Commissanes........Messrs.	and Miss Robinson
Lavancey & Savage	Donna Isabella...Mrs. Douvillier
Four Sailors.............Messrs.	Donna Sancha......Mrs. Rowson
Vandevelde, &c.	

First appearance of Mr. Challet, Mr. Corre [y] (or Corry), Mrs. Kendery, Messrs. Mengui, Moran, and Savage. Mr. Martin may have been John Martin, formerly with the Old American Co.; or he may have been "The Little Devil" (see Odell, I, 338); or he may have been a new performer.

July 22   Benefit of Mr. M'Donald The Clown   G. U. S.
Circus
* *The Sisters of the Rocks*—"Comic Pantomime"
"got up under direction of Mr. Sully."

July 27   Benefit of Mr. Pouble   G. U. S.
Circus
* *Modern Amazons*—"Pantomime in two acts"

1797

Last night of the season at Lailson's Circus from April 11 to July 27, 1797. New productions (pantomimes and farces): *La Belle Dorothé, The Death of Bucephalus, The Despairing Lover, The Four Travelling Brothers, The Fusilier, Harlequin Mariner, Harlequin Triumphant, Harlequin's Whim, Le Marechal des Logis, Mirza and Lindor, Modern Amazons, Pierre de Provençe, Les Preux Chevaliers, Les Quatres Fils Aymond, La Quinquette, The Sisters of the Rocks, The Two Huntsmen,* and *The Weird Sisters.* Reappearing afterpieces: *Blaize et Babet, Les Deux Petits Savoyards, Don Juan,* and *The Two Philosophers.*

New performers: Mr. Berg, M. Challet, Mr. Corre [y] (or Corry), Mrs. Devan, Mr., Mme., and Mlle. Douvilliers, Mr. Herman, Mr. Jaymond, Mrs. Kendery, Mr. and Mlle. Lailson, Messrs. Leger, Martin, Mengui, Moran, Nicholas, Pouble (or Prouble), Mrs. J. Rowson, Messrs. Saroie, Savage, Vandevelde, and Webber. Reappearing performers: Messrs. Langley, M'Donald, Poignand (or Poignard), Reano, Miss Robinson, Mr. St. Marc (or St. Mare), Miss Sophie, Mr. Sully, Mr. Sully, Jr., Miss Tesseire, and Mr. Viellard.

NEW THEATRE

Dec. 11   *Robin Hood*   Aurora

Robin Hood........Mr. Darley
Little John.........Mr. Wignell
Scarlet............Mr. Francis
Bowman...........Mr. Warrell
Archers...........Messrs. Blissett,
 T. Warrell, Doctor, Lafferty,
 Sully, etc.
Allen-a-Dale.....Mr. J. Warrell
Stella...........Miss L'Estrange
Clorinda..........Mrs. Warrell
Annette........Miss Milbourne

Shepherdesses.....Mrs. Harwood,
 Mrs. Doctor, Miss Oldfield, Miss
 Anderson, &c.
Ruttekin..........Mr. Bernard
 (being his first appearance in Philadelphia)
Friar Tuck........Mr. Warren
Edwin...........Mr. Marshall
 (being his first appearance here these
 twelve months)
Angelina........Mrs. Oldmixon

The Lyar

Old Wilding.......Mr. Warren
Young Wilding.....Mr. Bernard
Sir James Elliot...Mr. J. Warrell
Papillion.........Mr. Marshall

Servant.........Master Warrell
Miss Grantham.....Mrs. Francis
Miss Godfrey....Miss L'Estrange
Kitty.............Mrs. Doctor

Opening night (postponed from December 4) of the season at the New Theatre (Chesnut Street) from December 11, 1797, to May 5, 1798. First appearance of Miss Anderson, Mr. Bernard, Mrs. Harwood, and Mr. Lafferty.

1797

Dec. 13   *Wives as They Were, and*   G. U. S.
Maids as They Are—Mrs. Inchbald

Sir Wm. Dorillon..Mr. Harwood	James..........Mr. Warrell, Jr.
Lord Priory.......Mr. Warren	Servants.......Messrs. Lavancey,
Sir George Evelyn...Mr. Moreton	Lafferty, &c.
Mr. Norberry......Mr. Taylor	Miss Dorillon......Mrs. Merry
Nabson...........Mr. Warrell	Lady Mary Raffle..Mrs. Oldmixon
Oliver.............Mr. Blissett	Lady Priory........Mrs. Morris
Gaoler.............Mr. Sully	House-keeper........Mrs. Doctor
John..........Mr. T. Warrell	

The Adopted Child

Sir Bertram........Mr. Warren	Boy............Miss L'Estrange
Michael............Mr. Cooper	Clara.............Mrs. Warrell
Record............Mr. Francis	Nelly...........Mrs. Oldmixon
Spruce........Mr. Warrell, Jr.	Lucy.............Mrs. Francis
Le Sage............Mr. Darley	

First announcement of Mr. Taylor; but on December 23 he is announced as "first time on this stage." This may indicate a postponement of December 13's bill: more probably, Mr. Taylor did not then appear.

Dec. 15   *The Highland Reel*   G. U. S.

Laird of Col.......Mr. Warren	Sergeant Jack.......Mr. Darley
Laird of Ramsey.....Mr. Warrell	Apie............Mr. T. Warrell
M'Gilpin........Mr. Harwood	Benin........Master L'Estrange
Sandy............Mr. Marshall	Moggy M'Gilpin..Mrs. Marshall
Charley............Mr. Francis	(Being her first appearance these
Shelty............Mr. Bernard	twelve months.)
Crowdy...........Mr. Blissett	Jenny............Mrs. Warrell
Captain Dash......Mr. Moreton	

The Sultan

Soliman..........Mr. Moreton	Ismene...........Mrs. Warrell
Osmyn...........Mr. Harwood	Roxaland........Mrs. Marshall
Elmira.........Miss L'Estrange	

Dec. 16   ("By Desire")   G. U. S.
Venice Preserved

Cast as for Jan. 21, except:

(Spinosa not cast)

Rennault..........Mr. Wignell	Elliot...........Mr. T. Warrell
Durand..........Mr. Matthew	

1797

Dec. 16 (cont.)   *The Lying Valet*

Sharp	Mr. Bernard	Melissa	Mrs. Francis
Gayless	Mr. Warren	Mrs. Gadabout	Mrs. Doctor
Justice Guttle	Mr. Francis	Mrs. Trippet	Miss Milbourne
Beau Trippet	Mr. Warrell, Jr.	Kitty Pry	Mrs. Morris
Drunken Cook	Mr. Blissett		

First appearance of Mr. Matthew.

Dec. 18   *Wives as They Were*   G. U. S.
                Lock and Key

Brummagem	Mr. Francis	Ralph	Mr. Harwood
Cheerly	Mr. Marshall	Laura	Mrs. Warrell
Capt. Vain	Mr. Fox	Fanny	Mrs. Oldmixon

Dec. 20   *The Country Girl*   G. U. S.
       The Irishman in London

"In Which Mr. Hardinge will make his first appearance on this stage."

Dec. 22   *Every One Has His Fault*   G. U. S.

Lord Norland	Mr. Warren	Porter	Mr. Warrell
Sir Robert Ramble	Mr. Bernard	Edward	Miss Hardinge
(with the epilogue)		("being her first appearance on this	
Mr. Solus	Mr. Morris		stage")
Mr. Harmony	Mr. Harwood	Lady Eleanor Irwin	
Capt. Irwin	Mr. Cooper		Mrs. Hardinge
Mr. Placid	Mr. Moreton	("being her first appearance on this	
Hammond	Mr. Warrell, Jr.		stage")
Mrs. Placid	Mrs. Oldmixon	Miss Woburn	Mrs. Morris
Miss Spinster	Mrs. L'Estrange		

Three Weeks after Marriage

Sir Chas. Racket	Mr. Moreton	Lady Racket	Mrs. Hardinge
Drugget	Mr. Warren	Mrs. Drugget	Mrs. L'Estrange
Woodley	Mr. Fox	Nancy	Miss L'Estrange
Servant	Mr. T. Warrell	Dimity	Mrs. Francis

First appearance of Miss and Mrs. Hardinge.

Dec. 23   *The Mountaineers*   G. U. S.

Octavian—("first time on this stage") Mr. Taylor,
from the Theatre Boston [but see Dec. 13]

The Irish Widow

Widow Brady.....Mrs. Hardinge

1797

Dec. 26   *George Barnwell*   G. U. S.
* The Christmas Frolic; or, Harlequin's Gambols *

Dec. 27   *The Child of Nature*   G. U. S.
Dermot and Kathleen
The Castle of Andalusia

"Compressed into an afterpiece."

Dec. 29   *Columbus*   G. U. S.

Columbus........Mr. Hardinge   Dr. Dolores........Mr. Bernard

"To Conclude with a New Additional Scene, (Written by a
member of the Legislature of the United States.)"
Genius of Columbia—Mr. Marshall

The Lying Valet

Sharp..............Mr. Bernard

Dec. 30   *Columbus*   G. U. S.
The Farmer

1798

Jan. 1   * *A Cure for the Heartache*—Morton   Aurora
* *The Animated Statue*

Jan. 3   *The Revenge*   G. U. S.

Don Alonzo.......Mr. Moreton   Zanga.............Mr. Fennell
Don Carlos............Mr. Fox   (being his first appearance here these
Don Alvarez.......Mr. Warren   three years.)
Don Manuel....Mr. Warrell, Jr.   Isabella........Miss L'Estrange
Leonora...........Mrs. Merry

The Romp

Jan. 5   *A Cure for the Heartache*   G. U. S.
La Forêt Noire

Jan. 6   *Wives as They Were*   G. U. S.
The Devil to Pay

Jan. 8   *Othello*   G. U. S.

Othello............Mr. Fennell   Gratiano...........Mr. Warrell
Cassio............Mr. Moreton   Lodovico...........Mr. Taylor
Iago..............Mr. Warren   1st Officer......Mr. T. Warrell
Roderigo.........Mr. Bernard   2d Officer......Mr. Warrell, Jr.
Montano.............Mr. Fox   Desdemona.........Mrs. Merry
Duke of Venice...Mr. L'Estrange   Emelia.............Mrs. Francis
Brabantio..........Mr. Morris

1798

Jan. 8 (cont.)   *The Deserter*

Henry	Mr. Marshall	2d Soldier	Mr. Warrell
Russet	Mr. Darley	3d Soldier	Mr. Warrell, Jr.
Simkin	Mr. Francis	4th Soldier	Mr. T. Warrell
Skirmish	Mr. Bernard	Louisa	Mrs. Marshall
Flint	Mr. Blissett	Jenny	Mrs. Warrell
1st Soldier	Mr. Fox	Margaret	Mrs. L'Estrange

Jan. 10   *Columbus*   G. U. S.

Columbus..........Mr. Fennell

The Animated Statue

Jan. 12   * *Abroad and at Home—*Holman   G. U. S.

Sir Simon Flourish	Mr. Francis	Dickey	Mr. Blissett
Young Flourish	Mr. Harwood	Bluff	Mr. Warrell
Old Testy	Mr. Warren	Bailiff's Followers	Mr. Warrell, Jr., and Mr. T. Warrell
Young Testy	Mr. Bernard		
Capt. O'Neil	Mr. Hardinge	Lady Flourish	Mrs. Hardinge
Harcourt	Mr. Marshall	Kitty	Mrs. Oldmixon
Snare	Mr. Taylor	Miss Hartley	Mrs. Warrell

The Deaf Lover

Jan. 13   *The Revenge*   G. U. S.
    The Prize

Jan. 15   *Abroad and at Home*   G. U. S.
    The Midnight Hour

Marquis	Mr. Moreton	Ambrose	Mr. Warrell
General	Mr. Warren	Julia	Miss L'Estrange
Sebastian	Mr. Francis	Cecily	Mrs. L'Estrange
Nicholas	Mr. Harwood	Flora	Mrs. Francis
Mathias	Mr. Blissett		

Jan. 17   *A Cure for the Heartache*   G. U. S.
    The Spoilt Child

Jan. 19   *Isabella*   G. U. S.

Count Baldwin	Mr. Warren	Sampson	Mr. Francis
Biron	Mr. Fennell	Belford	Mr. Fox
Carlos	Mr. Wignell	Officer	Mr. Warrell
Villeroy	Mr. Moreton	Isabella	Mrs. Merry
Child	Master Warrell	Nurse	Mrs. L'Estrange

1798

Jan. 19 (cont.)   *Two Strings to Your Bow*

Don Pedro..........Mr. Francis
Don Sancho........Mr. Warrell
Octavio................Mr. Fox
Ferdinand.......Mr. Warrell, Jr.
Borachio..........Mr. Warren
Lazarillo..........Mr. Bernard

Drunken Porter......Mr. Blissett
Waiters......Messrs. T. Warrell,
                    Hunter, &c.
Donna Clara.......Mrs. Francis
Leonora.........Miss L'Estrange
Maid..............Mrs. Doctor

First appearance of Mr. Hunter.

Jan. 20   *The Jew*   G. U. S.
                       The Critic

Jan. 22   "By particular desire, and for the entertainment of the   G. U. S.
          Chiefs of the Wyandot Indians."

                     Romeo and Juliet

Romeo...........Mr. Moreton
Paris...........Mr. Warrell, Jr.
Montague..........Mr. Warrell
Capulet............Mr. Morris
Mercutio..........Mr. Bernard
Benvolio..............Mr. Fox
Tibalt.............Mr. Taylor
Friar Laurence.....Mr. Warren

Friar John..........Mr. Hunter
Balthazar.......Mr. T. Warrell
Apothecary..........Mr. Francis
Peter..............Mr. Blissett
Juliet..............Mrs. Merry
Lady Capulet....Mrs. L'Estrange
Nurse............Mrs. Francis

                 The Agreeable Surprize

Sir Felix Friendly...Mr. Warren
Compton............Mr. Darley
Eugene.........Mr. Warrell, Jr.
Chicane............Mr. Warrell
John...............Mr. Taylor
Thomas........Mr. T. Warrell

Cudden.............Mr. Blissett
Lingo..............Mr. Bernard
Laura..........Mrs. Oldmixon
Mrs. Cheshire...Mrs. L'Estrange
Cowslip..........Mrs. Warren
Fringe.........Mrs. L'Estrange

Jan. 24   * *The Will; or*   G. U. S.
                A School for Daughters—Reynolds

Sir Solomon Cynic...Mr. Bernard
Mandeville.........Mr. Warren
Howard..........Mr. Moreton
Veritas...........Mr. Wignell
Realize..........Mr. Harwood
Robert..............Mr. Fox
Old Copsley........Mr. Warrell

Servants.........Messrs. Hunter,
                    Lafferty, &c.
Albina Mandeville..Mrs. Marshall
Mrs. Rigid.....Mrs. L'Estrange
Cicely Copsley.....Mrs. Francis
Deborah..........Mrs. Doctor

1798

Jan. 24 (cont.)   *The Dead Alive*

Sir Walter Weathercock.........   Dennis............Mr. Warrell
                Mr. Warren   Grizley............Mr. Hunter
Edward..............Mr. Fox   Miss Hebe Wintertop..........
Sable..............Mr. Morris   Mrs. L'Estrange
Sheers...........Mr. Harwood   Comfit..........Mrs. Oldmixon
Motley..........Mr. Bernard   Caroline..........Mrs. Warrell

Jan. 26   *The Will*   G. U. S.

Cast as for Jan. 24, except:

Cicely Copsley..........Mrs. Bernard

Lock and Key

First appearance of Mrs. Bernard.

Jan. 27   *Abroad and at Home*   G. U. S.
                          Robinson Crusoe

"Compressed into one act"

Jan. 29   *The Fair Penitent*   G. U. S.

Sciolto............Mr. Warren   Rossano.........Mr. J. Warrell
Altamont..............Mr. Fox   Calista............Mrs. Merry
Horatio............Mr. Fennell   Lavinia...........Mrs. Francis
Lothario..........Mr. Moreton   Lucilla.........Miss L'Estrange

Robinson Crusoe

Jan. 30   *Wives as They Were*   G. U. S.
                       * *Hunt the Slipper*—Knapp

As the same plays were announced on the next day, this may have been postponed.

Jan. 31   *Wives as They Were*   G. U. S.
                          Hunt the Slipper

Feb. 2   "First time in America"   G. U. S.

* *Fenelon; or*
The Nuns of Cambray—Merry

"[Altered from a celebrated French Play of that name, performed at Paris with unbounded applause.]"

Fenelon (Archbishop of Cambroy)   Abbess..........Mrs. L'Estrange
.................Mr. Fennell   Friars..Messrs. Warrell, Warrell,

1798

Feb. 2 (cont.)

Delmance.........Mr. Warren
Officer of Household...........
         Mr. T. Warrell
Eloisa.............Mrs. Merry
Amelia..........Mrs. Marshall
Isaura............Mrs. Francis

Jr., Hunter, Lavancy, Doctor, Lafferty, Matthew, &c.
Nuns...Mrs. Doctor, Mrs. Harwood, Mrs. Stuart, Mrs. Warren, Mrs. Hunter, Miss Anderson, &c.

Inkle and Yarico

First appearance of Mrs. Hunter, Mrs. Stuart, and Mrs. Warren.

Feb. 3   *Fenelon*   G. U. S.

Cast as for Feb. 2.

Robin Hood

Feb. 5   *Henry IV*   G. U. S.

King Henry........Mr. Wignell
Prince of Wales.....Mr. Bernard
Prince John......Mr. T. Warrell
Worcester..............Mr. Fox
Northumberland.....Mr. Darley
Hotspur............Mr. Fennell
(being his first appearance in that character in America)
Douglass..........Mr. Marshall
Sir Richard Vernon...Mr. Taylor
Sir John Falstaff....Mr. Warren

Sir Walter Blunt..............
         Mr. Warrell, Jr.
Poins.............Mr. Harwood
Peto...............Mr. Hunter
Bardolph.........Mr. Matthews
Francis.............Mr. Blissett
Carriers..........Messrs. Francis & Morris
Lady Percy.....Miss L'Estrange
Hostess Quickly..Mrs. L'Estrange

Animal Magnetism

Feb. 7   *Abroad and at Home*   G. U. S.
                The Guardian

Mr. Heartly.......Mr. Marshall
Sir Chas. Clackit....Mr. Morris
Young Clackit......Mr. Bernard

Servant.........Mr. T. Warrell
Harriet...........Mrs. Marshall
Lucy..............Mrs. Bernard

Feb. 9   *Alexander the Great*   G. U. S.

Alexander..........Mr. Fennell
Hephestion......Mr. Warrell, Jr.
Lysimachus........Mr. Hardinge
Cassander..............Mr. Fox
Polyperchon........Mr. Taylor
Philip..............Mr. Hunter
Clytus.............Mr. Warren
Thessalus...........Mr. Warrell

Perdicas...........Mr. Blissett
Eumenes........Mr. T. Warrell
Slave............Mr. Matthew
Roxana............Mrs. Merry
Sysigambis......Mrs. L'Estrange
Parisatis........Miss L'Estrange
Statira..........Mrs. Marshall

1798

Feb. 9 (cont.)   *The Poor Soldier*

Capt. Fitzroy........Mr. Darley	Bagatelle..........Mr. Marshall
Father Luke........Mr. Warren	Boy............Master Warrell
Dermot...............Mr. Fox	Norah............Mrs. Warrell
Patrick..........Mr. Hardinge	Kathleen.........Mrs. Oldmixon
Darby............Mr. Bernard	

Feb. 10   *Fenelon*   G. U. S
The Highland Reel

Feb. 12   *Macbeth*   G. U. S.

Macbeth........Mr. Fennell	Seyton..........Mr. Warrell, Jr.
(being his first appearance in that	Doctor.............Mr. Warrell
character these four years)	Messenger..........Mr. Blissett
Duncan.........Mr. L'Estrange	Lady Macbeth....Mrs. Hardinge
Malcolm..............Mr. Fox	(first time)
Donalbaine......Mr. T. Warrell	Gentlewoman....Mrs. L'Estrange
Macduff...........Mr. Wignell	Hecate..............Mr. Darley
Banquo............Mr. Warren	1st Witch.........Mr. Bernard
Lenox...........Mr. Marshall	2nd Witch..........Mr. Francis
Siward.............Mr. Morris	3rd Witch........Mr. Harwood

The Padlock

Don Diego.........Mr. Darley	Mungo............Mr. Bernard
Leander..........Mr. Marshall	Leonora.........Mrs. Marshall
1st Scholar......Mr. Warrell, Jr.	Ursula.........Mrs. L'Estrange
2d Scholar......Mr. T. Warrell	

Feb. 15 (Elaborate preparations for *Oscar and Malvina* had post-   G. U. S.
    poned this from February 14.)

The Gamester

Beverly.............Mr. Fennell	Waiter.............Mr. Hunter
Stukely.............Mr. Warren	Mrs. Beverly........Mrs. Merry
Lewson............Mr. Wignell	(being her first appearance in that
Jarvis..............Mr. Morris	(character)
Bates...............Mr. Taylor	Charlotte...........Mrs. Francis
Dawson........Mr. Warrell, Jr.	Lucy..............Mrs. Doctor

"Heroic Pantomime Ballet and Spectacle"
Oscar and Malvina

"Composed by Mr. Byrne—and performed under his direction at the
Theatre, Covent Garden, upwards of two hundred nights."

Oscar................Mr. Byrne	Scotch Pedlar.......Mr. Francis
Carroi...........Mr. Hardinge	Scotch Lad.............Mr. Fox
Fingal.............Mr. Taylor	Scotch Lassie....Miss Milbourne

[355]

1798

Feb. 15 (cont.)

Marven...........Mr. Marshall   Malvina............Mrs. Byrne
Draco.........Mr. Warrell, Jr.   Principal Bard.......Mr. Darley

Feb. 16   *The Clandestine Marriage*   G. U. S.

Lord Ogleby.......Mr. Bernard   Trueman...........Mr. Warrell
Sir John Melville...Mr. Warren   Mrs. Heidelberg..Mrs. L'Estrange
Sterling.............Mr. Morris   Miss Sterling.......Mrs. Morris
Lovewell.........Mr. Marshall   Fanny............Mrs. Marshall
Canton..........Mr. Harwood   Betty...........Miss L'Estrange
Brush............Mr. Hardinge   Chambermaid.......Mrs. Francis
Sergeant Flower......Mr. Francis   Trusty............Mrs. Doctor
Travers............Mr. Taylor

Oscar and Malvina

Cast as for Feb. 15.

Feb. 17 (*The Orphan* announced, but changed on account of Mr.   G. U. S.
Fennell's "sudden indisposition.")

The Jew

Sheva.............Mr. Bernard   Eliza...........Mrs. Marshall
Frederick.........Mr. Marshall

Oscar and Malvina

Cast as for February 15.

Feb. 19   *The Orphan*   G. U. S.
     Oscar and Malvina

Feb. 26   *The Will*   G. U. S.
    The Children in the Wood

Sir Rowland.......Mr. Warren   Russian............Mr. Hunter
Lord Alford......Mr. Hardinge   Helen...........Mrs. Hardinge
Walter..........Mr. Harwood   Josephine........Mrs. Oldmixon
Apathy............Mr. Francis   Winifred..........Mrs. Doctor
Gabriel............Mr. Blissett   Boy.............Master Warren
Oliver.............Mr. Taylor   Girl.............Miss Hardinge

Feb. 28   *The Jew*   G. U. S.

Peeping Tom of Coventry

Peeping Tom........Mr. Harwood

March 2   *The Road to Ruin*   Aurora

Dornton............Mr. Warren   Tradesmen......Messrs. Hunter,
Harry Dornton....Mr. Marshall   Warrell, Jr.
Sulky...........Mr. L'Estrange   Jacob.............Mr. Blissett

1798

March 2 (cont.)

Silky	Mr. Francis	Widow Warren	Mrs. Oldmixon
Goldfinch	Mr. Bernard	Sophia	Mrs. Marshall
Milford	Mr. Fox	Jenny	Mrs. Francis
Smith	Mr. Warrell	Mrs. Ledger	Mrs. Doctor
Sheriff's Officer	Mr. Matthew		

The Shipwreck—comic opera—Colman, Jr.

Selwyn	Mr. Marshall	Dick	Mr. Fox
Harry Hawser	Mr. Harwood	1st Plunderer	Mr. Darley
Michael Goto	Mr. Warren	Angelica	Mrs. Warrell
Shark	Mr. Blissett	Fanny	Mrs. Marshall
Stave	Mr. Bernard	Sally Shamrock	Mrs. Oldmixon

March 3   *Henry IV*   Aurora
                 The Devil to Pay

March 5   *A Cure for the Heartache*   Aurora
                 The Shipwreck

March 7   * *The Author*—Foote   G. U. S.

Gov. Cape	Mr. Warren	Printer's Devil	Mr. Blissett
Young Cape	Mr. Fennell	Poet	Mr. Francis
Sprightly	Mr. Fox	Mrs. Cadwallader	Mrs. Bernard
Robin	Mr. Warrell	Arabella	Miss L'Estrange

Fenelon

Cast as for February 2, except that
Friars were not mentioned

* *The Generous Tars*—Byrne
"New Pantomime Ballet"

Gacelon..........Mr. Francis

The Mayor of Garratt
(reduced to one act)

Sir Jacob Jollup	Mr. Taylor	Bruin	Mr. Warrell
Major Sturgeon	Mr. Warren	Roger	Mr. Blissett
Jerry Sneak	Mr. Bernard	Mrs. Sneak	Mrs. Francis
Crispin Heeltap	Mr. Francis	Mrs. Bruin	Mrs. Doctor

LAILSON'S CIRCUS

March 8   * *The Whims of Galatea, or*
                        Pastoral Love—Francisqui   Daily Ad.
      "A Grand Pastoral Pantomime Ballet Dance"

Paris	Sig. Francisqui	Sylvia	Mrs. Rowson
Dorilas	Mr. Lapointe	Laura	Mrs. Tompkins

[357]

1798

March 8 (cont.)

Strephon	Mr. Tompkins	Phillis	Mrs. N. M.
Dametas	Mr. Lousier	Pastora	Mrs. Corre[y]
Alexis	Mr. Galton	Philinda	Miss Robinson
Palement	Mr. Glaise	Galatea	Mrs. Douvilliers
Cupid	Miss Lailson		

First appearance of Mrs. Corre[y] (or Corry), Sig. Francisqui, Mr. Galton, Mr. Lapointe, Mr. Lousier (or Louisier), and Mrs. "N. M."

First night of a short season at Lailson's Circus from March 8 till April 7, 1798.

NEW THEATRE

March 9   *The Orphan*   G. U. S.

Castalio	Mr. Wignell	Chamont	Mr. Marshall
			("being his first appearance in that (character")

The Shipwreck

LAILSON'S CIRCUS

March 10   *The Milliners, or the Jealous Husband*   Phila. Gaz.

NEW THEATRE

March 12   *Columbus*   G. U. S.
           The Spoiled Child

March 14   *The Country Girl*   G. U. S.
           The Prize

March 16   *Hamlet*   G. U. S.

Hamlet	Mr. Fennell	Francisco	Mr. Blissett
("being his first appearance in that character these four years")		Marcellus	Mr. T. Warrell
		Bernardo	Mr. Warrell
King	Mr. Warrell	Ostric	Mr. Francis
Ghost	Mr. Marshall	Lucianus	Mr. Blissett
Horatio	Mr. Fox	Rosencrans	Mr. Warrell, Jr.
Polonius	Mr. Morris	Grave Diggers	Messrs. Harwood
Laertes	Mr. Hardinge		and Blissett
Guildenstern	Mr. Taylor		

Lock and Key

March 17   *The Rage*   G. U. S.
           Oscar and Malvina

LAILSON'S CIRCUS

March 17   *The Milliners, or the Jealous Husband*   Phila. Gaz.

[358]

1798

NEW THEATRE

March 19   Mr. Wignell's Night   G. U. S.

The Way to Get Married
The Death of Captain Cook

March 21   Mrs. Merry's Night   G. U. S.

The School for Scandal

Sir Peter Teazle....Mr. Warren	Rowley............Mr. Warrell
Sir Oliver Surface...Mr. Morris	Snake..............Mr. Taylor
Joseph Surface......Mr. Wignell	Trip..........Mr. Warrell, Jr.
Charles Surface.....Mr. Bernard	Lady Teazle........Mrs. Merry
Sir Benjamin Backbite...Mr. Fox	("that night only")
Crabtree..........Mr. Harwood	Lady Sneerwell......Mrs. Francis
Careless...........Mr. Blissett	Mrs. Candour....Mrs. Oldmixon
Sir Harry..........Mr. Darley	Maria..........Miss L'Estrange
Moses..............Mr. Francis	

The Agreeable Surprize

Cast as for January 22, except:

Eugene...............Mr. Fox	Farmer Stump.....Mr. Matthew
Chicane...........Mr. Wignell	(not cast before)
John..........Mr. Warrell, Jr.	Cowslip...........Mrs. Merry
Thomas.............Mr. Taylor	

LAILSON'S CIRCUS

March 22   * *The New Deserter; or, Supposed Marriage*   Daily Ad.

There is no record of this before, though it is announced:
"For the second time, a grand Tragi-Comic Pantomime, in 3 acts."

NEW THEATRE

March 23   Mrs. Marshall's Night   G. U. S.

* Tancred and Sigismunda—Thomson

Tancred............Mr. Fennell	2d Officer.........Mr. Hunter
Earl Osmond.......Mr. Wignell	Guards.........Messrs. Lavancy,
Suffredi...........Mr. Warren	Lafferty, etc.
Rudolpho......Mr. Warrell, Jr.	Laura..........Miss L'Estrange
1st Officer......Mr. T. Warrell	Sigismunda........Mrs. Marshall

* Richard Cœur de Lion—Burgoyne

Richard...........Mr. Marshall	Capt. of Party...Mr. Warrell, Jr.
Sir Owen...........Mr. Darley	Anthonia........Miss Milbourne

[359]

1798

March 23 (cont.)

Blendel..........Mr. Hardinge	Matilda..........Mrs. Marshall
Florestan..............Mr. Fox	Laurette........Mrs. Oldmixon
Guillot............Mr. Blissett	Julie.............Miss Hardinge
Old Matthew.......Mr. Warrell	Dorcas........Mrs. L'Estrange
William........Mr. T. Warrell	Collette........Miss L'Estrange

LAILSON'S CIRCUS

March 24   * The Provençal Sailors   Phila. Gaz.
                    The Two Brother Taylors
          * The Cooper, or the Tutor Outwitted—Francisqui

NEW THEATRE

March 26   Mrs. Oldmixon's Night   G. U. S.

He Would Be a Soldier

Col. Talbot........Mr. Warren	Caleb..............Mr. Bernard
Sir Oliver Oldstock.............	Charlotte...........Mrs. Merry
Mr. Harwood	Lady Oldstock....Mrs. Oldmixon
Capt. Crevelt.......Mr. Fennell	Harriet..........Mrs. Marshall
Mandeville.............Mr. Fox	Mrs. Wilkins......Mrs. Francis
Capt. Pierpoint....Mr. Marshall	Betty.............Mrs. Doctor
Wilkins............Mr. Taylor	Nancy.........Miss Milbourne

Cymon and Sylvia

Cymon..........Mrs. Marshall	Sylvia...........Mrs. Oldmixon
(first time, and for that night only)	Urganda..........Mrs. Warrell
Merlin............Mr. Marshall	Fatima............Mrs. Francis
Dorus.............Mr. Morris	1st Shepherdess...Miss Milbourne
Linco............Mr. Harwood	2nd Shepherdess..Miss L'Estrange
Damon........Mr. Warrell, Jr.	Dorcas............Mr. Bernard
Dorilas........Mr. T. Warrell	

LAILSON'S CIRCUS

March 27   The Two Brother Taylors   Phila. Gaz.
                    Mirza and Lindor

Principal parts by Sig. Francisqui, Mr. Douvilliers, Mrs. Rowson;
Negro dancers by Messrs. Sully, Dubois, Gourville, and Lapointe;
         Savage dancers by the rest of the company.

First appearance of Messrs. Dubois and Gourville.

1798

NEW THEATRE

March 28   Mr. Bernard's Night   G. U. S.

The Adopted Child

Cast as for Dec. 13, 1797, except:

Michael............Mr. Bernard   Flint..............Mr. Blissett
                                   (not mentioned before)

* The Prodigal—Waldron

Belmour............Mr. Fennell   Bargrave.............Mr. Fox
Courtney...........Mr. Wignell   Louisa.............Mrs. Merry

The Generous Tars   ....

Galleon............Mr. Francis   Other principal characters by Mr.
                                   Byrne, Mr. Warrell, Jr., Mr.
                                   T. Warrell, etc.

* The American in London ("Musical Entertainment")

Freedom...........Mr. Warren   Mrs. Manners......Mrs. Warrell
Pample..............Mr. Fox   Mrs. Prattle......Mrs. Oldmixon
Brush............Mr. Harwood   Mrs. Freedom....Miss L'Estrange
1st Servant........Mr. Lafferty   Maria...........Mrs. Marshall
Barney Boar.......Mr. Bernard

LAILSON'S CIRCUS

March 29   The American Heroine   Aurora

("Grand Historic and Military Pantomime—Ornamented with
Military Evolutions and Fights.")

Chief of Savages.............   4th Savage...........Mr. Sully
                Mr. Douvilliers   Inkle.......... ...Mr. Francisqui
Commandant of Soldiers........   Soldiers......By Supernumeraries
                Mr. Prouble   Indian Savages..Messrs. Rowson,
Lieutenant.......Mr. Gourville   Tompkins, Correy, Robertson,
1st Savage...........Mr. Sully   Keindry, and Bonnaux.
2nd Savage......Mr. Tompkins   The American Heroine..........
3rd Savage........Mr. Lapointe   Madame Douvilliers

First appearance of Messrs. Bonnaux, Keindry, Robertson, and J. Rowson.

Mr. Lailson printed the following notice:
"Mr. Lailson Respectfully informs the Public, that by a fatality of circumstances, he has not contributed this Season, as much to their amusement
as he originally intended; circumstances which were the immediate causes of
depriving his Circus of its wonted splendor and elegance, impeded his pay-

1798

ing a continual personal attention to its amusements. He has lately had the happiness of surmounting all the difficulties which paralized his exertions, and in future his whole attention will be directed to give to the unprecedented variety of amusements daily exhibited at his Circus, all the beauties of which they are susceptible. The Dresses and Decorations of which he, till now, was deprived, are in his possession, which enables him to entertain the Public in a manner congenial to his wishes, and worthy of its support.

"The Lights with which the Circus shall be illuminated, will not prove disagreeable, as heretofore, to the Spectators."

NEW THEATRE

March 30   Mr. Moreton's Night   G. U. S.

The Roman Father

Tullus Hostilius.....Mr. Warren	1st Citizen.......Mr. T. Warrell
Horatius...........Mr. Fennell	2nd Citizen.........Mr. Blissett
Publius Horatius...Mr. Marshall	3rd Citizen.........Mr. Hunter
Valerius..............Mr. Fox	Valeria.........Miss L'Estrange
Volscinius......Mr. Warrell, Jr.	Horatia.............Mrs. Merry
Vendicius.......Mr. T. Warrell	

* The Honest Thieves—Knight

Col. Careless........Mr. Wignell	Bailiffs......Messrs. Warrell and
Capt. Manly......Mr. Marshall	Hunter.
Mr. Story............Mr. Fox	Coachman..........Mr. Lafferty
Justice Day.........Mr. Bernard	Ruth............Mrs. Marshall
Obadiah..........Mr. Harwood	Arabella..........Mrs. Francis
Teague..........Mr. Hardinge	Mrs. Day.......Mrs. Oldmixon

LAILSON'S CIRCUS

March 31   The Death of Harlequin   Aurora

April 2   Aurora

"The Public are Respectfully informed that the Amusements at the Circus will be for this week only on MONDAY [April 2], WEDNESDAY [April 4], and SATURDAY [April 7]: in consequence of the Performance at the THEATRE, on the usual Evenings of Entertainments at the Circus." This notice appears till and including April 7.

April 4   See April 2.

NEW THEATRE

April 5   Mr. Fennell's Night   G. U. S.

King Lear

Lear..............Mr. Fennell	Edmund..........Mr. Marshall
Burgundy......Mr. Warrell, Jr.	Gentleman Usher....Mr. Francis

1798

April 5 (cont.)

Cornwall	Mr. Hardinge	Oldman	Mr. Hunter
Albany	Mr. Fox	Goneril	Mrs. Hardinge
Gloster	Mr. Warrell	Regan	Mrs. Francis
Kent	Mr. Warren	Arante	Miss L'Estrange
Edgar	Mr. Wignell	Cordelia	Mrs. Merry

The Drunken Provençal

Ivre	Mr. Byrne	Dickey Gossip	Mr. T. Warrell
Will	Mr. Warrell, Jr.	Susan	Miss Milbourne
Vicar	Sig. Doctor	Jenny	Mrs. Byrne
Moses	Mr. Blissett		

* The Advertisement, or A New Way to Get Married—Fennell

Alderman Goswell	Mr. Warren	Thomas	Mr. Blissett
Young Goswell	Mr. Bernard	Mrs. Courtney	Mrs. Francis
O'Trigger	Mr. Hardinge	Mrs. Snip	Mrs. L'Estrange
Peruque	Mr. Fox	Betty	Miss L'Estrange
Harry	Mr. Harwood	Kitty	Mrs. Doctor

LAILSON'S CIRCUS

April 7   See April 2.

Last night of a short season at Lailson's Circus from March 8 to April 7, 1798. See April 24 for reappearance of many of the circus performers.

New afterpieces: *The Cooper, The New Deserter, The Provençal Sailors, The Two Brother Taylors,* and *The Whims of Galatea.* Reappearing afterpieces: *The American Heroine, The Death of Harlequin, The Milliners, Mirza and Lindor.*

New performers: Mr. Bonnaux, Mrs. Correy (or Corry), Mr. Dubois, Mr. (or Sig.) Francisqui, Mr. Galton, Mr. Gourville, Mr. Keindry, Mr. Lapointe, Mr. Louisier, Mrs. "N. M.," Mr. Robertson, and Mr. J. Rowson. Reappearing performers: Mr. Correy (or Corry), Mr. and Mme. Douvilliers, Mr. Glaize (or Gleise), Mlle. Lailson, Mr. Pouble (or Prouble), Miss Robinson, Mrs. J. Rowson, Mr. Sully, and Mr. and Mrs. Tompkins (or Tomkins).

NEW THEATRE

April 7   Mr. Harwood's Night   G. U. S.

The Widow of Malabar

Raymond	Mr. Marshall	Young Bramin	Mr. Fennell
Albert	Mr. Fox	Narrien	Mr. Warrell, Jr.
Chief Bramin	Mr. Warren	Indimora	Mrs. Merry
2nd Bramin	Mr. Warrell	Fatima	Miss L'Estrange

1798

April 7 (cont.) * *The Humorist, or Who's Who?*—Cobb

Sir Anthony Halfwit..Mr. Francis
Frolic..............Mr. Warren
Blunt..............Mr. Blissett
Beaumont............Mr. Fox
William........Mr. T. Warrell

Dabble...........Mr. Harwood
Mrs. Mattador....Mrs. Oldmixon
Diana..........Miss L'Estrange
Jenny..............Mrs. Doctor
Mrs. Meddle.......Mrs. Francis

* *The Wandering Jew, or*
Love's Masquerade—Franklin

Sir Solomon Swallow...........
Mr. Warren
Major Atall.......Mr. Harwood
Capt. Marrall......Mr. Hardinge
Toby..............Mr. Blissett
Cook..............Mr. Warrell

Porter............Mr. Hunter
Lady Swallow....Mrs. Oldmixon
Camilla..........Mrs. Marshall
Lydia...........Miss L'Estrange
Susan.............Mrs. Doctor

April 9 — *The Shipwreck* — G. U. S.
Columbus

April 11 — Mr. Morris's Night — G. U. S.

* *The Italian Monk*—Boaden

Schedoni...........Mr. Fennell
Vivaldi...............Mr. Fox
Ansaldo...........Mr. Warren
Spalatro..........Mr. Wignell
Paulo...........Mr. Harwood
Carlo.........Mr. Warrell, Jr.
Stiletto...........Mr. Francis
Corvino...........Mr. Darley

1st Officer.........Mr. Warrell
Ellena Rosalba.......Mrs. Merry
Marchioness........Mrs. Morris
Olivia...........Mrs. Hardinge
Lady Abbess.....Mrs. L'Estrange
Fionesca..........Mrs. Marshall
Gradisca...........Mrs. Francis
Margaritone........Mrs. Doctor

The Register Office

("an interlude taken from the Farce of that name")

Neck or Nothing

Stockwell..........Mr. Warren
Sir Harry Harlowe..Mr. Morris
Slip..............Mr. Bernard
Martin..........Mr. Harwood

Belford........Mr. Warrell, Jr.
Mrs. Stockwell..Mrs. L'Estrange
Nancy..........Miss L'Estrange
Jenny..........(no name given)

April 13 — Mr. Francis's Night — G. U. S.

The Deserted Daughter

Mordent.........Mr. Marshall
Chevril..........Mr. Bernard
Lennox...............Mr. Fox
Hem.............Mr. Francis

Donald............Mr. Warren
Mrs. Sarsult........Mrs. Francis
Mrs. Enfield.....Mrs. L'Estrange
Joanna...........Mrs. Marshall

[364]

1798

April 13 (cont.)

Grime	Mr. Harwood	Betty	Mrs. Doctor
Clement	Mr. Warrell, Jr.	Lady Ann	Mrs. Merry

* *The Rival Harlequins*

April 14   Mr. and Mrs. Byrne's Night   G. U. S.

The Earl of Essex

Essex	Mr. Fennell	Rutland	Mrs. Merry
Southampton	Mr. Marshall	Nottingham	Mrs. Francis
Burleigh	Mr. Warren	Queen Elizabeth	Mrs. Morris
Lieut. of Tower	Mr. Warrell		

* *The Origin of Harlequin*

Harlequin	Mr. Byrne	Hope	Mrs. Francis
Pero	Mr. Doctor	Charity	Mrs. Hardinge
Pantaloon	Mr. Lavancy	Justice	Mrs. Morris
Beau	Mr. Jr. Warrell	Mercy	Mrs. Oldmixon
Gypsy King	Mr. Warren	Temperance	Miss L'Estrange
Columbine	Mrs. Byrne	Hymer	Master Byrne
Faith	Mrs. Warrell		

"In the course of the Pantomime Mr. Byrne will Fly from the back of the Gallery to the further end of the Stage."

First appearance of Master Byrne.

April 16   Mr. Marshall's Night   Aurora

The Belle's Stratagem

Doricourt	Mr. Bernard	Sir George Touchwood	
Hardy	Mr. Morris		Mr. Warren
Flutter	Mr. Marshall	Servant	Mr. Hunter
Courtall	Mr. Harwood	Letitia Hardy	Mrs. Marshall
Villers	Mr. Warrell, Jr.	Mrs. Rockett	Mrs. Oldmixon
Gibson	Mr. Warrell	Miss Ogle	Miss L'Estrange
Dick	Mr. Blissett	Kitty Willis	Mrs. Doctor
Saville	Mr. Fennell	Lady Touchwood	Mrs. Hardinge

The Sailor's Landlady

Jack	Mr. Warrell, Jr.	Landlady	Mrs. Doctor
Midshipman	Mr. T. Warrell	Orange Girl	Miss Milbourne
Ned Halyard	Mr. Marshall		

* *The Gentle Shepherd*—Ramsay

Sir Wm. Worthy	Mr. Warrell	Bauldy	Mr. Bernard
Patie	Mr. Marshall	Peggy	Mrs. Marshall

1798

April 16 (cont.)

Roger	Mr. Fox	Jenny	Mrs. Warrell
Symon	Mr. Francis	Madge	Mrs. L'Estrange
Claud	Mr. Warren	Maude	Mrs. Oldmixon

April 18   Mr. Warren's Night   G. U. S.

* Fatal Curiosity—Lillo

Wilmot	Mr. Fennell	Servant	Mr. Hunter
Young Wilmot	Mr. Fox	Agnes	Mrs. Merry
Eustace	Mr. Warrell	Charlotte	Mrs. Marshall
Randall	Mr. Warrell, Jr.	Maria	Miss L'Estrange

Dr. Last's Examination

[taken from Foote's Comedy of The Devil Upon Two Sticks]

Dr. Last	Mr. Bernard	Secretary	Mr. Warrell
Dr. Hellebore	Mr. Warren	Doctors	Messrs. Lavancy, Hunter, Lafferty, &c.

* The Man of Quality, or
A Trip to Scarborough—Sheridan (this cast in Aurora)

Lord Foppington	Mr. Bernard	Taylor	Mr. Warrell
Young Fashion	Mr. Wignell	Jeweller	Mr. Hunter
Col. Townly	Mr. Fox	Postillion	Mr. T. Warrell
Sir Tunbelly Clumsy	Mr. Warren	Servants	Mr. Lavancy, etc.
		Miss Hayden	Mrs. Marshall
Lory	Mr. Francis	Nurse	Mrs. Francis
La Varole	Mr. Blissett	Mrs. Coupler	Mrs. Doctor
Shoemaker	Mr. Warrell, Jr.		

April 20   Mr. and Miss Hardinge's Night   G. U. S.

The West Indian

Stockwell	Mr. Warren	Varland	Mr. Francis
Belcour	Mr. Bernard	Sailor	Mr. Blissett
Capt. Dudley	Mr. Fennell	Lady Rusport	Mrs. L'Estrange
Chas. Dudley	Mr. Marshall	Charlotte Rusport	Mrs. Marshall
Major O'Flaherty	Mr. Hardinge	Louisa Dudley	Mrs. Hardinge
Stukely	Mr. Farrell, Jr.	Mrs. Fulmer	Mrs. Francis
Fulmer	Mr. Harwood	Lucy	Miss Milbourne

The Prisoner

Marcos	Mr. Marshall	Narcisso	Master Warrell
Bernard	Mr. Fox	Clara	Mrs. Warrell
Pasqual	Mr. Darley	Theresa	Miss Milbourne
Roberto	Mr. Blissett	Nina	Mrs. Marshall
Lewis	Mr. Harwood	Juliana	Miss Hardinge

1798

April 21   Mr. Darley's Night   G. U. S.

Isabella

Cast as for Jan. 19, except:

Carlos	Mr. Fox	Belford	Mr. Warrell, Jr.
Villeroy	Mr. Wignell		

* *Marian* (comic opera)—Mrs. Brooke

Sir Henry	Mr. Darley, Jr.	Oliver	Mr. Warrell
Edward	Mr. Marshall	Marian	Mrs. Oldmixon
Robin	Mr. Francis	Patty Clover	Mrs. Marshall
Thomas	Mr. Darley	Peggy	Mrs. Warrell
William	Mr. Blissett	Fanny	Miss Milbourne
Jamie	Mr. Warren	Kitty	Mrs. Hunter

April 23   Mrs. Warrell's Night   Aurora

* *The Spectre, or The Castle of the Forest*

Ferrand	Mr. Fennell	1st Fisherman	Mr. Blissett
Edwy	Mr. Bernard	2nd Fisherman	Mr. Darley
Sebastian	Mr. Warren	3rd Fisherman	Mr. Warrell
Reminez	Mr. Fox	Athold	Mr. Marshall
O'Leary	Mr. Hardinge	Juletta	Mrs. Warrell
Francisco	Mr. Harwood	Necombo	Miss Milbourne
Carlos	Mr. Warrell, Jr.	Elvina	Mrs. Merry

The Children in the Wood

Cast as for Feb. 26, except:

Sir Rowland	Mr. Fox	Josephine	Mrs. Warrell
Oliver	Mr. Warrell, Jr.	Boy	Master H. Warrell

PANTHEON

April 24   G. U. S. and Phila. Gaz.

Mr. Chalmers presented An Olio, or *The Whim of the Moment* (including songs and acrobatics), comprising:

The Critic, Act I

Puff	Mr. Chalmers	Sneer	Mr. Frederick "(his first
Dangle	Mrs. Sully		appearance in Philadelphia)"
Mrs. Dangle	Mrs. Rowson		

"The Gentleman Jockey, or a Trip from New-Market"
from *Love à la Mode*

Beau Mordecai	Mr. Sully	Charlotte	"By a Young Lady of
Squire Groom	Mr. Chalmers		this city" (Miss Corry)

1798

April 24 (cont.)   *"The Seven Ages of Shakespeare,* from his
As You Like It"—Mr. Chalmers
* *The Vagaries*—"A Pantomime Sketch"

Harlequin	Mr. Chalmers	Clown	Mr. Sully
Farmer	Mr. Frederick	Colombine	Mrs. Rowson

First appearance of Miss Corry and Mr. Frederick.

This was the first of a number of scattered performances at the circuses and the Southwark Theatre between April 24 and June 8, 1798.

NEW THEATRE

April 25   Mr. Fox's Night   G. U. S.

The Italian Monk

Cast as for April 11.

Rosina

Belville	Mr. Marshall	2d Irishman	Mr. Blissett
Capt. Belville	Mr. Darley, Jr.	Rosina	Mrs. Warrell
William	Mr. Fox	Dorcas	Mrs. L'Estrange
Rustic	Mr. Warrell	Phoebe	Mrs. Oldmixon
1st Irishman	Mr. Warren		

April 27   Mrs. Francis's Night   G. U. S.

* *Tit for Tat*—Colman

Old Meanwell	Mr. Warren	Stripwell	Mr. Hardinge
Young Meanwell	Mr. Fox	Florinda	Mrs. Marshall
Villamour	Mr. Marshall	Letty	Mrs. Francis

* *The Scotch Ghost, or Fanny's Love*—Comic Scotch Ballet

Principal characters by Mr. and Mrs. Byrne, Mr. Francis, Mr. Warrell, Jr., Master Byrne, Mme. Harwood, and Miss Milbourne.

* *All in Good Humour*—Oulton

Squire Hairbrain	Mr. Bernard	Bellamy	Mr. Fox
Robin	Mr. Blissett	Mrs. Chagrin	Mrs. L'Estrange
Crop	Mr. Warrell, Jr.	Sophia	Miss L'Estrange
Chagrin	Mr. Francis	Dorothy	Mrs. Francis

* *The Death of General Wolfe* (serious pantomime)

General Wolfe	Mr. Marshall	Surgeon Adair	Mr. Darley
General Monckton	Mr. Hardinge	Grenadier	Mr. Warrell, Jr.
Brig. General Townshend		Indian Chief	Mr. Doctor
	Mr. Warren		

[368]

1798

April 27 (cont.)   *The Adventures of a Wit*

Trifle...........Mr. Harwood	Corinna..........Mrs. Marshall
Trip...............Mr. Blissett	Fillett.............Mrs. Francis
Old Squaretoes......Mr. Francis	

April 28   Mr. Blissett and Mrs. Bernard's Night   G. U. S.

The Busy Body

Marplot...........Mr. Bernard	Servants........Messrs. Hunter,
Sir George.........Mr. Fennell	Lavancy, &c.
Charles............Mr. Wignell	Miranda.........Mrs. Marshall
Sir Jealous Traffic...Mr. Francis	Isabinda........Miss L'Estrange
Whisper.......Mr. Warrell, Jr.	Patch...........Mrs. Oldmixon
Butler.............Mr. Warrell	Scentwell...........Mrs. Doctor
Sir Francis Gripe....Mr. Morris	

The Scotch Ghost

Cast as for April 27.

Love in a Camp

Marshall Fehrbellin.....Mr. Fox	Officer.............Mr. Warrell
Patrick...........Mr. Marshall	Rupert........Mr. Warrell, Jr.
Darby.............Mr. Bernard	Mable Flourish..Mrs. L'Estrange
Quin Odbody........Mr. Blissett	Norah............Mrs. Warrell
Father Luke.......Mr. Hardinge	Flora...........Miss Milbourne
Olmutz...........Mr. Warren	

PANTHEON

April 30   Mr. Sully's Benefit   G. U. S.

Mr. Sully announced that as he had been deprived of his situation and his benefit at the New Circus, he would "venture to put his name up" now— "with the assistance of Mr. Chalmers and others."

The variety show included: *The Tatler* (taken from *The Deuce is in Him*).

Dr. Prattle.......Mr. Chalmers	Belle..."By a Young Lady of this
Emily............Mrs. Rowson	City"

Linco's Travels

Linco...............Mr. Sully	Dorcas...........Mrs. Rowson
Damon..........Mr. Frederick	

The Power of Love, or The Vicissitudes of Fortune
(pantomime)

Harlequin...........Mr. Sully

[369]

1798

NEW THEATRE

May 1   *Isabella*   Aurora

"An occasional interlude consisting of Songs, Dances, and Spectacle"
—* *St. Tammany's Festival in the Temple of Liberty* [sic!]
The Padlock

May 2   Mr. Warrell and Mr. Warrell, Jr.'s Night   G. U. S.

Lionel and Clarissa

Lionel	Mr. Marshall	Harman	Mr. Fox
Col. Oldboy	Mr. Warren	Clarissa	Mrs. Warrell
Sir John Flowerdale	Mr. Fennell	Lady Oldboy	Mrs. L'Estrange
Jessamy	Mr. Bernard	Jenny	Miss Milbourne
Jenkin	Mr. Darley	Diana	Mrs. Oldmixon

* *Fortunatus, or Harlequin's Wishing Cup* (pantomime)

Harlequin	Mr. Warrell, Jr.	Shoe Black	Mr. Hunter
Sir Toby Tipple (Pantaloon)	Mr. Francis	Lads	Messrs. Lavancy, Warrell, M'Lane, Mersier, &c.
Jemmy Jumps	Mr. Byrne	Lasses	Mrs. Doctor, Mrs. Hunter, Mme. Harwood, &c.
Pero	Mr. Doctor	Fortune	Miss L'Estrange
Clown	Mr. Blissett	Columbine	Miss Milbourne
Barber	Mr. Lavancy	Fisher Women	Mrs. Hunter, Mme. Harwood, &c.
Lamp-Lighter	Mr. Fox		
Cobbler	Mr. Warrell		
Waiter	Mr. Johnstone		

First appearance of Messrs. Johnstone, M'Lane, and Mersier.

May 4   G. U. S.
Mr. Milbourne, Scene Painter, and Miss Milbourne's Night

The Grecian Daughter
The Death of General Wolfe
* *Harlequin Junior; or,*
The Magic Cestus (pantomime)—("part new and part compiled")

May 5   Aurora
"The last Night of the Company's Performing this Season"

Wives as they Were
St. Tammany's Festival

In the season from December 11, 1797, to May 5, 1798, these new plays
were produced: *Abroad and at Home, The Author, A Cure for the Heartache, Fatal Curiosity, Fenelon, The Italian Monk, The Shipwreck* (Colman), *The Spectre, Tancred and Sigismunda, A Trip to Scarborough, The
Will,* and *Wives as They Were.* New afterpieces: *The Adventures of a Wit,
The Advertisement, All in Good Humour, The American in London, The*

1798

Animated Statue, The Christmas Frolick, The Death of General Wolfe, Fortunatus, The Generous Tars, The Gentle Shepherd, Harlequin Junior, The Honest Thieves, Hunt the Slipper, Marian, The Origin of Harlequin, The Prodigal, Richard Cœur de Lion, The Rival Harlequins, The Scotch Ghost, St. Tammany's Festival, Tit for Tat, and *The Wandering Jew.*

Reappearing plays: *Alexander the Great, The Belle's Stratagem, The Busy Body, The Child of Nature, The Clandestine Marriage, Columbus, The Country Girl, The Deserted Daughter, The Earl of Essex, Everyone Has His Fault, The Fair Penitent, The Gamester, George Barnwell, The Grecian Daughter, Hamlet, Henry IV (part one), He Would Be a Soldier, The Highland Reel, Isabella, The Jew, King Lear, Macbeth, The Mountaineers, The Orphan, Othello, The Rage, The Revenge, Robin Hood, The Roman Father, Romeo and Juliet, The School for Scandal, Venice Preserved, The Way to Get Married, The West Indian,* and *The Widow of Malabar.* Reappearing afterpieces: *The Adopted Child, The Agreeable Surprize, Animal Magnetism, The Castle of Andalusia, The Children in the Wood, The Critic, Cymon and Sylvia, The Dead Alive, The Deaf Lover, The Death of Captain Cook, Dermont and Kathleen, The Deserter, The Devil to Pay, Dr. Last's Examination* (from *The Devil Upon Two Sticks*), *The Drunken Provençal, The Farmer, La Forêt Noire, The Guardian, Inkle and Yarico, The Irishman in London, The Irish Widow, The Liar, Lock and Key, Love in a Camp, The Lying Valet, The Midnight Hour, Oscar and Malvina, The Padlock, Peeping Tom of Coventry, The Poor Soldier, The Prisoner, The Prize, The Register Office, Robinson Crusoe, The Romp, Rosina, The Spoiled Child, The Sultan, Three Weeks after Marriage,* and *Two Strings to Your Bow.*

New actors: Miss Anderson, Mr. and Mrs. Bernard, Master Byrne, Mr., Mrs., and Miss Hardinge, Mrs. (or Mme.) Harwood, Mr. and Mrs. Hunter, Messrs. Johnstone, Lafferty, M'Lane, Matthew, Mersier, Mrs. Stuart, Mr. Taylor, and Mrs. Warren. Reappearing actors: Mr. Blissett, Mr. and Mrs. Byrne, Mr. Cooper, Mr. Darley, Mr. Darley, Jr., Sig. and Mrs. Doctor, Mr. Fennell, Mr. Fox, Mr. and Mrs. Francis, Mr. Harwood, Mr. Lavancy, Mrs., Miss and Master L'Estrange, Mr. and Mrs. Marshall, Mrs. Merry, Miss Milbourne, Mr. Moreton, Mr. and Mrs. Morris, Miss Oldfield, Mrs. Oldmixon, Mr. Sully, Mr. and Mrs. Warrell, Mr. Warrell, Jr., Masters H. and T. Warrell, Mr. Warren, and Mr. Wignell.

"NEW CIRCUS"—SOUTH FIFTH STREET (LAILSON'S)

| May 14 | Mrs. Douvillier's Benefit | Aurora |

A French opera—music by Sedaine—never in America

* The Deserter

| Alexis..............M. Estinval | Courchemin..........Mr. Fieron |
| (first time in America) | Jailor.............Mr. Marshall |

1798

May 14 (cont.)

Jean-Louis........Mr. Douvillier   Louisa............Miss Tesseire
Mont au Ciel........Mr. Pouble   Jennette........Mme. Bonneau
Bertrand..........M. Francisqui   Aunt..........Mme. Douvillier

* *The Death of Major André, and Arnold's Treachery,*
or West Point Preserved

Grand pantomime in 3 acts—"Composed by a Citizen of Philadelphia."

George Arthur........   John Poulding...Mr. Poignan[d]
(no name)   David Williams....Mr. Tompkins
André..........Mr. Douvillier   Isaac Vanvert........Mr. Moran
Servant............Mr. Ronald   Corporal............Mr. Glaise
Honoria........Mrs. Tompkins   American Soldiery.....
Sophia..........Mrs. Douvillier   Two Sailors..........(no name)
Arnold (the traitor)...........   General Washington..Mr. Pouble
Mr. Francisqui   La Fayette........Mr. Francisqui
Col. Thompson......Mr. Lousier

First appearance of Mme. Bonneau, M. Estinval, and Mr. Ronald.

May 18   Mr. Francisqui's Benefit   Aurora

"French Comedy"
* *The Generous Englishman*

James Splin.......Mr. Douvillier   Bailiff..........Mr. Francisqui
Laurent........Mr. D'Estinval   Theresa........Mrs. Harwood
Jacob..........Mrs. Douvillier

The Bird Catcher

Collars..........Mr. Francisqui   Rose............Mrs. Douvillier
Four Hunters..Mr. Tomkins, &c.   Shepherdesses..Mrs. Tompkins, &c

GRAND HISTORICAL PANTOMIME
(Never performed in America)

* *The Sufferings of the Maddison Family, or*
The Generous Indian

Maddison, the American Planter..   Tipperary..........Mr. Dubois
Mr. Pouble   American Officer.....Mr. Lousier
Miami, the Generous Indian.....   Mary............Mrs. Harwood
Mr. Francisqui   Mrs. Maddison...............
Osego..........Mr. Douvilliers   [Mrs.?] Douvilliers

"The subject of this Pantomime is taken from the Memoirs of a Mr. Maddison, an American Planter."

1798

RICKETTS' CIRCUS

May 21   Benefit of Mr. Tompkins   Aurora

The Sailor's Landlady
The Independence of America

"Splendid Historical National Pantomime"

NEW CIRCUS (LAILSON'S)

May 25   Miss Tesseire's Benefit   Aurora

(French Comic opera)

* *La Servante Maîtresse, or*
The Servant Girl turned Mistress

Pandolphe	M. Douvillier	Scatin	M. Lavancy
Zerbine	Miss Tessiere		

La Melomanie

Geronte	M. Fieron	A notary	M. Lavancy
Crispin	M. Douvillier	Eliza	Miss Tesseire
St. Real	Mr. Pouble	Lisette	Mme. Bonneau
Christante	M. Lavalette		

June 1   Mr. Douvillier's Night   Aurora

(The last Benefit This Season)

Grand FRENCH OPERA

* *Zemire and Azor*

Azor	Mr. Douvilliers	Zemire	Miss Tesseire
Sander	Mr. Fieron	Tisbe	Mrs. Bonceau
Aly	Mr. Francisqui	Fatima	Mrs. Douvilliers

"A Grand, Allegorical, Pantomimical Ballet, to be dedicated to

THE PRESIDENT OF THE UNITED STATES;

composed by Mr. Francisqui". . .

Principal parts by Mr. Francisqui, a Child ten years old, and Mrs. Douvilliers. (No title mentioned.)

OLD THEATRE (SOUTHWARK)

June 4   Mr. Chalmers Presents   G. U. S.

"*The Tablature, or Just in Time*" [Variety show]
with ("Pantomimical Sketch") *The Whim*

Harlequin	Mr. Chalmers	Clown	Mr. Lulsy
Pantaloon	Mr. Rowson	Columbine	Mrs. Rowson

First appearance of Mr. Lulsy.

[373]

1798

June 6   *"The Tablature"* and *The Whim*   G. U. S.

Cast as for June 4.

NEW CIRCUS (LAILSON'S)

June 8   Aurora

"BENEFICENCE"

Mr. L. Gleise's Night

(Heroic pantomime in 3 acts)

* *The Intrigues of Bayard*—Gleise

Bayard..........Mr. Douvilliers	Mrs. De Randon..............	
Alonzo...........Mr. Francisqui	Mrs. Douvilliers	
Don Pedro.........Mr. Lavancy	Goddess of Honor..............	
Don Alvaro.......Mr. Louzier	Mrs. Tompkins	
Lucinde...........Mrs. Rowson	Her Knight.........Mr. Pouble	

* *Billy the Oysterman, Coachman, and Chimney-Sweeper;*
or, The Lover Disguised (pantomime)—Gleise

Billy...............Mr. Gleise	Watchman........Mr. Tompkins
Mary.............Mrs. Rowson	John..............Mr. Lavancy
Father..........Mr. Francisqui	Piters..............Mr. Moran
Mother.........Mrs. Tompkins	

(Pantomimical Ballet)
* *The Garden of Love, or*
The Fountain of Youth—Gleise

"Principal Characters by Mrs. Douvilliers, Mr. Francisqui, a child 10 years of age, and Gleise. . . . in Character of Clown."

("These 3 pantomimes by Mr. Gleise, as also Songs.")

Scattered performances were given between April 24 and June 8, 1798, at Ricketts' Circus, The "New Circus" (Lailson's), and The "Old Theatre" (Southwark). New productions: *Billy the Oysterman, The Death of Major André, The Deserter, The Garden of Love, The Generous Englishman, The Intrigues of Bayard, La Melomanie, The Power of Love, La Servante Maitresse, The Sufferings of the Maddison Family, The Tablature, The Tatler, The Vagaries, The Whim,* and *Zemire and Azor.* Reappearing productions: *The Bird Catcher, The Critic* (first act, as part of an "Olio"), *The Independence of America, Love à la Mode* (in part), *Linco's Travels,* and *The Sailor's Landlady.*

New performers: Mme. Bonneau (or Bonceau), Miss Corry, Messrs. Estinval, Frederick, Lulsy, Ronald. Reappearing performers: Mr. Chalmers, Mr. Dubois, Mr. and Mme. Douvilliers, Messrs. Fieron, Francisqui, Glaize (or Gleise), Mrs. Harwood, Messrs. La Valet (Lavalette), Lavancey, Louisier,

1798

Marshall, Moran, Poignan[d], Pouble, Mr. and Mrs. J. Rowson, Mr. Sully, Mlle. Tesseire, and Mr. Tompkins.

July 8   Durang, Series I,
                                                                    Chap. XXXIII.

The dome of Lailson's Circus fell in, "crushing the interior completely."

1799

RICKETTS' CIRCUS

Jan. 9   Circus   Aurora
                        "Pantomimical Ballet"

Harvest Home, or The Reapers' Frolick

Lord of the Manor....Mr. Manly   Reapers........Messrs. Hutchins,
William...........Mr. Durang   Richardson
Albert............Mr. Ricketts   Phebe............Mrs. Rowson
Rustic..........Mr. F. Ricketts   Dorcas.............Mrs. Bird
Rosina.........Mrs. M'Donald

First night (for which anything dramatic was announced—as *circus* it opened on December 26, 1798) at Ricketts' Circus (sometime The Amphitheatre and the Pantheon), season from January 9 to March 23, 1799. First appearance of Mrs. Bird, Mr. Manly, Mrs. M'Donald, and Mr. Richardson.

Jan. 10   Benefit of Poor Families   Aurora

                              Circus

                   "The beautiful Pantomime, called
                            Rosina"

Jan. 12   Circus   Aurora
                        Don Juan (Pantomime)

Don Juan.........Mr. Durang   Commandant.......Mr. Freeland
Lover............Mr. Ricketts   Donna Anna.......Mrs. Rowson
Scarmouch.......Mr. F. Ricketts   Confidant.......Mrs. M'Donald

First appearance of Mr. Freeland.

Jan. 14   Circus   Aurora
                             Don Juan

                      Cast as for Jan. 12.

Jan. 16   Circus   Aurora
                        (Pantomimical Ballet)

    The Shepherd of the Alps, or the Woodman—Dibdin[?]

[375]

1799

| Jan. 21 | Circus | Aurora |

"The Two Misers, or The Merry Girl
by Mr. Durang, Mr. Thompson, and Mrs. Rowson"

First appearance of Mr. Thompson.

| Jan. 23 | Circus | Aurora |

"A Representation of the Death of Miss McCrea"

This seems to have been a "spectacle" of some sort.

| Jan. 26 | Circus | Aurora |

The Death of Miss McCrea

| Jan. 30 | Circus | Aurora |

The Devil on Two Sticks

| Feb. 2 | Circus | Aurora |

The Death of Captain Cook

Capt. Cook........Mr. Durang	Koah..........Mr. F. Ricketts
Lieutenant...........Mr. Bird	High Priest........Mr. Freeland
Perrea.............Mr. Ricketts	Emai.............Mrs. Rowson
Tarreboa........Mr. Tompkins	

First appearance of Mr. Bird.

NEW THEATRE

| Feb. 5 | | Aurora |

"The public are respectfully informed, that the entertainments
for the season will commence This Evening."

Secrets Worth Knowing—Morton

Greville..........Mr. Wignell	Nicholas...........Mr. Morris
Egerton...........Mr. Marshall	Valet..........Mr. Warrell, Jr.
Rostrum...........Mr. Bernard	Butler.............Mr. Hunter
Undermine.........Mr. Francis	Cook.........Mr. Warrell
April.............Mr. Warren	Mrs. Greville.......Mrs. Merry
Plethora.............Mr. Wood	Roza Sydney.....Miss L'Estrange
(Being his first appearance on this Stage)	Sally Downright.....Mrs. Morris

The Farmer

Dormant..........Mr. Warren	Councillor Flummery...........
Capt. Valentine....Mr. Marshall	Mr. Blissett
Jemmy Jumps......Mr. Bernard	Louisa.........Miss L'Estrange
Farmer.............Mr. Darley	Betty Blackberry..Mrs. Hardinge
Rundy.............Mr. Francis	Molly Maybush....Mrs. Warrell

1799

Feb. 5 (cont.)

Fairly............Mr. Warrell   Landlady...........Mrs. Doctor
Farmer Stubble......Mr. Hunter

First appearance of William B. Wood, later manager of the theatre.

First night of the season at the New Theatre (Chesnut Street) from February 5 to May 27, 1799.

Feb. 6   *Secrets Worth Knowing*   Daily Ad.

Cast as for Feb. 5.

Rosina

Belville...........Mr. Marshall   2d Irishman.........Mr. Hunter
Capt. Belville......Mr. Hardinge   Rosina...........Mrs. Marshall
William............Mr. Francis   Dorcas.............Mrs. Doctor
Rustic.............Mr. Warrell   Phoebe............Mrs. Warrell
1st Irishman.......Mr. Blissett

RICKETTS' CIRCUS

Feb. 7   Circus   Aurora

The Death of Major André (pantomime)

Commander in Chief............   Major André........Mr. Durang
                 Mr. Tompkins   Lieutenant........Mrs. Rowson
General Arnold [sic]...........   Van Voort...........Mr. Bird
                 Mr. F. Ricketts   Paulding...........Mr. Ricketts
Country Women..............   William..........Mr. Freeland
         Mrs. M'Donald, etc.

NEW THEATRE

Feb. 8   *Secrets Worth Knowing*   Daily Ad.

Cast as for Feb. 5.

The Children in the Wood

Sir Rowland.......Mr. Warren   Russian............Mr. Hunter
Lord Alford.......Mr. Hardinge   Helen...........Mrs. Hardinge
Walter...........Mr. Wignell   Josephine.........Mrs. Marshall
Apathy............Mr. Francis   Winifred...........Mrs. Doctor
Gabriel............Mr. Blissett   Boy.........Master H. Warrell
Oliver.........Mr. Warrell, Jr.   Girl.............Miss Hardinge

RICKETTS' CIRCUS

Feb. 9   Circus   Aurora

Death of Major André

Commander in Chief..........   Van Voort........Mr. Hutchins
                 Mr. Tompkins   William...........Mr. Durang

1799

Feb. 9 (cont.)

General Arnold.....Mr. Ricketts   Aides de Camp...............
Paulding........Mr. F. Ricketts   Mr. Tappen, Mrs. M'Donald

First appearance of Mr. Tappen.

NEW THEATRE

Feb. 11   *Knave or Not*—Holcroft   G. U. S.

Monrose..Mr. Downie (from the   Oliver..............Mr. Wood
  Theatres of Edinburgh and   Servant............Mr. Hunter
  Boston)   Aurelia.........Miss L'Estrange
Sir Job Ferment....Mr. Bernard   Susan...........Mrs. Marshall
Sir Guy Taunton....Mr. Warren   Lady Ferment.....Mrs. Morris
Mr. Taunton........Mr. Francis   Mrs. Clock.....Mrs. L'Estrange
Jonas..............Mr. Blissett   Poor Woman.......Mrs. Doctor
Mr. Quake.........Mr. Warrell   Maid Servant......Mrs. Hunter
Scribe..........Mr. Warrell, Jr.

Barnaby Brittle

Barnaby Brittle......Mr. Warren   Sir Peter Pride......Mr. Downie
Clodpole...........Mr. Blissett   Lovermore..........Mr. Wood
Jeremy............Mr. Francis   Jeffry.........Mr. Warrell, Jr.

(This cast in *Philadelphia Gazette*)

First appearance of Mr. Downie.

RICKETTS' CIRCUS

Feb. 12   Circus   Daily Ad.
The Valiant Soldier

Valiant Soldier......Mr. Durang   Lord of the Manor............
Thieves.......Mr. Ricketts, Mr.   Mr. Tompkins
  Hutchins   Adeline..........Mrs. Rowson
Lucas..........Mr. F. Ricketts   Milk Maid.....Mrs. M'Donald

NEW THEATRE

Feb. 13   *The Heir at Law*—Colman, Jr.   Phila. Gaz.

Daniel Dowlas......Mr. Warren   Kenrich.........Mr. Hardinge
  (Baron Dubberly)   John..............Mr. Hunter
Dick Dowlas........Mr. Blissett   Waiter...........Mr. Warrell
Dr. Panglos.......Mr. Wignell   Lady Duberly......Mrs. Morris
Henry Morland......Mr. Wood   Caroline Dormer...Mrs. Marshall
Stedfast..........Mr. Marshall   Cicely Homespun....Mrs. Merry
Zekiel Homespun....Mr. Bernard

1799

Feb. 13 (cont.)   *The Romp*

Watty Cockney	Mr. Francis	Richard	Mr. Hunter
Barnacle	Mr. Blissett	Priscilla Tomboy	Mrs. Marshall
Old Cockney	Mr. Warrell	Penelope	Mrs. Hunter
Capt. Sightly	Mr. Marshall	Mme. La Blond	Miss L'Estrange

RICKETTS' CIRCUS

Feb. 14   Mr. Tomkin's Benefit   Aurora

The Battle of the Kegs

"The memorable Historical Representation"
"With all the Scenery of the Delaware, Front-Street, wharves,
flat-men, corders, carters, citizens, &c."

Sir William Howe	Mr. Tompkins	Sentry	Mr. F. Ricketts
Sir William Erskine	Mr. Durang	Sailor	Mr. Ricketts
		Mrs. Loring	Mrs. Rowson

* Harlequin's Vagaries

Harlequin	Mr. Durang	Dunderpay Devil	Mr. Tompkins
Pantaloon	Mr. F. Ricketts	Columbine	Mrs. Rowson

(This cast in *Daily Advertiser*)

NEW THEATRE

Feb. 15   *The Chapter of Accidents*   G. U. S.

Governor Harcourt	Mr. Warren	Servant	Mr. Hunter
Lord Glenmore	Mr. Downie	Jacob Gawkey	Mr. Bernard
Woodville	Mr. Marshall	Cecilia	Mrs. Marshall
Grey	Mr. Wignell	Miss Mortimer	Miss L'Estrange
Vane	Mr. Francis	Mrs. Warner	Mrs. Doctor
Capt. Harcourt	Mr. Wood	Bridget	Mrs. Bernard

(This cast in *Philadelphia Gazette,* Feb. 14)

All in Good Humour

Squire Hairbrain	Mr. Hardinge	Bellamy	Mr. Wood
Robin	Mr. Blissett	Mrs. Chagrin	Mrs. L'Estrange
Crop	Mr. Warrell	Sophia	Miss L'Estrange
Chagrin	Mr. Francis	Dorothy	Mrs. Francis

(This cast in *Philadelphia Gazette,* Feb. 14)

The Death of General Wolfe

General Wolfe..... Mr. Marshall

[379]

1799

Feb. 18   *The Heir at Law*   G. U. S.

Cast as for Feb. 13.

* *Diana and Actaeon*—Byrne

"A new, grand, Pantomimical Ballet dance."

Feb. 20   *Henry IV, part I*   G. U. S.

King Henry......Mr. L'Estrange	Sir Walter Blunt..............
Prince of Wales...Mr. Hardinge	Mr. Warrell, Jr.
Worcester..........Mr. Downie	Pains..............Mr. Wignell
Northumberland.....Mr. Darley	Bardolph.........Mr. Milbourne
Hotspur....·.......Mr. Marshall	Francis.............Mr. Blissett
Sir Richard Vernon...Mr. Wood	Carriers......Messrs. Morris and
Westmoreland......Mr. Warrell	Francis
Falstaff...........Mr. Warren	Lady Percy......Miss L'Estrange
	Hostess Quickly..Mrs. L'Estrange

(This cast in *Daily Advertiser*)

Doctor Last's Examination

Dr. Last..........Mr. Bernard	Secretary..........Mr. Warrell
Dr. Hellebore......Mr. Wignell	Doctors..Messrs. Lavancey, Wood,
	Doctor, etc.

Diana and Actaeon

Feb. 22   Daily Ad.

"Poetic Recitations, Accompanied by Music vocal and instrumental.

IN HONOR OF THE DAY."

The Vocal parts by Mr. Darley and Mrs. Warrell

Bon Ton

Lord Minikin.......Mr. Downie	Davy..............Mr. Francis
Sir John Trotley.....Mr. Warren	Lady Minikin....Mrs. Hardinge
Colonel.............Mr. Wood	Gymp.............Mrs. Doctor
Jeramy........Mr. Warrell, Jr.	Miss Tittup.....Miss L'Estrange
Mignon............Mr. Blissett	

Columbus

Columbus.........Mr. Hardinge	Moscoso............Mr. Blissett
Alonzo............Mr. Marshall	Captain.............Mr. Wood
Harry Herbert......Mr. Wignell	Orozimbo.........Mr. Warren
Doctor Dolores.....Mr. Bernard	Solasco..........Mr. L'Estrange
Bribon.............Mr. Francis	Catalpo...........Mr. Warrell
Rolda.............Mr. Downie	Cora..............Mrs. Merry

[380]

1799

Feb. 22 (cont.)

Valverdo...........Mr. Morris   Nelti.............Mrs. Francis
Cuto.........Mr. Warrell, Jr.

"To conclude with a new additional scene, (written by a
member of the Legislature of the United States.)"

Feb. 23   *The Heir at Law*   G. U. S.

Cast as for Feb. 13—in *Phila. Gazette*

The Death of General Wolfe

General Wolfe.........Mr. Marshall

Feb. 25   * Cheap Living—Reynolds   Daily Ad.

Old Woodland......Mr. Warren   Thomas............Mr. Warrell
Young Woodland.....Mr. Wood   Sir Edward Bromly...........
Scatter...........Mr. Wignell   *Mrs. Marshall*
Spunge............Mr. Bernard   Mrs. Scatter......Mrs. Hardinge
Farmer Cole.......Mr. Blissett   Stella..........Mrs. L'Estrange
William...........Mr. Downie   Elinor Bromly......Mrs. Merry
Harry........Mr. Warrell, Jr.

All the World's a Stage

Sir Gilbert Pumpkin...........   Cymon...........Mr. Warrell
                Mr. Francis   Miss Bridget Pumpkin.........
Charles Stanley.....Mr. Downie   Mrs. L'Estrange
Harry Stukely.......Mr. Wood   Miss Kitty Sprightly...........
William......Master L'Estrange   Mrs. Bernard
Waiter.........Mr. Warrell, Jr.   Jane.............Mrs. Francis
Diggory...........Mr. Blissett

RICKETTS' CIRCUS

Feb. 26   Mrs. M'Donald's Benefit   G. U. S., Feb. 25.

Circus
"A pastoral Scotch Pantomime ballad, called
* *Jockey and Jenny.*"

A Harlequin Pantomime, called
* *The Shipwreck; or, Neptune's Favor*

NEW THEATRE

Feb. 27   *Cheap Living*   G. U. S.

Cast as for Feb. 25

Two Strings to Your Bow

Don Octavio..........Mr. Fox   Lazarillo..........Mr. Bernard

[381]

1799

RICKETTS' CIRCUS

Feb. 28   Mrs. J. Rowson's Night   Aurora

Circus
The Sailor's Landlady, or
Jack in Distress

Ned Halyard..Miss C [sic] "with   Jack...............Mr. Durang
the Song of 'America, Com-   Mrs. Casey........Mrs. Rowson
merce, and Freedom,' written   Sailor's Lasses, "by several young
by Mrs. Rowson"   ladies of Philadelphia."

*Harlequin Everywhere, or
What Does It Signify ("new Pantomime")
"Harlequin (being the first attempt of any female in America) . . .
Mrs. Rowson." (G. U. S., Feb. 28)

NEW THEATRE

March 1   *The Heir at Law*   Daily Ad.

Harlequin Shipwreck'd

RICKETTS' CIRCUS

March 2 Benefit of Mrs. M'Donald and Master Hutchins   Aurora

Circus
The Sailor's Landlady

Jack in Distress.....Mr. Durang   Mrs. Casey........Mr. Rowson
Ned Halyard.......Mr. Ricketts   Orange Girl......Mrs. Rowson

Harlequin Everywhere, or
What Does It Signify

NEW THEATRE

March 6   ** Duplicity—Holcroft*   Phila. Gaz.

Sir Hornet Armstrong..........   Servant..........Mr. Lavancey
Mr. Warren   Osborne..........Mr. Wignell
Sir Harry Portland.....Mr. Fox   Clara Forrester......Mrs. Merry
Squire Turnbull.....Mr. Bernard   Melissa.........Miss L'Estrange
Scrip.............Mr. Warrell   Barbara Turnbull...Mrs. Francis
Timid.............Mr. Francis

The Drunken Provençal
A Trip to Scarborough

[382]

1799

March 8   *The Grecian Daughter*   Daily Ad.

Dionysius...........Mr. Warren   Phocion..........Mr. Hardinge
Philotas...............Mr. Fox   Evander..........Mr. Wignell
Melanthon........Mr. Downie   Euphrasia..........Mrs. Merry

Richard Cœur de Lion

March 11   (Never Acted)   Daily Ad.

* A Wedding in Wales

Sir Owen Meredith..Mr. Francis   Boy............Miss Hardinge
Sir Griffith Price....Mr. Warren   Augusta Meredith..Mrs. Marshall
Lambton.........Mr. Marshall   Miss Winifred Price............
Somers...............Mr. Fox   Mrs. Francis
Llewelyn..........Mr. Wignell   Charlotte Belmont..............
Ambrose..........Mr. Bernard   Miss L'Estrange
Davy.............Mr. Blissett   Maria.............Mrs. Merry

The Farmer

Cast as for Feb. 5, except that Farmer Stubble is not mentioned

RICKETTS' CIRCUS

March 12   Aurora
(The circus had been closed for ten days while this was in preparation)

"A Magnificent Representation of the Siege of Gaza, Battle of
Arbela, and The Triumphal Entry of * *Alexander The Great* into
the City of Babylon."

NEW THEATRE

March 13   *A Wedding in Wales*   Daily Ad.
Cast as for March 11.

Lock and Key

Brummagem........Mr. Francis   Laura.........Mrs. Gillingham
Cheerly...............Mr. Fox   Fanny............Mrs. Warrell
Capt. Vain......Mr. Warrell, Jr.   Selina...........Mrs. Lavancy
Ralph...........Mr. Hardinge   Dolly..........Miss L'Estrange

Mrs. Gillingham (wife of the orchestra leader) had appeared as a singer
on December 5, 1796; this is her first appearance as an actress.

RICKETTS' CIRCUS

March 14   *Alexander the Great*   Aurora
(as on March 12)
[383]

1799

NEW THEATRE

March 15   *The Deserted Daughter*   Daily Ad.

Mordent..........Mr. Marshall   Donald............Mr. Warren
Chevril...........Mr. Bernard   Joanna..........Mrs. Marshall
Lenox............Mr. Downie   Mrs. Sarsnet......Mrs. Francis
Hem..............Mr. Francis   Mrs. Enfield.......Mrs. Doctor
Grime............Mr. Blissett   Betty.............Mrs. Hunter
Clement.......Mr. Warrell, Jr.   Lady Ann........Mrs. Hardinge

The Deuce is in Him

Col. Tamper......Mr. Hardinge   Emily............Mrs. Hardinge
Major Belford.....Mr. Downie   Bell.............Mrs. Bernard
Dr. Prattle........Mr. Bernard   Florival...........Mrs. Francis

This was probably postponed to March 16—the same bill reappears.

March 16   ("Not acted this season")   Daily Ad.

The Deserted Daughter

Cast as for March 15

The Deuce is in Him

Cast as for March 15

This may have been a postponement from March 15.

March 18   *A Wedding in Wales*   Aurora

Cast as for March 11.

Miss in Her Teens

Capt. Loveit..........Mr. Fox   Tag..............Mrs. Francis
Fribble............Mr. Bernard   Miss Biddy Bellair...Miss Arnold
Capt. Flash........Mr. Wignell   "(from   the   Charleston
Puff..............Mr. Morris   theatre, being her first ap-
Jasper.............Mr. Francis   pearance on this stage)"

RICKETTS' CIRCUS

March 19   "Third and Last Time"   Aurora

Alexander the Great

NEW THEATRE

March 20   *The Grecian Daughter*   G. U. S.

Cast as for March 8, with addition of:

Arcas..........Mr. Warrell, Jr.   Greek Herald........Mr. Wood
Calippus..........,...Mr. Warrell   Erixene........Miss L'Estrange

[384]

1799

March 20 (cont.)   *The Constellation, or a Wreath for American Tars*

Drag..............Mr. Warren		2d Sailor..............Mr. Fox
Jack Heart-Oak....Mr. Bernard		3d Sailor..........Mr. Warrell
Buchram...........Mr. Blissett		Mrs. Drag..........Mr. Francis
1st Sailor...........Mr. Darley		Nancy..........Miss L'Estrange

"With a representation of the Chase and Action between The
Constellation and L'Insurgente Frigates."

March 21   *The Mountaineers*   G. U. S.
                            The Constellation

Cast as for March 20.

RICKETTS' CIRCUS

March 21   Circus   Aurora
                    Oscar and Malvina

NEW THEATRE

March 23   *The Grecian Daughter*   G. U. S.

Cast as for March 8.

The Spoiled Child

Little Pickle (with songs)....Miss Arnold

RICKETTS' CIRCUS

Circus
Oscar and Malvina

During the dramatic season at Ricketts' Circus from January 9 to March 23,
1799, these new productions were given: *Alexander the Great* ("a Magnificent
Representation"—not the tragedy), *The Battle of the Kegs, The Death of
Miss McCrea, Harlequin Everywhere; or What Does it Signify, Harlequin's
Vagaries, The Harvest Home, Jockey and Jenny, Rosina* (pantomime), *The
Shepherd of the Alps,* and *The Shipwreck; or Neptune's Favor* (pantomime).
Reappearing productions: *The Death of Major André, The Devil Upon Two
Sticks, Don Juan, Oscar and Malvina, The Sailor's Landlady,* and *The
Valiant Soldier.*

New performers: Mr. and Mrs. Bird, Mr. Freeland, Mr. Manly, Mrs.
M'Donald, Mr. Richardson, Mr. Tappen, and Mr. Thompson. Reappearing
performers: Mr. Durang, Mr. (or Master) Hutchins, Mr. F. Ricketts, Mr.
J. B. Ricketts, and Mr. and Mrs. J. Rowson.

1799

NEW THEATRE

March 25   *Jane Shore*   G. U. S.

Duke of Gloster..Mr. L'Estrange   Belmour............Mr. Downie
Lord Hastings.....Mr. Marshall   Dumont...........Mr. Warren
Catesby.............Mr. Wood   Earl of Derby......Mr. Francis
Sir Richard Ratcliffe............   Alicia.............Mrs. Merry
          Mr. Warrell   Jane Shore.......Mrs. Hardinge

The Constellation

March 27   *The Dramatist*   Phila. Gaz.

Lord Scratch........Mr. Warren   Vapid.............Mr. Bernard
Neville.............Mr. Wood   Servant............Mr. Doctor
Floriville..........Mr. Marshall   Miss Courtney......Mrs. Francis
Willoughby.........Mr. Downie   Lady Waitfort...Mrs. L'Estrange
Ennui..............Mr. Francis   Letty..........Miss L'Estrange
Peter..........Mr. Warrell, Jr.   Marianne........Mrs. Marshall

Harlequin's Invasion

March 29   *Every One Has His Fault*   Phila. Gaz., March 28

Lord Norland......Mr. Downie   Porter.............Mr. Warrell
Sir Robert Ramble..Mr. Bernard   Lady Eleanor Irwin..Mrs. Merry
Mr. Solus...........Mr. Morris   Mrs. Placid........Mrs. Francis
Mr. Harmony......Mr. Warren   Miss Spinster.......Mrs. Doctor
Capt. Irwin........Mr. Marshall   Miss Wooburn....Mrs. Hardinge
Mr. Placid..........Mr. Wood   Edward..........Miss Hardinge
Hammond......Mr. Warrell, Jr.

* Botheration—Oulton

Dr. Wisepate........Mr. Francis   Thady O'Blarney..Mr. Hardinge
Jack Hopeful...........Mr. Fox   Lady Apes.........Mrs. Francis
Mr. Varnish.......Mr. Downie   Mrs. Varnish.......Mr. Bernard
Robert............Mr. Blissett   Rose..........Miss L'Estrange

March 30   *Romeo and Juliet*   Phila. Gaz.
          The Constellation

April 1   Benefit of Mrs. Merry   G. U. S.

* The Stranger—Dunlap

The Stranger.......Mr. Wignell   William.........Master Harris
Count Wintersen....Mr. Downie   Children.....Master H. Warrell,
Baron Steinfort....Mr. Marshall   Miss Hardinge
Solomon...........Mr. Francis   Mrs. Haller........Mrs. Merry

[386]

1799

April 1 (cont.)

Peter	Mr. Blissett	Countess Wintersen	
Francis	Mr. Fox		Mrs. Hardinge
Old Man	Mr. Morris	Ann	Mrs. Francis

Dermot and Kathleen

Dermot	Mr. Byrne	Kathleen	Mrs. Byrne

The Adopted Child

Sir Bertrand	Mr. Warren	Boy (The Adopted Child with	
Le Sage	Mr. Darley	songs)	Miss Arnold
Record	Mr. Francis	Clara	Mrs. Warrell
Michael	Mr. Bernard	Nelly	Mrs. Hardinge
Spruce	Mr. Warrell, Jr.	Lucy	Mrs. Francis

April 3   Benefit of Mrs. Marshall   G. U. S.

* He's Much to Blame—Fenwick or Holcroft
* American True Blue, or
The Naval Procession
"An Occasional Interlude of Song, Dialogue, and Dance"
The Wedding Day

April 5   Benefit of Mr. Bernard   G. U. S.

* The Mysterious Marriage—Miss Lee

Count Roselva	Mr. Warren	Physician	Mr. Warrell
Lord Albert	Mr. Marshall	Matthias	Mr. Blissett
Segesmond	Mr. Wood	Uberto	Mr. Bernard
Prisoner	Mr. Wignell	Countess of Roselva	Mrs. Merry
Rodolphus	Mr. Downie	Theresa	Miss L'Estrange
Osmond	Mr. Fox	Constantia	Mrs. Marshall

"The History of John Gilpin, The Linen Draper. Shewing how he went
farther than he intended and came home safe at last."

Thomas and Sally

Thomas	Mr. Darley	Sally	Mrs. Warrell
Squire	Mr. Fox	Dorcas	Mrs. Francis

* Rival Soldiers—O'Keeffe

Capt. Cruizer	Mr. Downie	Sinclair	Mr. Hardinge
Lenox	Mr. Marshall	Nipperken	Mr. Bernard
Major Tactic	Mr. Darley	Corporal	Mr. Warrell, Jr.

[387]

1799

| April 6 | Benefit of Mr. Byrne | G. U. S. |

Dermot and Kathleen

Dermot..............Mr. Byrne   Kathleen...........Mrs. Byrne

The Disbanded Officer

Col. Holberg...........Mr. Fox
Paul Warmans......Mr. Wignell
Katzenbuckle........Mr. Francis
Roko..............Mr. Bernard
King's Messenger....Mr. Warrell
Boy.........Master L'Estrange

Count Bellin.......Mr. Marshall
Baroness of Bruschal............
           Mrs. Marshall
Lisetta.............Mrs. Francis
Lady in Mourning............
         Miss L'Estrange

"New Historical Pantomime"
* *William* Tell—Byrne

Wm. Tell..........Mr. Byrne
Tell's Wife.........Mrs. Byrne
Young Tell......Master Byrne

Tell's Friend........Mr. Francis
Tyrant............Mr. Downie
Tyrant's party..Messrs, Lavancy,
Gibbons, L'Estrange, Mercer, &c.

| April 8 | Mrs. Byrne's Night | Aurora |

The Beggar's Opera

Peachum...........Mr. Warren
Lockit..............Mr. Francis
Macheath.........Mr. Marshall
Fitch..............Mr. Blissett
Mat o'Mint........Mr. Darley
Ben Budge............Mr. Fox
Nimming Ned...Mr. Warrell, Jr.
Harry Paddington...Mr. Warrell
Wat Drearey.......Mr. Doctor

Jemmy Twitcher....Mr. Lavancy
Robin of Bagshot......Mr. Wood
Mrs. Peachum......Mrs. Morris
Polly...........Mrs. Marshall
Lucy.............Mrs. Warrell
Mrs. Coaxer.......Mrs. Hunter
Mrs. Vixen........Mrs. Lavancy
Mrs. Slamakin...Miss L'Estrange
Molly Brazen.......Mrs. Doctor

The Spoiled Child

Little Pickle........Miss Arnold
Old Pickle.........Mr. Warren
Tag..............Mr. Francis
John..............Mr. Blissett
Thomas...........Mr. Doctor

Maria..........Miss L'Estrange
Miss Pickle.....Mrs. L'Estrange
Margery..........Mrs. Doctor
Susan.............Mrs. Bernard

"Grand historical PANTOMIME"
* *The Battle of Trenton, and Death of General Mercer*

General Mercer.....Mr. Downie
Old Soldier.......Mr. Milbourne

Ladies and Lasses...Mrs. Doctor,
Mrs. Stuart, Mrs. Hunter,

1799

April 8 (cont.)

Old Soldier's Son.....Mr. Byrne
Officers....Messrs. Francis, War-
              rell, etc.
General.......Mr. Warrell, Jr.

Mrs. Warren, Mrs. Byrne, and
  Miss L'Estrange
Officers........Messrs. Lavancy,
              Doctor, &c.

First appearance of Mrs. Lavancey.

April 10   Mrs. Morris's Benefit   Daily Ad.
                              The Stranger
                          Cymon and Sylvia

April 12   Mr. Marshall's Benefit   G. U. S.
                          The Conscious Lovers

Sir John Bevil......Mr. Downie   Daniel.............Mr. Blissett
Mr. Sealand.......Mr. Warren   Mrs. Sealand.......Mrs. Doctor
Bevil, Jr..........Mr. Marshall   Isabella...........Mrs. Hunter
Myrtle...............Mr. Fox   Lucinda........Mrs. L'Estrange
Cimberton........Mr. Wignell   Phillis.............Mrs. Francis
Humphrey.........Mr. Warrell   Indiana...........Mrs. Merry
Tom.............Mr. Bernard

Highland Festivity

Sandy...............Mr. Byrne   Father Gibby........Mr. Blissett
Jamie.........Mr. Warrell, Jr.   Poggie.............Miss Arnold
Mother Gibby......Mr. Gibbons   Annie..............Mrs. Byrne
Young Pedlar......Master Byrne

The Rival Soldiers

Cast as for April 5, except:

Lenox......Mr. Fox

April 13   Mr. Francis's Benefit   G. U. S.
                       * *False and True*—Moultru

Count Benini.......Mr. Francis   O'Raparty........Mr. Hardinge
Marquis Caliari.......Mr. Fox   Nicolo............Mr. Wignell
Count Florenzi.......Mr. Wood   1st Assassin.....Mr. Warrell, Jr.
Lealto............Mr. Bernard   Juliana............Mrs. Merry
Lupo.............Mr. Warrell   Lauretta..........Miss Arnold
Thomaso..........Mr. Warren   Marchese Veteria....Mrs. Francis
Malivoli..........Mr. Downie   Janetta...........Mrs. Warrell

[389]

1799

April 13 (cont.)   "New Pantomimic Olio"
* *The Arabs of the Desert; or,*
Harlequin's Flight from Egypt

Mustapho Lightfootero (or Harle-
quin Turk)...............
Mr. Francis
Mahmond (Father of Columbine)
Mr. Lavancy

Queronibus (or Pero à la Turque).
Mr. Doctor
Zobeide (or Columbine à la
Turque). Mrs. Francis

April 15   Mr. Warren's Benefit   Daily Ad.

* *Mysteries of the Castle*—Andrews

Hilario	Mr. Bernard	Sergeant	Mr. Warrell
Carlos	Mr. Marshall	Capt. of Vessel	Mr. Doctor
Fractioso	Mr. Warren	Anthonio	Mr. Lavancy
Count Montoni	Mr. Downie	Julia	Mrs. Merry
Montaubun	Mr. Darley	Constantia	Mrs. Warrell
Bernardo	Mr. Milbourne	Annette	Miss L'Estrange
Cloddy	Mr. Blissett	Sicilian Girls	Mrs. Gillingham,
Valoury	Mr. Fox		Mrs. Lavancy, Mrs. Warren,
Fisherman	Mr. Morris		Miss Arnold, &c.
Centinel	Mr. Warrell, Jr.		

* *Blunders Repaired*—"Written by a citizen of Philadelphia (never acted
before)"

Tully O'Neal	Mr. Hardinge	Julia	Miss L'Estrange
Capt. Sinclair	Mr. Wood	Nannette	Miss Arnold
Col. Frankly	Mr. Downie		

"An Epilogue, in the Character of Sir John Falstaff, to be spoken by
Mr. Warren."
The Constellation
Drag.....Mr. Warren

April 17   Benefit of Mr., Mrs., and Miss Hardinge   Daily Ad.
* *Life Vagaries, or*
Innocence Protected—O'Keeffe

Lord Terrendal	Mr. Downie	Waiter	Mr. Warrell, Jr.
Lord Arthur	Mr. Bernard	Tradesmen	Messrs. Doctor and
Sir Hans Burges	Mr. Warren		Lavancy
Dickens	Mr. Francis	Lady Terrendal	Mrs. Merry
George Burges	Mr. Wignell	Augusta	Mrs. Hardinge
Timolin	Mr. Hardinge	Fanny	Miss L'Estrange
L'Oerllet	Mr. Fox	Miss Clare	Mrs. Gillingham
Robin	Mr. Blissett	Landlady	Mrs. Doctor
Coachman	Mr. Warrell		

1799

April 17 (cont.)

"End of the play an EPILOGUE, Written for the occasion, by a gentleman of Philadelphia, to be spoken by Miss Hardinge."

The Poor Soldier

Capt. Fitzroy.......Mr. Darley	Bagatelle.........Mr. Marshall
Father Luke........Mr. Warren	Boy...........Master Warrell
Dermot..............Mr. Fox	Norah.............Miss Arnold
Patrick..........Mr. Hardinge	Kathleen.........Mrs. Warrell
Darby............Mr. Wignell	

April 19   Mr. Darley's Benefit   G. U. S.

The Natural Son
The Castle of Andalusia

April 20   Mrs. Warrell's Benefit   Daily Ad.

Wives as They Were

Sir Wm. Dorrillon..Mr. Wignell	Oliver.............Mr. Blissett
Lord Priory........Mr. Warren	James........Master L'Estrange
Sir George Evelyn......Mr. Fox	Miss Dorrillon......Mrs. Merry
Mr. Norberry.......Mr. Downie	Lady Mary Raffle...Mrs. Francis
Bronzely..........Mr. Bernard	Lady Priory.......Mrs. Warrell
Nabson...........Mr. Warrell	House-keeper........Mrs. Doctor

The Sailor's Landlady

Jack..........Mr. Warrell, Jr.	Lasses.......Mrs. Warren, Mrs.
Ned Halyard..........Mr. Fox	Hunter, Mrs. Stuart, etc.
Sailors........Messrs. Lavancy,	Landlady..........Mrs. Doctor
Gibbons, etc.	Orange Girl........Mrs. Byrne

Tom Thumb the Great

Tom Thumb.....Master Warrell	Merlin & Ghost
King Arthur........Mr. Blissett	of Gaffer Thumb } Mr. Darley
Lord Grizzle......Mr. Marshall	Princess Huncamunca..........
Noodle............Mr. Francis	Miss L'Estrange
Doodle........Mr. Warrell, Jr.	Mustachia.........Mrs. Doctor
Queen Dollalollah..Mrs. Warrell	Glumdalca........Mr. Warren

April 22   Mr. Fox's Benefit   G. U. S.

He Would Be a Soldier
The Padlock

1799

April 24   Mr. Francis's Benefit   Daily Ad.

"Not acted these 14 years"

Edward and Eleonora

Edward...........Mr. Wignell   Selim.............Mr. Marshall
Earl of Gloster.....Mr. Warren   Officer.............Mr. Warrell
Theald...........Mr. Downie   Eleonora..........Mrs. Merry
Assassin........Mr. Warrell, Jr.   Daraza...........Mrs. Morris

* The Catch Club; or The Sons of Anacreon

(A Musical Interlude)

President..........Mr. Marshall   Harmonics..Messrs. Darley, Gill-
Sr. Vice President...Mr. Bernard   ingham, Francis, Warren, Fox,
Jr. Vice President..Mr. Hardinge   Warrell, Blissett, Warrell, Jr.

The Old Maid

Clerimont..........Mr. Bernard   Miss Harlow.......Mrs. Francis
Capt. Cape.........Mr. Morris   Mrs. Harlow.....Mrs. Hardinge
Mr. Harlow..........Mr. Fox   Trifle.............Mrs. Doctor
Footman...........Mr. Doctor

April 26   Messrs. Blissett & Downie's Benefit   G. U. S.

* The Robbers (taken from Schiller)

Maximilian, Count de Moor.....   Herman...........Mr. Downie
                 Mr. Wignell   Schusterle.........Mr. Blissett
Charles de Moor...Mr. Marshall   Razman...........Mr. Warrell
Francis de Moor.......Mr. Fox   Commissary........Mr. Darley
Spiegelberg.........Mr. Francis   Kozinski.........Mr. Hardinge
Switzer...........Mr. Warren   Amelia.............Mrs. Merry
Grim.........Mr. Warrell, Jr.   Robbers..Messrs. Doctor, Lavancy,
Roller............Mr. Bernard   &c.

The Midnight Hour

Marquis...........Mr. Downie   Ambrose..........Mr. Warrell
General...........Mr. Warren   Julia..........Miss L'Estrange
Sebastian..........Mr. Francis   Cecily............Mrs. Doctor
Nicholas..........Mr. Blissett   Flora.............Mrs. Francis
Matthias......Mr. Warrell, Jr.

April 27   "Miss L'Estrange and Mr. L'Estrange's (Prompter's)   G. U. S.
                        BENEFIT"

The Stranger

Cast as for April 1, except:

Countess Wintersen.............Miss L'Estrange

[392]

1799

April 27 (cont.) *All the World's a Stage*

Cast as for Feb. 25, except:

Harry Stukely..........Mr. Fox   Miss Kitty Sprightly............
Miss Bridget Pumpkin..........   Miss L'Estrange
        Mrs. Doctor

April 29   Benefit of Miss Arnold and Mr. Warrell, Jr.   Daily Ad.

The Highland Reel

Laird of Col.......Mr. Downie   Capt. Dash.............Mr. Fox
Laird of Raasay.....Mr. Warrell   Sergeant Jock........Mr. Darley
M'Gilpin...........Mr. Warren   Apie...............Mr. Doctor
Sandy............Mr. Marshall   Benin........Master L'Estrange
Charley........Mr. Warrell, Jr.   Moggy M'Gilpin....Miss Arnold
Shelty.............Mr. Bernard   Jenny............Mrs. Warrell
Crowdy...........Mr. Blissett

* *The Magic Fire* (new pantomime)

Harlequin.......Mr. Warrell, Jr.   Tinker.............Mr. Gibbons
Pantaloon.........Mr. Lavancy   Columbine...........Mrs. Byrne
Lord Lofty........Mr. Downie   King of the Gypsies..Mr. Warrell
Piero.............Mr. Doctor

May 1   Mr. Morris's Benefit   Daily Ad.

"Never Acted in America"

* *False Impressions*—Cumberland

Sir Oliver Monbrath.Mr. Warren   Jack.........Master L'Estrange
Algernon.............Mr. Fox   Frank.............Mr. Warrell
Scud.............Mr. Bernard   Lady Cypress.......Mrs. Morris
Earling...........Mr. Wignell   Emily Fitzallan......Mrs. Merry
Simon Single........Mr. Morris   Jenny Scud........Mrs. Francis
Farmer Gawdry.....Mr. Downie   Mrs. Buchran.......Mrs. Doctor
Isaac..............Mr. Blissett   Rachael Williams.Miss L'Estrange
Peter..........Mr. Warrell, Jr.

The Catch Club

Cast as for April 24

Love à la Mode

Sir Theodore Goodchild........   Sir Archy M'Sarcasm.Mr. Morris
       Mr. Downie   Squire Groom......Mr. Marshall
Sir Callaghan O'Brallaghan......   Beau Mordecai.......Mr. Francis
       Mr. Hardinge   The Lady.......Miss L'Estrange

[393]

1799

May 3   Mrs. Bernard's and Mr. Doctor's Benefit   Daily Ad.

The Way to Get Married

Toby Allspice........Mr. Francis   Julia Faulkner.......Mrs. Merry
Tangent...........Mr. Bernard   Miss Allspice.......Mrs. Francis
Caustic...........Mr. Warren   Lady Sorrell........Mrs. Doctor
Dick Dashall.......Mr. Wignell

The Catch Club

Cast as for April 24.

The Author

Mr. Cape.........Mr. Wignell   Poor Beckey.......Mrs. Bernard
Cadwallader........Mr. Bernard

May 4   Benefit of Mr. Wells, Box Book-Keeper   Daily Ad.

The Gamester

Beverly..........Mr. Marshall   Dawson........Mr. Warrell, Jr.
Stukely...........Mr. Warren   Mrs. Beverly.......Mrs. Merry
Lewson..........Mr. Hardinge   Charlotte..........Mrs. Francis
Jarvis.............Mr. Morris   Lucy.............Mrs. Doctor
Bates.............Mr. Downie

The Agreeable Surprize

Sir Felix Friendly....Mr. Warren   Lingo.............Mr. Bernard
Compton...........Mr. Darley   Laura............Mrs. Warrell
Eugene........Mr. Warrell, Jr.   Mrs. Cheshire.......Mrs. Doctor
Chicane..........Mr. Warrell   Cowslip........Miss L'Estrange
John...............Mr. Fox   Fringe............Mrs. Hunter
Thomas..........Mr. Blissett

May 6   Benefit of Mr. Marshall and Mr. Warren   G. U. S.

The Heir at Law

Cast as for Feb. 13, except:

Dick Dowlass.........Mr. Fox   John..............Mr. Doctor
Henry Morland.....Mr. Downie   Caroline Dormer.Miss L'Estrange
and in addition:

Waiter at the Blue Boar.........Mr. Warrell, Jr.

The Catch Club
The Critic

(Messrs. Marshall and Warren had "failed in their former benefits.")

1799

May 8   "Widows' Night"   Phila. Gaz.

Benefit of the Widows Hunter, Gray, and Saville

Miss in Her Teens

Capt. Loveit	Mr. Fox	Jasper	Mr. Warrell, Jr.
Fribble	Mr. Bernard	Tag	Mr. Francis
Capt. Flash	Mr. Wignell	Miss Biddy Bellair	Miss Arnold
Puff	Mr. Morris		

Columbus

May 10   Mr. Gillingham's Benefit   Phila. Gaz.

(Leader of the Orchestra)

The Child of Nature

Marquis of Almanza	Mr. Wignell	Grenada	Mr. Warrell, Jr.
Count Valentia	Mr. Bernard	1st Peasant	Mr. Marshall
Duke Mercia	Mr. Warren	Marchioness Merida	Mrs. Morris
Seville	Mr. Warrell	Amanthis	Mrs. Merry

The Scotch Ghost

Principal Characters by Mr. and Mrs. Byrne, Mr. Francis, Mr. Warrell, Jr., Master Byrne, Mrs. Doctor.

An Olio—of recitation and Music

May 11   Benefit of Mr. and Mrs. Warrell   Aurora

(Mrs. Warrell had "fallen short of the charge" in her previous night. Miss Broadhurst had promised to help her tonight.)

The Roman Father

Horatius...........Mr. Warren   Horatia.............Mrs. Merry

"The favorite SONG, of 'SWEET ECHO,' By Mrs. Warrell,

Echoed by Miss Broadhurst."

The Deserter

Louisa "(for that Night only, being her second appearance on this stage these 3 years)"........ Miss Broadhurst		Henry	Mr. Marshall
		Jenny	Mrs. Warrell

May 13   *The Stranger*   Daily Ad.
         The Constellation

[395]

1799

May 15   *Tancred and Sigismunda*   G. U. S.

Tancred......"by a young gentle- man, being his first appear- ance" [Mr. Cain]	Officer.............Mr. Warrell
	Guards.........Messrs. Lavancy, Doctor, &c.
Earl Osmond.......Mr. Marshall	Laura..........Miss L'Estrange
Siffredi.............Mr. Warren	Sigismunda..........Mrs. Merry
Rodolpho.......Mr. Warrell, Jr.	

The Shipwreck

Selwyn.........Mr. Warrell, Jr.	Dick..................Mr. Fox
Harry Hawser.....Mr. Hardinge	Angelica........Miss L'Estrange
Michael Goto.......Mr. Warren	Fanny..............Miss Arnold
Shark..............Mr. Blissett	Sally Shamrock.....Mrs. Warrell
Stave..............Mr. Bernard	

The "Young Gentleman" was Mr. Cain—see May 20.

May 17   *Tancred and Sigismunda*   Daily Ad.

Cast as for May 15

The Liar

Old Wilding........Mr. Warren	Servant.............Mr. Doctor
Young Wilding.....Mr. Bernard	Miss Grantham......Mrs. Francis
Sir James Elliot..Mr. Warrell, Jr.	Miss Godfrey....Miss L'Estrange
Papillion..........Mr. Marshall	Kitty..............Mrs. Doctor

May 20   "Last Week"   Daily Ad.

"Benefit of Mr. CAIN, The Young Gentleman who performed Tancred"

Isabella

Count Baldwin......Mr. Warren	Sampson............Mr. Francis
Biron (3d appearance)...Mr. Cain	Belford........Mr. Warrell, Jr.
Carlos.............Mr. Downie	Officer............Mr. Warrell
Villeroy...........Mr. Wignell	Isabella............Mrs. Merry
Child..........Master Warrell	Nurse.............Mrs. Francis

The Prisoner

Marcos...........Mr. Marshall	Clara.............Mrs. Warrell
Pasqual............Mr. Darley	Theresa........Miss L'Estrange
Roberto...........Mr. Downie	Nina.............Miss Arnold
Lewis.............Mr. Blissett	Juliana..........Miss Hardinge
Narcisso........Master Warrell	

1799

May 24	Mr. Wignell's Benefit	G. U. S.

(First announced for May 22, with *Secrets Worth Knowing* and *Blue Beard;* then postponed, as the scenery for *Blue Beard*—though in preparation for months—was not ready.)

* Lovers' Vows—Mrs. Inchbald

Count Wildenhaim...Mr. Warren	Cottager..........Mr. Wignell
Count Cassel......Mr. Hardinge	Landlord..........Mr. Francis
Anhalt...........Mr. Marshall	Agatha............Mrs. Merry
Verdun...........Mr. Bernard	Amelia..........Mrs. Marshall
Frederick...........Mr. Cain	Sally Downright.....Mrs. Morris

* Blue Beard—Colman, Jr. (this cast in Daily Ad.)

Abomelique (Blue Beard).......	Hassan............Mr. Blissett
Mr. Warren	Fatima..........Mrs. Marshall
Ibrahim...........Mr. Francis	Irene............Mrs. Warrell
Selim...........Mr. Marshall	Beda..............Miss Arnold
Shacabac..........Mr. Bernard	

May 25	Mr. Reinagle's Benefit	G. U. S.

Lovers' Vows

Cast as for May 24.

Blue Beard

Cast as for May 24.

May 27	*The Midnight Hour*	Daily Ad.

Blue Beard

Cast as for May 24.

During the season from February 5 to May 27, 1799, at the New Theatre (Chesnut Street) these new plays were given: *Cheap Living, Duplicity, False and True, False Impressions, The Heir at Law, Knave or Not, Life's Vagaries, Lovers' Vows, The Mysteries of the Castle, The Mysterious Marriage, The Robbers, Secrets Worth Knowing, The Stranger,* and *A Wedding in Wales.* New afterpieces: *American True Blue, The Arabs of the Desert, The Battle of Trenton, Blunders Repaired, Botheration, The Catch Club, The Constellation, Diana and Actaeon, He's Much to Blame, The History of John Gilpin, The Magic Fire, An Olio, The Rival Soldiers,* and *William Tell.*

Reappearing plays: *The Beggar's Opera, The Chapter of Accidents, The Child of Nature, Columbus, The Conscious Lovers, The Deserted Daughter, The Disbanded Officer, The Dramatist, Edward and Eleonora, Every One Has His Fault, The Gamester, The Grecian Daughter, He Would Be a*

1799

Soldier, The Highland Reel, Isabella, Jane Shore, The Natural Son, Romeo and Juliet, Tancred and Sigismunda, and *The Way to Get Married.* Reappearing afterpieces: *The Adopted Child, The Agreeable Surprize, All in Good Humour, All the World's a Stage, The Author, Barnaby Brittle, Bon Ton, The Castle of Andalusia, The Children in the Wood, The Critic, Cymon and Sylvia, The Death of General Wolfe, Dermot and Kathleen, The Deuce is in Him, Dr. Last's Examination, The Drunken Provençal, The Farmer, Harlequin Shipwrecked, Harlequin's Invasion, The Highland Festivity, The Liar, Lock and Key, Love à la Mode, The Midnight Hour, Miss in Her Teens, The Mountaineers, The Old Maid, The Padlock, The Poor Soldier, The Prisoner, Richard Cœur de Lion, The Romp, Rosina, The Sailor's Landlady, The Scotch Ghost, The Shipwreck, The Spoiled Child, Thomas and Sally, Tom Thumb the Great, A Trip to Scarborough, Two Strings to Your Bow,* and *The Wedding Day.*

New Actors: Miss Arnold, Mr. Cain, Mr. Downie, Master Harris, Mrs. Lavancey, and Mr. Wood. Reappearing actors: Mr. and Mrs. Bernard, Mr. Blissett, Miss Broadhurst, Mr. and Mrs. Byrne, Mr. Darley, Mr. and Mrs. Doctor, Mr. Fox, Mr. and Mrs. Francis, Mr. Gibbons, Mrs. Gillingham, Mr. and Mrs. Hunter, Miss, Mr., and Mrs. Hardinge, Mr. Lavancey, Mrs., Miss, and Master L'Estrange, Mr. and Mrs. Marshall, Mr. Mercer (or Mersier), Mrs. Merry, Mr. Milbourne, Mr. and Mrs. Morris, Mrs. Stuart, Mr. Warrell, Mr. Warrell, Jr., Master H. Warrell, (and a "Master Warrell," who *may* have been Master T. or Master Harry Warrell), Mr. and Mrs. Warren, and Mr. Wignell.

RICKETTS' CIRCUS

Nov. 21	Circus	Aurora
	The Valiant Soldier	

Ricketts' Pantheon opened for the winter on November 21, and burned down on December 17, 1799.

Nov. 23	Circus	G. U. S.
	The Valiant Soldier	
Nov. 25	Circus	Aurora
	Robinson Crusoe	
Nov. 28	Circus	Aurora
	* *The City of Philadelphia,*	
	or The Ship Launch ("an occasional pantomime")	
Dec. 3	Circus	Aurora
	* *The Witches' Cave* (pantomime)	

1799

NEW THEATRE

Dec. 4   *The Stranger*   Phila. Gaz.

The Stranger.......Mr. Wignell	Old Man..........Mr. Morris
Count Wintersen....Mr. Warren	William..........Master Harris
Baron Steinfort.....Mr. Marshall	Countess Wintersen..Mrs. Morris
Solomon...........Mr. Francis	Ann..............Mrs. Francis
Peter.............Mr. Blissett	Mrs. Haller........Mrs. Merry
Francis............Mr. Wood	

* The Jew and the Doctor—Dibdin

Old Bromley........Mr. Francis	Abednego (the Jew).Mr. Bernard
Dr. Specific........Mr. Warren	Mrs. Changeable....Mrs. Francis
Changeable........Mr. Marshall	Emily..........Miss L'Estrange
Charles.............Mr. Wood	Betty.............Mrs. Doctor
William...........Mr. Blissett	

The New Theatre (Chesnut Street) was open from December 4, 1799, to May 19, 1800 (*Daily Advertiser,* May 19). (The present record, however, ends with the eighteenth century.)

RICKETTS' CIRCUS

Dec. 5   Circus   Aurora
Poor Jack (The Sailor's Landlady)
Poor Jack, with a Hornpipe, Song, &c.....Mr. Durang

NEW THEATRE

Dec. 6   *Lovers' Vows*   Phila. Gaz.
Cast as for May 24, except:
Count Cassel........Mr. Wood

The Rival Soldiers

Capt. Cruizer.....Mr. L'Estrange	Nipperkin..........Mr. Bernard
Lenox...............Mr. Cain	The Little Midshipman..........
Major Tactic.......Mr. Darley	Miss Arnold
Sinclair..........Mr. Marshall	Mary Tactic.......Mrs. Warrell
Corporal..........Mr. Radcliff	

Mr. Radcliff may or may not have been the Mr. Ratcliff who was with the "K" Company at the Northern Liberties in 1791–2.

1799

RICKETTS' CIRCUS

Dec. 7   Circus   Daily Ad.
                    Poor Jack (The Sailor's Landlady)

Jack..............Mr. Durang		Bob Ratling........Mr. Harman	
Ned Halyard........Mr. Ricketts		Wapping Landlady..Mr. Rowson	
Boatswain........Mr. F. Ricketts		Polly...........Mrs. M'Donald	
Tom Tackle.........Mr. Lewis		Orange Girl........Mrs. Rowson	

First appearance of Messrs. Lewis and Harman.

NEW THEATRE

Dec. 9   * *Five Thousand a Year*—Dibdin   G. U. S.

George Fervid.......Mr. Bernard	Dick..............Mr. Radcliff
Frederick Fervid....Mr. Marshall	Officer.............Mr. Warrell
Truepenny..........Mr. Warren	Boy..........Master L'Estrange
Sir Matthew Maxim..Mr. Francis	Lady Maxim........Mrs. Morris
Mr. Goulding......Mr. Wignell	Lady Julia.........Mrs. Francis
Henry Hastings.......Mr. Wood	Maria............Mrs. Marshall
Paragraph..........Mr. Blissett	Aurelia.........Miss L'Estrange

Robin Hood

RICKETTS' CIRCUS

Dec. 10   Circus   Aurora
                    *The Triumph of Virtue—or
                    Harlequin in Philadelphia*

"originally brought out by Mr. Ricketts, and which met with much applause
from its very great variety of changes."

NEW THEATRE

Dec. 11   *Tancred and Sigismunda*   G. U. S.

Tancred..............Mr. Cain   Sigismunda..........Mrs. Merry

The Prize

Caroline........Mrs. Oldmixon   Lentive...........Mr. Wignell
        (Being her first appearance
        here these two years)

RICKETTS' CIRCUS

Dec. 12   Circus   Aurora
                    The Triumph of Virtue

Harlequin..........Mr. Ricketts	Gardener...........Mr. Stanley
Pantaloon.........Mr. Durang	Columbine........Mrs. Rowson

[400]

1799

Lover	Mr. F. Ricketts	Queen Mab	Mrs. M'Donald
Pero	Mr. Rowson	Punchinello	Mr. Lewis
Punch	Mr. Harman	Milk Maid	[blank]

First appearance of Mr. Stanley.

NEW THEATRE

Dec. 13   *The Heir at Law*   Phila. Gaz.

Baron Dubberly	Mr. Warren	John	Mr. Radcliff
Dick Dowlass	Mr. Wood	Waiter at Hotel	Mr. Warrell, Jr.
Dr. Panglos	Mr. Wignell	Waiter at Blue Boar	Mr. Warrell
Henry Moreland	Mr. Cain	Lady Dubberly	Mrs. Morris
Steadfast	Mr. Marshall	Caroline Dormer	Miss L'Estrange
Zekial Homespun	Mr. Bernard	Cicely Homespun	Mrs. Merry
Kenrick	Mr. Blissett		

The Jew and The Doctor

Cast as for Dec. 4.

Dec. 16   *A Trip to Scarborough*   Phila. Gaz.

Lord Foppington	Mr. Bernard	Taylor	Mr. Warrell
Young Fashion	Mr. Wignell	Jeweller	Mr. Warrell, Jr.
Col. Townley	Mr. Wood	Postillion	Master L'Estrange
Sir Tunbelly Clumsy	Mr. Warren	Miss Hayden	Mrs. Marshall
Lory	Mr. Francis	Nurse	Mrs. Francis
La Varole	Mr. Doctor	Mrs. Coupler	Mrs. Doctor
Shoemaker	Mr. Blissett	Milliner	Mrs. Gillingham

* *The Horse and The Widow*—Dibdin
The Adopted Child

RICKETTS' CIRCUS

Dec. 17   Circus   Aurora
Don Juan, or The Libertine Destroyed

Don Juan	Mr. Durang	Donna Anna	Mrs. Rowson
Don Frederick	Mr. Ricketts	Confidante	Mrs. M'Donald
Landlord	Mr. Rowson	Fisher Women with a Duett	
Pacho	Mr. Hutchins	Mrs. Decker and Mrs. M'Donald	
Fisherman	Mr. Harman		

"The last scene represents the Infernal Regions with a view of the mouth of Hell."

Mrs. Decker, who is new to our record, probably did not appear, as Ricketts' Pantheon burned down before *Don Juan* was finished—Durang says, before it was begun. (*Daily Advertiser*, December 18; Durang, Series I, Chap. XXXIII.)

1799

The new performances at the circus during its brief season from November 27 to December 17, 1799, were *The City of Philadelphia* and *The Witches' Cave.*

Reappearing: *Don Juan* (scheduled to appear at the Pantheon, which burned down), *Harlequin in Philadelphia, Poor Jack (The Sailor's Landlady), Robinson Crusoe,* and *The Valiant Soldier.* New performers: Mrs. Decker, Messrs. Harman, Lewis, and Stanley. Reappearing performers: Mr. Durang, Mr. Hutchins, Mr. J. B. Ricketts, Mr. F. Ricketts, Mrs. M'Donald, and Mr. and Mrs. J. Rowson.

NEW THEATRE

Dec. 18   *Secrets Worth Knowing*   Daily Ad.

Cast as for February 5, except:

Valet..............Mr. Radcliff   Coachman........Mr. Milbourne

Butler and Cook not cast

The Spoiled Child

Little Pickle.......Mrs. Marshall		Miss Pickle.........Mrs. Francis
Old Pickle.........Mr. Warren		Maria.........Miss L'Estrange
Tag...............Mr. Francis		Margery..........Mrs. Doctor
John..............Mr. Blissett		Susan............Mrs. Bernard
Thomas...........Mr. Doctor		

Dec. 23   G. U. S.

"New Theatre Will Re-open"—(Closed because of Washington's Death)—
with

* "*A Monody* on the Death of the much lamented the late Lieutenant General of the Armies of the United States (The Music composed by Mr. R. Taylor, and Mr. Reinagle.) The principal vocal parts by Mr. Darley, Miss Broadhurst, Mrs. Warrell, and Mrs. Oldmixon. The Recitation by Mr. Wignell. (With appropriate scenery and decorations, designed and executed by Mr. Milbourne, Mr. Holland and Mr. Barnalet.)"

The Roman Father

Horatius..........Mr. Warren   Horatia...........Mrs. Merry
Publius Horatius....Mr. Wignell

Dec. 26   *A Monody [on the Death of Washington]*   G. U. S.
                      The Stranger
                      The Constellation

"an appropriate Ballet Dance—Composed by Mr. Francis—Principal Characters, Miss Arnold, Miss Solomon, Mr. Francis, and Mr. Warrell, Jr."

1799

Dec. 27   *Secrets Worth Knowing*—Morton   G. U. S.

Greville............Mr. Wignell   Rostrum...........Mr. Bernard
Egerton..............Mr. Cain   Mrs. Greville........Mrs. Merry

A Monody [*on the Death of Washington*]

Dec. 30   Daily Ad.

"The President of the United States will honor the Theatre with his presence this evening."

A Monody [*on the Death of Washington*]
* *The Secret*
or, *Partnership Dissolved*—Morris

Mr. Dorville........Mr. Warren   Bailiff...........Mr. Milbourne
Sir Harry Fletley.....Mr. Wood   Steward..........Mr. Warrell
Lizard.............Mr. Bernard   Servants...Messrs. Hook, Doctor,
Jack Lizard........Mr. Wignell   T. Warrell
Mr. Torrid........Mr. Francis   Lady Esther Dorville.Mrs. Morris
Henry Torrid.........Mr. Cain   Rosa..............Mrs. Merry
Ralph.............Mr. Blissett   Susannah Lizard..Mrs. Oldmixon
Frank.............Mr. Morris

This was the last performance in Philadelphia in the eighteenth century. Mr. Hook made his first appearance. So far in the season which had begun at the New Theatre (Chesnut Street) on December 4 (it extended to May 19, 1800) the new plays were *Five Thousand a Year* and *The Secret*. New afterpieces: *The Horse and The Widow*, *The Jew and The Doctor*, and *The Monody on Washington's Death*. Reappearing plays: *The Heir at Law*, *Lovers' Vows*, *The Roman Father*, *Secrets Worth Knowing*, *The Stranger*, *Tancred and Sigismunda*, and *A Trip to Scarborough*. Reappearing afterpieces: *The Adopted Child*, *The Constellation*, *The Prize*, and *The Spoiled Child*.

The only new actor was Mr. Hook, unless Mr. Radcliff was not the actor of 1791–2. Reappearing actors: Miss Arnold, Mr. and Mrs. Bernard, Mr. Blissett, Miss Broadhurst, Mr. Cain, Mr. Darley, Mr. and Mrs. Doctor, Mr. and Mrs. Francis, Mrs. Gillingham, Master Harris, Mr., Master, and Miss L'Estrange, Mr. and Mrs. Marshall, Mrs. Merry, Mr. Milbourne, Mr. and Mrs. Morris, Mrs. Oldmixon, Mr. Radcliff (if he had been here in 1791–2), Mr. and Mrs. Warrell, Mr. Warrell, Jr., and Mr. T. Warrell, Mr. Warren, Mr. Wignell, and Mr. Wood. Mr. and Mrs. Morris were the only connecting links with the colonial theatre: Mrs. Morris had appeared in 1772, and Owen Morris had played in the Theatre on Society Hill in 1759.

FINIS

PLAY INDEX

In the Play Index, chronological reference is made to the *Day Book* for each recorded appearance of every play given in Philadelphia during the eighteenth century.

Abbey of St. Augustine, The: 1797, March 20, 22, 25.

Abroad and at Home: 1797, Jan. 27; 1798, Jan. 12, 15, 27, Feb. 7.

Adopted Child, The: 1797, April 3, 5, Dec. 13; 1798, March 28; 1799, April 1, Dec. 16.

Adventures of Half-an-Hour, The: 1759, July 20, Sept. 14.

Adventures of a Wit, The: 1798, April 27.

Advertisement, The: 1798, April 5.

Agreeable Surprize, The: 1787, Jan. 27, 30; 1790, July 7; 1792, Jan. 17, March 13, May 16, Dec. 14, 28; 1793, Jan. 2, Aug. 9; 1794, April 9, 14, Oct. 30; 1795, March 13; 1796, Feb. 23, Dec. 28; 1798, Jan. 22, March 21; 1799, May 4.

Alexander the Great ("Magnificent Representation"): 1799, March 12, 14, 19.

Alexander the Great; or The Rival Queens: 1768, Dec. 30; 1769, Jan. 6; 1770, April 16; 1790, May 3, 5; 1794, Nov. 17; 1796, May 9; 1797, April 3; 1798, Feb. 9.

All for Love: 1767, March 9, May 1; 1797, May 1.

All in Good Humour: 1798, April 27; 1799, Feb. 15.

All in the Wrong: 1790, Jan. 25; 1792, Dec. 3, 22; 1796, April 4, 11.

All the World's a Stage: 1790, June 3; 1792, June 22; 1795, June 19; 1796, Feb. 8; 1797, April 26; 1799, Feb. 25, April 27.

Alonzo and Imogen: 1797, April 17, May 3.

L'Americain: 1794, July 2.

American Heroine, The: 1797, April 20, May 2, 18, June 1, 24; 1798, March 29.

American in London, The: 1798, March 28.

American Shandyism: see *The Father.*

American Tar, The: 1796, June 17.

American True Blue: 1799, April 3.

Anatomist, The; or the Sham-Doctor: 1759, Aug. 3; 1797, July 10.

Ancient Day, An: 1797, May 3.

Animal Magnetism: 1793, July 25; 1796, Dec. 16; 1797, Jan. 2, Feb. 3, 27; 1798, Feb. 5.

Animated Statue, The: 1798, Jan. 1, 10.

Apprentice, The: 1767, May 4, July 6; 1790, April 22; 1791, Jan. 10, March 18; 1795, May 8.

Arabs of the Desert, The: 1799, April 13.

Armans d'Arcade, Les: 1795, June 12, 17, Dec. 18.

As It Should Be: 1791, May 19; 1796, Feb. 19.

As You Like It: 1794, May 30, Dec. 10; 1798, April 24.

Auld Robin Gray: 1795, May 4.

Author, The: 1798, March 7; 1799, May 3.

Banditti, The (see also *The Castle of Andalusia*): 1788, Nov. 5, 10; 1790, July 1; 1794, Feb. 17, March 19; 1795,

March 30; 1790, March 15; 1791, Aug. 8, 15, Oct. 14; 1795, Dec. 23.

Crotchet Lodge: 1796, June 24.

Cure for the Heartache, A: 1798, Jan. 1, 5, 17, March 5.

Cymbeline: 1767, May 25, June 29; 1768, Nov. 4; 1769, Dec. 8; 1770, May 24; 1772, Dec. 7; 1791, May 23; 1794, July 9; 1795, Feb. 7.

Cymon [and Sylvia]: 1773, March 3; 1790, May 20, June 7; 1793, Jan. 7; 1798, March 26; 1799, April 10.

Damon and Phillida: 1767, Feb. 16, 27; 1769, June 5; 1770, Feb. 9.

Danaides, The: 1794, Oct. 8, 10, 13.

Daphne and Amintor, or The Fairies: 1787, June 29.

Darby and Patrick: 1787, Jan. 22, 23, 24, 26, Feb. 2, July 11.

Darby's Return: 1790, May 24, June 14; 1791, June 6.

Dead Alive, The: 1790, Feb. 19, March 13; 1791, Jan. 26; 1797, May 1; 1798, Jan. 24.

Deaf Lover, The: 1796, Jan. 18, March 16; 1797, March 13; 1798, Jan. 12.

Death and Renovation of Harlequin, The: 1796, Oct. 12, 13, 15.

Death of Bucephalus: 1797, April 11.

Death of Captain Cook, The: 1796, Nov. 7, 9, 10, 12, 14, 23, Dec. 15; 1797, Jan. 2, 3, 21, Feb. 23, 24, 25, March 1; 1798, March 19; 1799, Feb. 2.

Death of General Wolfe, The: 1798, April 27, May 4; 1799, Feb. 15, 23.

Death of Harlequin, The: 1791, May 19; 1798, March 31.

Death of Major André, The: 1798, May 14; 1799, Feb. 7, 9.

Death of Miss McCrea, The: see *A Representation of the Death of Miss McCrea.*

Dermot and Kathleen: 1796, Dec. 7, 16, 26; 1797, Feb. 27, March 4, July 5, Dec. 27; 1799, April 1, 6.

Deserted Daughter, The: 1796, April 29, May 6, July 1; 1798, April 13; 1799, March 15, 16.

Deserter, The (Dibdin): 1787, July 11; 1790, July 19; 1791, May 9, June 30; 1792, Oct. 3, 8; 1793, July 31; 1794, March 21; 1795, Jan. 23; 1796, March 21; 1798, Jan. 8; 1799, May 11.

Deserter, The (French opera): 1798, May 14.

Deserter of Naples, The: 1796, May 9.

Despairing Lover, The: 1797, May 13.

Deuce is in Him, The: 1767, March 14; 1778, Jan. 9, 26; 1791, Dec. 1, 17; 1792, Feb. 6, April 26; 1795, March 31; 1798, April 30; 1799, March 15, 16.

Deux Chasseurs, Les: 1795, Dec. 21; 1796, March 4, Dec. 17.

Deux Petits Savoyards, Les: 1797, Jan. 16, May 20, 30.

Deux Sœurs, Les: 1796, June 15.

Devil in the Wine Cellar, The: 1795, June 15.

Devil to Pay, The; or The Wives Metamorphosed: 1766, Dec. 19; 1767, Jan. 16, April 27, Oct. 30, Nov. 3; 1770, March 20, April 27; 1772, Dec. 9; 1773, Jan. 11; 1790, May 10; 1791, Sept. 14, Nov. 26; 1792, Oct. 19, 31; 1793, July 5; 1795, March 27, 30, April 8; 1796, Feb. 1; 1798, Jan. 6, March 3.

Devil Upon Two Sticks The: 1789, Nov. 4, 7, 14; 1790, May 27; 1794, July 9; 1798, April 18; 1799, Jan. 30.

Dialogues at the College of Philadelphia: 1761, May 23; 1762, May 18; 1763, May 17; 1765, May 30; 1766, May 20; 1767, Nov. 17; 1770, June 5; 1775, May 17; 1790, June 7.

Diana and Actaeon: 1799, Feb. 18, 20.

Disappointment, The: 1767, April 13.

Disbanded Officer, The: 1796, June 17; 1799, April 6.

Dissertation on Hobby Horses, A: 1798, April 7; 1799, April 22.

1796, Dec. 12; 1797, Jan. 6; 1798, Jan. 29.

Fairies, The; or Daphne and Amintor: 1787, June 29.

False and True: 1799, April 13.

False Delicacy: 1768, Dec. 16; 1773, Jan. 25.

False Impressions: 1799, May 1.

Fandango Dance, The: 1796, March 23.

Fanny the Fantome: 1768, Dec. 30; 1769, Jan. 6.

Farm House, The: 1795, March 4, 9, June 26; 1796, May 18.

Farmer, The: 1792, Nov. 16, 19; 1793, Jan. 4, Aug. 16; 1794, March 12, 28; 1796, Jan. 8; 1797, March 25, Dec. 30; 1799, Feb. 5, March 11.

Fashionable Lover, The: 1772, Nov. 30; 1773, March 8; 1789, March 11, 21; 1792, Dec. 29.

Fatal Curiosity: 1798, April 18.

Fatal Deception, The: 1794, Oct. 29.

Father, The, or American Shandyism: 1790, Feb. 5; 1791, Jan. 26.

Female Heroism, or The Siege of Orleans: 1794, June 27.

Female Patriot, The: 1795, June 19.

Fenelon: 1798, Feb. 2, 3, 10, March 7.

First Floor, The: 1795, June 8; 1796, Jan. 29; 1797, March 6.

First Love: 1796, May 23.

Five Thousand A Year: 1799, Dec. 9.

Flitch of Bacon, The: 1787, Feb. 3; 1792, Oct. 1, 5, Nov. 26; 1794, Feb. 21, April 7, Dec. 24; 1795, Feb. 21; 1797, Jan. 23, Feb. 1.

Flora; or Hob in the Well: 1754, May 27; 1767, May 1; 1770, Jan. 9; 1773 March 10; 1790, Dec. 29; 1791, Jan. 7, 29; 1795, May 20; 1796, Feb. 3.

Florizel and Perdita: 1791, Dec. 20, 31; 1792, Jan. 14, 21, March 3; 1795, June 15; 1796, March 9.

Follies of a Day, The: 1795, June 15.

Fontainville Forest: 1795, March 13, 16, 23; 1796, Jan. 4.

Forêt Noire, La, or The Natural Son: 1794, April 26, 28, 30, May 3, 7, 12, June 20; 1795, Feb. 28, March 2; 1796, April 15; 1797, March 17, 22; 1798, Jan. 5.

Fortunatus, or Harlequin's Wishing Cap: 1798, May 2.

Four Sons of Aymond, The: see *Les Quatre Fils Aymond.*

Four Travelling Brothers, The: 1797, May 12, 30, June 17, 20, July 20.

"Fourth of July, The, or The Sailor's Festival": 1788, July 4, 21.

French Shoemaker, The: 1792, Jan. 4, Feb. 4, 11.

Fruitless Precaution, The: 1794, May 16, 26, 27.

Funeral, The; or Grief a-la-mode: 1770, Feb. 9, 19.

Fusilier, The, or The Clown Outwitted: 1797, May 23.

Gamester, The: 1754, June 10; 1759, Dec. 14; 1767, April 2, July 2, Oct. 23; 1769, Nov. 14; 1787, July 19, 26; 1788, July 7; 1790, Jan. 22; 1791, April 9; 1794, April 11, July 16, Nov. 12; 1795, Jan. 16, 21; 1796, March 2; 1798, Feb. 5; 1799, May 4.

Garden of Love, The: 1798, June 8.

Generous Englishman, The: 1798, May 18.

Generous Tars, The: 1798, March 7, 28.

Gentle Shepherd, The (see also *Patie and Roger*): 1798, April 16.

George Barnwell: 1759, Aug. 17, Dec. 27; 1767, Feb. 23; 1769, Dec. 29; 1772, Dec. 2; 1788, July 26, Oct. 25; 1790, March 27, April 6, 8; 1791, Aug. 8, 15; 1792, Feb. 14; 1793, July 8; 1794, Dec. 26; 1795, Dec. 26; 1796, March 30, Dec. 27; 1797, Dec. 26.

Ghost, The: 1789, March 16; 1790, April 8; 1791, Jan. 31, Feb. 14; 1792, April 9; 1796, May 30, Dec. 8, 15; 1797, Feb. 15.

Gil Blas: 1796, May 16; 1797, April 21.

1773, Jan. 6; 1790, April 22, July 19; 1791, March 16; 1795, April 22.

Tammany: 1794, Oct. 18, Nov. 10.

Tancred and Sigismunda: 1798, March 23; 1799, May 15, 17, Dec. 11.

Tempest, The: 1787, July 14, 17; 1770, Jan. 19, 23, 29, Feb. 2, March 5, 20; 1773, Feb. 1, 3, March 31; 1790, April 24; 1791, Feb. 2; 1793, Aug. 14; 1794 July 14; 1795, Feb. 24, March 14; 1796, March 24; 1797, March 11.

Tempest of Harlequin, The, or The Clown Turned Miller: 1792, Jan. 23, 28.

Tender Husband, The; or The Accomplished Fools: 1770, March 30.

Theodosius; or The Force of Love: 1759, Aug. 10, Nov. 16; 1766, Dec. 26; 1767, Nov. 13; 1773, Feb. 10; 1790, June 14.

Thomas and Sally: 1766, Nov. 14; 1767, Feb. 20; 1770, April 16; 1772, Dec. 23; 1791, June 2, Oct. 5, 10, Nov. 5; 1792, Jan. 27, July 11; 1799, April 5.

Three Weeks After Marriage: 1791, Nov. 18, 29; 1794, June 11, Oct. 17, 20; 1795, Feb. 20; 1796, June 13; 1797, Dec. 22.

Tit for Tat: 1798, April 27.

Tom Thumb the Great: 1767, June 1; 1795, April 22, 24, May 1, 22, June 24, July 3, Dec. 30; 1796, Feb. 20; 1797, April 19; 1799, April 20.

Toy, The: 1790, April 10, 19; 1791, June 13; 1795, May 29.

Toy-Shop, The: 1759, Oct. 5.

Travellers Preserved, The: 1795, June 19, 26.

Trip to Harrogate, A: see *Sir Flimsy Nervous.*

Trip to Scarborough, A; or, The Man of Quality: 1798, April 18; 1799, March 6, Dec. 16.

Trip to Scotland, A: 1778, April 20, May 1; 1791, Aug. 22, Sept. 14.

Triumph of Mirth, The: 1794, May 21.

Triumph of Virtue, The: see *Harlequin in Philadelphia.*

Triumphs of Love, The: 1795, May 22.

True-Born Irishman, The: 1788, July 26, Nov. 8; 1789, March 11; 1790, May 24; 1791, Jan. 3, June 2; 1794, June 9, Nov. 10.

Tunbridge Walks; or The Yeoman of Kent: 1754, May 27.

Two Brother Taylors, The: 1798, March 24, 27.

Two Huntsmen, The: 1796, Nov. 3, 5; 1797, May 16.

Two Misers, The: 1791, April 9, 12, 15, May 5; 1795, April 17, 18, 20, 29; 1799, Jan. 21.

Two Philosophers, The: 1794, Oct. 24, Dec. 4; 1796, Oct. 12, 13, Nov. 23; 1797, April 22.

Two Strings to Your Bow: 1796, April 22; 1798, Jan. 19; 1799, Feb. 27.

Upholsterer, The; or What News?: 1767, Jan. 23; 1770, Feb. 16, 19; 1772, Dec. 7.

Vagaries, The: 1798, April 24.

Valiant Officer, The: 1796, June 10.

Valiant Soldier, The: 1796, Oct. 24, Nov. 3, Dec. 26; 1799, Feb. 12, Nov. 21, 23.

Venice Preserved: 1767, Nov. 2, 5; 1790, March 1; 1791, Dec. 27; 1792, April 14, July 11; 1793, Jan. 4; 1794, Feb. 24, Dec. 8; 1797, Jan. 21, Feb. 3, March 15, Dec. 16.

Village Lawyer, The: 1794, March 7, 29, Dec. 19; 1796, April 13, Dec. 7; 1797, Feb. 20.

Vintner in the Suds, The: 1788, Oct. 25.

Virgin Unmasked, The: 1759, June 25, Dec. 7; 1791, Oct. 1; 1794, March 22.

Volunteers, The: 1795, Jan. 21, 26.

Vulcan's Gift: 1796, March 12, 15, 17, 19, 22, 24, 26, 29, April 2, 19.

PLAYER INDEX

In the Player Index, reference is made to the *Day Book* for the first mention of each actor recorded as appearing on the Philadelphia stage during the eighteenth century, for every season in which he appeared, and for any other item of importance in the history of the actor.

Adcock, Mr.: 1754, April 15; 1754, April 15–June 24.

Adcock, Mrs.: 1754, April 15; 1754, April 15–June 24.

Allen, Mr.: 1774, Sept. 19; 1784, Dec. 7.

Allen, Mr.: 1791, April 26; 1791, April 8–1792, May 16.

Allen, Mrs.: 1784, Dec. 7.

Allyn, Adam: 1759, July 20; 1759, June 25–Dec. 28; 1766, Nov. 14–1767, July 6; 1767, Oct. 6–Nov. 23.

Anderson, Master: 1791, Dec. 10; 1791, April 8–1792, May 16.

Anderson, Miss: 1797, Dec. 11; 1797, Dec. 11–1798, May 5.

Anderson, Mr.: 1791, Nov. 29; 1791, April 8–1792, May 16.

André, Major: 1778, Jan. 19–May 19.

André, Mr.: 1791, Feb. 4; 1790, Dec. 8–1791, July 11.

Apker, Miss: 1789, Nov. 11; 1789, Nov. 4–30.

Appleby, Mr.: 1767, March 3; 1766, Nov. 14–1767, July 6.

Arnold, Miss: 1799, March 18; 1799, Feb. 5–May 27; 1799, Dec. 4–1800, May 19.

Ashton, Mr.: 1792, May 28; 1792, May 28–July 2; 1792, Sept. 26–1793, Jan. 12; 1794, Sept 22–Dec. 4.

Barnard, Mr.: 1792, Jan. 26; 1791, April 8–1792, May 16.

Bason, Mr.: 1794, March 10; 1794, Feb. 17–July 18.

Bates, Master R.: 1796, June 22; 1795, Dec. 14–1796, July 1.

Bates, Mr.: 1794, Feb. 17; 1794, Feb. 17–July 18; 1794, Dec. 3–1795, July 4; 1795, Dec. 14–1796, July 1; 1796, Dec. 5–1797, July 14.

Bates, Mrs.: 1794, Feb. 17; 1794, Feb. 17–July 18; 1794, Dec. 3–1795, July 4; 1795, Dec. 14–1796, July 1.

Becceley, Mrs.: 1754, May 27; 1754, April 15–June 24.

Beete, Mr.: 1795, Dec. 21; 1795, Dec. 14–1796, July 1.

Bell, Mr.: 1754, June 12; 1754, April 15–June 24.

Bellona, M.: 1794, May 16; 1794, Feb. 17–July 18.

Berg, Mr.: 1797, May 13; 1797, April 11–July 27.

Bernard, John: 1797, Dec. 11; 1797, Dec. 11–1798, May 5; 1799, Feb. 5–May 27; 1799, Dec. 4–1800, May 19.

Bernard, Mrs.: 1798, Jan. 26; 1797, Dec. 11–1798, May 5; 1799, Feb. 5–May 27; 1799, Dec. 4–1800, May 19.

Berwick, Mr. (or Barkwick, or Barwick): 1794, Sept. 26; 1794, Sept. 22–Dec. 4.

Biddle, Charles: 1789, March 11; 1789, March 9–April 4; 1790, Jan. 6–July 19.

Bird, Mr.: 1799, Feb. 2; 1799, Jan. 9–March 23.

Bird, Mrs.: 1799, Jan. 9; 1799, Jan. 9–March 23.

Bisset, Mr.: 1792, Sept. 26; 1792, Sept. 26–1793, Jan. 12.

Blissett, Mr.: 1794, Feb. 17; 1794, Feb. 17–July 18; 1794, Dec. 3–1795, July

4; 1795, Dec. 14–1796, July 1; 1796, Dec. 5–1797, July 14; 1797, Dec. 11–1798, May 5; 1799, Feb. 5–1800, May 19.

Bonnaux, (or Bonneau, or Bonceau) Mr.: 1798, March 29; 1798, March 8–April 7.

Bonnaux (or Bonneau, or Bonceau), Mrs.: 1798, May 14; 1798, April 24–June 8.

Bouchoni, M.: 1796, Dec. 17; 1796, Dec. 5–1797, July 14.

Bradshaw, Master: 1792, Feb. 29; 1791, April 8–1792, May 16.

Bradshaw, Mrs.: 1791, Aug. 8; 1791, April 8–1792, May 16.

Broadbelt, Mr.: 1767, Feb. 2; 1766, Nov. 14–1767, July 6; 1769, Sept. 14–30.

Broadhurst, Miss: 1794, Feb. 17; 1794, Feb. 17–July 18; 1794, Dec. 3–1795, July 4; 1799, Feb. 5–May 27; 1799, Dec. 4–1800, May 19.

Brett, Miss: 1792, Oct. 22; 1792, Sept. 26–1793, Jan. 12.

Brett, Mr.: 1791, Aug. 8; 1791, April 8–1792, May 16.

Byerley, Mr.: 1768, Dec. 2; 1768, Oct. 4–1769, Jan. 6; 1769, Nov. 8–1770, June 1; 1772, Oct. 28–1773, March 31.

Byrne, James: 1796, Dec. 7; 1796, Dec. 5–1796, July 14; 1797, Dec. 11–1798, May 5; 1799, Feb. 5–May 27.

Byrne, Master: 1798, April 14; 1797, Dec. 11–1798, May 5.

Byrne, Mrs.: 1796, Dec. 7; 1796, Dec. 5–1797, July 14; 1797, Dec. 11–1798, May 5; 1795, Feb. 5–May 27.

Cain, Alexander: 1799, May 15; 1799, Feb. 5–May 27; 1799, Dec. 4–1800, May 19.

Carr, Benjamin: 1794, Sept. 20; 1794, Sept. 22–Dec. 4.

Challet, Mr.: 1797, July 20; 1797, April 11–July 27.

Chalmers, Mr.: 1794, Feb. 21; 1794, Feb. 17–July 18; 1794, Dec. 3–1795, July 4; 1795, Dec. 14–1796, July 1; 1798, April 24–June 8.

Chambers, Mr.: 1792, Oct. 24; 1792, Sept. 26–1793, Jan. 12; 1796, Oct. 10–1797, Feb. 23.

Chambers, Mrs.: 1796, Nov. 24; 1796, Oct. 10–1797, Feb. 23.

Cheer, Miss: 1766, Nov. 21; 1766, Nov. 14–1767, July 6; 1767, Oct. 6–Nov. 23; 1768, Oct. 4–1769, Jan. 6.

Chew, S., Mr.: 1757, Jan.

Clarkson, Mr.: 1754, April 15; 1754, April 15–June 24.

Clarkson, Mrs.: 1754, May 27; 1754, April 15–June 24.

Claypit, Mr.: 1790, Feb. 10; 1790, Jan. 6–July 19.

Cleveland, Mr.: 1794, Feb. 17; 1794, Feb. 17–July 18; 1794, Dec. 3–1795, July 4.

Cleveland, Mrs.: 1794, Feb. 21; 1794, Feb. 17–July 18; 1794, Dec. 3–1795, July 4.

Clumsy, Mr.: 1791, Dec. 23; 1791, April 8–1792, May 16.

Coffie, Mr.: 1796, Oct. 15; 1796, Oct. 10–1797, Feb. 23.

Cooper, Thomas A.: 1796, Dec. 9; 1796, Dec. 5–1797, July 14; 1797, Dec. 11–1798, May 5.

Correy (or Corry), Miss: 1798, April 24; 1798, April 24–June 8.

Correy (or Corry), Mr.: 1797, July 20; 1797, April 11–July 27; 1798, March 8–April 7.

Correy (or Corry), Mrs.: 1798, March 8; 1798, March 8–April 7.

Crosby, Richard: see Richards, Mr.

Crump, Mr.: 1796, Feb. 13; 1795, Dec. 22–1796, April 23.

Darby, Mr.: 1768, Oct. 4; 1768, Oct. 4–1769, Jan. 6.

Darley, Mr.: 1794, Feb. 17; 1794, Feb. 17–July 18; 1794, Dec. 3–1795, July 4; 1795, Dec. 14–1796, July 1; 1796,

Dec. 5–July 14; 1797, Dec. 11–1798, May 5; 1799, Feb. 5–May 27; 1799, Dec. 4–1800, May 19.

Darley, Jr., Mr. J.: 1794, Feb. 17; 1794, Feb. 17–July 18; 1794, Dec. 3–1795, July 4; 1795, Dec. 14–1796, July 1; 1796, Dec. 5–1797, July 14; 1797, Dec. 11–1798, May 5.

Decker, Mrs.: 1799, Dec. 17; 1799, Nov. 27–Dec. 17.

Deforrest, Masters: 1796, Feb. 6; 1795, Dec. 22–1796, April 23.

Delancey, Capt.: 1778, Jan. 19–May 19.

Dellroy, Mr.: 1791, Dec. 23; 1791, April 8–1792, May 16.

De Marque, Mrs.: 1794, Feb. 21; 1794, Feb. 17–July 18; 1794, Dec. 3–1795, July 4; 1795, Dec. 14–1796, July 1.

Dermot, Mr.: 1773, March 10; 1772, Oct. 28–1773, March 31; 1773, Nov. 1–15.

Derrick, Mr.: 1791, Sept. 17; 1791, April 8–1792, May 16.

Devan, Mrs.: 1797, June 17; 1797, April 11–July 27.

Dickson, Mr.: 1789, Nov. 11; 1789, Nov. 4–30.

Doctor, Mrs.: 1796, Jan. 20; 1795, Dec. 14–1796, July 1; 1796, Dec. 5–1797, July 14; 1797, Dec. 11–1798, May 5; 1799, Feb. 5–May 27; 1799, Dec. 4–1800, May 19.

Doctor, Sig. Joseph: 1795, Dec. 26; 1795, Dec. 14–1796, July 1; 1796, Dec. 5–1797, July 14; 1797, Dec. 11–1798, May 5; 1799, Feb. 5–May 27; 1799, Dec. 4–1800, May 19.

Douglass, David: 1759, June 25; 1759, June 25–Dec. 28; 1766, Nov. 14–1767, July 6; 1767, Oct. 6–Nov. 23; 1768, Oct. 4–1769, Jan. 6; 1769, Nov. 8–1770, June 1; 1772, Oct. 28–1773, March 31; 1773, Nov. 1–15.

Douglass, Mrs. David: see Mrs. Lewis Hallam, Sr.

Douvilliers, M.: 1797, April 11; 1797,

April 11–July 27; 1798, March 8–April 7; 1798, April 24–June 8.

Douvilliers, Mlle.: 1797, April 11; 1797, April 11–July 27.

Douvilliers, Mme.: 1797, April 11; 1797, April 11–July 27; 1798, March 8–April 7; 1798, April 24–June 8.

Downie, Mr.: 1799, Feb. 11; 1799, Feb. 5–May 27.

Dowthwait, Miss: 1766, Nov. 28; 1766, Nov. 14–1767, July 6.

Dubois, Mr.: 1798, March 27; 1798, March 8–April 7; 1798, April 24–June 8.

Duché, Jacob: 1757, Jan.

Dumas, M.: 1792, May 30; 1792, May 28–July 2.

Dumont, Mr.: 1791, Dec. 23; 1791, April 8–1792, May 16.

Du Moulin(s) (or De[s] Moulin[s]), Mr.: 1791, Nov. 26; 1791, April 8–1792, May 16; 1794, Feb. 17–July 18.

Durang, John: 1784, Dec. 7; 1789, March 9; 1789, March 9–April 4; 1789, Nov. 4–30; 1790, Jan. 6–July 19; 1790, Dec. 8–1791, July 11; 1792, May 28–July 2; 1792, Sept. 26–1793, Jan. 12; 1793, July 1–Aug. 23; 1794, Sept. 22–Dec. 4; 1796, Oct. 10–1797, Feb. 23; 1799, Jan. 9–March 23; 1799, Nov. 27–Dec. 17.

Durang, Master Ferdinand: 1791, July 11; 1790, Dec. 8–1791, July 11.

Durang, Miss Caroline: 1784, Dec. 7; 1789, March 11; 1789, March 9–April 4.

Durang, Mrs. John: 1789, March 11; 1789, March 9–April 4; 1790, Dec. 8–1791, July 11; 1796, Oct. 10–1797, Feb. 23.

Estinval, Mr.: 1798, May 14; 1798, April 24–June 8.

Fennell, James: 1794, Feb. 19; 1794, Feb. 17–July 18; 1797, Dec. 11–1798, May 5.

18; 1788, Nov. 12; 1789, Jan. 9; 1789, March 9–April 4; 1790, Jan. 6–July 19; 1790, Dec. 8–1791, July 11; 1792, May 28–July 2; 1792, Sept. 26–1793, Jan. 12; 1794, Sept. 22–Dec. 4.

Hallam, Marvin: 1794, Nov. 24; 1794, Sept. 22–Dec. 4.

Hallam, Master: 1767, March 9; 1766, Nov. 14–1767, July 6.

Hallam, Miss [Helen?]: 1754, April 15; 1754, April 15–June 24.

Hallam, Miss Nancy: 1759, June 29; 1759, June 25–Dec. 28.

Hallam, Miss Sarah: 1766, Dec. 5; 1766, Nov. 14–1767, July 6; 1767, Oct. 6–Nov. 23; 1768, Oct. 4–1769, Jan. 6; 1769, Sept 14–30; 1769, Nov. 8–1770, June 1; 1772, Oct. 28–1773, March 31; 1773, Nov. 1–15.

Hallam, Mrs. Lewis, Sr. (after 1754, Mrs. David Douglass): 1754, April 15; 1754, April 15–June 24; 1759, June 25–Dec. 28; 1766, Nov. 14–1767, July 6; 1767, Oct. 6–Nov. 23; 1768, Oct. 4–1769, Jan. 6; 1769, Sept. 14–30; 1769, Nov. 8–1770, June 1; 1772, Oct. 28–1773, March 31; 1773, Nov. 1–15.

Hallam, Mrs. Lewis, "The Younger": see Tuke, Miss.

Hamilton, Mr. W.: 1757, Jan.

Hamilton, Mrs.: 1790, Jan. 20; 1790, Jan. 6–July 19; 1790, Dec. 8–1791, July 11; 1792, May 28–July 2; 1792, Sept. 26–1793, Jan. 12; 1794, Sept. 22–Dec. 4.

Hammond, Mr.: 1791, April 27; 1790, Dec. 8–1791, July 11; 1792, May 28–July 2; 1792, Sept. 26–1793, Jan. 12; 1794, Sept 22–Dec. 4.

Hardinge, Miss: 1797, Dec. 22; 1797, Dec. 11–1798, May 5; 1799, Feb. 5–May 27.

Hardinge, Mr.: 1797, Dec. 20; 1797, Dec. 11–1798, May 5; 1799, Feb. 5–May 27.

Hardinge, Mrs.: 1797, Dec. 22; 1797,

Dec. 11–1798, May 5; 1799, Feb. 5–May 27.

Harman, Mr.: 1799, Dec. 7; 1799, Nov. 27–Dec. 17.

Harman, Mr.: 1759, June 25; 1759, June 25–Dec. 28.

Harman, Mrs. Catherine Maria: 1759, June 25; 1759, June 25–Dec. 28; 1766, Nov. 14–1767, July 6; 1768, Oct. 4–1769, Jan. 6; 1769, Nov. 8–1770, June 1.

Harper, Mr.: 1787, Jan. 15; 1787, Jan. 15–Feb. 3; 1789, Jan. 9; 1789, March 9–April 4; 1790, Jan. 6–July 19; 1790, Dec. 8–1791, July 11; 1792, May 28–July 2; 1792, July 11.

Harper, Mrs.: 1789, March 23; 1789, March 9–April 4; 1790, Jan. 6–July 19; 1790, Dec. 8–1791, July 11.

Harris, Master: 1799, April 1; 1799, Feb. 5–May 27; 1799, Dec. 4–1800, May 19.

Harwood, John E.: 1794, Feb. 17; 1794, Feb. 17–July 18; 1794, Dec. 3–1795, July 4; 1795, Dec. 14–1796, July 1; 1796, Dec. 5–1797, July 14; 1797, Dec. 11–1798, May 5.

Harwood, Mrs.: 1797, Dec. 11; 1797, Dec. 11–1798, May 5; 1798, April 24–June 8.

Hatton, Miss: 1794, Sept. 26; 1794, Sept. 22–Dec. 4.

Heard, Mr.: 1789, March 11; 1789, March 9–April 4; 1790, Jan. 6–July 19; 1790, Dec. 8–1791, July 11; 1792, May 28–July 2.

Henry, John: 1767, Oct. 6; 1767, Oct. 6–Nov. 23; 1768, Oct. 4–1769, Jan. 6; 1769, Sept. 14–30; 1769, Nov. 8–1770, June 1; 1772, Oct. 28–1773, March 31; 1773, Nov. 1–15; 1782, July 1; 1787, Jan. 15–Feb. 3; 1788, March 18; 1788, Nov. 12; 1789, Jan. 9; 1789, March 9–April 4; 1790, Jan. 6–July 19; 1790, Dec. 8–1791, July 11; 1792, Sept. 26–1793, Jan. 12.

Henry, Mrs. Ann: see Storer, Ann.

[427]

Lapointe, Mr.: 1798, March 8; 1798, March 8–April 7.

La Valet, Mr.: 1791, Nov. 29; 1791, April 8–1792, May 16; 1798, April 24–June 8.

Lavancey (or Lavencey), M.: 1796, Dec. 24; 1796, Dec. 5–1797, July 14; 1797, Dec. 11–1798, May 5; 1798, April 24–June 8; 1799, Feb. 5–May 27.

Lavancey (or Lavencey), Mrs.: 1799, April 8; 1799, Feb. 5–May 27.

Lee, Mr.: 1794, March 10; 1794, Feb. 17–July 18; 1794, Sept. 22–Dec. 4.

Lege, M.: ₋795, Dec. 14; 1795, Dec. 14–1796, July ₁.

Lege, Mrs.: 1796, April 22; 1795, Dec. 14–1796, July 1.

Leger, Mr.: 1797, May 13; 1797, April 11–July 27.

Leigh, Mrs.: 1749, Aug.–1750, Jan.

Leroy, Mr.: 1792, Jan. 23; 1791, April 8–1792, May 16.

L'Estrange, Master: 1797, Jan. 2; 1796, Dec. 5–1797, July 14; 1797, Dec. 11–1798, May 5; 1799, Feb. 5–May 27; 1799, Dec. 4–1800, May 19.

L'Estrange, Miss: 1796, Dec. 5; 1796, Dec. 5–1797, July 14; 1797, Dec. 11–1798, May 5; 1799, Feb. 5–May 27; 1799, Dec. 4–1800, May 19.

L'Estrange, Mr.: 1796, Dec. 5; 1796, Dec. 5–1797, July 14; 1799, Dec. 4–1800, May 19.

L'Estrange, Mrs.: 1796, Dec. 5; 1796, Dec. 5–1797, July 14; 1797, Dec. 11–1798, May 5; 1799, Feb. 5–May 27.

Lewis, Mr.: 1799, Dec. 7; 1799, Nov. 27–Dec. 17.

Little Devil, The: 1792, May 28; 1792, May 28–July 2.

Louisier (or Lousier), Mr.: 1798, March 8; 1798, March 8–April 7; 1798, April 24–June 8.

Love, Mrs.: 1759, June 25; 1759, June 25–Dec. 28.

Lulsy, Mr.: 1798, June 4; 1798, April 24–June 8.

Malone, Mr.: 1754, April 15; 1754, April 15–June 24; 1769, Aug. 11.

Manly, Mr.: 1799, Jan. 9; 1799, Jan. 9–March 23.

Marks, Mr.: 1749, Aug.–1750, Jan.

Marriott, Mr.: 1794, Sept. 20; 1794, Sept. 22–Dec. 4.

Marriott, Mrs.: 1794, Sept. 20; 1794, Sept. 22–Dec. 4.

Marshall, Mr.: 1794, Feb. 17; 1794, Feb. 17–July 18; 1794, Dec. 3–1795, July 4; 1795, Dec. 14–1796, July 1; 1797, Dec. 11–1798, May 5; 1798, April 24–June 8; 1799, Feb. 5–May 27; 1799, Dec. 4–1800, May 19.

Marshall, Mrs.: 1794, Feb. 17; 1794, Feb. 17–July 18; 1794, Dec. 3–1795, July 4; 1795, Dec. 14–1796, July 1; 1797, Dec. 11–1798, May 5; 1799, Feb. 5–May 27; 1799, Dec. 4–1800, May 19.

Martin, John: 1790, July 1; 1790, Jan. 6–July 19; 1790, Dec. 8–1791, July 11; 1792, May 28–July 2; 1792, Sept. 26–1793, Jan. 12; 1794, Sept. 22–Dec. 4. See also 1797, July 20.

Martin, Mr.: 1797, July 20; 1797, April 11–July 27.

Matthew, Mr.: 1797, Dec. 16; 1797, Dec. 11–1798, May 5.

Matthews, Mr.: 1766, Nov. 28; 1766, Nov. 14–1767, July 6.

McDonald, Mr.: 1795, Dec. 24; 1795, Dec. 22–1796, April 23; 1796, Dec. 5–1797, July 14; 1797, April 11–July 27.

McDonald, Mrs.: 1799, Jan. 9; 1799, Jan. 9–March 23; 1799, Nov. 27–Dec. 17.

Mechtler, Mrs.: 1796, Dec. 7; 1796, Dec. 5–1797, July 14.

Melmoth, Mrs. Charlotte: 1794, Sept. 20; 1794, Sept. 22–Dec. 4.

M'Elroy, Masters: 1796, Feb. 6; 1795, Dec. 22–1796, April 23.

Mengui, Mr.: 1797, July 20; 1797, April 11–July 27.

Mentges, Francis: 1773, Jan. 18; 1772, Oct. 28–1773, March 31.

Merry, Mrs. Ann: 1796, Dec. 5; 1796, Dec. 5–1797, July 14; 1797, Dec. 11–1798, May 5; 1799, Feb. 5–May 27; 1799, Dec. 4–1800, May 19.

Mersier (or Mercer), Mr.: 1798, May 2; 1797, Dec. 11–1798, May 5; 1799, Feb. 5–May 27.

Milbourne, Miss: 1795, Jan. 2; 1794, Dec. 3–1795, July 4; 1795, Dec. 14–1796, July 1; 1796, Dec. 5–1797, July 14; 1797, Dec. 11–1798, May 5.

Milbourne, Mr.: 1794, July 14; 1794, Feb. 17–July 18; 1794, Dec. 3–1795, July 4; 1795, Dec. 14–1796, July 1; 1796, Dec. 5–1797, July 14; 1799, Feb. 5–May 27; 1799, Dec. 4–1800, May 19.

Miller, Mr.: 1754, April 15; 1754, April 15–June 24.

Miller, Mrs.: 1794, Sept. 22; 1794, Sept. 22–Dec. 4.

Mills, Master: 1796, Feb. 6; 1795, Dec. 22–1796, April 23.

Mitchell, Mr.: 1795, Jan. 21; 1794, Dec. 3–1795, July 4; 1795, Dec. 14–1796, July 1; 1796, Dec. 5–1797, July 14.

M'Lane, Mr.: 1798, May 2; 1797, Dec. 11–1798, May 5.

Moore, Mr.: 1749, Aug.–1750, Jan.

Moran, Mr.: 1797, July 20; 1797, April 11–July 27; 1798, April 24–June 8.

Moreton, John Pollard: 1794, Feb. 17; 1794, Feb. 17–July 18; 1794, Dec. 3–1795, July 4; 1795, Dec. 14–1796, July 1; 1796, Dec. 5–1797, July 14; 1797, Dec. 11–1798, May 5.

Morgan, Mr.: 1796, Jan. 1; 1795, Dec. 14–1796, July 1; 1796, Dec. 5–1797, July 14.

Morris, Mrs. Owen ("The First"):

Morris, Mrs. Owen ("The Second"): 1772, Oct. 28; 1772, Oct. 28–1773, March 31; 1773, Nov. 1–15; 1789, Jan. 9; 1789, March 9–April 4; 1790, Jan. 6–July 19; 1790, Dec. 8–1791, July 11; 1794, Feb. 17–July 18; 1794, Dec. 3–1795, July 4; 1795, Dec. 14–1796, July 1; 1796, Dec. 5–1797, July 14; 1797, Dec. 11–1798, May 5; 1799, Feb. 5–May 27; 1799, Dec. 4–1800, May 19.

Morris, Owen: 1759, June 25; 1759, June 25–Dec. 28; 1766, Nov. 14–1767, July 6; 1767, Oct. 6–Nov. 23; 1768, Oct. 4–1769, Jan. 6; 1769, Nov. 8–1770, June 1; 1772, Oct. 28–1773, March 31; 1773, Nov. 1–15; 1787, June 25–Aug. 4; 1789, March 9–April 4; 1790, Jan. 6–July 19; 1790, Dec. 8–1791, July 11; 1794, Feb. 17–July 18; 1794, Dec. 3–1795, July 4; 1795, Dec. 14–1796, July 1; 1796, Dec. 5–1797, July 14; 1797, Dec. 11–1798, May 5; 1799, Feb. 5–May 27; 1799, Dec. 4–1800, May 19.

Munto, Mr.: 1794, June 25; 1794, Feb. 17–July 18; 1794, Sept. 22–Dec. 4.

Murray, Master Dicky: 1749, Aug.–1750, Jan.

Murray, Walter: 1749, Aug.–1750, Jan.

"N. M.," Mrs.: 1798, March 8; 1798, March 8–April 7.

Nelson, Mr.: 1794, Sept. 20; 1794, Sept. 22–Dec. 4.

Nicholas, Mr.: 1797, May 12; 1797, April 11–July 27.

Nugent, Mr.: 1795, Jan. 2; 1794, Dec. 3–1795, July 4.

Oldfield, Miss: 1794, April 21; 1794, Feb. 17–July 18; 1794, Dec. 3–1795, July 4; 1795, Dec. 14–1796, July 1; 1796, Dec. 5–1797, July 14; 1797, Dec. 11–1798, May 5.

11; 1789, Nov. 4–30; 1790, Jan. 6–
July 19; 1790, Dec. 8–1791, July 11;
1791, April 8–1792, May 16.

Velleroy, Mr.: 1792, Jan. 23; 1791,
April 8–1792, May 16.

Viellard, M.: 1796, Dec. 17; 1796, Dec.
5–1797, July 14; 1797, April 11–July
27.

Viller, Mme.: 1791, Dec. 23; 1791, April
8–1792, May 16.

Wainwright, Miss: 1766, Nov. 28;
1766, Nov. 14–1767, July 6; 1767,
Oct. 6–Nov. 23; 1773, Nov. 1–15.

Wall, Mr.: 1766, Nov. 28; 1766, Nov.
14–1767, July 6; 1767, Oct. 6–Nov.
23; 1768, Oct. 4–1769, Jan. 6; 1769,
Nov. 8–1770, June 1; 1770, June 6;
1772, Oct. 28–1773, March 31; 1773,
Nov. 1–15; 1773, Nov. 22.

Wall, Mrs.: 1767, Jan. 9; 1766, Nov.
14–1767, July 6; 1772, Oct. 28–1773,
March 31.

Warrell, Jr., J.: 1794, March 3; 1794,
Feb. 17–July 18; 1794, Dec. 3–1795,
July 4; 1795, Dec. 14–1796, July 1;
1796, Dec. 5–1797, July 14; 1797, Dec.
11–1798, May 5; 1799, Feb. 5–May
27; 1799, Dec. 4–1800, May 19.

Warrell, Master Harry: 1795, Jan. 2;
1794, Dec. 3–1795, July 4; 1796, Dec.
5–1797, July 14; 1797, Dec. 11–1798,
May 5; 1799, Feb. 5–May 27.

Warrell, Master T.: 1794, Feb. 26;
1794, Feb. 17–July 18; 1794, Dec. 3–
1795, July 4; 1795, Dec. 14–1796,
July 1; 1796, Dec. 5–1797, July 14;
1797, Dec. 11–1798, May 5; 1799,
Feb. 5–May 27; 1799, Dec. 4–1800,
May 19.

Warrell, Mr.: 1794, Feb. 17; 1794, Feb.
17–July 18; 1794, Dec. 3–1795, July
4; 1795, Dec. 14–1796, July 1; 1796,
Dec. 5–1797, July 14; 1797, Dec. 11–
1798, May 5; 1799, Feb. 5–May 27;
1799, Dec. 4–1800, May 19.

Warrell, Mrs.: 1794, Feb. 17; 1794, Feb.
17–July 18; 1794, Dec. 3–1795, July
4; 1795, Dec. 14–1796, July 1; 1796,
Dec. 5–1797, July 14; 1797, Dec. 11–
1798, May 5; 1799, Dec. 4–1800, May
19.

Warren, Mrs.: 1798, Feb. 2; 1797, Dec.
11–1798, May 5; 1799, Feb. 5–May
27.

Warren, William: 1796, Dec. 5; 1796,
Dec. 5–1797, July 14; 1797, Dec. 11–
1798, May 5; 1799, Feb. 5–May 27;
1799, Dec. 4–1800, May 19.

Webber, Mr.: 1797, May 12; 1797,
April 11–July 27.

Wells, Miss: 1795, July 1; 1794, Dec.
3–1795, July 4.

West, Mr.: 1792, Sept. 26; 1792, Sept.
26–1793, Jan. 12.

Whitlock, Mr.: 1794, Feb. 19; 1794,
Feb. 17–July 18; 1794, Dec. 3–1795,
July 4; 1795, Dec. 14–1796, July 1.

Whitlock, Mrs.: 1794, Feb. 19; 1794,
Feb. 17–July 18; 1794, Dec. 3–1795,
July 4; 1795, Dec. 14–1796, July 1.

Wignell, Thomas: 1787, Dec. 10; 1789,
Jan. 9, March 11; 1789, March 9–
April 4; 1790, Jan. 6–July 19; 1790,
Dec. 8–1791, July 11; 1794, Feb. 17–
July 18; 1794, Dec. 3–1795, July 4;
1795, Dec. 14–1796, July 1; 1796, Dec.
5–1797, July 14; 1797, Dec. 11–1798,
May 5; 1799, Feb. 5–May 27; 1799,
Dec. 4–1800, May 19.

Williams (or Willems), Miss (after
1796, June 24, Green, Mrs.): 1794,
Feb. 21; 1794, Feb. 17–July 18; 1794,
Dec. 3–1795, July 4; 1795, Dec. 14–
1796, July 1.

Williamson, Mrs.: 1789, March 11;
1789, March 9–April 4.

Wilson, Mrs.: 1791, March 16; 1790,
Dec. 8–1791, July 11; 1794, Sept. 22–
Dec. 4.

Wolf, Mr.: 1787, Jan. 15; 1787, Jan.
15–Feb. 3.

Wood, William B.: 1799, Feb. 5; 1799,

Feb. 5–May 27; 1799, Dec. 4–1800, May 19.

Woodham, Chas. Somerset: 1749, Aug.–1750, Jan.

Woolls, Stephen: 1766, Nov. 28; 1766, Nov. 14–1767, July 6; 1767, Oct. 6–Nov. 23; 1768, Oct. 4–1769, Jan. 6; 1769, Nov. 8–1770, June 1; 1772, Oct. 28–1773, March 31; 1773, Nov. 1–15; 1787, Jan. 15–Feb. 3; 1789, Jan. 9; 1789, March 9–April 4; 1790, Jan. 6–July 19; 1790, Dec. 8–1791, July 11; 1792, May 28–July 2; 1792, July 11; 1792, Sept. 26–1793, Jan. 12; 1794, Sept. 22–Dec. 4.

Wright, Mr.: 1789, Nov. 14; 1789, Nov. 4–30.

"Young Florentine, The": 1791, Nov. 26; 1791, April 8–1792, May 16.

PLAYWRIGHT INDEX

The Playwright Index includes all the known authors of the recorded plays produced in Philadelphia during the eighteenth century, listing each author's plays under his name. For further information about any of the plays, refer to the Play Index.

[435]

Coffey, Charles: *The Devil to Pay, or, The Wives Metamorphosed.*

Collier, Sir George: *Selima and Azor.*

Colman, George, Jr.: *The Battle of Hexham; Blue Beard; Comus; The English Merchant; The Heir at Law; Inkle and Yarico; The Iron Chest; The Mountaineers; New Hay at the Old Market; The Shipwreck; The Spanish Barber; The Suicide; The Surrender of Calais; Tit for Tat; Ways and Means.*

Colman, George, "The Elder": *The Clandestine Marriage; The Deuce is in Him; The Jealous Wife; Man and Wife, or, Shakespeare's Jubilee; The Musical Lady; Polly Honeycombe.*

Congreve, William: *Love for Love; The Mourning Bride.*

Coomb, Thos.: *Dialogue* (1767, Nov. 17).

Cowley, Mrs.: *The Belle's Stratagem; A Bold Stroke for a Husband; More Ways Than One; Which is the Man; Who's the Dupe?*

Cross, James C.: *The Purse.*

Cumberland, R.: *The Box-Lobby Challenge; The Carmelite; False Impressions; The Fashionable Lover; First Love; The Jew; The Mysterious Husband; The Natural Son; The Shipwreck, or, The Brothers; The West Indian; The Wheel of Fortune.*

Delpini, Carlo: *Don Juan.*

Dibdin, Charles: *The Deserter; The Fusilier, or, The Clown Outwitted; The Lucky Escape; Poor Vulcan; The Quaker; The Shepherd of the Alps; The Waterman; The Wedding Ring.*

Dibdin, Thomas John: *Alonzo and Imogen; Five Thousand a Year; The Horse and the Widow; The Jew and the Doctor.*

Dodsley, Robert: *The King and the Miller of Mansfield; The Toy-Shop.*

Dogget, Thomas: *Flora, or, Hob in the Well.*

Dryden, John: *All for Love; The Spanish Fryar, or, The Double Discovery.*

Duché, Jacob: *Dialogue* (1762, May 18).

Dudley, Sir H. B.: see Rev. Henry Bate.

Dunlap, William: *Darby's Return; The Fatal Deception; The Father; The Stranger.*

Durang, John: *The Country Frolic.*

Evans, Nathaniel: *Dialogue "On Peace"* (1763, May 17).

Farquhar, George: *The Beaux' Stratagem; The Constant Couple, or, A Trip to the Jubilee; The Inconstant, or, The Way to Win Him; The Recruiting Officer; The Stage Coach.*

Fennell, James: *The Advertisement.*

Fenwick: *He's Much to Blame.*

Fielding, Henry: *Don Quixote in England; The Intriguing Chambermaid; The Madcap; The Miser; The Mock Doctor; Tom Thumb the Great; The Virgin Unmasked.*

Fletcher, John: *Rule a Wife and Have a Wife.*

Foote, Samuel: *The Author; The Buck, or, The Englishman in Paris; The Devil on Two Sticks, or, Doctor Last's Examination; The Lyar; The Mayor of Garratt; The Minor.*

Francis, William: *The American Tar; Les Armands d'Arcade; The Easter Gift; The Fandango Dance; Fruitless Precaution; The Guardian Outwitted; Harlequin Dr. Faustus; Harlequin Hurry-Scurry; Harlequin's Club; Harlequin's Invitation; The Irish Lilt; The Irish Vagary; The Lucky Escape; The Miraculous Mill; Rural Merriment; Rural Revels; The Sailor's Return; The Schem-*

Pelisier: *The Danaides.*

Philips, Ambrose: *The Distressed Mother.*

Pilon, Frederick: *Barataria; The Deaf Lover; He Would Be a Soldier; The Invasion.*

Pope, Alexander: "Sappho to Phaon."

Quenet: *The Danaides.*

Ramsay, Allan: *The Gentle Shepherd.*

Ravenscroft, Edward: *The Anatomist, or, The Sham-Doctor.*

Reed, Joseph: *The Register Office.*

Reynolds, F.: *Cheap Living; The Dramatist; How to Grow Rich; Notoriety; The Rage; Speculation; Werter [and Charlotte]; The Will.*

Rich, John: *The Spirit of Contradiction.*

Ricketts: *Harlequin's Renovations.*

Robinson, J.: *Constitutional Follies; The Yorker's Stratagem.*

Rose, Rev. John: *The Prisoner; The Quality Binding.*

Rowe, Nicholas: *The Fair Penitent; Jane Shore; Tamerlane.*

Rowson, Mrs. S. H.: *The Female Patriot; Slaves in Algiers; The Volunteers.*

Schiller, von, J. C. F.: *The Robbers.*

Shadwell, Thomas: *The Tempest* (altered from Shakespeare).

Shakespeare, William: *As You Like It; Coriolanus; Cymbeline; Hamlet; Henry IV, Part I; Julius Cæsar; King John; King Lear; Macbeth; The Merchant of Venice; The Merry Wives of Windsor; Much Ado About Nothing; Othello; Richard III; Romeo and Juliet; The Taming of the Shrew*—see Garrick, *Catherine and Petruchio; The Tempest.*

Sheridan, Richard Brinsley: *The Critic; The Duenna; The Rivals; St. Patrick's Day; The School for Scandal; A Trip to Scarborough, or, The Man of Quality.*

Sheridan, Thomas: *The Brave Irishman, or, Captain O'Blunder.*

Shirley, William: *Edward the Black Prince; or, The Battle of Poictiers.*

Siddons, Henry: *The Sicilian Romance.*

Smith, William: *Dialogue* (1761, May 23); *The Masque of Alfred.*

Smollet, Tobias: *The Reprisal, or, The Tars of Old England.*

Southerne, Thomas: *Isabella; Oroonoko.*

Spinacuta: *Harlequin's Renovations; The Magic Fight.*

Steele, Sir Richard: *The Conscious Lovers; The Funeral, or, Grief à la Mode; The Tender Husband, or, The Accomplished Fools.*

Stevens, G. A.: *A Lecture on Heads; A Rhapsody.*

Sully: *Harlequin's Renovations; The Sisters of the Rocks.*

Tate, Nahum: *Duke and No Duke.*

Theobald, Lewis: *Orpheus and Eurydice.*

Thomson, James: *Coriolanus* (altered from Shakespeare); *Edward and Eleanora; The Masque of Alfred; Summer; Tancred and Sigismunda.*

Tickell, Richard: *Patie and Roger.*

Townley, James: *High Life Below Stairs.*

Tyler, Royall: *The Contrast.*

Vanbrugh, Sir John: *Like Master Like Man.*

Voltaire: "Folly on Both Sides."

Waldron, Francis Godolphin: *The Prodigal; Heigh Ho! for a Husband!*

Whitehead, William: *The Roman Father; The School for Lovers, or, Man of the Town; A Trip to Scotland.*

Young, Edward: *The Revenge.*

GENERAL INDEX

This General Index is primarily concerned with the chapters on Theatrical History. The Indices of Plays, Players, and Playwrights serve as detailed keys to the *Day Book*. However, the General Index includes also reference to important items in the *Day Book* not covered by the foregoing specialized indices.

[444]